LOOKING AFTER

John Daniel

LOOKING
AFTER

A Son's Memoir

COUNTERPOINT

WASHINGTON, D.C.

Portions of this book first appeared in *Eugene Weekly, Hope, Northwest Review, Southwest Review,* and *Wilderness.*

Reprint acknowledgments appear on page 263.

LIBRARY OF CONGRESS CATALOGING-IN-PUBLICATION DATA
Daniel, John, 1948–
Looking after: a son's memoir / John Daniel.
1. Daniel, John, 1948–   . 2. Parent and adult child—United States.
3. Mothers and sons—United States.   4. Adult children—United States—
Family relationships.   5. Aging parents—United States—
Family relationships.   6. Caregivers—United States.   I. Title.
HQ755.86.D35   1996   306.874'3—dc20   96-18627
ISBN 1-887178-23-6

FIRST PRINTING
Book design by David Bullen
Composition by Wilsted & Taylor
Printed in the United States of America on acid-free paper that meets the American National Standards Institute Z39-48 Standard.

COUNTERPOINT
P.O. Box 65793
Washington, D.C. 20035-5793

Distributed by Publishers Group West

FOR JIM DANIEL
AND HEATHER DANIEL

I have become to myself a piece of difficult ground,
not to be worked over without much labor.

SAINT AUGUSTINE

I am as convinced as I can be of anything that this
experience of ours is only a part of the experience that is,
and with which it has something to do; but *what* or *where*
the other parts are, I cannot guess. It only enables one to
say "behind the veil, behind the veil!"

WILLIAM JAMES

I shall pass beyond memory to find you—oh, where,
where shall I find you, my truly good and serene delight?
If I find you without memory, I shall not remember you.
And how shall I find you if I do not remember you?

SAINT AUGUSTINE

The Dogwood Tree

In my mother's last years she ate her breakfast and lunch at a small oak table in our kitchen, by a window that looks out on the limbs and leaves of a dogwood tree. With ferns below it, the tree makes a small, dapple-lighted garden of that side of the house, screening us from Tom the neighbor's place next door. The pink blossoms gave my mother pleasure in the spring—though, like me, she preferred dogwoods that bloom white—and she also enjoyed the sparrows and finches and chickadees that came to the bird feeder with a mossy roof that hung from the dogwood's central limbs. My mother took a long time with her meals. She looked out the window as she ate, and sometimes the food on her plate seemed to surprise her when she looked down and saw it. She usually sat at the table long after I had finished my meal and gone out back again to write or off in the car on errands. My mother spent many hours with that dogwood tree.

I can see her clearly as I write this, and I can smell her, too. It's a fresh and musty smell of sandalwood and damp sweat, of skin cream and urine, and it's as vivid in my memory as her stooped back and curling white hair, as clear as her slow, flat-footed shuffle in bare feet or slippers, her hands flying out sporadically to a wall or table edge to steady her on her way. That smell of her old age is as sure in my mind as her quick scowl and sharp remarks, her laughter and childlike smile, her frowning concentration as she tried to listen with her bad ears, the look of her reddened eyes behind her glasses as she dog-gedly tracked lines of print across page after page of the books and papers and magazines she kept piled beside her on her bed.

Her eyesight, unlike her hearing, stayed sharp until the end. As we drove in the car she would sometimes speak out loud the names she read on street signs and billboards, as if to fix our location in memory—or maybe simply for the exercise, for the pleasure of forming words, for the happiness of being out of the house and in motion through the streets of Portland. Her eyes saw clearly the birds that came to the kitchen feeder, but she often asked their names. Sometimes she asked about the same bird at breakfast and again at lunch, sometimes at the same meal.

"What *is* that one," she would say, intently, "with the bright red . . ." She gestured at her throat with her long, purpled fingers.

"That's the finch," I'd tell her.

"*Finch,*" she'd say. "That's what I thought."

A black tomcat, not ours, once in a while would rocket from the ferns and almost capture a finch or sparrow, upsetting the feeder in a spray of millet and sunflower seed. My usual response was to charge out the back door and throw a stick of firewood at the fleeing cat. My mother would watch through the window, looking at me and the wobbling feeder as if the scene had never occurred before and was as delightful as anything that had ever happened in the history of the world. And sometimes a particular image would come to her, a known shape of words, a recurrent visitation from the mists and shadows of the past.

"Do you remember," she would ask, in that way she had of giving each syllable its full enunciation, "when the cat brought a poor bird to the door, and I scolded it? And you were there, all of six"—she'd be smiling now—"and you said, 'Mother, it's a cat's *nature* to hunt birds.'"

"I remember," I'd tell her, though in truth I didn't remember saying it so much as I remembered hearing her tell the story about me. I remembered being remembered. But I cherished those moments, brief and infrequent as they were, when the two of us could pause together in the shared light of each other's recall. In those moments we were all at home—me, my mother, the family and friends we spoke of. I felt myself resting then, relaxing from some continuous effort I hadn't known I'd been engaged in and would shortly resume.

Sometimes when she brought up a glimpse of the past, I would try to draw her out, to enlarge the landscape of her recall. But memory for my mother was a thing of moments, as mutable as the lightplay in the dogwood tree. What I searched for with my questions usually wasn't there. She knew the names I spoke—my father's, my brother's, the places we had lived—but much of the time the names had come loose from their moorings, like boats adrift on the sea. If I told a family story she would recognize it with pleasure, but my mother in herself had few stories left.

In the hot summer months the dogwood leaves curled on the tree, and then as fall arrived and the light turned pale, the leaves took on a tinge of red—a subtle red, nothing vivid—and began to drop and gather on the ground. The gray Northwestern season that starts in mid October and lasts through late spring was hard on my mother's spirits. In the spring she could watch the dogwood twigs hopefully for evidence of buds. In the fall she could only watch the tree unleaving itself. By late November of her last autumn the branches shook in the wind with only a smattering of leaves still clinging, and there came a morning when only one was left, on a lower branch near the window at my mother's end of the breakfast table. She pointed it out to me, and again the next few mornings. "Still there," she said, smiling as if with a secret we shared.

One morning as I heard her feet begin to shuffle from her bedroom, I glanced at the window and saw that the leaf had fallen. I pointed as I poured her coffee. "It's gone," I said.

She gazed blankly out the window.

"The leaf is gone," I told her. "The last leaf."

"Oh," she answered vaguely. "The leaf."

Because it was absent from her present sight she had only the faintest memory of it. The leaf was profoundly gone for her, and soon would be absolutely gone, but in my own mind it still hangs on. I can see it now, I can't stop seeing it: a dark curled form infused with red, a beautiful ghost that by chance or willfulness still holds to its place in the world. In memory I circle and circle that leaf. I watch it much more carefully than I watched it before. I want to know what makes it hold on in the cold wind, how it somehow emerged out of sap and fiber and grew in the sun and remains now only by habit, by a spell of nature, by nothing at all. It's only memory that holds it now, and memory, at last, that lets it go.

It's October, the last clear days before the rains. The sun is warm and bright but paling, already retiring toward winter. There's a trace of wood smoke in the air. Crows have gathered in the park, as they usually do in the fall, poking around in the grass, raising querulous hubbubs as I walk by. I squish through a scatter of fallen plums, breathing in their sweet rotting aura, breathing it out. The birches lining the streets are yellowing, their leaves collecting in small drifts in the oil-stained gutters. Some of them scatter as the wind comes up, then settle to the street again.

I've been talking with a psychologist, and I'm gusting with memories. Or not whole memories so much as pieces, random leaves swirling, patches of bright color I haven't seen since childhood. Where have I been all my life? *Who* have I been? It's odd to think it, even odder to write it, but I don't feel whole. I'm a hodgepodge, a motley crowd I hardly know. This *me*, this whatever it is that I am, was passed one to another in a makeshift relay race, a race with no destination that happened to wind up here, me, walking the gridded streets of a North Portland neighborhood, three thousand miles and forty-five years from my birth. The others just drifted away once they'd carried me a while. They lost themselves in my memory's terrain.

But it's not them—*I'm* the one who's lost. I'm lost from them. Is this a midlife crisis? It feels too gray for that, too dull and sluggish. I'm not inspired to leave my wife or dump my career. How could I dump my career when I don't have one? I don't have an itch to bungee jump or hole up with video games or seek a guru in Nepal. And I'm glad, because that kind of thing is undignified for a man in his forties. It's the kind of thing Bob Bourgeois might do, if he had the courage. Bob's one of my selves who stuck around. He's the one who actually enjoys mowing the lawn, who worries that he should paint the rain gutters with Rustoleum, who ambles docile and well scrubbed through the cavernous spaces of Costco or Home Depot, gently henpecked by his smiling wife. You can see Bob's face on every sack of Kingsford charcoal briquets. He's a basket case, a swamp of quiet desperation. Let *him* have a midlife crisis.

Whatever's happening to me, I prefer to think of it in Dantean terms. I've lost the way in a dark wood. I've lost the way, I don't know where it was going, I don't think I ever knew. You get up in the morning, you drink your coffee, you read the paper, you set yourself in motion. You put one foot in front of the other and do what's next. You go ahead through your life like that and suddenly your life's half gone, and more than half. You're over halfway to those stars of no return.

My doctor says I'm suffering from depression, which is depressing in itself. What do you do about depression, give smiling lessons to your lips? Read *The Power of Positive Thinking*? My doctor prescribed pills, little red traffic cops to direct the chemistry of my brain. I take them dutifully, and maybe I feel better, but I think I need to do more than recalibrate my chemistry. That's why I'm seeing the psychologist. If I'm depressed there must be something I'm not seeing, or lots of things, things I need to understand. It's only in the last year, since my mother died, that I've been able to glimpse my depression, let alone see inside it. It's a gray weather that I've come to take for normal. I walk inside it for days or months and never see it, then the sun burns through and it slips out of me. I see its dark form, shaped like me, then the mist again.

Drinking lightens it, then makes it worse. Exercising helps, and so I take these fast walks with weights around my wrists and ankles, like some prisoner in a hurry. There's only one reliable medicine, and it's not here. It's out beyond the end of the road, in wind and rivers and ponderosa pines, silently offering itself in every leaf and stone. The gospel of the good sweet world, the beauty beyond all human moods. It never fails me, but I can't seem to bring it home. It fades like the colors of a caught trout. When I return, it's always to myself and my gray weather.

Power poles march next to me, two or three to a block. The dull-colored houses sit behind their fences, lawns clipped and edged, flowers weeded, roses mulched. So much care in keeping things in order, keeping things enclosed. Blank windows, shut front doors. I have a wild urge to stride in my shorts up a walkway, any walkway, and pound on the door with my weighted right hand until someone answers. Twenty-five years ago, frazzled by methamphetamine, I did just that . . . Someone's looking at me from his window. I imagine a gun in his hand. I wave and keep walking.

At the end of the block I turn left onto Willamette Avenue and there's Mount Hood, dark and streaked with old snow, floating in the southeast like a figure from a dream I can't quite recall. Not far from here, somewhere on this bluff above the river, William Clark looked south two centuries ago. He saw no bridges, no cranes or dry docks, no tankers or tugboats, none of the clustered oblong spires of downtown Portland. In the continental quiet he looked at wooded hills, the river surging in spring flood, maybe the huts and smokes of an Indian camp. Mount Hood floating in the distance as it floats for me. It thrills me to imagine what he must have felt—to have traversed the wild heart of North America to stand in that great solitude, to look upon a vista no man of European ancestry had ever seen.

It was for some tiny semblance of Clark's Voyage of Discovery that I used to climb mountains, and it's for that semblance that I now hike desert canyons and old-growth forests—always outward, away from the human world into the sanity of nature. But this time, I know, it's a different kind of journey that I need. I have it in my head that "crisis," in the Greek it comes from, means separation. So maybe this is a crisis. I'm separated from my life and whoever's been living it. From myself. From my selves.

There's one in particular who keeps calling me, one who's been hidden a long time. My psychologist says it might do me good to get to know him again, and I think she's right. I can't see him clearly, the boy I was, but I can smell the breeze on his face as the Appalachian Trail steepens beneath his feet, leading him to a rocky promontory where thick hardwoods give way to sparse pines, where nothing but distance obscures the view before him, a view he has glimpsed through trees but not seen in its wholeness until now. The brown Shenandoah River meanders through patched farmland and forest below him, and beyond the river valley the blue Allegheny Mountains range away, ridge after ridge, into the hazy West.

I wish I had the poem the boy wrote there. I know it sang with all the lonely passion of his fourteen years. I know it sang of wanderlust—that word was in the poem. It sang of the perfect peaceful looping of the Shenandoah, the blue grandeur of the mountains, and the pure formless possibility of that far distance where the mountains disappeared. I had traveled out there with my family, clear to the Golden Gate, but that had been motels and restaurants and the car. That had been my parents and their arguments. This was me, my life, and I absolutely knew that someday I would live out there. I sat for a long time with my arms around my knees, watching with a wild exaltation as the wind called in the pines and called in me.

It's crazy, this living of a life. You're never quite sure where you're going or what you're doing, and in the rearview mirror the most it makes is a chancy kind of sense. The boy was right. I did go west, and now I'm looking east across thirty-some years for that kid who looked this way with all his longing. We meant to stay together, but we got split up somehow. He got lost or I got lost and now he's back there on that Blue Ridge promontory, and I'm walking the circular squares of these Portland streets. This wasn't in the poem he wrote. This isn't what he had in mind when he looked west. And so I'm going in this time instead of out, I'm going back to find that boy, to find others if I can, to find anyone who might be me. If you've lost your way in the forest, how can you find it again except by going back?

*F*_{*ailing*} is the term we use. Failing health. Failing mind. As if life were a series of tests, and we have to keep our grades up right to the end. And failing whom? Oneself? Or those around oneself, those family and friends who know a person in certain ways and hope and expect that she will continue in those ways forever? To fail is to disappoint, to prove unreliable. When a bank fails, it proves unworthy of everyone who had faith in it. It ruins people—and behind the scenes, we suspect, someone got rich. "Fail" comes from the Latin *fallere*, which means, among other things, to deceive.

It's hard to say when my mother began to fail. My wife and I, and my brother too, were living in California during the 1980s, a continent away from my mother's home on the coast of Maine. Failings tend not to show in letters or phone calls, or even in occasional visits, especially to those who aren't looking for them. My mother had long been a vigorous and independent woman. In her twenties and early thirties she was a labor organizer, like my father, and later in life, after my brother and I had left home and she and my father had separated, she became a nomadic adventurer and seeker. She sailed on steamers, lived in a lakeside cabin in British Columbia, spent two years in the Findhorn spiritual community in Scotland. In her seventies she became a devotee of the Indian avatar Sai Baba and made two pilgrimages to his ashram, staying several weeks each time, sleeping on a thin mattress on a concrete floor. She had always gone her own way. She was tough as lobster shell, solid as New England granite, lively as the wind.

And she was living in her old age exactly where she wanted to be, in the same region of the central Maine coast where she had spent long stretches of her girlhood. Her father, a Unitarian minister, kept a modest summerhouse on Hancock Point, near Acadia National Park, and with her two sisters my mother did much of her growing up there. Tides and fogs and the clangor of the bell buoy became part of her being, as did the inland lakes (which New Englanders call ponds) where her father took the family on camping vacations. I have a photo of the teenaged girl who would become my mother as a Sea Scout, standing on the bowsprit of a two-masted schooner, one hand on the headstay, hair and bloomers flapping in the breeze. That is a true portrait of her spirit. The salt wind drew her back to Maine throughout her life for visits and vacations—my brother and I too did some growing up there—and in 1978, tired of roving, she settled in to stay, it seemed. She rented a plain wooden house in Brooklin and lived simply there, keeping a garden, reading and writing, working as a proofreader for *WoodenBoat* magazine.

In 1980, when she was seventy-two, my mother's Volvo station wagon left the road and almost plunged her into Blue Hill Harbor. She escaped with only a broken left arm, a lucky outcome that we too readily interpreted as another sign of her reliable durability. She didn't know or wouldn't say how the accident had happened. Two years later she passed out at the wheel of her car in her younger sister's driveway in Needham, Massachusetts. Only then did she go to a doctor, who immediately put her on a drug to control her high blood pressure. My mother's attitude toward illness was a simple one: she denied it. A friend who dropped by on an early spring day in 1983 found her sick with flu and chilled to sluggishness, too weak to keep a fire in the woodstove. She had a telephone but had called no one. I remember talking with her on the phone while she was recuperating with friends. She seemed baffled, mystified by what had happened—and, it occurs to me now, a little scared.

Such incidents put us on alert, I suppose, but she seemed to recover quickly and go on with her life. She was white-haired now and a little stooped, weaker in her left arm, but still Zilla Daniel, still my blithe mother. My father had died at seventy-two, and given what he had done to his body, he had been lucky to live out his biblical span. He smoked four packs of Chesterfields a day and was a hard-drinking alcoholic for four decades of his life. My mother had quit cigarettes long before and no longer drank heavily. She ate healthy food, and the same willfulness that caused her to deny illness filled her sails with an indomitable spirit. I remember when Marilyn and I saw her off at San Francisco Airport on her second trip to India, in the fall of 1986. In pants and sneakers and canvas vest, water bottle dangling from her belt, my mother resolutely pushed her baggage cart up the rampway of the international entrance, waving good-bye with her ticket in an upraised hand, looking back not once. We laughed at the wonder of it.

When she returned two months later, though, she seemed subdued and peaked. For the first time she fully looked her age, which then was seventy-eight. It turned out that she had brought home a well-developed staph infection in her leg. She had to stay with Marilyn and me in our tiny cottage, gradually regaining her strength as the antibiotics took hold and beat down the bacteria. She slept and rested in our bed; we flopped on a pad in the living room or in a tent on the gravel patio out back. I had a talk to give in our old hometown in Oregon, but she wasn't well enough to travel with us, so Marilyn had to stay home with her. This wasn't a happy alternative—Marilyn and I had been looking forward to the trip together—but there was nothing else to do. A new responsibility and a new kind of tension had entered our lives, a harbinger of what was to come.

My mother got well slowly in the weeks after my Oregon trip. When I was done teaching for the day I would drive her to the nearest almost-level road—we lived in the foothill country of the San Francisco Peninsula—and we would walk there, slowly, a little farther each afternoon. She breathed hard from the exertion. For the first time in my life my mother was leaning on my arm for support, and I wasn't comfortable with it. I had a life to live, things to do, little accomplished as a writer and a lot to prove. I didn't like the drift. Zilla Daniel was supposed to be strong. She was supposed to take care of herself. She was supposed to be leading her independent and presumably happy life three thousand miles away on the coast of Maine—where I could visit her once in a while, where we could feast on scallops and lobster together, where we could drive to Acadia Park or row in her boat off Naskeag Point and talk about those things we were able to talk about. Where, in our oblique ways, we could affirm our love for each other. And I could leave, knowing that my mother was living the life she wanted to live and was doing just fine.

I want to say that my first moment of awareness occurred in my mother's arms. The sense of the memory is vague, but I seem to remember the warmth and gentle pressure of arms and breast. And I seem to remember a voice speaking to me, drawing me out of myself into the world—I hear it murmuring like a stream moving easily over smooth stones, the words all dissolved now in the lilt and whisper of their flow. Maybe it was her heart and blood I was hearing, maybe it wasn't words at all.

But it's the stars that I remember most clearly from that moment, or that I think I remember. It's the stars that were my first seeing. Maybe my mother was talking about them, crooning about them. I saw, I think I saw, a scatter of light above me, and it was in seeing that scatter of light that I first distinguished a world separate from me and a me separate from the world. I think of it as my second birth, as profound as my first—more profound, because it was the birth of consciousness, of the point of view that I would come to know as myself, more *me* than arms or legs. And, of course, it was also a death. In that instant of seeing I fell from the cosmos I was born to and had been securely and unknowingly part of.

There are other details of that first experience that I want to say I remember: that the night air was warm and soft on my face, that the stars looked cold somehow, that crickets were sounding, that a dog barked. But how could I at two years old or less have been aware of anything I could identify and remember as the sound of crickets? A dog's bark, maybe, because we had one and I knew she barked, but crickets? And what did I know of the sensation of cold that I could identify it and extend it to the stars? Surely my mind has invented those details, remembering them *into* the memory of voice and warmth and scattered light. I'm a writer, after all, and I have a writer's instinct for artifice. I want to make the scene immediate for the reader, and that artifice of language is only an extension of a deeper, preverbal artifice. Something in my psyche wants to make the scene immediate for *me*, the me who distantly remembers it. Memory itself is a fabricator, a spinner of yarns, a poet and a liar.

Scientists for decades have been trying to discover the site or sites in the brain where memories are stored. Now, at last, they seem to have found the answer: there are no such sites. When we remember an experience, the brain does not somehow retrieve a record of it from storage, as a computer retrieves information from its memory banks. There is no record. The brain *re-creates* the experience, conjuring the image out of vast, labyrinthine loopings of neurons firing in a pattern similar to the one evoked by the original experience.

Similar, but not the same. The re-creation is not a photocopy. According to neurobiologist Gerald Edelman, there are ten billion neurons in the human cerebral cortex, and more potential connections between those neurons than there are subatomic particles in the entire estimated physical universe. It is a system of near-infinite complexity, a system that seems designed for revision as much as for replication, and that is what occurs in memory. Details from separate experiences weave together, so that the rememberer thinks of them as having happened together. The actual year or season shifts to a different one. Some details are lost; others are freely invented. We tend to remember in ways that suit the present self, not the self of ten or twenty or forty years ago. And even the fresh memory, the "original" memory, is unreliable. It happens all the time that two eyewitnesses to the same recent incident give widely divergent accounts. We remember not the story of what happened but always *a* story, not the truth but a version of the truth that fits our present understanding of the world and helps us get on with our lives. That story is subject to revision over time. The latest draft becomes for us *the* story, the clear and certain memory we would swear to.

And so how do I proceed? My memories are me, they live exactly at the center of who and what I think I am. If I can't know them to be true, how can I know who I am? How can I write a memoir if I can't trust memory? It disturbs me to acknowledge, as I must, that my recollection of seeing the stars from my mother's arms may be entirely fabricated. Like the cat and bird story, it may be an instance of remembering myself being remembered—my mother may have told me, when I was older, that she had carried me into the yard one night and I had seemed to take an interest in the stars. I may not have been in my mother's arms at all but in the arms of Nanny, the woman who helped with housekeeping when my brother and I were small. Or I may never have seen the stars from anyone's arms. It may all have come from stories, from songs, from who knows what or where.

It's even possible, I believe, that the memory I call my first may have come with me into the world. We are from the stars, after all. Every particle we are made of was formed in their unimaginable fire. The matter that we call ourselves and our world, the matter of our brains and bones and the eyes we see with, has been gathering, dispersing, and drifting the distances of space for billions of years before materializing in these familiar forms. Our nature and all of nature is a story of fire strewn through darkness, and that story must somehow be inscribed in us. To see the stars for the first time may be more an act of recognition than of learning, a dawning into consciousness of what in some sense we have always known.

But what I have, regardless of its origin, regardless of its veracity, is the memory. The image. I looked up from my mother's arms and saw the scattered stars in the black night sky. I have carried that glimpse for over forty years, and there are other glimpses I have carried nearly as long. The stars were on my mind as a young boy. When I was five or so, my mother was trying to explain the West Coast to me, a place called Oregon. I got it that the land went on from where we were and ended far away in Oregon, but for some reason I didn't see an ocean beyond the land. I saw trees and mountains, a last solid shore, and then the void of starry space. *Oregon.* And there was a recurrent nightmare I had throughout my childhood, my most terrifying experience. There was no story to it, just an image. I felt myself floating among icy stars, a dead and disembodied soul lost forever from my life. I would cry out until my mother came in to turn on the light and comfort me.

I still have an acute fear of death. It's liable to well up suddenly in any circumstance—in classroom or concert hall, talking at a party, alone at my desk, in bed with my wife. It isn't a fear so much as a certainty, an ultimate despair. It says: *I will die from this sweet world. I will vanish among the stars in the cold abyss of eternity. I will be nothing forever.*

I've sometimes thought that the glittering sky I saw from my mother's arms somehow burned me with a fear of death, but it makes no sense. Why would that moment have been fearful? What danger could I have sensed? What was death to the *I* who had just been born beneath those stars? My fear must have come later, from some other source that memory still withholds, something that subverted my original vision and turned the stars cold, turned them into emblems of extinction.

I don't recall any frightening experience involving the stars, but fire and bright light were threatening in a different context. In the late fifties and early sixties we lived in Glen Echo, Maryland, a semi-rural suburb of Washington, D.C. The firehouse was just down the street, and its siren was loud, an implacable shriek. When it went up and leveled off at its highest pitch I would stop everything and wait for it to go back down, because that would mean it was signaling only a fire. If it didn't go down it meant the worst. It meant that Russian missiles were on the way and nothing could be done to stop them and along with Congress and the president and my family and friends I would soon burn instantly to nothing in a blinding flash. I would be standing in the center of my blue-papered room, my Rand McNally world map on the wall, all my familiar things around me—and then I'd be gone. When the siren seemed to stay too many seconds at its top screaming pitch, I closed my eyes and *willed* it to go down, then pleaded, beating my fists against my thighs.

Light and dark, to be alive, then suddenly not even a body—is that what gave me the nightmare? Is that what caused me to see a terrifying brink at the end of America? I don't know, and I don't suppose I can know. But maybe it's enough to realize that the starry dark is a primary image for me, a riddle of my being—and so it makes sense that my memory should work and worry it, shape scenes and stories from it, tease it into words. There is something there to be discovered, some shape that memory both hides and wants to body forth from its darknesses. Something I need to know, and the only way to find it or let it be born is to follow this pencil, this circling, stuttering, scratching pencil that might know more than I do. I can't be sure that everything it writes will be true, but I can hope to approach the truth only by following it.

And by following my mother. It's she who stirred this up in me, first by living here and then by dying. Until she came, I had never thought much about my past or anybody's past. The past was past; I believed in now. But when she came, her memory falling from her like sediment from a slowing stream, I began to gather my own memory, gleaning the past as she let it go—as if I could save it for her, as if I could save her sense of self from its slow dissolution. And then she died, over a year ago now, and I haven't been able to stop grieving. I cry frequently, suddenly. I tell her how sorry I am. I miss her intensely despite my vivid memories of how hard it was to have her with us.

It's as though she has something still to teach me. She comes in dreams occasionally, and in one of them, a recent one, she asks to see the leafless tree. I take her to the deck behind the house where I live, where she too may live, though it's not our Portland house. I'm assisting her, but she doesn't need it—she's agile, steady on her feet, the Zilla of twenty years ago. She's wearing a navy blue sweater. She holds her cane vertically in front of her, grasping it just above the middle, raising it high and marching after it in high spirits. We pass two trees I've never seen before, a lemon and a grapefruit, both with glossy leaves. The tree we came to see is the third one, the last one. I suspect I was wrong about it, it might have leaves after all, but I can't bring myself to look at it. I don't know if my mother looks or not. She says she'll walk to a stream that runs through the forest behind the house, she'll walk to a pool in the stream and wet a handkerchief there. "You'll need help," I say, but I know that I'm the one being guided now. I'm the one who lives in the house but doesn't even know what's behind it—a stream in the forest all this time and I never knew.

It surprised us when my mother, after recovering from her infection and flying home to Maine, began to ask for money. She had never had a lot, and what she'd had she hadn't tried to save, but she lived cheaply. Between Social Security and Medicare and what she earned at *WoodenBoat*, she always seemed to have enough. When she didn't, her sisters helped her out. Now her letters were saying that she was a bit short this month, could we spare fifty or seventy-five or a hundred dollars to tide her over. She had a car payment due. She owed the dentist. The Bar Harbor Bank was dunning her about her VISA account.

We were concerned about the health of both her body and her finances, and so I flew to Maine in December of 1987 to spend Christmas with her. She was pleased—relieved, it seemed—to let me go through her bills and checking records. I found that she had enough income to cover her expenses, barely, but that she had been writing redundant checks. She had paid her rent twice in a month, made two car payments, and the like. Her checks were bouncing from Blue Hill to Bangor, and at the larcenous rates that banks charge to cover bad checks, or not to cover them, she had dug herself a sizable hole.

"Oh!" she said, in self-disgust, when I told her what the trouble was. "How absolutely *silly* of me."

"It's no big deal," I said. "I'll get you a record book to help you keep track."

"I shouldn't need one," said my mother, still scowling at herself.

I bought the record book and set it up for the year ahead, listing the checks she needed to write each month. My brother sent some money to get her out of the red, and things seemed squared away. But I remember, walking the bright snowy streets of Blue Hill—my mother had taken an apartment there—an inescapable knowledge dogging me: *My mother is old.* And I remember my discomfiture as I talked to the bank teller about my mother's account. I lowered my voice and leaned close over the counter, wishing other customers weren't around. My mother's check-bouncing was a sign of mental deterioration, of senility—at least I knew it was—and somehow that was shameful.

Her staph infection had caused me no embarrassment. Most bodily illness carries no stigma; the afflicted one is a victim, an unfortunate, a brave spirit let down by her flesh. But mental lapses, mental illness, mental *failing* are different. We don't extend the same sympathy and support. There's a suspicion that the failing one could do better if only she would try, that will or discipline, rather than health, is what's wanting. I felt it right away, and I would feel it again when I came back to Maine the following fall and saw that her entries in the record book had tailed off over the winter and disappeared in the spring. Her finances had bollixed up again. It's not her fault, I thought. And then I thought: All she had to do was follow the list.

I realized during my Christmas visit that my mother would eventually need to come west and live with Marilyn and me. Eventually, and maybe soon. Some of her many friends, most of them much younger than she, told me that the time was coming or had come, and her frailty was evident enough. She walked slowly, at moments a bit unsteadily. Her white head seemed too heavy for her neck, bowing of its own weight. But it was her way of getting groceries to her second-floor apartment that revealed her decline most graphically. I can see her now, coming in from the snow in her mackinaw and L. L. Bean boots, a bright wool cap on her head. She sets the grocery bag on the third step, hoists herself up two steps with the handrail, then lifts the bag ahead of her again and in that way follows her groceries up to the landing, where she hefts the bag with an effort and lugs it into her kitchen.

I felt a sharp prick of guilt that her life had become so hard and I had been so oblivious to it. She had never complained, of course. Her fierce willfulness had sustained her, and her devoted friends checked up on her, helping her as much as she would allow. She got the groceries up the stairs. She got by—and isn't that what parents are supposed to do? Parents care for you, not you for them. They raise you, they help you and hurt you, they see you on your way. They look on as your own life comes to the fore, and they recede gracefully, loving you, of course, as you love them. They are prudent and realistic. They plan for their old age. They take care of themselves.

But my mother, ever the nonconformist, didn't do what parents are supposed to do. Like me, she never planned very far ahead. She lived from day to day, from year to year, trusting in fortune and the gods. There was no retirement home awaiting her, no efficiency apartment reserved and paid for, no senior-citizen Elysian Fields of group dinners, organized activities, and medical staff at the ready. She had no money for such a thing and no desire. She would have hated it. She would have preferred to fail on her own and call it happiness, and maybe happiness is what it would have been.

"How would you feel about living out West?" I asked her on Christmas Eve, at dinner in a Blue Hill restaurant.

She took a long time to answer. "Well, I don't know," she finally said.

"It's pretty hard for you here."

"Oh, it's not hard. There's no need to talk about it now."

It wasn't easy for either of us to speak of personal matters. There's no tradition of it in our family. As I was growing up, personal discourse between my parents consisted often as not of shouted accusations and recriminations, followed when the liquor had worn off by grim silences. My brother and I learned to be little Stoics, novitiate monks in the Daniel Way. And my mother, in the two decades after her split with my father, had followed her own compass and kept her own counsel. She was not accustomed to discussing the course of her life with anyone. I don't know to what extent she discussed it with herself, but I do know that she frequently consulted her pendulum, a small steel weight she dangled from her fingers on a chain, watching for it to swing one way or another in answer to her questions. It was a practice she had learned from New England dowsers. And I do know that she, like me, subscribed to the vaguely Taoist sixties notion that not to decide is to decide. That things have a way of working out.

We went on to talk of subjects we were easier with—her friends, my brother and his daughter, the weather. Snow was drifting down in the lighted central street of Blue Hill. There was a candle set in a wreath of holly on the table between us. Talk and laughter and the smells of good food flowed warmly in the restaurant, and suddenly I felt an upwelling of Christmas as a child—the snugness and happy expectation, the tree with its bright lights, candle chimes whirling and tinkling in air that smelled like coffee and brandy, my mother and father genially drunk by the fire. A sense that all was well and would be well . . . I suppose we slip into childhood all the time, hardly aware, when circumstances trigger it. The restaurant cast a powerful spell. It was my mother who snapped me out of it. Not anything she said or did, but her face—her truly beautiful old woman's face, wreathed in white curls, smiling at me in the candlelight exactly like a child's.

Marilyn flew in a couple of days after Christmas. She agreed that my mother needed to live with us in the West, or near us at least. There was nothing to be done about it at the moment, since my mother couldn't possibly afford a Bay Area apartment even if she wanted one, and there was no room for her in our 470-square-foot cottage. But Marilyn and I were looking for jobs in Oregon, where both of us had lived before marrying and moving to California, and we decided that when we moved north we would ask my mother to join us.

If we had any doubts, they were extinguished at the Bangor airport, early on the icy morning we were to fly home. I had driven the three of us the sixty or so miles to Bangor in my mother's little blue Dodge, and now, after our farewells, my mother was setting off back to Blue Hill. Her stooped frame looked too small in the driver's seat, her jauntily capped head barely clearing the wheel. We watched from inside the terminal as she eased the car back and nudged the bumper of an empty sedan behind her. Then she swung the wheel and crept ahead, working for maneuvering room, and bumped the car in front of her not quite as gently. Suddenly I noticed the many small nicks and scrapes on the body of her year-old car. At last she swung it clear and steered slowly away, the rear wheels tossing up little spumes of snow behind her.

I was thirteen, I think, when I announced to my parents that I would attend the University of Oregon and study forestry. Forestry, because I liked the outdoors and because an aptitude test in school had shown that I should be a forest ranger. Oregon, because I had never been there, because I'd been reading Bernard De Voto on Lewis and Clark and the westward expansion, and because I liked the name (which at the time I must have pronounced ARE-uh-GAHN). I no longer believed that the world ended there, but even with an ocean beyond it instead of the starry void, Oregon had the allure of an Ultimate Place. It was more enticing than any of the foreign countries arranged in soft pastels on my Rand McNally World. I've never much cared about other countries, but I've always had a passion for America.

I got it right and got it wrong. In the late summer of 1966, eighteen years old, I did indeed steer the rattling blue-and-white Jeep my mother had given me across the country to the great state of my imagining. I had been turned down by Harvard, a stinging slap at the time that I now see as a fortunate fall, and had chosen Reed College over Cornell and Wesleyan. It wasn't a hard decision. I'd gotten into Reed on my good grades, a decent short story I'd written in lieu of an application essay, and the sheer force of my desire. At the end of my application I wrote, "Every train whistle in the night seems to pull me toward the Pacific." The admissions committee might have wondered how many train whistles one is likely to hear on Connecticut Avenue in Washington, D.C., but how could they refuse such eagerness? My brother had gone west the year before, to George Air Force Base in the Mojave Desert, and now it was my turn.

I cried as I drove away from the apartment my mother and I shared in D.C. I cried, and I was intensely happy. I had America and my whole life ahead of me—and, though it wasn't in my mind at the time, in the life I was leaving there was much I was glad to leave. Living with my mother had become a little strained. By my mere presence in a small apartment, I was interfering with her relationships with men. What's more, in my last two years of high school I had banged up one car and totaled another, her favorite, a black Studebaker station wagon with a sliding roof panel. The accidents were due partly to bad luck, partly to inattentiveness, and partly—the big wreck in particular, which could easily have killed me or the other driver—to my new and enthusiastic appreciation for beer and other forms of drink. I'm amazed my mother could still afford insurance. One night during my senior year when I once again came home late and loaded, she looked up from the book she was reading in bed and told me, scowling behind her glasses, "I'll be glad when you're gone."

Drinking was, of course, a tradition of the Daniel Way, and though my mother drank her share while I was growing up in the fifties, the standard setter was my father. When he was home—his work for the AFL-CIO took him frequently on the road—he was often drunk. He had an enormous capacity for beer and bourbon, and up to a point his drink made him wonderfully amiable, a delightful companion for playing cribbage, listening to Beethoven on the hi-fi, or watching the hapless Washington Senators on our black-and-white TV. With a ball game to absorb us, we could talk easily. We could laugh and groan, exult and brood, lean forward in tense anticipation. My father took great pleasure in my command of pitching and batting statistics, gleaned from books and baseball cards. He liked to show off my memory to his friends, and I was gratified to please him.

Franz Daniel was six feet two and two hundred twenty pounds, handsome in a full-faced Teutonic way, and invested with a charismatic past. He had started out to be a Presbyterian minister but found a more compelling religion in the late 1920s—the uplifting of industrial workers through the American labor movement. He followed that calling through a dedicated, tumultuous, and sometimes dangerous career, and liquor fed his zeal. As early as the 1930s, my mother once told me, he was drinking as much as a quart of bourbon or white lightning a day. He spent time in a sanatorium in the late thirties and at Menninger's Clinic in 1965. Though the father I knew was mostly affable in his drunkenness, at any moment he might do something that embarrassed me in front of my friends or the neighbors. He might stagger or slur a sentence or not have his bathrobe all the way closed. You never knew. And, I learned early on, he might at any time do battle with my mother. I lay awake listening more nights than I want to remember, rigidly alert to the rhythm of rising and falling tension, the urgent lowered voices and sudden curses, a hand slamming a table, my father's heavy footsteps on the hardwood floor.

After the split-up—they legally separated in the mid-sixties but never divorced—my father went to live with three of his sisters in Springfield, Missouri, in the country where he had been born and raised. In the summer of 1966, when I was setting out to Reed College, it happened that he had an assignment to organize oil workers in the Four Corners country, so I picked him up in Springfield and we chugged west together in the Jeep. My father had bourbon and water with dinner each night, and in the motels he sat on the side of his bed drinking beer as he read, chin propped on his thumb and a cigarette between his fingers, the ash growing in a long sagging curve and falling to the floor without him noticing. A few weeks after I left him in Farmington, New Mexico, he wandered down to the hotel lobby in his underwear, cursing and wrestling the alcoholic demon that wouldn't leave him be. I think that was his last drinking binge. After drying out in a New Mexico sanatorium, he started going to Alcoholics Anonymous meetings back home in Springfield and remade himself in the last ten years of his life.

But I was through with my father's drinking, through with family pain and acrimony, through with my past as I drove south from Farmington, hit U.S. 66 in Gallup, and turned west again. I was on my own at last, barreling along in a vibrating capsule of engine noise and exhilaration. The southwestern landscape wasn't beautiful to me then—to my eastern eyes it seemed bleak and glary, the vegetation too sparse and not green enough—but it was vast and open, and I was free. I sang Bob Dylan's "Mr. Tambourine Man" over and over, shouting the lyrics above the Jeep's blatting roar—the final verse especially, that extraordinary ode to pure ecstatic solitude.

I was on my way to see my brother in the desert and then to the Pacific Coast, to Big Sur and San Francisco, over the Golden Gate and up through the redwoods and on to Oregon, on to college and the future and the life, whatever it would be, that was supposed to be mine. It makes me smile to see him, that boy I was. He's got a hand on the wheel, a hand on the death's-head gearshift knob, a bucket of coins beside him from a summer of waiting tables, and he's singing himself without memory or fate down the hot asphalt ribbon of Route 66 that stretches ahead of him forever. Is he really me? He seems more like a son than like myself, a son who's reached the age where I don't know him anymore. I don't know him any better than he knows himself. But he's on his way to Oregon, I do know that, and Oregon is where I'm waiting, where I'm writing this spell to speed him on. I haven't seen him for a long time. I need him. But I fear him, too. I can't help feeling that all his hope and blithe enthusiasm should lead him to more than what I am. I can't help feeling that I've let him down.

In the spring of 1988 Marilyn got the job we'd been hoping she would get, with the Oregon Department of Environmental Quality, and we moved to Portland. My mother agreed—readily, it turned out—to come west in the fall and join us. Marilyn and I rented a green Victorian house in the Irvington district with an extra bedroom for my mother, should we need it. Our plan, though, and her preference as we understood it, was that she would live in an apartment in the neighborhood where we could watch after her without unnecessarily cramping her independence. Hunting a place for her was fun. We thought about how many steps she'd have to climb (it had to be none or few), how far she'd have to go for groceries, what kind of view she would have, what sort of people she'd be living among. And it had to be cheap enough that she could live and feed herself on her Social Security check.

We settled on a two-room efficiency in an older brick building only two blocks from our home. Its only drawback was the view, which was mostly of the blank, olive-drab siding of the house next door. Otherwise it seemed perfect—hardwood floors, breakfast nook, little flourishes of trim we knew she would like. She flew to Portland in September, and while I was driving west in a Ryder truck with her goods and furniture, the little Dodge in tow, Marilyn showed her the apartment. My mother didn't speak. She stared at the window, trying to put on a brave face, but clearly shaken. Her apartment in Blue Hill had looked out on spruces full of birds. Everywhere she had lived she'd had a view. And now not only had she been uprooted from one end of the continent to the other, from a landscape and community she loved to a place she knew nothing of, but for the first time in twenty years she was living in a big city.

Yet it was more than that. My mother, as she stood in that bare apartment, was more disoriented than we knew. I can say with some certainty that in that moment she probably couldn't have named the city she was in or what direction it was from the home she had left. She probably couldn't have given the date or day of the week. She would have had a hard time saying, except in very general terms, where her son Jim lived or what her son John was doing at the time. If asked by a stranger why she was there in that apartment in a strange city, she might have said she didn't know. She might not have remembered talking with her son and daughter-in-law about moving west. That new apartment, we know now, was barer and the view blanker than my mother could tell us, or even tell herself.

But with her familiar bed in place—it had been made for her by a friend from planks and timbers seasoned by seacoast weather—and whatever else of her furniture that would fit, she seemed tolerably content. I visited most days to help her arrange her nest—hang a picture, move a table, plug in a new extension cord so that a lamp could go in a different place. I took her grocery shopping, found her a doctor, got her registered to vote. Sometimes we walked a few blocks of the neighborhood. My mother hooted at the Lutheran church's open belfry—"It looks exactly like a *gallows*," she remarked—and she appreciated, as I did, the old maples and horse chestnut trees that had filled their enclosures and buckled the sidewalk slabs with their roots.

Occasionally for lunch we walked to the closest restaurant, the Metropolis on Broadway. It was a small, busy place with good salads and other light fare. We got to know the waitresses, who soon welcomed my mother happily when we appeared. The big black man who bussed dishes, always wearing a brightly colored African cap— bright like my mother's own eclectic clothing—would often stop at our table to talk. My mother's ears were pretty bad by then and she often missed what he said to her, but it didn't matter. She liked him, and she smiled at him, as at many people she knew only slightly or not at all, with a radiant childlike energy. She smiled utterly, from deep within herself, as if words were extraneous to that truer speaking of the spirit. No one who received that smile could fail to be moved by it.

When I see her smiling that way in memory, it's always someone else she's looking at—the dish busser, a doctor, a visitor in our house. Or else I see her delighted at a dog, a dandelion in a sidewalk crack, a robin splashing in a puddle, or something else in the natural world. I don't see her smiling that deepest smile at me, and I suppose I didn't give her my fullest smile either. When I was a baby and a toddler we must have exchanged in that way, but the truth is there wasn't a great deal of warmth between my mother and me as I was growing up. She was not a particularly tender or affectionate mother. I recall her as intense, frank, and aloof, given to gaiety and effusion usually with friends rather than family and usually under the limbering influence of liquor. I don't think I ever doubted her love for me, but she was not a mother—and we were not a family—much given to the demonstration of love.

Of the many things my mother taught me in the last years of her life, that deep smile of the spirit may be the most important. Or not the smile itself, which can't be taught or learned, but the need for it, the poverty of its absence.

But the first thing she taught me—and maybe it's prerequisite to the smile—was patience. The lesson is still far from complete, but my mother got me started. In the Metropolis she would close the menu and pick it up again, not sure what she had decided on; she'd open and close it, pull out her glasses and put them away again. And she would still be eating, glancing around the restaurant with a full fork suspended in air, when I had finished and was tired of drinking coffee and wanted us to be on our way. In Nature's, the grocery market, she dithered over the vegetables, poking among them with one hand as she held on to the cart with the other. And every time she prepared to leave the apartment with me, she would paw through her handbag to be sure her glasses and Kleenex were there, take a sip of cold coffee, look through the bag again, make her way to the bathroom one last time, and finally consent to put on the coat I held for her and walk out the door, her face still wondering if there was something she'd forgotten.

I suppose I had expected my mother to resume her capably independent existence once she had settled in to Portland and her new place. I found, instead, that I was spending considerable time each day taking her on errands and attending to her needs. I tried, not always successfully, to contain my irritation. She didn't know anyone in Portland, after all. She had left behind a loving and loyal band of friends. What's more, she couldn't walk far—especially if she was carrying a burden—and Marilyn and I had resolved that her driving days were over. When she spoke of using her car again, we pointed out how busy the streets were, how fast everyone drove, how different it was from little Blue Hill. "My dear," she sternly informed me, "I have been driving my entire life."

"Well," I told her finally, "to get an Oregon license you'll have to take a written test, you know." I gave her a copy of the driving manual from the Department of Motor Vehicles. She kept it at her bed-side, immersing herself periodically in its plaguing complexities, and after a while she let the issue die. On the surface, at least.

What I saw was my mother losing her powers of judgment, along with her hearing and her strength. What my mother saw, and proba-bly felt more keenly than Marilyn and I appreciated, was the loss of her independence. Of course she wanted to keep driving. To her the little blue Dodge meant freedom, release from her viewless apart-ment in gray and dreary Portland. It was her most tangible link not only to the life she had left in Maine but to her life in its entirety, the life that was slipping from her memory. This was a woman who had spent much of her sixties roaming North America in a Land Rover. A woman who fifty years ago, when the law was after my father for union agitation in Tennessee, had driven him on an eighty-miles-per-hour getaway attempt down a winding highway, pursued by a carful of sheriff's deputies brandishing guns. My father told her to pull over when he saw the deputies aiming at their tires. "*Like hell*," my mother said. He had to coax her into slowing and then stopping the car. As they took my father into custody, the sheriff of Roane County, Tennessee, said to Zilla Daniel in honest admiration: "Ma'am, you are the best woman driver I have ever seen in this county."

I'm certain it injured my mother to give up driving. And I'm equally certain that she and her nicked and scraped-up Dodge wouldn't have lasted a week or even a day on the streets of Portland. The city would have eaten her alive. And so, the child now more pow-erful than the parent, and the parent acting like a child, I enforced my will and tried to make it as palatable as I could. And vowed to myself that I would recognize when I should no longer drive. And knew I probably wouldn't.

My mother couldn't talk about the loneliness and disorientation she must have been feeling. She couldn't talk about it directly, that is. Her way of expressing it was to say flatly, "I think I'll go back home soon. You know, back where I came from."

"Mother," I'd tell her, "you live here now. All your things are here. You're a Portlander."

"But I don't *live* here," she said one day. "I'm only *staying* here."

"Mother, you live here. I know you miss Maine. Maybe we can go back for a visit next year."

"Oh, I don't miss it," she said, frowning her don't-be-silly frown and turning away. I could almost always count on her to deny any feeling I attributed to her, and sometimes that played to my advantage.

But she wasn't happy, I was running myself ragged, and she wasn't getting by very well. I found chicken in her refrigerator cooked on the outside and raw in the middle. When I came over, which usually wasn't till noon or after, she often was unsure if she had taken her blood pressure tablet. Undoubtedly there were days when she took several and days when she took none. I marked the bottle "Take One Every Morning" in big letters, but it didn't seem to help. She was sick a lot that fall, an easy mark for West Coast viruses she hadn't been exposed to before. In December she was so ill that Marilyn slept over in the apartment. Independent living wasn't working.

One evening around Christmas, after dinner at our house, my mother said again that she was ready to go back home.

"Well, Zilla," said Marilyn, "here's another idea. We have a room upstairs. Would you consider living with us?"

"Why *yes*," said my mother. "Why didn't we think of this before?"

I n January we moved my mother into our house. And in January Marilyn said to me, "I feel as though I'm carrying a little ball of light."

I remember lowering the *Atlantic* I'd been reading, looking at her in the glow of what she'd spoken. As I went to her I saw through the window the outspread arms of Douglas firs two blocks away, stirring fluidly, soundlessly, against the pewter sky. And later, on the way to the store to buy something for dinner, I drove slowly, splashing leisurely through puddles in my mother's car, my usual impatience with traffic entirely abolished. Let others rush if they needed to. I was slowing the world from within myself. What hurry could there possibly be? In such happiness, what hurry?

We'd been trying to have a baby for four years without a hint of luck. After the first year, as it became evident that merely forsaking birth control was not going to do the trick, we gave ourselves up to the techniques of fertility. We scheduled love for biologically propitious moments, developing a nuanced eye for the gradations of blue by which ovulation-detection kits measure the female cycle. For a time we relinquished the task of insemination to a nurse named Ruth, who capped Marilyn's cervix with a dose of semen I produced at home and Marilyn kept warm between her legs as she drove to the clinic. "Here's hubby!" chirped Ruth as she did her work. Back at home, smiling sweetly, my wife quipped that she and Ruth would make a lovely baby together.

To find out if her fallopian tubes were open and functioning, Marilyn first endured a procedure that shot her full of dye, and then a laparoscopy, in which a doctor actually pokes around the reproductive system with seeing-eye equipment, ascertaining firsthand the inner conditions and snipping away any troubles. Marilyn's system was fine, but she was left miserably nauseated by the anesthetic. For my part, I rendered samples on demand, learned a new word—"motility"—and had the satisfaction of knowing that my little swimmers had proven themselves capable of penetrating the ovum of a hamster. But my sperm count was marginally low, and so I switched to boxer shorts and had a varicosity removed from my scrotum. (Too much blood warmth kills sperm.) In the course of the operation I needed two additional shots of spinal anesthetic, and even with those I could feel the surgeon pressing and tugging as he discussed California wines with the anesthesiologist. Neither of them noticed, but I did, when the music system piped in Willie Nelson singing, *"All of me, why not take all-l-l of me . . ."*

Each new step in the process seemed to promise success, but the magical microscopic union never happened—or if it did, it didn't prosper. The experience was intensely frustrating. The gift that most couples receive merely by rolling over in bed was being withheld from us, like the fruit of Tantalus, even after we had engineered ourselves into the most efficient reproductive machines we could be. Marilyn had children already, two boys near adulthood by her first marriage, but I had none. In my twenties I had wanted none, but now, in my late thirties, married and at last with a sense of vocation, I wanted a child passionately. I felt aggrieved, unjustly denied. Most of my friends had children, my brother had a daughter, the streets of Portland were filled with laughing kids in bright clothing. I had the irrational sense that I'd been reduced to a cipher. Life comes of life, said the emotional logic—if you can't produce a life you aren't alive.

One night, in our third year of trying, I had a dream. A certain few of my dreams have a numinous presence by which I understand that something of primary value is being revealed. They usually occur soon after I fall asleep, and usually they are composed not of a narrative sequence but of a single image. I think of them as sleep visits, or visions, rather than as dreams. This was of that kind. I saw a baby with upraised arms, cradled in darkness, glowing with a soft light and loosely wrapped in glowing strands. When I woke—I wake immediately from these visions—I took it as a sign that a child was on its way to us, but instantly I doubted that interpretation. I had a troubling sense that my desire had awakened me too soon, a moment before the vision was fully born. I didn't know if it boded well or if I merely wanted it to bode well. The light around the baby might have been the holy spirit; it might have been the subdued glare of a hospital ward. It might, I felt for some reason, be radiation. The glowing strands could have been drawing the new life to this world. And they could have been the tubes and wires of life support.

And so, after four years of hope and frustration, in a new home in a new city, with my mother newly arrived in our household, we learned that we would have a child. Marilyn, who was forty-two at the time, knew the risks—Down's syndrome, spina bifida, the possible necessity of a late abortion. I knew them too, in my mind, but my excitement overwhelmed all worries. I was giddily eager. I read *A Child Is Born*, poring over the photographs of embryonic and fetal development, astonished at what happens as a conception evolves through fish and amphibian and reptile to the human. I bugled the news to all our friends and family. I hadn't been so happy since I was a boy. It felt as if I were on the threshold of completion, as if my family, fractured in my childhood, were verging on a rebirth into wholeness. I wished my father were alive, and almost felt he was.

I was cheerfully evasive in breaking the news to my mother. "Now that you're living here," I said one night at dinner, "how would you feel about more family moving in?"

"Jim?" she asked.

"No, I don't think Jim can leave California. Someone else."

She puzzled, looking at her plate and out the window, her jaw set.

"Someone new," I said. "Someone little."

"*John Daniel*," said my mother. "Don't be coy."

"You're going to be a grandmother again," I told her. "Marilyn and I are going to have a baby."

Her mouth opened. "You aren't," she said, looking back and forth between the two of us, smiling her deepest, childlike smile.

"We are," said Marilyn.

"Oh, that's wonderful," my mother said, lowering her eyes to her plate and eating again. Clearly she was touched, but I also felt a hesitance in her response, a joy withheld or absent—as if she didn't completely comprehend what we had told her, or as if she understood it all too well, as if she had glimpsed a future that I couldn't or wouldn't allow myself to see.

We couldn't see the baby's heartbeat when we went in for the first ultrasound examination, but the technician and the doctor weren't disturbed. It was nothing unusual. But then Marilyn began spotting, then cramping, and on Valentine's Day we lost the child. "The blood ran out of me," Marilyn would write in her journal. "A steady stream for a while—stop—a cramp and another stream. Soon I could feel the distorted rhythm of it. My late child. My Elizabeth slipping from me. February 14, 1989."

It's best she wasn't born, of course. It's best he wasn't born. Something was wrong in the making, something was flawed in the seed, something ended the life at six weeks. I dwell on possibilities. I think of the sixties propaganda about LSD damaging chromosomes and how I scoffed at it. I think of x-rays, of radiation from a thousand sources. I think of coffee, whiskey, tobacco, marijuana, pesticides, chlorine, all the billions of molecules that have entered my body and perhaps done nothing, perhaps done harm. And of course I remember that nature itself is flawed and lives by its mistakes. Nature itself is extravagant with conceptions, stingy with achieved lives. The story of an offspring that isn't to be is the commonest story in the world, a necessary story, a story that has to be true so that other stories, happier stories, can also turn out true. I know all that, but I also know what *nature* means. It's from the past participle of a Latin verb, and the verb means *to be born.*

We told my mother when we got home from the clinic. She reached out her hands, one to each of us, and we sat linked together in silence. I was feeling a kind of numb grief, but something else more strongly. It overcomes me whenever I suffer a major disappointment. It's the most debilitating feeling I know. It's not really a feeling at all but a lack of feeling, a repudiation, a cold mockery of feeling's failure. *This is the truth,* it tells me, *this is reality. Your hopes and expectations were foolish. You have deluded yourself again. Others may achieve their desires but you will not achieve yours, simply because you are you. You will not succeed because you are not worthy. You are not worthy. You are not worthy.*

It was in the late 1930s that my mother and father began to think of having children, or at least my mother did. They had been married since 1934 and had been involved with each other for another four years before that, but throughout the thirties they had lived together only intermittently. Both had been leading rootless, independent lives as labor agitators and organizers in the East and the South, constantly on the move from one unionizing campaign to another. My father had transferred his religious passion from Union Theological Seminary in New York, where he had studied with Reinhold Niebuhr, to the social gospel and the streets of working America. A man of books and opera and philosophical argument, his hands and body bore the scars of numerous fights with scab workers and company goons. His greatest gift, by all accounts, was as a speaker. Whether soapboxing to a few uncertain workers on a street corner or addressing a rally of two thousand, he could bring the brotherhood of man to life in his words. He was a catalyst, a pinch hitter, a man the union chiefs called in on their hardest campaigns and those that needed a shot of new fervor.

My father was a Socialist party organizer in Philadelphia when my mother met him, and she fell hard both for him and for the union cause. A descendant of Pennsylvania suffragists, she attended Kent Place School for Girls in Summit, New Jersey ("Where Manners Maketh Man," the motto went), and Vassar College, where she majored in English. After graduation she became interested in the labor movement and took a job in the necktie sweatshops of Philadelphia, at six dollars a week, to see what working-class life was like. She taught at Highlander Folk School in Tennessee, then as now a beacon of social activism, and along with my father she took up the challenge of organizing clothing and textile workers in the South. She would go into little mill towns in Tennessee and the Carolinas, frequently alone, and quietly make contacts, feeling out the chances for unionization. Decades later, when she was interviewed for an oral history called *Refuse to Stand Silently By*, she said that she hadn't been afraid for herself but for the workers, who risked being fired for the least taint of union activity. "So I tried to be careful and to be honest about it," she told the interviewer. "I was asking them to take a big chance. . . . The company almost owned many of them. Often there was a company store and they always owed something, so their pay was always goose eggs: zero, zero, zero. Week after week after week."

Her one great success came in 1933, at the Liebovitz plant in Knoxville, Tennessee, where she succeeded in organizing the first Amalgamated Clothing Workers local in the South. For the most part, though, her work could not overcome the very long odds against it. On several occasions she was arrested and jailed. Once, when she called for a union election in Greenville, South Carolina, crosses were burned on the lawns of local activists. And on an organizing mission in Anderson, another South Carolina town, my mother was fired on in her car by deputies with shotguns. *That* scared her. "My knees shook so much on the way back, I wasn't sure I could keep my foot on the accelerator," she told the interviewer. "But I think you can't function if you are going to allow yourself to be fearful. I didn't give it any thought because fear is a negative emotion."

My mother and father had no home base in those years and didn't organize together. They spent what time together they could, a week here and a day or two there. He had told her before they were married that the labor movement would always come first, and it did. In a letter I found recently, my mother mentions two abortions. She doesn't say when they occurred, but it must have been during that intense activism of the thirties, when caring for a baby would have been unthinkable. I have no idea where she went for the operations, who performed them, or how. Abortion was illegal then, very likely dangerous, and almost certainly a wretchedly degrading experience. My mother's letter gives no sense of how she felt about ending two pregnancies that way. My guess is that she saw it as part of the price one had to pay to be involved in a mission of grand idealistic purpose with a man she loved and admired, a man who expected her to be emotionally self-sufficient and all for the cause.

Soon after she turned thirty, though, my mother realized—or resolved—that she wanted to have children. It took her a while to convince my father, but in 1940, while he was troubleshooting for the Laundry Workers Union in New York and they were living in Greenwich Village, she became pregnant and quit the labor movement. The pregnancy ended in a miscarriage, and she fell into a deep depression—from losing the baby but also from losing her freewheeling labor career. "I remember being so depressed I sat in a chair and couldn't get out of it," she told me years later, when she was sixty-nine. A doctor recommended electric shock treatment, but my father vetoed that. His rising star in the labor movement carried them on to New Orleans, where they rented a second-floor apartment in the French Quarter with a wrought-iron balustrade and bedbugs in the mattress. There they lived happily in a circle of progressive intellectual bons vivants. "All those lovely bars," my mother recalled. "I just decided I'd try every one of them."

Before long she was pregnant again, and before long they were back in Philadelphia, where my father worked as a city organizer. George Hawes Daniel was born in the early morning of September 29, 1943, after a long labor during which my mother, as she would write to my father's sister Margaret, "raised a terrific ruckus. For once I lost all inhibitions, and kicked and howled and even bit my arm." The impatient obstetrician finally ended it by hauling little George out with a pair of forceps, raising a temporary knot on his head for which my father almost killed him. For a couple of days, every time the nurse brought George to my mother, she and he promptly fell asleep. It had been well worth the siege of labor, she wrote Margaret, to have produced a fine, blond-haired baby who resembled nothing so much as a small suckling pig.

The little pig grew into a happy and healthy child who delighted his parents. My mother's letters over the next few months give off a glow of satisfaction in the minutia of baby tending, and my father, for his part, absolutely doted on Georgie. The tough labor fighter rocked his son on one arm as he made formula, my mother wrote, and laughed with pure joy when the baby cracked a toothless smile. My father was not quite forty and in his prime when George was born. It's both lovely and a little painful, as I read his and my mother's letters, to imagine him dandling his child, cooing at him, showing him elephants at the circus, ducks and sheep in the Pennsylvania countryside. By the time I had arrived and was growing up, my father was turning fifty, an aging warrior nursing his many emotional wounds. He was reserved and remote, given to long brooding silences. I never knew—or at least I don't remember—the young fatherly zest, tender and a little goofy, that little George drew out of him. I don't think Jim knew it either. My mother once told me that George was the only human being my father ever loved absolutely, without stay or condition.

I love him too, in my own way. I think about him often; I think I might owe my life to him. I carry his picture in my wallet, as if he were not my brother but my son. And there are times, like tonight, when I get out all the pictures, all the curling, creased, black-and-white snapshots I'm grateful to my father and mother for taking. I spread them on my desk and try once again to see through their aging glossy surfaces into the boy himself, this golden-haired child who is not me, not Jim, but a whole other blending and reforming of my mother and father, a whole other Daniel starting out in his life, picking up the kindling my father splits and piling it into his wagon. It's fall and he has just turned three, he is wearing a light canvas jacket and a dark watch cap with his hair flowing down on his forehead almost to his eyes. His striped t-shirt is rumpled, one strap of his overalls is loose, his eyes are downcast and he is smiling a slightly off-center smile as if he has finished a long day's work that he thinks of now with both pleasure and pain. He is only a boy of three years, but there is something about him as old as anything alive.

He is loading his wagon in front of a white tenant's cottage in the country near Wellford, South Carolina, where his parents have moved from Philadelphia with him and his baby brother Jim— *Jimmy Dan'l*, as George likes to say—and a hound dog called South Caroline. They arrived in August and now it is fall. Oak leaves lie strewn on the ground, there must be a chill in the air as his father in a sweater splits kindling and he gathers it up. It's the end of October now, and in just a few days or perhaps today little George will cough and run a slight fever. He's fine, the pediatrician will say, he's fine, but four days later, on November 4, he will start to choke. His father has taken the car to work, there is no phone in the cottage, his mother will scream for Mrs. Ponder up at the big house and run there with George in a blanket, choking, and they will drive as fast as they can to a doctor ten miles away but always, every time she relives it the rest of her life, her firstborn child will die in her arms before they arrive.

Laryngeal tracheal bronchitis was the cause of death, as my mother remembered it. A common infection that in some few cases achieves a critical mass, an exponential explosion that rapidly overwhelms its host. A fulminating infection, one doctor called it—meaning, literally, an illness that strikes like lightning.

The doctor they had reached too late was the local mill doctor, and he refused to sign the death certificate. My mother and father had to find George's pediatrician for that. Numb with shock, they made phone calls to family and friends. The next day they arranged for a small service at a funeral home in Spartanburg. Labor friends drove down from Philadelphia, my father's sister Berthe arrived. Neighbors who despised my father's work came by with gifts of food. The local preacher stopped in several times and was very kind, my mother recalled, but mostly she remembered two things from the aftermath of George's death. She remembered sitting on the porch for hours at a time with little Jim in her arms, rocking and rocking. And she remembered the train. My father was out drinking with his friend Wes Cook, balming his pain in his usual way, when the train left town with George in his small coffin, bound for Atlanta and the crematorium. My mother knew what time it would leave, she heard it pass, and in that moment she felt herself collapse inside—she felt void, she said, just utterly void, as the train whistle sounded and died away.

It's like sleepiness without being tired. My eyes don't close but my awareness does; it folds up the way some flowers do at night. All it knows how to do is play the carousel of doubts and second-guessings. I'm forty-five years old. I have gray hair. I wear jeans and t-shirts as if I were a kid. I don't have a child. I call myself a poet, a writer. What have I written? I make less than twenty thousand. I weigh too much. I'm a writer but not a great writer. I don't know who I am. I wasn't patient enough with my mother. I didn't help her enough. I don't know what I feel. I sleep too late. I don't have a real job. I don't get enough done. I don't spend enough time with my wife. I don't have a child. I don't know what I'm doing. I have gray hair.

I'm angry at an editor for turning me down, but even my anger is dampened, dulled by a low gray sky. I'm sunk down inside myself. A chickadee takes a sunflower seed from the feeder, holds it against a birch limb, hammers it with his bill. I watch, but there's some screen, some invisible smoke between us. He lives on the birch limb, but he doesn't live in me. He takes another seed, hammers it, flies out of the window view. The chickadee is what I was. As lively. As gone.

Thoreau says in his journal that he values his melancholy moods. "Be as melancholy as you can be," he says, "and note the result." He says there's a "certain fertile sadness" that he seeks, a sadness that saves his life from being trivial. Well, fine for you, Henry. Mine must be a different kind—an infertile cross, a mule of a sadness. It makes my life seem trivial and nothing but. It's certainly not melancholy. It has nothing of the music of those four syllables, the minor-key chant they make in the mouth. It's flat, just plain flat and heavy. Old snow specked with dirt.

My psychologist has been asking about the part of me that doubts and second-guesses, that tells me I'm not worthy. Who's saying that, she wants to know. *I'm* saying it, I told her at first, and what's wrong with it? I hold myself to standards. Self-criticism helps me get things done, helps me do things better. But I knew the lie of it even as I said it. It's when I'm *happy* that I get things done, because I love doing them. This mood only dulls me. It leaves me slouched in my chair.

Listen to that voice, she says. How does it come to you? Whose voice is it? Well, it's a male voice. And it's someone older than me, someone in authority. Not my father, not any teacher or boss I've had. No one I've known at all. He's a stranger, and yet he knows everything about me. The more I pay attention, the more military he seems. (That's one of the things he nails me on: I never served, never proved myself in battle.) He's not a drill sergeant, not a general. Not even active duty—he's retired. Only a retired man would have so much time. He's always watching me. He observes, he remembers even the smallest things I've done wrong, or may have done wrong. Last night I lay awake till 3:00 A.M. watching a Halloween party ten years ago at Stanford University. The night was well along, I was two or three sheets to the wind, I climbed over a raised kitchen hearth to get around a clog of partiers to the living room. My sneaker hit a blue-and-white bowl, and glancing back, very quickly in my drunken hurry, I couldn't tell if I had broken it or only rattled it.

Why do I lie awake ten years later worrying—*worrying*—about a bowl I may or may not have broken at a party? Because I didn't go back to check, as I should have? Because I was drunker than I should have been? Because I need to learn that when I'm wildly happy I'm careless, and things get broken? Or what? The observer who insists I remember doesn't tell me why I should remember. He doesn't even know if I broke the bowl (or does he?). He only says that I was wrong, I was wrong, and he'd be derelict if he didn't call it to my attention. It's not his *job*, exactly. He doesn't work for anyone. But it seems to be his discipline, his preoccupation, his self-appointed office. It's what he does. I think I'll call him the Inspector.

The chickadee is at the feeder again. He has his own preoccupation, but his is natural and right. His gives him sustenance. The Inspector only wears me down.

But it's not the Inspector I want to think of now. I'm sitting at my desk in Henry Thoreau's spirit, trying to see if my sadness might be fertile after all. To see if it might grow something. What's coming to me is a winter afternoon by the Potomac River, near one of Washington's memorial parks. I think it's the Jefferson. I'm a senior in high school. My friend is taking pictures for the yearbook, of which I'm editor, and I'm watching the dark river with my hands in my pockets against the cold, watching the gray sky with its pale glow of late sun in the west. My face—*his* face, that boy of seventeen's face—is smooth and unlined. His curly brown hair is my hair, and there is no gray in it. His lean body is my own, thirty pounds lighter, and I know the familiar way it feels in the cold, the way it firms and tenses, scrotum tight, how shivers turn its tension to a shaky warmth.

I know some things about that boy. I know he reads a lot, he does his homework, he gets straight A's. His way of life is to please people, older people, and he's good at it. He cherishes the praise of teachers and fears he'll disappoint them, fears they'll see into the emptiness he covers with words and smiles. He smokes cigarettes, even though they made him sick at first. He's lonely. He doesn't talk much except when he's excited or drunk. He drinks at parties, dances in the warm melee with no one in particular, sometimes stumbles out to sprawl on the grass as everything spins and his stomach heaves. He's had a few dates but never had sex. He envies his friends who have, or who act like they have. If asked, he might tell you he wants to be a historian. Inside he wants to be a writer, but he worries he has nothing to write about. If he has a deep desire he doesn't know what it is. He has always been in school and assumes he'll go on in school, reading what he's told to read and bringing home the A's, riding the escalator his parents put him on when he was five—the escalator that surely is taking him somewhere, that surely will deliver him in the fullness of time to the life and career of a man who knows what he is doing and belongs in the world.

I know these things about the boy, but I don't know what he's thinking as he stands on a walkway above the Potomac in the wan light of a winter afternoon. I don't know whether he's happy or sad, whether he's content to be waiting as his friend takes pictures, or else bored and restless and wishing he could leave. But this is what he does. There is a figured stone parapet between him and the river, and his gaze lights where a little skiff of snow has caught in the carving. One shape of snow among several, unremarkable. But he stares at it. He stares harder. What he sees takes on a strangeness. Why should that shape of snow be just the way it is? He wants to burn the image into his memory, to photograph it. He wants to have it always, exactly as it is, just so. He feels a flood of light within him. He stares longer, his eyes watering. He wants to be absolutely sure the image is his, a part of him forever, exactly as it now lives in the world.

Why? Why did he want that? Why did that image glow so intensely for him? Why was he so concerned with clarity and permanence, perfection of memory? It's as though he had a message to send, and he could only send it coded in a clear image, perfectly preserved, through years and decades to the adult he could not know but knew he must become. But what? What was the message? He relied on me to understand, but I'm failing him. I'm standing there above the river, I'm staring at the parapet, the snow. I see tones of white and gray, snow and stone, I see the quality of light, I think, but I've let the image go out of focus. I don't see the exact shape of the little drift, I don't see the specific figuring of the parapet, the texture of the stone. It's murky, mocked up, like the scenery in a dream if you look at it hard. I have only a blurred estimate of a thing the boy wanted passionately to secure undiminished, undiffused.

Is it inevitable to lose like that? Does memory give up its clarity the same way hair gives up its color, skin gives up its moisture, muscle and bone give up their green resilience? Is memory losing focus as my outward vision has, forcing me to wear these twelve-dollar reading glasses that Bob Bourgeois bought at the drugstore, that keep slipping down my nose as I write and blurring the entire world when I look up from the page? What I want to believe is that the soul builds itself from the experience of life, that it makes a thing of lasting wholeness, a monument unseen from without, and memory is what we see from inside it. But what I feel isn't a building, it's a wearing down. My memories lie scattered in pieces. If it's a monument it's in poor repair, and the city where it stands is deserted.

I started noticing lapses about the time my mother came to live with us. I'd walk into the kitchen or my study and forget for a moment what I'd come for. I'd forget to tell Marilyn that her father called. I'd make a list and forget to take it to the store. I suppose memory does decline with age; I suppose it must, like everything else. And then, for some like my mother, it plunges near the end. And what about the end? Can all that living, all that accumulated seeing and doing of a lifetime, can it all go dark—lights out, gone? Surely there's at least a zone of fade, the mind slowly going dim like the light in a dying animal's eye. And maybe memory comes back at the end, maybe it's all restored, everything—but dissolving into gray form-lessness, a sea of shaped particulars melting down, moving vaguely with what was their life as all light ebbs away. Fog. Final fog, and nothing. And where then is this soul I want to have? Where does the monument stand? And what can it be made of?

A light rain is falling, slanting without sound. The chickadee's back, perky in his black cap. He takes one seed again, always one. He has a leisurely way of cracking it, a patient hammering: *tap . . . tap-tap*. The sparrows and finches feed in gangs, standing in the tray and spraying seed as they scratch and peck. I like the chickadee. He's a loner. He comes to the tray for one good seed, and that's enough. I did keep a promise to myself. Thirty years later, I did remember. The boy got through to me, and maybe it sounds a little silly, but I feel a kind of awe at that, and gratitude. The shape of snow on stone hardly mat-ters as much as he does, and though the image of what he saw has weathered in memory, the boy is true. Snow melts, stone wears away. Everything, including me, is made of time. But the boy stands faithfully by the dark Potomac, filled with a brilliant clarity, as intent and changeless as a god, pouring himself into the passion of his seeing.

D_{inner was the} one meal that my mother and Marilyn and I usually ate together, and it often began with a Sanskrit food prayer my mother had learned in India. We held hands as she sang. The prayer began with a long *Om* that started deep in her chest and slid up the scale to a soft, wavering height that she held as long as she had breath. After four short verses in that higher range the song ended with another *Om*, sung the same way, and then *Shanti* three times, the last syllable of the last *Shanti* taken up a tone, then trailing downward to silence. We held the peace of that silence a few seconds before squeezing hands and opening our eyes to dinner.

Though in her last years she forgot much of the life she had lived, many of the people she had known, and most of what she might have read an hour before in the newspaper, my mother never forgot that song of prayer. She never faltered in singing it. It seemed that she had taken it into her deepest being, and there it rested unassailable. I think that song was the culmination, the fruit and final harvest, of the spiritual journey of her life.

I don't know as much about that journey as I would like to know, but I did understand something of it as she was living it, and I've been gleaning more from her letters and writings. Her father being a minister, she must have grown up in at least a thin atmosphere of Christian spirituality—though Unitarianism, as I experienced it in the occasional services and Sunday school sessions my parents took me to, seemed more of an intellectual coffee klatch than a religion. My mother would eventually tell an interviewer that she had found it arid and uninspiring. As with my father, who was a confirmed agnostic, some of her spiritual energy went into the labor movement of the 1930s, but unionism didn't remain for her the all-consuming, millenarian mission it was for him. I think that she, as I would later do, followed her hunger outward into the natural world. For my father, nature was primarily the scenic backdrop to the drama of human history. For my mother it was a balm, an excitement, a mystery.

In 1953, the year I turned five, my father's work took us from Charlotte, North Carolina, out to Denver. My mother, then forty-five, had never seen the West before. I remember her driving Jim and me to the open amphitheater at Red Rocks for shows of one kind or another, and sometimes she took us up toward Loveland Pass for a dinner cooked in a cast-iron skillet and eaten under the stars. I remember, or I think I do, the pleasure she took in sandstone pinnacles and mountain vistas. If the coast of Maine was the first landscape my mother loved, the Colorado Rockies were the second. She told me once that the years following my birth in 1948, with Jim and me healthy and the awful grief at George's death subsiding, were the happiest of her marriage. To then come to a place of such sublime natural splendor must have made her joy complete.

But it wasn't to last. We had been in Colorado for not even a year when my father was appointed Assistant Director of Organization in the newly merged AFL-CIO, and we picked up and moved to Washington, D.C. My mother practically had a breakdown, she told me years later. She wept as she packed and wept as we moved, until my father finally told her to buck up because he didn't want his friends to see her that way. He made the same demand on several other occasions during their marriage—he was going through a difficult time, he would tell her, he was under a lot of stress and needed her to be strong. In my own memory I have a faded image from our Denver house of my mother leaning against a doorway, crying. The first harsh words I remember them exchanging came at that time. I didn't know then what the arguing was about. I only knew that they both were angry and my mother was sad.

She would return to the Rockies, though not to Colorado, nearly two decades later, after the marriage had foundered, Jim and I had left the broken nest, and she had reached the age when she could retire from the union work she had resumed but cared little for by then. The late sixties had a liberating effect on my mother. Unlike the many of her generation who reacted against the tumult and excesses of the counterculture, my mother learned from it and in her own way joined in. "If I have a cause these days," she wrote to my brother in 1967, "it is the young. We have nowhere to go, unless we follow your paths." When I told her, in the middle of my first year at Reed, that I had been taking LSD, she was intensely interested in my experiences. I don't think she ever took a psychedelic herself, but I think she may have smoked some grass along the way—though not habitually—and she was looking in the same direction we drug takers were looking. "I'm going to read *The Doors of Perception*," she wrote in a letter. "Opening those doors has attracted me for a long time. I try in many ways."

One way she tried was in writing poems. She read poetry throughout her life and worked at her own verses now and again for several decades. Her efforts didn't satisfy her, and few drafts remain. One that does, written probably when she was in her forties, expresses in uneasy union the passion of a sensualist and a spiritual seeker's yearning for transcendence:

> [My blood] runs with the grace of a mountain stream
> and my breath at dusk is a smoke of balsam
> to one whose arms are sinews of my love,
> whose hands know how to bless a thousand ways,
> whose lips are sweet and [illegible]
> in the blue-flamed candle melting time's deep fog.
>
> And so I cry with laughter at the clumsiness
> of death's bravado
> when a pale gold scimitar dangles above my window
> in a sea-green sky,
> for I have ample warmth for others
> but only a spark to fire the fences of my blindness,
> and in the beauty of their burning learn, perhaps,
> it is not death to die.

After retirement my mother took a long voyage on a freighter—to Africa, I think—and vagabonded around the U.S. and Canada in a Land Rover she called the Green Seal. In 1970 she settled for what would be five years in Kaslo, British Columbia, on Kootenay Lake in the Canadian Rockies. For two of those years she holed up in semi-seclusion in a small cottage accessible only by boat. I know she read and studied Carl Jung's collected writings during that time—"hard going," she wrote my brother, "and will become much harder because I intend to pursue it until I find the Self." In the handwriting of her letter, "Self" was first written with a small s, then corrected with a capital. The voyage of self-realization she saw herself launching was at the same time an act of self-reformation. Her reading of Jung persuaded her that the masculine side of her psyche, because she had refused to accept it, had been acting itself out in rebellious and some-times spiteful behavior throughout her life, perplexing her relationships with men—her father and husband especially. She vowed to soften her hard edges and tame her angers, a quest she would follow, with mixed results, the rest of her years.

Solitude, her reading, and no doubt the glory of her surroundings seem to have opened a mystical awareness in my mother, or at least set off a mystical seeking in words. The rebellious Vassar intellectual and gritty union organizer was now, in her sixties, meditating, reading the Upanishads and other sacred literatures of the East, and writing verses such as these:

> If I see something I dislike
>   let me look deeper
> if I hear something displeasing
>   let me listen with my inner ear
>
> for the Heart of all Being assumes
>   forms inconceivable to us
> and beats with an almost imperceptible
>   gentleness.

In 1975 her evolving religious imagination led her out of solitude to the Findhorn spiritual community on the north coast of Scotland, where she prepared meals, cleaned the Sanctuary, and worked in Publications—"with Boris the binder (who screeches) and Guinevere the guillotine paper cutter." I don't know specifically what attracted her there. She may not have known herself. I do think she was interested in reports that some individuals at Findhorn had communicated with the Devas, or nature spirits. And I think she probably felt a need for a church, a fellowship, some kind of shared structure for her religious feeling.

My mother's early letters from Findhorn teem with a thrilled excitement in the community and its setting—she was living near the sea, on a sparsely settled coast something like Maine's—and with a sense of inadequacy in the company of persons she considered more

spiritually advanced than she was. The feeling of inferiority seemed
to pass, though, in the course of group meditations she found enormously powerful. She wrote, "I sort of watch myself developing in
unexpected ways, and wonder, is this *me?*" Her new sense of wholeness, she wrote, "is not a passive state and cannot be experienced
alone, but a positive, irradiating process of entering into others and
interweaving with them in daily acts which thereby become fulfill-
ing; a process of discovering cracks and knotholes into openings of
communion with other realms."

A photograph in a 1976 issue of the Findhorn newsletter shows
her kneeling in a simple shift with a group of gardeners, both hands
on her spading fork, an easy laughing smile on her face. She looks
more relaxed and content than I remember ever seeing her. Typically, she is older by twenty or thirty years than anyone else in the
picture.

On my birthday that year, my mother wrote a card in which she
thanked me for choosing her and my father to be my parents. She
would express the same idea in various ways the rest of her life. Nothing, she came to believe, occurs by chance, and each of us is responsible for everything that happens to us. Human existence is a school
that the Self puts itself through, and the Self creates the curriculum
it needs for its own advancement. Little George came and died, my
mother now believed, to teach her humility and acceptance. Because
of her rebellious willfulness, the lesson had to be harshly dealt.
George had the look of age in his young face because he was an old
soul, a soul capable of enduring the wrenching transition of entering
and quickly departing the flesh. He had reincarnated into the world,
my mother was advised in a spiritual reading. She would very likely
meet and recognize him, and when she did she must say nothing.

A skeptic might argue that my mother had merely contrived a
shelter of spiritual trappings to help her endure the ongoing pain—
a pain that must have contained much guilt—of Georgie's death. It
may be so. But even though I don't believe in reincarnation—not in

any coherent way, at least—I find her view of the Self and its education compelling. Not illuminating, but compelling. I was twenty-eight in 1976. Within three months of my birthday and my mother's card thanking me for choosing her as my parent, I crushed my right ankle in a rock-climbing fall, my father died, and a five-year relationship with a girlfriend ended abruptly and painfully. What did I need to learn, I wondered, that required such devastating lessons so closely bunched? What in my education was I being a bonehead about? Something to do with loss, obviously. Something to do with limits. Something—if there's any lesson at all—I still don't see.

My mother, ever restless, returned to the States in 1977 and traveled for most of two years. "Will it ever end?" she wrote. "I am propelled, or drawn, and it is as it is. Innerly I'm beginning to create the little place 'to be.'" Findhorn friends and the power of her first love led her to the Maine coast in 1978, and there she settled. There, from my ample distance, she seemed to have found the wholeness of living that had been eluding her. Village life suited her independent disposition, yet she was part of a community of friends who loved and respected her. She worked at *WoodenBoat*, raised a garden, read much, wrote some, and rowed among loons and seals in her skiff, the *Lully Lulay*. She became ordained in a New Age church and performed wedding ceremonies for friends. In her letters she began to refer to herself as a Wager of Peace, and, inspired by a John Gould column in the *Christian Science Monitor*, she sometimes signed them "yr. Esteemed Old Geezer, Mom Zilla."

Spiritually, though, she was still seeking. She went to dowsers' meetings in Maine and Vermont and took up some of their techniques, including the use of a pendulum to receive guidance from energies transcending the personal. For a while—I don't know if this came from the dowsers or from a different source—she wrote me about "entities," or alien presences, that she had discovered and was clearing from her mind and also my mind and my brother's. Though I've known since the 1960s that I have plenty of strange things in my head, I had a hard time relating to this direction of her quest. It seemed too technical and negatively focused. My own diffuse sense of spirituality acknowledged no need for cleansing, no threat of anything alien. All of nature, all of being, was my church. What could be alien? Her talk of "entities" sounded like science fiction to me.

I had a hard time in the mideighties, too, when Findhorn folk told my mother of a holy man doing good works in India and she decided she must go to him. My own religious inclinations tilt away from gurus. I don't feel I need an anointed human to show me the sacredness of life and things, and I don't trust the fanatical devotion that arises around some gurus. Humans distort truth, sometimes deliberately, sometimes for gain. Nature distorts nothing. I'd sooner take a river or a Douglas fir for a spiritual teacher, and I had thought my mother felt the same.

But Sai Baba seemed to answer a hunger in her that nothing else had. She believed him to be a true avatar, a perfect realization of the Divine in human form. He was her final resting place, the end of her journey. Twice in her late seventies she traveled to his ashram, near Bangalore in southern India, and each time she stayed several weeks, living a monastic life. She and a traveling companion were granted a personal interview with Sai Baba, an infrequent occurence. Upon her return from each pilgrimage she wrote a series of remarkable devotional meditations, some of them in the form of letters addressed to "Satya Sai Baba" or "God" or "SSB." She thanks him, in some of the writings, for the help of his love in her efforts to make pure her "imperfect, flawed self." The flaws she notes have to do with prejudice and self-superiority, her tendency to respond to differences between her and others rather than to commonalities. But other meditations, such as this one, are psalms of pure joy:

Dawn outlines the window of my worship room. I go downstairs, and as I watch the sun come up and turn the bare trees into pillars of light, it comes over me, "He does this, the sun circling, the stars and galaxies in their courses." The flames of the fire begin to leap up, also His, warming the room where intriguing frost patterns, never two the same, are slow in fading from the window—His also. It is overwhelming, and I am awestruck, that mankind should be so fortunate, living on his parent-planet, to have also been created as the most perfected of animals, because You were lonely and needed an activity of this immensity to throw Your immeasurable energies into. It is unfathomable, but I make no attempt to even try. It is simply so. Furthermore, You made me with my own measure of Godhead, inscrutably estimated from my innumerable lives, for which infinite gratitude fills me with Your Love, which I humbly accept as Your most wonderful gift of all.

Until my mother became too weak, she attended meetings of Sai Baba's devotees in Portland. She read and reread her books of his talks and sayings, underlining passages in pen. She kept pictures of him in her room and in her wallet. She kept a vial of *vibhuti*—sacred ash from Sai Baba's ashram—in her purse, where it frequently spilled and made a mess; sometimes she placed a dab of it on her forehead between her eyes. And she sang her blessing song at dinner, surely, beautifully, from deep within.

My mother found something, something she needed. One night when I picked her up after a song session with other devotees, she was extraordinarily relaxed and effusive. I asked her what it was in her religion that gave her joy. "Oh," she answered happily, "we don't have to pretend God is something he isn't." In that kind of happiness, the happiness of her deepest smile, she seemed not only at peace but overflowing with spirit. She was ready to face anything, death included. But at other times she was agitated, at loose ends, discontent in ways she couldn't express, impatient with her failing body but fearful of dying too. She thought she ought to see the doctor for one thing or another. She worried that she'd had a stroke or a small heart attack. She seemed to be clutching at a world that no longer had a place for her, a world she was afraid to leave.

In the four years that she lived with us, my mother spent most of her time reading in bed. She read the *Oregonian* (Portland's daily newspaper), the *Monitor,* various magazines she subscribed to, appeals from conservation and social action groups, junk mail of all sorts, and stacks of books—not only her sacred texts but books of all kinds. She understood what she read, and I assume, from underlined passages I found after she died, that she found solace in some of it. But most of her reading seemed only to fill time for her, to take up hours every day that she had no other way to spend. Often I saw her pick up a book she had only recently finished and start it again, and usually when I asked her what she had been reading she couldn't talk about it—the pages she'd been immersed in only an hour before had turned virtually blank in her mind. The stillness I sensed in her most of the time seemed less like peace and more like vacancy, an emptiness into which her memory was dissolving, a void that swallowed her words and interposed itself between her thoughts and turned them in recurrent circles.

And so I don't know. Did she find the Self she had set out in search of a quarter century before? Or did she lose, toward the end, what sense of self she had? Did she leave with wind in her sails or merely drifting, becalmed on an empty sea?

One night in 1966, home at Christmas from my first year at Reed College, I became aware of myself sitting on a sofa with a matchbook in my fingers chattering incessantly at a dark-haired girl who had been listening with smiling interest that now had changed, I thought, to clinical detachment—the face one wears in the presence of the mentally disturbed. I *was* mentally disturbed. I was wearing a gold paisley short-sleeved shirt I had never seen before, I was fidgeting on a sofa tearing a matchbook to shreds, I was babbling everything that came into my head or came out of my head at a young woman who understood none of it because I was insane. I had once been a regular person—I *knew* this girl—but now I was crazy and wouldn't come to my senses again, if I ever did, until I was white-haired and toothless and my life was over. Maybe that's what I already was. Maybe I'd always been crazy.

Then three friends came into the room and I remembered we had all taken big hits of LSD. The girl was Debby, the sister of one of my friends. It was their house we were in. The four of us left her and drove around the neighborhood for a while, doing what teenagers in the suburbs had always done, just differently intoxicated. We ended up at Dulles Airport in northern Virginia. It was new then, a technological whizbang. Maybe we wanted to see with spaced-out eyes where the world was going, but really I don't know why we went there. If I had the sixties to do over, I would be more selective about where I went and what I did on psychedelic drugs. We sat at a little table in the terminal, and we may have had coffee. My friends seemed in perfect command of the situation, psychedelic connoisseurs, cracking jokes of uncontainable meanings that kept them rollicking and kept me worried. I was spooked by the disembodied announcement voices resounding through the terminal's vast bright spaces, and I was pretty sure the security guards knew all about us. About me, at least. Why else would they keep looking? And what were we even doing there?

On the way home from Dulles, near dawn, the car skidded on a patch of ice, spun, and smacked the guardrail. This was surprisingly undisturbing, except perhaps to the friend who had just crunched the fender of his parents' Volvo. No one was hurt. The car was drivable. What's a fender bender to young men with open minds? As the unlucky driver and another friend worked at clearing crumpled metal away from the front left tire, John Sterne and I drifted off a ways on the empty highway. We had known each other since junior high school and now were attending Reed together. With silent snowy fields around us we looked at the stars, the brightest ones shimmering like pools of liquid light, and after a while we glanced at each other in glad wonderment, as if to say, *Can this be us?* Sterne's spectacled scholar's face was tilted back, half smiling, his dark hair haloed with stars. *Yes,* said his eyes, *this is us, and this is the world we never knew.* We stood there laughing like two lords born to the realm, nothing between us and the infinite sky.

I've often wondered if my sense of fragmentation, of being separated from myself, came from LSD and the other drugs I took in the sixties. Sometimes I feel it's taken me twenty-five years just to gather myself together after bombing my brain with psychedelics. I put myself through some terrifying times, moments in which my normal sense of self broke up in a riotous sea and left me—whatever *me* was—desperately clinging to a piece of wreckage, certain that I was lost forever from my life. Those were moments of true insanity, the kind of insanity that caused one friend who had taken acid with me to crouch down and pound his head on the sidewalk and run away shrieking down Connecticut Avenue one overcast Friday afternoon in Washington, D.C.

I've lost touch with that friend, but I've heard from a reliable source that he is now a psychiatrist. Somehow we survived our self-induced insanity, most of us, and got on with our lives. The car was damaged but drivable. And maybe the only damage LSD really did was to show us, too suddenly and too vividly, the actual volatile complexity of the human psyche. Maybe I had always been fragmented and hadn't known it. A brain scientist I've been reading, Robert Ornstein, says that what we call mind, as if it were one thing, is really a loose tribe of many minds, many selves that shift into and out of control all the time, mostly without the knowledge of the conscious self. He thinks consciousness is a secondary phenomenon, not very strong and not very active, that comes to the fore only when the body is threatened or the tribe is in conflict about what to do. We experience a more or less consistent sense of self because the conscious self is mostly unaware of the others, and because the entire menagerie shares at least a weak sense of group identity.

So maybe psychedelic drugs only introduced me to my personal tribe—introduced and abandoned me to be devoured raw. It would probably profit me to get to know better my various selves. I do know a few of them, vaguely at least—Bob Bourgeois, the Inspector, the boy I used to be—but the self that interests me most is not of that tribe. It's a self that brain scientists don't believe in, but I do. I have discovered it more than once. It's a deep and calm and undivided self, the self I was in that moment at dawn with John Sterne, the self my mother sought and wrote with a capital S. That Self is utterly at home in the universe it was born to and shares in its numinous perfection. It is both immanent and transcendent, within and without the wraps of ego and personality, always newly born and thrilled with the adventure of being. It was to be that Self again, if only for a moment, that I kept taking psychedelics and enduring the insanity they wrought.

On my first acid trip, a month into my freshman year at Reed, I felt as though my mind had flowed forth from the cave of its confinement and now was infusing my body. It *was* my body. I was a field of conscious energy aflow in the world. I couldn't stop smiling. The sunny Reed lawn was clearly itself and completely transformed. Each tree, each blade of grass, shone with its own being—familiar, elusive, beautiful beyond words. I was walking in the first field on the first day. I climbed a tree, the smooth firm limbs approving the fit of my hands, and at the top I shouted laughter like a two-year-old. Later I lay in the grass, my eyes closed, and whatever I was opened up inside, opened deep and far as time itself. I felt some ancient presence within me, moving like a long slow wind, the father of all things. Delight deepened into awe, and I was trembling.

On LSD I was often unsure who I was, but when I was outdoors and alone, I always knew where I was. I was in the world, the luminous, palpable world itself, and what I felt was the mystery of its being. Among native peoples there are cultural means by which adolescents seek a guiding vision from beyond the realm of normal consciousness. Our own culture offers no such means. It does its best, in fact, to enforce the idea that there is no meaningful realm beyond, nothing to be learned that can't be taught in school or church or everyday experience. I believe that I and a lot of other young people in the sixties were trying to invent, mostly unaware, what our culture failed to provide. In our bumbling and haphazard ways, we were initiating ourselves into the sacred.

As a child I knew sacredness mostly as a vague aura around Christmas. My father would read in his baritone voice from the Gospels, which he still appreciated as literature, and the carols we sang and heard on the hi-fi—"Silent Night," "Away in the Manger," "O Little Town of Bethlehem"—seemed to confer a glow of holiness that meant as much to me, until Christmas morning anyway, as the presents beneath the tree. Then one Christmas Eve I stood on the open roof of the side porch of our Glen Echo house and watched snow come down in the light of the one street lamp. A white Christmas had been more than I dared hope for, but now it was here, the snow drifting down out of darkness to glint and waver as it settled to the street. I'd meant to stay only a minute, but something held me there, and the longer I stayed the stranger it seemed that all warmth and comfort and sacredness should be sealed in below, in our living room with its music and bright tree, while all the infinite universe was darkness and cold glinting light. The best-ever Christmas of my life seemed suddenly a paltry thing. I needed it to take in the night and the snow, the untold mystery that wouldn't let go of me, and I knew it couldn't. When I went downstairs to the fire, I was shaking from more than the cold.

What I started to see with the help of psychedelic drugs was sacredness in no enclosure, unless the enclosure of earth and sky, a sacredness more common and more precious than I had known. Some version of that realization was occurring to many of us in the sixties, but there was no ritual, no institution—except for the kind that recognized only the insanity—to interpret and validate our experience. We were lucky to have a few books for guides. *The Psychedelic Experience,* the five-dollar hardback by Leary, Metzner, and Alpert, based on *The Tibetan Book of the Dead.* Aldous Huxley's accounts in *The Doors of Perception* and *Island.* Alan Watts's books, William Blake, a few others.

Mostly we had ourselves for guides. In my small dorm at Reed there were six or seven of us who were experimenting, and it still moves me when I think of how we looked after one another. My friend Michael, whom I'd known only a few months, once sat with me for what must have been hours when a whole tab of Owsley acid had melted my body and left me a mass of disturbed protoplasm on the dorm-room floor. I can still see his smile, the friendly interest in his eyes as I talked at him, probably with little coherence. I kept saying the word *remember,* seeing for the first time what it meant: to put the pieces together again, to rebuild the familiar house of the world. Michael's narrow Irish face was boy and man and old gray listener, continuously shifting as it stayed the same. I recognized the Michael who lived upstairs in the dorm, and I recognized the one who wore Michael's being, an ageless and undying friend.

All of us knew a little of the wilds we were exploring, and we made sure that everyone who entered them came back out. We came out, and we went back in. The flaw in our ad hoc initiation through LSD was that it led only to itself again. We were dilettantes, mere tourists of the sacred, buying tablet or blotter square time after time for the big transformation ride, complete with horror show—conveniently located right on campus, right in the dorm, right in the mystery of our own minds. No preparation, no effort required. The wonder of a psychedelic drug is that it shows you the authentic Self—but it shows you the Self whether or not you are ready to see it, and always it takes the Self away, with no clue how to find it except by the tablet or blotter again. In one of the Grail stories, the boy Parsifal discovers on his journey a mysterious fire in the woods with a salmon roasting over it. He reaches for the salmon, burns his fingers, and thrusts them into his mouth. He wasn't ready for what he desired. The mystery was too strong for him. Like Parsifal, I was left with a taste of the sacred and a lingering hunger.

Timothy Leary visited Reed in the spring of 1967, and probably three out of four of us who came to hear him were on acid or mescaline. I had taken a small hit, just enough to feel along my spine, enough to loosen the gridwork I carried in my head but not enough to dissolve it away. Leary, dressed in white with a mandala pendant, sat among vases of flowers and paisley tapestries on a small lit stage in the darkened Old Commons. He smiled the knowing smile of the acidhead, and as he talked along in his sonorous way, his voice returned again and again to six carefully cadenced words he delivered with a dance of his hands: "Turn on . . . . . . tune in . . . . . . *drop out."*

I didn't need much encouragement. I had begun to realize, with the assistance of my chemical education, that all my reasons for being in college were actually other people's reasons—my parents', my relatives', my high school teachers'. I liked my classes well enough, but I couldn't see that they pertained very much to my life, and besides, I'd been working hard in school for many years. I'd been locked in a house of words, it seemed, looking out at life instead of living it. In the fall of 1967 I came back for my sophomore year, but I knew I wanted out. In November I went to Dean Dudman's office and told him I needed a leave of absence, and I suppose it was only fitting that I was high on mescaline when I did.

I cringe at the platitudes I must have spoken to explain myself. I probably told the dean that I was my own best teacher, that real learning couldn't happen in a classroom. Probably, like a million other teenagers in those years, I used the word "irrelevant." But still, though my thoughts were simplistic and unexamined, I was doing what I needed to do. I was in no shape for the academic rigors of Reed College, and I had the vague but sure sense that great adventures awaited me outside. In the spirit of openness that I had decided would characterize my new life, I told Dean Dudman that I was on mescaline. The dean, a good and generous man, showed immediate concern.

"Have you been treated?" he asked. "Have you had medication?"

I looked at him and smiled.

I never looked forward to helping my mother with her shower. She wasn't the least self-conscious about baring her body in my presence, but something in me shrank from it. To be with her in her nakedness seemed too intimate for a grown son. And some other part of me, the child who wants always to be cared for and never burdened with responsibility, felt put upon and put out. Why was I having to do this? It seemed an indignity, and it touched an open wound. I had no child to bathe, to make faces at, to splash and laugh with. Most likely I never would. What I had was a frail and failing old woman who couldn't take a shower on her own.

Talking her into it was the first challenge. "Oh, I don't need a shower," she would say. "I just had one yesterday, didn't I?"

"You haven't had one for a week."

"But I don't *do* anything. Why do I need a shower?"

It wasn't only bad memory and lapsing judgment that made her resist, of course. It was also that the shower was strenuous for her, and she didn't want to acknowledge, or couldn't, that she needed help with anything so simple. In her own mind, the mind I believe she inhabited most of the time, she was perfectly capable of taking a shower by herself if she wanted to. In this mind she was still the woman she had been five years ago, a woman who came and went and drove a car, a woman who lived on her own on the coast of Maine and was only temporarily exiled in a distant place. This woman was honestly perplexed when we bought her a cane and asked her, over and over again, to use it. What need had Zilla Daniel for a cane? Somewhere inside her she was not only an able-bodied woman but still a Sea Scout, climbing the rigging in a bright clear wind.

But in her present mind she knew, whenever she leaned far forward in a chair and tried to stiff-arm herself to her feet, whenever she steadied herself with a hand on the wall as she shuffled to the bathroom, just how incapable she had become. She knew, and she hated it. How could she not have hated it? And if she had to bear it, she didn't want me or Marilyn or anyone else to have to help her bear it. She wanted to carry herself on her own stooped shoulders. I can still hear her making her way to the toilet with her left hand pulling her nightgown tight behind her, disgustedly whispering *No, no* to her bladder that could not hold back what it should have held back. As if she were castigating an unbroken puppy, but without the tolerance she would have granted an innocent thing.

It's easy to see, watching my mother from this remove, how much I resemble her. George and Jim inherited straight hair with a slight wave; I got my mother's curls. I got her long, slender fingers rather than my father's thicker ones. I got the Hawes nose. But just as surely, just as strikingly, I got my mother's Inspector. She didn't drill it into me—she didn't play Inspector as a mother any more than most parents—but somehow it just appeared in me, along with the hair and fingers and nose. The irritability, the spites and sulks, the impatience and the sharp tongue—and never sharper, of course, than when directed inward, aimed at herself, aimed at myself, aimed at the only failings and shortcomings in the entire human world that absolutely cannot be forgiven.

Standing for any length of time was hard for my mother, and so the shower was a kind of siege. She would grip the soap tray with both hands as I got the water temperature right—"*Aaant!*" she would holler, "too cold!"—and soaped a washcloth to scrub her sway-spined back. Even the soap met resistance.

"Sai Baba says not to use soap," she informed me early on. "It's just one more thing that has to come off."

"Well, it does come off," I answered, peeling open a bar of Dial. "It rinses off."

"My dear, it leaves a *residue*. Plain water is enough."

"Mother, for God's sake. This isn't the ashram. You need soap to get clean."

"Yes, Father," she said with a scowl.

Eventually we worked out a mulish compromise. We used Ivory, which we both agreed was the most natural. I washed her back and buttocks with a soaped washcloth; she held the cloth a few seconds in the shower spray before washing her front. One hand on the soap tray for support, she briefly swabbed her sagging breasts, her abdomen, the thinly gray-haired pubic region from which I once emerged, and the smooth, still-young skin of her upper thighs. Then I helped her down to the bath stool, where she rested a while and washed her lower legs and feet. The skin of her shins was dry and papery, perpetually blotched with dark purple—not impact bruises but bruises of age.

As I lathered shampoo into her wet white curls, her head would bow from the pressure of my fingers. I'd ask her to hold it up and she would for a second or two, then it would slowly sink again. It must have taken a major effort just to hold herself as upright as she did in her last years. All the while she was slowly bending, slowly folding, curling toward the fetal comfort of the grave.

She squeezed her eyes shut as I rinsed her hair in the shower stream. She scrunched up her face, stuck her lips out, and sputtered through the soapy runoff. It was in that recurring moment of her life with us, her hair flattened to her head, darkened a little with the soaking spray, that I could almost see my mother as a girl—swimming the cold swells off Hancock Point, splashing and laughing, shouting something toward shore, laying into the water with strong even strokes that would take her where she wanted to go.

She would let me stop rinsing only when she could rub a bit of her hair between finger and thumb and make it squeak. Then I would steady her out of the shower stall, her two hands in mine. It felt at moments like a kind of dance, a dance that maybe I knew how to do and needed to do. Who was that, doing the dance? Who was it who allowed himself those moments of pleasure helping his mother from the shower? Bob Bourgeois, I suppose. Bob has time and patience for things that only irritate me. He enjoys them. But it was someone else, too. When I look back at that scene in the bathroom, I see a boy in my place. A solemn boy with a bit of a smile, a boy attending his mother out of love and duty blended as one. The boy was there, and he was there now and then at other times in those years my mother was with us. He was there when I'd let him be there.

I helped my mother down into a straight-backed chair and left her in the bathroom with towels, clean underwear, and a little space heater to keep her warm. She took her time, as with everything. Often it was half an hour or longer before she emerged in her dressing gown, her hair beginning to fluff, her face smiling. No matter how hard she might have resisted the idea, a bath or shower always seemed to renew her. Soap or no soap, the old woman came forth cleaner of spirit.

"She was pure as the driven snow," she usually quoted, gaily, then a pause: "But she drifted."

I guess I came out of the bathroom cleaner of spirit myself. Soap or no soap, whatever the tenor of our conversation, I appreciate now what a privilege it was to help my mother with her shower. I wish I'd seen it more clearly at the time. We don't get to choose our privileges, and the ones that come to us aren't always the ones we would choose, and each of them is as much burden as joy. But they do come, and it's important to know them for what they are.

One morning as my mother came out of her shower she paused at the bottom of the stairs. I was reading the paper in the living room.

"Do you feel them sprouting?" she said, smiling in her white gown.

"Do I feel what sprouting?"

"Your wings," she said. She stood there, barefooted and bright, smiling right at me and through me, smiling as though she weren't feeble of body and failing of mind but filled with an uncanny power that saw things I could only glimpse.

"Mother, I don't have wings," I said.

But she was still smiling as she headed up the stairs, gripping the banister hand over hand, hauling herself up fifteen carpeted steps to her room and her bed made of sea-weathered posts and boards, where she would read for a while, gaze out her window at sky and treetops, then drift into sleep.

I'm standing with one hand on the red brick wall at the bottom of the stairs, peeking around the corner to the left into what we call the recreation room—the cool and musty basement that holds the TV set, a foam-pad sofa and a chair or two, a few bookshelves, a file cabinet, and my father's safe. Behind me there's a door I can open and walk through into the morning of a bright spring day, but I haven't sneaked down the stairs for that. I heard something, and I've come to see what. Why am I even home? It must be a weekend. Or maybe it's summer, not spring, summer vacation after third grade. It doesn't matter. Baseball, mess around in the yard, go across the street to Bobby Bradley's, whatever I was planning to do before I heard a repetitive sound and started down the stairs, none of it matters.

My mother and father are in the room. They aren't speaking. My mother, in gray corduroy pants, is facing three-quarters away from my father, looking down, her hands clasped in front of her. Is she crying? I don't think she's crying. My father, stubble-cheeked and cold sober, his face drawn flat and gray, is wearing his bathrobe and brown leather slippers. He is taking a step with his left foot, swinging his right leg free of the bathrobe and kicking my mother's rear end. She doesn't move, except with the impact. She stands there, just stands there, as he steps back and forward and kicks her again, and kicks her again, the two of them together like a windup toy somebody started in the basement and nobody knows how to stop—certainly not me, not the boy staring through the mortar joints of the brick corner unable to stop staring, certainly not him.

I still can't stop it. The toy plays on and on, a perpetual-motion machine in a sealed glass chamber where nothing disturbs it, nothing interrupts the perfection of its motion. My father with his lips pursed tight, his right leg pale and sparsely haired, the creased brown slipper flopping slightly as his foot leaves the floor. My mother with steel gray in her dark curling hair, her eyes dark and downcast, her face contracted in something like anger, something like sorrow, something like resignation. I see them as if they stood in front of me now, and I see myself too, I see myself watching—my torso skinny in a white t-shirt, my hair curly like my mother's, brown with sun-bleached glints, my fingers on the brick wall narrow and delicate like hers. I see my closed mouth. I see myself crying.

But I don't know what I'm feeling. I know the boy, I know what he must have been feeling, the way I know what he looks like from photos, but I don't feel it inside me now. It's not inside me. It's inside him. It's clamped behind his skinny ribs, behind the flat wall of his belly. He's holding it, molding it to his familiar form, so it won't fly loose where who knows what it might do. He's trying to hold it where he can take care of it, keep it from scaring him, like the big flying beetle he used to keep in a coffee can punched with little holes.

The boy must have been afraid, of course. I must have been afraid, and in a new way. Their arguments always scared me, but they composed a kind of weather that had come to seem normal in our household. I could almost predict the storms and how bad they would be, but this was different. This was crazy. This had no words, shouted or whispered, to clarify it. No tears or slamming doors. This was silent and dead sober. It felt as though I'd stumbled upon a secret ritual of marriage, a ritual of hatred—and that's the missing word, isn't it. Hatred. In that moment I think I hated my parents. Hated my father for kicking my mother. Hated my mother for standing there, for letting him do it. I hated the stupid secret craziness they had made of our family, without even whiskey to explain it now, a shameful, rotten craziness at the heart of our home.

Gradually, over weeks and months, I learned enough to make some sense of what I had seen. I learned it all indirectly, of course, the way I gathered all my intelligence—overheard conversations between the two of them, between them and their friends. The word "affair" wouldn't have meant anything to me at the time, but I learned that my mother had done what husband and wife do with a man named Guy Pfoutz, and my father had found out about it. Most likely, knowing what I know about my mother's personality, she told him about it. Probably tossed it in his face, just as she had tossed her radical politics and liberated lifestyle in her father's proper Unitarian face in the 1920s, just as later she would choose a dinner party as the occasion to announce to her husband that she wanted a divorce. She probably told my father all about her affair so that she could feel honest if not pure and hurt him for the weeks and months she had spent alone, for the career she'd forsaken to traipse the country in the tow of his, for the Cause that was his highest love and the whiskey that was his closest friend, and for everything I don't know about and never will.

She hurt him and stood there taking the hurt back, the hurt that part of her felt she deserved. She hurt herself through him, he hurt himself through her, and so the broken toy of their marriage cranked on and on.

There must have been a time, I keep thinking, when it wasn't so. A time when their love for each other was full and fine and sufficient. Maybe the Carolina years of the late forties and early fifties, those summers of barbecues and homemade ice cream, friends flowing in from everywhere, scratchy seventy-eights of Verdi and Beethoven loud on the record player, the wound of Georgie's death healing and two lively boys running in the grass. And a few years earlier, too, when my mother was pregnant with George and confident at last that she wouldn't miscarry again. She wrote my father nearly every other day when he was on the road, and in all her letters her tone is never more tender. "You first, darling," she writes. "I especially love to hear from you 'en route' anywhere: the whir of wheels underneath, country racing by, something new ahead. It's a fine feeling." "Darling," she writes, "to have you set a date for coming is enough. I am tremendously excited . . ."

And they had their first years together, that time in the early thirties when they were new and fresh to each other and saw themselves as nothing less than revolutionaries, committed to a huge and impossible mission that maybe was possible after all, because the passion they shared with their fellow organizers was so intense and boundless. When Franz Daniel was a charismatic zealot from the seminary with an eloquence that made factory workers cheer and weep at rallies, that made Zilla Hawes weep in meetings, where she sat sometimes literally at his feet. And when Zilla Hawes herself was a daring firebrand of patrician manners whom one male friend described as an Athena from New England, a woman, if not beautiful, of such vibrant and virile intensity that she made him and many men feel like inarticulate clods.

My parents wrote their own wedding ceremony, and they incorporated this verse from a poem by Ralph Chaplin:

We shall be faithful though we march with Death
　And singing storm the battlements of Wrong,

For life is such a little thing to give.
We shall march on as long as we have breath—
Love in our hearts and on our lips a song.

Their marriage, early on, was a comradeship as much as a romantic union. I don't know if they would have called themselves happy in that tumultuous era. What they craved, it seems, was not happiness but *action*—they wanted to storm and sing to the utmost limits of their souls. Through most of the thirties, as they shifted independently around the South and East on various strikes and organizing drives—both before and after they were married—they explicitly granted each other sexual freedom. My own parents, it turns out, were experimenting with Free Love a full thirty years before the hippie culture of the sixties made it a catchphrase and a sporadic way of life. It didn't work out any better for them than it does for most who try it. My mother did indeed experiment—and my father, when he found out, raised holy hell in spite of their agreement. My mother, in later years, wasn't sure if he had had other relationships. She thought not, but a woman friend who lived with them in Philadelphia in those days tells me he certainly did.

"Franz and I never really gave ourselves a chance," my mother said to me in the 1970s. Their personal lives were so consumed in the cause that they didn't even take a honeymoon after their wedding—they threw a house party on the Maine coast instead, carousing with labor comrades, and then plunged quickly into work again. They hardly knew what it was like to spend long periods alone together. My mother was philosophical about that, and wistful, when she and I talked. I could feel her sadness, and though my father never spoke to me directly about their marriage, his sadness loomed enormously. I can't think of them as a couple without feeling sadness myself. They were powerful people, yet very nearly helpless to steer their own way together in the turbulence of their lives and times.

But their sadness, and my sadness for them, is not what I meant to write about. Sadness is not what I felt as I watched their windup toy in the basement when I was nine. And it was something more intense than sadness I felt later that year, or the next year, when they called Jim and me into the living room one night and told us they were going to divorce. I walked toward my father in my underwear, crying "Don't go." And later I lay awake a long time, staring out at the ceiling light in the hall through the bedroom doorway that I'd asked my mother to leave open. *This happens to a lot of kids,* I remember thinking, my head cocked on the pillow. *This happens all over America.* I stared at the light and kept thinking and thinking—already generalizing, already abstracting my pain, already withdrawing to a watchful distance where I could sit by myself, sit quiet and still, feeling not too happy, not too sad, and maybe—if I was quiet and watchful enough—maybe safe.

On a little bookcase not far from her bed, my mother kept a small framed black-and-white photograph of my father. She may have taken the picture herself, from the stern of a rowboat—her father's green-painted boat, probably, on a Maine lake or the easy tidal waters of Frenchman's Bay off Hancock Point. My father, in a sweater, is handling the oars. He is forty-something—possibly younger than I am now—and he's smiling. He looks as happy and easy as I ever saw him. Surely that's the reason my mother chose that picture to keep near her: it shows the joy her husband was capable of, the joy, maybe, that *they* were capable of. The remembered joy, intact and still alive in the wreckage of their marriage, that had made her wistful in 1977, a year after my father's death, when I asked her to talk about him and their life together.

I recorded those conversations, with my mother's consent, and

I'm glad I did. Those tapes, along with the interview in *Refuse to Stand Silently By* and her letters that I've been able to gather, form the basis of what I've written so far about her marriage and labor career. To her present mind, as she was living with Marilyn and me, very few of those memories were available—and then only sporadically, randomly, occasional leaves wavering briefly through the sundown light of her psyche. There were days when she knew the given name of the man she had spent half her life with, but there were many days when she didn't. *Your father,* she would sometimes say, after struggling in vain for the missing single syllable full of consonant sounds she must have spoken ten thousand times in the course of her life: *Franz.*

How could his name have vanished from her? How could *he* have vanished to the extent he did, the man she had worshiped and slept with and partied with and borne children by and betrayed and been kicked by and hated and pitied—and loved deeply, abidingly, through all of that and beyond?

Sometimes when I barbecued I remarked to my mother how Franz had taken great pride in his steaks.

"Oh yes," she would answer, smiling, taking a sip of her Scotch.

"He called his basting sauce his Persuader, remember?"

"Why yes, John, that's right," she'd reply, and on like that, as if my words ignited some light in her mind, a pleasurable glow, but there was little there for the light to illuminate, little to offer back in kind. There was recognition in her, but little recall.

What was missing in my mother as we conversed was not intelligence or caring and certainly not language ability. She retained an extensive vocabulary to the end of her life, she rattled off nursery rhymes and snatches of poetry, and she spoke her words with an elaborate precision. Her enunciation had always been clear, but in her last years she took even greater pains to form her syllables carefully and completely, practically sculpting them in their saying. She seemed to taste and savor her language as she spoke it, as if in that way at least to forestall the formlessness expanding within her, to enact upon her life in the world the one exactitude that still remained to her.

What was missing was her part in the *interplay* of human talk, the ready resilience we mostly take for granted that absorbs another's words and returns—ingeniously, without planning and often without thought—words of one's own that answer or expand upon or deflect from or turn in a new direction the language received. That, I can see now, is a substantial part of what irritated me, what tried me in a way I didn't understand. It was unusual for conversation with my mother to *go* anywhere. She would sink it or shut it off, as if weary of the subject. One of the phrases she spoke most frequently, held in mind sixty years from her undergraduate days at Vassar, was *Questo non far niente. This really doesn't matter.*

In her first year with us, before we understood her affliction, I thought my mother was being purposely evasive. I wanted to hear about her labor work, her college life, stories about me and Jim and George, her final thoughts about my father and the life they had shared. What I got instead, most of the time, were repeated comments and questions about the appearance of trees she spent hours looking at through the windows, about the arrangement of the furniture or the placement of a picture, about the food we ate. When was Jim coming to visit? What was the little bird with a black cap? What *good* strong coffee I had made. The remarks and questions recurred with maddening frequency, but it wasn't only the repetition that annoyed me. If she wasn't purposely withholding herself, it could only mean that she had no self to share. It's both baffling and an outrage when mental failing occurs in a loved one, because the ailment can't be located in leg or heart or liver. It's not the body but *she* who is failing, the person inhabiting the flesh, the one we have loved and trusted and thought we knew. When a loved one loses her health, it is a sadness. But when she even begins to lose her mind, it is a sadness and a betrayal, an emblem of our deepest fear.

It was usually while we were walking that my mother remembered my father, and it almost always was a dandelion that provoked the memory. The natural view of her old age, because of her stooped back and bowed head, was toward the ground. She noticed bugs, kids' chalk marks, the stamped imprints of the sidewalk makers, and all the flowers along our way. The small, low-lying blooms were her favorites—violets, saxifrage, others that neither of us could name—and none delighted her more than dandelions. She liked their plain bright faces; she liked the way they pop up anywhere, including sidewalk cracks; and she liked them, I think, because they're so commonly scorned. I can't count the times she told me, not spitefully or ruefully but still returning the dandelions' yellow smile, "Your father, you know, could not *abide* dandelions. He had to rid the lawn of every one."

I don't remember that myself, but it fits. Perhaps because of the German in him, my father did like to keep the yard well mowed and orderly. But I don't think my mother was remembering a mere fact of my father's lawn-tending habit. As she made the same remark many times over the months, I got the strange but certain feeling that all their bitter arguments through the years and decades, all the painful wrenching and tearing they inflicted on themselves for so long, that all of that—very little of which my mother specifically remembered—had distilled and resolved in her present mind to a difference over dandelions. It may have been a kind of oblique coming to terms, the best she may have been capable of as her past receded into what must have felt like a dream to her, a dream lived by someone who was and was not her, and the present—pain in her bones, a bird in the tree, the shining flowers—drew her deeper and deeper into its sheer unspoken mystery.

She wanted no part of argument in her life with us. At dinner sometimes, infrequently, Marilyn and I would bicker about one thing or another—an issue in the news, something that did or didn't need doing around the house—the kind of disagreement that generates a little heat but quickly passes. My mother couldn't stand it. She stared into her dinner, chewing hard, clanking her fork on the plate. "*Please,*" I remember her saying once in complete disgust. "Would you *please* behave yourselves." Looking back now it occurs to me that my mother didn't know, because she hadn't experienced it, that a husband and wife could argue casually. She didn't know what a healthy marriage was, what strains and turbulence it might absorb without suffering harm. Also, of course, she had been on her own for twenty years, living in the quiet of her own company—and, in recent years, absorbed in the teachings of her religion, which frowns on disagreement with others.

Dinner was difficult for all of us. My mother, because her hearing was bad and her new hearing aid, her first, remained semi-incomprehensible to her, had a hard time tracking Marilyn's voice, which is softer and projects less well than my own assertive foghorn. And so, to make herself understood, Marilyn had to speak directly at my mother in loud forced syllables—not exactly what she felt like doing, first thing home after a long day of office and meetings and bus. She wanted to talk about her day, but she and I couldn't converse in our usual easy way without my mother feeling left out. She would interrupt to ask us to repeat what we had said, sometimes reprimanding us for our rudeness. I would ask her to turn up her hearing aid, if she had it in; she would do it and complain that she heard herself chewing. Irritation flared in all of us. Conversation lurched in fits and starts. I felt very much in the middle, wanting my wife to enjoy herself, wanting my mother to enjoy herself, wanting the two of them to enjoy each other and the dinner I had made, wanting the peaceful aura of my mother's Sanskrit prayer with which the meal had begun.

Dinner, of course, was the social highlight of my mother's day. Usually, unless we went out to lunch or to an appointment with a doctor or on some other errand, she saw no one during the day but me. Often I didn't either, but that was by choice; I could break off writing or reading and leave the house any time. My mother was marooned in a comfortable but silent home without work to do or friends at the door, no coming or going except with me, few travels except out the window with her eyes and wherever she journeyed within herself. Sleep and wake, the same books and magazines beside her, the bathroom and back to her bedroom, drifting along with the changing light until maybe a walk in the afternoon, then a drink in the living room or in the kitchen as I fixed dinner.

Marilyn and I tried to find ways to get other people into my mother's life. I took her to the local senior center a few times, but she resisted from the beginning and clearly didn't care for it. She was a misfit among the bingo players and TV watchers. I felt like a parent forcing a reluctant child to attend day camp because it would be good for her. We arranged with a senior outreach program for a volunteer "friend" to come over now and then to visit with my mother. For a few weeks this seemed to please her, but she was well aware of the artificiality of the relationship, and both she and the visitor lost interest after a while. Her most satisfying friendship was with a colleague of Marilyn's, a young Socialist and labor activist, who occasionally took her to breakfast on a weekend. And she did attend her Sai Baba meetings, but only once in a while. When the evening of the meeting arrived she frequently didn't feel up to it. Because of her physical weakness, any outing, even the most pleasant, had a dimension of ordeal.

Worried about her isolation, her listlessness and lack of initiative, in the spring of 1990 Marilyn and I asked a psychiatric social worker who worked for the county mental health service to evaluate my mother. She came twice, asking questions that left my mother slightly but pleasantly bemused—any visitor perked her up. Marilyn and I had suspected that she was depressed, but the social worker thought not. Lonely for sure, somewhat resentful over having been moved from her home and having her car taken from her, but not medically depressed. The social worker thought she had detected something else, though, and referred us to a clinical psychologist.

My mother spent two long sessions in the psychologist's office, performing verbal and visual tests with names like the Pfeiffer Short Portable MSQ, Hooper Visual Organization Test, Porteus Maze, Trail-Making Tests A and B, Wechsler Memory Scale Subtests, Familiar Faces Test, Boston Naming Test, and the Geriatric Depression Scale. She emerged from the sessions fatigued but in a good mood. She liked the psychologist, a warm and sympathetic woman, very much; and the psychologist, like so many who encountered my mother, was instantly and thoroughly taken with her. She was nearly in tears as she told Marilyn and me that the test results pointed clearly to a primary progressive dementia probably of the Alzheimer's type. Another possibility was multi-infarct dementia, a disease of similar symptoms caused by multiple small strokes. I was standing outside her office, listening through the door, when she explained to my mother what she had found. She paused when she first said "Alzheimer's disease."

"Oh," said my mother, real fear in her voice. "I hope I don't have that."

Forgetfulness is what I'm fighting as I write this. I want to remember everything because I know it all counts, it's all important, it all composes the constellation I need to see. But I don't remember everything. It hasn't been two years since my mother died, and already my memory of our life with her is softening, going vague and filmy. I have a few intensely clear images, a few notes of things she said, a few of her personal things and items of clothing, a few photographs, and I work from those into the weeks and months of her nearly four years with us that are only a blur, a fogged-in landscape, an absence. From what I know I write my way into what I don't know, or don't think I know. I'm a restorer, rubbing at the weathered surfaces, looking for the shine of life.

But it isn't restoration. There was, there is, no finished work to be restored. No artist, no art. There is only my experience—*experience,* that oddly unruffled term that tries to subsume the prodigious flux and welter of a human life. I'm not restoring my experience, I'm forming it. I'm constructing it. Actually, I'm creating it. I just looked again at something John Burroughs wrote in *Riverby:* "It was not till I got home that I really went to Maine, or the Adirondacks, or to Canada. Out of the chaotic and nebulous impressions which these expeditions gave me, I evolved the real experience."

Evolved it, that is, by writing it. The real experience of the birch forest in Maine occurs not when he is walking through it but back home at Slabsides in his study, where he "compels that vague unconscious being within me, who absorbs so much and says so little, to unbosom himself at the point of a pen." If he means that last phrase as a joke, it's a serious joke. There *is* compulsion in it. My own vague unconscious being—and who could it be but Bob Bourgeois?— would rather poke around the hardware store or hike in the Cascades, he'd rather blow the afternoon watching the Forty-Niners on TV, he'd rather clean the lint filter on the dryer than unbosom himself at the point of anything. But I, whoever I am, need to evolve the real experience out of what I remember and what I don't. I need to make memory into something whole, a monument, a place where meaning can live. And where I can live, too. A home I can live in and leave behind, returning when I need to for the rest of my life.

But the Inspector has a concern. He has a question to ask. Am I telling the truth, or only a truth I can live with? There are parts of the story I would prefer to leave to my vague unconscious being, because they don't please me. They don't show me as I like to think of myself, as I like others to think of me. The point of the pen has to demand those too. To evolve the real experience, it has to demand the fullest truth memory can provide—memory the unreliable, memory the self-serving, memory the liar. It isn't just a matter of giving birth, of bodying forth the mystery. It's an examination, an interrogation. It's an act of will. I'm the one pointing the weapon—the necessary weapon—and I'm the one filing the report. It's got to be a full report. It's got to be a report I believe.

My mother had been a strong and vibrant woman. It grieved me to see her reduced to a stooped crone who dithered over vegetables at the store, who couldn't remember what she'd read half an hour before, who forgot to take the pills I placed directly in front of her at breakfast. It more than grieved me—it enraged me, and there was no one to be enraged at but her. The psychologist's diagnosis confirmed that she couldn't help the way she was. I knew she was blameless, and yet I blamed her. I hurried her when she couldn't hurry, I was short with her, I cut off conversations as often as she did—because she said something she'd said before, because I was in a rush, because I wanted to get away and do something else, because I was stuck with caring for a feeble old mother and didn't want to be. Because she was what I got for a child. A wizened old child growing the wrong way, growing into senile dementia, growing into death.

There were moments when I wanted her dead. It's hard to write that, but it's true. There were moments when I hated the house, hated Portland, hated my writing and myself and blamed her for all of it. Moments when I felt racked between mother and wife and imagined no relief for years and years. Moments when I felt so trapped I wanted just to keep walking, ankle weights and all, when I wanted to stride back to the sixties and stick out my thumb on I-5, slip down to Swan Island and hide myself on a rusty tanker and sail wherever it took me. There were many evenings I wanted to sling dinner in the sink and sit out back with George Dickel or Jack Daniel or whoever I could find in the liquor cupboard and just not care. Once I left the dinner table to fetch more wine and lay down on the kitchen floor, crying silently to the cutlery clicks and scrapes of my wife and mother eating silently in the next room. And once I burst into my study slamming the door behind me and screamed, "Just die then, *die*," and sat down sobbing at my desk.

You'd think I'd remember what set me off that time, but I don't. Usually it happened when she said something snappishly ungrateful about the caregiving things I had to do—take her blood pressure, make sure she took her medicines, remind her to use her cane and later her walker. I knew she wasn't ungrateful, and of course she hated all that. Why wouldn't she? Why wouldn't she chafe under the enforcing eye of her all too fatherly son—her son with more than a passing resemblance to her own reverend father? Why wouldn't she hate to take a diuretic when she was already partially incontinent? Why wouldn't she be jealous of the wife I wanted to spend time with? Why wouldn't she be going half crazy from the tedium of her changeless days? She felt as trapped as I did. Once, when she was going through the tests with the psychologist and had recently endured an exhaustive medical assessment—not her idea, of course— she and I had a small fracas over something and she told me, "Just leave me alone and let me *die*." She only said it once, but there must have been many moments when she felt it.

She *was* dying, of course. She was declining toward death the whole time she lived with us. If I could have seen that more clearly and accepted it, I could have been a better help to her than the dutiful blood pressure taker and moody cook and conversant I was. You don't get a second chance to live your mother's last years. She dies and it all freezes in place, everything you did and didn't do. I wish I could have been more patient with her, more supple, more willing to follow her lead instead of so often imposing my own will. And I wish I could have provided her with a ritual, a ceremony, some form or path for approaching death by which the troubles and longings of her spirit could have expressed themselves. I wish I could have found a way to talk with her about Franz, about little George. I wish she could have cried and laughed and worked it all through and come to something, to a final *Yes, this is what my life has been, and it's all right.*

She couldn't do that, because she didn't have the memory for it. But why do I think she had the need or the desire? Her memory loss, though it vexed and grieved me, didn't seem to disturb her all that much. She knew at least the gist of what was happening to her—she had come from Maine with homeopathic salts to improve her mem-

ory—and though sometimes she was impatient with her forgetfulness, by and large she took it with humor and her uniquely eloquent
grace. "My memory is so *slippery,*" I remember her exclaiming once.
And another time she volunteered, "I'm forgetting everything these
days. The only thing I don't forget is the fact that I'm alive!" It was
harder for Marilyn and me to take a laughing view, of course, because
it was harder for us to live with her and care for her if she didn't remember to use her hearing aid and take her pills, and her lapses could
be dangerous. Once, shortly after she moved in with us, we came
home from a movie to find the empty steel tea kettle rocking on a red-
hot burner, my mother sunk into a book in the living room.

But what do I know of what she finally came to, or didn't come to?
What do I know of what she experienced most deeply within, what
she couldn't or wouldn't speak? She had that photo of her husband
smiling at the oars of a boat—the man she had loved in his handsome
prime, his brightest mood—and maybe that was enough. There had
been much between them that surely she wouldn't have wanted to
remember even if she could have, and why did she need to? Why
wasn't a difference over dandelions, real or imagined, a sufficient
summary of their troubles? And how do I know she didn't come to
some similar resting point about the son who had died in her arms,
about the other pains of her long life? And if the only resolution was
forgetfulness, what's wrong with that? I keep thinking of her Alzheimer's or whatever it was as a robbery, an awful diminishment, but
maybe it was a kindness too. Maybe it did for her the necessary work
of winnowing the harvest of her life, leaving her a small but ample
nourishment as her soul started from the world. Maybe memory
loss among the aged is only an overflowing into life of the river Lethe, the water of forgetfulness, the good balm of oblivion in which
they and all of us bathe at last.

And that's what scares me, isn't it. That, underneath it all, is what
grieved and enraged me about my mother's condition. Forgetfulness
is what I'm fighting, all right, because forgetfulness is exactly what

I most fear. The oblivion of Lethe holds no balm for me. In that child-hood nightmare of floating dead among icy stars, what terrified me most was not the vision itself but waking and knowing that even the vision was a lie, that when I died there would be no me among the stars or anywhere, not ever again, not *ever*. I could stand to lose my family, my friends, the places I know, even my body, but to lose this awareness, this precious light, this way of looking at the world—to lose what I *am*, to know that I will not remember . . . I'm the one un-reconciled. I'm the one without a ritual or a path.

The diagnosis of Alzheimer's or multi-infarct dementia changed little in our relationship with my mother. She didn't mention it—it wasn't clear at all that she remembered it—and we didn't speak of it to her. Who wants to say those words aloud? *Alzheimer's* has a deadly, terrifying ring, and dementia—the broader term—is, if anything, worse. To be demented is to be de-minded, drained of one's inner life. I hate the word. In the last week of my mother's life, as she lay in the intensive care unit of Emanuel Hospital with a respirator pumping her lungs, a cardiologist I liked very much asked us to think about what further life-prolonging measures we wished them to take, given her age, her frailty, and her demented condition. It was a good question, a timely question, but I felt a jolt of rage when he said "demented." He knew my mother's body. What did he know of her mind, beyond the clinical language he had read in her medical history? What did he know of her life?

There really aren't any comfortable names for what happened to my mother and happens to many older persons—at present about four million, according to the National Institute on Aging. More than 10 percent of men and women over sixty-five have probable Alzheimer's or a related condition. Among those eighty-five and older, the figure approaches 50 percent. "Senility," the old generic term for deterioration with age, is used less these days as more specific conditions are identified and diagnosed. I'm glad, because I dislike it too. The very sound of the word is ugly, its connotations grotesque. "Second childishness and mere oblivion," wrote Shakespeare, "Sans teeth, sans eyes, sans taste, sans everything." Yet senility may after all be the fairest and most meaningful term. *Senex,* the Latin root of the word, means simply "old" or "old man." My brother Jim, who came up from California to care for our mother when Marilyn and I went on vacation, was unconvinced that the psychologist's arcane testing and analysis meant very much. "Don't you think maybe she's just *old?*" he asked.

In geology, I've learned, "senile" refers to a landform or landscape that has been worn away nearly to base level at the end of an erosion cycle. It helps me to look at aging that way. Time wears all of us down, and how well we last depends on what we are made of and what our weather has been. Some persist like fresh granite; some dissolve like limestone in the rain. My mother stood like a crag as she advanced into age, but eroded suddenly toward the end. There are many who slump and slide far more rapidly and drastically than she did, falling utterly from their own lives while still alive, beyond the reach of family and friends. In our boundless scientific optimism we like to think we will find a preventative or cure for senile dementia, but it may turn out to be as incurable as mortality. Death is not a point in time but a process of time. There are as many ways to die as there are ways to live, and all of them involve the psyche as well as the physical being.

My mother knew in her years with us that her death was near, and, as I'll relate, I have reason to believe she didn't fear it as much as

I fear mine. What she did fear, palpably, was something else—not the end of life but any major *change* in life. I became aware of this in the spring of 1990, shortly after the diagnosis, when Marilyn and I bought a house in a different Portland neighborhood and prepared to move. We hadn't owned a house before, and we were excited. The new place had a ground-floor bedroom and bathroom for my mother, a spacious upstairs for the two of us with a weaving room for Marilyn, and a detached garage I could convert into a writing study. There were birches, pines, and dogwood trees, rhododendrons front and back, and the house was in a quieter part of town than our neighborhood at the time.

Though my mother seemed agreeable enough when we talked about the move, she did wonder aloud why we needed to change homes. What was wrong with the house we lived in? The issue of owning versus renting didn't seem important to her, and—of course—she pooh-poohed the notion that she needed a ground-floor bedroom. But those doubts she voiced formed only the apparent surface of a deeper fear, a fear that became evident one night in the upstairs hallway. I looked up from the book I was reading in the den to see my mother in her white nightgown hovering in the doorway. I don't know how long she had been there. She was deeply agitated, almost in tears. "Remember," she said, her voice breaking, "I need something to hold on to."

I felt a flash of annoyance that she could say something so irrational—we were moving only a few miles, not around the world. But for once I restrained my irritation. I went to her and held her, my arms around her humped back, her thin bony shoulders against my chest. I tried to comfort her as I might have comforted a child. I told her that she was part of the household, that we were moving together, that I would be there to help her. All the while, I struggled to understand what she had said.

"Mother," I asked her, "what do you need to hold on to?"

"Oh, nothing," she said. "I was only being silly."

"But you weren't being silly. How can I help you if you don't tell me what you're feeling?"

"It's nothing," said my mother, her grayish-green eyes turning away from mine. "*Questo non far niente.*"

My mother spoke her fears only rarely, and to voice one with such open feeling was unprecedented. She may have forgotten, in the solitude of her bedroom, what she had understood in conversation with Marilyn and me a few hours before—that the three of us were moving together. She may have felt abandoned. But I think it's more likely that in her disoriented condition the prospect of another move was simply distressing. It had been only a year and a half since she had left her home and friends in Maine, a little over a year since she had moved from her apartment to live with Marilyn and me, and now it was out the door again to still another place.

Her room in the new house was small, big enough for her bed and not much more. We couldn't enlarge the room but we did open up her view, replacing a window that would have shown her only the patio roof with a sliding glass door that looked out into the trees and flower beds of the backyard. Marilyn arranged all the furniture that would fit as closely as possible to the way it had been in my mother's old bedroom: two beat-up bookcases; a small oak chest of drawers that held her clothing and jewelry; and her nightstand with its familiar lamp, pictures of Sai Baba and my father, and several bowls and boxes containing shells, crystals, and other treasures that had come to her along the way. When Marilyn drove her to the house and helped her into the room, my mother said nothing but sat down on the bed and wept—for joy.

It was to be her last room, her last house. I think she knew that, and I knew it too. It wasn't the perfect place. I'd like for her to have lived out her days in sight and sound of the ocean, the salt breeze on her face, or at least in the country rather than a city. But if it wasn't perfect, it was at least a good place. She had Marilyn's flowers and the birds that came to the feeders to look at, the changing weather and the changing light, the dogwood tree in the window by the kitchen table. She had the tall Douglas firs in the park just north of us she could watch from the living room. She had, when we walked, the alleyway out back with its profusion of dandelions and a redbud tree that reminded her of the South. She had our friendly neighbor Tom, she had Marilyn and me, she had Jim when they spoke on the phone or he visited. She had something to hold on to.

What she didn't have, of course, was a way to hold on to herself. That was what she had cried for the best way she could in the hallway of the old house. That was the fearful need that erupted into words through all the strata of her stoicism and self-reliance, the same need that spoke itself in a less emotional way when she talked about returning to Maine. She was referring to a real place, a real landscape and community of friends, but I believe it was also her way of wishing aloud that she could be herself again. People with Alzheimer's and the similar dementias characteristically want to go "home"—to a place where things made sense, where the compass of reality reliably guided them, where they were capable and useful and secure. The wandering that some of them are prone to may be an attempt to return to this place that is no place. They seek outwardly what they are losing within, trapped in a metaphor of their own unconscious making. The mind, though failing in cognitive function, does not give up its habit of trying to understand the world by connecting likenesses. Memory may become entirely unreliable, telling gaping lies of omission and misconstruing the facts and images it does recall, but the deep tendency to give *form* to memory doesn't die. It still finds analogues, still makes stories and imagines places, still cobbles together a raft of meaning to keep identity afloat in its own chaotic waters.

My mother was too frail to wander, and she probably wouldn't have even if she'd been able. Though it ravaged her memory and caused her much confusion, her condition never progressed to the extreme stage. She never permanently forgot why she couldn't go home again in either sense. She spoke of Maine only occasionally after the move to our new house. But once in a while she did mention a certain clock, a ship's clock, that she had left behind somewhere. It seemed very important to her. I can't say for certain that there wasn't such a clock, but I know her possessions fairly well and don't recall a ship's clock among them. I thought it wasn't a good idea to encourage delusions, and so at first I wasn't responsive when she mentioned the clock. But eventually, one evening as we had a drink before dinner, I engaged her about it instead of dismissing it.

"Did you leave the clock in Maine?" I asked.

"I don't remember their name," she said, frowning intently. "But you take the road *toward* the coast, not all the way there, and then you turn . . ." She put fingers to her forehead, trying to see the lay of the land, trying to find the forgotten way. "And then, well . . ."

"What was the clock like?"

"It was brass . . . not heavy but very substantial, you know."

"Was it used on a ship?"

"Oh yes, it's the real McCoy. A real ship's clock."

She sipped her whiskey, looked out the window at the trees in the park, and was silent for a while. She glanced quickly at me and out the window again. Then she went on.

"Sometime we might drive over there and maybe we could find it. You know, *toward* the coast. Not all the way there. It was a good clock, it rang the bells and kept good time."

CHAPTER SEVENTEEN

I like to see my life as a seeking, a moving toward, but if I squint my eyes a little it looks like one long running away. As a boy in Maryland I spent a lot of time outdoors, like most kids in semirural places. I poked around the little creek that ran between two sections of our suburb, catching frogs and water striders, failing to catch minnows, turning over stones to check for crayfish. Sometimes, alone or with a friend or two, I made an expedition down to the C & O Canal with its old wooden locks, and beyond the canal to the sloughs and muddy channels of the Potomac River. Occasionally I went to fish, but more frequently to explore— to wander the sycamore forests along the polluted river as if I were the first white person ever to walk there. I dreamed of discovery. After my parents bought an old cabin in northern Virginia when I was twelve, I spent much time fishing nearby farm ponds for bass and bluegills or hiking the Blue Ridge. I'd walk for hours or all day, taking in the woods, spying on animals, dreaming westward from that promontory on the Appalachian Trail.

It's no strange thing for a boy to be drawn to nature. We're born wild and with a love for the wild. But if I was attracted to the outdoors by affinity, I now see that I also ran to it for refuge. Trees don't stagger or erupt into argument. The creek runs evenly, always its mild self. The stones expect nothing from you and don't disappoint you. Nature is good company in part because it's no company at all: it's reliably unhuman. Its dangers are limited and comprehensible, or so they were in my natural worlds. If you scraped your knee or got stung by a hornet, at least you knew where you hurt and why. The pain was localized, it was treatable, and it went away.

None of this, of course, was in my awareness at the time. I don't know what was in the mind of that solitary hiker. It's amazing—all those thousands of hours being me as a kid, and I have only the vaguest idea of what I thought or felt. I know what I did but not who I was. But whatever I thought about, it certainly wasn't the troubles between my parents. What was there to think? They hadn't divorced over my mother's affair, in part perhaps because I had begged my father to stay. But if I'd succeeded in keeping them together, I failed at getting them to be happy together. The drinking and fighting went on, worsened if anything, and eventually I went to my father and told him they should separate if they were so unhappy. I think he took my statement as a rejection of him. They didn't separate, not for another four years. I failed at that too.

How much of my passion to go west, I wonder, was an unconscious desire to get as far away from my broken family as I could? I hardly considered Cornell or Wesleyan; it was Reed all the way. And even after I dropped out of Reed—which must have been partly a shot at my parents, who took great pride in my academic success—I never lived in the East again except as a temporary convenience. I didn't see myself as running away. I was being a hippie, transforming the world, in love with the western land—but now, thirty years later, the boy I was sure looks like a boy on the run.

I took up rock climbing and mountaineering with a fierce hunger that far exceeded my skill, continually pressing myself into danger-ous situations. Crags and clouds and glacial brilliance seemed a secret language I was always on the verge of understanding, and I sensed obscurely that the riddle of the mountains somehow was the riddle of myself, that in the wild hills if anywhere I might discover the sure and undivided human being I wanted to be. I climbed in an ecstasy of fearful exhilaration that simplified my confusions and uncertainties into snow and stone, a hand here and a foot there, rising toward the possibility of a clear-cut success that no one, not even I, could dis-pute. And the ease of an exhausted peace.

I've climbed little since injuring my ankle, but recently I went with a friend to Mount Washington in the central Oregon Cascades. The West Ridge, a route I first climbed in 1969, rises steeply at some points and at others narrows to a thin edge, a drop of hundreds of feet on either side. The volcanic rock is frequently loose. My friend led the hard sections, which I followed on the safe end of the rope, but still I struggled awkwardly, overgripping the holds, my knees trem-oring beneath me. As a twenty-one-year-old I climbed that ridge without a rope and without a partner, exulting in my own sufficiency and the blue brilliance of a summer afternoon—and so driven by a demon it scares me now to watch. He had a lot to prove, that young man. And he was lucky.

Back in the city—I shuttled back and forth between Portland and San Francisco—I sought my wholeness in other ways. I took LSD and mescaline and psilocybin, hoping to break through to a compel-ling spiritual enlightenment that would settle my life and give me peace. And I took hard drugs, which seemed safer in a way because they were so much more predictable—and the peace they gave me, though not very spiritual, was thorough while it lasted. I don't like to recall that part of my life, but like it or not there I am: alone in a room or with a using friend, tightening my belt around my upper left arm with the same kind of fearful ecstasy I found in climbing. When the vein stands out I slide in the needle, a little blood rises in the glass syringe, and I squeeze the solution into the vein, into my mind, easing back in the chair as the good stuff waves me away from all uncertainty and sadness.

I shot morphine and heroin for the dull oblivion they brought, but my drug of choice was methamphetamine, good father speed. Its tingling rush delivered me not to oblivion but to a vibrantly intense awareness that was itself a perfect sufficiency—an alertness such as the gods might know, I enthused with fellow users. An alertness, I suspect, closely akin to the seductive mania of the manic-depressive. An alertness requiring neither food nor sleep, clouded only by the progressively troubling question of how to get more speed. And when there is no more, body and mind crash-land together, plunging as deep as they had soared high. All that had glowed with self-meaning now falls inert and meaningless. Color has leached from the world. People are ugly, mechanical, and against you. It's an effort to move. I remember one night in my room in a Portland student house, exhausted and unable to sleep at the end of a three-day run, staring at the glow of a streetlight on the floor and thinking that happiness was there, was just that close, if only I could go to it and touch it. If only it could live in me again.

I wondered, in those deep depressions, if I was crazy. "I'm hopelessly divided from myself," I remember saying again and again one afternoon in a mountain meadow, where—strung out on speed—I had hyperventilated and collapsed on the way with friends to climb a Cascade peak. *Hopelessly divided from myself.* I saw my self-destruction clearly, and it frightened me. At home I spent hours drawing hierarchical diagrams of my broken mind, struggling to understand what was missing, what was wrong. I didn't know what I wanted except to be whole and happy, as whole and happy as I assumed other people were. But how? You either were or you weren't. I was too ashamed to see a psychiatrist. I sealed myself off from my friends behind an air of self-sufficiency, successfully practicing the Daniel Way. How could anyone help me with my troubles, I reasoned, when I didn't understand them myself? I knew only two remedies for my depression. One was to buy more drugs. The other was to venture into the mountains again, where I was lonely but enlivened by cliffs and glaciers, where I could prove myself once more and maybe scare some happiness into my head.

In the early 1970s I lived with friends in San Francisco, dabbled in Zen meditation, hiked and climbed in the Sierra, took drugs and sporadic college courses. I felt pulled in a thousand directions. Posters on storefronts and telephone poles announced encounter groups, political rallies, environmental causes, religious sects. Each one seemed a door behind which people were engaged in something authentic, and I was walking the hallway unable or unwilling to knock. I studied classical guitar, then dropped it when I realized it would take years to develop the skill I wanted right away. It had been in my mind since childhood that maybe I could write, but the few lines I forced out seemed merely contemptible. They confirmed what I'd known all along—I had nothing to write about. I had dropped out of college in order to live, but without my student identity I didn't know *how* to live except by drifting aimlessly from one job or interest to another.

There was no further west I could go. I had fled to land's end, to the very brink of the abyss I had imagined as a little boy. It came close to swallowing me. And even at the far edge of America, it turned out, I couldn't shake off the family pain that had set me in motion in the first place. My parents had both done well since their separation. My father had stopped drinking and launched a successful civic life in Springfield, Missouri. My mother had set out on her travels and her quest. They corresponded and had patched together a relationship at a distance. In the summer of 1971 they each came to Berkeley to see their granddaughter Heather, who had been born to my brother and his wife the fall before. The visit went fine for a couple of days, but then—of course—it went to hell. In the parking lot at Candlestick Park, after a Giants game, my mother wanted us to go to a party a friend of mine was throwing, my father didn't want to, and in a flash they were wrangling—he with his feelings hurt because no one respected his wishes, she alternately soothing and berating him, and me in the middle where I'd always been. I wanted them to be happy, I wanted to please them, I felt somehow to blame for the terrible discord when all had been fine just a minute ago.

I think it was the next evening, in the shabby duplex I was renting in Berkeley, that I blew up at my mother. I don't remember exactly what I said, but I know it erupted out of me. *Why do you have to come here from thousands of miles away and start this shit all over? Don't you think I had enough of it as a kid? Why do you and Franz do this? Why?*

My mother, taken aback and defensive, said something like "I didn't know you felt so strongly." And I suppose she didn't, since all my life I had been so successful in burying my feelings. But she did know, of course she knew. She knew very well how hard our family life had been on all of us, she wanted to make it right somehow, she thought this get-together would be a step in that direction, and she too was frustrated and regretful. My outburst must have raised up all of that, a load of thwarted love drenched in guilt.

They left the Bay Area soon, and I never saw them together again. My father died in 1976, and though we were on good terms in his last years, we visited infrequently and never found a way to talk about our feelings. I don't think either of us looked for one. My resentments toward him were buried so deeply beneath my love and admiration that I scarcely knew they existed. And even if I had been able to express them, I would have been afraid of hurting him and unsettling his hard-won sobriety. My father—the stirring orator, the tough strike leader—was emotionally a very vulnerable man. He carried some enormous painfulness within him, some ruined cathedral that no one, not even he, could enter. He could only shore it up with sad eyes and silences, and the many who were drawn to him, me included, helped him keep it safe. Talking baseball and Beethoven was as close to intimacy as we got.

I did get closer to my mother, but we never entered the dialogue that my explosion in Berkeley might have made possible. We communicated by letter mostly, and in hers she tended to write of our family troubles in terms of her religious ideas. She wrote that all of us were worthy souls struggling under the necessary burden of our personalities, the particular burdens each of us had entered the world to bear. That we loved one another deeply, purely, despite the deformations of personhood. That our strife and griefs all served to help us know ourselves, which is the soul's work in the world. It all seemed apt enough, right enough, but now when I look at those letters I'm struck by how general those terms *love* and *burden* and *personality* seem. I can't help thinking that my mother needed vessels, large and sturdy vessels, to hold harmless the many hot pains of her marriage, and in her spiritual beliefs she found those vessels.

Few of my letters to her survive, but I'm sure I wrote less about family matters than she did, and in terms no less general. I wish I could have—wish I *would* have—told my mother in a controlled way the strong feelings she both knew and didn't know I had. I wish I would have said, *You hurt me. You and Franz hurt me. You fought the whole time I was growing up, and it wasn't all his fault. It was your fault too.* I wish I could have found a way to say that. Not to revile her. Not to punish her. More than anything, to forgive her.

For many years she was probably capable of hearing that and responding to it. But by the time I became capable of saying it, she was losing her memory and clarity of thought. It would only have troubled her, unfairly clouded her mind with things she could not fully understand or deal with. And of course it's only now, a year and a half past her death, two decades past my father's, that I'm really capable of saying it, and saying it only to a sheet of paper. After running for all those years I double back now when everyone's gone, late as usual, late to my parents' lives and late to my own, I poke and worry through what I can find and make this vessel to hold it.

CHAPTER EIGHTEEN

I don't know why I should be tired," I can hear my mother saying. "I haven't *done* anything."

It runs through my mind like a tune that won't stop playing. She's lying on her bed as she says it, her head propped on pillows, or maybe sitting in the living room with a book or magazine in her hands. There's a certain laugh in her voice as she says *do* or *done*—a guilty, self-mocking laugh, as if she were derelict for not being busy, for spending her days eating meals, drinking tea, and reading. She doesn't need a bath, she says, she hasn't *done* anything. She really oughtn't to be hungry. What has she done all day to work up an appetite? It seemed almost as though she felt she didn't deserve to exist because she didn't do anything with her life.

When I had time and she was willing, we took short walks together. The exercise was good for her, I wanted her to keep in contact with the air and odors of the outdoors, and a walk was a break in her oppressively restful day. Sometimes we drove to a nearby park, where forsythias might be blooming in spring or maples turning in the fall, but usually we didn't drive. In the old house, when she was stronger, we walked around our home block—and sometimes an extra block or two if she was up to it—pausing to admire flower beds, shapely Victorian houses, the majestic copper beech on Hancock Street that was my mother's favorite tree. She leaned heavily on my arm, her wooden cane in her other hand, and every half block or so she stopped and had me change sides. She shuffled along in her sure-footed way, breathing rapidly, her white head bowed. Her circulation was poor—poorer than I knew—due to age and to heart valve damage from a childhood bout with rheumatic fever. Her lungs, like her feet, tended to collect fluid.

In our new neighborhood we would sometimes drive a few blocks to the University of Portland campus and walk there, usually to a bench that looks off the bluff to the Willamette River, which was likely to be busy with tugs and pleasure boats. The Swan Island shipyard would have a freighter or tanker in for repairs, maybe two or three. My mother loved ships and boats of all kinds, but I always sensed something uncertain, something unresolved in her attention, when we watched from the bench. I don't think she ever grasped the linkage of waterways, Willamette to Columbia to Pacific, so she may not have understood what big ships were doing in front of her. When I glanced at her face it looked as though she didn't quite know what she was seeing—as if she didn't truly believe that the ships were ships, as if she were playing along with the imposture only for me.

Walking was labor for my mother, harder and harder the longer she lived. When we returned she would be ready to lie down for a while or sit for a long time with a mug of tea. But though it taxed her physically, walking didn't make her feel useful. It wasn't *doing* something. We tried to involve her in the chores of the household, but because of her frailty there was little she could effectively do. For a while she was able to set the table for dinner, but before long it became too much effort for her, too many trips between table and kitchen with plates and silver and glasses, her balance precarious without her cane. Folding laundry was the only job she could consistently do. Marilyn or I would set a full basket by her chair in the living room, and by and by she sorted napkins and washcloths and dish towels into neat stacks on the footstool in front of her. Some days she would put off the folding for a while—mostly, I suspected, because it raised her spirits to have the prospect of work ahead of her. "I'll be back," she would say, shuffling into her bedroom. "I've got that basket of laundry to do." For me, the laundry became a rough barometer of my mother's health. If a load sat unfolded for more than a few hours, it probably meant that she was feeling poorly and I should try to find out what was going on.

When I had produce that needed preparation for cooking, I always asked my mother if she would like to help with it, and I can't remember that she ever declined. She would sit leaning forward at the oak kitchen table, a dish towel in her lap and concentration on her face, shelling peas or snapping beans or hulling strawberries or shucking corn. "Oh," she would say, "what fine red berries." Or "This corn looks *terribly* good." James Hillman has said that the fingers are the soul's means of involving itself in matter, of enacting its desires among the things of the world. And the connection, once opened, works both ways: the soul takes nourishment through the fingers even as it uses them to express itself. As she bent to her work, my mother was connected to old rhythms, irreducible truths. In those intervals of shucking and hulling she felt herself a contributing member of the household, redeemed from marginality. She belonged.

Back in my LSD days I was fond of saying that the purpose of existence is simply to be. What we do, I believed, doesn't matter much; that we are is everything. I thought scornfully of jobs and careers as nothing but servitude exchanged for money, blinders that obscured the shining truth of being. The world was perfect, if only we would pause from our busyness long enough to see it. Real fulfillment could occur only outside of what one did for a living. I had no idea what work actually was and how badly I needed it, as I drifted from place to place and job to job, looking for enlightenment beyond the horizon, my hands, except while climbing, almost as empty as my mother's in her last years. I revered freedom and a simplistic idea of love. What I wanted, and took years to find, was a necessary task to which I could bend myself.

My mother's life had been replete with meaningful work: her mission in the labor movement, the raising of children, the explorations of her quest for the Self, and lesser tasks along the way—learning Serbo-Croatian, making tile art from pieces of sea-smoothed glass, editing a friend's manuscript on Iran under the Shah, studying Haitian culture. But in her last years that energetic directedness melted away, along with her memory. Now and again as I straightened the books and papers on her bed I would find a note she had penned in a margin or on a scrap of wastepaper, a self-exhortation: *Get paper clips etc. Laurens van der Post book on Jung. Write Jim . . .* She missed that sense of engaged activity that had defined her, she wanted it back, but she never did retrieve it.

Like many with Alzheimer's or other dementias, my mother had trouble executing simple sequences that the rest of us take for granted. When she was done snapping beans, for instance, there would be bean ends among the beans and beans among the bean ends. She got fouled up stringing popcorn and cranberries at Christmas. She had to concentrate while dressing to put her clothes on in the right order. When she wrote checks at the beginning of the month—for her Medicare supplement insurance, her VISA account, her share of household expenses, and so on—I had to cue her at each step of the process: the date, the payee, the numerical amount, the written amount, her signature. Sometimes before writing the check she recorded it in the register, so she wouldn't forget.

Then she would pause, staring at the checkbook and the pen in her hand, and I would have to remind her to write the check itself, telling her the date that she had just written in the register. It was a long and tedious process for both of us. I could have made out the checks myself—we had a joint account—but I wanted her to retain as much control of her own affairs as she could. I thought it was good for her. Now I wonder if I wasn't inflicting a form of torture.

That trouble with sequences, along with her memory loss, made it impossible for my mother to pursue any kind of sustained research, any activity much more complicated than folding laundry. But something else was missing, too. My mother had a great many friends and relatives and received letters from most of them, but after her first year with us she almost never answered the letters. This puzzled and grieved me for a long time. An active correspondence was work she *could do,* I thought, work that could ease her isolation and help sustain her. She had been a letter writer her entire life, and she was still capable of writing. The lettering was labored, the lines of her clear cursive sometimes inked over two or three times, as if she didn't trust that the pen was making an impression on the page. But she could write, and in a voice recognizably hers. Her sister Adelaide received this postal card, a rarity, in 1991:

If this beat-up card reaches you
let me know. I am mostly very well.
I go nowhere, hardly; to the
Farmers' Market, across the
Willamette River, with John.
Marilyn is exhausted tonight,
from her full-time job. John is
working on his book of essays.
I just live, but glad to be alive.
　　Love always
　　Zilla

She wrote a few others, but the letters and cards mostly piled up on her nightstand. Gradually they mixed with her books and magazines, were rediscovered and read anew a month or six months later, and set aside once again. She wanted and intended to answer—"I *must* write the Gorskis," she would say as she read their letter. Her little card file of addresses was by her bed, and we made sure she had pads and envelopes and even stamps handy. I gave her a clipboard for writing in bed. She had time—God knows she had time. But she didn't write. Something in her had washed out, some canyon had formed between desire and action. I know that in the simplifying lens of her dementia, most things not physically present were essentially unreal to her. She saw the last leaf on the dogwood tree, but after it fell she could scarcely remember it. It may be that when she set herself to write she simply could not bring into focus the individual she was addressing, though that person's letter was before her. It amazes me—and frightens me now—how far the mind leaps and how broadly it casts its net in faithfully performing, for most of us, the simplest tasks of day-to-day doing.

Had my mother's will weathered away? Not the bulldog will that got her through her arduous walks with me but some less physical, more subtle form of it? She wanted to write, intended to write; maybe she simply could not will her desire and purpose into fulfill-ment. Maybe volition was not there. And what *is* volition? What spurs us into the actions of a lifetime, and then, at some point in some of us, quits? I know that something as quickly desired and accom-plished as getting up from a chair often took my mother many min-utes, and not only because of her physical weakness. Many times I watched her secure her purse strap across her shoulder, lean forward in her chair, look around, look at her lap, sit back a little, look around, start forward, scratch her shoulder, look at her lap, look out the win-dow, sit back, sit forward . . . It may have been simple distraction that delayed her, but I got the distinct impression that distraction was in-vading in the absence of will.

But probably it was something even deeper and more essential than will that failed. Alzheimer's dissolves the very core of an individual: the self, the identity. Maybe my mother's difficulty was not in bringing to mind her correspondent but in bringing to mind her own self. It's possible that "I go nowhere" and "I just live," along with a very few particulars, were the fullest accounts of herself that she was able to give. Writing a letter, like writing this book, is an act of mythologizing, an attempt to make from life lived a meaning that another might understand. But if the life makes little meaningful sense to the one who is living it, if life is essentially changeless, eventless, a vagueness unavailable to words . . . Was my mother's silence an inability to reflect? Or was there in her own inward view no substance, no firm matter of experience, no landscape of being to receive reflection and return it?

CHAPTER NINETEEN

Today I told my psychologist about a dream in which a dark-haired woman led me down a winding staircase—or I tried to tell her, but my psychologist was interested in something else. The dream began with two men arguing nearby while I dozed on a park bench. Then the woman came along and led me down the stairs, which seemed to me the important part. She had some work for me, and I wanted to find out what it was.

"But who are those two men?" my psychologist asked. "What are they arguing about?"

I thought about it—a bit irritably—and couldn't come up with anything. Just two guys arguing. Bit players, I told her. Bums probably. But they've been in my head all day and half the night, and I just realized I know them both. And I know what they were arguing about.

Bob Bourgeois will sometimes wake with a thought to prune the birches or split firewood or fix the leak in the washing machine, and he'll follow that thought right into the heart of the new day. It's easy to like Bob. He ruffs the fur of friendly dogs, he makes small talk with salesclerks. He greets shuffling geezers he passes on the sidewalk, causing them to light a smile and nod and mumble good day. Bob is pleasant. He's decent, he's cheerful, and the work he does he does pretty well.

The trouble is, there isn't a lot of depth to him. He hasn't earned his happy glow; he was born with it. He's a smiling cipher. He's comfortable being like everyone else, just another citizen in the grocery line, uncomplaining even when the checker yaks too long with customers ahead of him. He glides along on his even keel, soaking up sunshine, soaking up rain, soaking up anything that comes his way. He'll never be anything more than what he is, and he doesn't care. "I just live" could be his motto. "Hi, I'm Bob. I'm not going anywhere." Bob doesn't think very much. The truth is, he isn't very smart.

At least that's how the Inspector would have it. And it's the Inspector, as usual, who has my ear at 2:16 in the morning as I sit in my bathrobe at the kitchen table unable to sleep, as usual, the left side of my back hurting, as usual, a bowl of shredded wheat in front of me to ease the gnawing in my gut and settle my nervous mind. The Inspector may think *too* much, he acknowledges that, but he points out that a man in his position inevitably *will* think, and if he thinks excessively it is only a sign of his caring. *Someone* has to examine life lived. *Someone* must exert the discipline to stay awake and watchful, alert to the nuances. *Someone* must be willing to make the necessary judgments: *You should have behaved differently. Don't be so satisfied. How poor of you. Your work is flawed. You'll have to do better.*

And someone has to say, *You were selfish. You did not attend to her as she deserved. She gave birth to you, she raised you, and when she herself was a child in the last years of her life, you failed her.*

No one failed her, Bob says back. (Or is it me saying it back?) Nothing failed her except her body, her broken-down body of eighty-four years. Bob misses her. He mourns her. But when he thinks about her now, he's as likely to smile as to cry. She lived a good long life, after all. She lived most of it on her own terms. She did more than most people do. And she died pretty easily in the end, not in great pain.

Easily? snaps the Inspector. *What about the nightmare she had to endure in intensive care? And why were you out of the house when she fell? Why did you leave her alone so often? Why didn't you spend more time with her? Why did you make her feel unwanted in your home?*

She *didn't* feel unwanted, Bob insists. She said herself this house had been a real haven for her. She said she was lucky . . .

The Inspector only scowls at such evasion. He might as well be arguing with a child. *He* knows where responsibility resides, and he knows it is his duty to point it out. Responsibility must not be glossed over, and neither should pain. Pain must be felt. It must be contained and endured with dignity. With discipline and vigilance. The Inspector regrets that he has lost his digestion, but duty will exact its costs. He would like to get over his insomnia, but he suspects that ordinary sleep will always be an elusive thing for someone of his acuity and caring. Ordinary sleep is for the Bob Bourgeoises of the world. And depression? Of course the Inspector is depressed. Life is nothing trivial and nothing easy. To live is to be injured. Joy is possible in moments, perhaps, but happiness? Any fool can be happy, because any fool can fool himself.

Privilege inevitably has a price. And it *is* a privilege, the Inspector insists, to be night magistrate of the province. To be the only one awake in the house, likely the only one on the block, just him and the occasional teenager cruising slowly on Princeton Street with muffled bass beats thudding from his car. Of course it's a privilege. The province may be small, a limited territory, but who knows it as intimately as the Inspector? Who else has spent such time with it? Who else can nod and smile and bite his lip and shake his head so knowledgeably? Who else is capable of such caring? And who else, the Inspector points out with some pride, can look upon this province in the middle of the night and know it to be his, all his, as long as he shall live?

Bob and the Inspector hardly recognize that the other exists. They share nothing of temperament or inclination. Bob is a man of action and an optimist; the Inspector is a thinker, a brooder. Bob's a morning person. The Inspector begins to wake at dusk, with the owls. Bob spends little time in the past, the Inspector little in the present. They both drink, but differently. Bob quaffs a pint or two with friends, shares a bottle of wine with his wife. The Inspector drinks with himself. He likes the bite of whiskey, its measured burn, the confirmation of its glow. He lets the liquor cast his province in an amber afterlight, an aura that softens his criticisms—he knows that sometimes he's too harsh—and lightens his heart without impairing his watchfulness. He drinks not exactly to ease his pain, but because his pain, his position, entitles him to drink.

When they do encounter each other, Bob is noticeably less relaxed than he is in other company. He doesn't understand the Inspector and admits that he doesn't care for him. The Inspector, for his part, is abrupt and out of sorts. He's embarrassed to be seen with Bob. The boy is the only reason they meet at all. The boy is all they have in common now, and they disagree sharply about him. That's what they were arguing about, the boy asleep on the bench. The Inspector, you see, is terribly protective. He's a solitary man, an aging, childless man, and the boy means everything to him. It's for the boy, at heart, that he keeps his careful vigil, enduring the sleeplessness and knotted stomach that come with it like wounds of war. He wants the boy to live exactly as he's always lived, safely home in the province, undisturbed. The boy has had a painful childhood, and the Inspector feels he needs time to heal. He is delicate, unformed. To change his circumstances might only hurt him more.

Bob thinks those ideas are weird. He loves the boy but doesn't think he needs protection, at least not the way the Inspector does.

How can you protect him from life? And why would you want to? Is the Inspector looking out for the boy, Bob wonders, or for himself? If he cares so much about the boy, why does he keep him so far away, all the way back in what he calls his province? It isn't natural. It's not where the boy belongs anymore. Everyone's had some pain in his life—all the more reason the boy should get away. He ought to pack his knapsack, Bob believes. He ought to strap it to his skinny shoulders and come on out to Oregon.

CHAPTER TWENTY

I still argue with myself about my mother. Why should it have been so hard to care for her? She didn't have an advanced dementia, after all. In a bedrock way she knew who I was, who Marilyn was, who she was. She recognized the faces, though often she couldn't recall the names, of our friends. She didn't wander, didn't become belligerent, didn't fritter her money (which in any case amounted only to the six hundred and something a month she received from Social Security). She wasn't forthcoming in conversation but spoke well—so well it was hard for many who met her to believe she had a mental deficit at all. She could read. She was not confined to bed or a wheelchair. She couldn't cook but could feed herself. She did not require constant supervision or care. And when we lucked into the treatment half of a government study called the Medicare Alzheimer's Project, some of the care she did need—help with bathing and grooming, straightening her room, and so on—was provided by a nurse, Patty, who came for a few hours two or three times a week and became my mother's good friend.

So what was it? What made me mutter to myself, what made me yell or cry in the other room, what made me hide in irritable silence behind the morning paper? It was no one thing, no one task—not making meals or checking her blood pressure or driving her back and forth to doctor or dentist or Sai Baba group. More than what I did, it was what I didn't do. It was feeling that I should take her out to lunch, for an ice cream cone, for a drive in the country, feeling I owed her those things more often than I gave them. It was feeling that I should spend more time with her, time not directed to matters of her health or feeding—that I should sit in her bedroom and let her talk to me, if she would, and talk to her with no purpose in mind, to see if between us we might break out of the well-worn ruts of our daily exchanges about the quality of the breakfast fruit, the names of the birds, whether she had taken her morning medicines, and did she feel like a walk that day.

For Marilyn the chief daily irritant was my mother's bad hearing, the continual need to repeat herself in slow, loud, carefully enunciated syllables. For me it was my mother's eyes. The eyes whose gaze I felt on my back whenever I stood cooking at the stove or washing the pots and pans. The eyes that glanced away quickly, back to her plate or her reading, when I looked up from my newspaper. The eyes raised just enough to observe when I took a bite of French toast, when I took a sip of coffee, when I raised the blue cloth napkin to my face. When my mother and I were in the same room, I never felt free of those eyes. If I looked out the window she looked out. When I took another bite of breakfast she did too. At times I felt the rageful frustration of a kid in the copycat game, his every action mimed relentlessly by a friend.

It wasn't that my mother didn't know how to eat without having me or someone present, but the blankness inside her was extensive enough that she used a model when a model was there. The simple daily acts that most of us accomplish automatically weren't so automatic for my mother. She was lucky, and we were lucky, that her breakdown didn't progress further than it did. People with advanced Alzheimer's often lose the ability to feed themselves altogether. Plaques and nerve tangles in the brain scramble the intended movement—lifting fork to mouth, say—into a different one: scratching an ear, reaching for a purse. Eventually, if the individual lives long enough, there may be no outward motor activity at all, only the reflexive ability to swallow when food is placed in the mouth. And eventually not even that.

My mother lived out her life in an in-between state, partly enfeebled and partly quite capable. She was well enough to miss and desire the active life of her past, but not well enough to resume it. She wanted to go to poetry readings, but afterward she complained that she hadn't heard a thing and the seat had been uncomfortable. Movies were a little more successful—especially the seats—but it was a laborious trek for Marilyn and me to shepherd her through the crowded lobby and along the sloping dark aisles of the theater. Sometimes she leaned so heavily on my arm I was half carrying her. The best excursions I made with her were to the farmers' market on Sauvies Island in the Columbia, where my mother would sit in a chair apparently enjoying the quiet hubbub, watching with a smile as I drifted among the produce stalls filling a basket. Marilyn sometimes took her to Holladay Market in northeast Portland, where they would have *caffè lattes* and some pieces of bittersweet chocolate, for which they shared a passion. (My mother earned many credits in Marilyn's heart when she announced one day that eating chocolate was essential because it "grounded" her.)

Our trips to the coast were generally successful, too. A few times a year the three of us would drive to Oceanside and take a room where my mom could gaze at the gray or shining Pacific, the moonlit Pacific, the breakers rolling in from chartless reaches, the veering and crying gulls. I think she enjoyed that—surely she enjoyed it—

but those trips exhausted her, too. Walking down to the water to wet her feet required both Marilyn and me, one on each arm. As at home, my mother spent most of those weekends sleeping and reading. And when she looked at the sea—this other sea, this sea of final distances where the sun doesn't rise but only goes down—I sometimes thought I saw in her face the same disconnection, the same perceptual disbelief, that showed when she stared at the Swan Island tugs and freighters.

One of our hottest altercations occurred at the coast. The three of us, in my mother's Dodge—which Marilyn and I had bought from her by taking over the payments—pulled in to a state park and stopped by a curb where my mother would have a sea view while Marilyn and I walked a few minutes. When we came back she was livid.

"*John Daniel,*" she exploded. "Do not ever again leave me stranded in my own car without the keys."

"Mother," I said, "what happened?"

"Someone . . . a vehicle needed to get by . . ."

"Well, they must have *got* by. What was it, a motor home?"

"He got by with great difficulty. You were extremely inconsiderate. Don't ever again—"

"Jesus, Mother, you don't *drive* anymore."

"This is *my car.*"

I was so mad I clammed up, sulking like a reprimanded child as I drove us on to the motel. Silently I was writing her out of my life and welcoming her to drive her goddamn car off a cliff. My mother sulked in the passenger seat. Marilyn, in back, wove a peace between us once we both had cooled off a little, and the rest of the weekend went fine.

I don't know what happened in that parking lot, but I do know that my mother from time to time was prone to delusions. Her poor hearing contributed to these, along with the bitter fact that she was no longer in control of her life. When Marilyn and I tried to talk to each other at dinner, not speaking up for my mother's benefit, she was sure at times that we were talking about her, making some decision without consulting her. We weren't—though of course we were struggling with decisions all the time outside her presence, decisions about how to deal with her incontinence, how to relieve her boredom, how to find a good and affordable caregiver so that we could get away on our own for a while. My mother was wrong in the particular instance but right in the general fact.

Other delusions were more severe. One morning as I passed her door at the foot of the stairs, I saw her sitting in her nightgown on the edge of her bed, arms folded across her belly, rocking back and forth. She clearly was in some pain.

"What's wrong?" I asked.

"It's you," she said after a while.

"What do you mean? What's me?"

I sat down in the wicker chair in the corner of the room. She rocked on the bed, almost in tears.

Finally she said, "You're the one who gives them to me. You make me take them."

She meant, of course, her pills—the diuretic, the blood pressure pill, the antibiotic against urinary infections, the children's aspirin to thin her blood against clots—the pills whose sizes and colors she clearly saw but whose purposes she could never remember for more than a few seconds at a time and probably didn't believe in. The routine we went through every morning, the forced ritual that had come to symbolize for both of us the deterioration of her body and the failure of her freedom. I was the one who made her take them, who tracked her down if she left them on the breakfast table, and the cramps of constipation or indigestion that were hurting her this morning she believed to be the work of the pills. My mother thought I was poisoning her. I came near tears myself as I explained and explained to her, wondering all the while how long she'd been awake in the thrall of that idea, how many other mornings she might have thought it but held it unvoiced.

Another time she asked me, at lunch I think, "How is it back there? Your little house."

"My house?"

"You know, where you live back there."

"Mother, that's just where I *write*."

"Oh, I know that," she said quickly, but the moment before she hadn't known it. I took her out to see my garage-turned-study with its cluttered walnut desk, its puke-green carpet, its workbench layered with books and papers. No bed, I wanted her to see, and she did. But for how long did she understand? Staircases had become too much for her, and so she never saw the upper floor where Marilyn and I slept, where Marilyn did her weaving, where we read and watched TV. We described it to her, reminded her of what she could not see, but we never knew for sure just what she did see, we never knew how the house and its occupants mapped themselves in her mind.

Once in our first few months in the new house, Marilyn was unpacking extra linens into a closet in the hall outside my mom's bedroom. After a while, through the open door, she heard these words: "I know you and John are having trouble, and I'm sorry you have to leave. I wish you well." My mother's demeanor was grave. Marilyn, smiling, explained that we weren't having trouble, that she was unpacking, not packing, and that it was only a box of spare linens. My mother nodded, smiled without conviction, maybe convinced and maybe not.

Afterward Marilyn wondered if my mother's delusion expressed an unconscious wish. They had always gotten on well, often beautifully and deeply well, since the moment they first met in Marilyn's living room in 1982, when my mother, visiting from Maine, walked in and gave her a great hug before saying a word. But a household of husband and wife and mother is bound to know some tension, even in the best of circumstances. How could ours not? With or without delusions, a triangle is a triangle.

It was hardest when Marilyn and I went out for the evening. My mother was at times up to being a good sport about it, at others only capable of a grim acceptance. I remember all too clearly the way her eyes would frown when I told her we were going out for dinner and a movie, the way she wouldn't look at me as I reminded her that her dinner would be on the kitchen table, her tea in the steel thermos. I learned never to tell her until very late in the afternoon—if I told her earlier she might forget, and we'd have to go through the same little crisis all over again, or if she remembered she was likely to dwell for hours in a gloomy funk. I put off entering her room until I absolutely had to, dithering outside the door, finally forcing the breach. I hated it. And coming home was sometimes worse, because my mother— a night owl, like me—would rarely be asleep for the night. She'd be reading in bed, maybe dozing with her mouth open, and depending on what had passed through her mind in the time we were gone she might welcome us cheerily when we stopped by her room, or she might acknowledge us soberly, or she might snap, "I've been waiting here for *hours.*" And she had been.

CHAPTER TWENTY-ONE

I drew a picture when my mother died. Six strokes in red watercolor, a child waving good-bye. He is waving toward the right, one arm outstretched, upraised, the other at his side. The finality is what I was feeling. It made a child of me, a small child filled with sadness. *Good-bye.* I knew I would never hold again her veined and purpled hand, never touch her white hair, never feel the weight of her on my arm as we walked. All that is ashes now, and what isn't ashes rose into air and sky, into the ready emptiness of wind. And yet she lives. She is here as I write, interfused with what I am, strangely in me and around me. She is more present in this moment than anything I know. It's she who stirred my memory, and she whom memory bears forth.

But the other one. The other one who died, the one who never lived—how can I say good-bye to the one I never knew? A parent is supposed to die; a child is supposed to live. I knew only the earliest light my child sent before itself, the first wan light that comes to snowy fields before the break of day. *I feel as though I'm carrying a little ball of light*—and how the world slowed, how I slowed when Marilyn said that, how her face shone and the moment shone. The light of entrance to the world. A light all new to me. The light of yes.

I wanted what everyone must want. I wanted to see her face, I wanted to see his face—me and Marilyn stirred loose from ourselves, everything we are somehow swirled together like birds in a wind and formed again. To see that face, to welcome its cheeks and red scrunched brow, to welcome the gift that had been borne so far, to honor it from the tips of its tiny toes to the hairs of its head . . . To hold it to me, light and squalling—nothing to search for, nothing to be found, nothing like this unsure scratching at the page, this near-sighted groping, but *here*, achieved, alive. And knowing it good, knowing *this that has come of us is good.*

I wanted him to crawl and climb. I wanted her to shout, to run, to laugh in the rain so that I would laugh, cry so that I would cry. I wanted him to dash and tumble, to roll on the ground, I wanted his thin limbs to grow. I wanted to hear the syllables she would croon, the words she would speak, the words I would speak back to her. I wanted some best part of me to bound forth smiling, press footprints into frosted grass, saunter beneath arching trees and know the company of every rock and soul it met. I wanted a part of me to unfold that only she or he could have touched, I wanted to bloom this once like a century plant, to shower forth in a bright new body. I wanted to look into the clear eyes of my child. Not to seek my reflection there but to enter those eyes and discover my place to die.

How do I say good-bye? I knew the earliest light and only the light. Memory has nothing with which to conduct its ceremony—no image, no touch of hands, no slightest cry. Of my gone brother George I have photographs, accounts in my parents' letters, the living memories of my aunt and cousin. But of the one who was not

born there is only a slow pale shape rising from the depths, rising toward me, almost resolving into a form I recognize but not yet
formed, a face but not a face. It rises, wavering, the face of nothing
and of everything. It shimmers suspended on the verge of being and
wavers into formless light again, a sheen of motion, a stirring in the
clear dark sea that conceived it.

CHAPTER TWENTY-TWO

The cat showed up our first summer in the new house. Suddenly she was hanging around in back, rubbing up against the picnic table, curled in the beds between rhododendrons. She gave insistent chirpish cries like a bird. She didn't mind that we didn't feed her or invite her in—she stayed anyway. For a while we fancied that she liked us, but what she really cared for was the place, a fact we learned when a girl knocked one evening looking for her cat. The girl had grown up in our house; we had bought it from her parents. The cat had lived all seven of its years in and around the house, and now was with the girl elsewhere in the neighborhood—or had been. The cat kept returning to her old and only home, and after a few days we and the girl agreed that she was ours.

She was, and is, a black-and-tan tabby with a nervous disposition. The three of us never came up with a better name for her than Cat or

Kitty; when the vet had to have a name for his files, I called her Spook, short for Spookus Maximus or Spooky Spookissima. She is wary of strangers, starts at small noises, and does neurotic things like dash up the stairs as you walk down or down as you walk up. Turns up her nose at fish. Won't allow her front paws to be touched. And will not settle down when stroked but presses her face to your fingers in a purring agitation, demanding more and more, chirping birdlike all the while.

Puss, my mother called her. "Where's Puss?" she'd want to know, several times a day. She loved to watch the cat grooming herself— licking a paw and rubbing it across her ear, or licking her chest while propped indecorously in the easy chair, her buff-and-white under-region on general display. And she liked the way the Spooky One stretched after sleeping, reaching far forward with her front paws, her rear end high and the rest of her tapering low to the rug, as if she were performing some act of wild obeisance. And she delighted to see the cat smacking her chops as she sauntered through the kitchen af-ter breakfast.

But most of all it was the cat's tail that entranced my mother, her gray and black and brown-shaded tail that she almost never, while awake, held entirely still. Even when the cat and most of its tail lay flat on the floor, the tip, the last two inches, would be upraised and stirring, gently turning and flicking like a self-willed creature of its own. My mother would point it out to anyone who might be around, smiling her most delighted smile.

"It's a *semaphore,*" she exclaimed one afternoon. We were out back, enjoying an easy wind that stirred the hanging branchlets of the birches. The cat was sprawled on the concrete between Marilyn and my mother, the drifting tail-tip its only sign of life.

"What does it say?" I asked her.

She smiled steadily, captivated. "My dear," she said after a while, "it says what words cannot."

This time, I thought, it wasn't the blankness inside her covering for itself by cutting off conversation. This was one of those occasions when she spoke not from absence but from intense presence, an untranslatable richness, a seeing not diminished by her age but empowered by it. I suddenly remembered a morning twenty-five years in the past at Reed College when I had glanced down at wet yellow leaves on a concrete walkway, glowing in the rainy light, and suddenly knew them to be *signs.* Not symbols or types but signs, tokens of the tao, the spirit, the unspeakable meaning within and behind all things. I didn't know their meaning but felt it, understood it with my body. I almost rose off the walkway in my joy.

With that in mind I smiled at my mother and nodded, holding her eyes for a moment in mine.

The cat gave other signs, some of them annoying and some enchanting. Some evenings after dinner I would read aloud to my mother in the living room. Marilyn would join us if she felt like it; more often she would go to her weaving or a hot bath. We began with *Huckleberry Finn,* and from there took a vagrant path through *Moby Dick* and Joseph Conrad, P. G. Wodehouse, many weeks with the *Norton Anthology of Poetry,* J. R. R. Tolkien and Isak Dinesen, back to Twain for *Life on the Mississippi,* and on like that. My mother seemed to enjoy it all. She had always loved literature—she had been an English major at Vassar, and her father had wanted her to be a professor. It must have been a pleasure to relax and let the language come to her instead of having to pick it off the silent page, line after line, with her dogged, overworked eyes. She drank coffee as she listened, watching me like an attentive child, now and then asking to hear a sentence or short passage again.

The cat, it turned out, enjoyed the readings too. We couldn't predict when she would show up—she seemed to like e. e. cummings as well as Tennyson, Melville no more than Wodehouse—but when the mood struck her she would pad into the living room from upstairs or downstairs, hop into my lap, and proceed to rub herself all over me, turning in circles and purring loudly between me and the

book I was trying to read, fairly intoxicated with pleasure. This delighted my mother greatly and me a little less, since managing cat
and *Moby Dick* simultaneously could be a little tricky, but I hated to
shoo her off. My readings rarely elicit such adoration. All we could
figure was that my voice, a reasonably sonorous baritone, must have
tickled the cat's nerves at precisely the right frequency.

On other evenings the cat attended the reading with a less pas-
sionate interest. She might lie on her side in the middle of the room,
queen of the carpet, licking a paw and languidly taking in the verse
or prose of the hour. Or if we were lucky, she might decide that the
evening outdoors was of more interest than anything in the living
room. She would hop to a chest beneath the window, slip between the
closed, cream-colored drapes, and stare out from the sill, invisible to
us except for her tail with its roving semaphore tip. When she treated
us to this show, I stopped reading and we gave ourselves to the silly
wonder of it.

My mom never said it and would have denied it, but I think she
must have identified with the cat. They lived much alike in some
ways. Each of them napped in the day and spent many hours alone,
day and night. Each had to rely on others to let her in and out of the
house. Each had her meals prepared by others and placed before her.
Each was dependent and inveterately independent too. Each was a
creature of the moment. Each seemed to gaze through door or window toward things beyond my sight or knowing. And neither could
tell me in any thorough way about what she saw or what she wanted.
"She's picketing," my mom used to say sometimes when the cat
paced neurotically back and forth through the kitchen. I don't know
what the cat wanted—not food, because often she did this right after
eating—but after a while I discovered what my mother wanted and
could express only through comments on the cat. If I made her a
sandwich at such moments, she devoured it hungrily.

But if my mother identified with the cat, the cat did not identify
with my mother. She wasn't particularly affectionate to any of us,

but I could occasionally entice her into my lap and force her to submit to petting, gradually subduing her to a warm purring bundle—for about three minutes. She would accept the same from Marilyn, but usually she strode by with the merest glance or no glance at all when my mother patted a leg and urged her to hop up. I can see my mom now, leaning as far forward in her chair as her back would let her, extending her hand to the uninterested cat, or bending precariously from a standing position, balancing with her cane—and the cat would walk away or sit like a statue just out of reach, withholding her soft thick fur.

"She *simply* does not like me," my mom would say with a scowl. I reminded her that cats are wilder than dogs, domesticated a shorter time, aloof by genetic disposition. It's part of their charm, I told her, and to myself I wished the damned spookish thing would just once jump into her lap and warm her with rubs and purrs. I couldn't help thinking that the cat, with one of her keen senses, could sniff the chill of death on my mother and so carefully cut her a wide berth.

CHAPTER TWENTY-THREE

So when was I happy? It seems that all I'm remembering are the hard moments, the painful ones. I know I need to remember those, I need to dredge them up and see what they become in the light of consciousness. Anything can grow, even seeds trapped in caves for thousands of years. Anything, if you bring it to light, becomes something else.

But there's more to remember, and it's my infertile sadness that gets in the way. I've been reading about depression and memory, and I've learned two things that should have been obvious. The first is that depression dulls remembering, just as it dulls everything. Remembering is an active state, a dynamo of firing neurons—it's a fire in the mind (a fire of renewal, maybe), and depression is the damper in the stovepipe. It shuts the fire down to a smolder, clouding the mind with smoke. That's the Inspector's problem. Memory is his province, but his memory is depressed. His memory doesn't go anywhere. He patrols in the same ruts he's worn for years, sees the same views over and over, smiles and grimaces and goes on with his rounds.

The second thing is that it's not only the self trying to remember who's depressed—the self being remembered was probably depressed too. It didn't begin yesterday. Not with my mother, not with the miscarriage. It goes back at least to my drug days, and my psychologist keeps hinting that it goes back farther than that. I think she's right. It goes back to that boy with his feelings clamped inside his ribs. The boy who wanted to make things better and couldn't. The boy I can see but can't quite be. The boy still waiting.

He was vigilant, he was wary of the household weather, but vigilance and wariness don't necessarily make for sharp recall. They convert the mind to a defense system, a radar that wants to see nothing because the things it might see are threatening. Memory comes from attention, and attention is not a defense system, not a passive absorption, but an active reaching of the soul. Attention is the reason I remember the snowy parapet by the Potomac as well as I do. Depression cages the soul, ties it to a rock so it can't reach. Depression says, *There's nothing here I want to touch, nothing to keep.* And so I didn't, and so there are stretches of my life I recall poorly. I know where I was living, some of the people I was with and some of the things I was doing, but I recall few particular images, few certain feelings.

A friend asked once if I'd had a happy childhood. "I guess so," I answered. It seems strange to have to guess about your own past, your own youth, but I don't know that I have enough evidence in my memory to say anything more definitive. There was plenty of unhappiness, but there was happiness too. There was an afternoon when I dropped my bike and myself on a grassy bank and lay there writing a poem, the first I wrote outside. I don't have it, and I don't remember what it was about, but I remember being happy writing it. And other moments. When I caught a three-pound bass in a farm pond, when I tackled one of my brother's friends in a football game, when I tore around the yard full of steak and strawberry shortcake on my birthday.

And more, I'm sure, but where is happiness if you don't remember it? If you have to guess?

There's a certain form of happiness, a certain form of pleasure, that I remember best. It started early—a glow of satisfaction when my father showed off my baseball knowledge to his friends, when I danced with a tambourine to calypso music as my tipsy and delighted parents applauded on the sofa. After that it was mostly about my life in school. Being praised in class by my eighth-grade geography teacher, Mr. Fries. Opening a telegram from Lyndon Johnson telling me I was a Presidential Scholar for 1966. Being class president and valedictorian. As a kid I specialized in that kind of happiness, the happiness that comes from the approval of others. The pleasure of being a good boy in the eyes of parents and teachers and the world. That's not what I'm looking for now.

When was I happy for myself, happy in my own eyes? When, without drugs, was I happy to be alive? Driving west in the Jeep, singing to Route 66 and my unknown future. Seeing the glowing leaves, and *knowing* them, on the Reed College walkway. After making love with my girlfriend in my shabby Fillmore district room in San Francisco, having a vision in which she and I were perfect beings and everyone everywhere was a perfect being. Climbing straight into the noonday sun up the West Ridge of Mount Washington, alone and untethered, a gulf of space off either shoulder, my hands and feet in jubilant concert with the spirit surging within me.

But those were joyous moments, ecstatic moments, and what I want to find now isn't exactly joy or ecstasy. When I soar that high I always feel a devastation near, as if I've soared *too* high and can't accept that gift without also accepting a corresponding plunge. In Emerson's phrase, I am glad to the brink of fear. What I'm after now isn't that intensity of feeling but something more like garden-variety happiness—the "happiness" that's related in its roots to "happen," which comes from the Middle English "hap," meaning chance, fortune, that which occurs. Haps are what happen to you, and happiness means that you have it in you to be content, or at least reconciled, with the haps of your life.

Where can I find that? I can't, of course. By definition, it can't be sought. At any given moment it's either in you or it isn't. It's not seeking or striving. It's being.

Once at Reed I had an especially harrowing acid trip. I spent the night alone in a swampy wooded vale called the Canyon, trying to hold together not just myself but the world—the very firmament of reality was cracking open, actually splitting into jagged sections with a bright light shining through. The light was salvation or insanity; either way I didn't want it. Many hours of that night are lost to me. When I came back to myself, I was holding the trunk of a small tree. Birds were singing their liquid songs in the cool of the morning. All the waking green world was one, and I was both part of the one and outside it, the most privileged of beings. I walked around campus kicking pools of pink blossoms fallen from the trees, not ecstatic, not enlightened, but happy. Just happy. I kept saying, inside me, a four-word sentence that had come with me out of the Canyon: *I am this moment.*

It's been many years since I've said that sentence or even thought of it. I used to carry it with me and speak it sometimes as I might touch a lucky stone in my pocket, as I might feel the smooth touch of an amulet under my shirt. In the early 1970s, I remember now, when I was at loose ends in San Francisco, I would sometimes sit in a park, say the sentence, and try to let the doubts and confusions that burdened me fall away. I'd feel the ground beneath me, smell the eucalyptus, the sea tang in the air, and try to focus on my breathing in what I thought was Zen meditation. I didn't have to try to breathe, I told myself. It happened on its own, reliably, by some agency that had nothing to do with the loud cluttered rooms of my mind. The stillness of the trees was what I was after, the way their leaves stirred in the wind, or didn't stir.

I have a hunch that those moments of doing nothing might mean as much to my life as moments of decisive action or intense realization. There's something hard to define but very important they allow to happen, a way of remembering who you are. Not of knowing who you are, since consciously you may learn nothing, but of sensing your hidden dimensions—as a man alone in a small boat senses the depths of the sea and the great lives that move there, though he knows them not at all. LSD had shown me an extraordinary world dwelling in the ordinary one, and in those quiet sitting spells, without the tumultuous storms the drug was liable to set off, I could feel the presence of that world like the afterglow of sundown in the desert, when warmth still lingers in the stones. I could feel a larger Self within me, smiling.

It was LSD that taught me the value of such moments, but the moments didn't originate with drugs. I remember something that happened in the late summer of one of my high school years, when I was living with my mother in Washington, D.C. For a few weeks I'd been working graveyard shift in a Little Tavern hamburger shop on Connecticut Avenue, not far from the Twenty-eighth Street apartment we shared. One morning at first light I walked home with a piece of French apple pie in a white sack and climbed the iron fire escape to the roof of the little apartment building. I sat on a vent housing and ate the pie, which I had never tasted or even liked the looks of before that morning, when the night boss had offered it to me. It tasted wonderful. I scooped up bites with a plastic fork, taking great pleasure in the soft white icing, the few plump raisins mixed among sweet and spicy pieces of apple.

As I ate the pie the sun was rising, lighting an orange glow above the treetops, above the slopes and flats of various rooflines with their clutter of antennas and pipes. A few clouds were lit and shining. I was eating the sunrise along with the pie, happily taking in everything before me, swallowing the world, and then I stopped. How strange it all seemed. How familiar. How unlikely yet inevitable that I should be sitting on a graveled roof in Washington, D.C., eating French apple pie for the first time as the sun rose behind these particular trees and cluttered building tops and filled the sky with an orange glow. Why should the sunrise be orange? Why should I be here to see it? How unlikely, *impossible,* that I should be me. That I should exist at all. That anything should. A little sun rose inside me.

It sounds crazy to say it, but before that morning I don't think I believed that the world is real. Or I believed it, but I didn't *know* it. I'd forgotten it—because even as a young boy, it occurs to me now, I had a similar moment of knowing. (Memory amazes me. I walk its wilds and stumble upon place after place where I once camped.) I think I was eight. My shirt was a faded blue plaid, short-sleeved, a shirt I liked. I had just put it on, not tucking it into my jeans, and now I walked out my bedroom door and saw a broad shaft of sunlight slanting between the picture-window curtains and falling on the dark walnut table that had been my grandfather's legal desk. Flecks of dust drifted in the light. As I walked by the table I reached my left hand into the light and stopped to look at it, slowly closing then opening my fingers, extending them in the clear radiance. *This is my hand,* I thought. *This is a dream, and the dream is true.* I felt I'd been withdrawn from time. Then I walked on into the kitchen, the summer day, the rest of my life. That's all there was. That was everything.

CHAPTER TWENTY-FOUR

My mother kept a clock on her nightstand, a battery-powered portable that had accompanied her on many of her travels. She paid attention to it—when it stopped she asked me to replace the battery—but I don't know for sure that she could read the time on the clock, or if she could read it, I don't know if it meant to her what it meant to me or Marilyn. If I told her that she needed to be ready to leave the house at 11:00 A.M. for a doctor appointment or whatever, I'd be likely to find her sitting on the side of her bed, fully dressed with her purse strapped across her shoulder and cane at the ready, by 10:30. Maybe she knew how long it took her to dress and prepare herself, and she was overcompensating. Or maybe memory could give her no guidance on how long her preparations would take, and so she began right away to be safe. Maybe she didn't trust the clock to tell her, or herself to understand, when "11:00 A.M." would arrive. On a few occasions she wasn't ready when the departure time came and had to finish hurriedly as I stood holding her coat like an impatient husband.

Aside from her infrequent appointments, of which I always reminded her several times, clock time had little bearing on my mother's life. We had meals at no set hour; when the food was ready I came by her room, or else clanged the brass yacht bell she had ordered from a nautical catalog and I had mounted on the dining room wall. She didn't watch TV or listen to the radio, so she had no need to check program times. She didn't divide her day into various activities with budgeted time for each. She had, for the most part, drifted out of time's main channel and was turning slowly in the eddies.

She lived in an older kind of time. She saw the light changing in the shrubs and trees of the backyard, their shadows shifting, reconfiguring. I'm sure she saw the dawn of many mornings. She saw blocks of sunlight move across her room as the day progressed, she saw color in the western sky at sundown. She watched the beginning of rain and the end of rain, the gray sky brightening and darkening. She watched wind stir the birches and pines. She saw leaves drop away in the fall and watched closely, intently, for their reappearance in the spring. "We'll see the leaves soon, won't we?" I remember her asking as early as January, with two to three months of leaflessness still ahead. "You can tell by the twigs," she observed one late March morning, studying the dogwood tree at breakfast. "They're getting fatter. Don't you think they are?"

As the days and seasons turned around her, my mother gazed and drifted. She had no need to know what time it was. Her personal river of more than eighty years had borne her close to its mouth, to that great mingling of waters where the current slows, where the channel widens and deepens, where time itself is drowned in timelessness. One afternoon when I stopped by her room, she had just wakened from a nap, and she said, "I hope it's the same season. I feel as though I've lived a whole *life*." There was a tone of wonder in her voice.

"Since when?" I asked.

"Since I fell asleep."

Physicists from Einstein on have insisted that our sense of time as separable into past, present, and future is an illusion. A peculiarly tenacious illusion, but illusory all the same. Time does not happen incrementally, second by second. Like space, with which it came into being and from which it is inseparable, time is all here all the time. Past, present, and future are one. No one knows why we don't perceive them as one, but writer-physicists Paul Davies and John Gribbin have speculated that it may be something in the working of human memory that creates our certain sense of immersion in a moving present flowing out of the past into the future. We think of memory as a function of time. It may be truer to say that time, or our illusory sense of time, is a function of memory.

And if that's the case, it may well be that when memory fails, as it did in my mother, a physically more accurate sense of time may come to awareness. Who was experiencing the greater illusion? I as I worked at my desk with one eye on my digital clock, or my mother as she drifted, unmoored to the clock by her bed? It was as though eternity was opening to her, showing glimpses of itself as the ocean sometimes will, appearing and disappearing in fog. In medical and psychological terms, my mother was a cognitively impaired octogenarian suffering the confusions of senile dementia. But in terms of her own sense of being, in spiritual terms, I believe she lived parts of her last years in the presence of the eternal and in the eternal present.

I also believe she *saw* differently than I and most people do. At times at least I think she experienced a visionary kind of seeing, a seeing perhaps like the psychedelic awareness that many of us sought in the 1960s, a seeing-into-things that reveals a deeper level of identity than name or category. A seeing in which all things glow with the fullness of their being. Like me on LSD, my mother didn't always know who she was in a personal sense and couldn't always name the city she was in or the day of the week, but in her visionary moments she always knew *where* she was—deep in the world's unspeakable being.

On one of our walks in the rainy season she couldn't stop looking at the brilliant green moss that lined each crack in the sidewalk and lay in velvety waves here and there along its borders. "So green, so *green*," she said. She seemed transported, ravished, as if the beauty of it hurt her eyes. She reached a hand down, wanting to touch the moss, to feel its greenness with her fingers, but even with me to steady her she couldn't stoop that far. At the corner of the block, the sidewalk makers had stamped into concrete the date—1911, I think—and the name of their company: a partnership, Miller & Bauer. The lettering was filled with emerald moss. "If only they knew," my mother said. "Their names magnified in moss."

And then there was the morning I set a large nectarine on a saucer at her place at the breakfast table. It was an especially colorful fruit, its rich yellow shading into orange and a large splotch of deep purple. My mother shuffled in, got herself dropped into her chair and her cane hung on its hook, and when I scooted her chair into place she saw the nectarine. She stared disbelievingly, her mouth agape. She seemed horrified.

"Is it . . . *corrupt?*" she said.

"It's just a nectarine, Mom," I said in my let's-get-through-breakfast voice.

She ate her soft-boiled egg and toast but wouldn't touch the fruit. She stared at it, silently, for long intervals. It was not "just a nectarine" to her. I don't know what it was—vision fruit, ember of the other world, portent of her own consummation and decay—but it was no mere docile object. My mother may have been seeing in that moment as Van Gogh or William Blake must have seen. She was not looking at a thing. She was in a presence.

Very little was just a nectarine to my mother, and in a way this was the triumph of her late life. The diminishment that her dementia brought, though a very real impairment, allowed at the same time an enlargement of her spirit. It may have allowed, in a way she didn't foresee and wouldn't have chosen, a culmination of her spiritual quest. Her forgetfulness had an aspect of remembering—a religious remembering, a cleansing of the doors of perception. The conventional certainties we carry in common in our ordinary lives are themselves a forgetting of the primary world, the world we knew best as children and are in danger of never knowing again. The world, in the words of painter Harlan Hubbard, whose "radiant beauty should be an unending source of wonder and joy, yet most people live and die without noticing it." What could be more fitting, as one draws near death, than to slough off by one means or another the tired definitions we have imposed on the world and remember it in its unfathomable mystery? "The invariable mark of wisdom," wrote Emerson, "is to see the miraculous in the common." By that standard, my mother at the end of her life was a very wise woman indeed.

One evening in the fall of 1990, when my mother had just read an essay of mine about the limits of our visual perception of nature, she and I were having a drink in the living room. I argue in the essay that nature's chief beauty and value lie not in what we see of it but in what remains hidden and mysterious. It ends with an image of a desert canyon opening itself to a hiker but always withholding its further reaches in mystery.

My mother rarely commented on my work, but this time she had been moved. We had a conversation I think of often, a conversation I'm grateful for. She asked if I knew ahead of time where I was going in my writing, if I had a destination.

"Not usually," I told her. "Or if I do, I only see it in a nearsighted way."

"It's like the canyon?"

"It's like the canyon."

She seemed happy to hear that, and she seemed to have taken some kind of important inner step on her own journey. There was exaltation in her voice.

"I think we know too much now. And if we don't know everything, we *think* we do. We need more mysteries."

I asked her if she was afraid of dying.

"Not so much," she answered. "Not so much. I worry more about things I haven't done."

"But you've done so many things . . ."

"Oh, I think of what it would have been like to explore unknown terrain. I think of the explorers . . ."

"I think of them too," I told her. I wish I had told her that she was an explorer. I wish I had told her that I was proud of her. I hope she knew it.

We were silent for a time. We looked out the window at our neighbor's house across the street, glowing softly yellow in the failing October light. A man walked by, limping. Crows were flying among the tall trees of the park. After a while my mother raised her glass of whiskey.

"Here's to the Unknown!" she said.

CHAPTER TWENTY-FIVE

I'm thinking that maybe I've always had a faith in the unknown. As I was living my desultory life in the Bay Area in the early seventies, I was unsure about most everything. I had dropped out of college and landed only in more self-doubt and confusion. I didn't know what I wanted to do or what I could do. I was waiting for my life to find me, and wasting it as I waited. Looking back now, I can see that two unknowns sustained me in that time. One was the larger Self, the sure and undivided Self, whose smile I could sometimes sense. And the other was the greater West Coast itself, where I was certain, despite my uncertainties, that I somehow belonged. The mountains had told me this from my first year in Oregon, and so did the breezy streets and bright housefronts of San Francisco, the soaring exclamation of the Golden Gate Bridge —they raised a yearning for I wasn't sure what, a sense of tantalizing destiny never quite swimming into shape.

Eventually I got a job as mail clerk for a railroad inspection bureau with offices on Market Street. The bureau had field positions up and down the coast, and when an Oregon job came open I put in my bid. I was twenty-four and hoping for simplification, for a new beginning. And so one gray winter morning in 1973, my girlfriend and I awoke in our Volkswagen bug in a highway rest area on the outskirts of Klamath Falls, just east of the Cascade Range in the southern part of the state. The landscape puzzled us. No Douglas firs, no tumbling streams or emerald fields, no green at all . . . just sagebrush flats and barren hills studded with a few disconsolate junipers. In the nearly seven years since my first arrival in Oregon, I had missed the fact that two-thirds of it is desert and steppe. My girlfriend and I decided we wouldn't stay long in that bleak country.

Things didn't go well between us. We quarreled and stormed, as we had in California, and before too long she left for law school and we broke up. She told me what others had: I was too aloof, too self-enclosed, I didn't give enough of the me she loved. I knew it was true, and I knew my helplessness. What did I have to give? If I was holding out, I was holding out on myself as well.

I took refuge in my new job, which was criminally easy. For a handsome monthly salary I spent three or four hours a day in the Southern Pacific and Burlington Northern freight yards, opening boxcars of lumber to see if shippers were cheating for a lower rate by misdeclaring their loads. My nearest supervisor was four hundred miles away in San Francisco. I called in each morning to announce that I was working, drank coffee with the clerks in the freight office, cracked open a few boxcar doors, and passed time with the hoboes—who greatly admired my job—under the highway overpass. I could usually complete my paperwork and call it a day by noon. It amounted to an extended fellowship in fooling around.

The forested mountains I'd thought I was going to be living in weren't far away. I hiked and fished and skied the southern Cascades and, after meeting a few other climbers in town, made expeditions with them to Mount Shasta and other peaks. North of Klamath Falls we found a clean basalt rimrock, a perfect rock-climbing playground where we'd divert ourselves for an afternoon putting up new routes and then hit the taverns for pool, pinball, and many cold pitchers of beer. I loved the cool and cavelike beer halls with their lights and ready laughter, their swirling flow of life that I could join and drift with any time.

I also began to explore the drier country east and south of town. The openness of the land, though strange to me, was somehow inviting. I found I liked the way junipers apportioned themselves on the rocky slopes, how each shaggy tree stood solitary and whole. Even clumps of sage and crusty scab rocks came to seem not bleak but friendly as I walked among them. I'd sit and watch big cloud shadows traveling the hills, a light breeze stirring the bronco grass and the hair of my arms. There was something settling in all that spacious stillness. I didn't feel tugged in all directions, as I had in the city, and despite the turmoil with my girlfriend and the pain of our parting, I began to feel a kind of wholeness that was new. The great dry land seemed an open secret, a secret with room for me.

It was there in the Klamath Basin that I began to write. I built myself a stand-up desk (I'd read somewhere that Hemingway had used one), bought a Webster's Third International and a used Royal manual typewriter, enrolled in a correspondence course in story writing, started keeping a notebook, and put my fooling-around fellowship to use. My father, in a frank moment, had asked if I intended to be a railroad dick my entire life. That had goaded me, and so did the face I sometimes saw in the bathroom mirror after a long night in the taverns with my climbing friends. My twenties were waning, and I figured if I was ever going to try to be a writer it had better be now.

I was hoping for publication, fame, and money, none of which I found. What I did find, to my surprise, was a kind of difficult and pleasurable journeying that was a lot like rock climbing. Move by move, each one making possible the next, you pursue a route you

couldn't have planned in advance. You find your way only by step-
ping up, persisting, staying alert to the possibilities. Sometimes you
advance easily, sometimes you need the climber's almost tearfully
desperate grit. Sometimes you can get ahead only by changing
course. Sometimes you have to give up the attempt. And sometimes
you succeed—you achieve a height from which a landscape is revealed to you as you hadn't seen it before, a landscape limited but
whole. Along the way you're sustained to some extent by faith in
yourself but more by faith in the unknown, faith that there will be a
way for you in what at the moment lies beyond your vision.

I had resisted writing all those years because I felt I had nothing
to say. I felt I had to know something in order to write, had to have
achieved a clarity of thought and feeling that I could then present in
words. What I stumbled upon when I finally got myself to pick up a
pencil and keep it in my hand was not clarity but a way of stumbling
into clarity, if I worked at it and if I was lucky. And, as each sentence
made the next sentence possible, I gradually came to see that each
story, each poem, each notebook entry, each letter to the editor, un-
distinguished and shortfallen as it might be, makes possible the next
piece and the next. I was impatient with my progress, tossed between
scornful self-doubt and giddy inflation. Sometimes I ignored the
typewriter for a week or two at a time, but I left it on the desk or the
living room table (I wasn't always as good a man as Hemingway),
manuscript pages piled beside it. Drunk or sober, happy or sad, I
couldn't go through a day without seeing it, and eventually I had to
stand at the desk or sit at the table and have at it again. For years I refused to call myself a writer, but a writer I was. I had found an engage-
ment. I had found a necessary work.

As with climbing, I've picked up writing craft as I've gone along.
My work ways have become more efficient, my route finding
sharper. I bring to any passage the experience of past efforts; I bring
an informal ongoing study of how others have made their passages.
I think of it more like gardening now. I have some pretty good com-

post built up through the years, some seeds and cuttings that are likely to grow, and always some volunteers. But through it all, now as I write these pages just as twenty years ago in Klamath Falls, the essential predicament is the same: I make my way by not knowing what I'm doing, by scratching these lines on a green legal pad, sniffing my way in pursuit of the story I need to tell. I've been doing it long enough that I know to remind myself, when the writing goes poorly, to be patient. Something worthy may come of it yet. It's valid and necessary to write this way.

And I also remind myself, from time to time when my life isn't going so well, that it's valid and necessary to live life the same way—in the same uncertainty, the same faith that one thing leads to another, that confusion will settle into clarity, that incompletion will somehow give birth to wholeness. When I was teaching freshman English at Stanford I frequently counseled eighteen-year-olds who had their entire lives mapped out. It was hard not to advise them to take some acid and melt off the map. I've never set goals in life. My young dream of going to Oregon is about the only long-range plan I've ever made, certainly the only one I've ever carried out. I didn't plan to be a writer, didn't plan to get married, didn't plan to have my mother with us, didn't plan to write this book. Life can't be marshaled. You have to honor fortune or chance or providence. Or, as my mother used to say when I was managing her life a little too intensively, you have to "let go and let *God*."

On the other hand, maybe all I'm doing is spiffing up my drifting, desultory nature and presenting it as a Way of Life. And maybe I don't even believe in it. I've taken some losses for living the way I write. If I had planned to have children, I might have them. If I had planned to be a writer, I might have gotten a quicker start. If I had planned to make more than twenty thousand a year, I might be making it. If I had planned to live in the country, I might not be lying awake these nights listening to sirens, car alarms, and the college kids' bad taste in music from across the street.

And of course there's the final loss, the one I always come round to writing about. The trouble with honoring the unwritten future is that the end is already written. I know how the story of my life concludes. Or I think I do—I know how the ending looks from here—and I don't like it. That starry void off Oregon will swallow any wholeness, any knowing, any clarity I might achieve. Death surrounds the revealed landscape. Death *is* the landscape, finally. And though I don't seem to be as frightened as I used to be, not so submersed in terror, I'm still the kid who stood on the porch roof watching snow come down on Christmas Eve, knowing that the warm and festive room beneath him couldn't comprehend the universe of cold icy light. I want this faith of mine to comprehend the final mystery, but it sags and falters. I don't want to die. I want to seize the story, write a different ending. And what I really want is the grace and courage of the woman who was my mother, the old crone on her life's last shore who raised her whiskey glass and toasted her own extinction.

CHAPTER TWENTY-SIX

There's not a lot of night sky to see from our backyard, what with the tall birches and the impinging rooflines of our house and our neighbors'. The stars we do see are only a few wan specks, dulled by the diffused electric radiance of greater Portland. But the moon, riding high on clear nights or shining through thin overcast, sometimes with a coppery ring around it, the moon is something better. At some point in the fall of 1990 I started walking my mother out at night to see it, especially when it was full or near full. It seemed a small thing I could do to get her off her bed for a while, to keep her in touch with the life of nature beyond the walls and roof of her circumscribed world.

We stayed out only a minute or two. It was hard for her to stand for longer than that, hard for her to straighten her crooked neck and raise her eyes to the moon for long. She liked seeing it—it always made her smile. "Oh, yes," she'd say, "there it is." And I know she liked it that I took the time, that I thought of it and troubled to do it.

It made me feel quite virtuous, of course. It quieted, at least temporarily, my nagging sense of guilt that I didn't spend enough time with her. That Marilyn and I were just boarding and feeding her until she died. It was a nice way of sharing something we didn't have to talk about, a nice way of saying good night.

What I didn't know at the time, and wasn't even close to knowing, was that Marilyn was upstairs sobbing into her journal as I walked my mother out and walked her back.

"*I* want that," she finally told me one night. "I want that to be you and me."

I heard it not as a plea but as an unjust criticism. I was stung. "What do you mean you and me? We do things together. She's an old woman, she hardly gets out . . ."

"I know that. It's wonderful how devoted you are. But John, you're just consumed with caring for her."

"I'm not consumed. I'm just doing it the best I can, and I'm not even doing very much. What the hell is wrong with taking my mother out to see the moon?"

"There's nothing wrong with it. It moves me to hear you out there. But what about *us?*"

I couldn't understand why my wife, who was whole and healthy, couldn't make allowances for what I saw as my minimal attentions to my mother, who was old and declining. I couldn't see what Marilyn saw clearly: that the accumulation of those attentions had enveloped me and taken me over, so that between caring for my mother and trying to get my writing and teaching done I had little time or temper for anything else, including my wife of seven years. She tried in various ways, subtle and blunt, to make me see what was happening. "You have all the symptoms of a stressed housewife," she smilingly told me once. She knew the syndrome personally from her first marriage, when as a lawyer's wife she had been busy to bursting with two young children, entertaining, and various service boards. And she was right—I was rushed, crabby, defensive, and depressed.

But as I saw it, what were my options? My mother was with us.

She had certain unalterable needs and the right to such companion-
ship as I was able to give her. My writing needed all the time I could
give it and more. And so when Marilyn confronted me about the
moon watching, I took it as a gratuitous extra pressure. When she
complained that she couldn't take a bath in her own house—the only
tub was in the downstairs bathroom, the one my mother used frequently—I told her with some impatience to make do with showers.
When she said that the two of us needed to get away together, I said
sure we do, but we'll have to find a decent caregiver, the caregiver will
be expensive, she won't know my mother's needs and habits as I do,
it'll be confusing for my mother, we'll just worry about her, it's too
much. I appealed to Marilyn to be flexible. I told her I needed her support, it wouldn't last forever. Now when I listen to myself in memory
I hear my father telling my mother, all those years ago in the thirties
and forties and fifties, that he really needed her support just now in
this bad time, he had a lot of pressure on him, she simply had to buck
up and help with the cause.

Marilyn and I did take trips, but not very many, and each one had
to be planned in stifling detail. We couldn't decide on the spur of the
moment to go to the coast for the weekend or stay a third night when
we had planned only two. We made time for ourselves, some time,
but forfeited our spontaneity. And always we returned to a house
filled with tensions that no one desired but that seemed beyond our
control, tensions that brittled the feelings of all three of us and
turned us inward and dried up the generosity we were capable of.

Marilyn, to put it simply, felt crowded out of her house and her
marriage. She worked long days in her downtown office, came home
to an irritable husband and a difficult dinner with a hard-of-hearing
and sometimes sharp-tongued mother-in-law, then retired upstairs
to a usually solitary evening while I took time to read aloud to my
mother or show her the full moon and spent the rest of the evening
holed up in the sanctuary of my study. Guiltily holed up. There were
nights when I shuttled from the garage to one woman for a few min-

utes and then to the other, just to make contact and keep both ap-
peased, Bob Bourgeois being cheery to both as the Inspector made it
perfectly clear that I wasn't attentive enough to either.

A crisis reared when I was offered a one-semester writer-in-
residence job at a Tennessee university in the spring of 1991. The job
paid what to us was a small fortune. We talked it through and decided
that the extra money would be worth four months of separation,
four months in which Marilyn would have to care for my mother on
her own, with some additional help from Patty, my mother's regular
home-care nurse. We talked it through, but we didn't feel it through.
Marilyn felt underappreciated for the burden she would have to bear.
I—advanced practitioner of the Daniel Way that I am—didn't acknowledge the burden as fully as I might have and then felt our
agreement betrayed when she acted out her resentment. We had the
roughest passage of our marriage in the month before I left for Tennessee. Soon after my departure Marilyn dreamed that I had cut
down a huge deciduous tree. She knelt by the stump, caressing its cut
top, moving her hands along the gap where the trunk had split. I
looked on, shaken. Neighbors said we could plant another. Marilyn
cried and cried, stroking the moist stump.

She got through the four months with her strength and sanity intact by half-seriously imagining her task as an assignment to attend
to the Great Goddess as manifested in Zilla. "Some days she will get
great care," she wrote in her journal. And she also wrote, "Caring for
Zilla will make up for all the spiders I have ever killed." In one important way it turned out happier than she had expected: as a twosome
they got on much better than they did as members of our usual tense
triad. They had words at times—Marilyn learned firsthand that
managing my mom was sometimes like dragging a mule by the
ears—but by and large their natural liking for each other was able to
sprout and bloom in my absence. They huddled under quilts when
the furnace went out, enjoyed a sixty-dollar lunch now and then,
and kept the house well supplied with dark chocolate. The finest mo-

ment came when Marilyn, acting on many months of disgruntle-
ment with the dark vinyl living room wallpaper, sprang from her
chair one evening and started stripping it off in great noisy sheets as
my delighted mother cheered her on.

At the end of my teaching stint Marilyn joined me in Tennessee
for a slow and winding journey home. My brother Jim took leave
from his work in southern California and saw to our mother's care,
along with her friend Sarah Holmes, a fellow devotee of Sai Baba. It
was a joy for Marilyn to be free of the "dear old bird," and it must
have been a great joy for the bird herself to have her older son in the
house for an extended period. She asked about him all the time and
always relished his calls and visits. Jim had been little over a year old
when Georgie had died, and he grew up with the impossible task of
filling the golden shoes of perfection. He had a hard go of it through
his teenage years, clashing often with our father, while I secluded
myself in schoolish achievement and an air of self-sufficiency. Our
mother gave Jim key support when he needed it and developed a
closer relationship with him than with me—or so it sometimes
seemed and felt. There were moments as a boy when I felt a twinge
of jealousy and a spark of anger over that.

Our first days home, before Jim left, were very satisfying. It was a
pleasure to walk into a restaurant, two tall and graying sons with our
white-headed mother between us in her "Give thanks and be joyful"
dress, a bright red-and-green printed smock with an embroidered
collar. People looked at us, and I was proud. The core of the family
was arrayed as it ought to have been. I felt a simple happiness, a happiness I guess I didn't get enough of as a child. Healing means whol-
ing, and despite the pain and tensions of my mother's years with us,
she did bring the gift of healing. In her living and in her dying, she
made the family whole.

Marilyn and I felt the old pressures closing in as the household resumed its normal pattern, and I suppose my mother did too. There
was one element in the pattern that she particularly resisted. For

about a year she had been going two days a week to the Interlink Center of the Volunteers of America, a day-care program for frail older adults. We had started her there because we felt, and were advised by counselors, that she needed to be around other people, people her own age. When I picked her up at the end of a day at the center, she was worn out but usually in good spirits. She couldn't tell me much about the day. There was singing sometimes, which she liked, and she didn't mind the exercise routines. I know that she took part in recall and reminiscence sessions, but she remembered almost nothing of those. I'd like to have been an eavesdropper. The lunches and the occasional Bible talk were very much *not* to her liking.

For a while my mother went gamely, sometimes referring to her days at the center as her "work." I encouraged that notion, choosing to believe that she meant by it her concern for helping the other attendees, some of whom were wheelchair bound and variously infirm. She always wanted to help, never to be helped. But she also could have meant that going to the center felt like a job—a job she hadn't chosen, a not very pleasant or meaningful job that exhausted her. She took to saying, when I reminded her at bedtime that the next day was a center day, that she wasn't feeling strong and might not be up to it. "Let's see in the morning," she would say. And then some mornings, if I pressed her to go, she would emerge from her bedroom in her old burgundy jersey-knit nightshirt, maybe with a belt drawn around it, sandals or rubber boots on her feet, depending on the weather. I laugh now when I recall it, but at the time it gave me a spasm of intense annoyance.

"Mother," I'd say, "that's a nightshirt. You can't go to the center in that."

"It is also a *dress*," she'd come back at me, her eyes flat with anger.

"It's not a dress. It's what you wear around the house with your slippers. You can't go in that."

"All right, then," she'd say very slowly, "what *should* I wear? If you don't find this suitable."

And so we'd parade into her bedroom, and I would pull a dress or skirt and sweater from her closet, and she would dress and eat her breakfast, and we would troop to the car and drive in silence to the center. I always won that power struggle, and winning always felt crummy. It was a violation somehow. It wasn't right to be lecturing my mother as if she were a wayward girl who didn't want to go to school. It wasn't right to make her spend the day with people she didn't particularly care for, doing things she didn't find meaningful. It *was* good for her to get out of the house, to sing, to interact with others, but it wasn't my place to engineer good into her life. She mutinied over the center while Jim and Sarah were caring for her, and when I came back, I decided she would go only if she said she wanted to. She never did.

The other reason we had started her there, of course, was for *my* good. It got her out of my hair for a few hours two days a week. She knew that, and I don't like to think about how it made her feel. She knew many things, including the difference between a nightshirt and a dress. Sometimes I think she knew much more than I knew, and in the end she may have been braver in acting on it.

CHAPTER TWENTY-SEVEN

I see the bedroom clearly, my little bed facing the window, the window I used to watch with one eye open in the morning wondering what I was hungry for. (It wasn't pancakes or bacon or strawberry shortcake, it wasn't any kind of food I could think of but something outside, something in the songs the morning birds were singing, something still hidden in the world or maybe nowhere in the world at all.) I see the three-drawered dresser, the closet in the corner with its door open, the smooth scarred length of hardwood floor, my wooden top with a steel tip that I used to spin ferociously. It's the same room where I lay staring through the doorway at the ceiling light the night my parents told my brother and me they were going to divorce. And out the other doorway (like a woodchuck's burrow the room has an entrance and an exit) is the hall and the door to the basement where I had seen my parents as a windup toy, or would see them soon. This may have come before, maybe after.

This is my mother, standing in slacks and leather shoes—I think they're brown and white—just inside my bedroom, the door open behind her, the hallway lit with a kind of half-able glow from the ceiling light. It's dark outside my window. I think we're alone in the house. It's fall, October or November, sometime when night comes early and there's a chill in the air. My mother may have a hand on the doorknob, she may have both hands at her sides. She is turned part toward me, part away, looking down at me, her dark hair cut short, her lips dark with lipstick, the light burning behind her with the vague forms of dead moths in the bowl. I see everything, the entire tableau. I see even the mussed and rumpled bedspread made of ridgy cotton fabric, yellow *National Geographics* on the bed and the floor, my idle wooden top with the string that spins it—from time and again of going there, I know everything about this scene except the words my mother speaks.

I know they hurt me. Whatever she said was said to hurt, I feel sure of that. I know it from the look on her face. I know it because I felt it, I can feel it now, a kind of crumpling inside, a stiffening pain that contracts and arches my whole being and shrinks my eyes to the floor. She might have told me that she was moving out of the house—she did, for a time—but it couldn't have been only that, because whatever she said was personally wounding. So wounding, apparently, that my psyche has dissolved or obscured the language and won't let me hear it again—protecting me, maybe, the way some accident victims are protected by amnesia. In the absence of her words my imagination goes to the scene again and again, touching and probing the way the tongue tip moves to a missing tooth.

What did she say? I've tried and tried to remember, with my psychologist and by myself. I've even thought of undergoing hypnosis, but a little research convinced me not to. The hypnotized subject remembers with great confidence and in great detail, but many of the details are likely to be invented. Hypnosis heightens the confabulating power of memory, and it does so by inducing a condition of extreme suggestibility to intended or unintended cues from the questioner. It's for this reason that hypnotically "refreshed" testimony, common in the 1970s, is now disallowed in many courtrooms. Some of the adults who are now remembering being sexually abused as children are doing so under the influence of hypnosis, and in some cases their "recovered memories" are turning out to be wholly or partly false.

As I write this book I'm filling in details I can't be sure of. I'm adding to remembered events people and things that might not have been part of them. I'm filling out scenes with crickets and barking dogs. I'm even putting into mouths—Marilyn's, my mother's, my own—words that probably were never said. All this, yet I insist I'm telling the truth. I'm writing from what I remember into what I don't remember, not away from the truth but toward a fuller realization of it—or at least that is what I'm trying to do. Truth means conformity to fact, but it also means fidelity, faithfulness. I owe fidelity to events as they happened. I gather all I can; I wouldn't want to misrepresent them. But I also owe fidelity to the wholeness of the story of which those remembered events form only a part. I owe fidelity to what memory can't provide. I owe fidelity to imagination, and what can imagination be but memory entered with faith and encouraged in its form-seeking ways?

And yet there are certain liberties imagination must not take. When I was eight or nine my mother said something very hurtful to me. I know she did. Actually, I don't know she did. Memory may have conjured the entire scene, complete with a sense of something hurtful having been said, out of some childhood resentment, or out of nothing. But I have a sure belief that she did say something cruel, and to know what she said would help me understand who she was and who I am. It would be highly relevant to this story. But I simply don't remember, and in this instance it would be unfair to imagine words into her mouth. I don't recall, and I will have to be satisfied with that. The vague unconscious being I hold at the point of a pen will not relinquish what I want. What shall I do, threaten him? Run him through? If he's protecting me by withholding her words—or if, as it occurs to me, he's protecting *her*—well, maybe we need his protection. Maybe his recalcitrance is an act of discretion, an act of generosity. Maybe he too has judgments to make, and maybe he's making them.

And what would it really matter? Would I love my mother less if I remembered? Would I find it so hard to forgive her? She was far from a perfect mother. My father was far from a perfect father. They both hurt me. They both could have done better. And yet here I am almost half a century old, grown of body and still growing in spirit, carrying the hurt of my mother's words along with other hurts as a tree takes inside it by its own expansion a strand of barbed wire that once chafed its bark. My mother's words aren't lost. I can't recite them but they are remembered within me, part of what I am, part of what William Wordsworth called the dark inscrutable workmanship of the human spirit. Maybe Wordsworth was the best psychologist, the psychologist of wholeness, when he wrote this passage of *The Prelude:*

> How strange that all
> The terrors, pains, and early miseries,
> Regrets, vexations, lassitudes interfused
> Within my mind, should e'er have borne a part,
> And that a needful part, in making up
> The calm existence that is mine when I
> Am worthy of myself!

My passion to remember is coming to seem a bit excessive to me, a little overardent and compulsive. That's the way it feels these nights when I lie awake wishing I was asleep, the endless neuronal circuits of memory lit like a pinball machine I can't stop playing. The damn thing keeps giving me replays—how can I resist free games?—taking me back through looping passageways that eventually lead only to themselves again. I wish I could will myself away from the game, but you can't will yourself to sleep. You get there only by giving up. Who's playing the machine? Why can't he just close his eyes, let his fingers slip from the buttons? Because he—not me, but that wired, compulsive part of me—is afraid of losing control, afraid of letting go, so afraid of dying that he won't even give himself to the little death of sleep. For a while I thought he was another self I need to get to know, but now I realize I'm looking at the Inspector, hypnotically hitting the buttons, his eyes wide and glazed. The game's playing him as much as he's playing the game.

Maybe I should give Bob Bourgeois a little more credit. He forgets what he doesn't need to know. He forgets, he lives, he does what he does. And he would probably sleep a good sound sleep if the pinball wizard would let him.

What's so wrong with forgetfulness? Maybe my anger and repulsion at my mother's memory loss only reveal my own overvaluation of memory, my own inordinate desire to fix my every experience as I tried to fix the snow on that Potomac parapet—to batten down my life as lived in order to cling to it always, to make it keep me afloat in the sea that made me and would have me back. The sea that scares me, the sea of no land in sight. The sea where I will drown—or maybe, just maybe, find myself swimming from the wreck of my life in a way I didn't know possible.

Marilyn thinks there might be consciousness after death but no memory. The Greeks thought so too. Mortals crossing over drink from the fountain Lethe and remember no more. Only a very few, such as Tiresias, retain memory intact in Hades. A rare privilege, but what kind of privilege would it be? Tonight—this morning—it sounds like damnation, insomnia with no hope of ease. Oblivion would be better—sleep, perchance to dream. Or if indeed there's consciousness, why wouldn't it be best to drink as deeply of the fountain as you can, to wash this life entirely away and embrace what's there?

I've felt inklings, but I've never really believed in a soul that survives death, with memory or without. I've read about near-death experiences, I've read some of the spiritual teachers, I've wanted to believe, but I haven't been able to surmount the suspicion that it's all just wishful thinking, wishful imaginings projected onto that cold black void. But now I don't know. My mother threw the whole thing open for me. My mother with her hints and clues, my mother with her smiles and seeings, my mother whose forgetting looked a lot like remembering. My mother who came to Oregon bearing her death like one last gift, the gift that I most needed.

CHAPTER TWENTY-EIGHT

When my mother commented on a topic in the news, when she stated a preference of any kind, she almost always added, "But that's only *my* opinion," as if her view shouldn't count for much. The habit irked me because I *wanted* her opinions. I wanted her to pull out of her drift and assert herself in words. I wanted her to be engaged, to struggle against the dissolution of self wrought by the changes in her brain. But it wasn't only her dementia. In her last years she was purposefully curbing her ego, intentionally diminishing and separating from the person she had been.

Passages she marked in her books of Sai Baba's sayings repeatedly exhort the spiritual aspirant to "break the bonds of 'I' and 'Mine'" through concentrated meditation on the God within. In *Dharma Vahini* Sai Baba says this: "Whoever subdues his egoism, conquers his selfish desires, destroys his bestial feelings and impulses and gives up the natural tendency to regard the body as the self, he is surely on the path of Dharma; he knows that the goal of Dharma is the merging of the self in the over-self." My mother underlined in pencil almost every word in the long introductory clause.

This concern hadn't been new to her with Sai Baba; she had tried for decades to subdue or transform what she didn't like about herself. She had attempted—bridling all the way—to make herself the supportive and unquestioning helpmate her husband had wanted her to be. In the 1970s, when many women were striving to develop more assertiveness, my mother was trying to become less judgmental and outspoken. (Qualities she had sorely needed, she said in *Refuse to Stand Silently By,* as a woman always outnumbered by assertive male colleagues in the labor movement.) Even in 1988, when she was eighty years old, I know from a tape recording of a spiritual exploration guided by a friend in Maine that she wanted to round her edges, to make a more fluid and loving person of herself. This ongoing effort may have borne fruit in the childlike warmth—the warmth of her deepest, most irresistible smile—to which she was frequently given in her final years. But she never came close to shedding her old self completely. The frank and opinionated Zilla of old coexisted, within the same hour or even the same minute, with the Zilla who wished to be egoless, attentive only to the views and concerns of others.

If detachment from the ego was hard for her, detachment from the body was harder. It's clear enough why she would seek it. Who wants to identify with a vessel of hurt and incapacity? Her gut pained her, her neck scarcely supported her head, her ears heard indistinct risings and fallings of voice that resolved into human speech only through sly lip reading. To rise from a chair she had to thrust herself up by her straining arms in a several-second siege of uncertain outcome, like a weight lifter at her limit. Her urethra left little splash trails behind her as she shuffled her way to the toilet, lecturing herself under her breath. And it was her body with all its infirmities, the ones she understood and the ones she didn't, that caused her to be shuttled time and again to the doctor, to be examined and asked to give specimens and sometimes stood up by her son against a cold white panel as the x-ray technician aimed the crosshairs at her naked back and commanded, "*Holllld*" and "*Breeeathe.*"

So of course she put her pen to the page where Sai Baba writes, "But remember, you are not this body; this body cannot be you. Tat Tvam Asi. *Thou art that* . . . You are the indestructible *Atman* . . ." Of course she underlined in double pencil strokes, penciling an arrow where the passage breaks between pages, his commentary on the *Bhagavad Gita:* "But what is clear, what is clean, what is indestructible and what is effulgent and shining, is only one and that is the soul . . ." And of course, as her porous and slippery mind let her down as surely as her body did, she would find solace in a definition of atman that seems written for a senile dementia sufferer: "The *atman* is the unseen basis, the real self, one's divinity. . . . It is inherently devoid of attachment. It has no awareness of agency or of its own needs or nature or of its possessions. It has no 'I' or 'mine.' The *atman* does not die. Memory is a function of the intellect, not the *atman.* The *atman* is imperishable."

Try as she might to transcend them, though, my mother's pains and corruptions pressed continually on her awareness—kept her wincing at her bad knee, admonishing her bladder, and panting from the short walk between house and car. The body may not be the real self, but it knows real hurts and limits. Still, my mother was not easy at the prospect of leaving it. She became agitated when her blood pressure was up, asking nervously if it was time yet to take it again. She was concerned when Tom Harvey, her physician and mine, explained to her the danger of congestive heart failure—though after lunch and a nap she seemed to forget her worry, one of the many instances when her failing memory proved a blessing. Two or three times in her years with us she was convinced she'd just been visited by a small stroke or heart attack and wanted to go immediately to the doctor or the hospital. There must have been many stretches of her timeless time when fears for herself were stewing in her mind, fears she couldn't or wouldn't express.

There was one experience of my mother's body, though, that kept her pleasurably attached to it right up to the last week of her life. She loved to eat. She slurped her soup voluptuously and scraped the last film of it from the bowl. She sucked every slick fiber of goodness from the pits of plums and nectarines. She chomped her false teeth into corn on the cob, ate asparagus spears from her fingers. On nights of cracked crab she lingered at the table long after others were done, carefully licking her fingers as she picked through the mound of wreckage in front of her. My mother was gratifying to cook for because she wasn't picky; she just liked good food. (Once she exclaimed about Marilyn's cream of broccoli: "This is the best soup I ever stuck in my mouth!") Though mostly a vegetarian since first going to Sai Baba's ashram, she wasn't doctrinaire in the least. She ate chicken and fish and occasionally relished a plate of sautéed chicken livers. If very hungry she was quite capable of wolfing her meals, but more typically she ate at a stately pace, clearing her plate by small forkfuls and eventually leaving bones and other detritus in one neat pile on its polished empty surface. As Marilyn's mother once commented, "Zilla doesn't eat. She dines."

Another detachment my mother sought was from current events of the nation and the world, and in this, as in her other efforts, she was only moderately successful. The humanitarian and social activist in her was still alive and keenly interested. She read the *Oregonian* at breakfast, the *Christian Science Monitor* when it arrived in the midday mail. She read determinedly, often with a set mouth and a steady slight frown. By and large she seemed weary, more than weary, of the numbingly repetitive accounts of human meanness and misery that make up the great bulk of what we call, without a trace of irony, the news. She chuckled at lighter stories, the odd photo of traffic stopped for a goose and goslings, and she lit up at anything affirmative. She followed Nelson Mandela's release and triumph, the Earth Summit in Brazil, features on poets and artists and musicians. She clipped articles about cooperation, self-sacrifice, peaceableness between enemies. My mother was after the real news. She was gleaning hope.

One morning when she had arrived in the kitchen ahead of me, I found her in tears over the front page of the *Oregonian*. Her eyes and cheeks were red; she had been crying a long while. An intruder in a Portland home—a glue sniffer, as I remember—had taken a little boy hostage and held him with a knife to his throat. Police marksmen couldn't accurately fire through the house windows, and so three cops entered the house and confronted the intruder in a hallway. He was crazed, unpredictable, the edge of his knife on the boy's throat. Fearing he might cut any second, they opened fire. The knife man was killed, and one bullet killed the little boy.

I think my mother could comprehend, much as she hated it and despaired at it, the news of rape and torture and murder in Bosnia. She had had some experience in her own life with the ferocity of human passion. And she could accept, with sadness, the toll in human lives taken by hurricanes and earthquakes. Nature was vast and blameless in its power, human beings weak and small. But the death of an innocent boy at the hands of three innocent men doing exactly what they had to do to save him . . . What consolation is possible? How does one detach herself from that? How can it be reconciled with any notion of God or justice?

In the view of Hinduism, which in a general way became my mother's religion, God does not reward or punish. He only reflects. We humans create our own destinies, our deathless spirits born into bodies again and again in order to learn what they need to know, acting out the infinitely complex drama of karmic evolution. Seen in that way, the fates of boy and knife man and policemen were determined by the acts of their previous lives, as their acts in this life would contribute to the shaping of their lives to come.

My mother may have believed in karma, but if she did it gave her no solace as she cried her eyes red over the awful news that morning. Bound as we are in the joys and horrors of the flesh, the idea of karmic justice is just as abstract and ultimately as hapless as the Christian idea of a personally attentive God. It can explain, if held with faith, but it cannot justify. The pains and evils of this world may all be maya, illusion, but if so it is hard to imagine a crueler ruse. To the boy's parents and the policemen who killed him, and in a more distant but still painful way to my mother at the breakfast table, his death was an illusion as real as agony. Maybe it needs to be so. But the human soul must be an awfully poor learner to require such schooling.

The death of that boy made my mother readier to quit the world. I got the sure sense that morning, and at other times too, that she was saturated with the ills of humankind and wanted no more. But was her movement toward death only a fleeing, then? Were her religious ideas only an apparatus she borrowed and adapted to help her escape her fear of dying, the pains of her body, and the sufferings of humanity at large? I think she was fleeing those things, but I also think she was reaching toward something, toward a truth she experienced within and knew to be good. I believe she felt intimations at least of the clean fire of the soul, the light in which the contrarieties of mortal consciousness interblend as one. Deeper than her fears and ditherings and delusions, deeper than her smile and her tears of anguish, I believe my mother glimpsed her wholest and truest identity, that which her religion calls the atman, the Self that understands its own infinite nature and approaches with a smile the body's death.

In January of 1992 she told me she might not have much longer to live.

"How does that make you feel?" I asked.

"Thankful for everything I've had," she answered after a pause. "It's been a privilege."

Not long after that, a month or two maybe, she tried to show me something. She would try in the same way several times before she died. We were in the living room after dinner. I was about to read the next chapter of Tolkien's *Lord of the Rings.*

"Over there," my mother said with a smile, pointing out the window toward the park. "Do you see a bird in the top of the tree?"

I got up and stood next to her chair. "Which tree?"

"The tallest one," she said. She spoke very surely, very deliberately. "Do you see the bird?"

I didn't. The tallest Douglas fir stood like the others, clearly silhouetted against the twilit sky. There was no crow or hawk, and no smaller bird, perched on its point.

"I don't know," I said. "There could be a bird, I guess."

"Oh, yes," my mother said, smiling, watching with her sharp eyes. "It's a great bird, isn't it."

CHAPTER TWENTY-NINE

I think of branchings, forks in the trail, points of opportunity where I might have taken a different way. When my mother said she might not have much longer to live, that was such a point. I keep feeling that I missed my cue, or heard the cue but didn't step forward, didn't understand the part that was required of me. I keep feeling that having heard her say that, I should have set about building her a bower for her dying. I should have honored with more attention her sense of death's imminence, should have helped her prepare herself for the great departure, the great embarkation. It's not that I denied what she said. I took her at her word, asked how it made her feel, and was gratified, and moved, to hear her answer. But mostly, in the weeks and months that followed our conversation, I went about cooking and caring for her as I had always done, and our uneasy triadic household creaked along with its accustomed and increasing tensions.

A man from India I've corresponded with, a former Jain monk, tells a remarkable story about his own mother. When she was eighty or so she said to her family, "I'm now too old. I can't cook, I can't see, I can't do anything for you. What point is there in carrying on? From tomorrow, I'm going to start dying." She made the rounds of the village, stopping in to visit relatives, friends, everyone she knew. "I have come to say good-bye, because I am going to die," she told them. Then she began to fast. As she lay peacefully, bearing herself into death, villagers chanted, sang hymns, prayed and meditated around her. They did their part to launch her on the voyage she had chosen.

My mother made no such forthright decision—no decision, at least, that she communicated. I think she was much more ambivalent about dying than my correspondent's mother was. But she did sense, she did know, that death was near, and she did communicate that. And why didn't I respond, beyond asking how she felt? Why didn't I ask, at the very least, "What can I do? How can I help you?" I didn't know that she was right, of course. She was weak, but she was also tough. She might well have lived another five years. I suppose, too, that I didn't want still another duty, whatever it might be—caring for her failing life was a regimen quite full enough. And I had other things going on. My book of essays came out that spring, my first prose book and first with a New York publisher. I was giddy and fretting, fussing with one or another detail of the book's release. I was teaching part-time. I had minor surgery in late winter. I was occupied. I was busy.

And I was denying the prospect of my mother's death. I didn't want her to die (except in those private furies when I did). I loved my mother and didn't want her to go from the world, and I didn't want myself to feel what I would have to feel if she did. I didn't want my mother or Marilyn or myself or anyone to die. I didn't want to deal with death—and in that stonewalling, of course, I was acting out the deep denial of my culture.

Who dies in America? Certainly not us. Our birthdays conspire to prove that we age, but we defeat their perversity by devotedly making ourselves younger and younger. We dye our hair, plump out wrinkles, sweat off fat, tone muscles, condition heart and lungs, improve our diets, curb our vices, have great sex longer, and stay actively engaged in our jobs and hobbies and recreations. We can't possibly die! Only others do, those poor unfortunates who didn't care for themselves correctly, who didn't improve their lot if poor, who didn't see the doctor when they should have, whose self-esteem was too low or anger too high, who didn't laugh or meditate or play enough golf, who didn't see to their personal growth as they should have, who drove cars too fast or themselves too hard, who took too much whiskey or not enough garlic capsules, who should have drunk twelve glasses of water a day whether or not they were thirsty and attuned themselves to the universe through psychotherapy or deep massage.

And so, since it clearly doesn't involve us, there's no need to talk about death. Why would we? Where we live, the sun is shining with no end in sight. Death is elsewhere, in the backcountry maybe, in the deep wilderness, somewhere far outside our lives. Death is a backward thing, a primitive, apelike thing, a violence we may have lived with once but long ago, before progress delivered us to the modern world. It is only a quirk, due to a temporary imperfection in our technology, that death still lives anywhere. But that it survives at all is a sign that we must try still harder, we must rededicate ourselves to progress, we must fulfill our quest to eradicate death even from the margins of our human realm. It is outrageous that it still victimizes anyone, outrageous that dark uncivilized shadows should be able to breach our security every day and seize fellow humans, even people we know, who were innocently enjoying their lives.

In any case, we do not go gentle into that good night. When we cannot ignore death, we fight it, we stave it off, we hold out nobly against it. But how much nobler was my correspondent's mother in India. There came a point in her life, a point of sudden clarity, when she realized that to die was the next thing to do. To *do*, not to avoid or even to wait for. She recognized death and reached out her hand. She knew when and how to die in the same way that a hunter knows when to move or stand still, when to shoot or hold fire, in the same way that a farmer knows when to plant corn, that a wave knows when to curl and give itself to the shore. She exercised a natural intelligence that our technological world tends to stifle under thick wrappings of comfort, convenience, and relentless distraction.

My mother felt the promptings of that intelligence well before the day in January of 1992 that she told me she might not live much longer. In 1989 I started writing down some of the more striking things, all kinds of things, that she said. In February 1990, she told me with a sigh, "Sometimes I feel as ancient as the ancientest days." Later that year, in October, she said one afternoon, "It feels as though I were swimming, and it's hard to keep up." In 1991 I read to her from *Passwords*, William Stafford's latest book of poems. Like me, she loved Stafford's work. She kept the little hardback by her bed, and after she died I opened it to certain pages she had marked with torn strips of Kleenex. She had circled in pencil the title of a poem called "Four A.M.," which is about waking at night in the forest with a sense of ghostly figures floating among the trees. The poem ends:

> Some night I will breathe out and become
> part of the silent forest, floating as they do
> toward the thin lids of dawn,
> and like them, unknown.

The title of the poem on the facing page, "Security," also was circled. The poem compares each tomorrow of our lives to an island we always find, day after day, until there comes a tomorrow without an island:

> So to you, Friend, I confide my secret:
> to be a discoverer you hold close whatever

you find, and after a while you decide
what it is. Then, secure in where you have been,
you turn to the open sea and let go.

My mother had bracketed that final stanza in wavery pencil lines. Within a year she would be dead. And one year later, in August of 1993, William Stafford died suddenly of heart failure.

"Fear can arise only when there is another," my mother wrote on a yellow Post-it note within six months of her death. The full sentence, which she read in a book of quotations from Sai Baba's discourses, reads, "Get over fear by establishing your mind in the One, for fear can rise only when there is another." The idea goes back at least three thousand years to the *Brihadaranyaka*, the earliest of the Hindu spiritual treatises known as the Upanishads. According to Joseph Campbell's translation of the story, in the beginning there was only a Great Self that perceived nothing else. "This am I!" it said, and immediately it fell afraid, as anyone alone can be afraid. But then it thought, "If there is nothing but myself, of what, then, am I afraid?" And its fear vanished, because there was nothing, no other thing, to fear. That Great Self, as I understand the story, is the immortal Brahman, soul of the cosmos. When the spiritual aspirant recognizes that through the atman, or deepest human soul, she is part and parcel of the Brahman, all fear melts away. She sheds her body, which she thought she was, as a snake slides out of its skin.

I know this story now. If I had the privilege of turning back the tape of time, I would know it sooner. I would enter the world of my mother's religion at least far enough to help her, if she wished for help, to express her fear and locate herself in the One. I would offer to read Sai Baba's words to her. I would copy out his sayings in large letters and post them on her walls if that's what she wanted. I would find her tapes of sacred music in her boxes of possessions and play them for her. I would ask what she needed to help her pray. I would ask if there were friends, fellow devotees, she wanted to call.

She may have wanted none of this. She didn't like fusses made over her, and if I had been too forward with my attention to her dying she might have disavowed it—I might only have pushed her into denial. But still, if I could live those last months again, I would find time to make myself available to my mother and her dying. I would find room for death in the household, so that it wouldn't have to sneak in like a thief while I was away. I would do this for my mother, and I would do it for myself. What can I gain by locking the door? What can I learn at a distance? I would admit death to my company. I would eat and sleep with death, I would walk with death through all the rooms of the house, and maybe after a while I would recognize its face. Maybe I'd become easy enough in its presence to look into its eyes. Maybe I would ask to hear what death had come to tell me.

CHAPTER THIRTY

The waitress stands, waiting and waiting as my mother struggles with the menu, trying to choose, trying to know what she wants, her eyes shifting here and quickly there across the welter of print, the salads and sandwiches and hot entrées each with its brief description, the specials of the house set off in boxes. She clears her throat, she straightens in her chair as if to force concentration into her mind. Her eyes flit, she clears her throat. The waitress stands, pen in one hand, pad in the other, as I pick up the salt shaker and set it down, as I shift in my chair and tap the floor with my foot, as I stare out the window at the rush of traffic on rainy Burnside Street, as I wait and wait and wait in my flushed prickling impatience until I just can't bear it, and "*Mother,*" I say, "will you please *pick* something."

And she does. I don't remember what. I remember her helpless gray-green eyes, large in the lenses of her reading glasses, sad and earnest like the eyes of a child who has failed a parent, as she says, "I'm sorry, John," her voice breaking.

The remorse that stabbed me then is more painful now. My mother needed my patience, and in the end I just couldn't summon it. I couldn't take a deep breath, I couldn't smile, I couldn't make small talk with the waitress. I couldn't let my mother dither as she needed to dither. Or I could have, but I didn't. And I didn't smile and take a deep breath one evening later in the spring when she just couldn't get herself into her chair at the table on the back patio. One hand on the chair back and one on her walker, she couldn't see or get her limbs to see how to make the transfer. She stepped slightly forward, stepped back, regripped the walker, looked down, looked to the side, scraped the walker ahead an inch, reached into her purse, reset her feet . . . Finally I took her under the arms from behind, swung her forcibly into position, and lowered her into the padded chair.

Marilyn too lost her patience that spring—her patience with me. She loved and admired my mother, but she also had to live with her, and she absolutely resented that my mother had taken over our household and our lives. She saw me eaten up by caregiving and hated it. She didn't look forward to coming home in the evening, rarely enjoyed dinner, and could hardly bear to hear me reading to my mother or singing with her, as we had begun to do that year. And of course she felt guilty about her feelings, and of course when she tried to express them I didn't want to hear them. I was mired in my own guilt, my own sense of helplessness. I told her not to push me. One morning after I'd snapped short another conversation, she smashed her favorite tea mug on a rock in the garden, then threw the bed pillows hard and furious against the wall. She almost fled the house for the coast, Seattle, anywhere. "It took a lot of control and suddenly a huge burst of tears to keep me at home," she wrote in her journal.

Something had to change. Marilyn had known it for a year or longer, and finally, in the early summer of 1992, I recognized it too. I

saw that my mother would have to live somewhere else. For Marilyn, for our marriage, and—the hardest by far to acknowledge—for
me. I think it must have been my own behavior that persuaded me,
my impatient outburst at the restaurant, my roughness on the patio.
It was my behavior that finally tipped the scale against all the *shoulds*
that had piled up in my mind, all the evidence that we *should* have
been able to care for my mother and live our own lives too. We had
help from a good home-care nurse, we received a modest monthly
support check from Aging Services, she didn't require continuous
care, she was able to get herself to the bathroom and the dinner table,
I worked at home anyway, my brother spelled us several weeks a
year, she wouldn't live forever and she should have the right to live
out her days with family and the family should be willing to have
her, able to have her, happy to have her . . .

But no one was happy. I wasn't happy, my wife wasn't happy, my
mother didn't seem happy herself. Maybe, a wild hope tried to convince me, maybe she would bloom in a different home. Maybe she
would feel restored to some of her former independence, maybe it
would do her spirit good to be freed from the daily watchfulness of
her domineering father of a son, the daily presence of a daughter-in-
law who claimed more of her son than she could. We would visit her,
bring her food and flowers, take her for walks and drives, talk with
her like lively friends again instead of housemates stale and tense. I
even remembered something she had said two years before, when
we were thinking about moving from the old house—"I don't have
to live with you and Marilyn, you know." She had said it in a helpful
spirit, as if all options should be open. As if she might have been stat-
ing a preference, even, as openly as she could.

I knew the lie of it, though, even as I imagined it. We weren't moving her out for her sake. We were doing it for us, and I despised myself for it. We were doing it, the Inspector harangued me, because we
didn't have the generosity to make it work. We didn't have the simple
grit and decency to see out of the world the woman who had seen me

into it. I hate that America is a society of foster homes and nursing homes and retirement towers. I hate that we farm out our elders when they aren't useful anymore and can no longer do for themselves and begin to intrude on our precious convenience. I wanted us to be different. I wanted us to be able to say, "Such as we are, we are a family. We live here in this house, all together." Now I had to admit to myself that I was just another self-absorbed and self-regardful member of my generation and my culture. "We tried it," Marilyn and I rationalized to each other. "We tried it for three and a half years." And, we didn't say, *we failed.* Once again my family was falling apart. Once again I had tried to hold it together, once again I had come up wanting, and this time I was the reason for its failure.

I called Aging Services and got a list of adult foster homes in our part of town. It was a depressing document. Most of the homes had only shared rooms available, most of them were not interested in Alzheimer's clients, all of them had strict specifications as to mealtimes, bedtime, visiting hours, and the like. I imagined dormitory food, TVs blaring. Otha Cunningham and Helga Falconer and Dottie Lou Labenske probably were fine people, but what did they cook? What did they talk about? What would they think of a woman who dangled a pendulum to make decisions and came with pictures of an Indian holy man with a spreading Afro? No doubt they were fine people, but theirs were the foster homes that had contracted to accept Medicaid as payment—the homes at the lower end of the scale, the homes that my mother and we could afford. I drove by two or three of the ones closest by, drab Portland houses on streets where Marilyn and I wouldn't have wanted to live. I couldn't get myself to call and visit a single one. The list sat on my desk.

My mother, of course, knew nothing of this, unless she sensed it in the air. I could imagine, barely, finding a place we could afford where she might be comfortable and reasonably well attended. I could even imagine her eventually liking such an arrangement, but I couldn't begin to imagine telling her that she had to go. I could hardly bear to tell her when Marilyn and I were going out to dinner. I had to screw up my courage to face her inevitable disappointment when I was too busy to read to her after dinner. How could I possibly break the news to her that she had to move to a foster home? Marilyn felt the same way. We knew what we needed to do, and we felt perfectly incapable of doing it.

Then we made a discovery that seemed to answer everything. We heard of an outfit called ElderPlace, a program of Providence Medical Center for the frail elderly. It offered day care, comprehensive medical attention—and when the time came, social workers helped the family find a foster home or nursing home. The program was aimed precisely at clients with limited financial means. Alzheimer's people were welcome. Marilyn and I visited the center, met with the staff, and couldn't believe our luck. The initial commitment they asked of those joining the program was attendance twice a week at the day-care center. I took my mother to see it and appealed to her, very earnestly, to try it out. I framed it not as something that would be good for her—I had learned never to do that—but as something she could do to help *me*. I didn't go into specifics. I appealed to her generosity, her wanting to be helpful, and she agreed. The staff took to her immediately, as people usually did. She liked them and the ElderPlace setting better than the center she had gone to—and not gone to—before, or at least she seemed happier about the new arrangement.

Marilyn and I felt relieved to have entered a process that would make the necessary change much easier to handle. Nothing would happen right away, which privately comforted me. My mother would attend the center for a while, and eventually we would talk with the staff about locating a foster home. With their help we were certain to find the best place that could be had through Medicaid. There would still come the moment of truth when I would have to talk with her about leaving our home, but maybe by then her involvement with ElderPlace would have prepared her for it—and, I hoped, prepared me.

In the meantime I was still too busy, still too tense. I felt run into the ground by our repetitive routines. My mother's incontinence was worse. She forgot or refused to wear her protective pads, and I found myself sponging up her splash trails and cleaning seat cushions almost every day. I was irritable, short tempered, prone to cold silences and peremptory remarks. When I apologized she usually responded graciously, sometimes quizzically, as if she wasn't quite sure what I was apologizing for.

One evening I tried to go further than apology. I walked into my mother's room and sat down in the wicker chair in the corner, the visitor's chair, my elbows on my knees. "Mother," I said, "I know I'm often impatient and out of sorts with you, and I'm sorry. It's not your fault. I know that being old isn't a picnic. I appreciate the way you bear up under it. I admire your spirit."

"Oh, my dear," she said. "Thank you." She took off her reading glasses. She was choked up, and I was too. We shared a smile. Not an easy smile, not a relaxed smile, but a real one.

"What can I do to help you?" she asked me.

"Help me? Oh, I don't know . . . Just know that it's hard sometimes, you know, doing everything."

"You do a great deal, child."

"I don't do so much. But it really is hard sometimes . . ." I wanted to tell her more. I wanted to tell her why and how it was hard. I imagined us talking about where she should live, speaking easily, kindly and candidly, reasoning out the best thing to do, all the usual shunts and angers swept away. I heard us talking as easily as a river talks, the two of us resting beside it in no hurry and no need. I saw it and heard it, right there in the room, but I couldn't make it be. I was afraid to say more, afraid she wouldn't understand, afraid I would hurt her, afraid I would seem unworthy.

"What can I do?" my mother asked. "Are you sure there isn't something?"

I will forever remember her saying those words.

"Just be yourself, Mama."

I went to her and kissed her, her bony hands hugging my shoulders with all the tremulous power of her old body.

That conversation took place in late June, maybe early July. On July 14 my mother and I signed an agreement with ElderPlace confirming her participation in the program.

On July 23, early in the afternoon, I came home from coffee with a writer friend in downtown Portland. The cat shot out the front door as soon as I opened it. On my way to the kitchen I heard a voice from the bathroom—not words but a voice, a beseeching, close-mouthed call. My mother was on the floor, in her nightgown, her head propped against the base of the wall. She couldn't tell me anything. Her eyes were present, but she couldn't form words. I tried to lift her but quickly saw she couldn't sit or stand. I called 911 on the kitchen phone, looking down at the uneaten lunch I had left for her. I gave her a sip of water, and within five minutes the paramedics pulled up in front of the house. From the moment they came in, with their questions and instruments and friendly efficiency, the life I had looked after for nearly four years was no longer in my care. As they carried my mother out the front door on a stretcher, I was not leading but following. It had been no more than twenty minutes since I had come home.

CHAPTER THIRTY-ONE

I remember my father calling from the hospital, or maybe it was before he went to the hospital. He didn't know then how shot through with cancer he was. He may not have known he had cancer at all, but he knew something was wrong, something was badly wrong. He said, "I'm awful scared, Johnny," and there was a fear in his voice I had never heard. It was the most emotionally open thing he ever said to me. I don't recall exactly what I said in return, but it was something positive, something banal, something that returned us to our accustomed depth. "I bet you'll be fine," or something like that.

Now when I hear his voice in memory, I know that he knew he had come to his end—that the four packs a day of Chesterfields and the decades of hard drinking had caught up with him. But I didn't know it then. I was twenty-eight, he was seventy-two. I heard fear in his voice, but he was a tough and vigorous man, hale despite the long-time insults to his body. He was a veteran of countless picket-line fracases, severe beatings at the hands of company goons. And he had a rich vein of luck, too. Once in LaFollette, Tennessee, he had been shot point-blank in the chest by thugs from the United Mine Workers; when they left him for dead, he pulled his wallet from the inside coat pocket of his jacket, and the flattened slug fell to the floor. Surely, I told myself as we spoke on the phone, surely they would fix him up in the hospital and he would resume his reading and coin collecting, his AA meetings and his work on the public utilities board. He would go on growing his tomatoes and smoking his turkeys and living his retired warrior's life in the pastures of age.

Two days after we spoke he was dead. I would like our last conversation to have been something more than it was. I wish I had understood what he understood, at least in the depths of his being: that he was dying. I don't blame myself much, because there was no precedent between us for the kind of conversation I wish we had had. He was a reserved man, a patriarch of the Daniel Way, and I grew up his son. But he opened a little at the end, he confessed his fear to me, and I wish I could have opened myself just a little in answer. I wish I could have given him more than hackneyed cheerfulness in my last words to him in this world.

Death comes when it comes, of course. Who knows which words, which acts, will be the last? I think the dying person knows, with a glimmer of consciousness at least, that death is drawing near. The dying person must see in a kind of light of lastnesses, though he may not recognize the light. But even he won't know which words or acts will be his last—unless, like my correspondent's mother in India, he makes his death a voluntary act—and those around him won't know either. Death comes when it comes.

I have no clear recollection of my mother's last morning in our house. It must have been a morning like many others. I would have made coffee, scrambled or soft-boiled an egg for her, made oatmeal for myself or maybe French toast for both of us. We would have read the *Oregonian,* we would have talked a little. Later in the morning I made her lunch, I remember that—a sandwich with a sheet of plastic wrap laid over it, a bit of leftover something in a bowl, soup in the steel thermos—and I laid it at her place at the table. I stopped by her bedroom to tell her I'd be visiting a friend for a couple of hours and her lunch was ready when she wanted it. This was easy enough to tell her; she didn't resent me leaving during the day. She looked up from her book, smiling, thanked me for the lunch, and wished me a good visit. I don't *know* she did this on the morning of July 23, but it was her way to do it. I probably didn't kiss her; I usually kissed her only when saying good night. If she raised her left hand, I took it for a second, then left the house.

Death comes when it comes, the next thing that happens. We do not stop for it, most of us; it kindly stops for us. It calls at the door—not Jehovah's Witnesses this time, not a salesperson, not the Greenpeace canvasser, but the long-expected, half-forgotten guest. Or maybe the guest has already arrived and has been waiting, sitting in the chair in the corner, the visitor's chair, sitting still in meditation until one moment of one morning when its eyes open and it says, "Yes, it's time." And she slides one leg off the bed and then the other, straightens herself in her nightgown and sits a moment, looking around as if someone has called her, then leans far forward and pushes herself up from the edge of the quilt-covered mattress and stands on her two bare feet. She shuffles ahead, stiffly for the first two steps, steadying herself with her left hand on the nightstand, reaching with her right for the bedroom door frame. She doesn't take her walker because the bathroom is just around the corner, and the walker is hard to maneuver in the tight space by the toilet. She doesn't take her walker because she doesn't need it.

She knows and she doesn't know. She wants and she fears. Right hand on the bathroom doorway, left hand lifting her gown a little, it is only the familiar shuffle to relieve herself, the frequent trip her diuretic sends her on each morning. The same white walls, the worn hardwood of the hall giving way to dark linoleum, the green basin, tub, and toilet, gray light streaming through the one high window— all of it familiar but strange now too, a strangeness that will not resolve but opens inside her. Her feet scarcely feel the cold floor, the light streams through the window, her hand presses the bathroom wall, slides down, stops. Maybe something says, *It's time now*. Maybe something tells her, *Choose, choose*, or she tells herself. Maybe something asks, *How can I help? What can I do?* Or not those words, not any words, not a thought or a choice but a sense as sure as the streaming light that a choice has been made, that whatever she is is sliding past thought, past words and memory, that she herself has been the guest and visitor, that the endless, ending instant of her sojourn here was all to reach this moment, *this*, breaking in a flash of pain or dizziness, a buckling like a timber sheared, a slipping underneath and she is falling now, falling toward the heap of what she was and whatever she will be.

The emergency room x-ray showed what I assumed it would: my mother's right hip was broken. The angled neck of bone that connects the femur shaft to its head had been snapped when she hit the floor or else had fractured first, causing her to fall. In old people with osteoporosis, I learned later from Tom Harvey, the calcium-starved bones can become so thin and brittle that they sometimes break spontaneously. The neck of the femur, because it bears considerable weight and slants away from the vertical, is a prime candidate. My mother was surefooted in her unsteady way, unlikely to fall in a place where she could use her hands to steady herself, and the position I found her in suggested she may have slid down the wall in a semicontrolled fall rather than a sudden one. If it wasn't a sheared femur neck that sent her down, it may have been a stroke. She never spoke more than a syllable or two from the moment I found her, something at the time I attributed to shock. As I remember, one doctor who examined her thought she might have had a stroke; another thought she hadn't.

As I waited by my mother's gurney, first for her to be x-rayed and then for the x-ray to be processed and reviewed, her eyes trained on mine with a look of concentration as I talked to her, holding her hand. I think she smiled—slightly, quickly—once or twice. When I wasn't speaking she gazed up at the ice-cube-tray diffusing panels of the fluorescent lights, gazed with her brow gathered, as if trying to see something or to understand. She seemed absent to the sounds and bustle of her surroundings but very present to something in her awareness.

Marilyn was on her way from her office, a long cross-town trip by bus. The shift was changing in the emergency room. At least two doctors, maybe three, examined my mother and spoke briefly to me. Their names and faces and comments are filmy, insubstantial in my memory. Finally an orthopedist showed me the x-ray and recommended immediate surgery to repair the hip, either with a pin or a complete replacement. It was the only way she would have a chance of walking again, and if bedridden she was almost sure to die before long of pneumonia or some other infection. He said there really wasn't much choice. My mother couldn't speak her preference; it seemed unlikely she understood her situation well enough to have a preference. I agreed to the surgery—too readily, I think now. If I had it to do again, I would ask more questions, take more time. I would put off, at least for a while, the immensely authoritative specialists who run the hospital machine. I would try to collect myself, to consult with Marilyn and my brother, perhaps with another doctor. I would try to think of everything I knew and believed about my mother. I would try not to succumb to the helpless passivity of fear, the shocked panic that says to the experts *Yes, do everything, please do it now.*

When I left her side to try again to reach my brother, my mother herself gave a sign, though not in response to doctor or nurse or anything in the emergency room that I could see. She raised her right arm, her good arm, straight above her, her hand mostly open. Her eyes focused intently on whatever she was seeing, whatever she was reaching toward. They moved slowly side to side, tracking it, staying with it, her brow slightly bunched, her hand wavering. She reached and looked for minutes at a time, lowered her arm, and raised it again.

"Mother?" I bent over to ask. "What are you reaching toward? What do you see?"

She turned her head to me with no change in her expression. She tried to speak, I thought, just once. Or maybe not. She shook her head and returned her gaze above. She couldn't say, or didn't know. Or she knew that I couldn't know.

She was reaching and looking when Marilyn arrived. She was reaching and looking until they wheeled her away to surgery.

CHAPTER THIRTY-TWO

Wwe wouldn't hear for several hours how the surgery went, and so Marilyn and I, dazed and hopeful, went out for a bite to eat and then a movie for distraction. When we got home and I called the hospital, the news was good. My mother was not yet out of surgery, but everything seemed to be going well. Soon after I hung up, though, the phone rang. Near the end of surgery my mother's blood pressure had plummeted. A medical team in intensive care had worked desperately to save her. For now, at least, her condition had stabilized. We had better come to the hospital.

As I drove the car, crying, holding Marilyn's hand, the truth held still around me like a shock of cold air. *My mother is going to die.* In that way of seeming outside myself, I felt as I had in that moment long ago when I lay in my child's bed staring at the ceiling light, knowing that my parents were going to divorce. *This is really hap-*

pening. Such moments are like wakings from the sleep of normal life. But why does it take the prospect of death or separation to wake us?

I think there was a delay, maybe an hour, before we could go up to see her. Maybe they had to clean up, make her and the room presentable. A nurse or someone tried to prepare us for what we would see, but it was still a shock. It was worse than finding her fallen on the bathroom floor. A respirator billowed her lungs to a steady gasping beat through a tube inserted through her nose. She had an IV in one arm, she was catheterized for urine, she was wired to an EKG monitor through four patches on her chest, and some delicate high-tech sensor had actually been introduced through a vein in her shoulder into the right side of her heart and through the heart into her pulmonary artery, there to detect fluctuations in pressure and report the information to a monitor above the bed. My mother's eyes were closed, her mouth open, her head tilted to one side, shifting rhythmically with the rising and falling of her ventilated chest. She looked small, puny among the tubes and monitors, her white hair matted. She was there and she was nowhere.

Afterward in the hospital lobby we met with the cardiologist, the one who angered me by using the term "demented." But we both liked him. He told us it had been touch and go during the crisis. They had very nearly lost her, and she might destabilize again any time. He urged us to think about what procedures we might want to rule out if she did. The concentrated pressure of manual CPR sometimes breaks ribs, especially if the patient is old and osteoporotic. "I would not want it done to my mother," the cardiologist said. We told him we didn't want it either.

After I called Jim, there was nothing we could do but go to bed and try to sleep. I lay awake a long time. No one had said anything about my mother getting better—but no one had said she couldn't get better, either. We had a room of hope to wait in, a small but substantial shelter from our worst fears. But the room was no refuge from the second-guessings that plagued me. Maybe I shouldn't have consented to the surgery. I wished—and wish no less now—that someone in the emergency room had taken me aside and talked with me at length. I wish I had *made* someone talk with me. I wish I had at least asked why the operation had to be done immediately, why it couldn't have waited until my wife and brother and I had had a chance to seek further advice. It was a piece of very bad luck that my mother's doctor, Tom Harvey, was on vacation in the East that week. He and I weren't able to talk until after my mother died.

The orthopedist had put it simply: she wouldn't walk again without surgery, and if she couldn't get up and out of bed she would probably soon die. But he didn't assess for me, and I didn't ask about, my mother's chances of walking again *with* the surgery, given her age and frail condition and given the possibility that she had been felled by a stroke. And though of course I understood that any surgery posed a risk to an elderly patient, no one specifically addressed the *degree* of risk to the particular patient in question, a failing eighty-four-year-old woman with at least one damaged heart valve. I know the risk could not have been pinned down in numbers, but it should have been talked about. I let the intense inertia of the emergency room make the decision for me.

To have chosen against surgery would have consigned my mother to bed and death. Choosing for it gave her at least a chance and gave us a room of hope. She was tough and gritty, after all. In stubborn perseverance she outstripped everyone, maybe even me. She had been walking for eighty-some years up to the instant of her fall. Hip surgery works. Why couldn't she rise again to shuffle along behind her scraping walker, joking about the hardware in her hip? We couldn't ask her for her choice, of course. She couldn't speak, and even if she had been able to, what would we have made of her responses? At the very best, even if there had been no stroke, she would have been confused, disoriented, in pain, in shock. How could we have been sure that she fully knew what had happened to her and what could happen, what her choices and chances were?

We had to choose for her, and the hope of surgery may have been the best choice. If we had chosen against it, though, we would have spared her the stress of a major operation and an awful travail in intensive care. We would have spared her the machine existence of respirator and sensors in the heart. To have declined the operation would have consigned her to death, but once she had fallen, once she had broken her hip and very possibly suffered a stroke, wasn't she almost certainly consigned to death in any case? Wasn't death thoroughly written on her situation, there to be read by those with eyes to see? Was the little room of hope really only a room of denial? At the time, of course, the room seems the only place to be. It's a refuge; the weather outside is threatening. The technical prowess and expertise that take over while you wait in the room seem unquestionably right. Everyone wants only the best, everyone wants life. But were we—all of us, doctors and family—were we really serving my mother's life, my mother's whole being, by conspiring to prolong a physical existence that had arrived at its final passage?

I was the one who knew most about that being in her last years. I knew that she had said she wasn't much afraid of dying, that she had raised her glass to the Unknown. I knew she had volunteered, six months earlier, that she might not live much longer and that she felt considerable ease with that. I knew her religion's teaching that the death of the body is no extinction but a liberation of the real being, the soul. I knew she had meditated on her departure, worked at overcoming her fear, sought fortitude in poetry and scripture. I knew that she had recognized her death, had engaged with it, had at least occasionally *wanted* to die, and yet I did not acknowledge her death when it presented itself. I chose to have her forcibly restrained from it. I gave her care and keeping to technicians of the physical and took cover in the little room.

I didn't know, no one did, that her heart would go on strike. All of us did what seemed the right thing, the only thing; but it wasn't the only thing, and I'm not at all sure it was right. Death by pneumonia,

I know now, tends to be relatively comfortable for elderly patients—
a slow depression of all systems, a coma, and death. I don't know but
feel pretty sure that Marilyn and Jim and I would have stood a better
chance of communicating with our mother in her last days if she had
never gone into surgery. Even if she hadn't been able to speak, she
might have been able to communicate through hand squeezes, certainly through smiles and tears. Maybe, with her good right hand,
she would have been able to write. In any event, we might have had
more time with her before she slipped into a coma, time for the af-
firmations and regrets and the simple need to be together that the
death of a loved one evokes in us. And her time, *her* time, would have
been less troubled.

I don't brood much about this. I don't still kick myself much. But I
think about it, and I wish I'd thought about this kind of thing before
my mother fell into her dying. My thinking resolves into two images. My mother on the gurney reaching her hand, searching with
a concentrated gaze. And my mother wired and tubed and billowing
with mechanical wind in the awful clarity of intensive care. The doctors and nurses might not agree—I don't know that they even noticed it—but I am certain my mother was doing something
important in the emergency room, something crucial to her being.
Something I don't understand, something she didn't understand and
needed to. Something was there and she was reaching, seeking to
know it. My worst regret is not that I caused her a needless last ordeal. My worst regret is that I interrupted her encounter at the bor-
derland, her sighting of the great Unknown.

CHAPTER THIRTY-THREE

I don't remember how many days my mother was in intensive care—three, I think. She was briefly conscious from time to time, of what I can't say. I think she recognized Marilyn and me. The rest of it—the tubes, the respirator, the strange faces of doctors and nurses, her pain—the rest of it must have been a nightmare, a lighted nightmare she kept waking to. No day or night, nothing to see but the same muted light, the same metal and plastic surfaces, nothing to hear but the gasping respirator opening and closing like some big fist inside her. Any change was hard for her, and now to wake from surgery into this . . . If, as close to death as she was, she still needed something to hold on to, I hope she found it in our faces at visiting hours. I hope we gave her some kind of solace. I hope inside she wasn't pleading, *End this, please end this . . .*

Two messages, one from within and one from without, helped me accept the end. On what I think was my mother's second night in intensive care I paced around the house in my bathrobe, picking up books and magazines for distraction and quickly abandoning each. Finally I dropped to my knees in front of the sofa and prayed. To whom or to what I didn't know, I didn't even know what exactly I was asking. It was a plea for guidance addressed to anything outside the anguished chamber of my mind, anything that might know more than I did. Later I went to bed, and soon after falling asleep I had one of my numinous dreams, the kind I think of as sleep visits or visions. This one was a single image. I saw my mother as I had seen her at noon the day before her fall, leaning back in her chair by the kitchen table, wearing sandals, a faded orange blouse, and a lavender skirt. She had been relaxed and plucky that noon, her mood buoyant, and in my dream vision she seemed made of light—it shone in her clothing, her smiling face, her silvery white hair. Just that, no more. I woke with her image clear in memory, and with the image I knew a twofold truth: my mother couldn't live in her body anymore, but nevertheless she would live. My waking mind accepted neither aspect of the truth, but still it was there, planted in me, mute and certain as a flower that had opened overnight.

The other message came the following day from an internist at the hospital who took Marilyn and me aside to talk about my mother. We liked his manner, which was friendly and forthright. She might stay alive indefinitely on the respirator, he told us, but only alive. If she were going to recover she would have shown signs by now. The surgery had simply overtaxed her heart, which already carried the burden of forcing blood through a calcified aortic valve that had possibly been narrowed to less than the width of a pencil. She had no resilience, no resources in reserve. At this point, the internist told us, we might want to think about easing my mother's decline. We might want to think about taking her off the respirator.

"Will she die then?" I asked him.

"She could die very quickly, but she might not. I'm afraid it's not something I can predict."

"But there's really no chance she'll get better?"

"My opinion is there's really no chance."

It was hard news, but finally it was more reassuring than devastating. It confirmed what we secretly knew, what we could see and
sense but hadn't been able to acknowledge to each other or ourselves.
And hard as it was, it at least gave us the opportunity, for the first
time in my mother's hospitalization, to consider and choose a course
of action on our own instead of following and inquiring about and
hastily approving the actions of others. To choose a course that
would make my mom more comfortable. A course, we believed
without hesitation, that she herself would choose if she were able.

Jim agreed with us over the phone that taking her off the respirator was the right thing to do, and he wanted to be there for it. I met
his flight at the Portland airport the next day, Sunday, about noon.
We drove straight to the hospital and met Marilyn there. While Jim
spent some time with our mother, two friends arrived—Sarah
Holmes, fellow follower of Sai Baba, and Paulann Petersen, who had
known my mother through Marilyn and me for many years.

We each took a few minutes with her, said a few words. I thanked
her for being the person she was. I told her it had been a privilege to
know her. I told her that I loved her, that I knew she had a voyage to
make, that I sent my love with her whenever she decided to set sail.
It's funny, I can't remember if her eyes were open or closed.

Sarah sang my mother a devotional song, "Dance, Shiva, Dance in
Our Hearts," which the two of them had sung together in the past,
and "Don't Have a Worry in the World," a song she had written herself. Both were lively, upbeat celebrations. It was wonderful the way
they opened up the antiseptic room. I felt myself smiling. We stood
around the bed as the internist shut off the respirator and quickly
withdrew the breathing tube. My mother kept on breathing. Her
blood pressure, which had been weak, shifted for a while and then
stabilized at a stronger level. She even seemed to take on a bit of color
in her cheeks. My mother was still my mother—still alive, still dog-

ged, still, in a way, willful. I thought of something she had said a few
months before in a chipper mood: "My whole life I've been obstreperous, obnoxious, and oppositional!"

And so, as my mother settled back into life, we settled in to keep vigil
with her. Because she was no longer receiving major life support, she
was moved from the intensive care ward to a standard hospital room,
a narrow single with one window and space for a few chairs beside
her bed. I remember the room in a pale greenish light. My mother
lay on her back; sometimes, when the nurses turned her, on her left
side. Her right leg was propped with pillows to keep it slightly bent,
easing the pressure on her hip, which was enclosed in a plastic brace.
She had an IV in her arm to maintain her fluid balance and blood
sugar and wore a light oxygen cannula on her nose to help her lungs
get what they needed. It was nothing like the respirator. What we
heard was my mother's own breathing, her lungs inhaling and ex-
haling as they had for eighty-four years, doing what eons of evolution had designed them to do, what life itself urged and insisted
they do.

She drifted between sleep and wakefulness, though not a wakefulness of speech. I know of only one word my mother spoke in her
last days. When I leaned over her bed one morning and said, "Hi,
Mama," she quickly answered, "Hi." I felt a bolt of happiness, an instant of new hope, but right away I saw the concentrated effort of recognition dissolving from her pale eyes. If she didn't speak, though,
she most definitely heard and felt. When Paulann read a poem by
Rumi, her eyes opened wide. And when Marilyn, in a private moment, thanked my mother for her strong and inspiring example as a
woman, she saw tears flow down my mother's cheeks.

I spoke to her at times and read to her often. Because she couldn't
speak herself and because language had been so crucial to her, such a
passion and a solace, it seemed important to offer it to her now. I read
her poets, mainly—Wordsworth, Tennyson, Gerard Manley Hop-

kins, Christina Rossetti, D. H. Lawrence, Edna St. Vincent Millay, e. e. cummings, Theodore Roethke, William Stafford. I read from the Psalms, the *Tao Te Ching*, the Upanishads. I read for a while and stopped, looked at her eyes, listened to her breathing, read more when I was ready. Who knows what the poems meant to her? Who knows what *she*, her subjectivity, really was? But they were lines she had loved, lines that had moved her and moved me, lines she had marked in pencil or with Kleenex strips or had noted to me in our sessions of reading aloud. Lines about dying, departure, traveling, the presence of the holy. What can you do when your mother is dying? You give what you can. You give what might strengthen and clarify, you give what might serve. You give the best and most appropriate language you know, and you give it in the same spirit in which Neanderthal people, sixty thousand years ago, gave flints and axes and heaps of medicinal flowers to the graves of their dead. She is leaving now. She will not return. You help her on.

I spent most of the daylight hours at the hospital, joined by Marilyn when she got off work and before long by my mother's niece, Betty Wilson, who flew in from Missouri. My brother took the night shift, catching some fragments of sleep in one of the hospital lounge areas. Technically this wasn't permitted, but Jim struck up a friendly rapport with the night nurses and they looked the other way. Earlier in the year, as he had cared for our mother while Marilyn and I took vacation, he had played her a tape of an ancient mantra, Om Namah Shivaya, sung to a simple musical arrangement. She had liked it, and so he played it now in the hospital room, at low volume on the boom box. Soon we were playing it almost constantly. It soothed all of us, a steady peaceful tide washing through us as it washed through our mother. The phrase means "I bow in reverence before Shiva"— Shiva the Destroyer, the god who decays and dissolves all things, and thereby liberates the human soul from mortal ignorance and delusion.

One morning I walked into the room to a striking change. My

brother, with his sure sense of the appropriate, had turned our mother's bed around to face the window instead of the hallway door, repositioning her IV and other apparatus as necessary. She had the light of morning on her face, the green boughs of a tree moving in a breeze outside. One of the nurses, surprised and a little alarmed, had asked Jim why he'd done it. He told her simply that his mother was alive, and so why shouldn't she have a view? The nurse smiled and let it be.

It buoyed me instantly to see my mother facing the window, and who can say what difference it might have made to her? Clouds, blue sky, the waving boughs—she had known these all her life, and she carried in her genes their unknown influence on ancestors human and nonhuman clear back to the dawn of life. Whatever she recognized, whatever she perceived, whatever she sensed, she faced the good world she had loved and now was becoming again. The world flowed in through her window, flowed into her open eyes whatever they saw, even as she flowed forth to join the world from the personhood of her many days. Even after she fell into a sleep she wouldn't wake from, the sun's light still touched her as it always had, still moved upon her ancient face as it moved upon the face of Earth.

In the afternoon of July 31, her ninth day in the hospital, my mother's breathing changed to a pattern of short inhalations and louder, punctuated breathings out. My brother and I were alone with her. Her breaths grew further apart. At five minutes to eight in the evening there came a stillness of several seconds, and then a long, sighing exhalation—as if, exactly as if, she had finished a long labor and now could rest.

CHAPTER THIRTY-FOUR

M arilyn suggested that we wash my mother. She asked the nurse on duty to free the body of its IV and other paraphernalia while we waited in the hall, then the five of us went in and stood around her—Jim at her head, our cousin Betty at her feet, Marilyn and Paulann on her left, me on her right. We wet towels in a basin of warm water and gently wiped her skin, gently toweled her small breasts, her abdomen with its slanting hernia scar, the sparse silver hairs of her pubic area, her silky upper thighs, her dry and purpled shins and forearms, her feet with their crooked and callused toes, her hands of graceful fingers, her peaceful face. We washed my mother, her accomplished body, the full flowering of her eighty-four years. Somehow she seemed young to me, a girl, but I felt her whole unliving weight when we lifted her to slip on one of her dresses from India, white cotton with raised white embroidery. We placed a string of sandalwood beads around her neck, and then a small leather pouch containing a few items from her bed-side at home—a shell, a feather, a photograph of Sai Baba, a packet of his sacred ash. I read three poems she had asked me, at one time or another, to read upon her death: Tennyson's "Crossing the Bar," Christina Rossetti's "Song," and e. e. cummings's "anyone lived in a pretty how town." Then I read Robert Louis Stevenson's "Re-quiem," which she had occasionally recited from memory in her last years:

> Under the wide and starry sky
>   Dig the grave and let me lie:
> Glad did I live and gladly die,
>   And I laid me down with a will.
>
> This be the verse you 'grave for me:
>   *Here he lies where he long'd to be;*
> *Home is the sailor, home from the sea,*
>   *And the hunter home from the hill.*

Then we kissed her, and we left.

In the restaurant afterward we were spirited, talkative. We cele-brated the woman we had known. We remembered her. We rejoiced at the final ease of her passing. We drank wine, ate good food. And where, I wonder now as I watch us in that restaurant, as I feel again the warmth and spirit of our little table—where was she? Where was Zilla Daniel, my mother? Where was the soul I knew and didn't know? Was she watching somehow, in some way like the way I watch now in memory? Had she watched us bathe her body, as some who have entered death and returned to life report having watched the surgeons struggling to save them? Or was she absorbed into a reality utterly removed from the hospital room, utterly gone from the res-taurant in which we who loved her laughed and drank our wine and spoke of her? Was she anywhere? In our remembrances she walked and smiled, she cursed, she climbed the rigging as a Sea Scout girl, she strode in hat and elegant heels from a Carolina porch, she drove the West in a Land Rover built like a tank, she slurped her soup and shuffled along behind her walker—where was she now, and what? Could she see the landscape of her life? Could she think of us? Or was she anything at all but a stiffening corpse in the hospital morgue, a cold body with blood pooling in its under portions, a parcel of dumb brute flesh already falling to corruption?

Seven weeks after my father died, he came to me in a sleep visit. My memory is mainly of his voice speaking. He told me that instead of vegetables he raised flowers now, and I saw them, masses of radiant flowers in many colors, unlike any I knew. They were flowers of light, a garden of gathered light. He told me he was happy now. He told me he was glad for my good thoughts about him and understood why I had negative thoughts. It was all right to be happy, he told me, even to be happy he was dead. I was shocked that he knew my shameful secret, shocked and afraid, but my fear turned into gratitude. I thanked him and the vision ended.

I hadn't understood, in the weeks since his death, the joy I felt within the tumult of my grief. Did it mean I was glad he had died? That I hated him? I couldn't bear to believe I felt that way. After the sleep visit I was easier; I began to understand my feelings. I saw that I wasn't glad for my father's death but glad for my own life, glad to be walking in the world. I was joyous in my sorrow because I knew it was my world now, my moment to be alive, my time to hit the trail in the clean cold of morning with no one to report to, no one to expect me home. My father had died as he had to die to make room for me, and the joy that thrilled me was not ingratitude but my soul's thanks. It soared in me, I realized, exactly like the strings in the second movement of Beethoven's Seventh Symphony, the violins he had made me hear when I was a boy—the way, as the theme comes to full volume, they soar for a moment high and intensely alone above the orchestra's somber measured march.

My mother, then living in the Findhorn community in Scotland, was overjoyed to hear of the sleep visit from my father. "So many things occur to say," she wrote. "How open you were—and are—to experiencing across the veil. How very concerned Franz was that he found a way to come to you; the love on both sides making it possible. The flowers he is growing!" She went on about a book that had come to her, just after my letter, by a woman who had received messages by thought transference from a close friend who had died, a former Anglican nun. My mother wrote that the nun had been "counseled by guides on the other side to send back the messages to her friend to inform interested persons here what it is like there for a recent arrival. That is where it rings true for me—the eternal part of me says 'yes.' She too had a garden of flowers. She tells how those who wish to get 'through' to someone on this side go about it, and much more that establishes the continuity of life, the carrying on of our dearest pursuits after going over our life history here to learn from it, after understanding why we did this and not that."

I don't remember clearly how I felt when I first read my mother's letter. Glad for the confirmation, I think, but resistant too. Certain about my own experience, the sleep visit, but skeptical of her enthusiasm, her seeming knowledge. How did she know so much? I preferred to think of my vision in its own isolated mystery, not loaded up with metaphysical arcana.

We decided on a direct cremation, and once that was arranged I left Portland almost immediately for Idaho. I'd been assigned by a magazine to write about salmon in the Columbia River Basin. I had delayed the research trip to be with my mother in the hospital and considered delaying it further when she died, but I realized I didn't want to. I was grateful for something to do, grateful to be in motion. Driving east through the great open gorge of the Columbia, the broad river on my left, forested cliffs and white waterfalls to the right, I kept glancing through my tears at the rental car's passenger seat and smiling, as if my mother were riding with me—she who loved journeys, who loved to be moving on land or sea. I didn't see her but sensed her, and something she had said came back to me. As I was leaving the house one afternoon in my shorts and ankle weights, her voice had followed me out the door: "Going for a walk? Put me in your pocket."

Two days later I walked and sat for hours by a stream high in the Sawtooth Range, watching my first chinook salmon. They hovered in the shade of boulders and pine snags, slowly waving their tails, opening and closing their mouths, the biggest of them nearly three feet long in a stream just ten feet across. Their fins were frayed and torn, their dark backs splotched with white infection. They had journeyed thousands of miles in the North Pacific and nine hundred miles up the Columbia and the Snake and the Salmon, thrusting themselves up the ladders of eight dams on the way, to arrive in this stretch of meandering meadow stream where they had been born. Within a few weeks they would spawn, shuddering out the last of their lives to the cold creek gravel, and their bodies would slide downstream with the current they had fought, their ripened red flesh disappearing into bear and raccoon, becoming meadow grass and streamside pines. I couldn't stop watching. I lay on a rock reaching down as slowly as I could, trying to touch their dorsal fins and spotted backs.

That night in a Boise motel I had a dream about my mother. Dead, she was being walked around by friends I didn't recognize as if she were alive. Maybe it was their house we were in; it wasn't mine. She seemed an awkward weight. After they set her in a chair, though, she showed signs of life. She stretched a little and seemed to be trying to open her eyes, which were glued shut with sleep. I went to moisten a white washcloth in warm water, but when I brought it her eyes were already open. She was sitting at the kitchen table, talking and drinking coffee. I was pleased but not overjoyed. I felt a bit out of sorts that she had recovered without my help. She was talking intently with the persons who had walked and wakened her, people I didn't know. When I woke in the morning I wrote down the dream without great feeling.

Two nights later, in the same motel, my mother visited me in sleep. I didn't hear her voice, as I had heard my father's sixteen years before, and I didn't see her. I had just fallen asleep. Someone rang or knocked at the front door of our Portland house. Someone was expected. How can I describe what I saw? I opened the door on a Presence. Down on the sidewalk were bunches of roses arranged in a large loose ring, standing, tilted slightly back, a ring of white and dark red roses glowing softly, deeply, in the dusky light. Roses there and not there, glowing into and out of the dusk, blooms of light and blooms of darkness, a circle of roses somehow arranged, somehow placed there for me to see, wavering in the gathering dusk of Princeton Street on the sidewalk just to one side of the concrete steps that go down from our door.

I woke right away with a longing to keep the roses before me, within me. I took no certain message from the vision except that it *was* a message—that my mother had sent it or been sent in its form, that my mother was the ring of roses, that they expressed her new state of being. I was overcome with awe and happiness and grief. As I tried to get it down in words, I felt I was touching only the husk of it, not the living image. I had been with it, inside it, in its living Presence. Now it was something smaller, something contained within me. Now I was only remembering. And as numinously whole as the vision had been and still remained, I felt that there was yet something in it, something about it, that I didn't quite understand.

CHAPTER THIRTY-FIVE

A month after my mother died we had a small service in our backyard. Her older sister Adelaide, then eighty-nine, flew in from Michigan. She and Marilyn drove to a you-pick flower farm on Sauvies Island and came home with a truckful of blooms, which they placed in pots and vases all around the yard. Ten of us sat in a circle and recalled the mother, sister, and friend we had known. Adelaide told of the many travels she and my mother had shared, beginning in 1910 when the family sailed to Holland for a Unitarian convention. Adelaide, then seven, led her two-year-old sister around the deck on a leash and harness, certainly the last time my mother ever submitted to such restraint. Seventeen years later, as Vassar undergrads, they returned to Europe; they flirted with the one eligible bachelor on the SS *Minikahda*, and Adelaide, who didn't drink, remembered her sister buying and consuming whole bottles of wine alone. Almost half a

century later, on a ferry voyage up the Canadian and Alaskan Inside
Passage—Adelaide's treat—my mother at sixty-five spurned the
comfortable stateroom, spending all the time she could on deck with
her face in the weather, enjoying the company of backpackers,
coastal natives, and the amazing scenery.

Others at the service read poems, sang songs, made their own remembrances. Marilyn read some of my mother's recollections of her
organizing days in *Refuse to Stand Silently By*. When the book had
arrived in the mail, about a year before she died, my mother didn't
recall being interviewed for it several years earlier, and neither did
she remember most of the events she had recounted. She read her
own words with close interest, keeping the book on her bed or
nightstand and returning to it often. She seemed gratified by what
she read, even proud. I seem to remember her saying, at one point,
"I really *was* something, wasn't I."

I read a message from Jim, who wrote of the many places our
mother had lived and loved—Maine and Scotland, India, British Columbia, the Blue Ridge of Virginia, the hill country of Carolina and
Tennessee. "She truly belonged to the world," he wrote. "Feed the
birds, folks. Let the cats come around. She was of all of us." He quoted
from "Ripple," the great spiritual anthem written and sung by the
Grateful Dead:

> Reach out your hand
> if your cup be empty
> If your cup is full
> may it be again
> Let it be known
> there is a fountain
> that was not made
> by the hands of men
>
> There is a road
> no simple highway

between the dawn
and the dark of night
And if you go
no one may follow
That path is for
your steps alone

I read a short piece I had written about my mother's life, a piece that would become, though I didn't know it at the time, one of the seeds of this book. At the end of it, after describing her death, I told about something I had discovered only a few days before the service. I had opened my mother's small deer-hide purse, in which she had squirreled away various items from time to time—money, shells, packets of *vibhuti*, her hearing aid. It's common for those with Alzheimer's to stash money and other objects in hiding places. There were two items in the change purse when I unsnapped it, one in each of its two compartments. One was her pendulum: a small, bullet-shaped, stainless steel plumb bob on a six-inch chain. And the other, which must have come to her in one of the take-out Chinese dinners we occasionally had, was a fortune from a fortune cookie. It read, "Leave your boat and travel on firm ground."

"What can I do?" I remembered her asking. "Are you sure there isn't something?"

I knew she had been preparing herself for death, but had she *decided* to die when she did? She must have been troubled by the tension in the house, the tension in me, and she knew the source of the tension. She knew that ElderPlace meant a change, and she may even have surmised that the change would end with her living among strangers in a strange place. Part of her still feared death, but more of her may have feared the uncertainties of her life. Looking back, it's hard to put limits on what she might have felt, what she might have known, what she might have done. She may have been demented, but she was demented in a canny way. And, of course, she didn't want to be a burden. She wanted to be helpful. Did she choose the time and the way she could help the most? Did she, like my correspondent's mother in India, seize a propitious moment to step out of the failing boat of her body and walk the spirit's firm ground?

It seems unlikely. She fell, after all. There was no sign of an intentional act. But a few days after the service, when I opened the red nylon carrying pouch on her walker, another discovery startled me. Among the contents was a mailing from one of the local hospitals or health care centers, maybe from the AARP, about the dangers of falling—how commonly it occurs, how dire the consequences can be, how to minimize the risk. Such mailings on a host of topics came all the time. Most of them my mother placed in the ash bucket she used for a trash can, but this one she had singled out for her walker pouch. Had it given her an idea, or encouraged an idea? If she did want to end her life, a fall was probably the only means available to her. Could the dithering crone who sometimes couldn't decide whether to get up from a chair have decided to embrace her death by falling to the bathroom floor? Unlikely, I still think, but the answer may be yes. She may have decided through one final act to end the burden of making decisions—and to release herself from decisions made by others.

It seems more plausible that the weakened bone of her hip broke spontaneously or that she had a stroke, neither of which she could have willed, but how can I be sure? Stroke is not the only possible explanation for her wordlessness in the hospital. Her head was near the side of the tub when I found her—she might have hit it as she fell. It's even possible that she deliberately forsook speech as part of her resolve to forsake life, the better to keep her attention focused on what lay before her as the veil between worlds parted. The evidence is ambiguous, the possibilities open. My mother may have accidentally fallen and died as a consequence, or she may have dropped herself to the floor intentionally. Like the speaker of the poem she loved, she may have laid herself down with a will.

I can't find the mailing that came to my mother about the dangers of falling. I have the deer-hide purse, pendulum and fortune still in it, but the mailing isn't here. I have an uncertain memory of keeping it a while, then throwing it out, and I know—not vaguely at all—why I might have done that. Just as I know why, when I've broken down crying in the time since her death, I've found myself saying, "I'm sorry, Mama, I'm so sorry . . ." It's not merely grief at her dying. It's a fear and a guilt, fear and guilt with the force of a conviction, that I pushed her into her death. That I made her feel unwelcome in my house and my life. That snapping at her in the restaurant and treating her roughly on the patio and a hundred other acts of impatience and selfishness built a pressure that said *Go* to her, a pressure that forced her ultimately out of her life. I can't bear to think it, but it is what I have felt.

Two more clues, two more marked poems in William Stafford's *Passwords*. One of them, titled "Young," tells a brief generalized story of a childhood, blessed and vital, giving way to the disappointments of age. "The best of my roads went wrong," says the speaker:

> It was far, it was dim,
> toward the last. And nobody knew how
> heavy it was by the end,
> for that same being who lived back then.
>
> Don't you see how it was, for a child?
> Don't you understand?

For most of two years I've taken that last stanza, which is lined sides and bottom by my mother's pencil, as a reproach intended for me. And I have cringed to read the first three lines of the poem on the facing page:

> Someone you trusted has treated you bad.
> Someone has used you to vent their ill temper.
> Did you expect anything different?

Stafford goes on to imagine consolation for the injured "you" of the poem, and this section, the final five lines, my mother bracketed in wavery pencil:

> But just when the worst bears down
> you find a pretty bubble in your soup at noon,
> and outside at work a bird says, "Hi!"
> Slowly the sun creeps along the floor;
> it is coming your way. It touches your shoe.

Exactly the kind of solace available to a largely immobile, largely housebound, largely solitary being. And exactly the kind of solace my mother would have been likely to find and appreciate—the consolation of little things, the comfort of the ordinary. I'm glad she put her pencil to that part of the poem and not the first three lines, but it nearly breaks my heart to consider that she *needed* such solace and that I, more than anyone or anything else, must have caused her to need it.

Am I reading too much into a few pencil marks on a few poems? Maybe. I may be reading too much and writing too much into many of the events I'm stitching together. And it may be that I'm too hard on myself, as my psychologist believes. Marilyn believes so too. She tells me that my mother was lucky, that I did well by her, and I don't think she says that just to make me feel better. She believes it, and because she lived it all with me, because she next to me is the one in the best position to know the truth, her view counts. Her view comforts me.

But finally, I'm the one I have to satisfy. I'm the one holding the pen, and I'm the one held at the point of the pen. Bob Bourgeois would like me to put the pen down and be done with this. You can only analyze things so far, he says, after that you're just wallowing in it. Bob loved his mother and mourned her death. He cried because he missed her, because she was his mother, not because he might have done her any wrong. Bob cried a lot, but not so much lately. It's not that he's forgotten her, but somehow he's taken her inside him, her life and her death. Somehow he puts her in the ground with the ferns and flowers he plants; somehow when he whistles as he cleans the rain gutters it's her whistling too.

But there's someone else I have to satisfy, someone who isn't whistling. The Inspector says I failed my mother. He says I drove her from the world. He says it and says it and says it. He's so shrill and insistent that I try to change the channel when he's on, I try to tune him out. When he's got me awake and half-listening deep in the night, I'll turn on a light and stick my face in a book right in the middle of his harangue. Eventually I fall asleep. But it seems the more I ignore him the more persistent he becomes, the more I hear his muffled voice from that observation chamber where he keeps his eyes on the province. Maybe I need to try something different. He's in the chamber by his own choice, but lately he's been sounding like someone in confinement, someone shouting to be heard. He's not going to stop. He's not going to die or go away. And depressed and obsessive as he may be, he isn't any fool. He thinks too much, but he *is* a thinker. My psychologist says I haven't really met him yet. Maybe she's right. Maybe it's time to knock on his door and see if he'll answer.

CHAPTER THIRTY-SIX

At Sai Baba's ashram, Sarah's been telling me, devotees stay in small concrete apartments or set up camp in huge community sheds. They sleep on thin mattresses purchased in Puttaparthi, placed on rented cots or directly on the floor. The ashram charges a nominal fee, little more than pennies, for food and accommodations. Early, around 4:00 A.M., the devotees rise and enter the temple to sing twenty-one *Oms*, the sound of sounds from which the world was born. Then one or two women sing the *Suprabhatum*, the good-morning hymn. "It's like saying, 'Wake up, Lord, we're your devotees!'" Sarah tells me. A fifteen-minute meditation follows. Later in the morning the group walks singing through the ashram grounds. They are from many countries, many religious backgrounds. Sai Baba teaches that all faiths are facets of the truth. "I have not come to start a new religion," he has said, "but to deepen your experience of God in the religion of your choice or heritage." The name of his ashram is Prasanthi Nilayam—Abode of Peace.

After breakfast they wait in the courtyard, monkeys sometimes walking among them. Sarah sees light around Sai Baba when he comes, a halo off to one side or a tall, multicolored pillar. That is what absorbs her attention. "You get the feeling his human body is just a prop," she says. He walks among them, Sai (Divine Mother) Baba (Divine Father), walks in a plain orange robe, his kinky black hair spreading in a large aura around his head. His face, as I've seen it in photos, is broad, fleshy, affectionate. There's a crinkle at the bridge of his nose when he smiles. He might speak, might press a bit of *vibhuti* to someone's forehead as an act of healing. Whatever his actions, Sarah says, his presence is transcendent. She speaks of a long-lasting glow, a sense of peace and restoration—something utterly singular, utterly pure. She says, "The Lord is walking the earth, and you, whatever your age or circumstances, are lucky enough to be alive and know of him."

Sarah believes, as my mother did, that Sai Baba is that rare thing, a true avatar—an incarnation of the formless into human form, here to do service, in humility, to the world. He is not driven about in Rolls Royces, he does not proselytize, he does not launch crusades or jihads. Devotees in the ashram must follow rules—no meat, no smoking, no sex, and others—but are not forced to believe anything. No one summons them, no one makes them stay. "Going to Baba is like walking into a beautiful wilderness," Sarah says. "If you're called in your heart, you go."

Just a week ago I discovered the letter, from 1985, in which my mother first mentions Sai Baba. Findhorn acquaintances had told her "that an avatar has been revitalizing India for a quarter of a century—Sri Satya Sai Baba—setting up colleges for women and young people, schools for children, whose gospel is, simply, love." In the right margin, in red ink, she added an annotation: "*Not* a guru." She traveled to Prasanthi Nilayam later that year, then again in the winter of 1986–87. I wish she could have spoken more thoroughly of what she experienced there, what it meant to her. She tended to answer my questions with vaguenesses, and she responded to Sarah—who went for the first time a year after my mother's second trip—in the same way.

Yet I do know something of what her pilgrimages meant to her. I think she told it in the rapt, quavery, slightly phlegmy voice with which she sang her Sanskrit food prayer, that unfaltering soft soprano that rose to a transcendent height to leave its "*Shanti, shanti, shanti . . .*" hovering for a long moment before we ate. I've learned what the words of the prayer generally mean: God is the food, the eating of the food, the eater of the food. God through the food becomes the life-fire in the bodies of living things. By God the food is offered into the fire of God.

During her first sojourn at the ashram, my mother and a fellow-pilgrim friend had a personal interview with Sai Baba. She wrote briefly about it, as if there were little of it words could convey, in one of her letter-meditations a month later. Sai Baba would not allow her to kneel and kiss his feet. She sat to his side and held his hand. They exchanged a few words, but she doesn't specify what was said. She writes of the moment as a "sweetness," the sweetness of her brown rice lunch in Maine magnified a billionfold. She writes of feeling his "overwhelming Love."

In my own imagination I go farther. I see tears on my mother's face. I see the woman who had lived and formed herself by words now resting in a garden beyond words. I see the obstreperous woman, the woman of spite and rebellion, submitting herself utterly. I see the advocate of causes shedding all conflict like leaves in a wind. I see the mother whose firstborn died in her arms relieved for a moment of that fifty-year ache. I see the veteran of a tempestuous and painful marriage made whole in a greater marriage, a marriage of peace. And I see my mother the Inspector, she who lectured and drove herself, who could not abide her own failings and weaknesses,

I imagine that woman completely at ease, for one tireless moment, in the sufficiency of being.

I may have it wrong. I may be imagining my own wishfulness into my mother's experience, whatever it was. I may merely want her to have realized her spiritual quest at Sai Baba's ashram so that I can feel easier about her dying. But still—when I remember her toasting the Unknown, when I remember her showing me the great bird I couldn't see, when I remember her reaching and searching with her eyes in the emergency room, and especially when I remember the ring of glowing roses, when I touch their mystery within me, then I feel myself touching an authentic joy, a fulfillment I did not invent. It was in my mother, and it is in these words she wrote in 1987, home in Maine after her second pilgrimage to Sai Baba:

> The sense of joy radiating from me exceeds all bounds. I asked for expanded awareness, now it is here—it comes from within me, where lies the source of all life, all wonder. It has nothing to do with what my mind conceives. It is like gazing into a deep, clear well, where bottom and surface are the same, obliterating limits of physical nature. They do not exist except in my mind that has to define them for its own petty sake. If I cannot hold on to this, it will return—or I will return to it: one and the same, and other openings will occur, as my sense of infinite expandability stays within reach: spiritual reach, which does not turn in upon itself.

I found that meditation only a short time ago, long after my mother's death. Reading it now I imagine a candle burning in the seclusion of her soul in the years she lived with us, a still and solitary flame burning in a place where no dementia or bodily failing or travail with family could extinguish it. I see it burning behind my mother's closed eyes, and I feel it behind my own.

Someday I will make my own pilgrimage to Prasanthi Nilayam. I would like to feel the power that touched my mother there. I'm in no hurry, though, because closer to home I have other places of peace, other beautiful wilds.

What I love about the old-growth forest is not so much the size of the trees, their sheer grandeur of scale, but their complete development, their wholeness, and the wholeness of the forest they compose. Each long-rooted tree began as a stirring in the seed, a tiny remembering spurred by the touch of sun and water, and each as it spired from the ground in the weather of its place took inside itself all that occurred—each urging of moisture and mineral among its roots, each feathery touch of fungus, the rains and slanting sun its boughs received through all its days and seasons, the sudden slashes of lightning, the weight of snow that broke down branches, the awful weight of wind that broke more, the shock of ground fire that charred its bark and killed its smaller fellows but left it living, deepening into earth and air, dripping rainfall from its limbs and channeling it then from the dark of soil back into the sky, turning earth into light and light into earth again. The tree stands until it can stand no longer, until its burdened memory is more than roots and trunk can bear, until the achievement of its peculiar form must forget itself in formlessness, in the darkness of its deepest self, then to echo, rhyme, and remember itself in the forms of future trees.

Remembering, forgetting—mind, I'm starting to believe, is nothing exclusive to human beings and other animals. The neurons we believe to be the source of mind may merely receive the mind imbued in all of nature, the mind that urges from within toward form and wholeness, that opens toward dissolution and decay. Sarah says she senses Sai Baba in the air she breathes, the water she drinks. My mother sensed him in the light of dawn, in the patterned frost on her windowpanes. I don't use that name but I sense it too, I hearken to it, I feel a mindful stirring in the forest quiet. There is mind in the great Douglas firs, in the ferns and mosses that grow on and around them, in the miles and miles of fungal strands in every tablespoon of forest soil, and there is mind as well in the soil itself, that vast unconscious store of memory, and if in the soil, then in the very stones and seeping waters, in the rivers and clear streams where salmon spawn, in ocean storms that freshen the streams and raise the forest, in the ceaseless ocean itself, in the shifting, flowing, spuming volcanic planet formed from the ash of long-spent stars. And the stars. The stars I wonder at, the stars that have scared me so—what can they be, if I see them truly, but fierce and subtle shimmerings in the mind of all that is?

Thou art that, it says in my mother's book, and so she is. She has gone back to that which she always was, in mind as well as body. What was the quest of her last twenty-five years but her attempt to find, to remember, the greater mind she felt intimations of and yearned for? And what was her Alzheimer's, finally, but another nudge in that direction, a further opening of her infinitely expandable spirit? As her accustomed point of subjectivity began to soften, to curl, to droop from firmness of form like a wildflower gone by its time, that personal point of view slowly gave way to a larger subjectivity, a greater Self, not the flower but the field of flowers, the forest bounding the field, the wind touching every tree and every flower. I see her aged face expanding like her spirit—nose and lips and wrinkled skin, the achieved landscape we knew her by slowly extends itself, slowly enlarges, her features forgetting their human forms to remember themselves as mountain ranges, valleys in sun and shadow, forests and fields of wild unknown lives beneath the stars.

CHAPTER THIRTY-SEVEN

The house seemed huge in the months that followed my mother's death. I rattled around in the daytime hours while Marilyn was at work, finding small things to fix or fiddle with, reading, writing my article on salmon and some other magazine pieces. I found myself petting the cat a lot. Marilyn, just a few days after my mother died, had felt a strange intuition that my mother was the cat, the cat was my mother. I didn't feel it so strongly, but they always had seemed joined in many ways. I did feel more tender toward the cat, more tolerant of her quirks and nervousness.

From time to time I sat in my mother's bedroom and looked out the sliding glass door that she had looked out, watching the light change as she must have watched it. The backyard world went on as it always had: the birch leaves yellowed and fell, the dogwood leaves turned red and fell later, the rain came down, the gray sky lightened and darkened, the finches and chickadees came to the feeder. It all continued, unbrokenly alive, but my mother did not. She had breathed for eighty-four years and then one evening at five minutes to eight she didn't breathe again. Her heart had pumped along for however many millions of beats and then stopped. All that she had been in this world, all that could be touched or hugged, all that could sing and shuffle and lift a coffee mug, all of that was a small clay pot of ashes on the closet shelf. In my grief for her I also felt an awe transcending grief, awe that an embodied life could persist so far and then just halt, vanish absolutely, never to return.

We had removed my mother's bed and given a few of her winter clothes to charities (we knew it would have pleased her to make them useful to someone who needed them), but otherwise had left the room unchanged. We weren't ready to turn it into something other than my mother's bedroom. I opened and closed her books, touched her jewelry, sorted through her stacks of magazines and unanswered mail. I suppose I was trying to touch her somehow by laying hands on the things her own hands had touched. And I was looking for more clues, for glimpses of what she had thought and felt in her last weeks and days. I found one, though I didn't know how to interpret it: a small, sealed, unmarked white envelope containing the pit of a single cherry.

When I cried, which was frequently, I knew what I was crying about but not what I was crying for. I missed her, of course, but *what* did I miss? Not the tension, not my irritation, not the pressure of being watched for cues, not anguishing over leaving her alone for an evening, not sponging up her trails of urine. I had been relieved of those burdens and *felt* relief, which I wasn't able to accept. I chided myself for being small, ungenerous. I berated myself for not being strong enough to bear the modest office of caregiving. I blamed myself for my mother's irrevocable absence from the world. Even the numinous roses, which I held inside me, which still seemed—against all reason—an affirmation from my mother herself, couldn't console me when the passion of my remorse was upon me. I worried about what I was still missing in that vision, what I didn't yet understand. I thought in my thinking mind that she probably hadn't left the world resenting me, but that knowledge was tossed about like a little boat in the steep swells of my feelings. As the months passed and I continued to feel racked with guilt, I found myself asking her for another sign, something more than the roses, something more than a cherry pit in an envelope.

I started a new kind of writing during this time. I had never written about myself in any sustained way, had hardly looked inward at all except to find my feelings about something in nature. But now a tiny essay I had written for a magazine, about where I lived and why, turned into a longer piece about coming west and coming of age in the sixties. Even the longer piece, I realized, held potential paragraphs and pages captive within single sentences. I went further into the necessary unfolding, but after a while I floundered. I was turning up the stuff of my life, the stories by which I knew myself, but what was I to do with them? The material had no form. As my life had been, it was scattered, shapeless, a mess of clay. I was frustrated, but now I can see how important that writing was. I had entered upon the paths of memory and begun the work of imagining myself.

At some point I had a lucid dream that both affirmed what I was writing and demanded more from it. I became conscious within a dream and saw what looked like a familiar manuscript, the formless memoir I was working on. A voice—something like mine, my inner voice—was reading the language as it was meant to be, reading surely, steadily, with exact authority and feeling, but I couldn't understand the words. They were English and mine but not quite mine, they were a river moving through but not part of my limited knowing. And then I realized that the manuscript, though it was in my typeface and bore my penciled markings, was not mine either. It was not something I had made but something that was making me. The voice and manuscript were the unknown life inside my life, writing and revising me, unfolding the true and necessary story. I woke knowing that the story was there, that I needed both to find it and to let it find me.

Over a period of about a year I had many dreams about wholeness, work, and lower depths. In one of them, a woman friend called with stunning news that a volcanic island had just risen to the surface of Paradise Lake, a lake I knew. An island being born! I felt blessed beyond measure to know of it. In another dream I watched a miner pulling what he called his Iron Horse, a complex and heavy piece of archaic machinery. It came to me with the force of revelation that he could pull the thing because he and it—and I—were *underwater*, and the water made it lighter. He wouldn't be able to budge it up above, on land. And in the most detailed of these dreams, a woman woke me to ask if I needed a job. "No," I said, "I have work, I've just been sleeping," but I got up and followed her down the winding stairway of what seemed to be a school. I wanted to justify myself, to explain that she had misunderstood me, but I also wanted to ask if there was something she wanted me to build. I thought it might be a system of shelves she wanted, shelves for sorting things out. It seemed too complicated, far beyond my skills, and I was afraid. But maybe she has a plan, I thought. Maybe she knows how I could do it. I kept walking down the stairs, catching glimpses of the woman far below me.

I was being shown, I see now, the necessity of writing this book— the necessity of entering the depths of memory under the guidance of the feminine. But at the time, the dreams simply frustrated me. I woke from each with a glow of wholeness and well-being, but I woke always to my uncertainty about my writing, my grief and guilt about my mother. The dream, as I went about my day, seemed small and merely wistful, utterly separated from my bereaved and confused reality. I continued to cry, continued to speak to my mother, continued to beg her for a sign of her forgiveness, or a sign that no forgiveness was needed.

Maybe she couldn't get through to me at home. I may have been too charged there, the rooms and things of the house too constantly branding me with the reproach of her absence. Maybe she had to wait until enough time had passed. Or maybe she just likes Idaho. In March of 1994 I was spending the night with friends in Lewiston and had just fallen asleep. In what feels like an ordinary dream, my host-friend and I are climbing a rocky height to fly the hobby airplanes he builds. It's *too* high, though. I start to climb down but my friend steps on my hands and I'm falling, fast, hurtling with the full rushing sensation of speed, wondering when I'll hit the ground then realizing I won't hit, I won't die, I'm falling free in space now and there's nothing I *can* hit. I open my arms and turn, still zooming, I feel the hard torquing weight of the turn and I turn again, flying free and rising now in the starry dark, arcing upward toward an intensely joyous light veiled in smoke like a nebula, the bright clouds of creation. But the light is more than I'm ready for, or it's not ready for me, and now I fly toward a more subtle light, a form, a hooded face, a mask of light with shadow interfused, *my mother*—not as she was in life but her face of spirit, her face that is all I can know of her now, her face with the cosmos behind it, nothing and everything behind it, a face of light itself interfused with shadow, smiling the serenity of being.

I want to stay, to hover freely in that presence, but now I'm drifting down from space into the dense unmoving weight of my own body, sleeping on my left side, my hands together between the two pillows beneath my head, and slowly I rise from the immense weight of sleep as if from the core of the Earth because I know I have to, I have to remember, and I'm crying already as I awaken but in gratefulness now for the sign she has given me.

After a while I turned on the light and wrote it down the best I could. I sat thoughtlessly a long time, the image of my mother's light-and-shadow face hovering within me, a stillness around which I trembled. Her smile, which was no smile I had ever seen on her living face, denied no loss, denied no least speck of pain or evil. It was not a smile of joy or happiness. It was a smile of knowledge, and *All is well* is what it said.

The Inspector has his own smile, a quick contraction of his pale cheeks and mustached mouth that looks as much like pain as pleasure. His smiling grimace, his grimacing smile. The thing I never appreciated is how vulnerable he is. I never fully understood his position. He has no child and now no mother, no family or friends at all. He has no life, really. Bob can grow tomatoes and can hammer nails, I can write at least, but the Inspector can only patrol his province and react. He spends all his time in that lonely room, staring carefully and haggardly like some air traffic controller who won't go off his shift. Where can he go? What can he do? I always thought Bob was the one I pitied, but really it's the Inspector. He's no older than me, it turns out, but he looks and acts much older. He's a pale, lonely old man who never was young.

But I don't want to pity him or condescend to him. I want to understand him, I want to give him his due. And so I went to him and told him that I value his observations. I told him I appreciate his commitment and caring. I told him that even though I think he's wrong sometimes, his judgments too severe, I've realized that I'm not a writer without him. It's really for him more than anyone that I'm writing this book—to take his harsh rebukes and make an answer to them. I thanked him for the challenge. I looked into his tired eyes and thanked him for keeping me honest. I touched him on the shoulder, asked if he'd like to take a walk.

We went no place special, just stretched our legs in the Portland rain. We breathed the good wet air with its sour tang of pulp mill. We walked the bluff above Swan Island and looked at the big ships in dry dock. We watched the crows hopping and squawking in the park. We walked the streets among schoolkids getting off their buses, heading home by twos and threes in their bright colors, shouting their clear high laughter. The Inspector walked with a kind of wariness, his hat pulled down on his forehead, but he took it all in.

I told him he was right. I wasn't patient enough with our mother. I wasn't flexible or imaginative or generous enough. I was too self-absorbed. There were moments I'm not proud of, moments I'd revise if I could, moments I'd try hard to make different if she were still here. I'd make myself a bigger person if I could. But I'm in my mid-forties now, I reminded the Inspector, and I've reached limits I'm unlikely to transcend. I am the man I am, lesser than the one I'd like to be—and, like a poem or an essay or this book, lesser than the one that might have been. I'm like the work I do, flawed and good. And that's what I did for our mother, I told him. I took on something hard, something important, and I did a job both flawed and good.

The Inspector held his pale eyes on me as I spoke, and to my surprise, he didn't object. But maybe I shouldn't be surprised. He of all people knows about limits—he's their close observer, their careful noter, and now I know that he very much feels the pain of his own. What he mostly wanted, I see now, was to hear *me* acknowledge my limits, hear from *my* mouth what he's been saying all along. I did that, but I also got him to look at things from my side. I showed him that last poem our mother marked, the one that begins, "Someone you trusted has treated you bad." I told him my fear that she meant those lines for me and why she might have had reason to—nothing new to the Inspector, of course. But then I showed him the title of the poem, and I showed him how she circled it with her pencil. I told him I take that as a message too, for me and for whoever sees it. "It's All Right," the title says. It's all right. It sounds like one of the tunes Bob whistles as he does his work. I can't whistle, I confessed to the Inspector, but I can hum that tune, and I bet him a beer that he could pick it up too. He gave me one of his grimacing smiles. It's our mother's tune, I told him. It's all right. It's something she wanted us to have.

CHAPTER THIRTY-EIGHT

Maybe this is a senile landscape, this open tableland. It extends with a slightest roll, a merest wavering, clear to far blue mountains east in Idaho and south in Nevada, under a sky of dark-bottomed cumulus clouds. Sage and rabbitbrush, gray and green going silvery in the wind. Not one tree. A landscape made of distance, an immense presence made of absence. Shallow creases lined with scab rock wander the land as if at random, as if they have lost their way, and that's the way I follow. Long lazy curvings gather me in, furrow me into the tableland, lower me away from wind and endless distance. An inevitable winding way guides me down, slowly down. Little walls of volcanic rock echo the stones clattering beneath my boots. Bunchgrass, clumps of yellow flowers. Damp sand, water in pools, then a trickling stream flows next to me.

What gives the solace I feel here? There's no congeniality in sand or lichen, no warmth in canyon walls except what they hoard from the sun. Why do I feel so generously welcomed? Because everything is as it should be. Everything is as it needs to be, through no doing of my own. The blind hand of time is scouring this canyon as it must be scoured, slowly, incrementally deepening its way through old flows and spewings of lava. The flat-bottomed clouds slide overhead in a sky exactly as luminously blue as it needs to be. The wind blows, the grasses bow and rise. The stream flows with a thin lilt through the way it has made, the way it was given. I walk deeper, the walls high above me now. Blue sky and shouldering cliffs, a song of water, the winding way as it all must be.

My mother would have loved this place. Desert wasn't her favorite landscape, but she knew the joy of natural quiet anywhere, the silent celebration in all things. She knew the happiness of feeling small in nature's greatness. She thrilled to the Olympic rain forest, its green riot of moss and ferns and colossal trees, when she and I drove there in 1969. She was sixty-one, on the loose at last from her working life in D.C., setting out on the adventure of her old age in her Land Rover, the Green Seal. I was twenty-one, a college dropout, a backpacker and climber in love with the wilderness West. We hiked a long uphill trail to camp for the night—I remember waiting for her, worrying a few minutes until she appeared, smiling, leaning into her pack straps, making her way up the trail at her own measured pace. I never thought about her heart back then, never thought how hard it had to be working to get her up the hills.

We toured around Oregon on that same trip—Mount Hood, down 97 to Crater Lake, and west along the Coquille River to the southern coast, where we ate crab and slept in the Seal pulled off on a logging road. I remember the trip warmly now, but my mother and I couldn't spend much time together without friction. Part of my joy in the West was being away from my parents, and she and I were too much the same—same fingers, same hair, same nose, same moody and cranky disposition. As a child I felt, rightly or wrongly, a kind of restraint, even coldness from her—as if she thought I didn't need her affection, or she didn't have it to give me. My father had wanted another child right away after Georgie had died, my mother told me in one of the conversations I taped, but she refused; she worried that he wanted George reborn right away. When I did come along—I'm pretty sure I wouldn't have if George had lived—I was doted on by Nanny, our maid and helper, to such an extent that my mother had to speak firmly to her, fearing that Jim was being neglected. We grew up calling our parents not Mom and Dad but by their first names, Franz and Zilla—because, my mother explained, she thought that way they would have closer and more personal relationships with us. If anything, I think, it distanced us. It tended to turn Jim and me into autonomous little adults while still children.

Through my twenties and thirties I had a comfortable relationship at a distance with my mother. We wrote letters, we saw each other occasionally. Two or three years might pass between visits. And so I suppose it was inevitable that we would rub sparks from each other when she moved into the house. We were too little accustomed to being together, let alone living together. She was losing her fiercely cherished independence, and I, in having to care for her, was losing some of my own. We loved each other, resented each other, and neither of us had much skill in knowing and expressing our feelings.

And so we did the best we could. We got by, and there were times in those four years when we did much better than get by. If our personalities were hardened and deformed in some of the same ways, our spirits, at our best, were also alike. We shared the same kind of religious imagination. Now and then I wrote down and left by her bed a line or two I had come across in my reading, lines I knew she would appreciate. "All finite things reveal infinitude," from Roethke. "i thank You God for most this amazing day," from cummings. And this from Gerard Manley Hopkins: "All things therefore are charged with love, are charged with God and if we know how to touch them give off sparks and take fire, yield drops and flow, ring and tell of him." My mother always thanked me happily for these gifts. "Yes," I can hear her saying as she read the Hopkins, "oh, *yes.*"

On our walks sometimes, especially early on when she was stronger, we would delight together in such small wonders as the neighborhood provided us. We would stop to peer into a small cavern in the base of a certain maple. "Anyone home?" my mother liked to inquire, poking gently with her cane. We rejoiced at the fine job the roots and boles of the older trees were doing upheaving the sidewalk slabs. We were for the trees, for the spiny horse chestnuts that littered Hancock Street in the fall, for the moss that filled all cracks and corners with its emerald wealth, for the dandelions, for the squirrels that ran across our path—my mother greeted each one—and the tiny ferns that grew from a mossy crotch of one of the maples. We were for robins and chickadees, for each and every walker we encountered, for rain and sun, for the wind that shimmered my mother's favorite copper beech. "Think if each leaf were a bell!" she once exclaimed in jubilation.

We were in league with the good green conspiracy of the world. We were for and part of much more than we could say, more than we could know, but in our best moments—when she was feeling spry and spirited, when I stopped wanting to be somewhere else and gave myself to the walk—in our best moments we *felt* what we were for and part of, we felt what we were, without any need to speak it. We smiled it, laughed it, shared it between us like the roving tip of our spooky cat's tail. There's something King Lear says to Cordelia toward the end, when his ravaged mind is both mad and terribly sane:

> Come, let's away to prison.
> We two alone will sing like birds i' th' cage.
> When thou dost ask me blessing, I'll kneel down,
> And ask of thee forgiveness. So we'll live,
> And pray, and sing, and tell old tales. . . .

And take upon's the mystery of things,
As if we were God's spies. . . .

My mother and I, in those moments when we were most worthy of
ourselves, took upon us the mystery of things. We were God's spies.

And imprisoned as we were in our personalities, caged in our history, we did sing sometimes. I remember an afternoon walk when
my mother suddenly piped up, "I'll give you one ho, Green grow the
rushes ho," thumping the sidewalk with her cane. I piped in to join
her, following her lead, learning the verses that she remembered
better than I did. Arm in arm we sang our way around the sunlit
block in the company of trees and new spring flowers, stopping to
laugh when a neighborhood sheepdog briefly joined our chorus. As
I helped her into the house, my mother said, "They forgot to put it in
the Bible: *Have fun.*"

How strange that I should feel uneasy telling this—as if, in recounting a moment of blithe happiness with my mother, I were con-
fessing something embarrassing, something shameful. How very
strange that I should have to say to myself, it isn't shameful. It's as
natural as anything in the world, and it's important. It's what I
wanted at the beginning of my life and received at last at the end of
hers: to walk with my hand in my mother's hand, circling toward
home in the light of forsythia and the shading trees, singing the song
my mother sings in her glad voice.

The light of my fire plays up the canyon wall, a few sparks rising. It's
good to be here, good to be weary and resting, listening to the ru-
morous voice of the stream—the voice of a life bound up like ours
in time and consequence, changing and changeless, free and con-
strained, young and ancient and ageless.

My mother didn't get cheated. She lived in her human way as long
and thoroughly as the flooding and trickling waters have worked this
canyon. She wore her body down, played it out, scoured it away with

living. Maybe she did end her life on purpose. And maybe she did it not because she felt unwanted, not because of anything I did or didn't do, but because her boat was failing her, and like the stream singing in darkness, she wanted to go on. The decision might have come from the deep place her food prayer came from, the place of God offering itself to God. The place of her quavery but clear *shanti*.

And if she did feel pushed? Maybe, just maybe, that's all right too. Maybe, a friend wrote, she needed a boost to get over the Great Divide, and maybe it was my part to provide it. And as she probably understood far better than I did, I needed to move on too. The Navajo say that old people have to die in order to make room for the living. I have a life to live, my own boat to steer. I needed a shove into open water, and it would have been typically forthright and generous of my mother to give me one as she brought her own boat in to shore. I keep thinking of her plucky mood the day before she fell, as she sat in the kitchen dressed in orange and lavender. I keep seeing the smile on her face—not her deepest childlike smile, but the smile of someone content in her own mind, a woman capable of doing the necessary task.

I only wish she could have laid her bones down more easily. I wish she could have crossed the divide not in a hospital room but at home, or—if she could have expressed the wish and I could have heard it and honored it—in a place such as this, where she might have died by firelight with streamsong bearing her away. Or back on her beloved coast of Maine, there to forget herself in the lap and splash of the sea, in gull cries and the smell of salt air. I could have read to her there, we could have spoken when she wanted to speak, we could have sung like birds in the cage, and we and all those around her could have looked and listened for the very right thing, for the corroboration of earth and sea and sky, of the mind of nature that unites us all. Maybe the time will come when we will allow such deaths, such whole and beautiful deaths, for ourselves and those we love.

Death doesn't seem so frightening here. It seems a little thing, significant but small, like the nest of white bones I saw today in grasses by the canyon wall. Nothing here worries about its end. If I stayed long enough, death might come to seem only the next thing to happen, the next turn of the canyon, the river flowing into its future as it must and needs to flow. I can imagine a certain happiness—and maybe I even feel it, some slightest glow—in giving myself up to stones and coyotes, to the greatness of the desert sky. A happiness, a holiness, a remembering beyond measure.

But not yet, not nearly yet. I stumble into the night on my sore ankle and stiff legs to relieve myself, and the broad stripe of sky is a shock of smeared and scattered light. Great Milky Way, great smoky wheel, the specked and glittering trail of time . . . *Thou art that*, says the book, I am that light, I burn with the fire of all that is, and I need no lantern to find my way.

CHAPTER THIRTY-NINE

It wasn't trouble with his parents that made him leave the cottage they had rented. No fighting, nothing bad going on, but the cottage was small and all the talking was between his parents and their friends, stories he had heard before, their laughter not a laughter he shared in. It was their place, not his. But outside was the North Carolina coast, the Outer Banks, the boom of breakers in the moist night air. He slipped out when no one would notice and walked north in shorts and t-shirt, striding fast but easily fast, his bare feet striking the sand heels first and leaving their prints behind, the longshore breeze blowing cool on his face, the Atlantic waves traveling unimaginable distances to rumble and spume in luminous glory.

The beach is his, his alone. The damp sand giving to his feet, a few stars scattered on the trail of night. At sea a single light wavers, lost, alive, and in a sudden strangeness it seems he has always been walking here. It is all so uncannily familiar that he cannot imagine himself not here. His real self has forever been part of the rumbling night, has always known this wind and sand, this scatter of stars, and only now, having left the cottage and set out walking, has he joined himself. Only now has he remembered who he really is.

His own night sky lights within him, in the thrilled emptiness where his breath tides in and out and his heart thuds fast and sure. It lights with more than he understands, almost more than he can feel. He senses his life extending behind him far down the beach and ahead of him at the same time, far north on the Carolina coast and the night's long trail, and though he cannot see or even sense the grown-up he will be and often wonders about, he knows that somehow he is that man, somehow he is his entire life, though twelve years of it is all he has lived. He walks outside himself somehow, his full completeness whatever it will be, and inside himself as the boy he is.

It is strange but so calmly strange, so clearly and certainly real, that he wants to walk and walk and never stop walking. Such a long, long way, he thinks to himself. Such a friendliness that there is a way, that there is this trail of sand and stars, the ghostly ocean alive and roaring and he alive to hear it and see it, to smell the moist wind and know for the first time who he is, though it's nothing he could say or explain. He knows that the boy who left his parents' cottage will turn around in the night and walk back there, but he also knows that the one he is, the one he remembered only this night, will not turn back. That one will go on walking beside the sea, will walk on in stars and the cool shore wind and will not stop walking, not tonight, not tomorrow, not ever.

In truth, I don't recall turning back that night. The memory is entirely of setting out, striding fast in a calm exaltation. How could I have lost it? How could I have forgotten till now that mystery of wind and stars, that singular strangeness of knowing, *knowing* who I was? I didn't forget it. The memory was with me, reduced and stored for travel. It came to mind less frequently over the years—

thirty-five years—as the busyness of living piled over it and made it a thing among many, a childhood toy, a piece of the clutter. I forgot how true it was, how eerily exciting it was to the boy. Maybe it took this particular rhythm of walking, fast but easily fast, to bring it back in its wholeness. And these rumbling waves, sliding up the beach in snowy foam, this breeze, this scatter of stars—it took all of this, and it took the boy. The boy who made me remember. The boy who remembered me.

He set out one night on the Carolina coast, and here I am on the Oregon coast still walking, still setting forth on the night's long trail and glad for the journey. A few pains of body and soul the boy didn't have—and a few he did—but still setting forth, my sky still lit with more than I know, still knowing what I cannot explain, still with a heart thudding fast and sure. Tonight I walk with sand and stars and the wind in my face on the brink of my home continent, on the border of all I know, exactly in the center of what I love. I walk fast and easy, dunes to one side, Pacific to the other, a strew of stars behind and before me, an Earth underfoot where it's good to be.

Tonight, somewhere, I'll stop and walk back again, and when I turn from the sea at last I will listen as I leave it behind. I will listen until I no longer hear the foaming slide of the waves, their withdrawing hiss and trill of pebbles. Until I no longer hear wavelets slapping and sloshing, brief veering currents jostling in the shallows. Until the pounding of breakers is muted by the dunes to a pulsing rumble almost quiet, both near and distant, a murmuring fierce and gentle —and by that sound I will know her as I must have known her before I was, when the anthem of her blood played round and bathed me in power I breathed and breathed until at last she could not hold me, until at last she opened and gave me the world.

CHAPTER FORTY

E very once in a while I'll say in my head, "Better go to the post office now," and then answer aloud, "Yeah, I think so too." I've always been more than one person. I remember distinctly sitting on my bed in our house in Maryland, ten years old or so, talking to someone named Bob—and Bob answering through my mouth. I was a solitary and sometimes lonely kid, and I suppose Bob showed up to keep me company. In a house of volatile tensions, he was a friend unfailingly genial and even-tempered. He was *normal*. We talked about ball games and fishing. We weighed the relative merits of biking to Cabin John to buy baseball cards or walking to Glen Echo Amusement Park to play miniature golf. We always got along.

The Inspector didn't have his title back then, but he too was around. I've always had a sense of being both a person who does things and a person who observes that person. When I batted a wad of tin foil high off the side of the house with a badminton racket, keeping it alive as long as I could, I was both the player—a well-known professional—and the TV announcer doing play-by-play. I don't know when the observer became so critically judgmental, but it must have been early on. You have to watch yourself (there he is) in an unpredictable household, and when things go awry the watcher is in a position to blame—to blame especially the one he knows best, the only one he might be able control. I wet the bed until I was ten or eleven. It was the Inspector, I see now, who made me say "I won't wet the bed" hundreds of times as I lay waiting to fall asleep, and it was the Inspector who bitterly upbraided me each time I awakened, too late again, to the moist warmth of my failure. He blasted me for being a coward when I hid in the house from the neighborhood bullies. He told me I was lazy and unworthy when I let a grade slip from A to B.

Once I was old enough to understand vaguely that having more than one self might be unhealthy, I kept Bob and the Inspector under pretty close guard. But they were very loyal in their way. Despite my inattention and contempt, they stuck with me. They inserted themselves, unexpectedly, into the writing of this book. I'm glad they did. I know them better now.

Bob, in particular, I've misjudged badly. I think it must have been in my dropout hippie days when I turned on the trusted cohort of my childhood and reviled him as bland and conventional. It must have been then that I gave him his surname, as great an insult as I could imagine in the late 1960s. Now I appreciate his strengths. His steadiness evens my ups and downs. He knows how to take a job of work and get it done. He's easy to please—this morning he bought an extension ladder, and he's been delighted all day long. And that, of course, is what I like about him most. He's happy. Bob is *happy*. I never dreamed that happiness would turn out to be something I so badly need, and that I'd find it in the oldest friend of my childhood.

The Inspector, on the other hand, isn't happy. It's not his nature to be happy, but he has eased up his scrutiny since I took that walk with him. Like anyone, he likes to be acknowledged. I think he appreciates the attention I've given him in this book. But it's the boy, definitely the boy, who deserves most of the credit for lightening the Inspector's mood. As I was hoping, the old man has been charmed. Some of his emptiness seems to have been filled. He fancies himself a kindly uncle when the boy's around. He tells stories, and listens to stories the boy tells him. He gets out of his room more. He's even straightened up his manner a little. He doesn't drink as much now that the boy is here, and he's cleaned the spots of dried oatmeal off his bathrobe.

In truth, we're all doing better since the boy arrived. It's good to hear his laugh now and then. He's a studious and self-reliant kid, as kids ought to be. Like me, he doesn't mind spending hours in a book. He likes to write poems. But there are times, of course, when he needs to go out and have fun. I'm learning to sense those times. I'll get a feeling and put down my pencil or book, say good-bye to the Inspector if I'm with him. I'll lean back in my chair gazing out the window, watching the birds at the feeder, watching nothing. And then we'll go.

If we're hungry we might drive to Burgerville—I don't usually go there, but the boy likes it—or to El Burrito Loco for *carne asada* tacos till they're coming out our ears. There are plenty of places to go, things to do. Sometimes he wants to head down to the river, the not-too-polluted Willamette, and throw rocks into its quiet current. Maybe look for blackberries, if it's summer. Mess around in the Riedel International yard, checking out the wooden spools of cable, the huge pieces of rusty equipment. If there's a baseball game or soccer match at the University of Portland, we might wander over to watch. Or if the boy has a hankering to play pinball—he's an old-fashioned kid, he doesn't like video games—I know a tavern down on Lombard where they'll overlook the boy's age and we can work the flippers and push the box to its tilt limit all day long.

If we're away too long the Inspector usually lets me hear about it, but he doesn't have his heart in it. I get my work done. If anything, I get more done than I did before. And I'm happier. The boy seems happy himself, all in all—especially when I take him backpacking. (The Inspector never comes along.) He skinny-dips, climbs rocks, catches lizards, gets scratched and grimy-handed and sometimes shouts for joy, surprising me. We stare into the fire at night, if we have one, as I used to stare into the fireplace beside my father. Once in a while, when I catch him unawares, I get the feeling that the boy looks up to me. I get the feeling that he's proud.

And when he's sad? Well, then he's sad, and I am too. Sadness isn't the worst thing. Sometimes it's a good time to write—sometimes it is fertile, as Thoreau claimed—and sometimes it's a good time just to do nothing. We might lie in the grass over in the park, looking into the trees, the sky. We might walk a while, aimless as the blowing leaves. Or we might stay home, where we're safe and comfortable. We might just sit with our sadness, or we might sleep, and when we sleep in sadness usually we dream. *I dreamed a horse,* one of us says, *a blue horse . . .* "Where?" *He was running on the plains . . .* We talk like that, and sometimes the sadness passes. And even if it doesn't, pretty soon it's time to fix dinner.

Marilyn has always loved the boy. She's glad to be seeing more of him. She says he takes after Bob, or Bob takes after him, and she's right. She likes Bob too, even though he doesn't do the laundry often enough to suit her and still hasn't tiled the closet floor. She compliments him on his cooking and never fails to thank him for the work he does around the place. The Inspector is harder for her to like, because she's seen what he does to me, and because she too has been the victim of some of his harsh and unreasonable judgments. If he's in one of his grouchy funks when she comes home, he might snap at her before I can stop him. "The Inspector's digestion is off," I'll tell her by way of apology. Sometimes she'll smile at this and allow herself to be kissed. And sometimes she'll say, "The Inspector is an ass, my dear, and so are you."

And so we get along. We have spats and differences, like any family, but there's room for us all. I trust us, all of us, to be who we are and to do what we need to do. I trust my dreams and visions. I trust the pencil in my right hand, the little trails it makes across the page. I trust myself to follow them. I trust my sadness, and I'm learning, at last, to trust my happiness too. Many years ago, sometime in the 1970s, my mother wrote these words on a birthday card: "Each one brings you nearer the harmony which you will achieve between your selves, and diminishes the anguish, for you are learning love. May your way become clearer."

I've got that card in front of me now, along with a few photographs, a few of her poems and meditations, a few of her colorful dresses that Marilyn wants to make into a quilt. It's three in the morning and I can't sleep, but tonight I don't mind. I woke with a start an hour ago, remembering I hadn't set the garbage can out by the curb for the morning pickup. I was lugging the can around the corner of the house, in high-top sneakers and a rain parka over my bathrobe, when I stopped short and laughed out loud. I sat on the can in the pouring rain, looking at the sidewalk. It had come to me, finally, what I'd been missing in my vision of the roses. It was nothing about the ring of roses itself but where the ring was, where it had been placed for me to see as I opened the front door of the house. It was on the parking strip next to the curb, just to the left of the bottom of the front steps, the exact spot where once a week I place this garbage can—this vessel of husks and peels and empty containers, spent coffee grounds and typewriter ribbons, the things whose good we have taken and turned into our lives.

And so I came in here to my study, still laughing, to sit with the sound of rain on the roof and look again at some of her spirited words, look again at her canny and kindly and mischievous face. Soon I'll go in and upstairs and slip back into bed with Marilyn, who will stir in her sleep and murmur some glimpse of her dream. But before I go I will do one thing. I have on my desk the antique travel clock my mother inherited from her mother, a brass cabinet four inches high with glass walls and a carrying handle on top. Not the ship's clock she missed and couldn't track down in memory, but a clock she had with her wherever she lived, a brass clock with elegant black hands and Roman numerals on a white face, a clock of a kind not made in the world anymore. It stopped—which day we aren't sure—at five minutes to eight, the hour of my mother's death. When I'm ready I will open the glass door in back, I will fit the key to the crank and wind the spring, I will leave the clock ticking behind me.

The Wilds of Home

I'm waist-deep in blackberry vines looking for a cat who isn't here. Or if she is, she has an acre to be hiding in and she's ignoring me. It's my fault either way. When the carpet layers arrived at 8:30 I put her on the deck, harnessed and leashed, to keep her out of their way. I brought her food and water and stayed a minute to soothe her ragged nerves, then drove to Dixie's Café for breakfast and the newspaper. When I came back, the leash was wrapped around a rosebush, and the harness, still buckled, lay empty in the grass. She must have un-peeled herself into freedom. A feline Houdini. No sign of fur or blood. No sign of cat.

And so I'm wading the tangled, thorny biota of our new home in the country, calling *Here, kitty kitty kitty* in a falsetto voice—the only way I know how to do it—embarrassed that the carpet layers might hear me and worried sick that I'm singing to a long-gone cat. Maybe she's taking a nap, my head argues hopefully. But my heart has a mind of its own, and my heart knows she's gone. She's fled the noise and confusion of this unsettled place to find the home she remembers, the home on Princeton Street in Portland where she was raised and for which she jilted her owner to move in with us. The home she defended from every tom and puss in the neighborhood with fierce screeches and deep, vibrant, business-meaning yowls. If my heart is right, she has a hundred miles to go and she won't make it. The farms around us all have dogs, many dogs, and around the fringes of the farms are coons and coyotes, and not much deeper in the woods are mountain lions.

And roads, of course. The instant I saw the empty harness I remembered in panic that I'd just seen a dead tabby on the way back from Dixie's—but it was two or three miles from here, and the body had already begun to bloat.

Here, kitty kitty kitty . . . I thrash ahead, listening for her odd, birdlike chirp.

Since her miserable, boxed-up trip from Portland, we've kept her mostly inside, letting her get to know the new house. As we cleaned and spackled and painted, she made her rounds. She sniffed meticulously, as high on the walls and lower cabinets as her hind legs would lift her. She rubbed her scent against corners and doorways of special cat significance. At a particular nail head along one of the joints of bare subfloor, something drove her delirious—she licked and pawed and rolled on her side in a frenzy of sensuous attention. She sharpened her claws on the subfloor and on the driftwood posts of my mother's old bed.

Once or twice a day, Marilyn or I would take her outside to let her acquaint herself gradually with the grounds. It was wonderfully absurd. A cat no more belongs on a leash than that French poet's lobster. She would creep along in slow motion, drawing out the retractable leash with no regard for the human at the other end, immersed in whatever intensities her eyes and ears and nose were bringing her, abruptly turning now and then to try to lick the harness off her back. She crept, I now recall with sadness, inexorably away from the house. And once back inside, especially after dark, she would park herself by the screen door, listening into the night. She pawed at the screen and tried to squeeze through where the former owner's dog had torn it. We had to patch the hole with duct tape to keep her in.

I stumble loose from our thicket into the neighbor's trees, and as I turn around our new house startles my eyes. I've been glancing out its windows for ten days but have hardly seen *it* in that time. A plain, brown, slope-roofed, oblong box—and it's beautiful. It's almost surrounded in Douglas firs over a hundred feet tall. "We live here," I say out loud. Today the carpet, tomorrow our furniture and thousand boxes of things. We're out of the city at last, good city though it was. Maybe, just maybe, we've finally found our place. I'd be wildly happy, I realize, if I hadn't lost our cat.

She could be ten feet away, of course, and I'd never know it. She was relentlessly indifferent to my mother and well capable of the same indifference to me and Marilyn. Many times I've called her from the doorway late at night, wanting to get her in so I could go to bed, only to spy her sitting not twenty feet away, absorbed in the darkness beyond, not only uninterested in my vocalizations but utterly, entirely oblivious to me and to anything human.

Well, to hell with her. I trudge back to the house, scratched and sweaty, itching with nettles, taking no solace from the buttercups I walk through or the tiny pears on the pear tree. There's work to be done if we're going to be ready for the movers tomorrow. I'm hoping hard for the joke to be on me, for Spooky Houdini to have rematerialized by the front door, sleeping or idly licking a paw. But no cat. Inside, the carpet layers are tacking and slicing and gluing away, finishing off our fresh and empty rooms.

In the cool of evening, with Jimmie Dale Gilmore crooning on the boom box, I'm remounting switch plates on creamy fresh-painted walls, enjoying the smell and feel of the new carpet. Its dusty rose color is just right. Even my tilework in the entryways, which in the mortaring and grouting looked like a major disaster, has turned out, with a little cleanup, to be a minor success. Marilyn is on her way from Portland, having watched the furniture into the Bekins truck and said good-bye to our old house. I can't wait for her to get here, to see the work we've done made whole. A fresh start in the country. A creamy white and dusty rose beginning.

I've placed saucers of milk at all the entrances, and occasionally I go out to call—loudly, now that no human being can hear me. All I get in response are frogs chorusing by the stream and the raucous, ratchety cries of guinea hens from across the road.

When I called Marilyn to tell her about the cat, I was surprised to find myself choking up. For a while I could barely speak. I realized after we hung up that I was crying for more than the cat. I thought I was over my mother's death. I thought I had grieved my way through. It's been two years since she broke her hip and went to the hospital and didn't come home. Long enough, my mind declared. She lived eighty-four years, and most of them on her own terms. She lived a full life, a beautiful life.

But I miss her. I miss her very much, I realize, despite my sharp memories of the tensions of those years. As I screw the switch plates to their boxes, sometimes tightening too hard and cracking the plastic, I tell myself that I did all right by my mother in her old age, I did what I could. I tell myself, and I think I believe it. But losing the cat has opened up the emptiness again, renewed the callings of grief. I keep thinking how much she would have liked this place—the birds, the blackberries, the big trees. The garden I'm going to plant.

I drop my screwdriver and turn off Jimmie Dale's infinitely injured voice, his songs that cry so beautifully of loss, and put on Beethoven's *Violin Concerto*—the music whose opening timpani beats will forever wake me into Sunday mornings as a boy, when the hi-fi sometimes issued an ordered serenity into our home. My father, in glasses and bathrobe, would be reading in his rocking chair, my mother on the sofa, the cloth of love they wrung and tore between them momentarily at rest. The music seemed to gather us into its stately wholeness. It was an unspoken communion, a kind of Sabbath we shared.

I open a beer and stretch out on the carpet to listen as Beethoven rises into the authority of his allegro, working up the necessary tensions so that Isaac Stern's fiddle can slip free of them, dancing in a sky where joy and sadness mingle. *My mother and father made a life together,* it keeps coming to me. Despite everything, they made a life, and even after they couldn't live together they made a life for Jim and me. Phrases from my mother's letters pass through me, letters she wrote my father in the 1960s. *They miss you . . . We're behind on John's orthodonture. . . Jim is taking courses at the community college . . . They came from Springfield in fine fettle, as always after visiting you . . . Thank you for the extra check . . . Sorry I bawled you out so hard . . .* His letters to her from that time don't survive, but I know their gist and tone from reading hers.

What is it that so moves me? Their marriage lay in ruins, they each had wounds that wouldn't heal, spites they couldn't control, grievances that could never be redressed—yet this earnestness, this faithfulness, this wealth of caring for my brother and me. As best they could, they kept the broken family whole, so that we might live and grow and go on in the world.

They paid everything their love exacted. They paid willingly and at great cost. I honor them for it. And both of them now gone, and almost all their friends, all my relatives of their generation except for three aunts in their eighties and nineties. All that composed the family cosmos for me as a boy, all the talk and smiles and shouting and tears, all the meals and travels, the touching of hands, all of that gone from the world and yet not gone, all of it as present and vivid as Beethoven's measured exultances, here in the bare rooms of an Oregon house where no mother or father or child of mine will walk through the door. Here in the mystery of memory, the rising of love. I see no end to love. And, forty-six years old, very shaky with a waking joy, I see no end of coming of age.

The slow movement in Beethoven is almost always my favorite, when he wins through his despondencies and turbulent triumphs to the blessed interval, that timeless transitory moment when the soul knows itself and needs no more. Writing scarcely can touch that moment; Beethoven found it many times. I listen outside on the deck, in the company of stars and tall shadowy trees, until something goes wrong in the boom box or the CD. A low, discordant groan crescendoes under the tuneful sweetness of Stern's violin. It takes me several seconds to realize that the sound is coming not from the boom box but from my cat, and that I am looking at her. She's crouched in the spill of light from the kitchen window, her fur puffed up like Halloween, issuing an ominous low yowl to a second cat who has encroached too far into our territory.

I ought to let the drama play out, but I can't stop myself from going to her. The other cat slinks away; my own glances at me with what might be annoyance. She won't be held— too tensed, her awareness too charged—and so I stand nearby until she settles a little and begins to chew a spear of grass. "Spookus, you've been out all day," I inform her, and she lets me carry her into the house. There are burrs and little sticks in her underfur. As I pick them out I remember hidden mushrooms I found while searching the brambles this morning, a blue wildflower I'd never seen before, the sweet and dark and berry-rich smell of the moist ground.

The cat laps up a saucer of milk and pads to the screen door, where she waits to be let out. I tell her I won't have it, and after a while she folds her legs and sinks down on the carpet where she is. She stares out through the screen as my mother used to stare through her sliding glass door, toward things beyond my vision. Beethoven wraps up his sprightly conclusion. The quiet of the night floods in. Soon Marilyn will be here with a few last pieces of our old life. The cat and I will be waiting. We'll let the night breathe in with its quiet stirrings, its stillnesses that verge on speech, its rumors of that deepest wild where my mother and father have gone. We'll breathe the air, we'll keep our eyes open as long as we can, we'll listen for everything the night can tell us of this home where we now live.

ACKNOWLEDGMENTS

First I thank Marilyn, who knew the beauty and burden of those four years and lived them with me again as I read her the chapters-in-progress of this book. Her suggestions, and the portions of her journal she opened to me, helped make it whole. She would tell the story in a different way, a way as true and necessary as this one. I thank her for the love, forbearance, and support that made my telling possible.

Margaret Daniel, Adelaide Karsian, Betty Wilson, and Jim Daniel—two aunts, a cousin, and my brother—put their memories to work and provided correspondence to the book's benefit, as did three labor movement comrades of my parents: Alice Cook and Philip and Miriam Van Gelder. I am grateful for their help, and grateful also to the memory of Booton Herndon, whose letters and anecdotes over the years enriched my knowledge of the man and woman I was born to.

Jane Crosen helped with recollections of my mother in her Findhorn and *WoodenBoat* days, and Gordon Barton, my mother's spiritual cohort and fellow traveler, kindly and patiently answered my questions. Sarah Holmes, faithful friend to my mother in her last years, illuminated life in the beautiful wild of Prasanthi Nilayam. Paulann Petersen told me the story of her mother, and Satish Kumar allowed me to quote from the story of his; their accounts helped me write this one. John Sterne, my oldest friend, knowledgeably informed me on things Vedic (with the gracious permission of his spiritual masters, Lenora Lynx and Billy Puma).

Dr. Tom Harvey brought smiles to my mother's face and the best health he could to her faltering body. He helped her live well, and Dr. Dan Gilden gave us advice that helped her die well when that time came. Both offered clarifying counsel on medical matters during the writing of this book. (Any medical inaccuracies and all unattributed opinions are strictly my own.) I'm grateful also to the Medicare Alzheimer's Project, the Columbia-Willamette chapter of the Alzheimer's Association, the Volunteers of America Interlink Center, and Providence ElderPlace. Those organizations helped the three of us manage while my mother was with us, and they gave me, through mailings and lectures and conversations, an education in senile dementia.

The inner path that led to the writing of *Looking After* was opened in many sessions with Elizabeth Hendricks, Psy.D., a Jungian genius of listening and questioning. She is truly a doctor of the soul.

The writing grew from a little seed of an essay Annie Stine asked me to write for *Sierra*, when she was an editor there. Tim Schaffner, then my agent, persuaded me to try a book-length memoir. Lisa Ross, now my agent, encouraged me and found the perfect publisher for the book-to-be.

Jack Shoemaker, Counterpoint editor-in-chief, knew what this book needed to be long before I did and long before he had a contractual interest in it. He gave discreet clues to guide me along the way and edited the manuscript with a sure hand. I thank Patricia Hoard, Carole McCurdy, Jane Vandenburgh, and Nancy Palmer Jones for their suggestions and support. David Bullen, best in the business, designed a beautiful book, and Becky Clark, Jessica Kane, and Nicole Pagano helped see it into the world.

In the 1980s I dreamed of being published by North Point Press. In the 1990s it is a dream come true to join the Counterpoint venture in its beginnings. I thank publisher Frank Pearl for making Counterpoint possible and for the enthusiasm with which he embraced my book.

Black bears and pileated woodpeckers heard the first readings of the early drafts of *Looking After*. (Their reviews were indifferent.) The time and solitude I needed to write my way into the book were provided in the form of the 1994 Margery Davis Boyden Wilderness Writing Residency at Dutch Henry Ranch in the Rogue River country. I thank Frank Boyden, Bradley Boyden, and PEN Northwest for the unique privilege and good action of that seven-month stay in a fertile meadow far from town.

In early 1995 I was able to advance the book while teaching at Sweet Briar College and living in the nurturing pastures of the Virginia Center for the Creative Arts. An Oregon Literary Fellowship arrived with uncanny timing near the end of the year, just when I needed it to help me finish the book. My thanks to the staff and benefactors of Literary Arts, Incorporated. I made final revisions while living in the Thurber House in Columbus, Ohio, and teaching at Ohio State University as the James Thurber Writer-in-Residence.

I am grateful to the Walter P. Reuther Library at Wayne State University in Detroit for access to my father's and mother's papers and for generous help with photocopying expenses. The Knight Library of the University of Oregon and Fern Ridge Library in Veneta either had or found the books I needed.

Finally, I would like to acknowledge four women who won't be expecting it, each of them flowering uniquely with the gains and losses of age: Margery Boyden, Dorothy Stafford, Mary Stegner, and Ann Zwinger. In each of them I sense my mother's spirit.

In writing my book I found important help in the work of these authors:

Wendell Berry. *Harlan Hubbard: Life and Work.* Lexington, Ky.: University Press of Kentucky, 1990.

Edmund Blair Bolles. *Remembering and Forgetting: Inquiries into the Nature of Memory.* New York: Walker, 1988.

John Burroughs. *Riverby.* Boston: Houghton Mifflin, 1894.

Joseph Campbell. *Historical Atlas of World Mythology.* New York: Harper & Row, 1988.

Mary T. Clark, trans. *Augustine of Hippo: Selected Writings.* Mahwah, N.J.: Paulist Press, 1984.

Paul Davies and John Gribbin. *The Matter Myth.* New York: Simon & Schuster/Touchstone, 1992.

W. S. Di Piero. "Notes on Memory and Enthusiasm." In *Memory and Enthusiasm: Essays 1975–1985.* Princeton, N.J.: Princeton University Press, 1989.

Gerald M. Edelman. *Bright Air, Brilliant Fire: On the Matter of the Mind.* New York: Basic Books, 1992.

Mircea Eliade. "Mythologies of Memory and Forgetting." *Parabola* (Nov. 1986).

Ralph Waldo Emerson. *Essays and Lectures*. New York: The Library of America, 1983.

James Hillman. *A Blue Fire*. New York: Harper & Row, 1989.

James Hillman. "A Psyche the Size of the Earth." Foreword to *Ecopsychology: Restoring the Earth, Healing the Mind*. Eds. Theodore Roszak, Mary E. Gomes, Allen D. Kramer. San Francisco: Sierra Club Books, 1995.

Robert A. Johnson. *He: Understanding Masculine Psychology*. Rev. ed. New York: Harper & Row, 1989.

C. G. Jung. *Memories, Dreams, Reflections*. Trans. Richard and Clara Winston. Ed. Aniela Jaffé. New York: Vintage, 1989.

Satish Kumar. "An Interview with Satish Kumar." *Timeline* (Sept./Oct. 1995).

Stephen Levy. "Dr. Edelman's Brain." *New Yorker* (May 2, 1994).

Alan McGlashan. "The Translucence of Memory." *Parabola* (Nov. 1986).

Sherwin B. Nuland. *How We Die: Reflections on Life's Final Chapter*. New York: Alfred A. Knopf, 1993.

Robert Ornstein. *The Evolution of Consciousness*. New York: Prentice Hall, 1991.

William Stafford. *Passwords*. New York: HarperCollins, 1991.

Laurence Stapleton, ed. *H. D. Thoreau: A Writer's Journal*. New York: Dover, 1960.

Eliot Wigginton, ed. *Refuse to Stand Silently By: An Oral History of Grass Roots Social Activism in America, 1921–1964*. New York: Doubleday, 1991.

Philip and Carol Zaleski. "Walking on the Waves: An Interview with Keiji Nishitani." *Parabola* (Nov. 1986).

Between
the Bullet and the Lie

By the same author

Between the Bullet and the Lie

American Volunteers in the Spanish Civil War

by CECIL EBY

HOLT, RINEHART AND WINSTON
NEW YORK CHICAGO SAN FRANCISCO

Library of Congress Catalog Card Number: 69-11804
First Edition

Designer: Berry Eitel
SBN: 03-076410-6
Printed in the United States of America

Grateful acknowledgment is made to the following publishers who have so
generously granted permission to reprint from their publications:
Harcourt, Brace & World, Inc. for passages from *Homage to Catalonia* by
George Orwell, copyright 1952 by Sonia Brownell Orwell, reprinted by per-
mission of Brandt & Brandt; Hogarth Press, Ltd., for passages from "Jarama
Front" by T. A. R. Hyndman, included in *Poems from Spain* edited by
Stephen Spender, copyright 1939, reprinted by permission of T. A. R. Hynd-
man and Hogarth Press.

Acknowledgments

My major debts are to the Conference Board of Associated Research Councils for my appointment as lecturer at the University of Valencia in 1967–68, thereby providing me with an opportunity to travel and to work in Spain; to the Executive Committee of the Department of English for their recommendation and to the Regents of the University of Michigan for authorizing my leave of absence; and to the trustees of the Rackham School of Graduate Studies at the University of Michigan for a research grant. Moreover, I thank the staffs of the following libraries: the University of Michigan, the New York Public Library, and the Hemeroteca Municipal (Madrid).

I wish to thank, in particular, Mr. Robert Cowley of New York for valuable information derived from his personal notes about the Lincoln Battalion; Prof. Victor Hoar of London, Ontario, historian of the Mackenzie-Papineau Battalion, who generously offered me the fruits of his own labor in a parallel subject; to Sr. Ricardo de la Cierva y Hoces, chief of the Sección de los Estudios sobre la Guerra de España, Ministerio de Turismo y Información, Madrid, who made available the resources of the archives under his purview.

And to thank the following for assisting me with specific details pertaining to the American volunteers: Mr. Thomas R. Amlie of Madison, Wisconsin; Prof. Carlos Baker of Princeton, New Jersey; Mrs. Harriet Castle of Oxon Hill, Maryland; Mr. John Cope of the Department of State; Dr. William Franklin of the Department of State; Mr. Joseph Gibbons of Chicago; Prof. Allen Guttmann of Amherst, Massachusetts; Mr. William Jovanovich of New York; Dr. Morris Leider of New York; Mr. Herbert L. Matthews of New York; Prof. Warner G. Rice of Ann Arbor, Michigan; Mr. Woodruff W. Wallner of the Department of State.

I am also grateful for letters and enclosures from Miss Kathryn Bassett of Swarthmore, Pennsylvania; Mr. Alvah C. Bessie of San Francisco; Miss Sara Crist of Montgomery, Alabama; Mrs. Lora Dreher of Madison, Wisconsin; Miss Nancy Elliot of Hanover, New

Hampshire; Miss Pattie Haney of Auburn, Alabama; Prof. Milton Hindus of Newton Centre, Massachusetts; Miss Jean Madden of Columbia, Missouri; Mr. Kenneth Robbins of Reno, Nevada; Mrs. Owen S. Selby of Chestertown, Maryland; and Mr. Seymour S. Weisman of New York.

Acknowledgments are owed to three tireless campaigners of field trips in Spain: Mr. Edward Hempson of Valencia; Mr. William McKim of Kansas City, Missouri; and Mr. Edmund Parsons of the Department of State.

From beginning to end, this project has been supported by Perry H. Knowlton of Curtis Brown, Ltd.; by Thomas C. Wallace of Holt, Rinehart and Winston; and by my wife, Patricia M. Eby. I am particularly grateful to them and to the veterans of the Lincoln Battalion whose names appear at the end of my section titled "Sources."

C.E.

Ann Arbor, Michigan
January 1969

To the Memory
of
two truckloads of Americans
names unknown
faces unremembered
who vanished behind enemy lines
when their drivers
took the wrong turn
on the Titulcia road
while trying to reach the front lines
at Jarama
in February 1937

Contents

*8 pages of black and white photographs appear
following page 168.*

List of Maps

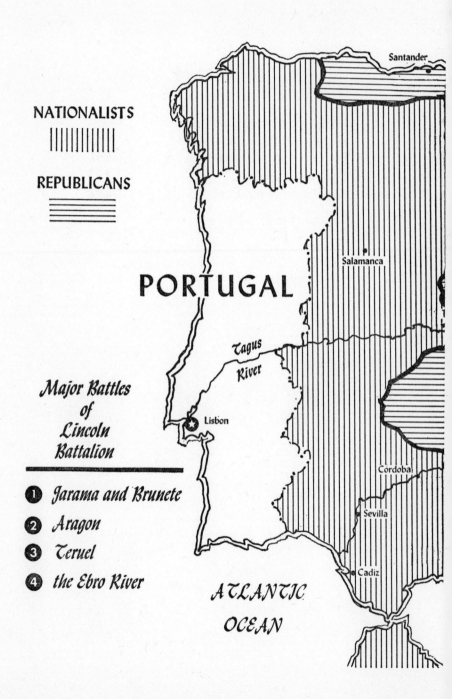

NATIONALISTS

REPUBLICANS

PORTUGAL

Major Battles
of
Lincoln
Battalion

1 *Jarama and Brunete*

2 *Aragon*

3 *Teruel*

4 *the Ebro River*

Santander

Salamanca

Tagus River

Lisbon

Cordoba

Sevilla

Cadiz

ATLANTIC
OCEAN

FRANCE

Perpignan •

Ceret •

Bilbao

Pyrenees Mts.

Ripoll •

Figueras

Ebro River

Burgos

Franco Capital

Zaragoza

Quinto

Barcelona

Castelldefells

Caspe   Marsa

Belchite

②

④

Tarragona

Segura de los Baños

Albares

③   Aquaviva

Madrid

①

Toledo

Villanueva de la Jara

Valencia

Republican Capital

Tarazona

Albacete

MINORCA

MAJORCA

Ibiza

Alicante

Murcia

**Spain
in the
Spring
1937**

Almeria

Malaga

Mediterranean Sea

Between the shadow and the ghost,
Between the white and the red,
Between the bullet and the lie,
Where would you hide your hide?

—George Orwell

Preface

July of 1936 was a month like any other. In the United States the corn crop was the worst since 1881. Thirty-one American cities reported temperatures above 100 degrees; seven hundred people in the nation were dead of heat prostration. The Secretary of Agriculture estimated that the drought would place two million more on relief during the winter. Hunger marchers occupied Harrisburg.

It was an election year. Stumping Colorado, the Republican presidential candidate, Governor Alf M. Landon of Kansas, called for a "return to old-fashioned Americanism" and did not demur when columnists labeled him a "horse-and-buggy governor." The vacationing incumbent, Franklin D. Roosevelt, was not to be heard from, for he had vanished in a dense fog off the coast of Nova Scotia. In order to save America from drifting into communism, Father Charles E. Coughlin—known as "The Radio Priest"—urged his vast Sunday afternoon audience to support Edward Lemke, the National Party candidate. Norman Thomas kicked off his presidential campaign on the Socialist ticket with a terse indictment of all other factions: "they are trying to cure tuberculosis with cough drops."

What Thomas called tuberculosis, retiring anthropologist Franz Boas of Columbia University called "sickness." Explaining why he had refused to attend the 550th anniversary of his alma mater, Heidelberg University, Boas cited Nazi theories of race as evidence that the whole world was sick, "with Germany the sickest of all." For years the League Against War and Fascism had been issuing the same strident warning: fascism was rapidly spreading without control throughout Europe, and in America the mentality, if not the political fact, of fascism was eroding the liberal tradition. The League pointed at the proliferation of such reactionary spurs as the Black Legion, the Sentinels of America, the Christian Vigilants, the Order of '76, and the Daughters of the American Revolution. It was not a time for sitting on the fence: people were scuttling Left and Right, frightened by the beast on the other side.

Compared with Europe, the United States was blooming and healthy. At Geneva in the Assembly of the League of Nations, Emperor Haile Selassie rose to denounce the Italians' use of poison gas against his people. His words were drowned out by a red-faced man who shrieked execrations from the Italian section of the press gallery. Others joined in, piping upon whistles. The Emperor waited patiently until guards had expelled ten *fascisti,* then continued reading his typewritten speech. From the Vatican, Pope Pius XII, always serenely quiet about the Ethiopian question, demonstrated his fervent opposition to sin by publishing an encyclical banning indecent motion pictures. Meanwhile, Berlin was preparing for its Olympiad. The editor of *Angriff,* official organ of the Nazi Party, urged all Germans to use this opportunity to dispel erroneous impressions of the Third Reich; but on the very same day, in a speech at Weimar, Joseph Goebbels, Minister of Propaganda, proclaimed that "the Ethiopian conflict was decided not by the League of Nations but by bombing squadrons." In France while twenty thousand veterans prayed for world peace during memorial services at Verdun, some ten thousand Rightists and Leftists battled in the streets of Nice. In Prague, Czechoslovakian authorities voiced skepticism about Hitler's pledge to honor Austrian independence. Gangs of *pistoleros,* Rightists and Leftists, patrolled the streets of Madrid trying unsuccessfully to exterminate each other. Moderates pleaded for time, reason, compromise; militants at either extreme demanded immediate confrontation.

In Spain no one expected a war. On July 17 a Rightist coalition sparked by officers of the regular army rose in rebellion against the Second Spanish Republic, and anticipated a swift victory. On the other hand, the Republic, with its tremendous human resources of the People's Army, also anticipated no great difficulty in containing the *coup.* Yet the civil insurrection in Spain seemed to be what the world was eagerly awaiting—an armed confrontation between ideologies of Left and Right. Germany and Italy supplied the Nationalists with armaments, advisers, and in the case of Italy, with "volunteers," many of whom came to Spain direct from Ethiopia. The western democracies, boggled at the prospect of annoying Hitler and Mussolini, eagerly signed a nonintervention agreement (also signed and immediately ignored by Germany and Italy) by which they could ignore the war in Spain and at the same time plume themselves upon their legal scrupulosity. Although the Spanish Republic had not recognized the Soviet Union prior to the war, it was forced to do so when, alone among European powers, Russia offered assistance. While the Red Army sent material of war to Spain (amply paid for by Republican gold reserves), the Comintern organized the International Brigades, recruited from non-Russian nationals in most western countries. In all, approximately fifty thousand men, of whom approximately thirty-two hundred (no exact figures exist) were Americans, came to Spain to fight for the Republic in the International Brigades. Most of the Americans were enlisted in the Abraham Lincoln Battalion; roughly half of these "volunteers for liberty" lost their lives in Spain.

On March 31, 1939, General Francisco Franco, commander of the Nationalist armies, announced the end of the Republic and the annihilation of its military forces. Hostilities had lasted nine hundred and eighty-seven days and had resulted in an estimated 410,000 violent deaths. But no one had expected a war.

In the early 1940s, while peace lay like a shroud over Spain, itinerant junk dealers set up scales in the villages lying near the battlefields. Peasants and townspeople learned how to harvest a new crop—husks of shells, fragments of bombs, broken implements of bygone battles. A kilogram of rusty iron was worth a few céntimos. So they spread out and scavenged across pitted fields and gashed hillsides where tons of human bones protruded from the earth like sinister roots and littered the ground like burnished flints. No one paid them to harvest bones. Metal is useful: bone is worthless until it pulverizes and fertilizes. Thirty years later, on the battlefields of Spain, most of the metal is gone, but the bones remain.

Between the Jarama and Tajuña rivers, less than twenty miles from downtown Madrid, lies a rolling plateau still fissured with trenches that wind through patchy vineyards and olive groves. A dirt road, mottled in places by strips of macadam not bombed off it during the war, meanders across the region linking the two rivers, even though the Jarama bridge runs one hundred feet out into the river and abruptly ends. Where this road joins the Republican trench line there is a shell-pitted, long fallow field of poisoned earth and dry nettles. Strewn about are scraps of belts and shoes (leather is more durable than might be supposed), rusty tins which resemble beer cans but which actually are Lafitte bombs, and bits of oxidized shell fragments the color and size of rat dung. Like most battlefields in Spain, this one is littered with human bones, femurs and pelvic arches, for the most part. There are no gravestones or markers of any kind which might indicate that a battle had ever been fought there. The site is desolate, swept in winter by bitter winds off the snowcapped Guadarrama Mountains and baked in summer by the hot sun of Castile. In springtime the place is bearable. The nettles put out pale lavender flowers. Madrileños drive out in their Seats, set up camp tables in the olive groves nearby, and add picnic refuse to the debris of the battlefield. They come not to commemorate anything (few of them even know that a battle was ever fought there), but to escape the city for a few hours and to refresh themselves in *el campo*.

On this desolate piece of Spanish earth are the mortal remains of one hundred and twenty-seven Americans killed while assaulting, without adequate covering fire, a well-entrenched Nationalist force located in an olive grove a few hundred meters to the west. Against a network of interlocking machine-gun fire they were as effective as a ripple against a breakwater. The most seasoned veterans among this group had been at the front less than two weeks; the newest recruits, less than two days. Collectively they represented more than three thousand years of human life expunged in less than an hour of fire by Fiat machine guns.

One spur of the American trench section is covered by limestone rocks about the size of melons. This cairn marks the mass grave of the Americans killed in the attack. Exposed to view is a human skull with sixteen teeth—impacted wisdoms but without a single filling. (The lower jaw is nowhere to be found.) The skull is nearly perfect except that an arc of bone is missing from the crown, much as though an eggshell were struck glancingly with a heavy object. This was a "volunteer for liberty," a nameless creature who perished in a hopeless attack buried in the moldering statistics of a lost war. There exists no memorandum nor roster, listing such minimal data as the names of the one hundred and twenty-seven dead Americans lying in this place. It may be true, as some have claimed, that they died for Liberty; but Liberty cannot know who they were.

The purpose of this book is to attempt to re-create—one might even say resurrect—the collective experience of what it meant to be an American volunteer in the Spanish Civil War. My method is descriptive rather than analytical: that is to say, it attempts to convey a sense of experiences as they happened to the men involved rather than to comment on them in the manner of a *post facto* historian. (After all, it is relatively simple to fit together the jigsaw pieces of a battle reconstructed thirty years later in tranquility—the real trick is to perform this chore in the field at a time when one's life depends on it.) It ought to be borne in mind that few of the American volunteers, or their commanders, ever had much more than a fragmented conception of developments beyond their own narrow field of vision. They were not manipulators of thumbtacks on a military map—they were the thumbtacks. On the other hand, without thumbtacks wars could not be fought at all. If, then, the reader discovers that his comprehension of a battle, like Jarama, falls short of encyclopedic thoroughness, he should consider that he probably knows a great deal more about it than the men who died there. By definition, a microcosm is a small sphere, yet it also contains the total experience.

Even after three decades, the conflict which Sir Anthony Eden characterized as "The War of the Spanish Obsession" continues to arouse somewhat heated debate. The present book has been written in a spirit neither defamatory nor laudatory. Hopefully it will fail to provide nourishment for fanatics, whether of the Right or the Left. From beginning to end, the reader ought to bear in mind that while the Comintern sponsored the International Brigade organization, it did so surreptitiously. Men who volunteered to fight in Spain were not necessarily informed of this sponsorship. Therefore evidence that an American fought with the Lincoln Battalion cannot be used to prove, to show, or to suggest that he was, at that time or subsequently, a member of the Communist Party or a Communist sympathizer. No less an authority than the Subversive Activities Control Board, which investigated this alleged connection during the McCarthy era, makes this point perfectly clear in its report of 1955: "The record shows that some Americans fought there on behalf of the Republic out of motivations alien to Communist purposes." To assume otherwise is to be cursed with the sin of oversimplicity.

Between
the Bullet and the Lie

I
ꭗ The Wines of Scranton

I wanted to go to Ethiopia and fight Mussolini.
. . . This ain't Ethiopia, but it'll do.

—Negro volunteer

After six months of war, parades and demonstrations barely ruffled the surface of downtown Barcelona. Whenever bands and cheering crowds occupied the Plaza de Cataluña and lightly shook the surrounding buildings with anthems and *vivas,* only a few clerks at the United States consulate abandoned their desks for the windows. The reason for these disturbances was ever the same: International volunteers were arriving from France or Catalan troops were departing for the front. But on January 6, 1937, Mahlon F. Perkins, the consul general, who idly watched the crowd teeming below, spotted an object that had never before appeared in marches and rallies. Coming up the street was the flag of the United States. Behind it ambled sixty men in 1918-doughboy uniforms. They were lined up in four-front squads with their leader out in front, a .45 automatic strapped to his hip. The United States Army in Barcelona? Impossible! Throwing open his window for a better look, Perkins watched in puzzlement as the group halted under the consulate window and began singing "The Star-Spangled Banner." They sang nearly as badly as they marched, but what must have astonished him as much as anything else was that they knew the words to the second, and even the third, stanzas.[1] It flashed upon him that the specter that had haunted the Department of State for the past three months had materialized under his very win-

---

[1] A common notion during the thirties was that if a man could recite the Declaration of Independence by heart or sing any stanza of "The Star-Spangled Banner" beyond the first one, he must be a member of the Communist Party.

dow. Despite "the most scrupulous policy of nonintervention" in Spanish affairs, a policy spelled out by President Franklin D. Roosevelt and underlined, many times, by Secretary of State Cordell Hull, the first group of American volunteers had arrived in Spain.

A clerk sent down to talk with the paramilitary band returned with the information that "they had come to fight for their principles." Some claimed to be veterans of the World War; others were callow youths barely out of high school. Their leader refused to say whether they possessed legitimate passports. As they marched off, one of them called out, "We're just the beginning!" Consul Perkins had reason to recall this impudent shout, for on the next day sixteen more Americans filed past his window. Then, on January 17, there appeared forty more, these carrying a blazing red banner marked AMERICAN BATTALION. A day later there were twenty new ones with a banner of the same color and size labeled ABRAHAM LINCOLN BATTALION.

As yet only a trickle of American volunteers was seeping across the French frontier. Hopeful that the leak could be promptly plugged and caulked, Consul Perkins cabled the information to Washington, which promptly commanded its consular representatives in France to board each incoming liner and to stamp American passports NOT VALID FOR TRAVEL TO SPAIN. It quickly became evident, however, that men willing to expose their flesh to Fascist bullets were not likely to be intimidated by American consuls brandishing rubber stamps. When Samuel A. Wiley, consul at Le Havre, warned sixty-five suspected volunteers arriving on the *Paris* that according to a 1909 statute, Americans who fought in a foreign war were liable to fines, prison sentences, and perhaps even loss of citizenship, some of the younger men laughed disrespectfully and someone to the rear of the group gave him a Bronx cheer. Even before these volunteers had disembarked, an impromptu ballad commemorated the confrontation:

> "The frontier's closed! You can't get through!"
> Were the words of the U.S. consul.
> But all of us laughed, because we knew
> He was only flapping his tonsils.

At Barcelona, Consul Perkins continued to be troubled. Powerless to prevent or dissuade them, he could do nothing more than count them as they trooped through the city, singing and laughing in their sheepskin jackets. He had learned that hundreds of French volunteers had deserted the front and had descended on Valencia and Barcelona, where they were demanding sanctuary from their consuls. At one time the Republican authorities had looked the other way when International volunteers attempted to flee from Spain, but recently they had threatened to punish foreign deserters exactly like their own. So far as Perkins knew, the Department of State had not formulated a policy to cover American volunteers: should they be accorded diplomatic protection, like other citizens, or had they forfeited this privilege when they agreed to serve a foreign power? He cabled Washington for clarification:

> In view of the hardships which they will soon undergo, I am apprehensive that some of them will be calling for assistance in the not distant future. I should be glad to be informed of the Department's general attitude toward the question of expatriation and loss of the right of protection of American citizens enlisting in the Loyalist armies.

In response, Secretary Hull cabled back, on February 1, that protection should not be extended to United States citizens who fought in Spain. Though the State Department had no power to prevent American citizens from traveling where they wished, it nevertheless had no obligation to protect those who violated the conditions of their passports. Did this mean, Perkins inquired, with bureaucratic thoroughness, that American volunteers were *not* to use the consulate as a mailing address? They most certainly were not. That was that.

By the end of January, three hundred Americans had crossed into Spain. The floodgates were open and the volunteers streamed south.

Throughout rainy October and chilly November of 1936, Spain had been front-page news, and for left-of-center readers in the United States that news was bad. The armies of Franco pushed through the outer *barrios* of Madrid, collecting their strength for a final thrust that would carry them into the city and deal a deathblow to the Second Spanish Republic. Neutral journalists took refuge in their embassies and predicted Madrid was doomed. General Emilio Mola, second-in-command of the besieging army, announced that while four Nationalist columns converged upon the capital from outside, a fifth column of armed sympathizers and *provocateurs* prepared to strike from within. The darkest day was November 7, 1936, when *Mundo Obrero,* the Communist Party daily of Madrid, printed in red ink the headlines:

ALL OUT TO THE BARRICADES
THE ENEMY IS ACROSS THE RIVER [2]

But in the days that followed, newspapers began to describe a phalanx of foreigners who had reached the trenches and barricades of the city. Forming well-disciplined lines, they hurled back the Nationalist attacks in Carabanchel, the Casa del Campo, and University City. The International Brigades, consisting of volunteers recruited by Comintern agencies in a dozen European countries, had come to the defense of Madrid, and, despite repeated attacks by the armies of General Franco to break the ring of defenders, the city held out.

Fascism, rampant elsewhere, had been halted at Madrid. For anti-Fascists the moment was galvanic, the mood contagious. In the United States, they asked what they could do to assist the Republic. The answer was simple and the apparatus ready: contribute to the North American Committee to Aid Spanish Democracy.[3] (Not, of course, to the National Spanish Relief Association, which supported Franco's Spain.) Young men who preferred a more activist role in defending Spanish liberty could enlist in the International Brigades, provided they knew the right people in Leftist political or trades-union organizations. No mere adventurers—or "romantics" as they were called in the Communist Party—need apply; nor, at this stage in the recruiting program, were bourgeois liberals desired. The ideal recruit was a youngish man with a proved, or at least promising, record in the Communist Party but, on the other hand, not so promising that his death in Spain would be a setback for the party. Although these first volunteers knew perfectly well that compiling a good record in Spain would enable them to have an inside track leading to the party hierarchy after they returned home, it would be foolish to suggest that political ambition was foremost in inducing them to fight in Spain.

[2] On the second page, in ordinary ink, a quarter-page ad announced that Charlie Chaplin's *Modern Times* was currently playing at the Capitol Theatre on the Gran Via.

[3] The list of sponsors of the North American Committee reads like a "Who's Who of the Thirties": Van Wyck Brooks, Edna Ferber, Martha Gellhorn, Rockwell Kent, Sinclair Lewis, Archibald MacLeish, Dorothy Parker, Elliot Paul, Elmer Rice, Upton Sinclair, to drop but a few names. It drew its support from old-fashioned liberals of the *Nation–New Republic* tradition, men and women of good will who deplored the rise of fascism. For well-wishers squeamish about knowingly contributing to war—any war—there existed a sister organization called The Medical Bureau to Aid Spanish Democracy. Contributors to the latter could be assured that their money would be used to combat Republican, not Fascist, gangrene.

There were easier ways to rise. What they possessed, beyond ordinary men, was an unusual willingness to sacrifice personal ambition to a political ideal. All of them were volunteers, in the most literal sense of that word. None were shanghaied into going.[4] And their mentality was so far removed from that of mercenaries that they registered surprise, in Spain, after learning they would receive regular military pay.

Just as the Comintern had approved and organized the International Brigades, setting up an International Control Committee in Paris, so the Communist Party of the United States (CPUSA) founded the Abraham Lincoln Battalion as its contribution to a worldwide effort to fight fascism in Spain. Every man accepted by the battalion had been tacitly approved by the party—a far cry from saying that every man was a Communist, however. The party had no intention of dipping into its coffers to finance the battalion. Money would be raised through "front" organizations like the North American Committee, whose membership would not know that they supported the battalion, much less that the CPUSA whistled the tune both of them danced to. It was a well-oiled, ball-bearing mechanism: in the interests of the Comintern, the CPUSA provided the expertise and apparatus for sending men to Spain—and would, in the end, accept the credit, provided there was credit to accept; in the name of anti-Fascist fervor, the "sympathizers" picked up the tab.

November was a month of strikes along the New York waterfront and in the garment workers' industry, and a large percentage of the first American volunteers were recruited from these trades. Recruitment was always low-key, even surreptitious. A second-generation Communist named Bill Harvey (*né* Horwitz), who worked in the furriers' union, happened to be talking with his union boss about the war in Spain and burst out with "I wish I was there." A week or so later Harvey received a letter in a plain envelope. Inside was an onionskin, without address or signature, which read: "Please appear on the Ninth Floor," adding a date. The ninth floor was the headquarters of the Central Committee of the CPUSA on 12th Street. At the appointed time Harvey entered that sanctum and faced a screening committee composed of five men. The leader seemed to be Fred

---

[4] The Soviet Union unloaded five or six hundred aliens into the International Brigades with the understanding that good work in Spain could result in eventual Russian citizenship. But this kind of trans-Siberian pressure was out of the question so far as Americans were concerned.

Brown (*né* Alpi), a former Italo-Austrian who had attended the
Lenin Institute in Moscow (where a classmate had been Bela Kun)
and who now served as the Comintern representative to the CPUSA.
Brown was a hearty bear of a man with a goatee trimmed in cosmo-
politan style who exuded the urbane charm of an old-world aristo-
crat. Beside him sat a dour figure wearing rimless spectacles who
peered intently from a prune-face bearing the scars of an ancient acne
battleground. This was the military adviser, Captain Allan Johnson
(*né* McNeil), a former United States Army officer with overseas experience (as payroll officer in the Philippines). Next came Charles
Krumbein of the Political Committee, a prime mover in the CPUSA.
The other two were easily forgettable party functionaries—little men
with high-sounding titles like Secretary of the New York Committee
of the Communist Party of the United States of America. They asked
Harvey a number of casual questions, making notes at suitable moments. Then Johnson shot a question at him, "Have you ever fired a
rifle?" "I have," Harvey replied promptly, fortunately recalling a
shooting gallery he had patronized at Coney Island. A few days later
he was notified, once again on an unsigned onionskin, that he had
been accepted.

Every night for several weeks the chosen men drilled in close-order
formation at the Eastside Ukrainian Hall. During rest periods, party
dignitaries like Earl R. Browder, the general secretary, and Jack
Stachel, director of the maritime section, made brief speeches explaining that they were the vanguard of an American working-class
army and relating the issues in Spain to a United Front against Fascists throughout the world. A special treat was the appearance of
Ralph Bates, an English novelist and International Brigade commissar, who alone among the visiting Red firemen had been to Spain.
Clad in a resplendent Republican uniform, Bates was a spellbinder.
"He was dramatic," recalled a recruit. "He almost made us feel that
we were being strafed by a Fiat and bombed by Capronis." Those not
weeded out were issued ten-dollar bills and instructed to purchase
passports. They invented fanciful reasons for traveling out of the
country—visiting an uncle in South Africa, completing art study in
Poland, undertaking theological studies in Palestine. Aliases were
common but by no means universal.

Then one night their leaders were introduced, both selected by
higher-ups in the party. Phil Bart, political commissar, would be in
charge of the group until they reached Spain and began to undergo

training, at which time James Harris, military commander, would take over. Bart was cartoonist for the *Young Worker,* the official newspaper of the Young Communist League, a position that somehow seemed more suitable for this quiet man in his waning twenties than leader of men shipping out to war. Pale, thin, and asthmatic, Bart produced antipathies among many volunteers cast from rougher molds. One of the seamen later complained that the world of Phil Bart was bounded "by a subway ride from the Bronx to Union Square, with an occasional trip to Brooklyn." This was not quite true, for Bart had once worked as a CP organizer in the Ohio National Guard—of all places. (He had been censured by the party when he sensibly refused to distribute some ridiculous antimilitarist leaflets that demanded that corporal punishment be abolished in the three-week summer camp, despite his protests that no such punishment existed in the National Guard.) James Harris (alias Jackson) was a Polish-American seaman said to be an ex-Marine sergeant who had fought in China as an adviser to the Red Army.[5] He was solidly built, sandy-haired, unassuming, and almost inarticulate. To the seamen he was an authentic proletarian, not a Union Square revolutionary.

By the middle of December, there were more than a hundred men drilling each evening at the Ukrainian Hall, and each day fresh recruits arrived to study the intricacies of about-face and parade arms. Out-of-towners began to arrive, largely from Boston and Philadelphia; they were put up at the 34th Street YMCA and given $1.50 per diem maintenance allowance. Shortly before Christmas, eighty of the most promising recruits were separated from the others and informed that they would sail in a few days on the *Normandie.* The hall seemed to burst with an eruption of thumping, stamping, and cheering. They were divided into ten squads. Absolute secrecy was to be maintained. Until instructed otherwise, men were not to communicate with volunteers in other squads, and only squad leaders were allowed to speak with Commissar Bart. No drinking would be tolerated under any circumstances. Following a timetable designed to space them at wide intervals—to confuse Federal "spies"—squads went to an Army-Navy store situated under the Third Avenue Elevated, near 14th Street, and

---

[5] Credentials more easily doubted than disproved. Repeated letters to the Military Personnel Records Center, requesting confirmation or repudiation of previous military service claimed by men who fought in Spain, bring nothing more fruitful than brochures like "Records in the National Archives Relating to Confederate Soldiers."

purchased fifty dollars' worth of equipment per man from the store owner, a party sympathizer not unwilling to mix profit with politics. In identical black imitation-leather suitcases, bound with yellow straps, the recruits packed away a random collection of army surplus —khaki-twill shirts, rubber-soled brogans, puttees, woolen mittens, and fleece-lined jackets. With their own money, some bought sheath knives and even long-tubed gas masks, musty with the smell of dead rubber. A few brazen souls went uptown and opened charge accounts at fancy men's stores. "The better the store, the more gullible they were," remembered a ringleader of this raiding party. A pair of boots from Abercrombie and Fitch lasted one volunteer the whole war.

The sailing date was fixed for December 26. Party leaders held a clandestine *bon voyage* celebration (*sans* alcohol) for them in a movie house near CP headquarters a few hours before they boarded ship. Each volunteer got a parcel containing a carton of Lucky Strikes, a Gillette razor, two cakes of Palmolive soap, and a tin— little white stars on a navy blue background—of G. Washington Coffee (an early-modern "instant"). They were handed third-class tickets issued by World Tourists, Inc., a Manhattan agency specializing in tours to the Soviet Union. (No one asked who was paying for their passage, because everyone knew.) Further, each man received a ten-dollar bill to cover shipboard expenses—*no drinking!*— including tipping, a repugnant bourgeois affectation necessary to reinforce the fiction that they were tourists. Before arriving at Le Havre, they were to receive fifteen dollars apiece to prove to port authorities they were not vagrants—but it was forcefully emphasized that this money had to be returned to Commissar Bart as soon as they cleared customs. As symbol of his ultimate authority, James Harris packed away a .45 automatic, but no one else was permitted to carry a weapon. In case they were asked where they were going, they should say that they were bound for the Paris Exposition. (It apparently occurred to no one that the exposition was not scheduled to open until summer.)

Like men jumping out of airplanes, they left the theater one by one at regular intervals. Earl Browder, an expensive cigar clamped in his jaws, stood near the door and shook each man's hand. One volunteer recalled his surprise when he discovered that Browder's hand was soft, warm, a little gummy—not the hand of a workingman. They went off to war on the uptown subway, the nickel coming from their own funds. No family or friends waited at the pier to see them off.

Most of them had not told anyone where they were going. At the last minute, four men changed their minds.

With the thermometer steady at sixty-two degrees, it was winter-cruise weather as the *Normandie* cast off its lines at midday on December 26, 1936, carrying the first group of American volunteers to the Spanish Civil War. In all, there were seventy-six men,[6] whose backgrounds defy glib generalization. Aboard were a former junior-high school principal from Alabama, a Negro county-fair wrestler from Providencetown, a Japanese-American cook from the West Coast, three Boston-Irish brothers, a one-time gunnery instructor at West Point, a *Daily Worker* columnist, an Armenian carpet-salesman, a City College soccer star, a U.S. Army deserter, a Texas redneck, and a Greenwich Village denizen who told everyone he wanted to die. (Despite rumors that circulated about them later, their ranks included no unemployed members of the old Capone mob.) [7] But this superficial characterization suggests only what they did, not what they believed. Most of this first group of volunteers were members of the Communist Party who despised fascism in all its myriad forms and wished to see the objectives of the Third International realized in Spain, and in the United States. Far from being the dregs of the lumpenproletariat, the volunteers for Spain were an activist elite. Temperamentally, they were the kind of men who had grown up taking the side of the runt in his schoolyard fight with the bully of the block.

Many of them had been to sea as deckhands, but the perspective afforded passengers was new to them. (The exception was Sam

---

[6] The count is variously given at twenty-six, seventy-six, ninety-six, and a hundred and six, but always at six-and-something. My number is based upon the scorecard of Consul Perkins, whose interest in this matter was professional.

[7] A Nationalist pamphlet, published in 1940, characterizes the Lincoln Battalion in this way: "Its armament was excellent; its equipment, perfect; its human material, deplorable. The combatants were Negroes from Broadway, Chinese from the ports of New York and Los Angeles, gangsters from Chicago, and militants from the Communist cells of Philadelphia. This battalion also included American Indians. For enlisting, each man was given a large sum of money—some four hundred dollars, at least."

Nationalist historians, immediately after the war, wallowed in a bog of irrationality and illogic whenever they attempted to evaluate the International Brigades. On the one hand, the Internationals were blamed for prolonging the war for two and a half years by saving Madrid; on the other hand, the Internationals were said to have been *canaille* raked up from the gutters of the Western democracies and packed off to Spain.

Levinger, a rabbi's son from Ohio, who at age fourteen had visited Hitler's Brown House wearing a Boy Scout uniform.) Nearly one-third of the first seventy-six were a worldly, hard-core group from maritime organizations, all of them fiercely loyal to one another and a little condescending to "the snot-noses of Union Square" who got their revolutionary fervor out of books read at City College and New York University. There was a handful or so who had obtained some military training in the lazy peacetime army. Douglas Seacord, the West Point gunnery instructor, had drilled them in bayonet technique back at the Ukrainian Hall. Martin Hourihan, the school principal, had served a year in the U.S. Cavalry before his mother bought him out, clinging to her devout hope that her oldest son would enter the priesthood. Joe Gordon (né Mendelowitz), a man's man and a Communist's Communist, had learned more about fighting in the Williamsburg district of Brooklyn, where he grew up, than in the U.S. Infantry, from which he had recently deserted. Among them, too, were many national guardsmen, although, for the most part, these were party infiltrators like Tiny Agostino, a sullen stalwart from upstate who never took his politics with a grain of salt—or humor. A few chaps had taken courses at The Workers' School, downstairs in the party headquarters, on "How to Organize Communist Party Cells in the U.S. Armed Forces." One graduate, a seaman named Robert Gladnick, had been in charge of this activity at Randolph and Kelley fields, in Texas.[8] Though he had never had military training, he had at least been briefly involved in a military environment.

Compared with these warriors, the large number of Jewish intellectuals aboard the *Normandie* were abysmally green. All had done their stint on picket lines and were up on party theory, but few had ever fired a rifle. A major reason they gave for volunteering was "to take a crack at Hitler." They had been told, and had seen the information repeatedly confirmed in the *Daily Worker,* that German storm troopers made up the bulk of Franco's army. They went to Spain to fight Hitler. This racial dimension of the war was lost upon the contingent from Boston, men like the three Flaherty brothers and their friend Paul Burns, a labor writer in his middle thirties. For them,

---

[8] Before this, Gladnick had propagandized the U.S. Fleet at San Pedro, California. One assignment involved sneaking copies of an anti-militarist, pro-Communist book titled *Kaiser's Coolies* aboard the U.S.S. *Pennsylvania*. On visitors' day, he accomplished his mission only to find that the book was already shelved in the ship library and stamped "Property of the U.S. Navy."

fascism was simply a reactionary political movement bent upon destroying the hard-won gains of the working class. It had to be turned back in Spain before it spread like a virus through the so-called Western democracies. They were weary of ballot boxes and picket lines; they wanted to confront the enemy headlong, with steel. The war in Spain offered a special taste for each palate. "Going was as natural as eating," one of them remembered.

A winter crossing in a Depression year: they pretty well had the boat to themselves. In tourist class there were only a dozen other passengers, one of whom was an athletic-looking man wearing a massive signet ring, the design always turned into his palm. Word got out that the seal was Annapolis and the suspect an agent from the ONI (Office of Naval Intelligence). Bart warned his volunteers not to engage in conversation with the "government spy." The NMU contingent fueled the spy theory, for it diverted Bart's mother-hennishness away from them. Having just left the strike kitchens of the New York waterfront, where they had dined on leftovers from the Fulton and Washington fish markets, they planned to enjoy the plush comforts of the *Normandie*. Ignoring Bart's strictures about drinking, they put away bottles of wine at meals and argued that the non-drinkers were arousing suspicion, not themselves. Moreover, they had scouted the ship and discovered that second class was filled with statuesque girls of the Folies Bergères. Despite Bart's admonition that these girls were thoroughly "bourgeois" parasites, and even his quoting a Leninesque bit of scripture about "never drinking from a public cup," the seamen proceeded to storm second class. More than one among the waterfront flock had served his time in the "Rough Riders Ward"—the VD clinic of the Marine Hospital on Staten Island. A dose was a dose was a dose. They had no money but soon established mutual interests among the Folies girls, many of whom had ancestors buried in the Communard cemetery. The seamen, if their tales contain even a grain or two of truth, broke records and made history on the *Normandie* crossing. Probably this was the only time in history when French girls bought drinks for American soldiers.

Even though it must have been perfectly clear to everyone aboard who they were and where they were going, Commissar Bart continued to behave as though the ship had been infiltrated by spies. Whenever his charges gathered together in groups of more than five, Bart dispatched Bobby Pieck, his eighteen-year-old assistant, to whisper commands to disperse. (Pieck was the nephew of Julius Deutsch,

commander of the private Austrian Socialist Army, the Schutzbund.)
They whiled away the hours at poker—playing for matches, not
money, because gambling was a capitalist vice—at muscle-building
exercises, and in thumbing through dog-eared, obsolescent ROTC
manuals, which circulated surreptitiously like choice bits of pornog-
raphy. A seaman volunteer named Virgil Morris dreamed up fantastic
practical jokes with which to needle Bart. He told him that the
French had a 300 percent duty on new shoes: this meant that the
four-dollar brogans would be taxed twelve dollars at Le Havre. "With
the ten bucks we got, that puts us two in the hole," Bart said. He
seemed to sag under the weight of this fresh burden. Then he passed
the word to the men to break in their shoes "so they will look second-
hand when we go through customs." On the next day seventy-six men
in business suits tramped the decks of the *Normandie,* shod in identical army boots. The girls from the Folies thought it hilarious. In their
effort to remain inconspicuous, the volunteers were most conspicuous
of all.

But halfway across, all of them were unnerved by a news flash
posted by the purser for their benefit:

> Chairman McReynolds of the House Foreign Affairs
> Committee declared he would urge the Department of Justice
> to apply the section of the Criminal Code providing $3,000
> or a year in prison for enlistment of Americans in a foreign
> war.

Bart's face bore a pained "I told you so" expression. To be arrested
at Le Havre and extradited to the United States would be an ignominious end to the volunteer movement. The men glared at the "ONI
spy," but he gave no sign of inward triumph, shame, or concern one
way or another. Infantry manuals and other incriminating documents
were tossed out of portholes.

At Le Havre, customs officers in pillbox caps winked at the volunteers and passed them through without looking inside their black suitcases. It was New Year's Eve, and they wondered how big a time
they could have in Paris on a couple of dollars. To their surprise, they
were dispersed to boardinghouses and dingy hotels in the port area
for two days.[9] They devoured newspapers left behind by the crew of

---

[9] Some men claimed that Bart held them from the Paris boat-train in
order to evade the "ONI spy" who unwittingly climbed aboard the train

the *Washington,* which had just sailed. Back home the birthrate was down and typhoid was up. They heard of the "sit-down" strike in Michigan, where 34,000 workers occupied seven General Motors plants and defied the capitalists to evict them. Later, they made sorties into the red-light quarter, where "women of all dimensions in fish-net robes and nothing else on" showed them that they, too, possessed union cards. (And calling cards as well.) Le Havre had no status as a tourist town, but the fifteen Americans who missed the Paris train on January 2 obviously found plenty to do. Kavorkian, a French-speaking Armenian who had once hawked "oriental" rugs of Belgian manufacture to bargain hunters in Paris, stayed behind to round up the stragglers, while Commissar Bart shepherded the main body to Paris.[10]

There were no hoped-for Paris leaves. After a free meal—bad enough to be commented on at the time and good enough to be recalled in the lean months ahead—they were shuttled across the city to the Gare du Lyon by an irascible guide and boarded the night train to Perpignan. The third-class compartments were jammed with hundreds of International volunteers. There were factory workers from Milan, purse-lipped refugees from Germany, cement-jawed Slavs, blonds with rucksacks from the Baltic. In many of these faces the Americans read silent tales of suffering and hunger: these were anti-Fascists forged from bitter alloys beyond the ken of most Americans. Everything they possessed after half a lifetime of labor lay wrapped in small paper parcels held between their knees. The babel of strange languages and heady disorder of men bound for war spilled over from the compartments to the platforms outside, where hundreds of French well-wishers saw them off. A foreign volunteer asked Joe Gordon his nationality. "Juif," he replied. As the train pulled out of the station nave, men were singing "The Internationale" in a dozen languages. The words were different, but the melody and the mood were identical. They were the wave of the future, discrete drops coalesced together in a sea of international identity. Strung from luggage racks, like a line of hanged men, long sausages wobbled from side to side as the train clicked south in the dark.

while the Americans remained in Le Havre. It is more likely that they were detained because great numbers of International volunteers had accumulated in Paris, and the Control Committee was unable to accommodate any more.

[10] This account of the stragglers, reported by a volunteer, squares with Consul Perkins' dispatch to the Department of State, for he counted sixty men on January 6 and sixteen on January 7.

At daybreak a vast river, the Rhone, appeared out of mist. In the frosted fields, workers wearing blue jackets and black berets pruned black vines that protruded from the earth like immense cloves. Bonfires of their cuttings lighted the way to Spain. Beyond Valence, they felt the nearness of the Mediterranean as the train glided past honey-colored villas on terraced hillsides and spiky palmettos dotting village squares. Leaning from open windows and basking in the warm sun, the volunteers raised the clenched fist of the Popular Front to bicyclists waiting at crossings as they clattered past. The dreamlike landscape flew by in kilometers. Avignon was a fleeting glimpse of a saw-toothed castle and a broken bridge. "Bridge bombed by the Germans in the World War," commented an American with a penchant for history. Béziers was a working-class town on a steep hill, like Wilkes-Barre, and here they bought bottles of red wine and huge sandwiches filled with an oleaginous substance that looked like raw ham but tasted like raw bacon. Beyond Narbonne, the tracks ran across salt flats beside the sea, and a lookout called from the window, "Hey, I see the Pyrenees!" And sure enough, he had. In this region, the populace, accustomed to volunteers and bored by everything about the Spanish Civil War except the profits to be made from it, seldom bothered to wave back. From the railroad yard at Perpignan they were led into a high-walled enclosure and told to keep out of sight. They were dirty, tired, hungry. Some sneaked out and brought back long loaves of bread, but no real food.

After nightfall they were loaded into battered schoolbuses, which bumped for several hours over a rutted road climbing into a gap in the looming mountains. Beyond the French frontier station, shut down for the night, their headlights illuminated a band of armed men wearing blankets. From a hut hung a red and black banner—the party flag of the Spanish Anarchists. Somebody on the bus shouted, "Viva la república!" and an Anarchist called back, "No! Viva la revolución proletaria!" The war meant one thing for a Communist and another for an Anarchist, but both agreed upon the clenched-fist salute. A fresh surge of international solidarity swept through the buses like an electric charge as they lurched across the frontier into Spain. By this time everyone was tired of "The Internationale," which they had sung countless times on the train, yet no one had the vaguest idea of what the anthem of the Republic was.

Dropping down from the mountains, they debused on the parade ground of the Castillo de San Fernando, a massive castle-fortress crowning the heights above the town of Figueras. Assigned a section of straw within a dark subterreanean casemate, they hung their suitcases on saddle hooks jutting from the wall. Commissar Bart spelled out the law with an authority borrowed from Spain: breaches in discipline would not be tolerated, particularly concerning drinking. "We are an army of the people, not an army of alcoholics!" Putting teeth in Bart's lecture, Harris added, "That means all you guys!" In a cavernous room lined with plank tables and lit by two weak lightbulbs, they were served goat chops from a skillet twenty-five feet wide and beans from steaming washtubs. Although there was no water, they obediently pushed aside the long-necked *purones* of wine sitting on the tables. A friendly Catalan came over to show the Americans how to drink from a *purón:* seizing the bottle, he flourished it above his head and poured a thin stream directly into his mouth. They admired his skill but still refused to drink. The mess officer had glasses and cups brought for them. Again they refused. The officer rapped the table for attention and delivered a plaintive speech: "Amcrican comrades, we Catalans are a poor people. We know our wine is a poor country product. We do not have the fine vineyards of your country. America is a rich country, and the wines of Scranton and Chicago are among the best in the world. This we know. But we ask that you not insult the poor products of Cataluña." Bart's interpreter tried to explain that the Americans refused wine on moral ground, but the officer saw no connection between wine and morality. With rising irritation, he said that in Spain a man who did not drink was a *maricón* (a homosexual): were the Americans *maricones?* Bart found himself impaled on the horns of a dilemma: sexual deviation was *ipso facto* fascism, yet party discipline demanded that an order, once given, had to be obeyed. It was Harris who cut his way through the dialectical impasse. Grabbing a *purón,* he shouted, "Drink—as guests!" With yells of jubilation, the Americans proved to the Catalans that they were not *maricones.* They drank.

A few days later the International volunteers marched down to the railroad station, led by the Americans, who were alphabetically first. As they passed through the streets of Figueras, townspeople lined the curbs, cheering and bombarding them with almonds. Because the washrooms at the station were inadequate, the French volunteers broke into a park to relieve themselves, despite the entreaties of the keeper that they use the road. Shouting *"C'est la guerre,"* they went down among the flowers. A train camouflaged with zigzag smears of green and yellow paint carried them to Barcelona. Already they had picked up two plagues which remained with them to the end, lice and dysentery.

It was midafternoon when they marched from North Station to the Plaza de Cataluña for their demonstration under the window of Consul General Mahlon F. Perkins. After they sang "The Star-Spangled Banner," a band burst forth with "Himno de Riego," the Republican anthem. The Americans began to laugh. The tune sounded like something they knew in the States as "Here Comes Barnum and Bailey— the Circus Is Coming to Town." They hummed and sang it, emphasizing the words "Barnum" and "Bailey." When the band had stopped playing, the crowd surged forward to congratulate the Americans, who alone among the International volunteers appeared to know the words of their anthem. No one divulged that Barnum and Bailey were not proletarian heroes like Tom Mooney or Big Bill Haywood.

Dawn found them south of Tarragona, the tracks running beside the Mediterranean—"as blue as everyone said it was"—or passing through hamlets—"unreal, like Hollywood villages." On southern slopes, almond trees were already in pink blossom. On tiny farms Spaniards clenched fists and called *"Salud!"* to the passing volunteers. A lookout at the window shouted, "Hey, I see orange trees!" Thereafter at every station, leather-faced *campesinos* tossed in oranges and the volunteers threw back cigarettes and loaves of bread. (The major granaries of Spain were in the Nationalist zone.) One man, who insisted upon paying for his fruit, found himself charged the equivalent of a penny for two dozen. For hours they gorged themselves, tossing the skins and pulp at dozing comrades and watching two Glasgow volunteers impale oranges in midair with stickblades. At Valencia, capital of the Republic since November, when the Government had fled Madrid in panic, they ate in the *plaza de toros,* across the street from the station, and emitted mock groans of agony when they saw their dessert—two oranges per man. Bullfight posters sagged and flapped in the wind. Since the outbreak of war no bulls worth mentioning had been fought in Spain. Spaniards of both sides had found more interesting animals to kill.

It was again night when the train wound up between jagged peaks of the coastal *sierras* to the Levantine *meseta,* an arid upland plateau beaten by winter winds that swept down from Aragon. In the springless carriages the wooden-slat benches grew harder. Window panes broken at the beginning of the war had not been replaced, and the men tried to plug the drafts with bundles of clothing and newspapers. (In Spain it was nearly always either too hot or too cold.) Some tried to sleep on the benches; others curled up in the aisles. In the blacked-out train, in the desolate wastes of Albacete province, four anonymous Americans and two Canadians composed what was termed the "official" marching song of the Lincoln Battalion. The tune was based upon a yet-to-be-identified college ditty plucked out on a guitar; the words, a conglomerate of collegiate hoopla and proletarian cliché:

> We march, Americans!
> To defend our working class,
> To uphold democracy
> And mow the Fascists down like grass;
> We're marching to vic-to-ry,
> Our hearts are set, our fists are clenched,
> A cause like ours can't help but win,
> The Fascists' steel will bend like tin.
> We give our word, they shall not pass,
> (shouted) NO PASARÁN!
> (again) WE GIVE OUR WORD THEY SHALL NOT PASS! [11]

With a few changes here and there—not so many, really—it might have been adopted by Fordham as a football song. The composers liked it and sent it to *New Masses,* which published it, of course. Most of the waterfront crowd, who had no appreciation of finer things, laughed at it. They preferred "The Caissons Go Rolling Along," which steadily pushed out the other. (After meeting Fascist steel in their first battle, no veteran ever sang the "Marching Song" again, unless sardonically.)

At gray dawn they looked through eyes grubby with lack of sleep across a tabletop plain with an African cast to it. There were fields where nothing seemed to be grown and occasional villages where nothing seemed to be made. Whenever the train halted at a huddle of roofs defining the site of human habitation, small boys raced to the platform, not to shower them with oranges and almonds, but to beg

[11] A defector later claimed that the song concluded with the lines "When we go back home once more / We'll do the same thing there." This was used as grist for the persecution mill among the American Right, who charged that men had enlisted in the International Brigades in order to obtain military training that would enable them to overthrow the United States Government when they returned. The CIO was mysteriously linked to this "conspiracy."

tobacco, bread, money. Romantic Spain was behind them. The volunteers had come to find and reclaim these miserable villages and these squalid lives. If their hearts were fuller than their pockets, there was nevertheless always something to pass through the train window.

At ten o'clock in the morning of January 8, the first American volunteers reached Albacete, saffron center of the world and headquarters of the International Brigades. A band heavy on the percussion side welcomed them with its repertoire of national anthems, including "The Star-Spangled Banner," "The Marseillaise," and "God Save the King." Pasted on the walls of the railroad station were posters advertising the IB, one of which featured a triad of heads—Caucasian, Negro, and Oriental—encased in French *poilu* helmets of the World War. They marched behind their band up the short Calle de Alfonso XII, past the blue-tiled pleasure domes of the Gran Hotel in the Plaza Altozano, and through the narrow streets of the *barrio chino,* where veteran shack rats with meaty arms peered at them from open windows. (Since the fifth column was rumored to be numerous in Albacete, each group of new arrivals was paraded ostentatiously as a display of IB strength.) Then doubling back, they were herded into a barracks known as the Guardia Nacional. Albacete was a provincial capital seemingly built by amateur architects, all of them with different tastes. Within the inner core of the city, for example, the railway station was Williamsburg Federal, the Gran Hotel was fin-de-siècle Monte Carlo, and the Guardia Nacional was West Point Gothic. Beyond these showpieces stretched the working-class quarters, a more uniform style, Castilian Slum. The Americans quickly decided it was the most God-awful place they had ever seen.

Their barracks had once housed the reactionary rural police-force, the awesome Guardia Civil. During the first week of war a fierce battle raged about the place. The Guardia had barricaded themselves in the edifice and held off Republican militia for eight days until subdued by a Bastille-like crowd. The walls were still pock-marked by small-arms fire, and the floors within stained by blood. Since these were the first traces of war the Americans had ever seen, they were examined minutely. Two theories existed to account for the bloodstains: one held that the Guardia had massacred their hostages, and the second maintained that the attackers had massacred the Guardia. Considering the fratricidal violence of the Spanish Civil War, one theory was as plausible as the other. Accepting one version did not preclude accepting the other.

The volunteers had not eaten since Valencia. Food awaited them, but first there were speeches. Cheers of recognition greeted the appearance of a walrus-looking Frenchman in "the largest black beret ever known to man." This was André Marty, the founding-father of the International Brigades and its supreme commander. He was a hero in his own time for his leadership of the French Black Sea mutiny in 1919, when the French Navy refused to support the White Russian armies. As a man who had refused to take up arms against the fledgling Soviet Union, he found favor with Josef V. Stalin and had become not a dedicated but a fanatical Communist. He had an obsession about spies. In his foghorn voice, he warned the new volunteers to guard themselves against Trotskyites and other "political deviates." Later, it would be claimed that Marty demonstrated more zeal in exterminating nonexistent Trotskyites than in prosecuting a war against real Fascists, but he had not yet earned his nickname "The Butcher of Albacete." Only a few of the Americans comprehended Marty's allusions to "political deviates" or sensed his threatening tone. One who did—or claimed he did—characterized him succinctly: "Marty, a bum of the first water." With Marty on an iron balcony surrounding the courtyard like a gallery in a prison cellblock were Luigi Longo, inspector general of the IB, and "Vidal," military commander of the base (subsequently removed on an embezzlement charge). They made short, reasonable speeches of welcome.

The arrivals were then lined up by nationality, photographed for their *livrets militaires,* and filled out questionnaires. Those who listed their political party as "Communist" were told to change it to "Anti-Fascist," even though no such antiparty existed, because of the Popular Front image of the International Brigades.[12] From a warehouse they received uniforms assembled from the surplus stocks of a half-dozen armies—primarily French—but no weapons. Clothes were given out on a catch-as-catch-can basis, the recruits trading to find the correct size. The Americans found that their doughboy regalia

---

[12] By underplaying the role of the Communist Party in the brigades, two ends were served: first, funds and men would be drawn into the IB from bourgeois sources; second, antagonism toward the IB from other parties in Republican Spain would be minimized. From beginning to end, the Anarchists believed that the IB existed in Spain in order to bring their country into the Soviet orbit after the war was terminated. They argued, with justification, that Republican Spain had all the manpower it required to wage the war. If the Soviet Union really wants to help—they were wont to ask—why doesn't it send us armaments?

was openly scorned by volunteers from other countries—they had come to Spain already clad in the uniforms of the most capitalistic country in the world! A few sensitive souls stuffed their conspicuous fleece jackets into garbage cans as proof of international fervor, only to be shocked, on the following day, to see them on the backs of French volunteers. Passports were taken up ostensibly for "safekeeping" at the base; the real reason was to minimize desertion and to make flight from Spain virtually impossible. If a man was killed, his passport was delivered to the Soviet military intelligence officer based at The Hague for possible use in espionage activities. But some men, vaguely smelling a rat, tucked their passports into their shoes and claimed that they were lost.

For a day or so, the recruits drilled earnestly in the arena of the Albacete bullring, a fanciful structure on the edge of town which looked as though it had been squeezed out of a confectioner's tube. Commands were barked out by French officers using French jargon that not even the French recruits seemed to understand. During a rest period, a Detroit auto-worker smudged a swastika onto his handkerchief and played *matador* to John Lenthier, a Boston actor who had once starred in an underground production of *Waiting for Lefty,* banned in his hometown. Cheers in a dozen tongues accompanied the contest, which ended when the bull tore the *muleta* to ribbons and gored the *matador.* On their time off, the recruits prowled the city, which turned into a sea of mud at the slightest drizzle; they sampled the local *coñac,* said to have been blended from equal parts of rancid olive oil and low-octane gasoline; and they bought the local specialty, jackknives with handsome mother-of-pearl handles and worthless tin blades. There was little else to buy, unless one wanted to queue up outside a door in the *barrio chino;* but the female wares, recalled a volunteer, were "pretty awful." Particularly after Le Havre. In Albacete, the IB hierarchy billeted at the Gran Hotel held *droit de seigneur* over every available girl who possessed either beauty or spunk. There was even a rumor around Albacete that André Marty had a private harem in a villa outside town. Nobody seemed really to believe it, but they enjoyed thinking about it. Posted in shop windows was a ubiquitous sign that said, NO HAY TABAC, which meant "There's No Tobacco," though one American comrade remarked, with deep disgust, "Well, if they make cigarettes out of hay over here, I wouldn't wanta smoke 'em." They soon learned to hoard butt ends for rerolling later and not to pass a pack around. Some of the stouter proletarians felt the authorities ought to prohibit Internationals from panhandling the new arrivals for cigarettes and from picking up butts from the streets, in the manner of Bowery bums.

Perhaps the most depressing place in town was the Plaza de Al-tozano. The municipal and provincial buildings had been taken over by Brigade bureaucrats, pouter pigeons in swank uniforms and in perpetual motion. There were fleeting glimpses of Marty himself, popping in and out of his chauffeured limousine decked with tiny flags. Hovering around him were his next-in-powers, section heads and *jefes* of something-or-other, bundled up in shaggy coats. They were long-striding fellows with lopes "that made them seem wolves in sheep's clothing." If an officer ranked high enough, his wife could join him in Albacete. (Madame Marty was there; privileged subalterns like Gustav Regler, the German writer, received invitations to visit her room privately in order to examine the collection of automatic pistols that she spread out neatly on her bed.) There was nothing about the Gran Hotel reminiscent of the give-and-take of an American union hall. Guards with machine guns stood at the revolving door and turned away those without special passes. In Albacete only one man had the right to cast a vote—André Marty, Soviet-planted czar, the French-nurtured grand marshal of the International Brigades. It was ironical that he had risen to power in the French Communist Party on a platform of antimilitarism.

The Americans had little time to study the intricacies of rear-guard politicking and in-fighting. During the second week of January they left for their training camp. They were glad to go. Albacete could make a working stiff feel pretty small.

2
卍 Villanueva de la Jara

I'm living better than I ever did in America. . . . The stomach has practically disappeared and biceps are fast forming. . . . I heartily recommend Spain to all those intellectuals who need a change and rest for their jaded nerves. And I must admit that the kick so lacking in America is here at an ever-increasing pace.

—American volunteer (early phase)

Had the Americans come to Spain as anthropologists rather than as soldiers, they would have found the small village of Villanueva de la Jara an ideal laboratory for their studies. Located thirty-five miles northwest of Albacete, it was the most remote of all the villages used by the International Brigades as training camps and billet areas—so remote, in fact, that it belonged to the province of Cuenca, not Albacete. At Villanueva, farmers plowed with oxen, women carried jars of water on their heads, and privileged guests were served roasted goat-testicles. The heaviest industry was a chocolate factory, but the product contained more carob than cacao. With its cobbled streets, whitewashed houses, and grated windows it was pleasant enough, but for Americans arriving there from Eastern industrial cities, Villanueva seemed like the end of the world, and beyond.

The townspeople distrusted, even despised, the Internationals. Earlier, an overflow group of French volunteers, most of them "uncontrollables," had been billeted in the Convent of Santa Clara. Before pulling out, they had peppered the floors with excrement and decorated the walls with obscene art. This desecration had not especially upset the villagers, who had decapitated religious statuary in a rampage of their own at the beginning of the war. What they had disliked about the French were seizures of wine cellars, drunken brawls, and affronts to their womenfolk. Therefore when the Americans disembarked from their municipal-green trucks in the tiny *plaza mayor,* they heard doors banging and windows slamming shut throughout the village. The mayor, flanked by his town-hall claque, appeared and proclaimed that he held no political beliefs whatever.[1] Then he led them to the Convent of Santa Clara, which still bore the traces of French occupation. "Garbage clogged the drain, crap was piled on the floor, the whole place was flooded," recalled an American. Cursing the French, they turned to with switch brooms and slop buckets to make the place habitable. They had arrived at dusk; it was after midnight when they finished.

Having shunted them to Villanueva, the Albacete base largely ignored them. Officially they were the 17th Battalion, XV (International) Brigade; unofficially they called themselves the Abraham Lincoln Battalion. Truckloads of new faces arrived nearly every day, adding to the confusion of leaderless men drifting about the village without specific knowledge of what they should be doing. Since Philip Bart had remained at Albacete as their representative at the base, James Harris assumed command. Their table of organization called for the formation of two rifle and one machine-gun company. Since the seamen were the most cohesive faction, they set themselves up as future machine-gunners and named themselves the Tom Mooney Company.[2] They freely chose whom they wanted to belong and hustled out some men foisted on them. They became a kind of supercompany with the best *esprit de corps* in the battalion, but many men left out resented the Mooneys. "The guys in that company were tough guys," complained one. "You couldn't get in if you weren't a hardcore something-or-other." They got the best military commander in the outfit, a Tennessean named Douglas Seacord, a soft-spoken man with a smiling, pirate's face. Gathering about him party stalwarts like Joe Gordon, Douglas Roach, a Negro wrestler nearly as wide as tall, and Ray Steele, a seaman who could outrun most men in the battal-

---

[1] In 1939, Juan de Dios Pérez Alvarillo, mayor of Villanueva de la Jara, was executed as a war criminal by the Franco government, having been convicted for the murder of twenty Nationalist sympathizers.

[2] Thomas Jeremiah Mooney, a militant working-class leader in San Francisco, was imprisoned on a trumped-up charge that he was responsible for a bomb explosion, killing ten bystanders, at the Preparedness Day parade in July, 1916. Jailed until 1939, Mooney was wooed by the Communists and eventually captivated by them.

ion despite his clubfoot, they began training with two machine guns obsolescent at the time of the First World War. Soon they were deep in such gunnery problems as "inverse section fire to secure oblique fire," insulated by hard work from the bickering factionalism rapidly developing in the other companies.

Now that Bart was gone, many volunteers wished he were back again, for he had been a link, however weak, in the chain leading back to the party organization in New York. Authority had broken down. Harris earnestly wished to establish a training program but could not cope with the anarchy already plaguing his battalion and compounded almost daily by the arrival of fresh recruits. A power struggle developed over the vacant post of political commissar with Philip Cooperman (*né* Kuppermann), the secretary, pitted against Marvin Stern, a stocky college soccer-player. Since Cooperman's convention-hall mannerisms did not wear well ("He was a rah-rah boy scout"), Stern was installed as commissar and proceeded to place Harris under arrest on charges to be preferred at a later time. Dumbfounded, Harris ordered Stern's arrest for insubordination, only to discover that in the International Brigades a commissar could overrule a commander but not the other way around. Part of the trouble stemmed from an age-old feud between trade-union men and Marxist intellectuals, the doers and the thinkers. In the end a grievance committee mediated. Thereafter the commissar slot was filled by the *troika*—Cooperman, Stern, and a third man representing the grievance committee-at-large.

The Americans were not unique in their garbled efforts to forge a chain of command and to create a training camp. At Madrigueras the British Battalion suffered similar problems. One of the earliest company commanders had to be dismissed when he refused to send away the French girl who had followed him from Paris; another of like rank proved to be so lackluster that he was made transport officer, even though no battalion transport existed at the time. The training was comprised largely of an improvised war-game in which an officer stood atop a hill blowing his whistle—the signal for his men to "attack," over open country, an entrenched "enemy" company, which could have wiped them out to a man at four hundred yards. The battalion commander was Wilfred McCartney, a paunchy *grand boulevardier* who, even in Spain, drank nothing other than good champagne and plain water. He had had experience in the World War as a staff officer, but he was not a Communist. McCartney had become so involved with the corridor cliques in Albacete—which were attempting to get rid of him—that he had little time to supervise the Madrigueras program. Therefore he sent out Tom Wintringham, a balding radical poet, to whip into shape the two British companies originally numbering about seventy-five men each. With them was a lone American, Joseph Selligman, who had slipped away from Swarthmore College on December 3, paid his own way to Spain, and joined the British before the Lincolns had left New York.

The British Battalion was far more unruly and divisive than the American. Having taken no teetotaling pledges, they drank what they liked, which was everything. Worse than drink, however, were the disruptive intranational rivalries among men who had come from the far corners of the British Empire. Armed with a sense of humor, Wintringham plunged into this imperial melting-pot containing English, Scots, Welsh, Egyptians, Cypriots, Maltese, and Irish. At once he earned their respect for his military lore—Wintringham was a World War veteran and former military editor of the London *Worker* —but his upper-crust speech and patrician bearing were not lost upon his coarser-grained men, who dubbed him "Bleedin' Lord of the King's Cock Horse." On one occasion, seeking a comrade in the recreation room, he interrupted a BBC broadcast and was shouted down by a roomful of the rank and file. They had the satisfaction of seeing their commander "creep out like a mouse," as one of them expressed it in a letter to chums back home. Efforts to institute discipline by jail sentences failed—because the lockup had an iron stove and was the warmest spot in town. No one saluted, because recognition of rank was "bourgeois," or even "Fascist." In this atmosphere of egalitarianism, an order had to be prefaced by "Comrade, as one man to another . . ."

For machine-gun instruction, Wintringham had twelve old Colts, which worked well enough when fed factory-loaded belts but not at all when the belts were loaded by hand. The most minuscule speck of dirt jammed a gun. The men had to spread linen altar-cloths from the church on the ground whenever the guns were stripped down. As a swagger stick Wintringham adopted a steel ramrod, useful in clearing burst cartridges from the breeches of the Colts. By his count, these machine guns averaged 120 shots an hour—a rate of fire slower than that of an ordinary rifle. Rifle oil was nonexistent. He tried to borrow some axle grease from local farmers but learned they never used it on their big wooden carts. Whenever a motor vehicle strayed into

Madrigueras, one of Wintringham's men crawled underneath to milk
it for transmission oil.

As though parodying their national character, the Irish badgered
the English by adopting emerald-green berets, despite the IB prohibition against national and sectarian emblems. (Since there were more
than thirty countries represented in the Brigades, chauvinism was always a major problem.) Battalion officers winked at the berets but
had to crack down when some of the Irish began speaking Gaelic to
one another. A few old-timers claimed to have ambushed English soldiers in the Irish Rebellion. When they heard that Americans had arrived at Villanueva de la Jara, half the Irish resigned from the British
Battalion and went over to the Americans. With great *élan,* they told
the Lincolns how they had forced the British officers to accede to
their transfer by surrounding headquarters with a ring of machine-
guns. Since most of the Irish were Roman Catholics, the *troika,*
afraid of wounding their religious sensibilities, had confiscated and
neatly stored away all the convent prayer-books, which the men had
been tearing up and using as toilet paper. Much to their surprise,
however, the Irish brought with them quantities of identical books,
which they employed for the same purpose.

The Irish formed their own section in the Lincoln Battalion with
their own commander and commissar (the latter from Liverpool, unknown to them at the time). "Long on blarney and short on recruits,"
recalled one American, they filled their spotty ranks with new arrivals
fresh from Brooklyn or The Bronx and fitted them out with names
like O'Greenberg and O'Goldstein. They were full of military strata-
gems and opinions, invariably introduced by "Here's how we used to
do it when fighting the Black and Tans . . ." And their maudlin
anthem engraved itself in the memory of the Americans:

> 'Twas early on a Sunday mornin',
> High above the gallows tree,
> Kevin Barry gave his young life
> So that Ireland may be free.

By strict party standards, the Irish were hopelessly "romantic," but
they were comic relief necessary in humanizing the Lincoln Battalion,
which all too often took itself with monolithic seriousness.

Adding to the difficulties at Villanueva de la Jara was the insouci-
ance of the French-dominated bureaucracy at Albacete. Directives,
whenever they arrived, were written in French and had to be labori-
ously translated. (Complaints netted only a few copies of French-

Spanish dictionaries, but French-English were unavailable.) Since rations were inadequate, the men had to forage in the village and purchase supplies with their own money. Cartons of cigarettes listed on invoices vanished on the road between Albacete and Villanueva, but the French truck-drivers merely shrugged their shoulders when confronted by curses and accusations. The Americans made some progress in drilling with eight-man squads until a French inspector demanded that they scrap this inferior American system in favor of twelve-man squads. He showed them a complicated diamond-formation of open-field maneuver in which the squad leader hand-signaled groups of three men to advance, much as a conductor batons an orchestra. Though beautiful to watch, it was so purely theoretical that probably no army in history could have employed it in battle without being exterminated. Perhaps the apex of French arrogance was reached when French Jews told American Jews that their own Yiddish was linguistically rich and pure, while the American variety was vulgar. "The French were the scum of the International Brigades," concluded one American, whose terse summary was echoed by countless other volunteers.

Complaints from Villanueva piled up in Bart's office at Albacete: where was their training equipment? what happened to mail from the States? when would overnight leaves be authorized; why couldn't they be billeted closer to Albacete? But Bart had no weight whatever with the IB bosses at the Base. The CPUSA was only a microscopic part of a completely capitalistic power, and Bart was a nobody in it. He represented a nation that in the view of the Comintern was slightly more politically developed than Albania but was considerably less so than Bulgaria. André Marty publicly expressed his disgust with those "spoiled cry-babies," those "arrogant Americans." It was the Marshal Foch–General Pershing situation all over again, but Bart lacked the financial leverage of Pershing. In Spain, Americans were debtors, not creditors. Marty warned that unless the American volunteers stopped whining, he would send them home in disgrace. Supported by no one and scorned by both the men at Villaneuva and the cliques at Albacete, Bart agonized in solitude, waiting the time (not very far off, as events proved) when his asthmatic condition would render him eligible for repatriation. The CPUSA had committed a grave error in not sending a better-credentialed man to represent the volunteers at the Base, for the Americans were, at least initially, treated like second-class citizens of the world revolution.

The men at Villanueva de la Jara did not endure their banishment stoically. Their greatest enemy, for the moment, was boredom. The *troika* tried to organize soccer matches, but these were little more than shin-kicking contests that "ended in draws because all played it differently." Ray Steele had brought an American football to Spain. Their games of "tackle" always drew a crowd of villagers, who marveled at the performance without fathoming the purpose of the game. Once on a Sunday they marched over to Motilla del Palancar, eight miles distant, to see an amateur bullfight held in a crumbling arena that "looked like it was a thousand years old." They were fascinated by the starkness of the drama but a little ashamed of its frivolity. "It proved to be an odd and interesting day," wrote a volunteer, not an *aficionado*, "though some of the boys expressed it as being a rather cruel sport." (This from a youth who had volunteered to kill Fascists.) Most of all, however, they wanted overnight passes. The *troika* issued a few for dental work in Albacete, but not everyone was lucky enough to have bad teeth. When grumbling over the paucity of leaves reached a danger point, a meeting was called in the church to explain that motor vehicles had to be used for transporting men and supplies to the front, etc. But the men were not impressed: they had heard this countless times before. Finally the battalion doctor got up, resolved to cut through the soapbox rhetoric and lay the truth on the line. "Comrades," he began, "I know you guys want to go to Albacete to get laid. But if you went, you'd get a dose and be unfit for the front. Yet there's one thing you can do." He paused, and the men listened eagerly. "You can masturbate." Some laughs rang out, but when they realized that Doc was absolutely serious, there was an uproar of jeering and hooting, which terminated the session.

Despite their desire to escape from Villanueva de la Jara, the Americans were nonetheless successful in winning back the good will of the villagers lost by their French predecessors. The 17th Battalion hospital, installed in a barn-sized villa fronting on the *plaza mayor,* opened its doors to the civilian population and became the first (and only) free clinic in Villanueva history. One of the battalion doctors, Eugene Fogarty of British Columbia, married a local girl half his age and tried to acquire Spanish citizenship.[3] The battalion movie-

---

[3] "Eugenio Furgarte" still has inlaws in Villanueva who remember him well. At the end of the war, he took up practice at nearby Iniesta, but as a former International fearing *depuración* by Franco authorities, he fled Spain, leaving his wife and children behind. After World War II, Jacoba Moreno y Fogarty was notified by the Canadian Government that her husband had

projector ran three times a day, one showing given over to the townspeople, who seemed to enjoy equally well such films as *The Sailors of
Kronstadt,* a Soviet classic, and *How to Operate a Maxim Machine-
gun.* The Cubans, who called themselves the "Antonio Guiterras
Column" (including half a dozen Puerto Ricans and one Mexican),
were extremely popular with the natives because of their ability to
converse fluently with them. Originally the villagers had been frightened of the American Negroes, believing them somehow connected
with the feared Moors of the Franco armies. Douglas Roach changed
all this when he performed acrobatics that astonished the local children, who thereafter waited devoutly for him at the convent door and
tagged his heels like a pack of loyal terriers. Volunteers amused
themselves by teaching the tots revolutionary songs and listening to
them sing

> On the line, on the line,
> On the peek-it, peek-it line . . .

John Lenthier produced an elaborate musicale for battalion and villagers alike which featured a Jewish truck-driver's songs in Irish
brogue, a former Wobbly crooning Joe Hill's "Scissorbill," a Harlem
Negro chanting Langston Hughes's "Scottsboro," topped off by his
rendition of "Marching Song of the Lincoln Battalion." During their
stay at Villanueva only one man, Ray Steele, had to be locked up for
being drunk and disorderly. The Americans so far surpassed the
French in establishing rapport with the populace that a few men,
mostly Cubans, even stole away in the evenings to savor an omelette
and to split a pack of Lucky Strikes in the high-vaulted medieval
kitchens of the village. Yet the local folk always retained a wary reserve toward the *extranjeros* who had come from places far away to
fight in their war. Some nights they heard shots being fired in the convent and a rumor swept the village, a whispered word—*executions.*[4]
It was only target shooting in the long-aisled chapel.

been killed in the Far East and she received a small lump-sum pension. No
other marriages are recorded in the registers of Villanueva. Of the half-dozen
British volunteers marrying local girls at Madrigueras, all were nullified by
religious authorities after the war save one, who still summers in the locality.
    [4] Thirty years later, the middle-aged villagers recall the French volunteers
far more vividly than the Americans. "Big drunks, the Frenchmen!" they say
laughingly. One of the boys who used to follow Douglas Roach is today the
mayor's assistant. He always assumed that the Americans were a trained army
waiting to be sent to the front, for he recalls no training program whatever.
He liked the Americans and wonders what happened to them in the war, and

Apart from building a respectable image among the citizenry of Villanueva, the Lincolns failed to acquire even a minimal knowledge of military art. Some of the men blamed Harris, saying he had the mentality of a sergeant—a first-rate sergeant, to be true, but a sergeant nonetheless. He seemed to know what he was talking about, but he talked so little! At lectures he posed, in technical jargon, abstruse tactical problems and then wheeled to ask a recruit, "What would you do in that case?" No matter what the recruit would reply, Harris was apt to shake his head and say, "No good. You'd kill off all your men that way." What the answer should have been, they never learned. It seemed, at such times, that Harris' store of knowledge was so vast and so valuable that he had locked the door and thrown the key away.

The wind of change began to blow in late January, when there appeared two figures destined to lead the Lincoln Battalion out of confusion and into catastrophe. Sam Stember came from Philadelphia, Robert Hale Merriman from the Soviet Union.

Both Stember and Merriman were in their thirties—but at that point their resemblance ended. Sam Stember was a loser. He was a sagging man with the mien of someone who had spent the best years of his life sitting behind a beat-up desk in a dingy office, organizing for the party. He seemed to the volunteers like a used-up hack slipping backward after a long uphill climb toward the higher ranks of the party bureaucracy. He emitted, almost like a body odor, a weariness and dreariness that led the men to nickname him "Last-Chance" Stember. Others alluded to him as "The Jello." Presumably he had been sent on a temporary basis by the New York office to develop political leadership and to put some snap in the battalion commissariat. At his inaugural meeting, the *troika* asked the men to give Comrade Stember a vote of confidence. A lone voice cried out, "Does it have to be unanimous?" Tiny Agostino, the New York tough functioning as self-appointed strongman of the inner cadre, stood up and glowered at the dissident. "It has to be *unanimous,*" he said. "You want your goddamn head broken?" So it came to pass that Sam Stember became political commissar of the Lincoln Battalion. Marvin Stern promptly resigned from the commissariat and entered the ranks.

he thinks America is the hope of the world—particularly if it would join with the Soviet Union and destroy China.

Ever afterward, the Lincolns would allude to an unpopular commissar as a "comic-star."

Robert Hale Merriman, on the other hand, was a winner. If Spain was the last chance for Stember, it provided the first chance for this Californian whose dossier was probably the best recruiting poster the Lincoln Battalion ever had. Magnetic leader, studious intellectual, devout proletarian—it all seemed almost too good to be true, yet it was. And even Ernest Hemingway, reluctant to admit military prowess in Americans fighting in Spain, found Merriman irresistible. Hemingway changed Merriman's name to Robert Jordan, gave him a sleeping bag, and made him the hero of his pastoral romance, *For Whom the Bell Tolls.*[5]

Born in 1906 at Eureka, California, Merriman grew up in half a dozen logging towns in the redwood country. His father was a lumberjack and his mother a schoolteacher with literary aspirations. After high school, he felled trees and fed pulp in a paper mill. Here he fell in with an old Irish radical, who forced him to question some of his *laissez-faire* assumptions. Young Merriman was intrigued by the theory that the strong ought to do something for the weak beyond exploiting them, but after he had saved enough money to matriculate at the University of Nevada as a twenty-three-year-old freshman, his ambition was still to rise out of his economic class rather than to carry this class upward with him. One month after he arrived in Reno, the stock market crashed.

At the university, Merriman quickly became a campus wheelhorse and the beau-ideal of fraternity row. Standing six-feet-two and weighing in at 190 pounds, he was a clean-cut, Anglo-Saxon go-getter. The Depression nipped the college careers of classmates, but not Merriman's. He picked up pin money as an end on the football team, ran the business end of the college newspaper, commanded a company of the ROTC (seven-fifty per month), and served as house manager of

---

[5] Hemingway's novel, which excoriated André Marty and "La Pasionaria" (Dolores Ibarruri, a leader of the Spanish Communist Party), has repeatedly been condemned by members of the Lincoln Battalion for dwelling upon trivial aspects of the war. It was a novel, wrote Alvah Bessie, a Lincoln veteran and veteran writer, "where the shattering struggle of 28 million people for survival and decency was subordinated to an endless episode in a sleeping bag, and the phrase 'the earth moved' was quoted by bohemians and bourgeoisie with a leer on their faces." Of their own love making such people quipped, "How come the earth didn't move, only the bedsprings?"

his fraternity, the prestigious Sigma Nu. Campus photographs of the time reveal a well-scrubbed, all-American boy who looks as though he had just stepped out of the pages of *Frank Merriwell at Yale.* "He was very ambitious," recalls a Nevada classmate with a gift for understatement.

Yet grafted onto Merriman was a rebellious quality that made him balk at establishments, canons, and taboos. His professors found him an omnivorous student: apparently the only courses he disliked were those that were required for a degree. On one occasion, when he refused to enroll in a course, the president himself intervened and demanded that he take it. After some research in Nevada statutes, Merriman found a forgotten law supporting his right to waive the requirements. (The law was subsequently changed, but Merriman had defeated the educational system.) Later, in an editorial he denounced compulsory ROTC as incompatible with American democracy, much to the surprise of the military staff, which regarded him as a superior officer, and to the consternation of the president, who made a public speech about "rabble-rousers" on campus but apparently feared to use Merriman's name. Yet on graduation day of 1932, the campus radical married Marion Stone, a sorority queen and drum majorette, and took a job in the corset department of a local department store.

In the fall Merriman found a post as assistant instructor of economics at the University of California. Conditions were so bad in the country that he had to support his wife's parents. All of them lived in a single room of a Berkeley lodging house. He moonlighted as a body polisher at a Ford assembly plant, where he helped publish an illicit union-shop newspaper. When the plant went out on strike and the Cal football team was recruited as strikebreakers, Merriman led demonstrations demanding that they return to the gridiron where they belonged. In 1934 he won a Newton Booth Travelling Fellowship for his research project dealing with collective farming in the Soviet Union. When the Spanish War broke out, he and his wife (*sans* inlaws) were in Russia, where he was completing a thesis at the Moscow Institute of Economics.[6] He said that he decided to go to Spain

---

[6] Some volunteers who knew Merriman well insist that the collective-farming story was a cover for his real activities—studies at the Lenin Institute for a major post in the CPUSA. Others steadfastly claim that Merriman was apolitical, not a member of the Communist Party, but this seems difficult to accept. That he kept clear of party meetings in the Lincoln Battalion might well have been in accordance with a preconceived plan to mask his political identity.

only after he had been reproached for the absence of Americans in the International Brigades and that he had not heard of the existence of the Lincoln Battalion until he arrived at Valencia by Soviet freighter in mid-January. His wife followed him a short time later.

It is not known what, if any, connection Merriman had with the Comintern. In the Soviet Union the *Yezhovshchina,* purges that would ultimately sweep away three-quarters of the Central Committee, were getting under way, and it is likely that the André Marty faction at Albacete, never entirely certain who or what stood behind Merriman, accorded him kid-glove treatment. In any event, they saw immediately that he was the ideal successor to James Harris. The problem was how to remove Harris without arousing the ire of his followers and adding thereby to the divisiveness already existing in the battalion. For the moment, Merriman was installed as battalion adjutant on the basis of his "experience" in the ROTC, an appointment that did not upset the delicate ecological balance existing at Villanueva de la Jara. (Merriman later told Sandor Voros of the IB Historical Section that his instructions were "to beef up" Harris.[7])

The American volunteers received Robert Merriman with mixed feelings. The intellectuals and student revolutionaries regarded him as one of "their kind"—an efficient (but not ruthless) college man with military training to boot. Yet many of the seamen and old-timers thought they saw ambition written all over him and guessed that the days of Jim Harris were numbered. "At first I liked his big, open smile," remembers one of these, "until I noticed that he never *stopped* smiling." With steel-rimmed spectacles drooping down his well-chiseled nose, Merriman suggested a young professor as interpreted by Hollywood. But when he began to move, he moved fast. First, he took over Harris' lectures on tactics. Next he relieved him of drafting daily orders—for Harris wrote as badly as he spoke. Then came frequent trips to Albacete, ostensibly to obtain promised equipment and to confer with the Base powers—all of these duties performed tactfully with the object of "saving" Harris. No one ever recalled a trace of friction between the commander and his adjutant, but some men did observe that Commissar Stember began to bypass

---

[7] In his book *American Commissar* Voros, a CP defector, often harshly criticized the Lincoln Battalion leadership. However, Merriman charmed him so absolutely that he accepted as gospel everything Merriman told him about the early days of the battalion. Ironically, those "stalwarts" who dismiss Voros as a self-apologetic liar nonetheless use his account of the Merriman epoch without questioning a word.

Harris for a direct hookup with Merriman. Imperceptibly Robert Merriman took over control of the Lincoln Battalion, proving that Horatio Alger and Karl Marx were not strange bedfellows, after all.

Yet most men did agree that after the arrival of Merriman, there seemed to be more zip in the drilling, gunnery, and lectures. Because live ammunition was required at the front, there was seldom opportunity for target practice. The few Steyr and Ross rifles on hand tended to jam after each shot, and the bolts often had to be knocked open with a rock. (No individual rifles had yet been issued to the men.) A few defused Mills-bombs were passed around to give the men a sense of their heft. Trench mortars were nonexistent, although a few tired Maxim water-cooled machine guns arrived. To simulate the sound of gunfire, Merriman ran a stick across wooden slats, in the manner of a boy rattling a paling fence. Attacking across open terrain, the Americans always tended to bunch together rather than to disperse. Parade-ground maneuvers remained beyond—or beneath—the capacity of the Lincolns, who never learned to march in step like the German and Slavic volunteers.

One night Albacete was bombed by enemy aviation. The war was coming closer to the Lincoln Battalion. Maneuvers through the sunny hillsides around Villanueva de la Jara took on a more serious purpose. Motley groups in khaki ski-pants, carrying imaginary weapons, attacked imaginary enemies. On the skyline, solitary umbrella pines stuck up from the plain like green barrage balloons.

Early in February rumors reached Villanueva that the Nationalists had launched a new offensive against Madrid, slashing across the Jarama River east of the city in an effort to cut the Valencia road, the principal artery feeding the nearly surrounded former capital. Yet nothing was confirmed. Few newspapers ever reached Villanueva other than the French-Communist *L'Humanité,* which few Americans were able to translate. (Outdated copies of the *Daily Worker* arrived, from time to time; *The New York Times* was banned from Albacete, along with other "Fascist propaganda.") [8] Nevertheless it was impossible not to detect that something big was in the offing. Couriers hinted that Albacete and the ancillary training-villages of

---

[8] Purists at Albacete even objected to the *Daily Worker,* primarily because it sold advertising space to obviously capitalistic firms, restaurants, and such. Members of the Soviet Military Mission to Spain were warned that the *Daily Worker* was a bourgeois newspaper.

the Interbrigades were being sucked dry of able-bodied men. Three sister battalions of the XV Brigade—the Saklatvala (British), the Dimitrov (Yugoslav), and the Sixth of February (French) [9]—had vanished overnight from their camps. But the Lincolns received no word. They chafed with impatience: they had come to Spain to fight fascism, not to play war games in a time-forgotten pueblo.

On February 12 the Lincolns were alerted and ordered to prepare to move, not to the front but to a new training camp in the piny woods at Pozorubio, a few miles north of Albacete. They were furious, blaming their call-up delay on lingering anti-Americanism at the brigade base. At least one man in the battalion was relieved. Douglas Seacord knew they were too green to be committed to battle at that time. Normally sober and steady, he had recently been drinking so heavily that his runner, Bill Harvey, had been forced to cover for him. As a professional army man, Seacord doubtless guessed what lay ahead for the Lincoln Battalion when it went into action led by a former sergeant and a ROTC shavetail.

At that moment, the afternoon of February 12, one other American in Spain might have comprehended what was troubling Seacord. Joseph Selligman of Louisville, Kentucky, was with the British Battalion, which was trying to beat back an attack by Moors in the olive groves of Jarama. A few months previously, at a Swarthmore party, a classmate had toasted, "Here's to the good life," and Selligman had replied, "No, here's to life." But for Selligman there would be no good life, nor long. Before the sun set on his first day of battle, he was dead.[10]

[9] Saklatvala was the name of an Indian Communist, but the word was so difficult to pronounce and the allusion so obscure that they were always known as the British Battalion. Georgi Dimitrov was secretary of the Comintern. On February 6, 1934, French workers went into the streets of Paris to put down a public disturbance provoked by Rightists.

On the day the British Battalion departed for the front, its commander, Wilfred McCartney, was called for a brigade conference. While traveling to it with an unidentified commissar, he was "accidentally shot" and went to the hospital while Thomas Wintringham took over as commander. McCartney never rejoined his battalion.

[10] Selligman, nineteen years old, had reached the Spanish frontier in mid-December but was turned back by French border guards. Somehow he obtained the passport of one Frank Neary and got across. Wanting to be the first American to see action, he refused to be transferred into the Lincoln Battalion. The *Halcyon*, Swarthmore's yearbook, in print before news arrived of his death, reads: "A quiet, thoughtful, literary atmosphere allowing many hours of repose . . . would be Joe's ideal habitat."

3

ꗑ The Yanks Are Coming

I think Sherman said, "War is hell," but he
never had to stand up against the International
Brigades or else he'd have put it much stronger
than that.

—American volunteer (early phase)

In midmorning of February 15, 1937, a convoy of empty trucks,
no two exactly alike, rumbled into Villanueva de la Jara and parked
in the *plaza mayor*. The American volunteers drilling on the hillsides
immediately returned to town and were instructed to assemble their
field kits and to leave behind nonessentials. They began to suspect
that they were not going to Pozorubio. A kid from New York carried
along a sack of crucifixes that he had collected because he liked them.
And a Texan whom everybody called "Peanuts" grinned when he
showed his squad leader a knapsack crammed with goobers and
almonds. "Best nourishment in the world," he said. Women from the
village came out, tears in their eyes, to see them off. "I think they
were genuine tears," a seaman remembered, "even though they never
knew us really."

Trailed by a brand-new ambulance, the trucks drifted downhill
past the queer bangkok-spire of the parish church (the battalion garage and gasoline warehouse), crossed the ditch-sized Valdemembra
River, and turned south on the Albacete road. Because troop movements were supposed to be made at nighttime, they killed time. After
Madrigueras, a solitary gasoline pump along the highway with a dusty
village beyond, they passed through flat prairie country that suggested
to the midwesterners patches of Iowa or Illinois. The convoy contained approximately four hundred North Americans. The original
group had received less than five weeks of haphazard military train-

ing; the latest arrivals, a group from the Bronx Young Communist League, less than three days.

It was dark when the convoy parked in the arena of the Albacete bullring, the assembly point for all Internationals bound for the front. In the bandstand, floodlit by headlights of the trucks and surrounded by his entourage, stood André Marty. Shaking his fist, he explained that the Republican front along the Jarama River had caved in; once again the Internationals must save Madrid. The time had arrived for the Americans to show what they could do. *"No pasarán!"* Every American understood that much Spanish. *"No pasarán!"* they thundered back. Then Peter Kerrigan, British representative at the Base, delivered a short exhortation. British lads had engaged the Fascists and had passed the word among one another that "The Yanks Are Coming." His peroration annoyed some of the Americans: Kerrigan urged them to hurl back the "Boche" just as their fathers had done on the battlefields of France. Considering the thousands of Germans fighting in the International Brigades, the remark sounded jingoistic. Phil Bart made no speech because he was not in the bandstand. Perhaps he had not even been told that the Lincoln Battalion was moving up to the front.

In the chill February evening, they lined up before a supply truck and unloaded heavy coffin-shaped boxes. They broke them open and pulled out Remington-style rifles, each wrapped in Mexico City newspapers and oozing cosmoline. Having no solvent to clean them, they used rags, handkerchiefs, and shirttails. The rifles were all of a kind, except that some barrels were stamped with the Czarist spread-eagle, others with the Soviet hammer and sickle. The latter were several inches shorter and a few ounces lighter, but their bolts were apt to jam when the metal overheated. (Some rifles were stamped only with "Made in Connecticut.") Because of their reputed origin—made in the United States, sent to the Czar in 1914, copied and fabricated by Bolshevik artisans, sold to Mexico for revolutionary work, and donated to the Spanish Republic—they were christened *mexicanskis.*[1] Each man got 150 rounds of ammunition, all the Mills bombs he wanted, and a vicious-looking needle bayonet with a triangulated

---

[1] Folklore surrounding the rifles (Steyrs?) issued to the British was even more imaginative. They were said to have been made in Austria for export to Afghanistan in 1913, used by the Turks, captured by English, given to the King of Iraq, who sold them to gunrunners before the Italo-Ethiopian war, but when the Ethiopians refused to buy them, they were then sold to Spain.

blade that could stick a pig but not cut a throat. There was no time to test-fire the rifles, which in many cases lacked locking attachments for the bayonets. Each man received a metal helmet. Nine men out of ten got the French *poilu* style of the World War, nearly worthless objects that might have done for construction-workers but proved to be metallic eggshells when struck by steel or lead. A fortunate few got an ugly chamber-pot helmet manufactured in Czechoslovakia from a superb quality of steel.[2]

Orders came down from Colonel "Vidal" confirming James Harris as commander, Robert Merriman as battalion adjutant, and Sam Stember as commissar.[3] As captains, they were issued field glasses, sidearms, and cloth map-cases (without maps). First Company, which included the Irish and Cuban sections, was commanded by John Scott (*né* Inver Marlow), a volatile Englishman of the Byronic school who gave the impression of more acquaintance with the cigars of a West End club than the fog and clamor of a union hall. (The only known photograph of Scott shows a husky, curly-haired man in Bermuda shorts seated in front of a chessboard, about to be checkmated.) Yet Scott was devoutly committed to the working-class movement. Having been outraged by living conditions in China and India, he had joined the Communist Party and gone to New York as a book reviewer and columnist for the *Daily Worker*. He had slipped away from his desk without a word to anyone and joined the first seventy-six aboard the *Normandie*.

Second Company was allegedly commanded by Steve Daduk, who had been hanging around Albacete since late fall recuperating from a wound. He claimed to have been shot down over Madrid while flying for the Malraux International Squadron during the early months of the war. (On the other hand, some Americans recall his recounting stories of fighting in the Thaelmann Battalion.) He was a peppery

---

[2] Specimens of these two kinds of helmet, found in a dugout at Jarama, where they had lain side by side for thirty years, show the French ones pitted and corroded and the Czech ones, only thinly layered with rust, as sound as ever.

[3] Merriman told Voros a strange story about Harris' becoming "unnerved" in the bullring, where he "grabbed rifles out of the men's hands saying he was a rifle inspector" and had to be ordered away by Stember. Harris having disappeared, "Vidal" then placed Merriman in command of the battalion. No other source alludes to this altercation. Three men in that convoy with whom I have talked remember Harris in the bullring when they pulled out and in Chinchon when the trucks stopped. Probably Merriman wished to make more plausible his hypothesis that Harris was mentally ill.

redhead of five feet six who wore, instead of the regulation IB uniform, a blue *miliciano* boiler suit with a red bandanna around his neck. Originally he had been sent to Villanueva on a temporary basis to assist with the training program. Some volunteers opined that Daduk's autobiographical war-tales improved with each retelling. "A luster-bluster," recalls one of them.

Third Company, the backbone of the battalion, remained under Douglas Seacord, the most respected officer among the Americans. Though his gunners were intractable and independent, Seacord was never known to raise his voice or lose his temper. "We behaved like a bunch of Anarchists," one of the men says, "but we loved that man." This company received half a dozen water-cooled Maxims, guns so heavy that they rested upon wheeled carriages and were pulled about like toy cannon.

At midnight the battalion climbed aboard the trucks, which rolled out of the bullring and up the road to Madrid, 150 miles northwest. Of the approximately 450 British who had left Albacete seven nights before, less than a hundred remained in their shallow trenches under the olive trees of Jarama.

The night was bitter cold and moonless. Lacking space to sit down comfortably, they stood up, balancing one another as they whammed over potholes and cursing the drivers steadily. Before leaving Albacete they were warned that anyone showing a light would be shot, so drivers flashed on their headlights only when dimly sensing that a curve, or another truck, loomed ahead. Men reported that their greatest fear was that the trucks would overturn and they would be squashed by tons of machinery and comrades-in-arms. There were no bladder stops: the best one could do was to edge through the press to the tailgate and let go. Then it became nearly impossible to work back, for every man quickly learned that suffocation in the center was preferable to freezing on the edges. Many men later claimed that an airplane motor droned overhead throughout the night, but whether true, or collective hallucination, they never found out.

The first streaks of daylight found them blunted by exhaustion and numbed by a bone-deep cold at the village of Chinchon, which perched on a ridge overlooking a lush, green valley—the Tajuña. Beyond the valley floor rose another ridge, or smallish mountain, topped by a wide plateau dotted with olive trees. This plateau was the extreme southern flank of the Battle of Jarama, then being fought along a twelve-mile front. (The Jarama River was out of sight, beyond the far plateau.) Ten days before, the Nationalists had launched their offensive, which had as its objective the cutting of the Madrid-Valencia highway in order to starve Madrid into submission. The main thrust had been halted farther north, and now both armies snaked their lines southward, hoping to discover a soft sector for penetration. Since both were vastly overextended, the front was liquid. On the plateau across from the Americans, the enemy occupied most of the higher ground and had pressed the Republicans backward toward steep ravines that dropped down into the Tajuña Valley. If they broke through, they would be able to blanket the valley floor with dominating fire and push the Republican lines back to the Chinchon ridge.

The rumble of distant artillery reverberated across the valley as the men climbed down from their trucks with orders to test-fire their *mexicanskis*. They loaded their clips with five cartridges and gingerly opened fire upon the limestone walls of a cement quarry. Although still gummy with cosmoline, no rifles exploded. Because of their light weight, they kicked like mules and the shots tended to throw high. Though a few summer-camp campaigners of the National Guard complained that the butts were fashioned from wood too soft for hand-to-hand fighting, the Americans were pleased with their weapons and eager to use them. For the newest recruits, the target practice in the quarry outside Chinchon was the first time they had fired a rifle in their lives. Captain Harris told the company officers that they would move up to a third-reserve position in late afternoon. They were safe where they were, but could expect shelling or air attacks when they descended into the valley.

While the Lincolns catnapped in the olive groves near Chinchon, two trucks of the convoy, separated from the others, bumped along a country road far to the southwest. Since the drivers had not been provided with maps, much less briefed upon the status of the lines, they missed a turn somewhere and meandered into the Nationalist positions near Titulcia. The trucks contained about forty men, most of them so recently arrived at Villanueva de la Jara that the other Lincolns had not had time to learn their names or to remember their faces. They vanished as completely as though they had never existed. Doubtless at some point they were stopped by surprised Moorish sentries scouting the extreme south flank of the Nationalist Army. Perhaps there was a brief exchange of queries as each group tried to

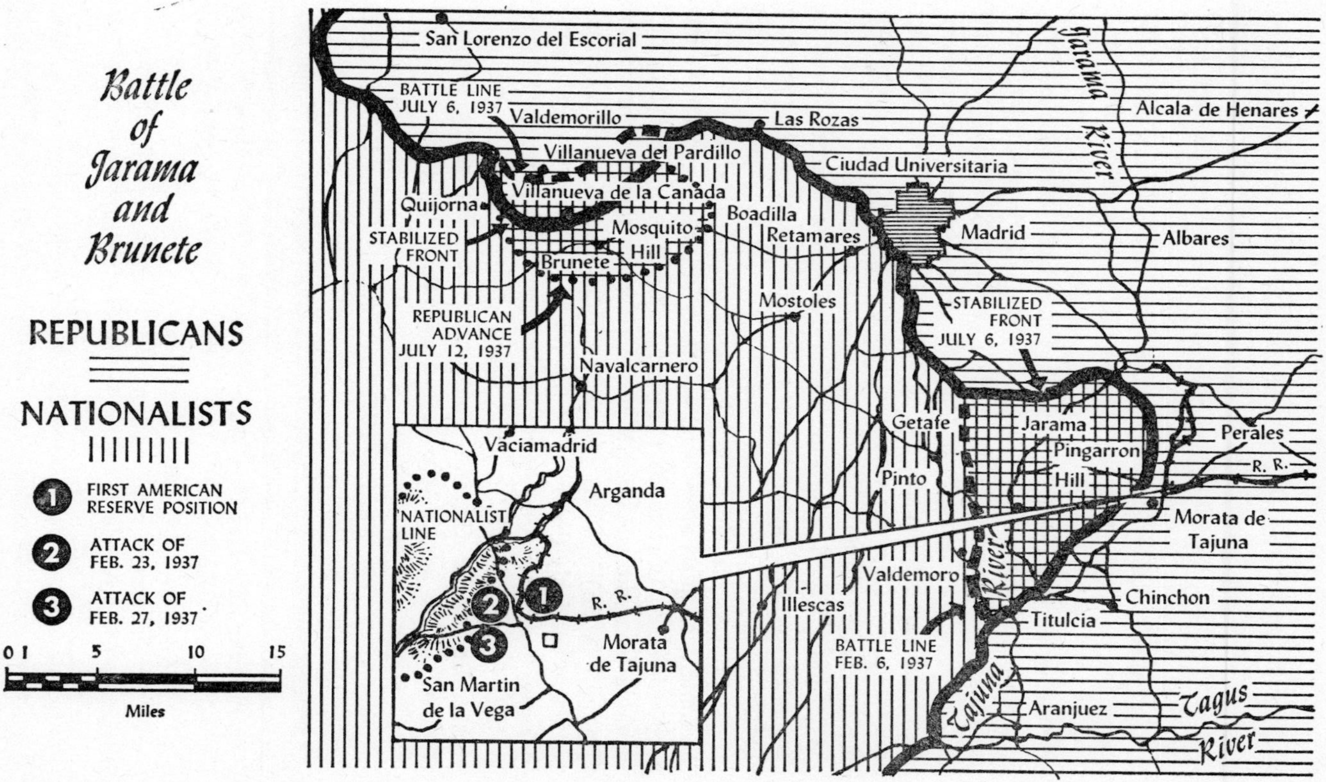

Battle of Jarama and Brunete
REPUBLICANS
NATIONALISTS
1 FIRST AMERICAN RESERVE POSITION
2 ATTACK OF FEB. 23, 1937
3 ATTACK OF FEB. 27, 1937
0 1 5 10 15
Miles
San Lorenzo del Escorial
BATTLE LINE JULY 6, 1937
Valdemorillo
Las Rozas
Villanueva del Pardillo
Ciudad Universitaria
Villanueva de la Canada
Quijorna
Boadilla
STABILIZED FRONT
Mosquito Hill
Retamares
Madrid
Brunete
REPUBLICAN ADVANCE JULY 12, 1937
Mostoles
STABILIZED FRONT JULY 6, 1937
Navalcarnero
Jarama River
Alcala de Henares
Albares
Vaciamadrid
Arganda
NATIONALIST LINE
R. R.
Morata de Tajuna
San Martin de la Vega
Getafe
Jarama
Pingarron Hill
Perales
Pinto
Valdemoro
Illescas
BATTLE LINE FEB. 6, 1937
Chinchon
Titulcia
Aranjuez
Tajuna River
Tagus River

identify the other in the half-light of morning, followed by increasing numbers of Moors jumping catlike from rock outcroppings—ever surrounding the trucks and grinning, as though in welcome, at their good luck in taking alive, quite by accident, such a large number of the hated Internationals. And we can guess that on the trucks the Americans, suddenly wide awake, tentatively groped for rifles that they had never fired, even as dry throats and thumping heartbeats told them that it was too late for guns, too late for innocence. It is unlikely that any of these forty-odd Americans had the satisfaction of firing a shot, or even raising his voice, in anger. Since none of them turned up on prisoner-of-war lists, they must have been executed, after some cat-and-mouse ritual that the Moors practiced with barbaric delicacy. Their three-thousand-mile pilgrimage to destroy fascism terminated abruptly with a bang and a whimper.[4]

Oblivious of the fate of the missing trucks, the Lincoln Battalion descended into the Tajuña Valley in late afternoon. Overturned and charred vehicles littered the ditches, but in the fields peasants thrashed olive trees with long poles, harvesting the fruit and ignoring the convoy, to them mechanical nuisances interrupting the more important business of producing food and oil. No sooner had they dismounted from the trucks in Morata de Tajuña than a squadron of Caproni (Italian) bombers emerged over the western ridge. They appeared so suddenly that most of the Americans stood frozen on the highway, looking up slack-jawed, as the first bombs screamed down. Wide of their mark, the bombs exploded in an olive grove outside the village. Before the Capronis could return for a strafing run, six *"Chatos"* (Snub noses)—the souped-up Russian version of a Boeing P-26—pounced upon them and dispersed the formation. Two Capronis erupted into brilliant celluloid flames and drifted down, trailing greasy black smoke. As they exploded dully behind distant hills, Americans joined other Republican soldiers in cheering and pummeling each other, shouting *"Nuestros!"* (Ours!). Two German Interbrigaders congratulated the Americans who had remained on the road for their *sangfroid*. One Lincoln began firing his rifle at the empty sky. Their initiation into battle was glorious.

Morata, the major road-junction of the sector, resembled a Hollywood set for a World War movie. Beside the field kitchen in the

---

[4] Because the battalion records were alleged to have been carried in these captured trucks, it was never possible to identify, much less commemorate, the missing men.

bombed *plaza mayor* a disabled Russian tank squatted heavily like a prehistoric toad. There were houses without walls (revealing interior rooms in the manner of dollhouses), houses without roofs, and in a few places nearly intact roofs without houses. The stork nest on the gable of the town hall had not been disturbed, but the storks were gone. Morata was the hub for operations on the plateau. Seven miles north lay Arganda, the original objective of the enemy offensive; five miles east lay Perales de Tajuña, headquarters of the Russian tank battalion (close enough to lend support but far enough away to insure that their valuable, experimental vehicles would not be captured, if the front collapsed). The western road wound up to the plateau, two miles distant, where the battle raged. Time and history would prove that the front existing at that moment was fixed until the end of the war and that the Battle of Jarama was in its last phase, but neither Nationalists nor Republicans were yet prepared to acknowledge this as they battered and probed one another, always hopeful of a significant "breakthrough."

Guided by an impassive German Interbrigader, the Lincolns filed on foot up the dark mountain starkly silhouetted against a blood red sunset that made the entire western horizon appear to be on fire. Yet the view back into the valley was incongruously pastoral with its whitewashed farms and mills, white-blossomed pear trees, and river marked by a line of feathery poplars. A line of Russian tanks clanked down the macadam road like threshing machines headed for home after a workday in the fields. Oil-smeared heads peered at them from open hatches. "These were the only Red Army men I ever saw in Spain," recalled an American. The noise made by the tanks drew a sporadic shelling of the road. Everyone looked for cover, but the German grinned and said, *"Das ist der wein. Das fleisch kommt noch."* It was completely dark when he led them up a mule path crossing a railroad track and then over loose stones and briers to a flat-topped knoll. They had no idea where they were and could see nothing. The German explained that the enemy held a ridge on higher ground, a mile or so west. Advising them to dig in, he vanished. A few machine-gun bullets crackled overhead.

"Dig in!" commanded the Lincoln officers. Nobody had remembered to bring up picks and shovels. Cursing Stember, they dropped on their knees and stabbed the rocky ground with bayonets and shoveled dirt with their helmets and bare hands. Water froze on these hills at night; digging kept them warm. By daybreak they had scratched out a wobbly circle of trench, deep enough to lie in but too shallow for standing, along the top of their knoll.[5] Drenched in sweat, they rolled up in blankets and awaited enough light to see the battlefield and to position themselves in it.

The first objects to materialize were a row of apple trees bordering the mine railroad that looped around their knoll on three sides. To the west rose a much higher ridge, structured like an ocean swell, irregular and buckled. Enemy trenches and outposts were hidden among a thick stand of olive trees, a thousand yards off. The road from Morata to San Martin de la Vega twisted between folds of hills directly in front and led upward into enemy territory. On their left, the Lincolns had a bird's-eye view of the Tajuña Valley. Mules with food and ammunition were being coaxed up trails to the plateau. Snuggled in a verdant hollow below them was a whitewashed country inn, taken over as the XV Brigade cookhouse.

Their first mistake, digging trenches on a skyline, was immediately exploited by the enemy spotters. At six o'clock a few shells lumbered overhead and exploded harmlessly beyond them. An American voice called out, "What the hell are they trying to do—kill us?" But jokes vanished when subsequent explosions crept gradually up the hillside toward their position. Grabbing bayonets and helmets, they frantically dug deeper. A line of machine-gun tracers now drifted toward them from the western ridge, the bullets cracking overhead like clapping hands. A young man named Charles Edwards was given a pair of binoculars and told to locate the machine gun, but he was pestered by other men begging to look through his glasses. "Keep your heads down," Edwards snapped. "There's a sniper up there." "What about you?" "F . . k you! I'm an observer," replied Edwards. The next moment a bullet smashed his head, killing him instantly. Shells exploded about their hilltop. A voice shouted through the dust, "Don't worry, Comrades! They're only 75s!" A piece of shrapnel sliced through the head of Misak Chelebian, a New York Armenian. He died without a groan. Few knew him well. He was the oldest man in the battalion, spoke nearly unintelligible English, and had recently lost his wife. These two deaths put an end to spectatorial curiosity about the battle.

---

[5] These trenches still remain on the hilltop. The circular arrangement seems to suggest that they conceived modern battle to be fought in the manner of pioneers beating off Indian attacks from their wagon train. What is more likely, however, is that in the darkness they were not certain where the enemy was and therefore dug a circular trench to protect all flanks.

Stember managed to get up thirty-five picks and shovels, which they employed while lying on their bellies.

Douglas Seacord was cursing mad. They had been assigned a position overlooked by the enemy and had dug in against the skyline. Furthermore, Oliver Law, a latecomer to his company, had been appointed his adjutant, a promotion passing over half a dozen abler men. Law was a sulky Chicago Negro, born in Texas, who claimed to have been a sergeant in the American Army. No sooner had the artillery barrage stopped than a flight of Capronis came over, flying so low that the Lincolns could see their bomb bays opening. Above them was the glint of objects dropping down. Law shouted, "It's all right! They're dropping leaflets!" Seacord shouted back, "Not leaflets—bombs! Hang on!" As they gazed up in horror, the bombs wobbled down, seemed to bore in on a horizontal plane, screeched over their heads, and exploded well beyond them. Before the Capronis returned, a Cuban section-leader ran amuck: whipping out his pistol he ran up and down the trench lip shouting, "I'll kill the first man who moves!" Before he could precipitate a panic, he was tackled and beaten to the ground. The bombers returned and missed again.

By nightfall two Americans had shot toes off to be evacuated, one man had deserted,[6] and a half dozen others were lightly wounded. They named their summit Suicide Hill.[7] Here they remained for four days subjected to light barrage and sniper fire but sustaining no further fatalities.

During the night of February 19 or 20 there occurred the controversial "Moonlight March" of the Lincoln Battalion, an episode that has raised more questions, with the passage of time, than it has provided answers. The unvarnished, raw facts are these. On his own authority, Captain Harris assembled the battalion behind Suicide Hill and led them on a march toward the enemy lines. After wandering

---

[6] A. R. reached the U.S. consulate at Valencia on February 23 and applied for sanctuary against arrest and for assistance in returning home. This was denied, although he was sheltered at the consulate on a temporary basis for several days. Early in March he left his uniform at the consulate and attempted to reach Barcelona dressed as a civilian. Whether he escaped Spain is not known. His uniform was returned to Washington as formal evidence to show that Americans were serving with a foreign power.

[7] Coincidentally, the British Battalion dubbed their first position at Jarama Suicide Hill, though with greater justification. It had been attacked and seized by Moors after a fierce fire-fight that accounted for many English and enemy dead. This Suicide Hill was located on the plateau, about a mile west of the American position.

about for a short time, they returned to their point of origin. That same evening Merriman replaced Harris. (Three months later, two Lincolns met Harris on the streets of Murcia, the site of an Interbrigade hospital in southern Spain. He talked gibberish.) No one ever learned what happened to him.

The pro-Merriman faction embellishes the story with lively details. Merriman was at brigade headquarters when Harris, absent since the convoy left Albacete, "appeared on the scene from nowhere" and told the men that he was moving them to a new position. He led them two kilometers northwest into no man's land. Harassed by enemy machine guns, they wandered about in great confusion, though they lost only one man. When Stember and others asked where they were going, Harris replied, "Follow the North Star." (Another version reports that he became delirious and told the men that he had seen "fifty thousand Fascists ready to attack.") About this time Merriman caught up with the column, ordered them to return, and had Harris removed in an ambulance. The pro-Merrimans claimed that Harris was either shell-shocked or mentally deranged.[8]

The anti-Merriman faction pooh-pooh this interpretation. They point out that the "Moonlight March" was a culmination of night maneuvers, which Harris had instituted at Villanueva de la Jara. Had he not repeatedly said that frontal attacks against an entrenched enemy were invitations to suicide and that soldiers accustomed to movements in darkness, like Chinese Communist guerrillas, had overthrown the trench-warfare tactics of the World War? The march encountered no enemy fire, and the force was recalled after it had proceeded less than three hundred yards. Moreover, Merriman himself accompanied them (and later informed brigade of the unauthorized movement). The incident, as they interpret it, provided brigade with a long-awaited opportunity to install Merriman as commander without raising mutinous outcries from followers of Harris. Later, a rumor scurried underground among the Lincoln Battalion that James Harris had been killed while fighting in the Dombrowsky (Polish) Battalion. Whatever the truth really was, Robert Merriman was indisputably commander of the Lincoln Battalion.

[8] The three major sources for Harris-insanity theory were not entirely disinterested parties: 1) Robert Thompson, in later years General Secretary of the CPUSA, who did not even arrive at Jarama until February 23; 2) William Wheeler, a New York teamster, who was later Merriman's closest personal friend at La Pasionaria Hospital in Murcia; and 3) Merriman himself, who passed on his interpretation to Sandor Voros in July, 1937.

Because the machine guns of the Lincoln Battalion were not needed in their third-reserve position on Suicide Hill, brigade loaned some of the guns and crews to the Sixth of February Battalion, which held a vulnerable section of the front lines south of the San Martin road. Seacord welcomed this chance to test his Maxims. Among the squads he assigned to this duty were those of Joe Gordon and Bill Harvey. Before they left, he gave Harvey an immense automatic pistol. Harvey was delighted until he discovered it had a broken hammer. "Wear it," said Seacord laughingly, "it'll look good on your hip." The crews moved out on the night of February 21, set up their guns behind terrace walls overlooking a deep ravine, and were told to expect an attack in the morning. These squads were the first units of the Lincoln Battalion to be employed in the Spanish Civil War.[9]

The sun was already high when the Mooneys heard weird wailing and singing coming from behind the opposite hill. Captain Van der Berghe, the Belgian commander of the Sixth of February, passed down the word to receive an attack. As though ordered to fix bayonets, the Franco-Belge pulled out and lit foul-smelling cigars, which the Americans interpreted as a phony gesture of Gallic nonchalance performed for their benefit. Captain Van der Berghe commanded them not to fire until ordered. Suddenly, like an awesome rush of stampeded cattle, a Moorish *tabor* burst over the far crest and sprinted down the slope. Their turbans, faces, and tunics were the color of dirt. Without pausing to fire, they plunged straight down, their cloaks winged out behind them. Squatting on his hams and smoking a stogy, Van der Berghe watched them with the calm absorption of someone who had paid good money for a ringside seat and was determined to see how the spectacle turned out. Everyone else fidgeted. The running figures had nearly reached the trough between the two hills when Van der Berghe sprang to his feet and shouted something. As though a switch had been pulled, the Franco-Belge let loose a stunning volley. The Moors out in front looked as though they had tripped over a wire. Harvey pulled the trigger of his Maxim. It fired one shot and jammed: "It curled up like a one-shot penis." The Moors reached the

---

[9] Harvey's squad consisted of the following men: Kavorkian, Shimrak, Cuban, Tsermanges, Manendidis, Skepastiotis, Wagulevich, and Tannenhaus. Ethnically it was typical of others in the Lincoln Battalion at this time— Americans, to be sure, but a far cry from the "old American stock" that recruiters and fund raisers in the United States alluded to when they discussed the national origins of Americans fighting in Spain.

bottom and surged up. Then the Americans learned why the Franco-Belge were smoking cigars. They picked up sticks of dynamite, fused them with the cigars, and flung them down the slope. Within ten minutes it was all over, except for sniping at Moorish bodies that still writhed or moved.

The experience of Bill Harvey with his machine gun had been duplicated by the other Maxim squads. Their guns were worthless rejects purchased from armory bone-yards, and most of them had to be sent to the rear for reconditioning. One or two squad leaders begged for permission to dismantle and reassemble them for another try, but most of the Mooney Company weapons were taken from them.

Meanwhile, on Washington's Birthday, the Lincoln Battalion moved from Suicide Hill to front-line trenches. The Republican command had resolved to pinch the enemy lines at half a dozen places simultaneously to find a soft spot, and the Lincolns were to deliver a frontal attack in the sector just north of the San Martin road. For five days they had peered at the olive groves on the upper plateau, hoping in vain to catch a glimpse of invisible snipers hidden by trees so far away that they resembled silver-green puffs and not trees at all. They moved up at night, in single file, into sandbagged trenches on the plateau. It was an eerie place. Shells had split open trees and created nightmarish shapes. Yet some trees were unscathed, their limbs thickly festooned with black olives, which rained down whenever a burst of machine-gun fire whipped the grove. Gusts of wind swaying the trees set off nervous rifle-fire from sentries convinced that they had detected Moors flitting through the grove. From higher ground the enemy occasionally sprayed the battalion trenches, which were much too shallow, with a withering fire. Sick and tired of crouching, crawling, and stooping like infants or old men, the Lincolns yearned to cross this last four-hundred-yard gap and meet the Fascists in a head-on fair fight.

In the morning of February 23, Merriman went over the attack plan with his company commanders and section leaders. An hour prior to sunset, Russian tanks were to push through the grove to the enemy trenches. While these knocked out strongpoints already charted by observers, the Lincolns were to seize the trenches, from which a harrowing fire could be laid down against enemy positions south of the San Martin road. Four hundred yards was no distance at all: a man in good shape ought to be able to cover it in a few minutes. Merriman hoped that the Mooney guns would come up during

the day: if they did not, the company would go over as riflemen.
Baskets of Mills bombs arrived. No one knew whether a stray bullet
could detonate them, so to be on the safe side they dug deep holes
for the baskets. Because of "complications from an old wound" Steve
Daduk had returned to Albacete,[10] and Eugene Morse, one-time
New York cabdriver, took over Second Company.

Time passed slowly, yet somehow too fast. In their trenches the
men fitted, unfitted, and refitted their bayonets. Out of earshot, Merriman and Seacord stood together, apparently arguing. Merriman was
listening with professorial tolerance, from time to time wiping his
glasses, while Seacord was leaning forward, his body tight and his face
angry. It made the men uncomfortable to see this quarrel—but probably not as uncomfortable as they would have been if they had known
what it was about. At such times it was better to listen to the Battalion Falstaff, Paul Burns, a pudgy labor writer from Boston. "Thun-
dercap" Burns was proud of his Vandyke beard, and he enjoyed mis-
quoting poets. "A tree that may in summer wear," he would begin,
intoning like W. C. Fields, "a nest of Maxims in her hair." Over on
the left Bill Harvey debated with himself where to set up his useless
machine, hoping that he could get it to work. As he stepped into the
open, a sniper bullet felled him like a punch, lodging in his neck, next
to his spine. He was paralyzed. They pulled him to safety, and in a
barely audible whisper he said, "Long . . . live . . . third . . .
International." Someone said, "Poor Bill. He's dead." (He was not,
but he never fought again.)

Exactly on schedule two Soviet fifteen-ton tanks clanked up the
San Martin road just before sundown and spun into the grove in front
of the Lincoln trenches. Their 45-mm cannon and Dichterev machine
guns hammered the enemy parapets. The Lincolns went over not as a
collective wave but by sections, the Cubans and Irish out in front.
Cursing and yelling, the others climbed out of their trench and advanced into the grove. Kneeling from time to time to fire a round at
distant piles of red dirt marking the enemy trench, the Americans
abandoned half-learned squad maneuvers in favor of an indigenous instinct to fight from tree to tree. It was easier than anyone had imagined, for the enemy was at the moment too busy fighting off the tanks

---

[10] Within six weeks, Daduk's wounds had improved sufficiently to allow
him to participate in coast-to-coast fund drives back in the United States.
Some men have no recollection of having seen him after the Albacete bullring.

to bother with clusters of unarmored humanity seeping through the grove. But there was too much sidewinding, bunching, and backtracking. The Lincolns pecked at, but did not threaten, the enemy.

All at once everything seemed to go wrong. There was an explosion, and a geyser of liquid fire shot up as one of the tanks burst into flames. The grove was suddenly illuminated by a garish light, dazzling to the oncoming men. While the sister tank scuttled back to the safety of the road, the Lincolns swept around the burning vehicle. They must have been perfect targets: those behind the bonfire were floodlit, those ahead were silhouetted. As bullets lashed the grove, numbers of attackers took refuge behind trees. Those in the lead learned with dismay that the olive grove ended. Ahead of them, sloping slightly upward lay a vineyard, naked and open, perhaps two hundred yards wide. No cover existed in that wide emptiness except gnarled vines protruding from the ground like hundreds of agonized, arthritic hands. Small groups gamely started across.

A few feet out, Lieutenant John Scott tried to rally his company after its momentum had stopped. He shouted, "Continue the advance," and fell with three slugs in his body. Still alive, Scott passed on his command to William Henry, a Dubliner, who lay down beside him and began scooping dirt in front of Scott's head with the illusion that it would provide protection. Other men trapped in the vineyard dug in with helmets, bayonets, rifle clips, and bare hands, trying to scratch a hole to salvation. Fascist gunners raked the vineyard, concentrating their fire on those places where they heard stricken cries, "First aid!" and "Stretcher-bearer!" Men pinned down in the open learned not to fire back, for the tiny spurt of flame from their rifle muzzle attracted a massive counterfire. The attack fizzled out. The major contribution of Captain Merriman to this skirmish was sending forward the Tom Mooney Company with picks and shovels to dig a trench in no man's land.

One of these sappers, Joe Gordon, found Scott lying on his belly where he had fallen in the vineyard. No one had attempted to evacuate him. Gordon promised to get help. "Don't do it, it's a waste of time," Scott said weakly. "What the hell do you mean, waste of time?" barked Gordon, squeezing his hand. "You're a human being, ain't you, and besides you're Captain [sic] Scott, see, and besides Joe Strysand will never talk to you again if you died." Scott managed a weak smile: Strysand was his runner and closest friend. Gordon crawled over to the road, which the Nationalists sprayed periodically with machine-gun bursts, and sprinted back to the first-aid station. "Captain Scott's wounded. He's dying! Where's a stretcher? Hurry up!" he shouted. The medics were French and Dutch who understood no English; besides, Gordon spoke in a wet lisp that few of his best friends readily understood. He tried the sign language and his twelve words of Spanish, all of which made the medics nervous. They thought he had gone crazy. Minutes later an interpreter came in and wrung Gordon's story from him. They collected two first-aid men and filed up the road to retrieve Lieutenant Scott.

Because their stretcher was gleaming white, they attracted fire as they moved across the vineyard. One medic dug into the ground and refused to proceed until the interpreter pulled out a pistol and threatened to shoot him on the spot. Scott was groaning slightly when they pulled him onto the stretcher. "He couldn't groan any harder if he wanted to, he was so weak." Paul Burns and a volunteer named Shapiro helped to carry him to the road, but as they climbed down an embankment a burst of machine-gun fire wounded everyone except Gordon, who again had to return to the rear for help. "What a hell of a situation," he said afterward. "You go after one wounded man and now look at the mess!" At the first-aid station he begged help from Cooperman, the battalion secretary, who relayed him to battalion headquarters, where Merriman sent him back to Cooperman.

Failing to find an ambulance driver willing to drive up the road, Gordon collected four Lincolns and set out again. Halfway up they found Burns and a Cuban dragging Scott in, a yard at a time. When they carried Scott to the station, he was still breathing. Going back to retrieve the others, Ralph Greenleaf was killed instantly when a bullet penetrated his helmet as easily as if it had been made of cardboard. Farther on, they found Shapiro, whose loud groaning attracted enemy fire as they carried him back down the road. He had a smashed ankle and his foot wobbled like a pendulum. "What a night! Killing can be a pleasure compared with the saving of a life," said Gordon. But everyone was sure that Scott would live: Joe Strysand threw his arms around Gordon's neck and kissed him.

Bloody and exhausted, Gordon staggered over to the American trenches. Too punch-drunk to see, he tripped over something soft. The object moved, and a white face peered up and asked, in a frightened voice, "What's up?" Gordon was too disgusted to kick or curse.

This shirker had lain there all night with a woolen blanket pulled up over his head. A short time later, word came down that Lieutenant Scott had bled to death.

It was nearly midnight before the Americans were recalled to their trenches. By this time the grove was so quiet that the men were able to walk back upright without a single bullet being fired at them. Many of them never received the order to retire and found themselves at dawn alone on the battlefield with the rest of the battalion a quarter-mile to the rear. Although individual volunteers combed the grove looking for particular missing comrades, there was little systematic effort to recover the wounded. Almost all cohesiveness and organization had utterly broken down. Ignoring regulations, commands, and threats, the men broke up ammunition boxes and built fires in the trenches to brew helmetfuls of G. Washington coffee. It was an unusual squad that posted a sentry. "If the Fascists had counterattacked," confessed a sectionleader, "they'd have walked right through us."

By daylight most of the cries and groans from the battle ground had ceased: there was nothing out there but scattered lumps of dead. Stronger than pity was the secret thought—"better him than me." Enemy snipers hammered at the American trenches. For the first time, the Lincolns were able to see the enemy, all of them Moors, who walked, not ran, across the unprotected gaps in their trench line. "Seeing them was like confronting an abstraction," said an American. Joe Gordon stood up to take a look and was hit by a bullet, which entered his left eye and came out behind his ear, but he walked under his own power to the dressing station. No food came up till midday, when stewpots of cold coffee and kettles of rice sludge were passed down the trench from man to man. Robert Taylor, a section leader from Boston, ladled out a cup of coffee and handed the pot to his WPA friend, Bob Norwood of Brewer, Maine. Norwood's head fleetingly passed in front of a loophole. A bullet whined through the opening, clubbing Norwood across the trench and splashing his brains into the pot. Taylor jumped back in horror, threw his cup away, and retched convulsively. This scene was nearly repeated in Marty Hourihan's section. A runner stood up to spoon rice into their messkits and was struck in the face by a sniper bullet. Blood spattered the trench wall and the hungry men. Looking down at his plate, one of them wailed, "The dirty son of a bitch! He got blood on my pudding!" But he scraped off the red part and devoured the rest.

News filtering into the line was bad. Eugene Morse, Second Company commander, was reported dead—a false alarm, as it proved. Rudolfo Armas, leader of the Cubans and anti-Batista revolutionary, was dead. Commissar Stember was said to be missing—but not in action. ("I swore that I'd kill the 'Comic-Star' when he came back," said a volunteer. "Unfortunately I didn't.") Casualties were estimated at twenty dead and forty wounded.[11] For what purpose? The men could not say. "Upstairs they called it a probe. To us it was a shaft," complained one. On the division or brigade level, sixty men amounted to nothing—it might even have sounded impressive to lose so many—but on their level, these sixty men were flesh and bone, known well enough to be admired or despised or loved. The world was not changed. That patch of vineyard laced with interlocking machine-gun fire was still there. They had met Fascist steel, and it had not bent like tin, as their song had promised.

The prevailing mood in the battalion was one of anger and frustration rather than of fear and dejection. The men built sniper boxes and fired at the Moors crossing the open spaces. (By the end of the day the Moors no longer walked across—they ran.) But the volunteers were haunted by a feeling, still very much undefined, that their first attack had failed because the leadership had not known, or had failed to explain, what was supposed to be accomplished. Perhaps more chilling than recollection of actual losses was the thought of what these might have been, had the battalion attacked in daylight and been pinned down, in plain view, between the lines. One thing they knew: to defeat fascism would take more time and be much more difficult than they had originally supposed. At Villanueva, Yale Stuart (né Skolnik), former lifeguard at Camp Unity, had fretted that the war might end before they got a crack at the Fascists. That no longer figured among the volunteers' present worries.

The skirmish of February 23 took the bloom off the rose. But the Lincoln Battalion was not demoralized. Not yet.

---

[11] This may be the only battle in the history of the Lincoln Battalion where the losses were overestimated. Brigade was very disappointed with the initial performance of the Americans, and it would be natural for Merriman to overcount his casualties in order to support his claim that the men had made a "supreme effort," etc.

4

ㅢ The Massacre

I tore his coat
It was easy—
Shrapnel had helped.
But he was dying
And the blanket sagged.
"God Bless you, Comrades.
He will thank you."
That was all.
No slogan,
No clenched fist
Except in pain.

—T. A. R. Hyndman
("Jarama Front")

The newly formed "B" Division, made up of the XI and XV (International) Brigades, was commanded by General "Gal" (often "Gall"), the most mysterious—and by far the most incompetent—of the International general officers in Spain. No one knew his given name, and "Gal" was, of course, a *nom de guerre*. He spoke German with a Slavic accent; he spoke Russian with a Teutonic accent. Apparently he thrived upon this aura of mystery concerning himself, encouraging it whenever he could. During the World War he had fought in the Austro-Hungarian Army until captured by Russians. Later he fought in the Red Army as a minor officer. Packed off to Spain, Gal had commanded the XV Brigade as a colonel during the opening days of the Jarama fighting. Now a divisional general, he possessed definite ideas of how generals should treat their inferiors, ideas based upon how, for the past twenty years, generals had treated *him*. He had a staff so slavish that any Balkan potentate might have envied him. It was not uncommon for Gal to receive minor functionaries while lying on a couch. (He was the sort of commander who would have left his desk for his cot seconds before a minion arrived to see him.) His staff saluted their general—and one another—incessantly, and they spoke only when their general spoke to them. (Gal forbade conversation at table: in the byways of Bukovina, or wherever he had come from, food was eaten, not talked over.) No doubt Gal had once had the compassionate heart and stubborn head of a Central-European peasant; but in his dizzy climb to exalted rank, the heart had been left somewhere behind. Gal was an unmagnetic, quick-stepping little man whose boots had the highest gloss ever found at Jarama. Probably the only first-rate thing about him was his tailor.[1]

His record at Jarama had been better than average. He had established a stable defensive line on the plateau, and several times he had rallied retreats by personal appearances among the men in the manner of old-style revolutionaries or minor Hellenic deities. But Gal was a foreigner in the Red Army during a period in Soviet history when outsiders were becoming increasingly unwelcome. Doubtless he reasoned that the Comintern would be more impressed by a stunning offensive, brilliantly conceived and executed, than by his defensive role, however vital this had been. Even though each side had thrown up a nearly invulnerable system of front-line and reserve trenches zig-zagging all the way from Arganda to Titulcia, General Gal pored over his charts and reports, searching for a magic key. Always he came back to Hill 693, called Pingarrón, the highest point in the plateau between the Jarama and Tajuña rivers. During the first days of the battle, a *tabor* of Moors had seized Pingarrón and fortified it. Gal desperately wanted it back, for he believed that by its recapture he could drive the enemy back across the Jarama. It mattered little to Gal that his division was plagued by desertions,[2] that he lacked ade-

---

[1] One ransacks the literature of the Spanish Civil War without finding any favorable treatment of General Gal. Even fellow commanders of the Inter-brigades seem to have repudiated, or despised, him. Herbert L. Matthews of *The New York Times,* experienced in evaluating the competence of Republican leaders, described Gal as "a Hungarian fighting for the Comintern rather than Spain." Ernest Hemingway, who had a good ear, claimed that conditions in Gal's sector were "deplorable," that "he should have been shot."

[2] By the end of February, 1937, the French consul at Valencia had supervised the evacuation of four hundred French deserters aboard French warships. The Spanish authorities made no attempt to impede this evacuation. However, when the French closed their frontier on March 3, the Republic seized sixty more deserters at Valencia and returned them to Albacete, arguing that since the French were permitting no International recruits to

quate artillery, tanks, and planes to support his attack properly, or
that the Nationalist offensive had already been stopped in its tracks.
For General Gal, Pingarrón had become, in Herbert L. Matthews'
phrase, "a fetish of position." He avowed that it must be taken "at all
costs" by an overwhelming surge of sheer manpower.

One rung below General Gal stood Lieutenant Colonel Vladimir
Copic, Yugoslavian commander of the XV Brigade. A thick-set man
of forty-six with sausage fingers and cleft chin, he exuded a grass-
roots charm whenever he inspected the line, festooned with a complex network of straps, belts, and other harness supporting map case,
pistol case, binocular case, and other implements of battle. Like Gal,
Copic had also been a conscript in the Austro-Hungarian Army, captured by the Russians, and "liberated" through loyal service in the
Red Army. After returning to Croatia after the war, he published a
radical newspaper and was sentenced to a three-year term for political conspiracy. Exiled from Yugoslavia, he lived in the Soviet Union
as one of a large group of unwanted foreigners who were dispatched
to Spain when the International Brigade was formed. It was understood that if a man proved his mettle, he might be allowed to reenter
the Soviet Union. Copic arrived at Albacete while Gal was organizing
the XV Brigade. Gal pulled him from the Dimitrovs and made him
brigade commissar. (The International Brigades were something of a
family affair for the Copics; his brother ran the Marty prison outside
Albacete for a long time.) Copic performed well as a commissar: he
understood political organizing, he had had experience writing propaganda, and he was an able psychologist. Indeed, he did so well that
after Gal went up to divisional commander, Copic succeeded him as
XV Brigade commander, a position far beyond his experience. Well
aware of his ignorance of military affairs, Copic became a yea-sayer
who realized that his sole pathway to personal salvation lay in unquestioning obedience to his superiors and in passing the buck when
conditions got out of hand. This man was destined to be the brigade
commander of the Americans for the next eighteen months—a man
whose most obvious talent was an uncanny ability in being lightly
wounded or absent whenever disaster struck.

As part of the Pingarrón offensive, the XV Brigade would create a
diversion by attacking the enemy lines along the San Martin road.
Since the Dimitrovs, the Sixth of February, and the British battalians

cross into Spain, they were no longer tolerating desertions from the International Brigades. Henceforth deserting was less common among Interbrigaders,
because they had no place to desert to.

had been nearly decimated by the fighting of the past two weeks, the Lincoln Battalion was assigned the main role in this diversionary move, while Gal's major attack developed at Pingarrón, a flattish summit two miles to the southwest. Gal and Copic let it be known that they were displeased with the Americans, in part because of their poor performance on February 23, and in part because, like the British, they tolerated debate and demanded explanations. General Gal had no intention of explaining anything to anyone—except, of course, to his own superior officers. And we may be reasonably certain that Copic, never inclined to deviationism of any sort, concurred in his general's plan of attack.

While General Gal and Colonel Copic powpowed in the valley, Captain Merriman labored to reorganize the Lincoln Battalion on the plateau. Desperate for someone with military experience to assist him, he pulled Seacord from the Tom Mooney Company and made him battalion adjutant. This helped him regain some support lost for his rear-guard part in the February 23 attack. Many men were muttering that Merriman was a coward, but they unanimously admired Seacord. Officers in the battalion were coming and going so quickly that the men began to lose track of them; to this day, for example, no one knows who filled the company-commander slots vacated by Scott, Morse, and Seacord.[3] It is not surprising. The three days that they had to prepare for a second attack were so frenzied and cluttered, and the attack itself so catastrophic, that recollections of any details beyond those of a man's own squad or section have been blotted out by time and by trauma. In effect, company apparatus all but disappeared: the Americans fragmented into small clans of armed men who began to suspect that mutinous rumblings among the French and English were not just complaints by "demoralized elements" and "Trotskyite wreckers." It was said that the French openly boasted about self-inflicted wounds that took them from the front.[4]

[3] It is very likely that William Henry of the Irish Section held on to First Company. The "official history" of the Lincoln Battalion puts Martin Hourihan at the head of Second Company, but Hourihan's own testimony denies that he commanded any unit higher than a section during the February 27 attack. Oliver Law may have taken over the Tom Mooney Company, although one veteran with an excellent memory categorically denies this, averring that Law had been demoted to the cookhouse.

[4] A Detroit volunteer says he saw a Frenchman stick his hand above a parapet and hold it there until a bullet penetrated the palm. Then he flourished it in the faces of his companions, who became so angry that they bayoneted him.

Meanwhile the Americans moved to trenches south of the San Martin road. The ground was uneven, and the Nationalist and Republican trenches writhed and bulged toward each other, following the contours of the land. Just ahead was a shell-wracked olive grove extending into no man's land perhaps fifty yards. Beyond it lay a forbidding hollow containing stunted vines that stretched two hundred yards across. On a far hillside, faintly visible through torn olive trees, was the enemy trench line. The British, who had once occupied this position, had vacated it eagerly, and the Americans soon discovered why. Not only was it raked by head-on fire from the opposing trenches, but also it was battered by angle fire from machine-gun nests on higher ground both to the south, toward Pingarrón, and to the north, beyond the San Martin road. Yet the British had been required only to hold it, not to press an attack from it.

On the day before the attack, about seventy new American faces arrived at the front, many of them still clad in the street clothes they had worn aboard ship. (The New York committee no longer provided volunteers with fifty dollars' worth of surplus uniforms.) Before they climbed up to the plateau from the cookhouse, a one-week veteran named Robert Gladnick gave them an hour's worth of rifle instruction. They received no other training at all. Some of the newcomers were seventeen years old. One of them was so green that he mistook a trench mortar for a stove pipe.

Unable to obtain maps for his officers, Merriman had pencil sketches drawn from the battalion chart, a cartographical wonder of such antiquity that elevations were marked not by contour lines but by brown hatching resembling millipedes. Yet this was vastly better than the Michelin road-maps used by many of the first Republican commanders at Jarama. Among the battalion issue there were so many different makes, models, and calibers of weapons that Merriman kept on his headquarters table a wooden plank with a specimen cartridge of every weapon taped to it. No more than four machine guns were "operational," which is to say that they functioned some of the time. But the terrain was very poor for placing the guns, cut up as it was by ravines behind the lines. Thus the Maxims were placed closely together on a battered hillock beside the road. These guns might be able to spray the enemy trenches in the manner of a fireman with a hose, but they would not be able to establish a cross fire or converge upon a single enemy point from two directions. To deliver the attack the Lincoln Battalion numbered about 450 men.

On February 26, Captain Merriman was called to the picturesque mill beside the Tajuña River, where Gal had installed his headquarters. Surrounded by charts, telephones, and Napoleonic protocol, the General explained the role of the Lincoln Battalion in the gathering battle. Precisely at 7:00 A.M. Republican aircraft were to bomb and strafe the enemy lines. This was to be followed by an artillery barrage. Finally a company of tanks would grind down the enemy barbed wire and clear a swath for the American attack. A Spanish brigade situated just north of the San Martin road would go over the top from its position a few hundred yards to the rear of the Lincoln Battalion—trenches occupied by the Americans when they delivered their February 23 attack. After the Spaniards had drawn up even with the Americans, Captain Merriman would lead his men swiftly ahead and seize the enemy trenches. Once this objective were attained, reinforcements could be hurled into the gaping salient. As a piece of paper work, Gal's war-college plan accounted for everything except the obvious: specific instructions on what to do if the promised airplanes, artillery, and tanks failed to materialize.

Dawn of February 27 revealed an overcast sky, with the low ceiling of imminent rain. The men breakfasted on three cups of tepid coffee each and a thick hunk of bread. Clamped on their heads were their brown French helmets with the cowlick crest. Fitted on their *mexicanskis* were the long needle bayonets, which, it was said, the Moors feared to see. It was a bronchitic day—damp and cold. Most of them wore greatcoats or sheep-lined jackets. The newest arrivals had strapped knapsacks and blanket rolls to their shoulders as though they planned to camp out in enemy trenches at sundown. Peering through firing apertures, they looked into a silent world, motionless except for wisps of fog drifting across no man's land. From time to time a machine gun clattered briefly, sounding a little like an outboard motor with a defective exhaust.

On a lee slope behind the lines, Captain Merriman briefed his officers. He spoke of discipline and timing, and as always, he spoke well. To the leader of the reconnaissance squad he said, "You go over last. Shoot anyone who fails to precede you." A few officers glanced briefly at one another, wiggled eyebrows, but made no comment. Absent from this group was Commissar Stember, who for the last few days had been preoccupied with morale-building tasks like bringing hot coffee up to the line. Then, as though he were playing the lead in

What Price Glory?, Merriman said, "We will now synchronize our watches." [5] A couple of men fumbled at their wrists; others pulled out dollar Ingersolls and began winding stems.

Zero hour came and went. Nothing happened. Merriman shook his watch, but there was still no sound of shell, tank, or plane. Half an hour later, sporadic rifle-fire broke out north of the road in the vicinity of the Spanish brigade scheduled to lead the attack. The Lincolns opened fire through their sandbagged apertures and drew upon themselves a devastating reply. Within minutes the enemy had obtained dominance of fire, and bullets were slashing open the Lincolns' sandbags. They huddled and waited. Time wore on and the mist burned off. A Republican battery fired a few salvos; some of the shells fell into the British lines farther south. They hoped this was the signal for a massive barrage, but the .75's abruptly ceased.

Captain Merriman called Colonel Copic to inquire whether air and tank support would be forthcoming and was told there would be a brief delay. The voice on the phone inquired whether he had laid down an aviation signal on the road. A what? Merriman said no one told him anything about an aviation signal. With rising impatience, the voice explained that a large white T must be laid down so that pilots would know where to unload their bombs. A simple task to perform at night, it was now extremely hazardous, for the road was under heavy fire. Dutifully Merriman assembled an assortment of underwear, shirts, and towels pinned together to form a T. The two men who "volunteered" to place it on the bullet-swept road were universal favorites, both of them battalion runners: Joe Strysand, a thirty-year-old organizer in the New York teachers' union,[6] and Bobby Pieck, once Phil Bart's assistant on the *Normandie*. They dashed out with their signal, which looked like laundry on a clothesline, and succeeded in placing it. Both were chopped down, blotting the cloth red. No one tried to retrieve the bodies, one of which smoldered from an incendiary slug. Apparently the signal underscored, for the enemy's benefit, that the main thrust would come up the San Martin road, for their fire intensified in this sector.

[5] The Spanish Civil War was the first major war in history in which the combatants adopted mannerisms and even a code of behavior from motion pictures. Literature of the war is packed with allusions to men undergoing moments of *déjà vu*, the source being "just like in the movies."

[6] An organizer in the teachers' union should not be confused with a teacher. By trade Strysand was an agent for theater tickets, bankrupted during the Depression. He graduated from the Hebrew Orphan Asylum of New York but never attended college.

A short time later, two fifteen-ton Soviet tanks climbed up from Morata, fired a few rounds from a road cut, and backed off. Encouraged by their appearance, the Spanish brigade north of the road climbed out of their trenches, advanced a few yards, and fell back virtually in rout. Were more tanks coming up, or were these two the extent of their armored "support"? No one knew. Just then Copic rang up the Lincoln headquarters. Why had not Merriman sent his men into the attack? The Spanish brigade, according to Copic, had already advanced seven hundred yards and were being cut to pieces because the Americans refused to move to their support. Merriman must have been astonished at this fantastic lie. He told Copic that the Spanish had already retreated to their original line.

"Don't contradict me!" bawled Copic. "Move your men out!" He gave the Lincoln Battalion ten minutes to come up with the position, on his headquarters chart, where the Spanish Brigade was supposed to be. Reluctant to expose his men without support, Merriman contested Copic's order, warning that the battalion would be wiped out.[7] Copic rang off angrily. He then dispatched two Britishers on his staff by motorcycle with instructions to remove Merriman from command if he refused to attack. Commissar D. F. Springhall and Lieutenant George Wattis raced up a mountain path and reached the communication trench just as three Republican planes dipped over the lines and dropped a light packet of bombs far beyond the enemy lines. According to one volunteer, they were not *"La Gloriosa,* but some sort of hangovers from Hell's Angels of the World War." (The planes came and went so rapidly that many Americans never saw them at all.) The Britishers learned that Merriman had already requested covering fire from the British Battalion on his left. The Tom Mooney machine guns fired a belt or so, then broke down. Enemy bullets were ricocheting off their armored shields with great slamming clangs.

Doubtless Springhall and Wattis were appalled by the prospect of attacking under such conditions, but they had no authority to call off the assault. Merriman met them with a grim smile. He was peeling off his field glasses and preparing to lead the attack in person. It is not known whether this heroic gesture was dictated to him by conscience or by Copic. Impressed by Merriman's example, the British staffers resolved to follow it. Even before the attack began, enemy bullets

---

[7] Some survivors claim that Merriman stalled Copic for over an hour; others, that he never questioned the attack order. It is likely that Merriman had enough moral courage to dispute an order but not enough to disobey one.

runner was laced from head to foot before he could rise to his feet, and seconds later he himself was struck unconscious by a mortar explosion that wrapped his helmet so tightly around his ears that it had to be hacksawed off.

Another man thinks he got fifty yards into the vineyard before he was hit. "I thought someone kicked me in the leg. Went down surprised and plenty sore. Got up again only to flop once more." He found some shelter and waited for a stretcher-bearer. None came. He lay there all day, received two more wounds, and crawled back at night. Elsewhere, men tumbled down convinced they had been hit only to find they had tripped over the claw-shaped vines reaching out of the ground.

To advance was as impossible as swimming up a waterfall. Those men farther back gathered some protection from olive trunks and opened fire against the enemy trenches. One rifleman found, however, that whenever he lowered his head to sight down the barrel, his hunching shoulder tipped the helmet over his eyes, spoiling the shot. Another heard a deafening explosion in his ear and found a comrade had used his shoulder as a rest for his rifle barrel. Lieutenant Wattis, upright and cool, paced the battlefield examining prostrate figures to make certain they were either dead or wounded, not shamming. Though a perfect target, he was not hit and never lost his *sangfroid* or his swagger stick. By this time none of the Maxims was operational.

Within ten minutes the attack had ceased. It had not been halted by official order; it had simply been crushingly stopped. Before being evacuated to a dressing station, Merriman passed on his command to Philip Cooperman, who repudiated it at once.[8] The weight of disaster was too heavy for his shoulders. The men out in front could advance or retreat, shoot or be shot. Cooperman wanted no part of it.

Meanwhile, the men out in no man's land were being exterminated. Those pinned down could not tell who was living or who was dead. As in a feverish dream, images were vivid yet cognition was elusive. One volunteer recalled a feeling as though he were play-acting: the director would soon say, "All right, let's try that scene again." Then on his left a man cried out, "Oh!," less in pain than in surprise. "Is that man hurt?" he heard himself ask. Back came an emotionless re-

---

[8] It is said that on his way down the mountain, Merriman insisted upon being carried to Copic's headquarters. Copic refused to talk with him, saying that Merriman was too weak to be permitted to speak.

ply, "He's dead." Out in front a body caught fire; the breeze brought a smell worse than that of burning hair.

Enemy snipers picked over the field. Trapped men lay as immobile as they could. One flicked up handfuls of dirt in front of his head, hoping to build a wall between himself and a bullet. Another recalled, "I had convulsions. My bowels let go. I was scared." The field seemed to be covered with men dead or dying. Dutch stretcher-bearers were shot down whenever they attempted to drag in the wounded. A single American is said to have reached the enemy wire, where he was gunned down and lay for days like a spattered statue with an unexploded grenade clutched in his rigid hand.

In the middle of the afternoon it began to rain. As visibility dropped, men ventured to crawl back and to pull in the nearer wounded. The narrow, shallow communication trench leading down to the dressing station became clogged with men bleeding, vomiting, coughing, and dying. Too exhausted to drag the dead from the passageway, the living ground them underfoot. Some of the badly wounded cases drowned in puddles of red mud and cold water forming in the bottom of the trench. There was no food, no medicine, no doctors. The ditch teemed with sobbing, broken creatures, shaking with cold, shock, rage, and fear. A youth wailed over and over, "They killed my buddy—they killed my buddy!" Coated with Jarama muck, the lucky ones leaned against the trench wall, gasping like exhausted swamp animals. The unlucky ones lay "with their curious ruffled look, like dead birds" among the vines and under the olive trees.

The light faded quickly, and the ditch blackened. The walking wounded continued to trickle to the rear, slithering down off the plateau in the darkness. There were not enough able men to move the stretcher cases. The best they could do was to crawl under blankets with them to give them some warmth and to shield them from the freezing rain. (Since no stretcher-bearers arrived until daylight most of the badly wounded died.)

At that moment the Lincoln Battalion consisted of eighty effectives. All the others were killed, wounded, or missing.[9] They had been in front-line positions less than six days.

---

[9] The Lincoln Battalion archives disappeared at the end of the war. Records were slipshod at best, and present statistics are only quasi-statistical. In mid-March, Herbert L. Matthews was told that 127 men were killed and 175 were wounded during the February 27 attack, figures subsequently canonized by

It was nearly daylight before gunnysacks of goat chops and demijohns of *coñac* came up to the trenches. A Hungarian captain took charge and ordered the Americans to clear their trenches of the dead.[10] Digging graves was out of the question. Instead, they dragged the torn bodies into a disused spur and pulled down rocks and earth on top of them to form a collective grave. Mutilated helmets were stacked on top of this limestone cairn. The bodies were neither counted nor identified, and the dead lying about no man's land were not retrieved. A Franco-Belge "labor battalion," consisting of Interbrigaders serving sentences for desertion and drunkenness, went out every night until March 10 and brought back cadavers; but many were never retrieved or buried. They lay scattered on the slope leading up to the Nationalist lines like flotsam stranded on an ebbing tide.

Shoveling and *coñac* converted the survivors from a leaden, lethargic mass into an angry, mutinous mob. As soon as Hungarian Interbrigaders took over their trench section, large groups slipped away, desertion *en masse* forming in their minds. By the time they reached the cookhouse, they were a formidable horde, still carrying rifles, shouting, "On to France!" The British and the Franco-Belge had already mutinied; now it was the turn of the Americans. But as they approached Morata de Tajuña, a squadron of French cavalry blocked their route with lances and machine guns. These horsemen, White Russian émigrés who had joined the International Brigades to earn the right to return to the motherland, ranged through the territory behind the lines, rounding up deserters. The Americans, having survived the ghastly slaughter on the plateau, had no wish to be massacred in the valley. They allowed themselves to be disarmed and herded back to the purlieus administered by Colonel Copic, who put them at once on trial for "cowardice and desertion in the face of the enemy." On the way back, Robert Gladnick struck up a conversation with the one-time Cossack commander of the troop. Smaller groups of Americans were caught and turned back after fleeing six to eight miles.[11]

repetition. The "official history" of the battalion uses Matthews' figure for the number of dead, adds twenty-five more wounded, and estimates a hundred effectives holding the line. Robert Gladnick, a survivor of the attack, estimates that eighty Lincolns were in the trenches on the morning after the attack.

[10] This captain is believed to have been Rajk, in later years the Hungarian Minister of Interior executed about 1949 for Titoism.

[11] The number of deserters among the Americans is not known. One survivor estimates that more than three-quarters of the survivors were involved

The trial took place in a high-vaulted cave, one of the numerous *bodegas* that honeycomb the foothills of Tajuña Valley.[12] Colonel Copic arrived in the afternoon with half a dozen of his staff and set up his kangaroo court. His chief of operations, Lieutenant Colonel Claus, a meticulous ex-Kaiser soldier, served as prosecutor. It is alleged that Copic asked for the death penalty for every tenth man, the rest to be relegated to a "labor battalion." The defendants had no counsel beyond one of their own group who was able to pick out a few words of German from the long-winded spiel of Colonel Claus, who spent most of the afternoon summarizing the history of the labor movement in Germany and relating its achievements to the proletarian revolution. Since the proceedings had to be translated into French, Spanish, and English for the principals in the court-martial, the trial promised to be a long one, even though the final verdict was never in question.

The trial was interrupted suddenly when General "Pavlov," commander of the Soviet tank corps in Spain, entered with his entourage and demanded to know what was going on. The tribunal bolted out of their chairs, and Copic explained that American volunteers were being court-martialed for desertion. Pavlov had been informed that a Russian-born American was being tried by the International Brigades. This effrontery had infuriated him, for Red Army officers customarily regarded Internationals as the sweepings of the Comintern. That Copic dared to place a "Russian" on trial touched Pavlov to the quick. He kicked over the table in front of Claus, brushed aside the sycophantic apologies of Copic, and ordered the tribunal dissolved. Though, strictly speaking, Pavlov had no authority over and little interest in the Lincoln Battalion, his élitist contempt for Copic and his flunkeys may have saved a handful of Americans from summary execution.

The mutineers then filed back to the plateau, where they were rearrested and incorporated into a labor battalion employed in digging trenches in no man's land. Events of the past forty-eight hours proved

with the mutiny. Five Americans, still in uniform, stormed the American consulate in Valencia, where asylum was denied. Then they fled toward Barcelona, beyond the purview of the consular officers. It may be that some men listed as dead by the Battalion were actually deserters who escaped from Spain.

12 In one of these caves, a large number of mutineers from the British Battalion had hidden after deserting the line on their first day of battle. They had been rooted out by a company officer who threatened to bowl in some grenades.

to be too much for one volunteer, who tied his belt to an olive tree and attempted to hang himself. (The limb was rotten and broke off.) Throughout the battalion men swore they would never go into battle again or obey the orders of men like Merriman, now called "Captain Murderman." Commissar Stember, whom no one had ever seen on February 27, reappeared to cajole, lecture, and threaten; but they glared at and cursed him openly. Stember mimeographed a leaflet designed to silence those who questioned or complained. It warned that "Those who challenge the military or political authority of Company, Battalion, or Brigade Commanders are self-seekers who are no less guilty than the deserters who have been sentenced to hard labor in the Labor Battalion at a recent trial." But the men scoffed at the leaflet. A succession of commissars—English, French, and German—visited the Americans to talk about grand strategy and noble sacrifice, but their speeches sounded like what they were—rationalizations, excuses, fabrications.[13] Repeatedly the men raised a question that no one in the hierarchy cared, or dared, to answer: why had not the suicidal attack been called off when it had become obvious that success was impossible? No weight of propaganda could counterbalance the conviction that 127 comrades had died in vain. If the attack proved anything, so far as they were concerned, it demonstrated the abject incompetence of officers who planned and pressed the massacre, officers who now begged them to respond to words like "discipline" and "courage." Moreover, they had begun to question the legal assumptions underpinning their act of volunteering to serve in the International Brigades. They had taken no oath to uphold the Spanish government nor vow to defend its flag. These brigades were extraterritorial, entirely separate from the regular Republican Army. A volunteer who wished to terminate his service argued that since he had come to Spain on his own free will, he thereby had the right to depart when he pleased. If he "deserted" what, on legal grounds, had he deserted from?

[13] The level of political development among the men of the Lincoln Battalion was probably higher than that of any other American military group in history. The political commissar system originated in peasant armies as a means of indoctrinating illiterates with the reasons for fighting (and of watching over military officers whose loyalty was suspect). When Americans balked at the system of "comic-stars" they were quarreling with means, not ends. They were not peasant fodder but men who, while agreeing with the objectives of the anti-Fascist struggle, had keen noses for smelling out hypocrisy and lies.

Pingarrón had not been taken. It and the trenches attacked by the Lincoln Battalion remained in Nationalist hands permanently. The Battle of Jarama had played itself out, but the scars of the massacre of February 27 remained under tissue that never completely healed. Never again would the American volunteers accept, with unwavering trust, the decisions of rear-line commanders, for they had learned that these men, despite glittering assurances, actually knew as little about the realities of war as they. And that amounted to nothing.

5

⌸ Waiting . . . Waiting

Oh, the Lincoln boys fought at Jarama,
They made the Fascis-ti cry "Ma-ma,"
They held down the line—
For months at a time.
And for sport they would play with a bomb-a.

—Battalion song

During the first days of March, the remnants of the Lincoln Battalion, fewer than a hundred men, assembled under a cliff behind their trenches in order to select a new commander. Because mutinous feelings still smoldered beneath the surface of the battalion, not even the imperious Colonel Copic dared appoint a commander without the men's approval. When he recommended that someone with military experience, like Lieutenant Wattis, be brought over from the British to assume command, his suggestion was shouted down by angry cries originating with the Irish and echoed by the others. They demanded to be led by one of their own, even though no one was qualified to lead. The choice narrowed to two men, both of them alleged to have been noncoms in the U.S. Army. The rank and file wanted Martin Hourihan; the party cadre supported Oliver Law. In view of the widespread campaign in the United States to recruit more Negroes into the Communist Party, the selection of Law would have been an excellent advertisement of racial equality in the Lincoln Battalion.[1] But, as we have seen, Law already had been appointed adjutant of the Tom Mooney Company over the heads of men better

[1] In 1936 the CPUSA had run James W. Ford, a Negro, as its vice presidential candidate. To vote for the Communist candidates was to absolve oneself from the taint of "racism." Since Ford was due to visit the Lincoln Battalion in April, the Party was doubtless especially eager to install Law as commander.

qualified. Most of the Lincolns disliked Law, not because he was a Negro (this would have stood in his favor, if a factor at all), but because they regarded him as sulky, narrow-minded, and incompetent. Even other Negroes addressed him mockingly as "Comrade Law." Having been chewed to pieces in a tragic battle, the Lincolns demanded someone whom they could depend upon—the devil take his press cuttings.

The stormy forum behind the lines lasted for half a day before Hourihan was installed as the fifth commander of the Lincoln Battalion. Commissar Stember and others of the hardcore were distressed. After all, Hourihan was something of a political maverick who indicated so little interest in bending to the party line that at times he seemed not to know what the line was. Hourihan acquiesced in Law's appointment as his adjutant but promptly ignored him. The party hacks mumbled that he was a racist, as might be expected, and bided their time until they could find provocation to oust him.

Martin Hourihan was a lean, toothy, boyish-looking man of twenty-seven. Of Irish descent, he had grown up in Towanda, Pennsylvania, in a pious Roman Catholic family. His father ran an inn and kept a stable of trotting horses. His mother hoped that Marty would become a priest like her dear older brother, but he was always better known to the football coach at St. Agnes High than to the chaplain. On the day after his graduation he left the Susquehanna Valley for good, running off to join the Army. A year later his mother, doubtless hoping for a miracle, collected the money and paid his way out. Instead of returning home, Hourihan made his way south, where he alternated odd jobs with courses at David Lipscomb College in Nashville and Troy State in Alabama. By 1935 he had married a southern girl, had joined the Church of Christ, and had settled down as principal of a rural school in Greenshaw County.[2] After domestic problems put him on the road again, he took a job in the stewards' department on United Fruit boats shuttling between New Orleans and the banana republics.

In 1936 Hourihan was beached by the maritime strikes along the Eastern Seaboard. Mussolini's invasion of Ethiopia convinced him of

[2] Battalion publicists, embarrassed by Hourihan's apolitical record, embellished it by claiming that he had gone into the South to organize sharecroppers! They also added that he had spent six years in the army and that he was a graduate in engineering from Alabama Polytechnic Institute. None of this was true. (In 1959, at the age of forty-nine, Hourihan received a B.A. from Huntingdon College in Alabama, where he was an honor student.)

the menace of fascism, and when the war broke out in Spain he volunteered to drive an ambulance. Because he was told by his contact man that no nonspecialized medics were needed in Spain, Hourihan joined as a rifleman and sailed on the *Normandie* with the first load of volunteers. At Villanueva de la Jara, the leaders were not impressed by Hourihan—a feeling he reciprocated. Neither the Union Square revolutionaries nor the urban industrial workers cottoned to Alabama recruits with southern drawls. Hourihan did not even command a squad until his squad leader was killed on February 23. In the attack four days later he led the same group into the fatal hollow but managed somehow to bring them all back alive.[3] Three days later he commanded the Lincoln Battalion under the tutelage of Captain Van der Berghe, a Belgian.

Looking over his men, Hourihan must have seen not the much vaunted International "shock troops" making such good copy in newsrooms throughout the world but a poorly armed and badly trained civilian mob—"shocked troops" was more accurate—ready to hang up their helmets and go home. What they needed was time to plug gaps and to rebuild morale. Above all, they needed protection from the cannon-fodder theorists like Gal and Copic, who defined a good soldier as one who obeyed commands as unquestioningly as a lead ox. Hourihan was a pragmatist who had repudiated miracles long since. ("One time I read the Bible. It was just a book.") The slaughter of February 27 had nothing to do with courage, or lack of it, and everything to do with the contrast between the International commanders, who did not know what they were doing, and the Nationalist officers, who did.

Behind his easy manner lay the independent, and at times intractable, soul of an Irishman. For days the Franco-Belge had been slipping into the Lincoln trenches and stealing everything they could lay their hands on, particularly blankets and cigarettes. Hourihan drove them out at pistol point and established sentries on both flanks to see that they kept away. When there were shocked outcries that such measures were incompatible with international solidarity, Hourihan said tersely, "They're not Internationals. They're bums." When Brigade ignored his requests to be briefed on developments elsewhere along

---

[3] Years later, when Hourihan was being denounced in the *Daily Worker* as "an enemy of the working-class," party stalwarts were to condemn him for not having lost men during the February 27 attack. This showed that he had been more interested in saving his men than in exterminating Fascists!

the Jarama front, Hourihan dispatched his Cuban volunteers to infiltrate units north and south and to bring back intelligence reports. His
spies learned that both sides had settled into a holding phase.

At times it seemed that Captain Hourihan had written his own version of a declaration of independence for the Americans in Spain, but
he made it clear to the powers above that the Lincoln Battalion
would not be crucified a second time on an altar spuriously labeled
"international solidarity." Far less malleable than Merriman, Hourihan was an effective interim commander during a period when the
Americans desperately needed assurance that someone with backbone stood as a buffer between them and the ruthless despotism of
the Copic-Gal clan. Perhaps the Jarama survivors had earned the
right to a portion of chauvinism and self-interest.

Having no intention of publicizing his debacle, General Gal spread
a tight net of secrecy about the American role at Jarama and forbade
journalists from entering his sector. Yet the cries of hundreds of
wounded at Interbrigade hospitals at Saelices, Murcia, and Orihuela
could not be silenced, and from them Anglo-American newsmen
learned that the Lincoln Battalion had gone into battle and lost over
half its men. But descending upon Morata for specifics, they were
told that the plateau was bracketed with artillery fire and that visitors
were prohibited because of the danger. When Herbert L. Matthews of
The New York Times expressed his willingness to incur this risk, Gal
parried skillfully: it was not that he personally cared what happened
to war correspondents but that he feared their movements might draw
fire upon his volunteers. Later, when the front "stabilized," the Americans could be interviewed. In this way was a scandal averted.

Party cards carried more weight with Gal than press credentials.
Newsmen representing quasi-propaganda media of the Left were allowed to visit the Americans, though even they were restrained for a
ten-day cooling-off period. The first outside visitor was James Hawthorne, a *New Masses* writer, who arrived at Jarama on March
9. He was genuinely impressed by good food, courageous dead, and
symboliste landscape. He examined the unkempt men in trash-infested
trenches and wrote about "the décor of hell"; and he peered through
a loophole at gashed olive trees and lumpish corpses and wrote about
"a garden of death." The divisional and brigade staff lavished praise
upon the Americans, and Hawthorne took it all down. A Hungarian
surgeon told him, "I remember a Negro with a bullet right through

his stomach who could still manage a wide smile. And they are all like that." And no less a personage than General Gal remarked, "The Americans covered themselves with glory. They are good soldiers." The general went on to observe that whenever American bodies were recovered from no man's land their fists were found clenched as though in Popular Front salute.

James Hawthorne was enthusiastic about what he found at Jarama, though not enthusiastic enough to enlist in the battalion. However acceptable such blatant propaganda was to the stay-at-homes who read *New Masses,* the men were enraged when they read his story. Having relinquished romance, they found nothing glorious about the bloated creatures scattered along the far slope. And months later, when another reporter from *New Masses* arrived at Jarama, they protested that they were "sore about being described as the tin-Jesuses of the proletariat."

Just one day after Hawthorne's visit, the English poet Stephen Spender, at that time a Communist, toured the trenches of the XV Brigade. Led by Major George Nathan, a cane-twirling Englishman of brigade staff, and followed by a nervous Indian writer, Spender climbed up mule paths to the plateau where stray bullets whipped overhead "like shrieking starlings." As they entered the communication trench, the elegant, battle-loving Nathan advised them to stoop low because they had attracted enemy snipers. Then, seeing their crestfallen expressions, he added jovially, "We make a point of not allowing our front-line visitors to be killed." Bent nearly double, the six-foot Spender and five-foot Indian filed down the trench like Mutt and Jeff, while Major Nathan breezily pointed out the sights. At one point the Indian stopped Spender to remark oratorically, "I can see Death's great question-mark hovering between the trenches." The metaphor annoyed Spender, who felt the environment better suited to dialectical materialism than to grotesque personification.

A machine gunner invited Spender to fire a burst at the enemy trenches. Though he was reluctant to do so, the men flocking around him seemed so disappointed in England's best-known proletarian poet, that he finally closed his eyes and fired a few rounds—"positively praying that I might not by any chance hit an Arab." Out in no man's land, unrecovered bodies lay in inert clusters resembling "ungathered wax fruit."

The most distressing event of the day was his conversation with a forlorn eighteen-year-old, who guided him back down the valley. The

youth said he had run off from school because he had been told that
the Spanish Republic was synonymous with liberalism. Now he was
bitterly disillusioned because the International Brigades were run by
Communists. When Spender pointed out that the defense of the Republic was nonetheless a liberal cause, the boy replied, "I don't know
about that. All I see are the Communist bosses of the brigade." Here
was a pattern that Spender found repeating itself among the younger
volunteers—an initial flood of romantic idealism ebbing away to mud
flats of barren disenchantment. Moved by this confession, he promised to see if he could arrange for his companion to be shifted to a
noncombatant position somewhere else, but the boy interrupted, "No,
my life is to walk up to the ridge here every day until I am killed."
(Spender learned six weeks later that the youth was killed, on a
different walk.) Yet when Spender wrote in a *New Statesman* column
that all recruits should be informed, in advance, that the Communists
controlled the International Brigades, he was rebuked by a party man
who argued that the ends justified the deception. For Spender this
kind of equivocation was as bone-chilling as the matter-of-factness of
the Yugoslav judges at an Interbrigade prison who had said to him,
without irony, "We are always happy when our friends are sent to
[detention] camps. It is so good for their education."

As truckloads of rookies arrived at the front and diluted the number of embittered survivors, General Gal allowed into his sector journalists friendly to the Republic though officially neutral. In mid-
March a tall blonde strode through the American trenches, picking up
a gaping flock as she passed through. Martha Gellhorn of *Collier's*
blithely explained that she had come down to Morata in a Ford station wagon "camouflaged in such a way that you could see it ten
miles off." Since the front was quiet, men lay along lee slopes trying
to obtain suntans. She talked with Hourihan, "a lean, slow-talking
boy who had been a schoolteacher in Alabama," and she asked some
of the others if they ever got homesick. Edward Flaherty of Boston
said he never did, because he had brought two of his brothers to
Spain with him. The volunteers' trenches reminded her of flimsy
ditches found in empty city blocks, where slum children played. Down
at the cookhouse she found a Cockney who claimed that he had once
worked in Lyon's Corner House in London. He argued that Lyon's
had "more class" than Childs, although his coffee tasted like mud.

In Morata, flies swarmed over the soldiers and trucks in the littered
plaza mayor. The field hospital, a white farmhouse covered with vines

and invaded by bees, lay seven kilometers away. Here Miss Gellhorn found two doctors pouring peroxide on the shoulder of a wounded youth. The liquid foamed on a long shrapnel wound that resembled soil erosion, "ridged and jagged and eaten in." Although his stomach shook with pain, he did not cry out. The place reeked of ether and sweat. All the serious cases had been evacuated to hospitals in the south of Spain. There were incongruities: an English nurse wearing long ribbon bandages to keep her hair out of her eyes looked like an illustration from *Alice in Wonderland* and in one bed a French soldier wore an artificial leather flying cap exactly like those in vogue among American grammar school boys. Everyone seemed "desperately tired." There was little romance and no glory at Jarama.

Nothing seemed to go right for Virginia Cowles of the London *Sunday Times*. A cloud of suspicion attached itself to her when she arrived in Republican Spain wearing a hat, an emblem of patrician privilege, and carrying a suitcase with red and yellow stripes, the Franco colors. A short time later, while wandering half-lost with her interpreter in the Tajuña sector, she stumbled upon General Gal's headquarters. Taken under guard to the General, she was refused permission to visit the American trenches. With sullen green eyes, Gal viewed her upper-class mannerisms, her stylish clothes, and her *Times* press card with undisguised loathing. To make matters worse, his visitors asked such questions as "Have many Fascist planes been over here?" and "Do you think the enemy will make another drive soon?" It was as though he had been introduced, in the flesh, to Mata Hari. Breaking off a spray of roses from his garden, he handed them to her, saying curtly, "You can write your story from the garden. No one will know the difference, and here is a souvenir to remind you of your adventures at the front." Miss Cowles abandoned hope of interviewing the Anglo-Americans of the XV Brigade.

To her great surprise, she received an invitation a week later to lunch with Gal at his headquarters. His staff car carried her out to Morata on the following morning. It was raining, and orderlies ran about the messroom collecting rain water from the leaking roof. By wartime standards, the lunch was lavish—partridges, vegetables, bread, butter, and strawberries—but it was a solemn rite. No one spoke, because General Gal regarded dinner conversation as bourgeois foolishness. After lunch he spoke to her through his interpreter David Jarrett (*né* Zorat), a New York City court translator. "I may take you to the front this afternoon, but first you will have to remove those gold bracelets you are wearing. The enemy would be sure to spot them." His staff laughed uproariously at this witticism. Then, looking at her black suede shoes, he added, "You are too soft. You would get tired and want someone to carry you."

The rain had stopped when they drove up the dark mountain to the plateau. The road was lined with tanks squatting, half-hidden, among dripping olive trees. Over the crest were distant artillery flashes like lightning. When shells burst nearby, Miss Cowles wanted to run, but thinking of how this would only confirm Gal's theory about her, she restrained herself. At the top stretched deep, muddy trenches that twisted beyond her vision through fields of red clay. Soldiers fired through sandbagged openings. They had no overcoats. Soaked clothes hung on them like loose layers of skin. General Gal passed regally down the line, patting riflemen on the back and shaking hands with officers. Asked how he enjoyed the front, an American Negro, just up from training camp, replied, "Ah appreciates de glory, suh, but to tell de truth, ah was puffickly satisfied in de rear." Although the men played a cheerful, light-comedy role for their visitors, their faces were lined and worn and their bodies ravaged by colds and dysentery. To Miss Cowles they lacked the swagger of legionaries fighting for the joy of adventure; they were idealists and down-and-outs, many of them ill-suited for soldiering. One weary American said, "You might suggest to the General we get a vacation. Not that we have any kick about the neighborhood, but the view is getting monotonous." They knew, of course, that Gal kept them in the line to teach them "discipline."

Returning to Gal's *finca* in the valley, Miss Cowles learned, to her great surprise, that she was to be kept there, virtually a captive, for three days so that she might understand, as Gal phrased it, "what we are fighting for." Perhaps he had other goals as well. She was assigned a room not distant from the General's and issued two filthy blankets, toothpaste, a comb, and eau de Cologne. After dinner Gal noisily broke open a bottle of champagne and emptied its contents into thick glass tumblers, which he passed round the table. Then he toasted his guest, "Here's to the bourgeoisie! May we cut their throats and live as they do." He seemed a little put down when she raised her tumbler mockingly. "I suppose in your bourgeois world you were taught that Bolsheviks were lacking in culture," he added. "It is untrue. We often drink champagne in Moscow." At this point a young officer broke in with a remark that convulsed the table. Jarrett translated it for her, "He says champagne is good but vodka is quicker."

A husky blond Russian proudly showed her a snapshot featuring a woman with thick black curls in a knee-length skirt lying on a rug with a rose dangling from her mouth. Miss Cowles thought at first that it must be a joke—a burlesque of a "degenerate" Hollywood vamp of two decades before. But the youth was quite serious; he said it was a picture of his wife. After examining the photo with a critical eye, General Gal pronounced that the Soviet Union need never be ashamed of its womenfolk. The youth blushed with pleasure. Afterward they sat in the garden while a soldier serenaded them with Russian love songs. An orderly appeared out of the gloom, reporting that the Fascists wanted to borrow some books and magazines. Gal forbade it. He explained that during the day literature was often exchanged under a white flag in no man's land, even though the emissaries often wound up hurling insults at one another. Fearing trickery, he prohibited these interchanges by night.

During the day General Gal allowed Miss Cowles to poke around headquarters and the village. At night he worked earnestly to convert her. Even though he regarded her now and again with the superstitious awe of a Central European peasant for an acknowledged vampire, he nevertheless took a certain glee in regaling her with bits of his autobiography. Once he confessed that heretofore he had considered it sinful even to speak to the bourgeoisie, but that now he had concluded that she had been misled by her background and education. Speaking of his life before the Russian Revolution, he said bitterly, "I used to live like an animal. Now I live like a human being." Then, in almost the same breath, he boasted of the private automobile at his disposal whenever he visited Moscow—never aware of the contradictions lurking within his confessions. He regarded it as inconceivable that anyone exposed to communism would not embrace it, and the idea that another economic system had merit was beyond his ken. In his fidelity to his faith, Gal had the one-sidedness of a Bible-thumping fundamentalist. When he saw that his arguments made no inroads upon Miss Cowles, he did not despair. "Read the works of Lenin—all thirty-seven volumes," he said. "When you are well instructed, join the party. You will be useful as an undercover agent." It was as simple as that.

When her three days expired, a staff car arrived to carry her back to Madrid. Gal invited her to return whenever she liked. Then he added roguishly, "You won't return, but you will boast to your friends that a Red Army general took a fancy to you." At such a moment it was possible to discern, buried beneath the crust of poorly assimilated Marxism, the earthiness of a simple peasant who had climbed a long way. Gal was a child-man spooked by garbled tales of capitalist ogres and bourgeois bogeymen. It was not, as the Americans believed, that General Gal was malign or stupid; it was just that he was incredibly sectarian and abysmally ignorant. Miss Cowles never saw him again. A few months later he was summoned to the Soviet Union, where his automobile was taken from him—then his life.

Of all the journalists who visited the Lincoln Battalion during the spring of 1937, the most popular was Josephine Herbst. She had arrived in Madrid carrying a heavy knapsack and battered typewriter and had settled down among the *tertulia* Hemingway at the Hotel Florida. But annoyed by the superficial cliques of highly paid correspondents in cutthroat competition with one another, she went down to Morata and took a room over the local cafe. On her first trip to the front, she was dropped off at the battalion cookhouse, where she found in the courtyard only a cat sitting under a wooden rake and a few hens scratching through a wet hayrick. Inside were two Americans in cinnamon-colored uniforms sitting around a bone-white table, peeling potatoes. When she explained who she was, they nodded without interest, so she helped them peel and all of them discussed the weather. Soon a heavy-duty truck came by to carry her up to the plateau. The driver explained that the road had been recently graded in order to transport supplies to the front without being seen by the Fascists. As they neared the top, bullets zipped overhead and brought down a light rain of olive leaves. Up in this region there were no birds. The Lincoln headquarters consisted of a deep dugout furnished with bare table, telephone stand, cot, and first-aid cabinet. Men popped out of holes little larger than the lairs of wolves to examine the "female" in tan tweed suit and brown woolen topcoat. A near-sighted Ohioan who regularly rubbed his breakfast bread with garlic, shouldered through the pack shouting, "Hey, who'll introduce me to the bitch."

Miss Herbst felt that the Jarama soldiers lacked a "heroic scale." Within the best was resignation or fatalism; within the worst, masochism or apprehension. When she asked about newspaper reports of their "victories" that she had read about, they disparaged them. One volunteer mentioned with contempt a newspaper story about a Cuban baseball pitcher in the Lincoln Battalion who had allegedly thrown grenades like baseballs at the enemy trenches, whereas the truth was that he hadn't been close enough to a Fascist to hurl anything at all. Why, they demanded to know, had no reporter written the truth—that, for example, out of the sixty-four Cubans originally mustered into the battalion only twelve remained? Even more irritating than news stories were a certain style of letter from the United States which egged them on "like the cries of cheerleaders roaring away to enhance a game they were not playing." They were sick and tired of big words.

The presence of Miss Herbst loosened tongues. Not that they talked about the war; nor were there ghoulish accounts of corpses, that conversational staple among Hemingway's crowd in Madrid. Rather their conversation tried to penetrate the hopelessly complex labyrinth of responsibility for the ghastly horror of February 27. Merriman was now "Murderman"; Seacord was the leader they liked to think about. What they seemed to like best, however, was to talk about dreams, reveries, vivid images of home. Jarama was an interlude between two other realities.

Poor morale was endemic to Jarama—the Lincoln Battalion had no monopoly on it. If anything, the British seemed more dispirited than the Americans. An outbreak of typhoid was expected, but despite pleas and threats by brigade physicians, many Britons refused to be inoculated. They argued that they had been promised relief from the front and that they were "striking" to obtain what the bosses promised. Moreover, as one of them told Miss Herbst, if the Moors attacked while their arms were immobilized by serum, they would not have a chance. Whenever you fought Moors, he added, "you always keep a bullet for yourself."

Miss Herbst thought the men at Jarama were very innocent and very young. If they were gloomy it was because of a legitimate instinct that conditions were apt less to get better than to get worse. Three lady journalists visiting the Lincoln Battalion at three different times came to roughly the same conclusion: the men had been badly jarred by a brutal initiation into battle and by a sequence of events that were incomprehensible to them. Who could blame them for feeling a little sorry for themselves?

March was very bad. "Always it rained," wrote one volunteer. "The mud clogged our rifles. The rain came down. The icy wind from the Guadarramas froze us in our trenches." It was never cold enough to freeze the ankle-deep mud and never warm enough to dry it up. Since their cartridges were primarily refills, easily spoiled by moisture, the men blew their noses between their fingers and saved handkerchiefs for more important things, like wiping off ammunition and rifle bolts. From the cookhouse half a mile below, coffee had to be brought up, on foot, in urns suspended from poles. No coffee was often as welcome as cold coffee, and always it was cold. Mud penetrated their food, their tobacco, their blankets. It was weeks before fortifications officers taught them how to prepare decent dugouts; before this, they stood day and night in open ditches without duckboards. Tin helmets shed rain but refrigerated sinuses. The best way to get warm was to work up a sweat with pick and shovel, provided one did not contract pneumonia while cooling off. In the lush Tajuña Valley, which lay behind them like a picture postcard labeled "Sunny Spain," apple blossoms came and went, but the plateau was swept by icy winds. Morale dropped lower than the thermometer.

During the first week in March a van appeared in the courtyard of the cookhouse enclosure. Lettered on the outside was COMISARIA POLITICIA—PASAREMOS! Inside were supplies of reading matter—party pamphlets and throwaways, for the most part—and a mimeograph machine for printing a front-line newspaper. Over the editor's stick-leg table were tacked two pinups, one of La Pasionaria and the other of Stalin. The newspaper, *Our Fight,* contained two pages chronicling successful industrial strikes in the United States, soccer scores from England, and appeals for discipline and unity. Leftover space was filled by a scruffy column called "Learn Spain" (*sic*) followed by lists of Spanish verbs (without conjugations):

To eat	comer	komehr
To drink	beber	behbehr
To speak	hablar	ahblahr

Commissar Sam Stember, a regular columnist, reported that such prominent Hollywood stars as Chaplin, Muni, Gable, B. Davis, and Crawford stood behind the Spanish Republican Government (without explaining how); and he wrote that such Americans as Ernest Hemingway and Sinclair Lewis were on their way to Spain to drive ambulances! He implored the men to support the newspaper by contributing to it—which they did not. And he railed against the mushrooming grievance committees "which were making demands in the Brigade as if they were forming demands against Capitalist class"—which they were, indeed. *Our Fight* seemed to be Stember's way of communicating with the men without being compelled to face their hostility in the flesh. "Comrades," began one of his editorials, "let us not grumble, let us carry on. Can we use a rest? Yes! But it must not be as a result of committees, but when our comrades in the BRIGADE can get it for us." They had heard all of this superloyal drivel too many times before.

Despite the editor's claim that *Our Fight* was "striking a blow at the Fascist enemy," the news sheet made more noise than sense so far as most of the men were concerned. If it was ludicrous to read that "A. Toscanini, famous conductor of the New York Philharmonic orchestra, has spit in Mussolini's face by refusing to attend the 70th anniversary of the opera La Scala," it was merely depressing to be told that "olive trees symbolize peace because men are buried under them." But party jargon became unintentional comic art when the battalion doctor, alarmed by unburied excrement in the trenches, attempted to make latrine digging an exalted proof of proletarian fervor, by proclaiming:

> Upon this foundation of collective effort, a superstructure of individual care can be erected, resulting in healthier bodies, saner minds, working together for the good that brought us together, the overthrow of fascism, the triumph of democracy.

It would have been wonderful had the doctor been spoofing them, but the fact was that he was deadly in earnest.

Weary of this treacle of propaganda oozing from each issue of *Our Fight,* the men themselves got up an opposition newspaper consisting of snippets and fragments tacked to a bulletin board just behind their trench. It was called *The Daily Mañana,* edited by "Manual Labor," and featured "All the fits that news can print." It was a zany publication, influenced more by Harpo Marx than Karl. There was a column written by General Nuisance, who predicted that "the war will be over as soon as we win," and there were news bulletins like "Flash! We see where the government has ordered the devaluation of the Franco." It poked fun at the machine gunner who had taken a bite of Spanish bread and demolished his bridge, and at the volunteer who had written his mother that the boat bringing him to Spain had docked at Albacete. Occasionally there were poems. Sam Levinger, the rabbi's son, was typical of dozens of other volunteers who found themselves with the time and the desire to versify:

> Comrades, the battle is bloody and the war is long,
> Still let us climb the gray hill and charge the guns,
> Pressing with lean bayonets toward the slope beyond.
> Soon those who are living will see green grass,
> A free bright country shining with a star;
> And those who charge the guns will be remembered,
> And from red blood white pinnacles will tower.

Dismal fatalism protrudes from the wrenched metaphors of his poem, which reflects the dilemma of a youth whose beliefs have been sorely tried by experiences too shocking to render adequately.[4] Levinger was a "Yipsel"—the slurring name Communists gave to members of the Young Socialist League—killed, a few months later, before he reached his twenty-first birthday.

In the afternoon of March 14 the front suddenly erupted again as Moors, preceded by Fiat tanks, attacked the trenches south of the XV Brigade, a sector held by skittish recruits of the "La Pasionaria" Battalion, who fled. Headed by a British officer who yelled, "Follow me in formation!," the British Battalion broke and scurried to the rear. At this particular moment there was a meeting of the big brass at brigade headquarters; therefore the line was held largely by unofficered men, for the most part the "demoralized elements" of the labor battalion. They dropped picks and shovels, grabbed rifles, and began blazing at the Moors sweeping into the trenches on their left flank. The attack had been so unexpected that no one had time for the luxury of fear. Shouting absurd, euphoric slogans like "Don't fire till you see the whites of their eyes" and *"No pasarán!,"* they peppered the Moors while Soviet tanks hovering in the vicinity beat back the Fiats.[5] Although the vanguard of Moors seized the "La Pasionaria" trenches, their support was rolled back, thus leaving a two-hundred-yard segment of Republican trench in the possession of an enemy that could move neither forward nor backward.

---

[4] Murray Kempton, who discovered this poem, finds in it the confessions of an idealist who had learned what it meant to become a target.

[5] Soviet tankists contemptuously alluded to Fiats as "the riot patrol."

Within minutes Captain Jock Cunningham, the ferocious, bushy-browed commander of the British,[6] came dashing up the hill shouting, "You bloody Yanks! Goddamn you—we won't leave you in the lurch!" Behind him was his adjutant, Fred Copeman, a gigantic ex-seaman (a ringleader in the Invergordon Mutiny of the Royal Navy in 1931) who had been known to pick up skulkers by the seat of their pants and hurl them toward the enemy. Grabbing handfuls of Mills bombs, a mixed force of Americans and British stormed down the length of trench, flushing out Moors in fine style. While someone tossed a grenade into a blind corner of a trench zigzag, the others quail-shot the Moors who tried to scramble out. The enemy had run out of grenades, and the nearly subterranean nature of the fighting made it impossible for them to know that they were being pushed back by a raiding party, not a battalion. At one point Cunningham ran along the trench edge sowing grenades like seeds. The counterattack ended when a Moor bagged Cunningham with a machine-gun burst that somersaulted him into the trench, his chest and arms spurting blood like a pump. Copeman dragged him back a hundred yards to where the "La Pasionarias," partially rallied, were throwing up a cross-ditch.

Casualties in the Brigade were light, and the encounter lifted the spirits of everyone, especially the former deserters of the labor battalion, who were at once transmogrified from "cowards" into "heroes." Even Colonel Copic embraced them. For the first time in Spain they could look out into no man's land and see mounds of the enemy dead, not their own.

One of the wounded men became the most celebrated American casualty of the Spanish Civil War. Robert Raven, a youngish but balding dropout from the University of Pittsburgh, was handed, in the melée, a grenade with the pin already pulled.[7] A concussion in front of him burned out his eyes, forcing him to drop his own grenade, which exploded at his feet. After the battle he was found miraculously alive and rushed to the hospital at Villa Paz, outside Saelices. He was disfigured from head to foot, and his agony came to be dreaded by orderlies, one of whom recalled that if they pulled back his bedclothes and a sheet brushed his foot, Raven would scream,

---

[6] Cunningham, a former seaman, took over the battalion after Wintringham was wounded on the second day at Jarama.

[7] Less foolish than it sounds. Some grenades had two pins, one so loose it could be shaken out, the other so tight it could barely be pulled out at all. In emergencies, soldiers often pulled out the tight pin ahead of time.

"My toes! My toes! Damn you!" The point was that these toes had been amputated, but as a doctor told a distinguished visitor, "He doesn't know that." "I wonder if he'll ever know it," asked Ernest Hemingway. "Oh, sure he will. He's going to get well." Not only did Raven get well, he also became one of the best fund raisers the Abraham Lincoln Battalion ever had. Crowds in Madison Square Garden wildly shouted, *"No Pasarán!"* as Robert Raven (promoted to the rank of "lieutenant" by his sponsors) rose eyeless to address them. Who could say no to a man who had given his eyes to the Spanish Republic?[8]

The short, happy flash-battle of March 14 seemed to support the conclusion that the Lincoln Battalion fought better when their officers were absent. After it had died down, the staff arrived, Commissar Stember at the rear with a stack of *Our Fight,* just off the press. "Don't that beat all?" commented one veteran. "While we killed Moors, he fetched the funny papers!" This was the third time that Stember had missed seeing action. A fourth opportunity never arrived for him. The outcry against him was so vociferous that he was removed from his post and took his *via dolorosa* back to Philadelphia. There were no send-off speeches for Sam Stember; he vanished as mysteriously and as suddenly as he had appeared in Villanueva de la Jara. "Probably sent home and buried somewhere," opined one volunteer. Originally nothing more than a well-intentioned but run-of-the-mill bureaucrat, Stember had become a symbol of all the disasters that had overtaken the battalion. He had had his last chance and had muffed it.[9]

Late in March, Captain Hourihan began to issue twenty-four-hour passes for Madrid. The first group left in an empty munition truck amid whoops and hollers of the men left behind, who seemed nearly as excited as those who went. Always the lure of what one might find

---

[8] Raven told Hemingway, "It was quite a bad fight, you know, but we beat them and then someone threw this grenade at me." At first, Hemingway, a shrewd judge of character, did not believe the story because "it was the sort of way everyone would like to have been wounded. But I wanted him to think I believed it." But Cunningham, whom he trusted, confirmed it and Hemingway wrote a syndicated dispatch about Raven.

[9] Stember's place was taken by David Jones, a New Englander remembered as a revolutionary purist rather than a party man. His younger brother Sheldon was attached to the John Brown Battery, training at Almansa. When Jones was wounded while bringing in a comrade from no man's land, his place was taken by Fred Lutz, a tractable long-server in Spain.

in the city was greater than what was there. Cigarettes had disappeared long since, the food was worse than that at the front, and the liquor tasted like varnish remover laced with vanilla extract. (Lieutenant Robert Taylor once claimed he found three bottles of Johnny Walker Red Label, but few men accepted this tale as gospel.) Worst of all, the sexual mores of Spanish girls were so impeccable that they would have earned hosannas from a Mother Superior, for despite their veneer of liberalism, their core was *catolicismo español.* "Every time you go out with one of them," griped one volunteer, "she holds a wedding ring in one hand and her mama in the other." The sleeker class of prostitutes, those whose blonde hair was now becoming black at the roots because peroxide was commandeered for hospital use, had left the public domain for private arrangements. "Black widows" abounded, but a goodly proportion of the Americans objected to liaisons with women older than their mothers. Besides, prostitution was regarded by many of them as a degenerate relic of capitalism.

Madrid was a schizoid city in which revolution and reaction coexisted happily. In the hand of the equestrian statue of Charles IV in the *plaza mayor* hung a red-black Anarchist flag. Women queued up in front of bakeries to be told what they already knew—that there was no bread that day; but a few doors away smart shops featured Schiaparelli perfume and silver fox furs. Movie houses showed Greta Garbo in *Anna Karenina,* the Marx Brothers in *A Night at the Opera,* and Al Jolson in *Casino de Paris.* For those seeking edification, there was always Charlie Chaplin's *Modern Times,* a satire on assembly-line industrialism, which had the longest run of its history at the Capitol on the Gran Via. Less than two miles distant, enemy batteries on Mount Garibitas fired shells down this avenue—dubbed Shell Alley—at the exact minute when the feature let out at the Capitol. (The theater manager could have changed the time of the showing, but it would not have helped—for Fascists also subscribed to the morning newspapers.) Like the *madrileños,* inured to these shellings, visiting Lincolns learned to hug the comparative safety of the southernside of the Gran Via or to infiltrate rapidly into the narrow maze of back streets leading to the Puerta del Sol. One Jarama veteran recorded that he once saw a *madrileño* leaning against a wall during a barrage, picking his teeth with complete absorption. And it was a favorite trick of veteran journalists, like Ernest Hemingway, to frighten the wits out of newcomers by taking them on a stroll down the lee side of the Gran Via at the moment when the Garibitas batteries opened fire.

As a center of tourism, wartime Madrid had lost its stars. Paintings in the Prado had been packed up for safekeeping and the façade boarded up. The famous Sybil and Neptune fountains were hidden by a deep layer of bricks and sandbags. Republican snipers fired with impunity from the windows of the National Palace, which overlooked enemy trenches in the Casa de Campo, since they knew that monarchist officers of Franco's army were reluctant to damage such an august Bourbon shrine. The Retiro Gardens, having been converted into an artillery park, was decidedly no place to get away from it all. In the zoo, the carnivores were dead or were starving by degrees. (It is said that when the elephant died, strange cuts of meat appeared in the butcher stalls of Madrid—but this same story is told of Barcelona.) The fancy hotels like the Ritz and the Palace had been converted into hospitals—an appropriate use for them because their chalk-white exteriors had always made them resemble rich men's sanatoria. Under the gilt and glass chandeliers of the once-regal dining room of the former stretched rows of white cots filled with unshaven men, and on the walls around hung multicolored posters that read BEAT FASCISM BY LEARNING HOW TO READ AND WRITE. Many an American came to Spain, only to die at the Ritz.

Evenings in Madrid were better. An Anarchist committee had taken over the famous Miami Bar on the Gran Via. In this wild cabaret anything could happen and often did. Like the time a drunken *miliciano* amused himself by table-hopping and shooting guests with a Flit can filled with lavender water, until he was shot dead by another soldier with a real pistol and dragged out by his heels, his fingers still locked around the Flit can. Or the time an American employee at the censor bureau, a dowdy girl with piano legs and cement-sack breasts, got drunk and put on a striptease pantomime called "The Widow of General Mola," commemorating Franco's second-in-command, who had recently died in an airplane crash. (General Mola was the patron devil of Madrid, best known nowadays for coining the term "fifth column.") For the Americans, the Miami Bar was a bit of home in old Madrid. A record player scratched out "You Are My Lucky Star." The fresco behind the bar featured languid boys and girls surfing in a blue sea while a yacht heeled down in the faded background.

Lincolns on leave always received a welcome at the Hotel Florida on Plaza del Callao, headquarters of Anglo-American journalists and official visitors, all of whom were on the lookout for interviewees who might save them the jolting trip out to Morata. Ignoring Don Cristobal, the Pecksniffian reception clerk who pored over his stamp collection trying to forget how low his hotel had sunk, the men camped out in overstuffed chairs in the lobby under a travel poster that read VISIT CUBA. It was at the Florida that they rubbed shoulders with everybody who was anybody in Republican Spain. John Dos Passos stayed there while he studied collective farming in nearby villages. Professor J. B. S. Haldane, the British gas-warfare expert, came and went always with his "Tommy" tin hat, his gas mask, and a leather jacket unbuttonable around his middle girth. Asked what he was doing in Spain, Haldane replied, "Enjoyed the last war so much I thought I'd come down here for a holiday." Herbert L. Matthews, whom the pros admitted was the best war correspondent in Spain, had a room at the Florida; his companion Sefton Delmer of the *Daily Mail* had two rooms, a sunny large one on the front exposed to shellfire, and a dank but safe hole on the back which he used for sleeping. Delmer had bought up a supply of Chateau Yquem 1904 looted from the wine cellars of the National Palace. A few doors away was Claud Cockburn of the London *Daily Worker,* a prolific genius who had once written, on party order, a book about Spain in seven days. Cockburn had never visited the Soviet Union and had no interest in going there, because as he put it, "I am not interested in watching revolutions; my job is *making* them." Even Errol Flynn breezed into the Florida one April day, announced he had come to fight fascism, and breezed out the next while his publicity agent claimed that he had been wounded on the Madrid front. (Flynn was publicly denounced by the Defense Junta for his presumptuous opportunism, but by this time he had crossed into France.)

But the innermost circle of privilege and patronage at the Hotel Florida was presided over by Ernest Hemingway, who cabled dispatches to the North American Newspaper Alliance at a dollar per word. Regular members of his *circulo* were Martha Gellhorn (Hemingway's third wife to-be), Herbert L. Matthews, and Sidney Franklin, a bullfighter from Brooklyn, New York. On an alcohol stove in his room, Hemingway prepared the most appetizing meals to be had in wartime Madrid. Visiting Lincolns soaked in his tub. (It was said that the Florida was the only hotel in wartime Madrid with hot water.) He had no use whatever for *politicos* or "comic-stars." He once told Joe North of the New York *Daily Worker,* "I like the Communists when they're soldiers; when they're priests I hate them. Yes, priests, the commissars who hand down the papal bulls. . . . That

air of authority your leaders wear, like cassocks." High on his list of
unspeakable obscenities were the names of André Marty and General
Gal—farther down was Colonel Copic. Best of all, he seemed to admire those who fought in Spain without political commitments of any
kind. These were American fliers like Frank Tinker, who shot down
Nationalist planes for fifteen hundred dollars per month (plus
bonus), and Harold "Whitey" Dahl,[10] who sought his advice about
the monetary value and artistic worth of a "Van Dick" painting that
he had pilfered from a *castillo* somewhere. The only contact the Lincolns ever had in Spain with the American pilots came through the
crap games on the floor of Hemingway's room. Tinker was aghast
when he learned the Lincolns made only ten pesetas a day. That was
no money at all! Moreover, Arkansanian to the bone, he was baffled
by the designation "Lincoln" Battalion. "Why not a Jeff Davis Battalion?" he once asked.[11]

Hemingway, perhaps irritated by the demoralization of the Americans at Jarama, preferred the businesslike German volunteers of the
XI Brigade, a unit that always took the heaviest casualties yet managed, like a bloodied fighter with great heart, to bore in once again.
On one occasion, he became furious when two Americans picked the
lock of his *armoire* and filched two jars of marmalade from his stock

[10] Shot down in July, 1937, during the Battle of Brunete, Dahl was captured
by the Nationalists, tried in Salamanca, and sentenced to death. After his wife,
Edith, an orchestra leader living at Cannes, wrote Franco a letter (enclosing a
picture of herself in a low-cut dress) averring that Whitey fought only for
money, not politics, his sentence was commuted to life imprisonment. It was
reported that Dahl offered to fly for the Nationalists if they would release
him from prison. The offer—if made—was rejected. He spent the duration of
the war in a Salamanca military hospital. In March, 1940, he was released and
returned to the United States, where he told reporters that he was "fed up with
war." As soon as he stepped off the boat in New York, he was arrested as a
fugitive from justice because of bad checks passed four years before in Los
Angeles. Charges were dropped, however, because extradition costs were
greater than Dahl's debts. Meanwhile, Mrs. Dahl, billed as "the blond who
spiked the guns of General Franco's firing squad" toured the United States
with her orchestra. A year later both confessed that they had never been legally married. During the Second World War, Dahl flew for the Canadian Air
Force until 1945, when he was dismissed after conviction on four charges of
selling equipment to Brazilian junk dealers. His chequered career ended in
1956 when he crashed a commercial plane eight hundred miles north of Que-
bec.

[11] It is astonishing to find in a recently published "official history" of the
Abraham Lincoln "Brigade" an account of these American pilots, all of them
mercenaries, as though they were somehow politically involved with the war in
Spain.

of foodstuffs imported from France. His anger stemmed less from stinginess than from his "soldier-complex," as Josephine Herbst described it. Hemingway had dipped into his own pocket to donate an ambulance to the Republic, but someone who stole from a friend was a thief, not a soldier. Some of the Lincolns worked up a strong dislike of Hemingway for his privileged status as a noncombatant. On one occasion a Jarama veteran (in later years TASS correspondent at the United Nations) blurted out, "You write pretty good stuff. But if you really wanted to help, you'd get yourself a rifle." This outburst was presumptuous and foolish, and Hemingway let it pass. After all, they had volunteered—he had not. What were they fussing about? [12]

The conversational patter of Hemingway's squire, Sidney Franklin, depressed the Lincolns because of his cynicism. He enjoyed telling how he had decided to come to Spain. One day Ernest had rung him up and said, "Lo, kid, want to go to the war in Spain," to which Franklin had replied, "Sure, Pop. Which side we on?" Since almost all of his *matador* pals had sided with Franco, Republican propagandists made much of Franklin, apolitical though he was. He rattled away that sex was no more important than a glass of water—"take it or leave it." And when he declaimed that nobody really cared about anything, deep down, except money and security, a Lincoln man whispered to Josephine Herbst that it was untrue: "What they want is happiness, and something to believe in." They hated to be in the lobby when the Madrid vice squad hauled away the prostitutes from the Florida. "Just when she was giving a little comfort to some poor guy," one man said. One American youth haunted the corridors of the hotel, convinced that he was deeply in love with one of these girls. He tortured himself and his companions with an unending query, "Do you think she *really* loves me?"

The girls at the Florida were a remarkable group. Lolita of the round, innocent face was the mistress of a counterintelligence officer; whenever they quarreled—which was often—he locked her up for a few days. Carminea, a buxom Amazon with black eyes, wore a towering, spangled comb in her hair, Andalusian style, and claimed to be the women's wrestling champion of Spain before the war. Whenever the vice squad broke into her room at five in the morning, she always

---

[12] Hemingway told a former commander of the Lincoln Battalion after the war, ". . . you guys sort of bought this anyway. You hired out to be tough and then somebody gets hurt and says they can't do this to me." His attitude toward them was generally—more fighting and less whining.

had the same excuse—she was keeping in shape for the return of peace. The two most popular girls were Farida and Fatima, Moorish sisters, both of them suspected of fifth-column tendencies. When Malaga fell to Franco's army, Fatima unwisely announced, *"We* have taken Malaga!" After they had been carried off to jail temporarily, Dr. Hewlett Johnson, Dean of Canterbury, was assigned to their room. A group of Anglo-American volunteers, led by a Scotsman, saw the "Red Dean" enter the room in his shorts and assumed he was a client. When he failed to emerge again, the Scotsman reeled up to the door and battered it with his fists, "Come oot, yer old bastard! Ye've been mair ane twenty minutes in there! Yer time's oop. Come oot!" Since all the girls at the Florida regularly donated blood to the Red Cross, the volunteers assumed that this certified their purity in other areas—a scientific fallacy, as they learned.

Because the Florida took a stray shell now and then, it was a poor place for sleeping. One morning ten Americans stretched out in the lobby were jarred awake at six o'clock. Unable to return to sleep, they commenced singing and woke up the paying guests, for the acoustics of the Florida were miraculous. (From the lobby the bedroom stories rose, tier upon tier, in the manner of old-fashioned Paris department stores.) In the midst of "Sewanee River" a shell struck the building, sending the elevator cables crashing to the basement and setting off the screams of Don Cristobal, "They're trying to ruin my business!" Herbert Matthews came down and asked the Jarama veterans how Madrid bombardment compared with those at the front. "This is worse!" exclaimed one man. Another chimed in, "Out at the front we know what they are trying to hit and how to avoid it, but here we feel trapped like rats." "Yeah," broke in a farmer from the Middle West, "We come here to have a good time, and now look at us. We can't even get out of the hotel."

Disappointing though Madrid often was, many volunteers overstayed their leaves and ended up in the labor battalion when they got back to Jarama. The brief passes were so prized that Captain Hourihan rigorously punished anyone failing to return on time.

April was benign. On the shell-pitted slopes at Jarama, spiky plants put out dainty yellow and purple blossoms, which when crushed in the hand smelled like Vicks Salve. Stumpy, dead-looking vines between the lines sprouted long, green shoots. An agricultural student from Farmingdale, Long Island, set out hand-lettered signs

along his trench: CARE FOR THE GRAPES—THEY SUFFER WHEN YOU
HIT THEM. The earth revived, and wounded men were returning from
hospitals. They were Rip Van Winkles looking at faces unfamiliar.
Even the terrain of the February 27 holocaust looked changed. The
replacements had heard about the attack so many times that they
were bored by it. For them it was as remote from their personal experience as Gettysburg or Thermopylae. Even the men who had suffered
through it found that specific details were time-eroded.

A dialogue between a returnee and an old-timer might have gone
like this. "Tiny? Transferred into transport. Heard he had joined the
IB police at Albacete. . . . Peanuts? He got it—never knew how.
. . . Remember his buddy, that guy that collected all those crucifixes? Killed by a machine-gun burst. Crucifixes spilled out like seeds
from a pod. . . . Mickey? That lucky bastard got a job broadcasting
for *Voice of Madrid*. . . . Lenthier? The actor? A Frog labor battalion brought in his body on March 9 or 10. At least somebody said it
sort of looked like Lenthier. . . . Bernie? He's in a bad way. After
he tried to hang himself, they sent him down to Almansa to train with
the artillery. . . . Bob? He got transferred into a Soviet tank battalion. He speaks the language, you know. . . . Oscar? Got a letter
from him saying he'd run into Merriman down at Murcia hospital.
Merriman has a private ward. . . . Max? You'd never believe it. His
daddy came over from the States and got him discharged. Said he was
only seventeen. . . . Andy? Nerves gone to hell. He was always
drunk up here so they sent him back to Albacete and I hear he's
drunk down there, too. . . . Marvin? I wouldn't bring that up, if I
was you. He was ordered to brigade one morning and hasn't been
seen since. You know how Marvin was—always asking questions.
. . . Parks? Wasn't he on one of the trucks that got lost? The name
sounds kind of familiar." [13]

In March they had bailed out and drained trenches; in April they
swept out fine, red dust that covered everything like velveteen. The
back slopes at Jarama resembled Hoovervilles, but they were home.
Like hedgehogs, the men had dug subterranean chambers containing
sleeping alcoves and chiseled staircases. Some dugouts had corru-
gated iron roofs camouflaged by olive branches and sod. A New York
Irishman grinned at a visiting journalist and cracked, "We ain't going
to pay any rent after this war. We'll just build dugouts in Battery

[13] A dialogue cast as fiction, the details of which are factual.

Park." A few carpenters, perfectionists who scorned iron as a conductor of heat, erected clapboard doghouses with plank flooring. At the battalion headquarters, cool and deep like a bootleg Pennsylvania mine, a typist pounded the keys with two index fingers while a windup Victrola played "Night and Day." Every morning between nine and nine fifteen an enemy battery shelled the San Martin road. "Our alarm clock," explained a veteran. "You can set your watch by it."

Despite Marx, private domains were springing up along the trench line, staked off by signs like JOE'S PLACE—PASS AT YOUR OWN RISK. Another read KEEP OUT! PROPERTY OF CHARLIE THE SNIPER. Charlie Regan kept a careful tally of every Fascist he shot. He squinted and fired at an enemy too far away and too deeply entrenched to be seen at all, and hollered in triumph, "Just got one!" When pressed for details, he backed down a little. "Well, if I had one o' those Zeiss telescopic sights, it'd be a cinch. Then I could count their lice and rats. The way it is, they're a little far off for me—my eyes are sore, strainin' at 'em."

Every twenty yards a sentry kept watch while his buddies lay in hivelike hollows scraped out of the trench wall, snoozing, reading, or writing hundreds of letters. Letters! At times the men seemed to live only to write them and to wait for them. Whimsical, boasting, ironical, sentimental letters chronicled the inner thoughts of men along a "dead" front.

> Dear Joe—It felt like the millennium when I heard a bunch of school-kids singing the Internationale and to see little tots of two or three raise their clenched fists in salute. It will be a grand place to live when we finish what the fascists started, and I'm almost convinced I shall remain here. . . .

> Dear Dave—After the war is won we will gladly supply you with fascist helmets which you can use for flower pots and an armored tank or so to use for collecting dues or transporting MacCallum's Scotch Whiskey.

> Dear Mr. Editor—These murderers are not satisfied with the use of bullets. They use dum-dums. And recently they have perfected a new brain child of the civilized scientists from Heidelberg University—an exploding bullet!

> Dear Hattie—When a heavy bomb explodes nearby it almost raises you from the ground and you feel as tho your guts were being sucked clean out. . . . One fellow was

creased between his stump and artificial leg. The poor horrified *medico* almost fainted when the leg came off in his hand. . . .

Dear Marge—The unpicked olives age in the trees and drop to the ground, literally covering it. The juice is wine-like purple when the olives rot. In the past we have learned lots about olives from the most intimate association, lying among them or on the ground until we were all over purple-red color. It makes you feel something like a salad. . . .

By May, Ping-Pong and baseball had replaced sniping and grenade throwing at Jarama. The prevailing idea was no longer to shoot the enemy but to induce him to desert. Each side battered the other with loudspeakers invariably advising men to shoot their officers and cross over. The Internationals guffawed at these invitations, but the broadcasts set off a flurry of desertions among Spanish-born troops of both sides.[14] The Republicans drowned out their enemy when they brought up a public-address system so vast that it had to be transported by two trucks, the first containing electrical equipment and a bulletproof room for the announcer and the second supporting the speaker, an apparatus twenty feet long and six feet wide at the mouth. "I could hardly believe my eyes," remembered an American. "It was a street-corner speaker's nightmare." This demonic contraption frayed the nerve ends of friend and foe alike as it blared forth endless surrender harangues, interspersed with recordings of "Ave Maria" pitched so high that individual words were submerged under ear-splitting noise. The consensus was that "it would do pretty well for Union Square gatherings," but its presence came to be a torment for the Americans.

They waited. They were bored. They complained. They became obsessed with cigarettes. The first two questions that Lincolns asked American visitors were "How are the strikes coming?" and "How about a cigarette?" They became convinced that American brands, shipped through Barcelona, had been confiscated by Anarchists and Trotskyites. (By far the most popular brand was Lucky Strike, per-

[14] A small number of Cubans did desert to the Nationalists about this time. (One American volunteer claims that the political development among many Cubans was not high. According to him, voodoo was practiced by a few of them.) It is not likely that any American went over to the enemy, although there were, of course, a dozen or so Americans serving in Franco's Army of Morocco as legionnaires.

haps because of the talismanic effect of the name, although good proletarians preferred Twenty Grand because they were union made.)
Spanish brands were insufferable. The loose, black grains that came
in paper "pillow-slips" were supposed to be rerolled but usually
crumbled into dust in the process. The tailor-made Spanish type were
dubbed "anti-tanks" because of their lung-piercing potency. Veterans
descended upon new men and lectured them on the merits of sharing,
but the latter quickly learned the necessity of hogging. The cigarette
shortage affected the brigade hierarchs. On a visit, Colonel Copic was
tagged by an American whose eye had fastened upon the Colonel's
cigar, but when Copic neared the end of his smoke he borrowed a pin
so that he could impale the stub for a few more drags.

The stew ladled out from galvanized washtubs earned its portion of
abuse. Perhaps the staple ingredient, mule meat, had something to do
with it. "The flavor wasn't so bad," remembered a veteran. "It was
the texture. I could never swallow a piece of it, no matter how small.
The more you'd chew it, the bigger it would get, until your mouth felt
like it was full of rubber bands." Part of the problem came from rele-
gating battalion washouts to the cookhouse, where their worthlessness
was apparent in every meal. Complaints about the cooks sometimes
attained verbal art. "Them left-handed half-wits in the kitchen,"
groused one man. "They don't know . . . from boilin' water. Like
the other day, we got half a sheep sent up, prime meat, and damned if
they didn't leave it lay in the sun till it got up and walked off with the
maggots in it. I saw that, too. And a cook runnin' after it with a
lasso." In time, Jack Shirai, a Japanese-American cook from the
West Coast, was put in charge of the kitchen and given his pick of the
best men in the battalion. But Shirai, one of the best riflemen among
the Americans, demanded and obtained an assurance that he would
be allowed to return to the firing line whenever the Lincoln Battalion
went into action again.

During their long trench vigil, which lasted from March through
June, the Lincoln Battalion left the line for a rest only one time. At
the end of April they went over to Alcala de Henares to march in the
May Day parade sponsored by the Soviet tank battalions. (The Soviet
tankists denied they were Russians; they were always "Serbians.")
After an overnight billet in an icy church, they marched through narrow, arcaded streets under banners that read PASAREMOS (We shall
pass), a new slogan replacing the old No PASARÁN. The Republic was
swinging from defensive to offensive roles. Observers at the parade

noted that although the Lincolns failed to glitter, they nonetheless had a competent look about them. The high point of the celebration was a review in an open field. "Men with mud of Jarama still in their ears, men with their behinds sticking out of their pants" stood at attention while dapper officers cantered past on horses that looked recently dry cleaned. After a series of speeches in a language none of them comprehended, they marched back to their barracks-church, only to be told, "Assemble at six. Full pack. We're moving out tonight." Their destination—the old trenches at Jarama. They grumbled a little, but not much. Said one, "Jarama's home. A hell of a lot more comfortable than this joint. Not so draughty." Yet there was an undercurrent of disappointment that the Red Army had called them to Alcala merely to fill up spaces in their parade. After all, they were fighting in the same war.

So they waited, wrote more letters, sniped at an invisible enemy, played more Ping-Pong, and waited. To this period belongs "The Valley of Jarama," a ballad composed by a Glasgow volunteer for the British Battalion but adopted by the Lincolns and Dimitrovs. Sung to the tune of "The Red River Valley," it spoke not of the horror of Jarama fighting but the resigned monotony of the waiting.

> There's a valley in Spain called Jarama,
> That's a place that we all know so well,
> For 'tis there that we wasted our manhood,
> And most of our old age as well.
>
> From this valley they tell us we're leaving,
> But don't hasten to bid us adieu,
> For e'en though we make our departure,
> We'll be back in an hour or two.
>
> Oh, we're proud of our Lincoln Battalion,
> And the marathon record it's made,
> Please do us this little favor,
> And take this last word to brigade:
>
> "You will never be happy with strangers,
> "They would not understand you as we,
> "So remember the Jarama Valley
> "And the old men who wait patiently." [15]

---

[15] The words were entirely unacceptable for home-front patriots in Great Britain and in the United States, and were changed. A London mass meeting

They did not know it, but the long trench vigil was drawing to a close. In their war rooms at Madrid, the Republican Army of the Center was mapping out a major offensive that called for hard use of the International Brigades. In this flood of new experiences, "The Valley of Jarama" would soon be as irrelevant as a song about the Lincoln Battalion. Yet it caught something of the spirit of what it was like to serve in the battalion, and it still remains the most haunting, and wistful, ballad sung by American volunteers in the Spanish Civil War.

sang a revised version that included these stanzas:

> We are proud of our British Battalion,
> And the stand for Madrid that they made,
> For they fought like true Sons of the Soil,
> As part of the Fifteenth Brigade.

> With the rest of the International Column,
> In the stand for the Freedom of Spain
> We swore in that Valley of Jarama
> That fascism never would reign.

6

🜂 The Torrents of Spring

On the front of Albacete
Meet the Generals of the rear.
Oh! They fight the grandest battles
Though the shells they never hear.
Oh, the floor is red and gory,
As the vino bottles flow.
To the front they say they're coming,
"Mañana or next day."
See them strolling in the evening
To the grogshops for their wine,
For they are the brave defenders
Of the Albacete line.

> —Battalion song (tune: "On the Road
> to Mandalay")

With whoops of jubilation, the New York *Daily Worker* broke the news that an American unit was fighting in Spain with the International Brigades. Even reading between the lines of this Communist Party newspaper, one found only chronicles of glory and no hint whatever of catastrophe. In its first battle the Lincoln Battalion had advanced "almost half a mile" into territory disputed not only by the armies of General Franco but also by mercenaries of Mussolini and butchers of Hitler. Other newspapers in the United States quickly discovered that the presence of American volunteers in Spain made sensational copy, although their stories never seemed to reach the dramatic heights of the *Worker*'s, for the simple reason that columnists of the latter were not required to limit themselves to the bare-boned facts.[1]

[1] Vincent Sheean, correspondent for the *Herald Tribune,* touring the front lines with Joe North of the *Daily Worker,* was at first astonished to find that his fellow reporter took little interest in military operations or in verifying

Elsewhere, too, the performance of the Communist Party in publicizing the Lincoln Battalion was wondrous to behold. In essence, it consisted of taking credit for a wildly popular cause without taking responsibility for a venture illegal and, in the end, disastrous. Even while denying that the party recruited for Spain or that the Comintern directed the International Brigade, Earl Browder as Party mouthpiece reported that 60 per cent of the American volunteers were Communists. This percentage was, of course, understated in order to elicit support from anti-Fascists of all creeds.[2] What Browder was trying to convey was that the Spanish Republic was defended by men of good will and democratic zeal, the majority of whom just happened to be Communists. If one granted the premises, did not the conclusion follow?

> The Republic is supported by adherents of democracy;
> The Communist Party supports the Republic;
> Therefore the Communist Party adheres to democracy.

This policy accorded with the Popular Front strategy laid down by the Seventh World Congress in 1935, by which the goal of world revolution would be temporarily shelved in favor of a coalition with all political parties opposing fascism. The American public tacitly supported the Spanish Republic, although officially it opposed lifting the arms embargo, which could have allowed the Republic to win.[3] However muddy this attitude may appear to be in retrospect, there was nothing inconsistent about it at the time: Americans distrusted fascism and admired democracies, but they did not distrust the one or admire the other enough to abandon their preference for neutrality. The Popular Front policy delighted them, because it suggested that

information. Eventually it occurred to him why: what need had he for facts when his column in the *Worker* would glowingly report Republican victories no matter what happened?

   [2] Among the Jarama group, probably 90 per cent or more were Communists. But Browder's soft-sell worked admirably, since the percentage decreased as the war went on and greater numbers of "liberals" joined the Lincoln Battalion.

   [3] According to a public-opinion poll of December, 1938, 76 per cent favored the Republicans over the Nationalists, yet 79 per cent favored retention of the arms embargo to both sides. Early in 1937 the joint resolution prohibiting shipment of arms to either side in Spain passed the Senate by a vote of 81 to 0, and the House by 406 to 1. (The only congressman to vote against it was John T. Bernard, Farm-Labor partyman from Minnesota, who later toured the Republic and visited the Lincoln Battalion.)

the other great political bugaboo, communism, was swinging to the support of democratic regimes.

Nevertheless, as Earl Browder well knew, no fund drive in the United States would get anywhere at all if it urged heartland Americans to assist Republican Spain and the Lincoln Battalion by mailing checks to the Communist cell of their choice. The machinery had to operate noiselessly at a level hidden from the naked eye. As we have seen, there already existed the North American Committee to Aid Democratic Spain,[4] which in its heyday employed twenty-five people full time in its national office and had branches in 131 American cities. Membership consisted primarily of liberal, not necessarily radical, men and women who supported the Republic with heart and pocketbook and who probably assumed that funds collected purchased woolen mittens and condensed milk for Spanish orphans. They probably would not have believed, had they been told (which they had not), that their money was administered by the CPUSA. As a matter of record, in some cities—Milwaukee, to mention only one—the executive director of the North American Committee and the recruiter at the Communist Party headquarters turned out to be the same man.[5] The North American Committee functioned as a clearing house for dozens of subsidiary front organizations that ranged from the Ben Leider Memorial Fund, which collected to bring back the body of an American flier shot down near Madrid in the spring of 1937,[6] to the Lawyers Committee on American Relations

[4] Not to be confused with the granddaddy of them all, the North American Committee for the Defense of Democratic Spain, an earlier one-shot organization, allegedly initiated by a Spanish Republican delegation, which held ninety meetings and collected $100,000 in seven weeks.

[5] At times this duality of roles approximated Restoration comedy. In Milwaukee, a would-be recruit was turned away at the committee office by Mr. X, who advised him in a whisper to try the party headquarters a few blocks away. Arriving there, the recruit found Mr. X, here known as Comrade Y, who asked a few perfunctory questions about politics and accepted him as a rifleman in the Lincoln Battalion. Comrade Y then sent him to the committee office, where Mr. X reappeared to provide an application form so that the recruit could be sent to Spain as a "social worker." In most places, however, the recruiting procedures were infinitely less crude.

[6] Ben Leider, a former reporter for the New York *Post,* was the only American pilot who flew for the Republic because of political convictions rather than money. (What he did with his fifteen hundred dollars per month is not known.) Before going to Spain he told Ruth McKenny, "Jesus, I never cover a story in Williamsburg or walk down Catherine Street without watching the dirty, hungry little kids. I think 'Never mind, we'll fix it up for you.' And

were hammering the Lincoln sandbags "like the heavy pounding of a riveting machine." It was about ten o'clock.

At the whistle, the Americans climbed up the trench wall, some of them dashing forward with animal yells while others peered cautiously toward the enemy lines. Merriman walked up and down the parapet waving the men out and shouting. Lieutenant Wattis, an officer famous for his cool style, strode through the trench, tapping lingerers on the shoulder with a swagger stick and prodding armpits with an automatic pistol. The new arrivals went over with full packs. One of these, a boy in muddy tennis shoes, slipped back as though he had lost his footing, his forehead against the trench wall as though faint or sleepy. A companion shook him, until he saw a stream of red ooze pouring from under his helmet and filling his collar. Yet few men were hit as they clambered out of the trench. The enemy fire fell off, if anything. For about thirty seconds, Nationalist officers allowed the Americans to emerge from their burrows so that they could be butchered in the open. Then they let go.

The sudden volley caught Merriman in the act of raising his arm to wave the men forward. He was knocked back into the trench by a bullet which broke his left shoulder in five places. As he turned to look at Merriman, Springhall was struck by a bullet that carried away his upper teeth from ear to ear. Seacord had fallen heir to the Lincoln Battalion, but he never learned of this honor. With hundreds of others he was dashing through the hollow. Seconds later he and two companions were killed by the same machine-gun burst.

Four men running side by side fell to the ground the instant the enemy volley lashed the hollow. A seaman just behind was impressed by their training-manual responses, until he crawled up and found them dead. By this time bullets were spewing up tiny geysers of earth around him. Therefore he used his dead companions—all of them YCL men from The Bronx—as a barricade. Not far away, an American wandered about unharmed, squinting at the enemy trenches and apparently undecided whether to run forward or backward.

One volunteer recalled reaching the hollow, where he saw a network of red stripes hovering a few feet above the ground like surveyor's strings. Although he had never before seen this phenomenon, he knew it was an interlocking crossfire from enemy machine guns on the flanks. Men who did not know what it was were plunging into it and dropping in swarms. He dispatched a runner to instruct the Lincoln gunners to concentrate their fire on the enemy flanks, but the with Spain, a group whose real purpose was to find loopholes in the law through which military aid could be funneled to Spain. Hundreds of thousands of pamphlets and leaflets were disseminated through the network of the committee, which also maintained a speakers' bureau and issued press releases almost daily. It sponsored and distributed films, some of them of excellent quality, such as *Heart of Spain, Spain in Flames, Madrid Document,* and *Spanish Earth* (script by Hemingway).

Funds were raised through dances, bazaars, rallies, fairs, auctions, picnics, shooting matches, and tag days. A dinner of the League of American Writers, chaired by Malcolm Cowley, cleared $1,650 and concluded with the auction of an autographed manuscript donated by Theodore Dreiser, guest speaker. Advertisements like the following appeared in left-of-center periodicals:

HEAR THE VOICE OF THE LINCOLN BRIGADE
BROADCAST DIRECT FROM MADRID

(Arranged by Friends of the Brigade, Political leader of the Brigade, John Dos Passos, Josephine Herbst, Joris Ivens, Sidney Franklin, Father Leocadio Lobo and others.)

MECCA TEMPLE
April 24 at 8:00 P.M.
Admission 30¢ and 25¢
(This ad is good for 20% reduction on price of your ticket.)

One could attend a "Barricades Barbecue" in a warehouse on West 17th Street to dance and listen to Leadbelly, or a "Lincoln Birthday Party" featuring Lillian Hellman, or a "Farewell Dinner to Ludwig Renn (Baron Veith von Golzenau)" at the Claridge Hotel. For those less politically intense, there were many opportunities to help the boys in Spain and to have a good time, too. Even Liberty Leaguers or

we will, too, by God!" He told her that he had two loves, the Communist Party and flying, in that order.

His body was exhumed from an Air Force cemetery at Colmenar Viejo and returned to New York in August, 1938. A funeral procession of two thousand marched from Times Square to Carnegie Hall, where services were held prior to burial at Mount Hebron Cemetery in Flushing. Although Leider had no connection whatever with either the International Brigades or the Lincoln Battalion, his guard of honor consisted of 125 Lincoln veterans.

American Legionnaires might have been attracted by this announcement in *New Masses*:

MOONLIGHT CRUISE
July 23
FEATURING
Dick Carroll and his International Swing Band
and
The "No Pasaran" Singers
"every ticket sold helps buy smokes
for our boys in Spain." [7]

Never before in its history had the CPUSA sponsored a program that aroused so many supporters or enjoyed so much snowballing publicity. For the American public, the crusade against fascism in Spain often attracted the sort of person who would have been horrified by an allusion to "dictatorship of the proletariat." And when it is remembered that the CPUSA had lost 20 per cent of its following during the four years between 1932 and 1936, one can imagine the intoxicating effect upon the party leaders.[8] They were shrewd enough to know, however, that sympathy for the good fight in Spain was not the same as affection for the Soviet Union. Rather, Americans were responding to a historical nostalgia for a period in their past when Thirteen Colonies struggled for self-determinism against an autocratic "oppressor." Communist propaganda exploited this tenuous parallel. Under the slogan "Communism is Twentieth Century Americanism," cartoonists depicted battle-hardened men of the Lincoln Battalion marching behind the drum and fife of the "Spirit of '76." Americans were redeeming long-overdue debts to Lafayette, Kosciusko, and von Steuben. The struggle in Spain was compared with Valley Forge. A poet wrote a poem entitled "Bunker Hill Is Now Madrid." Propagandists raided American history to show that the International Brigades were "the Lafayettes of the modern industrial age" or the "Paul Reveres waking the drowsy world to the midnight threat of Fascism." Who, then, was Franco? "Cornwallis" and "Benedict Arnold." In Madison Square Garden, Earl Browder explained that the Commu-

[7] The men of the Lincoln Battalion would have enjoyed this patriotic outing. They were, at the time, being hammered by the Nationalist counteroffensive at Brunete after seventeen days in the line.

[8] The Communist candidate for President polled 102,991 votes in 1932 against 80,159 in 1936.

nist Party revered "the spirit of the frontier, the covered wagon, Buffalo Bill, Steve Brady, Casey Jones and other heroic figures in our nation's copybook past." Then he went on to compare Thomas Jefferson with Cordell Hull, somewhat to the disadvantage of the latter. Who, in the present age, most resembled Jefferson? Lenin, of course.

Viewed under the chill light of practical politics, the policy of the Communist Party was ingenious. Such was the manipulative skill of Browder and other "Sages of Twelfth Street" that whether the outcome in Spain was win, lose, or draw, the party itself had to gain. If the Republic defeated fascism, the victory belonged to the International Brigade for its work at Madrid and to the Soviet Union, which alone among major powers had repudiated the hypocrisy of nonintervention. On the other hand, if fascism triumphed, the defeat could be blamed upon the effete democracies that had refused to assist the Republic. The stakes were high, and the Communists did not have to ante-up anything, for the costs would be borne by the other parties of the Popular Front.

By the spring of 1937, the CPUSA was prepared to cut loose from the sheltering lee of the North American Committee, which had become too large for effective exercise of control and which tried to adhere to the objectives of a "relief" organization like the International Red Cross. To channel funds directly into the Lincoln Battalion, a new organization was chartered that called itself Friends of the Abraham Lincoln Brigade (FALB). The name itself was a clever deception. "Friends" suggested a nonviolent order like the Society of Friends; "Brigade" implied that the Americans in Spain were more numerous than, in fact, they were. Henceforth, on this side of the Atlantic, one never heard of the Lincoln *Battalion;* always it was the Lincoln *Brigade,* a military unit that existed nowhere except in the minds of the publicists who coined the term. No matter: fiction was more marketable than truth. And the truth was that American volunteers reached brigade numbers only by counting the dead. FALB took charge of recruitment, transportation, and rehabilitation of American volunteers.[9] Under its auspices, returned veterans toured the country,

---

[9] Late in 1939 the FALB was assimilated by VALB (Veterans of the Abraham Lincoln Battalion), which had been organized in 1937 and which continues to function. In accordance with the hagiography of the American Revolutionary War, the VALB symbol consists of a Liberty Bell (cracked) inscribed with "For Liberty in Spain."

speaking at union halls, at universities, at *soirées*—whenever there was an audience ready to listen and willing to pay. Recruits for the Lincoln Battalion were never publicly sought, but if a likely youth cornered a speaker privately, he might obtain a street address or a telephone number where contact could be made. It is worth noting, however, that in the beginning there were always more applicants than places for them. It was an accolade apt to turn a young man's head to be accepted for service in Spain.

Eternally vigilant, officers of Federal, state, and municipal agencies donned cloak-and-dagger costumes in order to seek out and destroy nefarious pockets of "Red Army" recruitment and support. Acting on a tip from a Minneapolis bricklayer who defected from a group of Lincoln Battalion recruits in Paris, the sheriff of Sullivan County, New York, assembled a posse and beat the bushes between Fallsburgh and Woodridge seeking a "Spanish Camp" where recruits allegedly received military training. When he discovered a small farm owned by a former employee of the North American Committee, the sheriff was exultant, until he found that the "secret camp" was overlooked by a large resort hotel. In Detroit, Sergeant Maciosek of the "Red Squad" sensationally announced that the Communist Party "quota" for Michigan called for five hundred recruits. But when the House Un-American Activities Committee (HUAC) later put him on the witness stand, the Sergeant was able to submit the names of only twenty-two men known to be in Spain. At times, the Red hunt got rough. Police in Detroit broke into the house of the FALB executive secretary and carried off his files. Eleven people were jailed at Milan Prison on charges of having recruited for a foreign power, charges dropped after five or six days. Among the "incriminating" evidence never returned to the local executive secretary were a Communist Party card (Spanish branch) and a broken pistol (donated to the Lincoln Battalion by a Lansing schoolteacher).

Whether one wished it, or even believed it, to support the Spanish Republic was to be fastened, however haphazardly, to one or more jerrybuilt offshoots of the Comintern. No other bloc, alliance, or party employed weapons mightier than wet mouths or dry ink. Letters to congressmen might as well have been addressed to the Dead Letter Office, for Washington marshaled itself behind its own slogan "Scrupulous Nonintervention in Spain," a scrupulosity never evident in Berlin or Rome. While others dragged their feet, the Communists rode in the bandwagon, whipping up massive rallies and arranging mammoth parades in which wounded veterans (in tailor-made uniforms) led euphoric crowds in singing "The Star-Spangled Banner" beneath gigantesque portraits of Abraham Lincoln and George Washington. (One wonders whether jobbers in the photographic trades sold the same portraits to the German-American Bund when they held their meetings in the same halls and in the same streets.)

Jealous of the Communist success in cornering the market in Spanish aid, the American Socialist Party called for the formation of a "Eugene V. Debs Column" to fight in Spain. They managed to stage a kickoff march down Fifth Avenue before disappearing into oblivion. The pacifist wing of the party was outraged that Debs' name would be used in abetting militarism, in much the same way that a Quaker group might have protested against an outfit calling itself "The Jesus Christ Artillerists." Their efforts were farcical. It is alleged that only five would-be members of the Debs Column reached Paris, where they were stranded with neither the funds nor the know-how to cross into Spain. Tails between their legs, the recruits either returned home bitterly or, swallowing their pride, enlisted in the Lincoln Battalion. The Communists were, of course, exultant at this ignominious performance of their old competitor for the proletarian vote. It might be noted that when Norman Thomas, the Socialist leader, visited Spain in the spring of 1937, he did not pay his respects to the Albacete leadership or drop in for a chat with the Lincoln Battalion at Jarama.

Months before the Lincoln Battalion had been dreamed of, a group of Americans sympathetic to the Anarchists had been fighting with militia units on the Aragon front under the name "The Sacco-Vanzetti Column." They received no support, no plaudits, no publicity. Those not killed at the front by Fascists were doubtless gunned down by the Communists during the Barcelona purge of May, 1937. Or, if they escaped both enemies, they returned home to be swallowed up in the anonymity of American life.[10]

Efforts of the Roman Catholic Church to enlist support for Nationalist Spain were significant only in a negative sense: that is to say, the hierarchy was able to exert sufficient political pressure upon the Administration to block all moves to lift the arms embargo. (In the long run, this negative pressure might have influenced the outcome of the war far more than any other single event.) But attempts to engage

---

[10] There is reason to believe that some of them were athletes and spectators who had come to Barcelona in the summer of 1936 to participate in the Workers Olympiad (a boycott of the Olympiad at Berlin). George Orwell, in *Homage to Catalonia,* briefly alludes to them.

popular support for Franco were a dismal failure.[11] To begin with, 48 per cent of Roman Catholics in the United States favored the Republic, despite the anticlericism of the Republican government. And the lay organization known as the American Committee for Spanish Relief folded up before it had collected thirty thousand dollars—all of which had to be used for administrative expenses!

The conclusion is unmistakably clear. Only the Communist Party knew how to assess, engage, and mobilize public opinion in the United States with respect to the Spanish question.

Behind the fanfare and trumpetry, however, the Central Committee of the CPUSA was deeply troubled. It knew what the American public and general party members had no inkling of—that Jarama had been a disaster for the Lincoln Battalion. An exposé revealing the presence of mutinies, labor battalions, and massacres in Spain would damage party unity and credibility. The error, as they now saw it, was in sending over undisciplined volunteers lacking in experienced party leadership. Beginning in March, they sent to Spain many nationally known figures in addition to the "expendables." Robert Minor, a slightly deaf, white-haired former cartoonist, became the Central Committee representative to the International Control Committee (roughly equivalent to the board of directors of the International Brigades). Another prominent partyman, Steve Nelson, was sent to fill the slot vacated by Sam Stember. William Lawrence took over Bart's old post as American representative to the Albacete base. Allan Johnson took command of the new American training camp at Tarazona de la Mancha, near Albacete.[12] In addition to this galaxy, there

[11] One of the few Franco volunteers was Guy Castle of Oxon Hill, Maryland, who entered Spain in August, 1936, and joined the legion. A few weeks later he was badly wounded near Teruel and hospitalized at Calatayud, where his mother joined him. Unable to obtain a discharge from the legion, Castle attempted to swim from La Linea to Gibraltar but was washed back and sentenced to be executed. Through the appeals of his mother and the intercession of British citizens at Gibraltar—the U.S. consul having refused aid—Castle obtained a *salvo conducto* to leave Spain, which he did, in March, 1938. Subsequently Castle, who became a Washington reporter, had "nothing but praise" for the reckless daring of his fellow legionaries. In World War II he was wounded at Guadalcanal while serving with the First Raider Battalion. At the time of his death in 1965, Castle was a member of the Columbia Historical Society, Lords of the Maryland Manor, the Mayflower Society, and the Pilgrims of St. Mary.

[12] Johnson might have been slated to take over the military command of the Lincoln Battalion from Hourihan. He came up to Jarama in March and helped with trench fortifications for a short time. Hourihan disliked and dis-

were lesser luminaries like Joe Dallet, an organizer from Youngstown who had once run for mayor on the Communist Party ticket; Dave Doran, a national officer of the Young Communist League; Sandor Voros, erstwhile cadet in the Austro-Hungarian Army and more recently a political writer for Earl Browder.

The Jarama fiasco was such a tight secret that not even a party man as well placed as Voros had heard about it. Though a writer of party propaganda for years, he had been taken in by the published version of the Lincoln Battalion victory at Jarama. When a Central Committeeman briefed him at party headquarters prior to his departure, Voros listened to him in stunned surprise: "The Party is in trouble, Voros. All that stuff you've been reading about the heroic Lincoln Brigade in the *Daily Worker* is crap. If the truth comes out and the enemies of the Party pick it up, we're going to have a scandal. The truth is that the Lincoln Brigade mutinied the first day it was sent into action and had to be driven at pistol point into attack. The comrades in Spain are completely demoralized. They want to come home and many of them are deserting." Since no one seemed to know how many Americans were in Spain, where they were, whether they were living or dead, Voros was given the job of establishing an archives and historical commission. When he was handed a silk ribbon and instructed to sew it into the lining of his coat, Voros felt very important indeed. That innocuous-looking piece of silk identified him as a Comintern agent. His father was not impressed. When he learned where his son was going, he cried out, "Bums fighting bums. I can smell a bum from a mile. Hitler and Stalin, they both smell the same to me." Choking back tears, Voros senior went on, "You are my eldest son! Stay away from those bums. . . . You're disgracing the family." It took months for Sandor Voros to learn what the old man meant.

The roundhouse for the traffic in international volunteers was the Maison des Syndicats, a trade-union hall not far from the Metro stop "Place du Combat" in the heart of the "Red" arrondissements of Paris. Behind a high wall on the Rue Mathurin-Moreau, lines of dingy offices looked out upon a cobblestone courtyard that was always either muddy or dusty, depending upon the weather. This was the headquarters of the secret railway that transported volunteers to

trusted him, perhaps detecting that the Harris-Merriman situation was about to be recapitulated. Johnson then moved on to Tarazona, and the story was given out that he had been wounded on the Jarama front.

Spain across a frontier officially closed. Behind one unmarked door was the office of "Jack" and "Eric" (surnames never used), who made arrangements for the Americans. "Police spies," Jack reported, "were thicker'n rats in a sewer." If a volunteer was caught, it meant a jail term and deportation. Bottlenecked in Paris, during the spring of 1937, were several hundred Americans and Canadians who had been scattered about in lofts, boardinghouses, and private homes in the Batignolles quarter. Since lists of names and addresses could fall into the hands of the wrong people, Jack and Eric carried the whole business in their heads. The first volunteers had crossed the frontier into Spain cheering and singing; Rightist sympathizers in France had changed all that. Nowadays men had to hike by night over the Pyrenees or slip across in small boats.

Jack was a Marxist missionary whose real name was Arnold Reid. A New York Jew of twenty-four, he had quit the University of Wisconsin to organize for the party in Mexico and Cuba. He had married a Cuban schoolteacher, spoke Spanish fluently, and had an almost mystical affection for things Spanish. Tough and zealous, Reid had been primed for a commissar post in the International Brigades, but at the last minute he was held in Paris to unravel the difficulties that the Americans were having with their French comrades. Much of the trouble stemmed from an absurd notion that American volunteers were "lousy with money," that they were "proletarian millionaires." French comrades went out of their way to obstruct and inconvenience their American counterparts on these grounds. (At the same time, with remarkable inconsistency, they looked down upon German and Italian volunteers as lumpenproletariat forced to go to Spain in order to avoid prisons and firing squads in their own countries.) Employing a brusque frontal assault against the bickering factionalism of the Paris committee, Reid had obtained their grudging cooperation. But with his *permis de séjour* long expired, he was weary of dodging down back alleys one step ahead of the police, tired of picayunish infighting with Party hacks, and frustrated by his shepherd's role in herding volunteers over the frontier. Paris was muck and mire; Reid passionately wanted to go to Spain.

Eric, his assistant, was a Harvard man in his late twenties whose real name was DeWitt Parker. An esthete as well as a Marxist, he was as much at home in the Latin Quarter as in the Rue Mathurin-Moreau. He was open-hearted, intelligent, dedicated. His French was so good and his wit so keen that he was a great favorite among the plainclothesmen and gendarmes who snooped around the Maison des Syndicats. Both Parker and Reid repeatedly begged party leaders to send them to Spain. Their wish came true many months later, with very sad results.

Nearly every boat-train brought fresh volunteers into Paris, most of them eager for a last spree before going off to war. They were intrigued by the sawdust saloons lining the Boulevard Jean Jaurès where girls in pairs sat under signs marked

15 FRANCS, EVERYTHING INCLUDED
SOLDIERS ON LEAVE FROM ALGIERS, 12 FRANCS

To circumvent the dangers of brawling, drinking, and whoring—any of which could expose the entire operation to the police and endanger the whole *rite de passage*—Reid confiscated their money, returning them enough for cigarettes and a couple of beers. At the Maison he briefed them on the necessity for secrecy, while Mrs. Charlotte Haldane (the wife of J. B. S.) lectured upon the ravages of advanced syphilis. Because suitcases could not be carried over Pyrenean goat trails, they had to be left behind at the hall. Each volunteer was issued a blue beret on the theory that this would gallicize his unmistakably American appearance.

Not the least among the worries of Reid and Parker was a Detroit volunteer named Albert Wallach. On the boat Wallach had ruptured himself while doing calisthenics. When the French Communists refused to place him in one of their hospitals, Reid had no alternative but to send him to the expensive Anglo-American Hospital at Neuilly. After six weeks and an operation to boot, Wallach's bill was so vast that it exceeded Reid's small budget. Nothing could be done except to command Wallach to climb out of a window and flee for sanctuary in a friendly boardinghouse. The police followed close behind and searched the room in which Wallach was hiding. Fortunately he had climbed into a wardrobe and was overlooked. Eventually Reid was able to smuggle him to Marseilles.[13]

---

[13] The bad luck of Albert Wallach was only beginning. He was aboard the *Ciudad de Barcelona* when it was torpedoed off the coast of Cataluña. He fought in the Lincoln Battalion until the spring of 1938, when he went to pieces and deserted. Returned to the line in a labor battalion, Wallach deserted a second time. His luck seemed to turn. He hid aboard the *Oregon,* a merchant ship moored in Barcelona. Just before the vessel sailed for New York, Wallach went ashore on an unknown errand and fell into the hands of Tiny Agostino, then an IB policeman. He was taken to the IB prison at Castelldefels, on the

By late spring a trickle of men, wounded for the most part, began to turn up at the Maison. They had been discharged from the International Brigades and waited for a chance to work their passage back to the States. Since Reid had no money to buy them clothes, he broke open suitcases of men who had just departed for Spain, in order to clothe those homeward bound. (There was only a fifty-fifty chance that a Spanish volunteer would ever return to claim his suitcase.) From time to time these tatterdemalions, the visionary gleam long gone from their eyes, overlapped recruits en route to Spain. Such encounters seldom uplifted the morale of the recruits. There was, to mention but one example, the laconic exchange between a new volunteer and a veteran whose rigid leather glove obviously concealed an artificial hand. "You guys just get back?" asked the vet. "No, we're just going." "Oh," replied the vet with disappointment, "more suckers."

Since none of the Americans—not even Robert Minor, the principal party man in Spain [14]—rated either the submarine or private plane used to carry high-priority personnel to Spain, they waited their turn to slip aboard a fishing boat or to follow a guide over the Pyrenees. In May the backlog of waiting volunteers was so great that the Control Committee put five hundred men aboard the *Ciudad de Barcelona* at Marseilles. The vessel was torpedoed by an unidentified submarine twenty miles north of Barcelona. Knocked on one side, it sank at once, carrying perhaps half the volunteers to their deaths. (Lifeboats had been locked in their davits and could not be freed.) For weeks the fishermen of Malgrat separated unidentifiable bodies from a thick beach scum of oil, hemp, and lumber.

An opaque curtain of censorship was immediately dropped over the *Barcelona* disaster. The survivors were warned not to talk about it and were rushed south to Valencia. Sandor Voros, who came across them there, quite by accident, saw an opportunity to publicize a bona fide "Fascist atrocity" story in American newspapers. He col-

---

Tarragona road, and dropped into an empty cistern. Fellow prisoners heard his groans but could do nothing. Probably he had been reruptured. On the following morning the cistern was empty. Albert Wallach was never seen again. A few years later Wallach's father showed Agostino a snapshot of his son and asked whether he had ever seen that face before. Agostino looked at it and remarked that it looked a little like Cary Grant.

[14] Attempting to minimize the role of the Communist Party in the International Brigades, the "official history" of the Lincoln Battalion mentions Robert Minor's name only once, in a passing reference.

lected the name and hometown of every American known to be aboard—the forty-three American survivors estimated that eighty or ninety had perished—and in his mind's eye saw the headline LOCAL BOY TORPEDOED BY FASCIST SUBMARINE. Excitedly he sought Bob Minor and demanded a typewriter. But Minor became "livid with anger." Snatching the notes from Voros' hand, he shouted, "What are you trying to do, demoralize the people back home?" Eventually the news leaked out. And ultimately the steamship company admitted that the vessel had been sunk. The official announcement declared that the *Ciudad de Barcelona* had carried no passengers at all— nothing more than a cargo of fish, bread, and vegetables for hungry Spain.

A group of fifteen Americans led by Steve Nelson became legendary figures even before they arrived in Spain. They had tried to slip across the frontier in a fishing boat but were boarded at sea by a French patrol boat, which towed them back to Port Vendres. Nelson's identity had to be concealed. Fortunately he was traveling on a passport issued to "Joseph Fleischinger" (the name of his uncle) and was able to slip into the ranks. Joe Dallet of Youngstown took command. Before they docked, he distributed all incriminating documents to his men and ordered them to chew them into paste. (One man exceeded the order by swallowing his portion.) At dockside each man proclaimed that he was merely a tourist. This answer enraged the port authorities, who knew that not even crazy Americans toured Europe lying in the hold of a fishing boat, their clothes saturated with a filthy ooze of motor oil, salt water, and fish krawm. As the police herded them off to the provincial prison at Perpignan, villagers and captives turned the procession into a victory march, shouting *"Vive le republique!"* and *"Vive le front populaire!"* at one another.

The *gendarmerie* speedily learned that these were not ordinary prisoners. On the bus ride to Perpignan, an American picked the lock of his handcuffs and smilingly presented them to his guard at the journey's end. When the prison doctor tried to inoculate them against small pox, the Americans rebelled. "You can't shoot your Hitler germs into us!" they shouted. Once locked inside, they turned the prison into a bedlam of noise, door pounding, and outraged demands for immediate penal reform. A turnkey burst into their cell, cursing them in French, but drew back intimidated when Dallet cursed him back in French, in English, and in Yiddish. Alarmed that their mood of insurrection might spread to other prisoners, the warden transferred them to a separate wing and gave them carbolic acid to disinfect the cell and quicklime for the open-trough latrine. They adhered to their tourist story and refused to answer any questions unless Dallet was present. Meanwhile, Popular Front organizations in Perpignan rallied to their support, sending in baskets of food. Newsmen descended upon Perpignan to see whether the French government would enforce the Nonintervention Agreement or would allow the prisoners to go free. Mopping his forehead, the warden exclaimed, "Nothing like this has ever before happened in Perpignan prison. Nothing!" An American vice consul hurried down from Marseilles to confiscate their passports, but the French authorities refused to give them up, saying they were part of the permanent records of the case.[15] The identity of "Joseph Fleischinger" was not discovered.

In view of the volatility of crowds demonstrating in favor of the captives, the trial was held in Ceret, a somnolent village located in the foothills of the Pyrenees, eighteen miles south of Perpignan. Advised that six months would be automatically added to their sentence for contempt of court unless they abandoned their tourist pose, Dallet agreed to drop it. Personally he was delighted by the opportunity thus afforded to publicize the determination of International volunteers to reach Spain despite the barriers of the Nonintervention Agreement. With the help of an attorney from Béziers sent to him by the Comité d'Entre Aide Franco-Espagnol, Dallet set about his task with the instinct of a born showman who knew how to wring the last ounce of sympathy from every groan.

Underneath the do-or-die, hard-crust manner of Joe Dallet lay soft tissue oozy with bourgeois fat that he had never been able to burn off. Unlike the men he led, Dallet had not been suckled on poverty and revolution. Class war had not been bred in the bone but acquired, like a taste for caviar. The father of Joe Dallet did not work in a sweatshop: he ran one.

Joe Dallet, Jr., was born in Cleveland in 1907 but grew up in Woodmere, Long Island, a parvenu suburb of New York. As the only male child he was treated like an heir apparent by his adoring mother and sisters. At Lawrence High School he received a rigorous bourgeois education, where he was encouraged to take the right courses,

---

[15] The Department of State ordered its consul to arrest these men and arrange for their deportation. At the same time, it refused liability for expenses of escort, transportation, and maintenance!

read the right books, and entertain opinions as far right as an American education would allow. He became infatuated with modern poetry and advanced to intermediate Chopin on the piano. Joseph Dallet, Sr., a silk manufacturer, was a first generation American with expectations that his son might become something wholly different— a first-generation Episcopalian, perhaps. Fearing the radicalism of Harvard, he enrolled his son at Dartmouth in 1923 (at age sixteen). The Anglo-Saxon flippancy of Hanover appalled and suffocated Joe, Jr. (Dartmouth students of the time were the sort who looked down their noses at Babbittry not because it was boorish but because it was middle-class, too much like themselves.[16])

Perhaps in self-defense, he championed proletarian ideas and a classless society, ideas that did not shock his classmates as much as mystify them. At Harvard this hebetic radicalism would doubtless have found a channel, but at Dartmouth it was treated as perversity. Dallet was scorned, laughed at, and—worst of all—ignored. On weekends he drove down to New York City in his canary-yellow roadster to confer with labor leaders, or so he claimed. Yet when he was dropped from Dartmouth in the middle of his sophomore year, he took a job with Massachusetts Mutual Life. In 1928 he made the grand tour of Europe in the grand style but seemed to have had no working-class fervor at this time. As he told Steve Nelson, "Waiters were just flunkeys. That they were human beings, that they had wives and families and problems, that they were alive and worth knowing— it just never occurred to me." The Crash of twenty-nine brought communism to him with the impact of a religious conversion.

A Dartmouth dropout and rich man's son would have made good publicity material for the party, but Dallet refused to permit his shameful background to be aired. Plunging into organizing for the Steel and Metal Workers Industrial Union in McKeesport, South Chicago, and Youngstown, he ruthlessly tried to stamp out every lingering trace within himself of bourgeois pollution. His language became so ungrammatical and his manners so coarse that authentic proletarians, men with natural dignity, were at times shocked by Dallet. And sometimes his speeches were so rabidly partisan that they won-

---

[16] In the forties, Joe Dallet was "discovered" by Dartmouth students, who established The Dallet Memorial Committee to commemorate "the first Dartmouth man to be killed in World War II." They were able to find only one classmate, an assistant librarian, who remembered him. He recalled a "rather belligerent crust," a "champion of proletarian ideals," and "an utter misfit in college."

dered whether he was having a secret joke at their expense. Such suspicions were groundless: Dallet was entirely convinced that real proletarians behaved this way. In certain areas he drew the line. He married the daughter of a college professor, not a steelworker. In 1936, while his wife, Katherine Harrison Dallet (Joe was her first husband, J. Robert Oppenheimer her third), ground out campaign throwaways on the mimeograph machine, he ran for mayor of Youngstown on the Communist ticket. Though defeated at the polls, his hot and sassy campaign made him a folk hero among the Ohio Left.[17] Clearly Joe Dallet was bound somewhere in the party. At the Ceret trial he blossomed like a sinister plant.

The letters that Joe Dallet wrote his wife from Perpignan reflect the temperament of a man satisfied by nothing less than adoration from her, from the crowds, from his men. Of the trial he wrote: "We go in chains. . . . Everyone stares and we raise our right fists in salute and more than half of them return the salute. It's swell. My picture was in the Perpignan *Independent* today, taken as I came out of jail, fist raised." Then, a few days later: "The lawyer tells me the papers are full of it and he volunteered to send you a copy. Did he ever send you that picture of me? The photographer yesterday also agreed to send you a picture of yesterday's demonstration." Noble purpose and revolutionary dedication vanished amid the popping of flashbulbs as Joe Dallet clenched his fist for photographers. Why, we may ask, did his ego need all this spurious gratification? In a quieter mood, he confided to his wife, "Some day you and I must travel this land together and hire a small sailing boat and sail along the coast." Here was the true voice: a Woodmere yachtsman, not a Youngstown organizer.

Yet none of Dallet's unconscious mental equivocation or emotional insecurity appeared to rub off upon the men with him at Perpignan prison. They followed, and he led. If Dartmouth had taught him anything, it was how to needle the bourgeoisie. When more volunteers, captured in the Pyrenees, were brought to Perpignan, Dallet organized a "jail soviet," which won them privileges unheard of in French prisons. He established classes in politics and in Spanish, and he con-

---

[17] According to Sandor Voros, who wrote Communist propaganda in Ohio during this period, the party succeeded in electing a Communist mayor of Yorktown. "The only Communist mayor ever elected in the United States" had promised two irresistible reforms: 1) the abolishment of all debts and mortgages, and 2) no taxes on liquor—ever.

ducted thunderous songathons that thrilled the crowds milling about outside hoping to catch a glimpse of *les voluntaires*.

With informers, scabs, and weaklings Dallet took a dictatorial line. Some of the more recent prisoners were foreign volunteers who had undergone police torture in Italy and tended to "confess" to anything the authorities demanded. One day Dallet overheard a badly frightened Italian telling the police that he had volunteered because the Communist Party promised him ten thousand francs—a confession so absurd that even the public prosecutor discounted it. But Dallet did not. In front of the other men he denounced and insulted the informer. Proudly he explained the aftermath to his wife: "He hung his head and was too scared to speak. We all threatened him and I was surprised how well I could curse in French. I found out yesterday that when they got him back to jail they beat him up and completely ostracized him." This same Joe Dallet sat down before the piano in the home of the Ceret police inspector to play Chopin from memory in order to demonstrate that Communists were men of culture. The reporters loved it. Once more flashbulbs popped. Afterward Dallet begged Nelson, the only American witness, not to tell the guys about it, for he did not want to be mistaken for a "bloody bourgeois intellectual."

The Ceret trial resulted in an empty victory for the prosecution. The Nonintervention Agreement was upheld legally when the captives were found guilty of frontier violations. But the sentence mocked the verdict: they were given twenty-day jail terms, with credit for fifteen days already served. Before their release, Dallet ordered his men to decorate the cell with so many slogans and hammer-sickle emblems that the walls had to be whitewashed after they had gone. It was good college-boy fun. Their exit from prison was triumphant. "Crowds gather around us in the streets," he wrote his wife. "We are the idols of the YCLers and the Pioneers." People "begged" him to come back again and offered "to turn their places inside out" if he and his wife would return for a visit. (He did not mention that three American volunteers got drunk at a Popular Front dance and were sent back to the States as "disruptive elements.")

The only route to Spain was up. They climbed the Pyrenees by creekbeds and mule paths, skirting French border patrols at night. For seven hours they climbed this cruel ladder behind a Spanish guide who whispered, *"Camaradas, Adelante! Adelante!"* The worst moment came when the stars faded and the cold sky turned blue-gray with coming dawn. Border guards would be able to spot them. Dallet described their passage: "The last peak was a 5000-foot climb over loose and jagged rock, through thick stiff underbrush. And we had to race against sunrise to get over without being seen. I carried a 165-pound guy practically by myself that whole climb. Christ! When we crossed the line we almost cried for happiness—some people did cry and I had a hell of a job restraining myself." (In the Dallet canon, tough guys never cried—and somehow they knew the exact weight of the man they carried.) Concluding his letter, a surge of masculine strength swept through Joe Dallet: "It was a most interesting trip— and so successful I could holler for joy and if you were here I'd crush the breath out of you."

Dartmouth man, Youngstown hero, Perpignan martyr—Dallet stood erect at dawn in the snowy wastes of the Pyrenees among the exhausted shapes of weaker men. A proletarian artist might have done much with this vignette. From such an eminence there was nowhere to go except down. And it is important to picture Joe Dallet at this moment in order to appreciate how far down he would eventually sink.

American volunteers reaching Spain during the spring of 1937 were sent out to the new training camp at Tarazona de la Mancha, twenty miles northwest of Albacete. (Villanueva de la Jara had been abandoned.) It was a grubby town of middle size with dirt streets that washed out in spring freshets and with blanched wooden balconies hanging precariously over the *plaza mayor*. The unheated barracks was a former convent containing a vine-covered courtyard. Recruits were awakened before dawn and marched to the local cinema used as a mess hall. Covering one wall was a large sign, DO NOT WASTE BREAD. IT HELPS OUR ENEMY. At eight sharp they formed in the *plaza* to salute the red-gold-mauve flag of the Republic. Then followed instruction in close-order drill, infiltration, fortifications, camouflage, riflery, first aid, and topography. Once each day they attended Spanish lessons in the parish church, where the townspeople had hung a streamer across the nave, LONG LIVE THE SOVIET UNION, BEST FRIEND OF THE SPANISH PEOPLE. (Many men were irked by this banner, since it ignored the American contribution.) When off duty there was a *bodega* known as Sloppy Joe's. If a man drank too much, he cooled off in a little stone hut up the hill about a stone's throw from the cemetery. In the *plaza* a hand-cranked barrel organ endlessly played "Popeye the Sailor Man" and "The Music Goes Round and Round." (The organ-grinder in Albacete had more get-up-and-go; he adapted his instrument to play "The Internationale.") About the only diversion in Tarazona was a semi-monthly delousing with vinegar and alcohol—it stung—followed by a hot bath.

The training camp was commanded by the mysterious Captain Allan Johnson (né McNeil). He was a man of about forty with a face like wilted lettuce. His uniform never varied: heavily starched American army issue, except for a brown beret and engineering boots laced up to his knees. Around Tarazona the story was that he was a World War veteran, a graduate of the U.S. War College, and an ex-captain of the U.S. Army. But one volunteer, whose father was a professional army man, claimed that Johnson had left the service hastily after the books failed to balance in the Thirty-first Infantry. Johnson was a fast man with clichés. His favorite military maxim, "What is captured by the gun must be held by the spade," became a Lincoln Battalion joke—some of the Jarama vets muttering that they never saw *him* dig with anything except his spoon. In his office hung an American flag with a yellow hammer and sickle sewn across the stripes. "The flag of the future," he said. "Someday you'll see this in the United States, too." Considering the paucity of training material available at Tarazona, Johnson achieved considerable success. His lectures—and his clichés—saved many lives.

By the first of April, the Lincoln Battalion had been completely restocked with men, and there were enough Americans left over at Tarazona to commence the organization of a second battalion, which took the name George Washington Battalion.[18] Perhaps because of Colonel Copic's proclivity for Yugoslavs, the commander was Mirko Markovicz, a Croat-American from Chicago. Markovicz had almost become an American citizen in 1930 but failed to take out his final papers. It was said that he had had military training in Yugoslavia. He was a tough, no-quarter scrapper—better on the battlefield than the parade ground. His Croatian was better than his English, which was so atrocious that his men—no grammarians themselves—found it difficult not to laugh whenever Markovicz opened his mouth. Politi-

---

[18] There was also an Anglo-American company fighting in the 20th (International) Battalion on the Cordoba front. This was an experimental battalion consisting of men from half a dozen national groups. The idea was to minimize chauvinism by mixing them up. But it was hopelessly impracticable in moments of crisis, when communication all but vanished.

cal commissar of the new battalion was Dave Mates, who had been, during the worst years of the Depression, city secretary of the Unemployed Councils of Chicago. The *Tribune* had branded him "the most dangerous Anarchist since the Haymarket Riots," a singularly inept label. To call Mates an Anarchist was to miss the point entirely.

The plan for the Washington Battalion, as outlined by Bob Minor and Bill Lawrence, was to hold them at Tarazona for training as long as possible. Despite Hourihan's entreaty that the Washingtons take over the Lincoln trenches—held by them since February—Minor refused. When the Washingtons went to the front, he said, they would be the best-trained battalion in the International Brigades. Moreover, the new unit was isolated from contact with the "demoralized elements" of the Lincoln Battalion. On one occasion, three wounded Jarama vets—Joe Gordon, Bill Harvey, and Doug Roach—hitched a ride from Albacete to Tarazona to visit Gordon's brother, who was training there. At the barracks door a minor commissar told them, "No Lincoln bastards are coming in here to demoralize *our* men." They bulled past the comic-star and raised a ruction: Leo Gordon was in there, and they demanded to see him. The Tarazona commanders extracted a promise from them that they would not discuss Jarama, only innocuous matters like friends at home, the weather, and so forth. At dinner the visitors were assigned a table conspicuously isolated from the others. Bob Minor made a speech, in his rolling Texas drawl, that alluded to the Moors as "those *black* men from Africa." Roach, a Negro, was on his feet like a shot, glowering at Minor. Gordon, his eye socket swathed in a bandage, and Harvey, his neck in a giraffian cast, had to pull him back. The three of them then stamped out, while Minor, who was hard of hearing, continued his speech. Much more acceptable at Tarazona was Captain Robert Merriman, who arrived with his shoulder in a plaster cast and who assisted with the training program. His wife, Marion, had come from the Soviet Union to nurse him and to establish a ménage. Joe Dallet was deeply impressed by Merriman, who had "a political approach to every military question" (which was exactly what was wrong with the International Brigades).

The political mood of the International Brigades intensified after May, 1937, when a civil-war-within-the-civil-war broke out in Barcelona between factions of the Republican Government. The result was that the Communists, who presumably engineered the civil conflict, obtained greater power in the government and proceeded to ex-

terminate the POUM, the Trotskyite party of Spain.[19] The poison of
the POUM-purge seeped down to Albacete. Desertion, disobedience,
and even grumbling were no longer considered as human frailties but
as overt acts of Trotskyism, which the Communist loosely defined as
any belief or attitude not conforming to their own. Since the International Brigades were an autonomous military structure, volunteers
found themselves completely at the mercy of their commissars, without recourse to either the Republican Ministry of War or their respective consulates. Punishments were meted out, the severity of which
had no relationship to the actual crime. Zygmund Piasecki, a volunteer from Toledo, Ohio, was among the first to discover the hardening
mood of the party. Fueled by Albacete *coñac,* he hopped aboard a
locomotive and throttled for Valencia. A few miles out of town he
was apprehended when he lost his head of steam. Tried and convicted
of "espionage," Piasecki was given the death sentence, later commuted to a twenty-year prison term. Foolish though his act was, he
was nevertheless not tried for foolishness, theft, and drunkenness—but
for a *political* crime.[20] An officer of the Lincoln Battalion, in later
years, expressed it this way: "In February the enemy was Franco—
that's why I went to Spain; by June it was Trotsky—that's what I
never understood."

The Interbrigade prison was situated six miles out of Albacete,
near Chinchilla. Its nucleus was a farmhouse on a windswept plain,
around which additional buildings had been constructed. As early as
May, 1937, it housed two hundred International prisoners, most of
them French. Normally a prisoner was detained without a specific
charge. Every night certain ones were called and taken away; those
remaining behind never learned whether they had been shot, returned
to the front, released, or sent home. (A favorite means of execution
was to send a man to the front and shoot him from behind; his "death
in battle" drummed up support from friends and relatives at home.)
Some men were impounded here for months on end. As regularly as a

[19] George Orwell returned to Barcelona late in April after having fought in
the POUM militia around Huesca. Like most front-line soldiers he was unaware of the pressure building up against the Trotskyites. Caught in the middle
of the political conflict, he was forced to flee across the frontier to escape execution. Ironically, he was taking steps to enroll in the International Brigades at
the time the purge broke out.

[20] Piasecki remained in prison until April, 1939, when the Nationalist armies
were converging upon Valencia. Woodruff W. Wallner, the U.S. consul, appealed to the authorities, which relented at the last moment, and succeeded in
conveying Piasecki to France.

clock, a Polish-American prisoner (believed by some to have been James Harris) pounded on his cell door every night, shouting, "Copic, you low type, get f . . . . d by the Pope, and s . . . in the milk of your mother! *Let us out!*" The volunteers despised the brigade police as much as they did any goon squad at home. They made up a song about the BPs which they sang to the tune "I'm Popeye the Sailor Man":

> I'm BP the fighting man, pop-pop.
> I'm BP the fighting man, whack-whack.
> My muscles all ripple,
> When I hit a cripple.
> I'm BP the fighting man, pop-pop.

It was never sung in the detention camp, of course.

No army survives very long without discipline, and discipline if not based upon force is worthless. The real issue, however, is whether witch-hunting is an efficacious instrument in building unity or is, in the long run, destructive of the unity it attempts to build. Drunks, deserters, malingerers, and thieves had to be punished, but when they were punished in the name of such an ambiguous heresy as "Trotskyism," the leaders themselves undermined their own credibility and exacerbated the symptoms of general demoralization.

Imperceptibly the mood of the International Brigades began to change after the Barcelona insurrection. One began to hear less about "liberty" and more about "discipline." The clenched-fist gesture of solidarity was superseded by the military salute. The fiction that a commissar was a "delegate" of the men began to fade. Power was a pollutant, and it corrupted men who, under normal circumstances, might have been immune to it. There was the case, to mention but one example, of an English writer attached to the International Brigades as a commissar-at-large. He bragged to Stephen Spender that he had persuaded a young deserter to return to battle, even though he had secretly arranged for him to be sent to a place at the front where he would certainly be killed. He added pompously, "I have just had a message to say that he is dead. Of course, I am a little upset, but . . . I did right." Spender was shocked, not because this revelation was true, but because it was utterly false. This particular commissar did not have enough authority to make his victim shine his boots, much less to arrange for his execution. It was the fabricated story of a literary man who had tasted power and who wished another literary man to envy his activist role in the war. The same commissar stood before the Writers Congress in Madrid (July, 1937) and announced, "You will notice that I am dressed as a private, but really have a rank corresponding to that of general." War coined strange lies. Perhaps it was this kind of malignancy infecting ordinary people which compelled Spender to record that his experiences among the International Brigades were "frightening."

The ranks of the George Washington Battalion were quickly filled, and an overflow of volunteers began to spill over into a third battalion, commanded by Robert Merriman and commissared by Joe Dallet. What to call this third North American unit resulted in a prolonged hassle between adherents of "Tom Paine Battalion" and "Patrick Henry Battalion." (The politics of Patrick Henry were questionable—but everyone liked the slogan "Liberty or Death.") The stalemate was broken by a group of Canadians who protested that their countrymen had fought in the Lincoln Battalion and had been mustered into the George Washington, yet their presence in Spain had never been acknowledged. Their minority-group argument eventually won them the privilege of naming the third unit the Mackenzie-Papineau Battalion, after two nineteenth-century Canadian revolutionaries. Originally it was hoped that all Canadians in Spain would join the Mac Paps, but this proved unfeasible. Americans always outnumbered Canadians in the Canadian Battalion.

Training for the Washingtons came to an end in the middle of June. Early in the morning, trucks pulled into the *plaza* of Tarrazona. Five hundred men quietly and quickly packed their kits and climbed aboard. The whole loading took less than half an hour. The Mac Paps, who were left behind for further training, were awakened by the throbbing of the trucks outside. They came out to watch the departure of their comrades for the front. Where these were bound, they did not know, but by the time dawn lighted the little plaza, the Washingtons were gone.

7

⌐ Brunete

There you were lying naked.
And where was our anti-air-
craft, where were our planes,
where were our guns. . . . The
Fascists had everything, and we
had nothing. We never had a
chance. We lost this war long
ago.

—A "demoralized element"
at Brunete

"We are the anti-Fascists of the XV Brigade," Colonel Copic
shouted. "We are styled 'The Brigade that does not retreat.' Together
we will crush the enemy of Spain and of the whole human race!" It
sounded like a rather large assignment, and the peroration of the
Colonel's speech was met with scattered hand-clapping rather than
throaty *vivas*. The occasion was a welcome speech to the 24th (International) Battalion, consisting entirely of Spaniards, all of whom
looked either too young or too old. They were led by a Captain Mar-
tínez, a fifty-year-old career officer whose pistol always dragged his
belt far down under his vast belly. The dilution of the International
Brigades had begun. Foreigners were being killed off so rapidly that
their places were being taken by Spaniards. The induction of the 24th
Battalion into the XV Brigade marked the first step, soon to be followed by the adding of Spanish companies to foreign battalions, then
by the placing of Spanish platoons into foreign companies, and finally
by the disappearance of foreigners altogether.

A Republican offensive was scheduled for July, and the XV Brigade was reshuffled. A new table of organization called for two regi-
ments: the first composed of the Dimitrovs, the Sixth of February,
and the 24th (Spanish) Battalion; the second, of the British, the Lin-

coln, and the Washington. The Anglo-American regiment, entirely English-speaking, was commanded by Jock Cunningham, former British commander. Martin Hourihan of the Lincolns was kicked upstairs as his adjutant. This left the leadership of the Lincoln Battalion up for grabs. But not for long. As many men had feared, Oliver Law took command. Party publicists could at last proclaim that Law was the first Negro in history to command a battalion of predominantly white Americans. When they learned of Law's appointment, Douglas Roach and another Negro marched through the Jarama trenches with a placard reading WE WANT EQUAL RIGHTS FOR WHITES. Others inwardly shuddered at the thought of being led into battle by Oliver Law.

The party claimed that Oliver Law was born in Chicago. Actually he was born on a Texas cotton-farm, circa 1904. It is presumed that he joined the U.S. Army after the World War and made his way to Chicago after receiving his discharge. He is said to have been an employee in the meat-packing industry, a restaurant owner and slumlord, and a militant in the Negro movement on the South Side. The reasons for his skyrocketing rise to prominence are unaccountable. "Why Law?" the men asked over and over. If the party insisted upon a Negro commander, there were half a dozen superb candidates. "Law was not a Negro as I thought of Negroes," recalled a furrier. "Law was an illiterate, southern darkie. The kind you picture with a watermelon." Thirty years later, a Negro volunteer said of Law, "A tragic character. I took him over there; over there he took me over. The guys running the battalion made him a figurehead." [1] Even though Law was a hapless victim, a puppet manipulated on strings fingered by powers elsewhere, authority did not sit gracefully on his shoulders. He seemed to have, remembered another veteran, "this big chip on his shoulder that he was daring you to knock off." Yet whenever a newsman appeared in the neighborhood, Law was trotted out to deliver a set speech: "We came to wipe out the Fascists. . . . The Spanish people have the same aim as the Negro people—we are both fighting for our national independence." As counterweight to Oliver Law, Steve Nelson replaced Lutz as Lincoln commissar.

Steve Nelson was by all odds the most effective leader of the Amer-

---

[1] Although the "official history" of the Lincoln Battalion credits Law's machine gun with fine work during the February 27 attack, a survivor reports that when he crawled back late at night to bring food up to the line he found Law in the cookhouse.

icans during the Spanish Civil War. His great magnetism had nothing to do with credentials, appearance, or military experience, for most of the Lincolns were unimpressed by rank and soured on politicians. In a crowd he would have been overlooked. He was a small man of thirty-four with thinning hair and a button nose. His voice was gentle but had weight to it. Beyond reading a single book by A. Liddell Hart, he knew nothing of battle or war.[2] But the difference between Nelson and a lesser mortal was his quick intelligence and his unflagging self-confidence. He was a natural-born psychologist among natural-born fools of the IB commissariat. Although he demonstrated an uncanny ability in arousing loyalty—one might even say hero worship—among any group of men he led for a short time, he did not require admiration to gratify his ego. Men sensed that he could be trusted and that he had not come to Spain to build a reputation for himself. While others had to threaten and bully, Nelson led by conveying a sense that he expected the best, even from the worst. Dedicated to the principles of the Communist Party, Nelson seemed to know more about human nature than the fine print in *Das Capital*.

The first time Steve Nelson (*né* Mesarosh) had ever pondered a sociopolitical question was as an eleven-year-old in Chaglich, Croatia. A few weeks after the assassination at Sarajevo, he had to drive his father and four neighbors, in a peasant cart, to the district mobilization camp, and he never forgot the sight of hundreds of sad-faced, perplexed peasants milling about the barbed-wire enclosure. Nelson had no more knowledge of what the war was about than these men, but he set out to comprehend it. From Chaglich, great throngs of apathetic men departed for war—broken handfuls drifted back. If the issues of the war were inscrutable, why did they go? If a war had to be fought, why not collect together and destroy the real enemy—not Italian or Bulgarian peasants identical to themselves?

In 1919, Nelson, or Mesarosh, migrated to the United States and found work in a Pittsburgh slaughter-house on an eleven-hour workday. The job was not oppressive in the summertime, but during the winter the jabbing contrasts in temperature between the freezer and smokehouse broke down the health of strong men. One icy day he heard that the owner wintered in Florida. Most of his fellow workers accepted this fact complacently: it was the way of the system. Nelson was outraged. They worked, the boss did not, yet he prospered, they

2 He might have witnessed some fighting with the Chinese Communists in 1933.

did not. Where, in this arrangement, was justice? Seeking an answer, Nelson joined the Socialist Labor Party, but annoyed by the do-nothing forensics of this working-class debating society, he left it for the Communist Party in 1928. Three years later, it has been alleged, Nelson studied at the Lenin Institute in Moscow, and on his return to the States he became a prominent figure in the CPUSA. For him communism was a religion of hard work and social justice welded onto results—not theory. He became the kind of leader who could make a rousing speech and disappear from the platform before any-one quite realized he was gone. He was not a conventioneer.

When Nelson assumed his duties as commissar in May, he found the men at Jarama still demoralized by the February massacre. Their idea of a worthwhile task was constructing a monument to commem-orate the dead, not digging trenches for the living. Nelson believed in persuasion, not compulsion. One day he watched a volunteer deep-ening his dugout and remarked to bystanders, "What a fine com-rade!" Somebody asked why he said that. Without taking his eyes off the man with the shovel, Nelson explained the importance of strong fortifications. The digger probably had not intended to take out more than a few shovelfuls, but under the eyes of the others, he worked up an honest sweat. A voice in the crowd said, "What's so special about that guy? Hell, I can dig better'n that." Soon all of them were heaving out dirt. Thirty years later those trenches are still there. Nelson was a wizard, like Tom Sawyer at the fence.

The Lincolns delegated to Nelson the sticky job of requesting from General Gal that they be relieved from the line. Clad in oversize ski pants tied at the ankle with twine, a rusty brown shirt, and a shape-less brown beret, Nelson arrived at Gal's manor, where even orderlies and chauffeurs wore steam-pressed uniforms. Gal sat behind a massive desk, coldly eying Nelson as though he were a creature from an inferior phylum. On the wall behind Gal was a life-sized portrait of himself in the uniform, garnished with epaulettes, of a Spanish Re-publican general. "The whole thing floored me," Nelson later re-marked. When he explained that he wanted to speak "man to man," Gal cut in stingingly, "*I* am commander of the division. *You* are in that division." Changing tack, Nelson said that he represented the men of the Lincoln Battalion. Again Gal interrupted, "There are no delegations!" Nelson went on to say that his men thought their com-manders had let them down: in a People's Army, if leaders proved inadequate they could be removed. At this impious innuendo, Gal became "very upset." He unleashed a storm of invective upon the Americans, accusing them of "imperialist" contamination. Nelson listened, in his earnest manner, to this diatribe until there was a moment of relative calm, when he proposed that the Washington Battalion replace the Lincoln in the trenches. Gal swung on the defensive, arguing he could not spare the gasoline. Nelson countered by saying this excuse was senseless. Gal shouted, "You are talking to a *general!*" Nothing came of this meeting, but Nelson had at least put Gal on the defensive, showing him that American commissars intended to stand up for the rights of their men.

In the middle of June the Lincoln Battalion was withdrawn from the trenches at Jarama. Someone counted it up—they had been 116 days in the line. Trucks carried them to Albares, a time-forgotten village of three hundred souls tucked away in hill country east of Madrid. From the highway, a hundred stone steps wound up to the packed-earth *plaza mayor,* where a maize-colored church in fortress-gothic style overlooked a maize-colored convent, where they were billeted. Pockets bulged with nearly four months' pay. Nine men made a beeline for the only *bodega* in town. There was no whiskey and no *coñac,* but there was a vat of *anis,* a licorish-tasting distillate as clear as mountain water and as potent as grain alcohol. "Sissy stuff!" declared their ringleader. "Gimme a liter." Fifteen minutes later they had taken the *bodega* apart and were closing on the town itself when Paul Burns subdued them with a squad from First Company. The townspeople were alarmed. Worried about public relations, Nelson assembled the battalion in the *plaza* and sentenced the hangdog nine to five days in the brig—a stone shed near the convent, built to house tools but more often used as a *pissoir.* The leader, a revolutionary of twenty years' standing, wept with shame.

Early the next morning, Nelson was awakened by a delegation of villagers, hats in hand and pitchforks in arm. "More trouble," thought Nelson, wondering what his men had done now. But the spokesman explained, with great courtesy: "We think you know better than we how to run the army . . . but we all felt sorry for the man who cried and the other men you put in jail. They were so long in the trenches and they did no harm to anybody. . . . And so, *Señores,* in the name of the people of our village we ask you, we beg you not to be too hard on these men." Delighted with this turn, Nelson released the prisoners. A few days later the battalion turned out to help harvest the barley crop. (Lamed and blistered by the unaccustomed labor of cutting grain with short sickles, they wasted such prodigious amounts that the villagers had to beg the *señores* not to trouble themselves with the menial chores of a poor *pueblo*.) The straightest path to the heart of a Spaniard lies through his children. When the battalion doctor removed a sliver of glass from the eye of a small boy whose father was too poor to pay for a Madrid specialist, Albares belonged to the men of the Lincoln Battalion.[3] Later Nelson held a *fiesta* for them in the poplar grove below the village.

For two weeks they rested at Albares, dozing during the heat of midday among the sacks of flour at a mill in the valley. There were communal shower-baths from a special water truck, which had collapsible nozzles protruding from the tank like fragile legs of a gigantic insect. There was tooth pulling and filling by the brigade dentist, who had a lab mounted in the van of a Matford truck. This was a popular spectator sport always drawing an appreciative crowd of villagers and soldiers alike. (The story is told that Aris Hodges, a Kentuckian, known as the laziest man in the battalion, had most of his teeth pulled when he fell asleep in the chair.) Nelson arranged a series of intercompany baseball games (won by the seamen) and swimming contests (lost by the seamen). The arrival of a hundred new men brought the battalion up to pre-Jarama strength. There were now four companies instead of three. Though word came down that a Republican offensive was in the offing, it was too hot for intensive training. Besides, they were vets.

News drifted in from the States, via the *Worker*. Police had shot down unarmed strikers at Republic Steel in South Chicago. At Lansing a mob of reactionary students at Michigan State nearly drowned eight CIO organizers in Cedar Creek. Troops had been deployed in Youngstown to subdue strikers. Jean Harlow had died, and tacked on to an account of her obsequies was this astonishing item—"for years she worked toward the unionization of the motion picture industry." The *Worker* continued to caricature public enemies like Franco, Hitler, Mussolini, Trotsky, and Henry V-8 (Henry Ford). At Albares there were the usual complaints about the exaggerated virtue of the local sex goddesses, who never seemed to stir out-of-doors unless

---

[3] Thirty years later a mill worker at Albares affectionately recalled an American Negro—clearly Doug Roach—who rode children on his back and whose pockets were always loaded with candy for them. "He was the kindest man I have ever known." When asked whether the Americans were good men or bad, a fellow worker replied, "They were all good men. There were no bad men in *el batallón Lincoln.*"

guarded by one or two chaperons. "It ain't Lolly's grandma bothers me," confessed an American. "I don't mind her taggin' along. Only I do wish they'd leave the Goddamn *burro* at home once in a while!" The only man who had any luck with the village girls was Ray Steele, the club-footed machine gunner, who became engaged to one of them.

The summer idyll at Albares ended on July 2 when a dispatch rider arrived, followed a few hours afterward by a truck convoy. A bugler sounded "Assembly." By sundown Albares was emptied of the Americans. The big offensive was beginning

Wheeling its army around Madrid on a wide arc to the north and west, the Republican command concentrated fifty thousand men out of sight in the pine barrens and craggy foothills of the Guadarrama Mountains, fifteen miles west of the city. The offensive called for a surprise thrust southward through the lightly garrisoned Guadarrama Valley to the village of Brunete, a major crossroads eight miles from the jumping-off point, to be followed by a swing to the southeast in order to seize the Estremadura Highway, which supplied the Nationalist armies at the southern edge of Madrid. The offensive had a twofold purpose: to force the enemy to lift its siege of Madrid, and to divert troops from Franco's campaign in the Basque country. Communist cadres of the Republican Army, along with four out of five of the International Brigades, had been assigned the most important roles in the offensive and promised to benefit enormously in the event the offensive proved to be successful.[4]

The Republic had already proved its capacity for defense, but never had it initiated a successful offensive upon a major Nationalist army. It counted upon surprise and rapidity of movement to break through the enemy positions. Once the element of surprise had been dissipated, they could expect jarring counterattacks by a desperate enemy bottled up in its narrow salient just south of Madrid. The specific assignment of General Gal's newly formed 15th Division, which included the XIII (Slavic) and XV Brigades, was to descend into the Guadarrama Valley and, veering east, secure a hilltop forest called

---

[4] Prime Minister Largo Caballero (Socialist) favored an offensive in Estremadura, which was weakly held by the Nationalists, in order to cut Nationalist Spain in half. The Soviet military mission refused artillery, tank, or aircraft support for this offensive, so Caballero had to acquiesce in the Brunete Valley master plan.

Romanillas Heights (better known as Mosquito Ridge). Because Mosquito Ridge commanded the whole of the Guadarrama Valley, it had to be taken and fortified before the Nationalists could seize it and thereby blanket the valley floor with artillery fire. When the Nationalist counterattack came, it would be a drive due west, toward Mosquito Ridge.

As the Republican troops marched to their attack positions, morale was high. To avoid observation, they moved at night through the deep ilex forests of El Pardo, once the hunting lodge of the Bourbon kings, and ascended the foothills of the Guadarramas. Revolutionary songs swept back and forth along a ten-mile stream of human beings toiling up toward the mountains. Yet by dawn this immense body of men and machines lay hidden and invisible to enemy observation planes in the sector. Several times the Nationalists spotted movements on the El Escorial road, but these they falsely interpreted as an attempt to strengthen mountain garrisons. Of the projected offensive they had no warning whatever.

For the Americans, the Fourth of July meant a double ration of Hershey bars and packs of Lucky Strikes. They talked of a possible breakthrough that might carry them as far as Toledo, or beyond. It might even be possible to tie a drawstring around the pocket of Fascists near Madrid and to garrote them to death. On the following day they moved closer to Valdemorillo and camped around an Edenic mountaintop *finca,* the agricultural toy of some absent Madrid weekender. A modern swimming pool, filled with green slime, lay next to a medieval chicken-house. It was here, among pines and juniper, that the Lincolns mingled with the Washingtons for the first time. Accustomed to trench warfare, the Jarama vets, haunted by agoraphobia, threw up rifle pits of fieldstones around the house. The afternoon was hot but the night was crisp and clear, cooled by winds from the mountains. On their high peak it was like sleeping in an observatory, or in heaven. They nicknamed this farm "The Pearly Gates."

Battle orders arrived at 2:30 A.M. on July 6. Within half an hour the two American battalions were moving downhill to their takeoff points—knolls overlooking the valley floor. In this straggling, blind march the Lincolns became lost and arrived an hour late. As soon as the sky lightened, Republican artillery split the profound mountain silence and the echo of explosions reverberated up from the valley floor.

For the first hours, the Americans played only a spectatorial role in the battle under them, which was spread out like a model on a topographical table. To the south the full length of the Guadarrama Valley lay open in prismatic outline. Tanks wallowed across the flattish, treeless plain ahead of dark specks marking the first wave of infantry. Four miles south was a white village, Villanueva de la Cañada, threaded by the arrow-straight highway that passed on to Brunete, four miles farther south. Paralleling this black ribbon of macadam, three miles to the east, ran the Guadarrama River. Mosquito Ridge, flecked with trees, lay just beyond the river. The sky was filled with Republican airplanes gliding down and unloading bombs upon the garrisoned villages. Far to the southwest, greasy black smoke billowed up from a knocked-out munitions dump at Quijorna. The mounting sun quenched the mountain breeze. A noxious, furnace heat rose from the valley floor. Canteens were emptied even before the Americans descended to the plain.

Even as they watched the developing battle, things went wrong. The tanks and infantry surrounded Villanueva de la Cañada but failed to take it. Inexplicably they collected together like filings before a magnet and veered off to the east. The original orders had declared that the XV Brigade should not descend into the valley until Villanueva had fallen. Now General Gal countermanded it. Instead of proceeding to Mosquito Ridge, the Brigade should first subdue the town. Led by the Dimitrovs, one of the best battalions in the International Brigades, the XV Brigade plunged down the long slope and into the sun-scorched plain.

The valley, which from above had seemed undulating, turned out to be pimpled with hillocks and gouged by *barrancas*—rain-water gullies. Although there was better cover than anyone had expected, the broken topography caused dispersion. Streams clearly marked in blue lines on the charts were bone dry during summer months. It was not possible to refill canteens, already drained. ("Guadarrama" is an Arabic word meaning "river of sand"—knowledge of this obscure etymological point might have altered the course of the whole campaign.) Men were passing out with heat exhaustion even before they came within bullet range of Villanueva de la Cañada. The village was situated on the crest of a slight slope, and the houses were built so low and close together that machine gunners in the church tower had a 360-degree field of fire.[5] Four hundred yards out, as the XV Bri-

---

[5] According to Robert Gladnick, at this time a technician of the Fifth (Soviet) Tank Battalion, there was also a German officer with a 37-mm

gade advanced through knee-high wheat fields, these gunners halted the advance and forced those in the advance to use their helmets to rake out burrows in sun-baked ground "so hard you couldn't make a dent in it." Nowhere was there a spot of shade. And in the 100-degree heat what scant supply of water was on hand had to go to the water-cooled Maxims, which were in danger of burning out their barrels.

By noon the six battalions had completed their encirclement of the town and were pouring a heavy fire at the outer ring of houses. But their forward motion had stopped utterly. Hourihan came on the field with orders for the Anglo-American battalion commanders to rush the town. He found that Law had failed to send out patrols and had blundered into a blind draw from which he could neither retreat nor advance. The men were bunched up together, none of them knowing what to do. Law, according to one Lincoln, was so "paralyzed with fear" that he "thumbed his map unable to move." Hourihan, enraged, put Law under arrest and sent him back to brigade headquarters.[6] Then he led the Lincoln vanguard out of the cul-de-sac and placed them in a position of assault to the west of town. While reconnoitering the territory ahead, Hourihan was felled by a slug from the church tower which smashed his leg bone and terminated his military service in Spain. Since Vincent Usera, Law's adjutant (alleged to have been a former U.S. Marine Corps officer), could not be found, Steve Nelson took command of the Lincoln Battalion, which by this time had broken up into small pockets firing from the *barrancas.*

The sun crept westward. Valuable time was being wasted. Yet the XV Brigade foundered in a frustrating eddy of the battle, the main current of which had swept past Villanueva hours ago. A single artillery battery could have razed the stubborn little town, but the Republicans were employing their cannon against Brunete and Quijorna, miles away, where the major fighting was. Nelson resolved to sit tight

antitank gun in the tower. This gun knocked out more than a dozen Russian tanks and deflected the initial attack upon Cañada. After the battle, Gladnick found the German officer in Colonel Zveriev's headquarters tent and asked whether he would be shot. Zveriev said, "That Fritz is going to the Soviet Union ahead of me. He will teach us all about German antitank tactics, and after that we will exchange him for some of our men which Franco has."

   [6] The first study of the Lincoln Battalion, written in 1939 by Edwin Rolfe, a member of the party cadre in Spain, mentions the name of Oliver Law only once, saying that he had been "killed in the attack on Villanueva de la Cañada." Since that time Law has been rehabilitated. The "official history," published in 1967, contains fourteen items about him, all of them glowing.

and clean out the enemy garrison in the morning. The men had no water, no food, and were running short of ammunition. The dust and glare had reduced their eyes to powdered slits.

It was nearly sundown when runners from brigade demanded that Villanueva be stormed immediately. Battalion commanders were blamed for disrupting the timetable of the offensive—an unreasonable bit of buck-passing since the original plan called for no activity whatever by the XV Brigade at Villanueva. "What the hell!" exclaimed Nelson's assistant when he read the order. "We're doing all right. We'll get into a mess if we try anything. The guys are tired." But Nelson readied Paul Burns' First Company. At this minute, heavy firing and yelling broke out on the opposite side of town as the Dimitrovs, assisted by a fresh Republican brigade, bored into the town. Prodded by this stimulus, the Lincolns and Washingtons pressed through the barbed wire and swept over the sandbags of the Fascist line. The enemy garrison fled into private houses, while the attackers converged upon the center of town so rapidly that they briefly exchanged shots with each other in the dark alleyways near the main square.

Squeezed from the center of town, a desperate group of Falangists of the Bandera of Faith seized a dozen hostages from the village and pressed down the road toward Brunete in the darkness. A hundred yards outside of town they ran head-on into the British Battalion, which was filing into town from the south. Assuming that they were civilian refugees, a Briton ordered them to halt. Seconds later he was killed by a grenade. Then, as the screaming hostages scattered into the fields, the Falangists fired machine guns into clusters of the British. For ten minutes the fighting was ferocious, until the Falangists had been wiped out to the man. Several women were killed when impact grenades, carried by the enemy, were detonated by bullets. A British company commander leaned down to help a wounded Falangist, who shot him through the heart. This surprise attack from behind the skirts of women, combined with the loss of a popular commander, filled the British with a bitter rage. They swarmed into Villanueva, now illuminated garishly by burning buildings, and eradicated scattered groups of the enemy holed up in hayricks and cattle sheds. Fearing prisoners would be murdered in cold blood, Captain Fred Copeman had to order his battalion out of town and allow other battalions to clear out the enemy. The machine gunners in the church tower were eliminated by setting the tower on fire.

By daybreak of July 7, Villanueva was a gutted, silent husk, reminiscent of a Somme town in 1916. The Americans were exhausted but pleased with themselves: for the first time in Spain they had attacked and taken an enemy position. Now they dozed in shady corners, munched red-pepper sausages captured from enemy stores, and peeked through crannies in the barn on the edge of town where the prisoners had been lodged temporarily. The prisoners were disappointing: nothing like Fascists depicted in *Worker* cartoons, merely wretched creatures—unkempt, dirty, terribly frightened. Burial squads disposed of forty Americans killed during the fighting. By midmorning, contradictory orders were coming down from brigade headquarters: hold Villanueva until relieved—march south to join the major attack near Brunete—move east to Mosquito Ridge. So nothing was done, and time was lost. Only later did the men learn that brigade was feuding with division about the change in orders of the day before.

When the XV Brigade finally filed out of Villanueva in early afternoon, artillery batteries behind Mosquito Ridge had begun to shell the village. They pushed eastward toward the river, crossing open country where men were visible at great distances. Troops of cavalry ranged the meadows to their rear, prodding stragglers forward. In the lead was the George Washington Battalion, which marched in a tight arrow-formation, despite warnings from Lincolns that they should split up. Suddenly four Nationalist bombers, flying almost at ground level, burst upon the column and dropped a load of bombs. The men had no time to scatter. Seconds later, the bodies of twenty-odd Washingtons lay scattered around bomb craters. They smoked and turned black. After this ghastly tragedy, the Washingtons went to the opposite extreme, fanning out so far apart that they became separated from one another.

As they neared the river, the terrain became ragged. From confusing networks of *barrancas* and patches of forest, enemy ambush parties fired a few rounds to slow the advance and then melted to the rear. The Americans behaved more like hunters than soldiers. Instead of sweeping around these ambush pockets they responded to cries of "Fascist! Let's get 'em!" At the end of the second day of the offensive, the XV Brigade had not reached the river. Contact between battalions, companies, and sections had broken down. The skein of command was hopelessly snarled. A whole day had been wasted in aimless meandering. And time was running out.

In the morning of July 8, Soviet tanks splashed across the shallow Guadarrama River and pushed through the canebrake and poplars on the far shore. Filling their canteens in the brackish water, the men of the XV Brigade followed them across. Less than a mile ahead lay the summit of Mosquito Ridge. The terrain in front was, according to one volunteer, "a Goddamn roller-coaster." The ground rolled upward through a thick stand of ilex trees. It looked exactly like what it was —the private hunting preserve of the Duke of Alba. Pheasant whirred from undergrowth; skulls of rabbits littered the forest floor. The park-like enclosure was infested with invisible snipers, who forced the Interbrigaders to advance warily.

One group of advancing Americans flushed some Nationalists out of their cover and sent them fleeing up the hill. "It was a fox hunt," recalled a veteran. The enemy threw away rifles, mess kits, and blankets. While some of the Americans steadied their *mexicanskis* on one knee and fired at them, others shouted "*Adelante!*" and pursued them. Yet in most places the enemy gave up ground stubbornly. Hanging on trees were white cloth markers. Wallace Burton, who had spent some time in the French Foreign Legion, explained that these measured the exact distance that the Moors retreated—useful information for artillerists and mortarmen.

Captain Oliver Law had been restored to command, although the Belgian Captain Van der Berghe had been assigned to help him. Twice, Van der Berghe warned Law about likely ambushes, but each time Law pushed squads ahead and saw them cut to pieces. Men lagged behind or fanned out on the flanks. Fighting in a forest provides many opportunities to avoid combat without really deserting the line. Captain Copeman estimated that the British Battalion lost a hundred men in this fashion, and doubtless the figures for the American battalions, if known, would be comparable. But the stalwarts fought up Mosquito Ridge at a rate of a hundred yards per hour.

Tank units nearly reached the crest, but instead of breaking the enemy line by mechanical weight, they waited for the infantry, which never arrived in sufficient quantity to hold the top even had it been seized. Republican troops bunched up in *barrancas* a few hundred yards from the crest watched tanks fire off their stock of 45-mm shells and then turn back. A massive rush to the top was all that was needed, but without coordination such an attack was suicidal. They had outrun the lines of communication and supply long ago. Officers had difficulty in positioning themselves on their charts, because one *barranca* looked exactly like any other, and they were located in a position from which they could not see the forest for the trees. Even hospital tents now lay two or three miles to the rear, which meant that "light" wounds often proved to be fatal. The heat was suffocating —it was as though oxygen had disappeared from the air. By late afternoon men dispatched to the Guadarrama River with empty canteens found that the stream had run dry. For a day or so one could dig a hoe in the riverbed to unearth a pool of water, but even this source quickly vanished. Through the night the Republican commanders worked to collect their dispersed units and to launch a final, overwhelming attack upon Mosquito Ridge in the morning. Meanwhile, the Nationalists threw every man they could spare into the trenches being scraped out along the five-mile line.

The morning of July 9 dawned hotter than any of the preceding. Taking advantage of the deep gulches leading upward, men of the XV Brigade pushed forward. Among the Washingtons, Captain Markovicz, waving an automatic pistol, ranged the line shouting words that sounded like "On to Madrid!" Among the Lincolns, Nelson led the left wing, Law the right. For the second time, the battalion adjutant was missing. Later it was learned that he had returned to brigade headquarters to call up the reserves. (A perfectly sound idea, except that reserves did not exist.) But nowhere was there a semblance of battalion or company organization remaining. Mosquito Ridge came under assault by armed bands of brave men who lacked proper briefing, preparation, and support. That was the way of the International Brigades.

After advancing perhaps a hundred yards, Oliver Law's group ran into another ambush. "Over there!" yelled a volunteer, pointing to a clump of undergrowth on their left flank. Law turned his head to see and dropped with a bullet in the belly. There are two irreconcilable accounts of the aftermath. The "official" version argues that Jerry Weinberg, Law's runner, pulled him behind a tree. Law ordered him to take off his boots (an anti-Texan gesture?) and his Sam Browne, then lapsed into a coma from which he did not recover. Half an hour elapsed before he could be evacuated. Weinberg inherited his leather goods. Subsequently Law was buried near the river under the inscription "Here lies the first Negro commander of white Americans" or, according to a variant report, under his surname and approximate age. The "anti-official" version claims that a Negro machine-gunner swooped forward and performed a joyous dance of death around the

body. Others spat and urinated on it. Law's body was left where it
had fallen and was bloated by the sun into a horrible balloon.[7] Because both versions are sworn to, the truth, in this instance, seems to
consist of whatever one wishes to believe.

Meanwhile the Washington Battalion fared better. A lanky Texan
named Philip Detro, a company commander, was able to collect
about fifteen of his men for a push toward the summit. They filed
through a sinuous *barranca* and reached a slope perhaps a hundred
yards from the crest of Mosquito Ridge. All around them were soldiers working up the slope toward "that big black hill." The attack,
said a survivor, was "utterly chaotic." It pitted human will and brittle
bone against a mesh barrier of shrapnel and lead. The Americans
pushed on a little farther before taking refuge behind an ilex tree.[8]
Detro ordered them to open fire with rifles and a pan-fed Dichterev
machine gun at the dominating knoll above them. Then he sent a runner to find Markovicz and to ask where the rest of the battalion was.
Markovicz, who was trying to rally his men, sent back word that Detro
should hold on until the tanks came up. "Until the tanks came up"—
that phrase was always good for a scornful laugh. The first tank to
pop over a hillock at their rear exploded from a direct hit by an antitank gun, while the others—if there were others—promptly turned
back. Meanwhile eight of the fifteen Americans gathered together below the brow of Mosquito Ridge had been killed. "It was terrible up
there," remembered one of them. "I had all the fear symptoms—
palpitations of the heart, bulged eyes, pissed pants." This was the
high-water mark, literally as well as figuratively, of the Battle of
Brunete.

---

[7] Some veterans aver that the bullet that killed Oliver Law was fired by a
disgruntled Lincoln who was convinced, after two previous ambushes, that
Law had to be removed from command before he got all of them killed. This
former volunteer is still living but is "not available" for an interview.

Boris Todrin, a rear-guard poetaster, promptly beatified Law in a poem
concluding with these lines:

> Lord, Lord, loving Lord!
> This is the answer of the seed star fallen—
> This is the fruit of the lynching tree
> Growing in the cotton fields and risen free!

The poem would contain an ironic dimension if Law had evaded the
lynching tree only to be shot down by a "volunteer for liberty."

[8] Accounts of the battle are full of allusions to olive trees on the field of
battle. This is an error, for no olives are grown in this part of Spain. One
veteran even thought they were orange trees!

For three more days the XV Brigade held stubbornly to its line scratched out below Mosquito Ridge. With each passing hour the Nationalists became stronger. By day the forest was a holocaust. Mortars stalked the *barrancas* with fearsome accuracy; high-velocity shells tumbled trees on top of men dug in among the roots. At night, Moors on the summit barked and howled like jackals. A Tarazona troupe known as The Convulsionaries went through its repertoire of noisier songs to drown out the yelping above them.

On July 11, the Nationalists obtained mastery of the air, forcing the Republicans to abandon their hope of ever taking the summit. Enemy pilots in light commercial airplanes flew with impunity above Republican positions and unloaded boxes of impact grenades upon the clusters of men in the forest. As the tide of battle turned, the enemy probed with cautious counterattacks. Nelson, worried about an armored attack, brought up two antitank guns and concealed them from observation planes. Commanding them was Lieutenant Malcolm Dunbar, reputedly an English squire from Trinity College, Cambridge. (Actually he was a homosexual Scotsman from the University of London.[9]) Dunbar, a strikingly handsome officer with great style, watched coolly as eight tanks and a battalion of Moors attacked down Mosquito Ridge. He held his fire until the tanks got within five hundred yards, when both antitanks went off simultaneously. The lead tank burst into flame and the second revolved in a circle like a paralyzed insect. The others wheeled about and scurried back up the hill. But the Moors came on, bounding downhill with fantastically long strides. Ray Steele, the head Lincoln machine gunner shouted, "Give 'em twenty-five yards. Keep your shirts on." Steele was worried lest one of his gunners fire too soon, thus giving the Moors time to take cover. When they were a hundred yards off, Steele's Maxim opened fire with his trademark, a clattering "shave-and-a-haircut, two-bits." The other Mooney guns joined in and halted the Moors on a red dime.

Fighting, or even moving, in the heat of the day under a broiling Castilian sun became a torment. The sun was so intense that it caused a kind of snow blindness in which the color of all objects was molten white. The dry grass crinkled under foot. Trees turned into

[9] No generalizations should be made because Dunbar (and Major George Nathan, of the XV Brigade staff) was homosexual. No evidence exists to show that the incidence of sexual perversion was higher in the International Brigades than in any other military unit selected at random like, let us say, the U.S. Marine Corps.

dust balls. Down at the river, long dry, water details dug desperately in the streambed. At a depth of ten feet enough water seeped through the sand to form a shallow pool, but it tasted like an uncooked chowder of rotten fish. In one such waterhole stood a corpse, killed none could say how. A Detroit volunteer remembered, "We drank the slime at the bottom of the hole without dragging out the stiff—we never even thought about dragging it out." Dr. Harold Robbins, in saner times a Hollywood physician, filled a gasoline truck with disinfected well water. Fearing the precious liquid might be hijacked by another outfit, he drove it himself to the front. On the way an enemy plane dropped a bomb that blew out the rear end of the vehicle. The water poured out upon the ground and disappeared like a drop of ink on a blotter. Dr. Robbins lay slumped over the steering wheel, dead of concussion without a mark on his body.

On July 13 the two American battalions were withdrawn west of the Guadarrama River for a rest. Yet there was little rest, for they moved three times to back-stop threatened lines. (Trenches were seldom dug during the Brunete campaign: movement was much too rapid to bother with digging them.) Casualty figures were shocking. In eight days some 800 Americans had been reduced to 500 effectives. The British were down to 185 out of 600 who went in.[10] Lovable Jackie Shirai, probably the only native-born Japanese to fight in Spain, had been killed with a rifle, not a kitchen pot, in his hands. Even Colonel Copic had been hospitalized by a piece of bomb shrapnel. Five deserters checked in at the U.S. consulate in Barcelona, but for every one who reached Barcelona there must have been twenty who deserted the line at one point or another. The two American battalions were joined together and renamed the Lincoln-Washington Battalion with Markovicz as military commander and Nelson as commissar.

On July 18 word came down that the enemy were about to break the Republican line at Villanueva del Pardillo, a village located six

[10] After the Washingtons had been bombed on their march east from Cañada, the British had been assigned to lead the column and to occupy the southernmost flank in the Mosquito Ridge attack. Bracketed by artillery fire and too remote to be adequately supplied, they took such a buffeting that Wally Tapsell, their commissar, went to brigade headquarters to complain. He was arrested. When he failed to return, Captain Copeman went to investigate. Before departing, he told his machine-gun commander that if he failed to come back in two hours, the company and their guns should be brought to headquarters. The difficulty was resolved, but not before the British had been nearly decimated.

miles north near the river. The Nationalist counteroffensive was commencing in earnest, and Pardillo anchored the Republican left flank. The Lincoln-Washington was dispatched there to help hold the town. Henceforth orders would emphasize "holding," not "taking." As the verb changed so did the Battle of Brunete.

No transport was available. They marched all night through the riverbed in ankle-deep sand. Grains sifted into shoes and abraded socks and flesh. Some men tied their shoes around their necks and tried to walk barefoot, but the sand packed raw, open blisters. Whenever the head of the column stopped, those behind staggered into one another and fell asleep. Officers moved up and down the line kicking and cuffing them awake. Some men swore that on the night hike to Pardillo they learned to sleep while marching. The Mooneys had to dismantle their Maxims and carry them on their backs. Ray Steele, now company adjutant, "organized" a horse somehow and piled on guns and ammunition cans. When Nelson found out, he dressed Steele down: Fascists, he said, robbed peasants and stole horses, a People's Army did not. Then, his lecture done, he urged them forward, horse and all.

At sunrise they crawled out of the riverbed and were handed, to their great surprise, hard-boiled eggs. "The first—and last—taste of chicken food I had in dear old Spain," said one volunteer. It was a day of miracles. Next came what seemed, in retrospect, like a collective hallucination. Leaning against an ambulance parked off the Cañada-Pardillo highway was a beautiful, bobbed-hair English girl who smiled as they filed by. This was the first woman they had seen in over two weeks, and they were too much in awe to whistle. A half-mile from Pardillo they were assigned a deep, cancer-shaped *barranca* lying in a hollow below the town. Forests had been left behind: this was open country of pinched mesquite and parched barley. The rank and file had no clear idea of where they were or what they were doing.[11] A rumor passed through that they were on a guerrilla expedition, to take the enemy from the rear.

Through most of the day they lay in their *barranca*. Brief argu-

[11] Sense of time and place became confused after Mosquito Ridge. Heat prostration and physical exhaustion induced "nightmarish wanderings" and "dreamlike sequences." In retrospect it became nearly impossible to reconstruct a chronology of events unless a volunteer had written something down, and few of them had.

ments and ephemeral monologues flared up and died in the suffocating heat. John Cookson, a Ph.D. candidate in physics at the University of Wisconsin, expounded in his nasal twang his *idée fixe,* a dam across the Strait of Gibraltar. He went on to say that Lenin's *Materialism and Empirio-Criticism* bore upon this problem. Somebody asked a New York schoolteacher what he thought of Granville Hicks' writing, a queerishly irrelevant question, considering where they were. The teacher eyed his questioner as though he were insane, and replied, "That's a dumb thing to ask." A Chicago volunteer argued that what they needed were a couple of really tough *hombres* like Al Capone: he'd show the Fascists a thing or two. But a Brooklyn volunteer contested this. He said, "Capone was only a big stiff who got his break with prohibition and was a yellow rat who'd have turned tail here in half an hour." Others limply agreed with him. The heat made everyone feel punchy and drained.

Suddenly a shell exploded a hundred yards away. In their hollow they felt safe, but everyone quit talking. High above them hovered a tiny speck. A World War vet yelled, "Look out, Comrades. It's an observation plane!" Everyone ducked down, but the plane flew away. Half an hour later there was a noise overhead like threshing machines. "Get down! Bombers!" men shouted. Seconds later the bombers unloaded over the *barranca* as easily as dropping pebbles in a well. The men clawed downward, but it felt as though the ground were pushing them upward into the lethal, open air: "I was hugging the earth, pressing into it with my hands, my feet, my face . . . but the ground was pushing you up higher. . . . I felt I was perched up high and knew that they could spot me for miles. . . . You knew there was a shaft pointing to the small of your back and the bomb would hit you right there and blow you into a million pieces." They were caught, bunched up together, in a death trap.

The earth shook with a cataclysmic upheaval. There was an impression of being hurled high into the air: "We had a helluva time just staying on the ground. . . . We had to hold onto the grass to keep from rising." White-hot pieces of shrapnel whizzed through the *barranca* and set fire to the grass. Black smoke billowed from the pit, and they choked on the brimstone smell of cordite. When the planes had droned away, Nelson crawled out and ran along the lip of the ditch with sinking heart. He assumed his men had been annihilated. Heads popped out and looked about. Apparently lifeless bodies lifted themselves up. All were as black as coal heavers. "You sat up, you looked around—your whole section, the whole company, everybody alive, not a single one hurt." Not strictly true—but only nine were dead and sixteen wounded. It was, said Nelson, "The miracle of the war." The dead were not bloody; shrapnel had gouged out openings in them like biscuit cutters in thick dough.

The Republicans on the high ground around Pardillo had had a bird's-eye view of the bombs falling in the *barranca*. When they saw nearly the entire battalion crowding out of the ravine and running up-hill toward them, they broke into exuberant cheers and met the Lincoln-Washingtons with wine skins. Minutes later the Nationalists attacked Pardillo and the Americans helped beat them back. A group of the enemy hid behind a pock-marked house between the lines until a tank shell brought down the walls. The Lincoln-Washington gun-ners then had the satisfaction of chopping them down as they tried to flee back to their line.

For the next three days the reconstituted Lincoln Battalion—the name Lincoln-Washington quickly faded away—occupied trenches little bigger than ditches around the once-whitewashed village of Vil-lanueva del Pardillo. It was a comparatively placid by-way of the bat-tle, for the main Nationalist counterattacks were directed toward Brunete, far to the south. The men felt lucky to be where they were. Cigarettes and chocolate arrived from the FALB; there were even hot meals. In this sector it was a sniper's war. During this lull an order came down requesting Ray Steele to report to officers' school at Pozorubio, and Nelson arranged for him to stop off at Albares to see his *novia*. Too happy for caution, Steele went down the ditch to bid his men good-bye and walked into a sniper bullet. He was dead be-fore he hit the ground.

On July 22 the Lincolns were ordered to return to their old positions under Mosquito Ridge. Once again they slogged through the sand dunes of the Guadarrama River in total darkness. In the morning, while sleeping in canebrakes beside the river, bands of retreating Re-publicans brought news that the front had broken. Collecting three tanks, the Lincolns disputed the enemy at the riverbank, but retaking the lost positions was now out of the question. Airplanes dropped in-cendiary bombs; parched grass and dried cane burned like tinder and forced them back into the open country toward Villanueva de la Cañada. For the next two days, the Americans kept trying to form a defensive line only to discover that Spanish units supposed to cover their flanks had disappeared. Yet they learned bitter lessons of retreating without panic or disorganization. Contesting each ridge, each copse, each sunken path, they withdrew to other ridges, other copses, other paths.

Behind them, three miles southwest, black smoke hung a thousand feet in the air as the village of Brunete burned. Through black fumes and ocher dust the sun turned into a "blood-red ball." The black crosses painted on the rudders of Nationalist aircraft completely dominated the air. As the enemy steadily advanced, the Republican command resolved to fortify Villanueva de la Cañada as its front line, and in the evening of July 25 the Lincolns were relieved from the line. In the moonlight they filed through a macabre pile of stones, which threw up silhouettes like those unearthed by an archaeologist's shovel. A battered tile plaque identified the place as VILL—NUEVA DE LA—AÑ———. Nineteen days before, they had dropped down from cool hillsides into an infernal valley to seize this village. Of the eight hundred who had come down, only three hundred went back up. They trudged through a destroyed village that should have been familiar but was not.

Daylight caught them on the open road winding into the foothills near Valdemorillo. With thousands of other soldiers they toiled upward, passing thousands of others on their way down to the scorched valley. Fresh meat for the cauldron of Brunete. "Beside those fresh shaved faces," said an American, "we must have looked like the House of David, or a line of bums using rifles as crutches." What the veterans feared, came into view. A dozen Junkers trimotors droned up the long valley, following the ribbon of highway. Antiaircraft batteries began popping from the higher hills to the west. Panic-driven men scattered into ditches and *barrancas*. Suddenly the lead Junkers exploded softly in a brief effulgence of orange flame and black smoke. Debris drifted down "like falling leaves—bits of metal, fabric, and men." The other trimotors swerved like startled birds and dropped their bombs on empty fields. Thousands of soldiers on the hillsides burst into frenzied cheers at this million-to-one shot of an anonymous Republican gunner.

Near "The Pearly Gates" a cold mountain brook trickled into a dammed pond. Around it poplars grew so close together that they blocked off the sun. The green grass, deliciously cool, grew a foot high. What remained of the Lincoln-Washingtons bivouacked in the green shade beside the first running water they had seen since the Guadarrama had run dry. Far, far below them the Battle of Brunete gasped to a spasmodic inconclusion. The men looked ahead to trucks that would carry them back to Albares. To look behind them, into the past, was to remember the names and faces of comrades left forever in that valley of the dead and the damned, that baking valley of non-shadows.

On the second night at "The Pearly Gates" Nelson summoned the battalion to a meeting in the grove. He had bad news: Republican divisions at Quijorna, eight miles to the south, had been surrounded. The XV Brigade was the nearest support. They had to go back. Out of the darkness came a wailing cry, "For Chri' sake, Steve, you're not going to tell us to go back!" Nelson tried to explain to men he could not see. "If the lines break, you are not going to be able to stay here. . . . We will either be driven out of here or we will die here. We don't have a chance except to go back." Not even Steve Nelson dared tell his men that at a brigade meeting the British (37 men left out of 360), the Dimitrovs (93 out of 450), the 24th (125 out of 400), and the Sixth of February (88 out of 360) had adamantly refused to return to battle.[12]

Nelson expected catcalls and curses. But there was a deep stillness in the grove. A lone voice said, "You're right." The men moved off to collect their equipment and then followed Nelson through the white-washed gates of the farm. On the highway a dispatch rider intercepted them and passed Nelson a written order: "The Spanish comrades have extricated themselves and have the situation in hand. The XV Brigade will remain in camp." No one cheered. It was like a reprieve from a death sentence. Some veterans later said that the supreme moment of their service in Spain came when they complied with the order that they return to battle.[13]

The Battle of Brunete had ended. Like so many other battles in

[12] At some point after Villanueva del Pardillo, Markovicz was removed of his command because he refused to order his men into a counterattack that he regarded as purposeless. It might have been at this time. Contemporary accounts allude to his "illness," the "official history" does not mention his removal at all, but Nelson himself has confessed that it occurred for the reason stated above. Markovicz transferred into a Slavic brigade and served out the war with distinction. Early in 1939 he was held on Ellis Island for failure to establish his citizenship. It is alleged that he was later deported.

[13] Unfortunately for the sublimity of this sacrificial moment which has been historicized by repetition, an earlier version relates that the men were in the process of voting whether to return to the line when the counterorder arrived. There is a vast difference between doing and voting whether or not to do. On the other hand, one ought not jump to the other side by concluding that they would not have gone.

history, both sides claimed the victory for themselves, although the Nationalists muster the strongest arguments: the offensive had not broken the siege of Madrid, nor had it impaired the progress of the war in the Basque country. These avowed objectives of the Republic had been frustrated. The Republican claimed the seizure of seventy-five square kilometers of territory. Within the XV Brigade there was an indirect result of the battle. Since they emerged with fewer losses and more men, the Americans began to dominate brigade leadership. Not least among the achievements of the battle was the recall to the Soviet Union of General Gal to answer charges of military incompetence and eventually to be swallowed up in the purges. This was not much—but it was something.

8

⊞ The Road to Zaragoza

Since I had seen them last spring, they have
become soldiers. The romantics have pulled
out, the cowards have gone home with the
badly wounded. . . . Those who are left are
tough, with blackened, matter-of-fact faces,
and after seven months, they know their
trade.

—Ernest Hemingway (Aragon Front)

After a year of war, nothing of great consequence had transpired
on the Aragon front, a sector of fortified villages and sandbagged
highpoints extending southward from Huesca and Zaragoza to Belchite and Teruel. Many months before, Anarchist militia with flam-
boyant names like the "Iron Column" and the "Battalion of Death"
had left Valencia and Barcelona amid shouts of "On to Zaragoza!"
But the slogan had withered on the blighted upland plateaux, a moon-
like place of empty spaces and uncertain vegetation. The front in
Aragon was so sparsely garrisoned that in some sectors it barely existed at all. Once roadblocks had been thrown up and bunkers built
on the higher hilltops, there seemed little else to do. The terrain itself
fostered a defensive mentality. Where it was not gouged by serpentine
canyons, extinct tributaries of the Ebro River, it was pressed flat by
the weight of a prehistoric sea. Almost anything that stirred in this
nearly treeless region could be spotted by an enemy often miles away.
Therefore the idea, in Aragon, was not to stir.

For war correspondents, the Aragon front had a folklore all its
own. Troops were said to be so bored by inactivity that their commanders attempted to bolster their morale by spreading false rumors
that a battle was in the offing. It was accepted as a fact that Fascists
and Anarchists competed in soccer games between the lines. George

Orwell, who served with the militia in this region, called this front "a comic opera with an occasional death." Militia harbored the illusion that they were performing useful work when they engaged in rifle duels with an enemy entrenched half a mile away. Barcelona newspapers repeatedly published aerial views of Zaragoza "under attack by Republican aviation." (The same prewar picture postcards could be purchased at any kiosk for a few *centimos.*) Among the apocrypha of the Aragon front is the story of a Madrid general inspecting a field hospital. "How many cases have you treated in the past six months?" he asked the chief surgeon. "One, my General." "Ah," mused the general, "he fell out of bed, I suppose."

Through this backwash the Republican commanders planned to send an army of eighty thousand men in a massive assault upon Zaragoza. As at Brunete, it was hoped that Franco would be forced to stall his offensive in the north of Spain in order to rush men and material to Aragon. Moreover, there were other considerations, less pragmatic than symbolic. Zaragoza was a kind of Jerusalem *español,* a holy city that had been visited by the Virgin Mary on January 2, A.D. 40. Her shrine, known as Nuestra Señora del Pilar, had been consecrated by St. James (who, among other duties, was patron saint of the Spanish infantry) and had long been a notable place of pilgrimage for Spanish Catholics. Were it to fall into the hands of the godless hosts of the Republic, the ramifications would be terrible for Nationalist morale. To take it, General Sebastian Pozas planned a rapid sweep up both sides of the Ebro River, bypassing fortified towns like Quinto and Belchite, which could be subdued after being surrounded. Unable to depend upon the Anarchists who occupied the region, Pozas summoned the best troops from the Madrid sector, including the International Brigades. The offensive was scheduled to commence on August 22, less than a month after the last salvos of Brunete.

Paradoxically, the forgotten Aragon front would prove in the end to be the region where the war was won, and lost.

At Albares and nearby villages, the XV Brigade reshuffled its table of organization. The dual-regimental system disappeared. Since the Sixth of February had been reduced to a bare company, it was dissolved altogether and the men absorbed into the French-speaking XIV Brigade. Thus were left four battalions, the Lincoln-Washington, the British, the Dimitrov, and the 24th (Spanish). The British had been so badly mauled that Jock Cunningham, Fred Copeman, George Aitken (brigade commissar), and Wally Tapsell (battalion commissar) were summoned to London to answer charges of misfeasance by the British Communist Party.[1] As soon as the guns of Brunete ceased firing, Lieutenant Colonel Copic magically reappeared from the hospital to assume command of the XV Brigade. Steve Nelson was made brigade commissar, and Robert Merriman returned to active service as chief of staff of brigade. Dilution of the Internationals continued, one entirely Spanish company being integrated into each of the four battalions.

Within the Republican cabinet, the shaky coalition between Socialists, Anarchists, and Communists began to show signs of breaking apart. Minister of War Indalecio Prieto (a Right Socialist) was alarmed by the proliferation of Communists in high posts within the Army and Government, for he took it for granted that they intended to seize power if the Republic won the war. The most effective units of the army—those of Lister, Modesto, and El Campesino—were already cadred by Communists; the International Brigade was an autonomous army of the Comintern; and the notorious S.I.M. *Servicio de Investigación Militar,* a secret imperium that functioned underground to ferret out "defeatism," was Communist dominated. Beginning in June, 1937, Prieto moved to break down political activism within the military arm. As a first step, he prohibited party propaganda of all kinds in the army and forbade officers from proselytizing among civilian populations. Next he turned upon the International Brigades to make them an equivalent of the Foreign Legion (*Tercio*) fighting on the Nationalist side.

By a decree promulgated on September 23, 1937, the International Brigade became assimilated into the Republican Army and the Albacete base subordinated to the Foreigners Bureau of the Ministry of War. Henceforth the brigades were supposed to consist of equal parts of foreign and Spanish volunteers. Half of all promotions beyond the rank of sergeant were to be made by the ministry, the other half by Albacete. The Interbrigades would continue to train foreign volun-

---

[1] Cunningham, who had been hailed as "the British Lenin" in the *Daily Worker* a few weeks before, was accused of "Fascist tendencies" and "temporary insanity." He became the scapegoat for the British difficulties in Spain and was not returned there. Among other things he had opposed tighter Communist control of the battalion. Aitken was given a clerical post in England. Copeman and Tapsell returned to Spain, but their former influence had been weakened by the party.

teers, but once they had been dispatched to their respective brigades, the ministry would determine how and where they would be employed. Uniforms would be identical, except that Internationals could wear a special emblem—a three-pointed star slightly fatter than the Mercedes trademark—on the right side of their jackets or shirts. Supposedly the Albacete base was reduced to a processing center, a clearing house for gifts arriving from abroad, and an archive for the dossiers and records pertaining to foreign volunteers. Yet there were compensations. Internationals were accorded the same privileges and rights as those in the Regular Army with respect to pensions, death benefits, and domestic leaves. Any volunteer with a year of service and a clean record would be issued a certificate, if requested, entitling him to eventual Spanish citizenship.[2]

Although publication of this ukase was not tantamount to its implementation, the Government made clear that while it would tolerate the presence of "anti-Fascist" foreigners, it would nevertheless not accept any meddling in domestic affairs by outsiders. Moderates like Prieto (who were wildly denounced, as might be expected, by the Communists) had no intention of ousting fascism only to fall prey to communism. In effect, the decree hinted that the golden period of the International Brigades had passed. No longer was the Republic boggled by the organizational problems of creating an army from a human mass, or pinned against the walls of Madrid and dependent upon foreign volunteers. Now there was hope that the war could be won. The Brunete offensive had proved that the Republic no longer waited until the enemy delivered a blow before countering with one of its own. And the hope existed that the Western democracies might be ready to intervene in Spain if the Republic could just gain a decisive victory somewhere. What all this came to was a phasing out of the International Brigades. In the months ahead they would provide news copy but not make headlines.

As though to show hands unincarnidine, the Albacete faction appointed Hans Amlie as commander of the Lincoln Battalion. Oliver Law had been their civil-rights plank; Amlie was their Popular Front candidate. Hans Amlie was a man of about forty with a lined Baltic

[2] The offer of citizenship was especially attractive to volunteers who had come from Fascist countries like Germany and Italy, because they had no hope of returning home. Few Americans expressed interest in remaining in Spain except for several Negroes attracted by the prospect of living in a nonracist society. If the Republic is ever restored in Spain, presumably International volunteers would be legally eligible for Spanish citizenship.

face and spiky, graying hair. He had been born and reared at Binford, North Dakota, where his father was a prosperous wheat-farmer who dabbled in unsuccessful inventions. Politically he was a late flowering of the Populist movement that swept the upper Middle West during the La Follette era. After attending school in nearby Cooperstown, Amlie joined the Regular Army and fought in the World War. Following his discharge, he drifted west and worked as a miner and prospector. Conditions in mining towns conjoined with stories of the "Ludlow Massacre" contrived to place him always on the workers' side of picket lines. As he later said to Herbert L. Matthews, "They sent men down to work where silicosis was inevitable. Two years' work, one year of dying, and no compensation—that was their career. I've always fought for them, and so I lost job after job, for the owners got to know me." During the thirties he was involved with strikes up and down the Pacific Coast, but he seems to have avoided political commitments. When his friends began drifting off to join the Lincoln Battalion, Amlie hung back, distrusting the Communist flavor of the International Brigades. But when the Socialists organized their ill-starred Eugene Debs Column, he joined them and was slated to be their commander. When this paper organization died a-borning, Amlie enlisted in the Lincoln Battalion as a protest against Socialist apathy. (He never forgave them for their do-nothing attitude toward Spain.)

At Tarazona, Hans Amlie helped to train the George Washington Battalion, and when they attacked Villanueva de la Cañada, he commanded First Company. After his men were pinned down by sniper fire from the church, he tried to lead them into a *barranca* but was hit in the hip by a shot that paralyzed him from the waist down. Before he was pulled to safety, his knapsack was perforated by fourteen sniper bullets. After being hospitalized at the Ritz, he turned up at Albares, his face pale and drawn, and was immediately promoted to Lincoln commander.

It was by no means coincidental that the older brother of the new commander of the Lincoln Battalion was the Honorable Thomas R. Amlie, former Republican congressman of Wisconsin.[3] Not unex-

[3] Thomas R. Amlie had been appointed to fill a death vacancy in the House of Representatives between 1931 and 1933. Subsequently he ran for the senate as a third-party candidate but failed to be elected. Convinced that capitalism had failed and that communism was "dialectics adrift," he hoped to find the middle ground with his American Commonwealth Political Federation, a farmer-labor bloc.

pectedly the party publicists and fund raisers made assiduous use of this family relationship. Here was the ultimate in Popular Front respectability. Poor Hans Amlie, let down by the Socialists and now logrolled by the Communists. Probably he comprehended that he was being used as an expendable news release but acquiesced because he felt that it would assist, in some modest way, the cause of the Republic, in which he believed. Having come prepared to give his life, Amlie did not scruple at the use of his name.[4] He was an earnest, almost saintly man, incapable of ruthlessness or cruelty, for whom Spain was a crusade. But he was stooped and haggard, outward features that seemed to mirror the inner man. His first order of business was to obtain extra spectacles for each man obliged to wear them. He wrote his brother that he feared their glasses might get broken in battle and they would be functionally blind. Always he worried about his men, a solicitude rarely returned. The party stalwarts viewed him with contempt and nicknamed him "The Hick."

As ballast for Captain Amlie, the new Lincoln commissar was John Quigley Robinson, a Belfast-born seaman forty years old. For many years he had been a wheelhorse in the International Seaman's Union, and he had arrived in Spain with enough of his men to start a private army of his own. The seamen were inclined to be roistering troublemakers at Tarazona. They said they had come to fight, not to salute party martinets like Joe Dallet. Only Robinson seemed to know how to handle them. He was a little man who walked with a rolling gait and whose brogue came out of the corner of his mouth. Whereas Nelson wooed dissidents with the mien of a shrewd man listening attentively to the trite mumblings of others, Robinson floored them with his bluntness. His profanity was rich and metaphorical; his delivery, deadpan. No spectator ever forgot his confrontation with a husky seaman, twice his size, who hulked above him and brandished

---

[4] During Amlie's tenure Colonel Stephen O. Fuqua (ret.), the U.S. military attaché in Spain, visited the Lincoln Battalion and allowed himself to be photographed with Amlie and other officers. Obviously Fuqua did not regard his visit as official or unofficial recognition by the United States of the Lincoln Battalion, but the photographs were widely circulated by party propagandists to suggest such recognition. The photograph continues to embarrass the United States Government. Nowadays in Spain it is trotted out and reprinted in order to "document" that the Lincoln Battalion was supported by the United States in much the same way that the Condor Legion was supported by Hitler's Germany. Moreover, as a final irony, the caption fails to make clear that Fuqua (in mufti) is not the figure wearing a Spanish Republican uniform (Amlie).

his fist under the little commissar's nose. The seaman finished his diatribe with a string of oaths, spat at Robinson's feet for emphasis, and snarled, "What have you got to say to *that?*" Looking him up and down for a moment, Robinson replied, "I think you're full of hops!"—or words to that effect. Onlookers gathered round to break up a fight, but the complainer appeared less bellicose. "So what!" he finally bawled out. Still looking him up and down, Robinson retorted, "So, go f . . . yourself." The sailor seemed to consider this point thoughtfully before saying, "Well, if that's the way *you* look at it, it's perfectly O.K. with me." Then he slunk away. If Robinson's wit was not subtle, it was nevertheless formidable. After this, the men called him "Popeye," but not to his face. Publicly he was "Robbie."

When, in the evening of August 18, Major Merriman received orders to transport the XV Brigade to the Aragon front, he discovered, to his dismay that 197 men were on leave in Madrid, swallowed up in boardinghouses and *pensiones* from the Retiro Park to the Puerta del Sol. He requisitioned trucks from the Interbrigade Auto-Park and dispatched every file clerk and night guard he could find with orders to round up the absent men. Edwin Rolfe (*né* Fishback), a Leftish poet who edited the brigade newspaper *The Volunteer for Liberty,* found himself speeding down empty streets at four in the morning, pounding on the doors of darkened hotels, demanding guestbooks from grumpy concierges, and rousing volunteers from all manner of nocturnal lair. Within six hours Merriman's night watch had collected rations (sardines and bread) and all but five of the absent men. By ten in the morning the trucks were on their way to Albares to meet the main convoy.

Two days later the XV Brigade detrained at Hijar, a ramshackle town of dried brick huts, the concentration point for troops assigned to sweep up to Zaragoza along the southern bank of the Ebro. From here they marched to Azaila, the last village within Republican lines, a wretched place on an escarpment that looked as though it had been constructed by cliff swallows. To the west stretched a colorless dust bowl, blindingly brilliant, without shrub or tree. From the flaking church tower of Azaila, brigade officers focused their binoculars upon the church tower at Quinto, ten miles distant. They had been ordered to take Quinto as soon as the offensive opened and had been allotted three days to do the job. Between these two high points there was no sign of human creature or human habitation other than a deserted

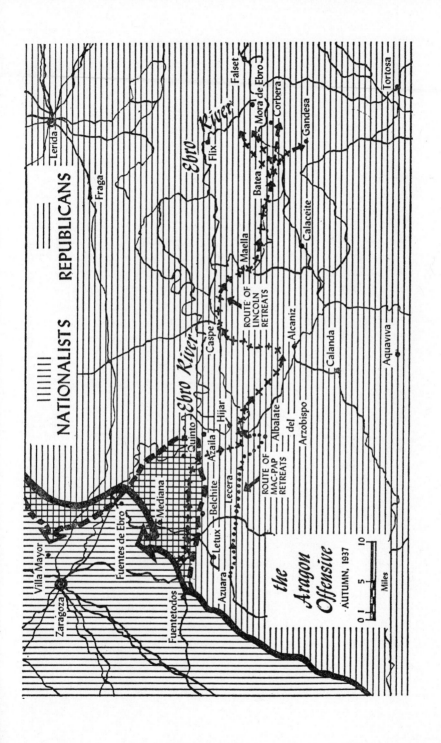

road-menders' shack located at what seemed an infinite distance. To their right the Ebro, a snaking green ribbon, scored a path through russet canyons to the sea.

Steve Nelson went forward with a small group to the most advanced Republican blockhouse and found the outgoing Anarchist commander, wearing a black and red ascot, supervising the withdrawal of his men. Making no comment upon conditions of the front, he saluted the International officers with icy formality and strolled off to the touring bus that would carry him and his men back to Barcelona. Lashed to the roof of the bus were mattresses, suitcases, two wine kegs, a wind-up phonograph, and a tennis set—paraphernalia that aroused scornful comment from Americans who found it convenient to forget that at Jarama their field equipment included Ping-Pong tables, checkers, softballs, and a wind-up phonograph. Coming back to town, Nelson stopped at a tiny farm tucked away in an irrigated ravine and offered to buy the farmer's entire stock of green vegetables. The old peasant, tight-lipped and suspicious, outlined his terms—cash and carry. But when Nelson pulled out a wad of Republican bills, he pushed them away contemptuously. "You call *that* money?" he asked. Paper trash issued by the Republic. Crops were real—politics and paper were meaningless. Looking north toward Fascist-held territory, the *campesino* articulated his long-view theory of history: "There has been no fighting—all has been peaceful. And now it's going to change. Why couldn't you let us alone? Fight your own war at Madrid. The Fascists let us alone, and we let them alone." Such attitudes angered the Internationals. The Aragonese drastically needed "education."

In the predawn hours of August 24, 1937, Republican armored units quickly battered through enemy roadblocks along a front forty miles wide and plunged ahead toward their point of convergence, Zaragoza. In their wake, the XV Brigade moved across the open plain toward Quinto, bypassed by the vanguard. The village lay upon a slope between the high plateau and the valley bottom. One mile south was a cliffside fortification called Pulburrel Hill, which beetled over the valley but which was at an elevation lower than the plateau to the west. It was perfectly designed to command the Barcelona-Zaragoza railroad paralleling the Ebro. While the Dimitrovs feigned an attack upon Pulburrel Hill from the plateau, the other battalions moved through gulleys to positions south and west of Quinto, thereby severing communication between the hill and the town.

The Lincolns infiltrated across the dust-whipped highlands west of Quinto and moved downhill toward their first objective, a line of fortified ditches and barbed wire strung out around the whitewashed cemetery enclosure. Except for the blunt tower of the parish church, the village itself was almost out of sight in the valley. Framed against a vivid blue sky, the Americans were exposed at once to a waspish small-arms fire from the cemetery and church tower. Captain Amlie quickly pulled them back. From Pulburrel Hill came intermittent rifle and machine-gun fire, but the distance was much too great for any effect other than mild psychological harassment. (The Nationalists had withdrawn all their artillery from Quinto but not their garrison; cannon, it is presumed, being of greater value than men.) The attack stalled while nine Republican guns battered the enemy positions. Meanwhile, the Dimitrovs swung to the north of town to cut off a Nationalist retreat.

In midafternoon the barrage ceased. Half a dozen fifteen-ton Soviet tanks clanked through the American lines, their 45-mm guns peppering the enemy strongpoints, anthill cones strewn about the downslope. Having no antitank weapons, the Nationalist line collapsed at once. Exultant Americans, some of whom had shaved their heads in Iroquois fashion, dashed forward with war whoops. Resistance was short-lived. Those Nationalist soldiers not in rabbit flight toward the village cowered in their parapets with hands over their heads. For several minutes the scene resembled a marathon. Even after the Lincolns had swept through the flattened wire, enemy soldiers were popping out of their burrows and bounding away in all directions. The tanks continued as far as the municipal dump, a multitiered escarpment hanging over the western edge of Quinto, from which they bounced shells off the church tower looming above them. As at Villanueva de la Cañada, the parish church was the most heavily fortified place in town. The tanks could advance no farther, for the arabesque alleyways of Quinto were deathtraps for vehicles. Ferreting out the enemy snipers was the job of foot soldiers. Thus far Quinto had been more a lark than a military operation. The number of American dead could have been counted on two hands with fingers left over. Captain Amlie pulled his men back to the cemetery for the night, reserving the next morning for a mop-up of the village.

The Nationalists had had a bad day, but their night was disastrous. Somehow their munition dump caught on fire and went off like a gigantic fireworks display, the big stuff last. Then a Lincoln patrol found a pipeline that led out of town and into the hillsides to the south. They smashed it and thereby cut the waterline supplying the garrison on Pulburrel Hill—"Purple Hill" as the men called it. This garrison had remained so sluggish and inconspicuous throughout the day that Major Merriman had concluded that the force up there was insignificant. He ordered the British to storm the heights in the morning.

At dawn the street fighting in Quinto began in earnest. While the Mooney machine guns kept the bell tower occupied, the rifle companies entered the town. They were inexperienced at house-to-house fighting. One American dashed into a doorway and staggered back outside with a bayonet gash in his leg; a soldier lurking inside had nearly pinned him against the hall. Thereafter they bombed every house and watched oaken doors cartwheel down cobblestone streets. Companies were now armed with Dichterev machine guns, light, air-cooled weapons firing sixty-three bullets per pan, which were employed with great effect. Yet many men were undertrained. A Lincoln section leader watched one of his new men nicely lob a Mills bomb through an open window, but no explosion ensued. "Did you pull the pin all the way out?" The recruit replied, "Pin? What pin d'ya mean?"

Unlike the telescopic impersonality of Brunete or Jarama, the fight at Quinto was a confrontation against an enemy that had tangible identity. Flaring up and dying down, the fighting raged through squalid alleys flanked by one-story adobe huts and stables. One American recalled dashing across a street in one direction at the instant an enemy soldier dashed across in the other. He ran back just as the enemy decided to do the same thing, and they nearly collided in the road. Unable to decide who was pursuing whom, both decided to remain where they were. The enemy took advantage of interconnecting cellars under the houses to make subterranean maneuvers within the town. The church tower seemed to overlook every wall and hovel in Quinto. Although the brigade antitank guns caromed one-inch shells off its massive brick surface, the tower was infested with snipers, who fought with the desperation of trapped animals. At Quinto the Lincolns learned to respect the killing power of a church.

Quinto held its portion of psychological terrors. One American, running across an open space, had to vault the body of his best friend, shot down in front of him. Ducking into a walled enclosure he found himself between two houses, one of them gutted and the other intact with the windows open, as though someone inside were airing the room in the warm sunshine. Through this window he could see a kitchen table, freshly laid out with linen, crockery, and silver. Beyond the table was a calendar on the wall. What he next saw unnerved him. Next to this window was what appeared to be a pantry or alcove containing a tiny, smudged pane, behind which he could not see. Suddenly it occurred to him that someone hiding in the alcove was watching him. To rush out into the bullet-swept street was suicidal. Keeping his eye on the blackened window, he rolled a cigarette, but his hands shook so badly he could not light it. In rigid movements he began to crawl across the courtyard toward the ruined house, never taking his eye from the ominous window. All at once something exploded beside him "with a roar louder than the loudest aerial bomb." He had disturbed a cat, which scuttered away over the loose rubble. Hours later, he brought his squad back and bombed the house before entering it. The alcove was empty. The other room was filled with bits of broken crockery, and splintered furniture, but the calendar still hung undamaged upon the wall.

A major fire-fight broke out around a valuable prize abandoned in a square—a water truck supplying the village garrison. While the Lincolns pushed the enemy back, Dave Doran, one of Nelson's junior commissars, climbed aboard and drove it out of town to the Brigade kitchen, where its contents eventually reappeared in the evening stew. It was somehow appropriate that Doran, a street fighter from Albany, should first draw attention to himself in Spain by hijacking a truck, but this was only the prologue to a series of dramatic spectacles authored and staged by Dave Doran.

The battle inside Quinto continued all day as the Nationalists fell back to the houses surrounding the church. At nightfall, Amlie once again pulled the Lincolns back to the cemetery. The British attack up Pulburrel had been beaten off easily when the attackers discovered that the position Merriman had called "lightly held" contained about five hundred men—that is to say, more than the number of Britons climbing the forty-degree slope. The British commander, Peter Daly, an Irishman, had been mortally wounded, and the battalion conceivably could have been massacred had the Nationalists not become excited and tipped their hand by opening fire prematurely. The British were down on Merriman, who promised to soften "Purple Hill" in the morning.

On August 26, the third day, the battle centered upon the parish church. Inside were two hundred die-hards whose desire to resist had been fortified by lurid stories, recounted by their officers, of how *los internacionales* tortured their prisoners. They set up barricades in windows located eighteen feet off the ground and fired at anything, human or animal, that moved in the town. Machine gunners remained in the belfry, although by this time it looked like rotten cheese. It is alleged that Steve Nelson wormed up to the esplanade and walked completely around the church, his back pressed against the walls. He had proved that it could be done, even though two of his runners were killed and another wounded. While XV Brigade snipers kept the enemy away from the windows, a group of Dimitrovs battered down the west door with an immense beam and opened fire into the murky interior. They obtained a foothold in the vestibule, where they came under fire from the baptismal font and the high altar. By this time the hard core of the defense had ascended into the organ loft, from which they dropped grenades into the nave. Then began a Sisyphean labor to smoke them out. Bundles of straw were tossed inside and grenades pitched in to ignite them, but this chore took a long time because the grenades blew the straw to smithereens without setting it on fire.

While the Internationals were breaking into the western end of the church, Nationalists were pouring out the windows and surrendering. The terrace quickly became a babel of *vivas!* shouted by frightened prisoners who seemed to believe that survival depended upon combining the right slogan with the correct lung volume. Eager to please everyone, they cried, *"Viva la república!" "Viva el gobierno!"* and *"Viva Rusia!"* Many Americans were flattered to be mistaken for Russians; others were annoyed by it. The prisoners were turned over to the Lincoln Second Company, almost entirely Spanish, and herded out of town. Some of the captives, having regained their confidence, hurled insults at their guards, who promptly yanked them out of the column and shot them down in the road.[5] The Nationalist officers, none of whom surrendered, had to be stalked through the gothic half light of the church and gunned down one by one. By midafternoon the village of Quinto had been secured by the Brigade.

While the Lincolns and Dimitrovs were rolling drums of gasoline into the last enemy strongholds in Quinto and flushing Fascists out of the church, the rest of the brigade was surrounding Pulburrel Hill.

---

[5] Purportedly the American volunteers were indignant when they learned what their comrades in *el batallón lincoln* had done. They were already sore at the Second Company for having been trigger-happy at the fighting around the church, where they had accidentally shot some Yugoslavs and Americans near the main portal.

The three antitank guns of the brigade shelled enemy parapets from slightly higher ground along the Azaila road. The British attacked the mound from the north, the 24th from the east, and the Lincoln Third Company from the western plain. In the middle of this maneuvering, a dozen Nationalist bombers came down from Zaragoza and unloaded over them. By some mischance, the airplanes had unloaded on top of Pulburrel! Black smoke purled over the summit. Jarred by concussion, and surrounded by an enemy force closing in from all sides, the Nationalists stuck handkerchiefs on bayonets and waved them. As the hilltop sprouted white flags, the attackers surged upward. Then, as suddenly as they had appeared, the white streamers vanished and a rattle of rifle fire came down from the top. (It was learned later that the soldiers had attempted to surrender but had been forced to resume the battle by their officers, who shot those who had hung out the flags.) The British, by this time nearly halfway to the summit, dug holes in the plum-pudding soil as grenades tumbled down the slope. The enemy even rolled down boulders, which accelerated to fantastic speeds.

The antitank battery again picked at the elongated line of trenches rimming the edge of the plateau. In late afternoon resistance fell off and white flags again fluttered along the crest. The XV Brigade hurried up, pushed aside the wire, and jumped into the trenches. The first attackers to reach the top saw Nationalist recruits throwing their rifles far down the slope so they could not be forced to resume fighting. For two days they had been without water. Ignoring the bayonets of the Internationals, they swirled around them, pointing to their tongues and croaking, *"Agua! Agua!"* Internationals who had scaled the hill enraged at the false surrender now poured water down the cracked throats of men they had sworn to kill to the last man. The accidental bombing as well as the high-velocity shelling from the one-inch antitank guns had turned the trenches into a horrid butcher shop, strewn with "pieces of meat everywhere, lying around, covered with dust and dir

The Nationalist officers had run through the trench to their headquarters bunker at the northeastern promontory of Pulburrel Hill. None surrendered. One of the last ones to be hunted down was a White Russian officer who brandished his pistol and screamed "Red Pigs! Red Pigs!" As a group of Anglo-Americans approached him warily, he placed his pistol against his temple and blew his brains out. On his body they found a Cyrillic Bible and a Czarist sword.

Quinto had been taken in three days, exactly on schedule. By any standard this was the most spectacular action in which the Americans had taken part in Spain. Their divisional commander, General "Walter" (Karol Swierczewski, a Pole), estimated that only thirty men in the entire XV Brigade had been killed, whereas the enemy had lost three hundred dead and nearly a thousand prisoners.[6] The Lincolns emerged from a battle at full strength and with an élan never present before. For the first time in their six-month history they had functioned as a *batallón de choque* (a shock battalion), which was what the Internationals were designed to be. None of them could have foreseen that Quinto was a crest in their military annals and that henceforth they would be carried by a draining tide.

On the day that Quinto fell, Nationalist reinforcements from the Madrid front arrived in Zaragoza on trains so crowded that great numbers of soldiers had suffocated to death in the cars. At the same time artillery and aircraft (but no men) were detached from Franco's offensive in the north and sped to Aragon. Santander had fallen, and those Republicans not captured in the city were fleeing westward into the Asturias. Meanwhile, General Pozas' offensive had stalled twelve miles short of Zaragoza at a place along the river called Fuentes de Ebro. The Nationalists also held on to a mountain chain extending southward from the Ebro to the western edge of the Belchite plain. Having occupied hundreds of square miles of scorched wasteland, the Republic seemed unable to maintain its momentum of attack. And with each passing hour the enemy massed enormous fire-power behind a line increasingly formidable. In Republican circles there was as much talk about repelling counterattacks as taking Zaragoza.

A major trouble-spot had developed at Belchite, a fortified town eighteen miles southwest of Quinto. There a Nationalist force of about two thousand men had been bypassed and subsequently surrounded during the first days of the offensive, but after a week of intense barrage and repeated frontal attacks, the garrison still held out under conditions of siege. Although their ring of concrete artillery bunkers had been smashed, they had fortified the churches, factories, and outer houses of the town and seemed prepared to resist to the

---

[6] It is worth noting that these "statistics" are based upon a summary of the divisional report published in *The Volunteer for Liberty*, a periodical designed to be a propaganda organ of the XV Brigade. As might be expected, the Republicans make much ado about Quinto, while the Nationalists rarely allude to it at all.

end. Egging them on, Nationalist radio alluded to Belchite as a second Alcázar [7] and promised that a relief column would be sent to aid the beleaguered garrison. On the other hand, the Republic, embarrassed by the existence of an enemy force deep inside its newly gained territory, repeatedly announced that Belchite was about to surrender. Both sides devoted more news space to Belchite than its tactical importance warranted, for a mere two thousand Nationalists isolated inside of Republican territory constituted no menace to anyone except themselves. Yet newspapers made Belchite sound as though the outcome of the war would be determined by its fate. During the Peninsular Wars, it was pointed out, not even the army of Napoleon had been able to subdue Belchite. Now the Nationalists demanded that dead history be repeated and the Republicans that it be rewritten. The result was that the XV Brigade was rushed from the Ebro to assist in its capture.

On September 1 the Brigade marched south across a wide plain along a road as straight as a taut rope. It was a landscape of immense emptiness, awesome and African. From behind pastel-colored mountains to the west came the rumble of artillery. They scanned the sky for signs of Fascist airplanes, for there was no cover in this open plain. But they marched unmolested, except by the heat. Even the wind was hot, like the exhaust of an engine. They passed through Codo, a hamlet populated only by waxlike cadavers of Nationalist soldiers. Magpies pecked at the bodies. One soldier lay dead with an equally dead rabbit tucked under his arm. Scattered about were leaflets that had been dropped by Nationalist planes days before—Carlist propaganda featuring a portrait of Christ with bloody face, flanked by photographs of General Franco, his face wreathed with a smile, and General Mola, peering froglike from thick eyeglasses.

Two miles north of Belchite, they entered an imposing olive forest, a natural cathedral composed of gnarled trees centuries old. (Six months later this same grove would save the Lincoln Battalion from annihilation.) The deep woods seemed to be filled with camions, tanks, and bivouacked troops, all of which had been employed, at one time or another, against the encircled town. The last mile to the northern edge of Belchite consisted of a slight ascent across wide terraces, each of which was supported by a rock wall. Through the trees

---

[7] During the summer of 1936 a Nationalist force had been besieged in the Alcázar, a military school in Toledo, for seventy days until relieved by a Nationalist column.

came fleeting glimpses of two church towers silhouetted above the town: San Agustín, a chimney-shaped belfry guarding the northern approach, and the parish church, a cone-topped tower commanding the eastern side. The most advanced Republican line consisted of a drainage ditch four hundred yards from the first houses of the town. While the Dimitrovs swung off to the northwest, Amlie pushed the Lincolns beyond the Republican ditch.[8] It was a bold maneuver, born of misinformation and overconfidence. The Americans infiltrated across a succession of artichoke and cabbage gardens lying between the olive forest and Belchite, taking advantage of terrace walls. In the growing twilight, some Lincolns reached ditches within a hundred yards of San Agustín and dueled with snipers in the belfry. Very quickly they learned that Belchite would not be a scrimmage like Quinto. Houses tightly ringed the town with the compactness of solid wall, and each window harbored a sniper. Within minutes a harrowing fire beat down upon them and stopped their advance. One of the first Americans killed was Sam Levinger, YIPSEL poet from Ohio.

Captain Amlie recalled his men to the Republican trench. Meanwhile, Commissar Robinson heard his field telephone ringing. Picking up the receiver, he heard the voice of John Cookson, his sergeant of *transmissiones,* who wondered how the telephone sounded. "It works fine," said Robinson. "Where are you guys?" "In Belchite," replied Cookson, in his matter-of-fact, Cobb (Wisconsin) twang. "Belchite!" Robinson yelled. "Get out of there—you're surrounded!" Cookson lost no time in returning to the battalion, although he brought all his apparatus and wire with him. Ironically, it would take the Lincoln Battalion four days to fight their way to the place from which Cookson telephoned them.

Large numbers of Americans received no order to withdraw. Daylight of September 2 found them pinned down in shallow ditches by a lashing hail of fire from San Agustín and the houses on the northern perimeter of Belchite. Unable to move forward or backward, they waited for the torrent to subside. Only the Jarama vets among them could remember having seen such textbook patterns of interlocking machine-gun fire, which seemed to emanate from all directions simultaneously. A couple of men bolted toward the rear and were shot down among the artichokes and cabbages.

---

[8] The British Battalion had been dispatched into the mountains west of Belchite to assist in repelling Nationalist counterattacks; the 24th Battalion was placed on "standby reserve," whatever that means.

When Amlie notified brigade headquarters that large numbers of his men were trapped, Major Merriman ordered him to advance the battalion and to seize the church and surrounding houses. Amlie was aghast: in effect, he had been commanded to lead his men into a deathtrap. He refused to obey the order. Merriman began yelling through the telephone, "You've got to, you hear! You go or face court-martial!" (The words of a man with a short memory: had Merriman forgotten February 27?) Merriman promised artillery support, a promise fulfilled a short time later when shells began exploding, not in the town but upon the Lincoln positions! They were only 75s, but no one complained of boredom.[9] More effective was a sheltering barrage against the houses and church laid down by the brigade anti-tank battery commanded by Hugh Slater, an English writer.[10] Slater was very proud of his guns: at a distance of a mile he could place a shell through an individual window. He could badger the snipers in Belchite, but it was up to the Lincolns to root them out.

Meanwhile, Amlie pushed his men across half a dozen terraces to within two hundred yards of San Agustín. In between lay an open field. By this time he had lost two company commanders and enough men to make him appalled. No one doubted that to cross that field meant certain death. Again Merriman rang him up and demanded that he assault the church. Turning to his staff, Amlie groaned, "What am I going to do? Court-martial at the front means *execution!*" The solution was simple, rejoined one man, "You order us to go and then we'll refuse. Then you tell them to come down here and we'll follow *them!*" Robinson endorsed Amlie: if Brigade intended to employ firing squads, they could arrange one for him, too. Steve Nelson came over to oil the troubled waters and found the usually placid Amlie simmering with outrage. "What the hell is the matter with you guys?" snarled Amlie. "That town's bristling with machine guns, thick as hair on a dog's back, and you want to send infantry against them! You want to slaughter the whole damn battalion?" Not even the presence of Nelson prevailed to move the men forward.

To their right was an olive factory, a long, low building shaped like

[9] It is by no means clear whether the shelling was intended to force the battalion into action or the result of inaccuracy and incompetence.

[10] Slater had come to Spain as correspondent for a Communist news agency in 1936 and joined the International Brigades. His real name was Humphrey Slater, but he adopted Hugh because it sounded more proletarian. After the war his novel *The Heretics* (1947), part of which was based upon his experiences in the Spanish Civil War, attacked Communist orthodoxy.

an airplane hangar. Nelson observed that despite the bodies of Republican soldiers strewn about the factory, no fire flashes came from the windows. He collected a small group, slithered down the road to it, and peeked in through a hole smashed through the wall by shellfire. Inexplicably the place had been abandoned. Nelson passed down the word and within a few minutes the Lincolns occupied the factory, which ran up to the first houses of Belchite. Quickly setting up a Dichterev at a far window, Lincoln gunners engaged the Nationalist snipers in the belfry, less than fifty yards away. Nelson had discovered the vulnerable underbelly of Belchite. Hundreds of men could be massed here, under cover, to press their attack upon the town.[11]

Provisioned by airdrops, the defenders read about their heroic defense in Zaragoza newspapers and fought on. Their planes dropped leaflets promising that relief columns were converging upon the city. They threw up barricades of cobblestones and mattresses along every alleyway leading toward the center of the city and fought with the desperation of men who believed what their officers told them about the Internationals massacring prisoners. The leaders urged their men on with the cry, "Die like men today—not like rabbits tomorrow!"

For two days the Lincolns dueled with snipers without making a significant inroad into the town. The antitank guns of the XV Brigade alone battered sniper nests with nearly three thousand one-inch shells. But each time the Americans moved forward, snipers popped up again and drove them back. For a time the men labored to advance through houses by knocking out connecting walls, but the results were unsatisfactory. (In the twenties, Belchite house-owners had been introduced to Portland cement—a brand appropriately known as "Samson"—which proved to be nearly impervious to pick-axes wielded by hand.) The Republican command seemed unable to coordinate massive assaults: units attacked individually and were cut down piecemeal. Heavy artillery eroded the strong points but did not pulverize them.

Finally, on September 5, the thirteenth day of the siege, the Republicans broke into Belchite behind six tanks. Prisoners had already charted the town and pinpointed enemy barricades and communica-

---

[11] According to an account of the battle written by Emanuel Lanzer, an American machine gunner, a few weeks after the event, it was the Dimitrovs rather than Nelson's party that first occupied the factory. More recent accounts invariably credit Nelson with the occupation. Since there are no Dimitrovs nearby to dispute such claims, one suspects that Lincoln historians often appropriated Dimitrov military accomplishments as their own.

tion lines. Bombing parties proceeded to destroy every house on their route to the Nationalist *comandancia,* a five-story concrete building in the *plaza mayor.* A XV Brigade antitank gun was wheeled up to the city gate facing the Plaza de Goya and fired point-blank up the long Calle Mayor, the only straight street in Belchite. Late in the afternoon, while tanks and artillery converted the nearby houses into rubbish, two waves of the Lincoln Battalion converged upon San Agustín, one from the factory and the other from the artichoke fields. They broke into the rear of the church and bombed their way through the nave to the west portal, where they set up a Dichterev and beat off a counterattack. Even with the church occupied, a lone sniper held out in the belfry above for another twenty-four hours. A short time later he shot Nelson in the thigh, when, in a moment of carelessness, the commissar walked past a window in the olive factory. Nelson's life was saved, but his career in Spain was ended.

Throughout the remaining daylight hours of September 5, the battle for the center district of Belchite wavered back and forth. At one point a band of Lincolns built a barricade across an alley out of sacks of grain. Then a barrel-chested Colorado miner, picking up the sacks one by one and carrying them in front of him like shields, advanced the barricade toward the enemy fire. Nearby lay the body of Charlie Regan—"Charlie the Sniper"—who never got that Zeiss scope for his *mexicanski.* On the wall of a house near this barricade hung a hand-lettered sign that read FORBIDDEN TO PLAY HANDBALL HERE. Doubtless the owner had been a person sensitive to noise and vibration.

During the night Belchite burned with a ghastly realism "no Hollywood film could ever give." Tongues of flame were reflected off the black pall of smoke hanging above the dying town. Spectators a mile away smelled the stench of putrescent, roasted carrion. Two hundred Nationalists tried to break out. Stumbling over one another as they dashed down an alley, they were caught in a devastating fire and driven back to the center of town. A half-dozen or so managed to escape to the olive grove north of town and eventually beyond the mountains to Nationalist lines.

With ultimate victory no longer in doubt, Republican soldiers bombed their way through smoking houses on the morning of September 6. Major Robert Merriman and Lieutenant Philip Detro personally led bombing parties across rooftops, dropping grenades into chimneys and courtyards. Carl Geiser, an assistant commissar who had left Ohio State University to come to Spain, and Ralph Thornton, a Pittsburgh Negro, found a civilian hiding in a garret. The citizen, who held a rifle in his hands, explained that he had seven children and that he had always supported the Republic in word and in deed. Geiser took the rifle from him and felt the barrel: it was hot. He turned the sniper over to some Spanish soldiers, who executed him, probably in the middle of his monologue about his seven children.

The steepled church on the eastern side of town had become the nerve center of the resistance, other pockets of fighting having become little more than twitching ganglia. The parish church had been converted into a hospital-fort containing several hundred wounded men, most of them armed. No one relished the prospect of storming this church. It would cost the lives of many good men, friend and foe alike.

While the military commanders worked out a plan of attack, Dave Doran, the upstart commissar who had hijacked the water truck at Quinto, stole their thunder. He wrote out a short speech and brought a propaganda truck to within a block of the church. An interpreter translated it and read it over the loudspeaker. Doran did not promise pie in the sky; he had a single theme—quit or die:

> Come over to us and live. . . . We have you surrounded on all sides. . . . Drop your arms and come over the barricades one by one. . . . All who come over will live. . . . If you don't come over, you will all be killed in the morning. . . .

The loudspeaker voice, as booming as the voice of God, suddenly shut off. Minutes passed. It was growing dark. Then, in the gloom, a lone figure crawled out of the church. He was wounded and begged for a doctor. Doran collared him and ordered him back inside to fetch his companions. The soldier crawled back and for half an hour nothing happened. All at once rifles clattered on the cobblestones and the street next to the church was filled with shouts of *"Viva la república!"* as the maimed, the crippled, and their able-bodied comrades poured out of the church. After fourteen days of siege, Belchite had surrendered.

The Americans were dog-tired. They were sapped of strength, drugged by sleepless days and nights, devoid of enthusiasm for the "victory." Every sixth man was *hors de combat* (twenty-three killed and sixty wounded). So great was the fear of an epidemic that the dead were soaked with gasoline, piled in stacks, and burned. The living were grateful when the order came for them to bivouac in the olive grove outside of town, for Carl Geiser doubtless spoke for all of them when he said, "Belchite—the stinkingest town I was ever in." As they filed out of Belchite they passed an advertisement, illuminated by the smoky light of funeral pyre which read ZETSO—EXTERMINATOR. Whether Zetso was a man's name or a brand name they never found out. Either way, it was appropriate.

In the olive grove the men built cane lean-tos as protection against the orange dust, stirred by the endless caravans crossing the plain and trapped by eyebrows and hair. Ernest Hemingway, Martha Gellhorn, and Herbert L. Matthews arrived to inspect Belchite and found a town so totally ruined that often one could not tell where the streets had been. People were digging under piles of mortar, bricks, and beams searching for the dead. Mule carcasses, cooking pots, framed lithographs, sewing machines—all covered with flies—suggested a surrealist collage. Belchite was less a town than an unpleasant smell.[12] The visitors dropped in on the Lincoln Battalion in the olive grove and wrote dispatches about Merriman, who outlined the campaign for them "as carefully as if we were his freshman class in economics back in California." A freckled redhead from Brooklyn told them, "You ought to of seen us at Belchite. Boy! The marines got nothing on us." Even Hemingway was impressed by their accounts of fighting, which seemed to be "the sort you never know whether to classify as hysterical or the ultimate in bravery." But he admitted that the Americans were beginning to look like real soldiers. Missing was the defeatistic self-pity of the Jarama period. But missing, too, were most of the faces of that faraway time.

Captain Amlie and Commissar Robinson were assigned the role of playing scapegoats for the delay in taking Belchite. Amlie, who had been lightly wounded, received an indefinite hospital leave while his repatriation papers were being prepared by the Albacete base. For a few weeks he hung about the battalion, a brooding Lazarus-figure, hoping to be of help yet invariably shunned like an unclean creature.

[12] The destruction at Belchite was so enormous that in the forties an entirely new town was constructed one mile west of the ruins. Except for clearing the rubble from the streets, Old Belchite was left as it was on the day the armies moved out of it. Today it is an uninhabited ghost town.

Finally he was packed off to Valencia, where he met and married a middle-aged American newswoman named Mildred Bennett.[13] The party was able to wring a few more drops from Amlie before discarding him: in the United States he traveled as a fund raiser and critic of the Socialist position toward Spain. After this, oblivion.[14] Removing Robinson was much simpler: he was "recalled" by his union.

The new commander of the Lincoln Battalion, Philip Leighton Detro, was one of the most anomalous Americans ever to fight in Spain. This lanky, six-foot-four Texan seemed to take few things seriously, least of all himself. He told everyone that he had originally come to Spain to collect fifteen hundred dollars a month as a pilot and that he had crossed the frontier on April Fools' Day. While others tried to eradicate all hints of bourgeois upbringing, Detro boasted openly of his WASP heritage. Among pious proletarians Detro was a blasphemer. Not only did he flaunt Texan attitudes, but also he claimed to be a spiritual Mississippian. While in training at Tarazona he was suspected, at various times, of being a romantic, a nincompoop, and a spy. Way back when, or so he spun his yarn, the Detros had been Mississippi planters. As a matter of fact, one of his mother's kinfolk had been a general in the Civil War—"on the Confederate side, of course." ("Of course," echoed lads from The Bronx.) When Reconstruction brought misery, poverty, and "nigra problems," the Detros moved west to Conroe, Texas, to grow up with the country. But times were bad, and the Detros were always genteel-poor. His mother had to teach school. After graduation from David Crockett High School in 1928 he began working his way through nearby Rice Institute but quit after a year to ship out of the Gulf ports on a tanker. On shore leave in Germany he heard Hitler deliver a speech in 1932, and in the street brawl that followed, Detro lost a shirt sleeve. Politics was not the issue: "I didn't like getting pushed around."

---

[13] There seems to be no truth in the rumor, circulated by newsmen in Spain, that Miss Bennett had previously married three other American volunteers, all of whom had been killed in battle.

[14] During World War II, Amlie managed a War Food Administration camp in California housing seven thousand itinerant workers. After the war he continued to run the camp for private growers. The septic tank clogged up regularly and had to be repaired by lowering a man to free the exit pipe from within. Since this job was dangerous, Amlie always insisted upon doing it himself. In 1950 he was asphyxiated by sewer gas before his men could pull him to safety. With him died a workman, also overcome, who had climbed down the rope to save him.

Aboard ship Detro began to fancy himself a writer. (At age nine he had written a novel but had never published anything.) In 1934 he quit the merchant marine and enrolled at the University of Missouri. He joined Alpha Tau Omega, a fraternity for Southern Gentlemen, and took flying lessons at Columbia Field. His classmates felt he was "a restless, soldier-of-fortune type." In one semester he completed third-year Spanish and flunked creative writing. At the end of the year Detro was "excused from the university" for having accumulated seventy-seven overcuts in his classes—something of a local record. For a year he worked in New York for a writers' syndicate.

When Detro heard that the Republic was recruiting fliers at fancy prices, he submitted an application to the Spanish consulate but was rejected because he had not logged enough hours. He then tried to join the Lincoln Battalion, but the party turned him down, probably because he seemed like a poor political risk. After the Jarama fiasco he was accepted because of his National Guard and ROTC experience. On the boat going over, when another volunteer asked him what he thought of the Spanish situation, the gangly Texan drawled, "Back where I come from, they think Spain is too far away to affect the price of cotton." He enjoyed the role of political dummy. Once he alluded to the "class struggle" as though it had something to do with the tribulations of getting from class to class at the University of Missouri.[15]

At Tarazona he commanded a squad. At Brunete he took over Amlie's company and led them up Mosquito Ridge, where he was wounded by mortar fragments while tending his dysentery. He missed Quinto but was released from hospital in time to lead a bombing party at Belchite. He was not a fashion-plate officer. At a time when others were turning up in tailored uniforms, Detro invariably wore a faded beret and a turtleneck sweater several sizes too large. His only badge denoting officer rank was a big automatic—his "shootin'-iron" —strapped with leather thongs, Texas-style, halfway down his right thigh. He had grown a thin mustache, barely visible except in certain angles of light. In manner he affected an ironically chipper style favoring phrases like "m'boy" and "right-o" in the tradition of Hollywood Englishmen. At twenty-six Detro was the youngest commander the Lincoln Brigade had yet had.

[15] One ought not to rule out the possibility that Detro pretended to be more apolitical than he really was in order to conform to the Popular Front image of the International Brigades.

Meanwhile, the battalion spent September in a series of moves back and forth along the Aragon front, bivouacking near wretched villages of consequence only to census takers and cartographers. There was no fighting, only moving. The breakthrough to Zaragoza had failed to materialize. Among the men, the rumor was that the fighting was over until the spring campaigns, and this theory seemed strengthened when the Republican newspapers began referring to recent developments in Aragon as the "Belchite Offensive," no longer as the "Zaragoza Offensive." A quarter-loaf was better than none.

International Volunteer raising clenched fist of the Popular Front

Left: Colonel Vladmir Copic who commanded XV International Brigade throughout most of the fighting at Jarama. His companion is unidentified. *Center:* Purportedly an International Volunteer. Hammer-sickle emblem may be spurious (i.e., a "plant" by National publicists). *Right:* Republican spying terrain at Jarama.

Left: Goya Gate, after the Americans broke into Belchite, September 1937.
Right: Shattered tank on slope leading up to Mosquito Crest, Brunete.

Internationals moving to attack at Jarama

Fighting in the bitter cold at Teruel

Lincoln grave on the battleground at Jarama

Crossing the Ebro, July 1938

The return *back* across the Ebro

OUR ⋀ FIGHT

NUESTRO COMBATE

JOURNAL OF THE XV INTERNATIONAL BRIGADE

THIS YEAR - THE FINAL VICTORY OVER FASCISM

RESOLVED

LOOKING TOWARD A NEW YEAR 1938 WHICH WILL SHOW, BEFORE IT RUNS ITS TIME, WHETHER DEMOCRACY SHALL LIVE ON THE FACE OF THE EARTH, OR WHETHER THE PEOPLES OF THE WORLD SHALL BOW UNDER THE VICIOUS WHIP OF FASCISM.

**Peace
On Earth
-Good Will
To Men**

Copy of XV International Brigade house organ

After a 20 kilometer breakthrough at Ebro, the Republicans ran into heavy resistance at Villalba and advanced no farther

Internationals captured by the Nationalists, April 1938, forced to give the Nationalist salute before boarding trains to prison camp

Left to right: An American prisoner arriving at San Pedro and American prisoners at San Pedro

Chow line at San Pedro. On good days there was a sardine on top of the stew.

"Education" classes at San Pedro. Nationalist officers attempted to "de-Marx" their prisoners.

9

⌐⌐ Truth in Steel—Fuentes de Ebro

All the dirty work you did for years, cranking leaflets, passing
them out in snow and sun, visiting contacts, etc. was not in
vain. Everything we worked for for years is coming true in steel.

—Joe Dallet to wife

Life insurance rates for American volunteers in Spain, had such
policies been written, would not have been cheap. As we have seen,
the Lincoln Battalion had lost most of its men in a single battle, and
the Washington Battalion had ceased to exist as a separate unit after
two weeks in the line at Brunete. By comparison with other battalions
in the International Brigades, these were not extraordinary losses:
probably they were on the light side, if anything. No doubt the
Comintern ignored the long lists of battle casualties (after all, these
men were not good Russians) as the price someone else had to pay
for shipping poorly wrapped produce into disturbed areas. And the
customary response from the in-faction at Albacete whenever deci-
mation or disaster was the order of business was to hold an investigation seeking evidences of "sabotage." Foolish as this might sound,
it was surely no more naïve than the interpretation offered by the
American representatives at the Albacete base, Robert Minor and
William Lawrence, who theorized that American losses were directly
attributable to improper training. (One might as well attempt to cure
lung cancer by deep-breathing exercises.)

To head off a fresh disaster, they insisted that the Mackenzie-
Papineau Battalion, the third North American unit, be held from the
front until they had completed the most thorough training program
that could be devised for them. Pouring replacements into the gaps of
the Lincolns was like pouring putty into a rathole. Instead, the Mac
Paps should become an exemplar battalion that would arrive in the
line superbly trained and officered, a model of discipline and effi-

ciency around which the other so-called "veteran" battalions could rally. Americans are great believers in formulas and panaceas, in seeking simplistic answers for pluralistic questions, and nowhere did Minor and Lawrence reveal their homespun Americanism more clearly than in the Mac Pap case. It is to their credit that they wished to do something about the prevailing slaughter of their countrymen, but they were confusing cause with result: the Lincoln Battalion was demoralized and casualty-ridden not because of some perverse inward defect but because of a congeries of external factors that the addition of the best battalion in the world could not help. The Republic had the more viable cause, but the Nationalists had dominance of the air and superiority of fire. So far as the men at the front were concerned, it was as simple as that.

All the while, the training camp at Tarazona de la Mancha ticked like a well-oiled clock. Jarama and Brunete veterans arriving there from hospitals roamed through an unremembered world. Most of them disliked what they found, even if they admitted that the changes might be necessary. The ugly little town bustled with an air of supervised activity, half war college and half boys' camp. There seemed to be schools or classes in just about everything—map reading, armaments, transmissions, sniping, fortification, Spanish history, first aid. The old tribal methods of selecting chiefs had given way to bureaucratic procedures of appointing officers, most of whom possessed certificates of achievement from the officers' training school at Pozorubio, where a few *sovietniks* (Russian advisers) beefed up the faculty. Nowadays there was even a school for corporals. The days when a volunteer was handed a rifle and ordered to fire five rounds at a hillside on the eve of battle belonged to the past, and no one regretted their passing. But some veterans sensed that the easy comradery of the early days was absent from the formalized regimen at Tarazona, and they wondered whether all the emphasis upon saluting, badges of rank, and specialized functions was really as important as the commissars seemed to think it was. Steve Nelson had not known the front of his helmet from the back—but he had been the best commander the Americans had ever had. Instead of Nelson, they had Dallet.

Complaints against Joe Dallet were a daily chorus among the men at Tarazona. The gloss of the Ceret Trial had worn off rapidly enough. All sorts of adjectives were used to describe him—cocksure, dictatorial, conceited, megalomaniacal, boy-scoutish—and no end of unprintable nouns. With his sleeves rolled up nearly to his armpits, a big .45 dangling from his Sam Browne belt (originally buckled on him by Robert Merriman in a quasi-knighthood ceremony), and a big Sherlock Holmes pipe clamped in his teeth, Joe Dallet was the monarch of all he surveyed. In the name of "discipline" he supported the segregation of officers from rank and file at mess. If a man neglected to salute him, he could count upon a string of insults at best or a cooling-off period in the brig at worst. But with Dallet it was not so much what he did as how he did it that raised the dander of his men. He wore the proprietory air of an overseer inspecting a gang of migratory workers who had come to work in his grove, not theirs. They sensed that his authority emanated not from the inner strength of a man they could admire but from the delegated power of the Party; he was a warden, not a leader.

Spain suited Joe Dallet to a T. To his absent wife, he confided that he had acquired "a pretty good tan from drilling without a shirt," that the Lincolns "sang popular songs, smoked and joked" while they were being cut to pieces on February 27, and that "one sector of the front is only 90 miles [sic] west." And he shared with her his experience of playing war on the shooting range:

> Man, what a feeling of power you have when entrenched behind a heavy machine gun! You know how I always enjoyed gangster movies for the mere sound of the machine guns. Then you can imagine my joy at finally being on the business end of one.

Every line he wrote and every move he made seemed calculated to impress someone—his wife, his friends, his men. He boasted about his accommodations at Tarazona, in which he lived "like a real bureaucrat" in a big room all to himself. Between the lines, his message was clear: a nobody in Youngstown had become a big shot in Spain. Obscurely Dallet understood this change within himself and stood ready with a rationalization. As he told his wife:

> You probably have noticed that since I left Paris I have lost some of the rank-and-filest tendencies that I had there and before leaving the States. However, the situation does not permit having them and it's a question of jumping in wherever you can do the most good, no matter what your personal inclination might be.

What this meant, apart from his implied but nowhere demonstrated reluctance to assume power, was that the "rank and file" had become pawns in his maneuvers along king row.

No one detected the change in Joe Dallet more quickly than the men of the Mackenzie Papineau Battalion. They were mystified by his mercurial behavior: bullyragging and harsh punishments one moment were as often as not followed by fawning and flattery the next. Dallet flew into tantrums that derived from his upbringing as a spoiled child but that unsettled men from wholly different milieus. The truth was that when his men failed to gratify his psychotic need to be worshiped, Dallet behaved ruthlessly and irrationally. No one ever doubted that he drove himself harder than the men he commanded, but often his ideas for improving their training were based upon nursery games. He instituted, for example, a military game patterned on a spelling bee, in which recruits competed for prizes by answering such questions as: how many bullets does a Maxim fire per minute? how many seconds elapse between pulling the pin of a Mills bomb and its explosion? how many machine guns are necessary to set up a cross fire? He encouraged gala fiestas and was delighted by the table decoration at a party held by the machine-gun company:

> Tables and walls decorated with slogans, and in the center of a square of tables, freshly cleaned and beautifully draped in red, was their pride and joy, their love, their machine gun.

As proof that one was a "right guy," Dallet insisted that every man participate in the horseshoe tournament he organized, and he demonstrated the right attitude by advancing to the semifinals himself. (One wonders whether he was a natural horseshoe athlete or whether his competitors sensed his *need* to win.) Many men could not decide whether Tarazona was patterned upon Fort Leavenworth or Camp Unity.

By May, Dallet was doing so well for himself that his wife wanted to come to Spain to join him. At this stage, Dallet still retained enough egalitarian scruples to make him veto the idea:

> It's this way—the boys up in the front lines are naturally prey to all rumors that at the base the officers are eating, drinking, smoking, etc., that they have their wives or other women, etc., etc. Actually the boys up front get better food, they get first crack at cigarettes, etc., but we must lean over almost backward to deprive them of any excuse for the above stories.

But Joe Dallet did not lean over backward very long. Two months later, in mid-July, he had lost his squeamishness about exercising the prerogatives of his power. Eagerly he wrote his wife:

> Wonderful news. You can come. Get in touch with Jack [Arnold Reid] in Paris, for whom I enclose a note, and he will put you through.

Part of the reason for this change stemmed from a hardening of opposition toward him on the part of the men of the battalion. A grievance committee, supported by many officers and junior commissars, attempted to depose him. Deeply shaken, Dallet sought the advice of Steve Nelson. He wanted to tender his resignation, but doubtless Nelson reassured him. Although his lacquer was as tough as ever, Dallet was inwardly bruised. Since his men had repudiated him, he needed his wife to buttress his sagging ego. A sober, even morbid, tone intruded into his letters. A visit to Madrid prompted his comment:

> There was no bombing at all except for some three shells that landed many kilometers away. I don't want Madrid bombarded at all, but if it *must* happen, I hope it happens while I am there.

It was as though he were courting the violence of battle as a way of proving to his men how wrong they were about him. He must have known that men were openly betting that he would turn yellow at the first sound of a gun fired in anger. Joe Dallet knew that the motto of a good commissar was "first to advance, last to retreat." But he did not know what he would do when battle became an actuality, divested of abstract considerations. Would he advance—or would he turn tail and run?

The time soon came for him to find out. Three days after the fall of Belchite, the Mackenzie Papineau Battalion was called to the Aragon Front. His wife, delayed in Paris with an appendectomy, failed to reach Tarazona in time to see him off. Joe Dallet went to war alone.

For five weeks after the fall of Belchite, the Lincoln Battalion milled about Aragon. Camions shuttled men, armaments, and supplies from one dusty village to another in a series of moves that bewildered them. Even the names of these clay-daubed towns were quickly forgotten, if ever known. Once they prepared for an offensive near Huesca, which was called off on account of rain. Logistics, however, had never been better: for the first time in their history, the Lincolns moved rapidly and comfortably in motorized convoys. Even though they went in circles, they traveled in style. (The men called this rigmarole "maneuvering to confuse the enemy.") One night a motion-picture van arrived. On the flickering screen set up among olive trees, the XV Brigade watched themselves taking Belchite for Paramount Pictures.

As an occasional chill wind, harbinger of autumn, swept down from the Pyrenees, applications for release and repatriation by six-month veterans began to pile up at brigade headquarters and at Albacete, but there were only two ways to obtain a discharge—bad wounds or party pull. A group of twenty-five disgruntled Americans left Aragon without permission and turned up in the office of Bill Lawrence in Albacete, where they claimed their "contracts" had expired and demanded repatriation. Since it was feared that if they got away with their high-handed demands massive desertions would follow among the remaining Americans, these men were promptly court-martialed and sent back to Aragon under guard.[1] A smaller group, whose number included a volunteer purportedly a direct descendant of John Quincy Adams, stole an ambulance and made for the French frontier but were caught and returned to the brigade for trial. Dave Doran, who had taken Nelson's place as brigade commissar, demanded that they be shot. Loath to assume this responsibility on his own, he called a meeting of battalion and company commissars and urged them to convince the rank and file that execution had been carried out by unanimous consent of the men themselves. But the men used this lingering vestige of union-hall democracy to vote down Doran's recommendation. The deserters received sentences of hard labor and were eventually reinstated in the brigade. Doran, who was more stalinist than parliamentarian, was unhappy about the outcome. Henceforth he would take this responsibility upon himself. With the advent of Doran the XV Brigade entered a despotic phase.

Dave Doran (*né* Dransky) had grown up as the toughest kid on his block, a tenement dead-end in Albany. Unlike Joe Dallet, Doran

---

[1] According to three witnesses (including the ill-starred Albert Wallach) who unsuccessfully tried to obtain refuge in the U.S. consulate at Barcelona, these men were later executed. These three were terrified: they tried to make a deal with the consul whereby they would set forth the names of recruiters in the United States in return for safe custody to the French frontier. The offer was declined, and they were subsequently picked up by IB policemen and returned to the line.

was a grass-roots proletarian whose ideas of class war were picked up on the streets, not culled from books. His father had emigrated from Russia in 1907 to the Lower East Side of New York City, where he worked as cigar maker and photographer's assistant. Hating the ghetto, he had moved upriver to Albany in 1910, the year his second child was born. Before he was out of short pants, Dave was hawking the Albany *Times* on street corners and delivering groceries for the A & P. While his father babbled about the glories of the Old Country, to which he made no effort to return, his son learned to fend for himself in the New. He was good with his fists and accurate with a rock: no one called him David except his mother. He dropped out of school at sixteen and later claimed that his only pleasant memories of Albany High were of geography class and Joseph Conrad. Doran was short and husky. When he smiled, his mouth twisted sidewise into a strange leer.

Doran shipped out of New York on a tanker owned by Morgan Line, a company said to be so rough on seamen that experienced men avoided it whenever they could. His family got no letters and heard no news of him until one day when he showed up in Albany with a broken nose and jaw, fruits of shore leave in Sweden. The jaw never healed properly, and his twisted face froze into a scowl. At sea he read a lot—especially Gorky, Ibsen, Sinclair, and Galsworthy. But Conrad was his favorite writer. Like Lord Jim, Dave Doran seemed to be waiting for a supreme test.

Scurvy put him on the beach in 1929. For a time he worked as an apprentice to his uncle, a New York paperhanger and sign painter. In his free time he hung around the Hungarian Workers Club on 59th Street and First Avenue, where he picked up radical ideas of a Wobbly nature. The turning point in his life, so it is said, came in 1930 when he found his landlord evicting a destitute family. Although Doran barely knew the victims, he demanded that they be permitted to remain. The slumlord waved his hands futilely and whined, "What do you expect of me—charity?" Doran replied, "Not charity—justice!" Two months later he joined the Young Communist League.

The League sent him into the South to build membership among the unemployed, particularly among Negroes. This was regarded as an impossible assignment, because few of Doran's prospective members had sufficient political development to comprehend trade unionism, much less communism. He arrived in Chattanooga on a freight train with a total budget, for personal maintenance and operational expenses, of three dollars a week. Probably no one at YCL headquarters expected to see Dave Doran again. (Sending a new organizer into the South was roughly the same as sending a machinist apprentice for a left-hand monkey wrench.) For a year he kept on the move, doggedly following strikes and riots. Trouble always germinated recruits. In Scottsboro, Alabama, he was beaten up for protesting the innocence of the Negroes accused of having raped a white woman. During the Gastonia textile strike, Doran built membership from zero to two hundred in three months. Police dragged him off the steps of Charlotte City Hall for alternately reading the Declaration of Independence and a petition demanding unemployment relief. He worked with other groups in the Black Belt trying to organize a Soviet Negro Republic, although he cynically remarked to another recruiter, "Do anything you want, just be sure to get plenty of publicity."

It was soon apparent to Gil Green and other leaders of the YCL that Doran was too good a man to be wasted in the South, where no one really anticipated much beyond token penetration by the party. By 1933 he had been recalled to organize steel workers in Allegheny County, Pennsylvania. In the Pittsburgh area "Red Squads" ruthlessly warred with "agitators," and Doran had to work underground, regularly changing both his residence and his name. Before he was twenty-five, he was a member of the Central Committee of the Young Communist League. By this time he was becoming bored with the grinding, picayunish details of his job. He repeatedly asked permission to go to Spain but was rejected on the grounds that he was married and was too important in the party hierarchy. But after the fizzle at Jarama, he was sent over to bolster party leadership among demoralized American volunteers.

Unlike Joe Dallet, Dave Doran was a proletarian by instinct rather than by acculturation. And the letters that he wrote to his wife from Spain were as blunt as a party throwaway. From Tarazona he wrote:

> Trying hard to be a good soldier and fill some Fascist bellies with lead. Feel certain that I can more than hold my own when we meet the bastards out there. . . . The tough training has really hardened and toughened me. Just what a guy needs after being a functionary of the League a number of years. . . .

In three sentences he used the words "hard" and "tough" four times, and these words conveyed the core of his world view. Unlike Dallet, he had not been contaminated by a bourgeois prose-style. He talked tough because he was tough. A machine gun was an implement for filling "Fascist bellies with lead," it was not a power fetish, charged with phallic symbolism. And for Doran a clenched fist had less to do with Popular Front solidarity than a simple means of converting a hand into a club. Issues, like colors, were for him either black or white. No doubt in his single-dimensioned view of the war, Franco's armies were composed of Fascist mercenaries, financed by obese capitalists and commanded by Gestapo degenerates. Fine shadings were lost upon Dave Doran.

Going into battle at Quinto as one of Nelson's assistant commissars, Doran was quickly confounded by the intricacies of attack patterns and field position. The firing line was not the picket line. In battle, something more was required than collecting scrawls on a petition or nailing a placard to a pole. It is significant that Doran's contribution to this battle lay in his hijacking the water truck and driving it into the American lines, for this is exactly what a dead-end kid could be expected to do properly. Although Doran must have been proud of his exploit, he did not allude to his derring-do in the letter written shortly afterward to his wife:

> The thing I like best is that I have gone into action against the enemy and have had ample opportunity to work under rather sharp and direct fire. Always did want to test myself and am not entirely disappointed with myself.

"To test myself"—Joseph Conrad said it all before.

Following Nelson's wound at Belchite and Doran's stunt with the loudspeaker at the parish church (his speech was later called "the heavy artillery of the science of politics"), Doran succeeded Nelson as XV Brigade commissar. He had done well, indeed. Within four months of his arrival in Spain, he had become the highest ranking American in the International Brigade, for as political adviser to Copic he held a rank equivalent to lieutenant colonel. He was only twenty-six. What no one knew at this time—and how they would have shuddered had they known!—was that Doran's ambition was to assume military command of his brigade. That moment would arrive, but in September, 1937, it was still far in the future. For the moment, he had to be content with a nearly absolute political power. Men had followed Nelson because they believed in him; [2] they would obey

[2] During the Quinto-Belchite offensive, the cry "Don't let 'em get Steve" passed down the line. When they learned that he had been wounded the men were shocked, but when word came that his wound was not serious, they cursed him roundly—for not staying in a safe place behind the lines.

Doran because they feared him. Most of the oppressive measures, the persecutions, and the executions carried out within the Lincoln Battalion belong to the Doran period.

In mid-September there was a parade outside the XV Brigade campground at Azaila to bid farewell to the Dimitrov Battalion and to welcome the Mackenzie Papineau. Everybody admitted that the Dimitrovs had been "our crack battalion." From Jarama to Belchite they had been the backbone and sinews of the brigade, and the others felt an emptiness, as though a vital organ or bone had been removed, as the gaunt, gallant Slavs formed a pathetically thin line and marched away. Colonel Copic remained in command of the XV Brigade, which was now predominantly Anglo-American.

As the Mac Paps marched by to take their place, a Briton shouted, in falsetto, "Aren't they darlin'!" They appeared to be too sleek, too natty, too young—more like cadets than soldiers. The old-timers were visibly cynical about the credentials of "the best trained battalion of the International Brigades." And the Mac Paps were shocked at their first sight of the Lincoln Battalion: "thin to the point of emaciation, bloodshot, pus-running eyes, facial bones sticking out, brusque to the point of rudeness." On the first night they camped together, the Lincolns stole the Mac Pap bugle, stamped it flat, and flung it back. Aragon was no parade ground. And at the first staff meeting, Doran, whose enmity toward Dallet seemed to be instinctive, ground him down at every opportunity. Aragon was no scout camp. The aura of special privilege that had surrounded the Mac Paps in Tarazona was soon dispersed by the dust, lice, dysentery, and pleurisy of Aragon.

On October 10, the XV Brigade bivouacked around the cemetery overlooking the old battleground of Quinto. In the moonlight the shattered houses shone like the jagged silhouette of an iceberg. The village was so depopulated that a new man observed that "the cemetery was the liveliest place in town." Even though the sky buzzed with airplanes, mostly Nationalist, and sounds came to them of a massive artillery barrage upriver at Fuentes de Ebro, no one quite believed the rumors that the Zaragoza offensive would be resumed. Carl Geiser, the new Lincoln commissar, set up headquarters in a vacated house in Quinto. No sooner had he settled back luxuriously on his first mattress since training days when a runner arrived. The brigade was moving up to the front immediately.

In late afternoon of October 12, while the men were being loaded on the trucks, General Walter called a divisional meeting to explain the reactivated drive toward Zaragoza. The XV Brigade would assault Fuentes de Ebro at dawn, opening a gap for reserve units to rush through. The British were to deploy on the right, near the Ebro River; the Lincolns in the middle, along the Quinto-Fuentes road; the Mac Paps on the left flank, an open plain. A routine plan? Not at all. Walter then played his trump card. Fuentes de Ebro had been so heavily garrisoned and fortified during the past six weeks that it was assumed to be impregnable to infantry assault. Therefore several companies of the 24th (Spanish) Battalion would be mounted on top of forty-eight Soviet "Christie" tanks, which would drive right through the Republican trenches, sweep across a mile of no man's land, and crush down the enemy wire and barricades. As soon as the tanks had penetrated Fuentes de Ebro, the infantry would jump down and attack the town from the rear, like a guerrilla force, while the Anglo-Americans moved against the place frontally. The Russian tank commander, Colonel Kondratyev, was eager to experiment with this tactic.[3] If it worked, the Colonel might revolutionize modern warfare. What he failed to take into account was that the ground between the lines was scored by *barrancas* and gouged by irrigation ditches, none of which showed on his charts.

The plan was conceived in such haste that the Anglo-American officers had only a few hours in which to reconnoiter the terrain and to prepare their men for battle. General Walter regretted that tactical details would have to be worked out after the brigade moved into position—that is to say, between nightfall and daybreak. There was not even time to provide company commanders with maps indicating enemy strongpoints; doubtless the officers would be able to discover these places for themselves—after the attack had begun.

As though the jerry-built plans of Walter and Kondratyev were not problems enough for the eve of battle, Commissar Doran called a special meeting of the brigade commissariat to discuss whether Dallet ought to be removed from his post. From sundown until two in the morning they discussed, grilled, and analyzed Joe Dallet. Outside their barn, had they listened, the commissars could have heard the movements of trucks and men up the highway toward Fuentes de Ebro; but

---

[3] During the summer of 1937, the French Army had experimented with parachuting infantry behind enemy lines as part of their military maneuvers. It is generally assumed that Kondratyev's inspiration for a tank drop derived from this.

the war outside was somehow less absorbing than the political hassle raging within. Acting as an awesome referee was Robert Minor, Comintern representative among the Americans in Spain. After nearly six hours of denunciation and dissection, Dallet begged for permission to resign. This was refused for reasons unknown.[4] It is alleged that Dallet's only defender was Saul Wellman, his assistant commissar, a young truck driver from Elizabeth, New Jersey. While the others flayed Dallet alive, Wellman tried to patch him up. By the time this stormy session ended, most of the brigade had long since departed from Quinto. As they returned to their men Wellman tried to buck up Dallet; the others avoided him as though he were leprous.

It was nearly dawn when Dallet reached the Mac Paps. Although the attack was just hours away, he scratched out a letter to his wife:

> Kitty Darling: I've been a louse about writing but there was no sure way to reach you and anyway we've been on the jump. Now we're waiting for the convoy—by the time you get this we'll be in action. We are in shape and will do our best. Writing this by flashlight. I hope that by the time we get out of the lines you'll be in the country to spend a few days leave with me.
>
> Until we meet—
> Joe

What Dave Doran wrote his wife is not recorded. More likely than not he went straight to bed and slept the sleep of the just. A rival had been destroyed.

Behind the Republican lines at Fuentes de Ebro there was a two-mile logjam of vehicles, which meant that most of the men of the XV Brigade had a long walk even before they reached their jumping-off positions. The British, first in line, entered their assigned section of trench without disturbing the enemy opposite them a mile distant. But the Lincolns, next in line, were spotted in the lightening dawn and set off a chain reaction of small-arms fire. Ricocheting bullets sparkled against the flint of the highway. Finally came the Mac Paps, who

---

[4] The ostensible reason, of course, was that his dismissal on the eve of battle would have a terrible effect upon the Mac Paps—hardly convincing when one considers how the men loathed Dallet. It is sometimes conjectured that Dallet was "back-sliding" from the party and that he had been fingered for execution in the middle of the battle (to make it appear as though he had died valiantly while fighting the Fascists).

were etched against the skyline as they moved over a crest and baptized into the Spanish War with the blood of a dozen men shot before they reached their attack positions. Within minutes the "best trained battalion" had turned into a "mad jumble of wildly running men, running any Goddamn direction to get out of the way of the fire," as one survivor remembered it. Those scrambling ahead ran headlong into twisted coils of barbed wire inexplicably blocking access to the Republican communication trenches. Thus the battle for Fuentes de Ebro commenced with a bizarre scene—Mac Paps burrowing under or cutting through their own wire. In the confusion the machine-gun company abandoned their Maxims and later had to be ordered out to fetch them in. A surprise attack was now out of the question.

The tanks, scheduled to appear at dawn, failed to show up. Actually, through some staff error, they had been spread out so far on the flanks that it required most of the morning for them to work back to the center of the front. In order to avoid detection by the enemy, most of the tanks had covered twelve to eighteen miles of rough country before they went into attack. As a result, their bogies and other mechanical equipment had been jarred out of alignment. Yet there was no time left for even cursory adjustments. As soon as they had been refueled they picked up their infantry "riders" and massed behind the Republican lines. The artillery barrage, supposed to have been synchronized with the attack, had ceased hours before. Training binoculars on the enemy trenches located on the edge of Fuentes de Ebro, brigade observers had watched with satisfaction as distant antlike creatures fled into town under the opening barrage and with dismay as the same antlike figures dashed back to their trenches as soon as the barrage ended. Captain Robert Thompson, the twenty-three-year-old Oregonian who commanded the Mac Paps, had been wounded in the February 27 fiasco at Jarama. As the battle for Fuentes de Ebro got under way he must have had an unsettling sensation that history was repeating itself.

It was well past one in the afternoon when the "Christies" swept forward at top speed in a wide spread-eagle formation. The tanks were driving ahead at twenty-five miles per hour and more when they churned through the hip-deep trenches of the XV Brigade. The foundations of the earth seemed to shake. In some cases the ground not only shook but caved in, crushing Anglo-Americans beneath the steel treads. Hanging on for dear life were the riders of the 24th Battalion— four men to each tank—few of whom had ever ridden on a vehicle more formidable than a tractor, if that. As they passed through, some of them bravely managed clenched-fist salutes. Others, their brains perhaps addled by the jarring ride, opened fire upon the Anglo-Americans, having mistaken them for the enemy. None of them had received special training for service with an armored column.

The passage of the tanks through the trenches of the XV Brigade created confusion and, in some instances, hysteria. One squad of Spanish recruits incorporated into the Lincoln Second Company assumed that the monstrous machines belonged to a Nationalist column that was attacking them from the rear. They opened fire gamely upon the riders; fortunately they were poor shots. Another one threw down his rifle and attempted to surrender to an onrushing tank, barely escaping being crushed beneath the treads.

The XV Brigade followed in the wake of the tanks, which before the dust had settled were "long gone," recalled an American. Few of the riders survived the toboggan ride across no man's land. They were picked off, fell off, or jumped off long before they reached the enemy lines. Fully half of the tanks plummeted into deep *barrancas* or ditches and were unable to climb out. Others ground down enemy wire and swept along the single main street of Fuentes de Ebro, where they were knocked out by antitank guns. A crippled tank dammed the flow of those behind and forced the others to back out or to bypass the town. Of the forty-eight Soviet tanks employed in the attack, less than half made it back to Republican lines.

What all of this amounted to was that the armored attack had no liaison with and no relation to the infantry attack following it. The Anglo-Americans were, in effect, abandoned on a wide plain and forced to advance against enemy positions known to be impregnable to an assault by infantry. They stepped into an enfilade fire that was "simply shocking." To the right, the British were halted within minutes of going over the top after both their commander and commissar had been killed.[5] In the middle, Captain Detro led the Lincolns forward under cover of burning tanks, whose oily smoke drifted across the battlefield, to ravines approximately halfway between the lines.

---

[5] The commander, Captain Harold Fry, once a sergeant of His Majesty's Brigade of Guards, had commanded a machine-gun company in the first action of the British at Jarama. Captured by Moors on the second day of battle, he miraculously escaped execution and even more miraculously was exchanged and returned to England. He was probably the only Anglo-American volunteer to return to fight in Spain after having been held as a prisoner of war. Fry ran out of miracles at Fuentes de Ebro.

Seeing that further attack was hopeless, he ordered his men to dig in and wait for a counterattack that he could not doubt would follow.

To the left, the Mac Paps paid an enormous price for their naïve élan. Too inexperienced to know that the plan had been botched, they advanced against a lashing fire with the mechanical precision of training maneuvers—kneeling, firing, rising, advancing. "This training was useless," said a survivor, "only we didn't know it at the time." Men were falling like cornstalks, but they seemed to believe this was how battles should be fought.

When the commander of First Company fell, Joe Dallet took his place. With pipe clamped tightly in his mouth and automatic pistol flourished in his hand,[6] he walked into the storm. Picking his way through the harvest of writhing and motionless bodies, every one of which he knew by name (he made a point of that), he overtook the company and sauntered past them. Was it true, what some men have said, that he walked like a man dazed, drugged, or dead—without human expression? Did he perhaps wonder whether the bullet that had to kill him would come from the front or the back—or was he indifferent to academic speculations? It is alleged that a machine-gun burst killed him. For Joe Dallet everything had at last "come true in steel."

Within a half-hour the Mac Paps were following the example of other battalions less well trained: they were falling back to their lines or were attempting to scoop out holes in the open plain. "The ground in Aragon is hard," remembered one man, "and a tin dinner plate a poor shovel—but machine-gun fire is a good persuader." Over the high-pitched racket of small-arms fire, they could hear the boiler-like explosions of disabled tanks scattered about the white plain. Five men caught in the open took refuge in a hole that might have accommodated two, with crowding. They lay stacked on one another in the manner of a club sandwich. The bottom man was nearly crushed by the weight of flesh on top of him, but, protectively sheathed, he did not complain.

In the middle of the afternoon, long after the attack had been flung back, squadrons of Republican bombers, two-wingers resembling phlegmatic dragonflies, unloaded sticks of bombs upon the Nationalist lines. They had arrived many hours too late. Vile curses greeted

[6] Dallet was very proud of his automatic, which he called his "side-cannon." As he told his wife, while in training camp, "you don't need ammunition, for the other guy sees it pointing at him and runs."

them from the men on the ground. Obscurely they felt betrayed.

Only after the fall of night were the men pinned down between the lines able to crawl back to their positions. The wounded were dragged in and the dead counted. Despite the claims of the brigade staff that the Republican lines had been pushed forward several hundred yards toward Fuentes de Ebro, the men were not so readily fooled. They knew that the battle had achieved nothing. The only statistics relevant to this death rattle of the Zaragoza offensive pertained to casualties. It was astonishing that so many men had been killed or wounded to achieve so little. With sixty dead and a hundred wounded, the Mac Paps had lost approximately one man out of every three. The Lincolns, who had long since developed a sharp nose for smelling out trouble, fared better—eighteen dead and fifty wounded. Most of these had been hit by small-arms fire, for the Nationalist artillery had fortunately been located elsewhere during the battle. The officers of the Mac Paps had all but disappeared: Captain Robert Thompson was near collapse "from a prolonged fever," Dallet was dead, one company commander killed outright, another fatally wounded, and a third badly wounded. An olive warehouse behind the lines was taken over as dressing station, although there was almost no surgical attention. The railroad had been destroyed, so large-scale evacuation of the wounded was impossible. In "that pitiful shed of horrors" Anglo-Americans begged for water and morphine while wounded Soviet tankists were evacuated to Barcelona hospitals by airplane.

Perhaps the indelible reminder of failure was a pastel-blue sign painted on the road-menders' hut used by enemy snipers:

FUENTES DE EBRO   1 km
ZARAGOZA   23 kms.

It was an appropriate epitaph for a dead offensive.

For the next ten days the XV Brigade occupied their trenches opposite Fuentes de Ebro, participating in the sporadic fighting to retrieve disabled tanks strewn like junked automobiles about no man's land. A replacement arriving at this period found that the favorite subject of conversation among the men was the death of Joe Dallet. These discussions inevitably concluded with the same peroration: "Joe had guts." He had proved that much. Even Dave Doran eloquently served up an oration treating his heroic death on the field of battle. Nearly everyone was full of extravagant praise for Joe Dallet —now that he was dead.

10

⌐╓ Teruel—The North Pole

We're a bunch of bastards,
   Bastards are we;
We'd rather f . . . than fight
   For Liber-tee.
Aye, Brother, aye—and up your ass!

—Battalion song

It was early November before trucks carrying the XV Brigade crept back to the rest villages of the Tajuña Valley. For the third time, the Lincoln Battalion was billeted in Albares for reorganization and "reeducation" while replacements—most of them Spaniards—came up from Tarazona to replace men lost in the Aragon campaign. Looking back upon what they had just gone through, the men felt that Quinto had been lucky, Belchite grueling, and Fuentes calamitous. Applications for repatriation from volunteers with plus-six months' service piled up in Albacete and were rejected. As if to underline his personal dissatisfaction with the Americans, General Walter adopted two sheep as divisional mascots and named them "Lincoln" and "Washington." [1] This joke was enjoyed enormously in Albacete among factions that on other occasions denounced chauvinism and called for "international solidarity." Colonel Copic took to absenting himself from the brigade and threw the burden of rebuilding upon Dave Doran, who willingly shouldered it.

In just two months Doran had advanced from an unseasoned junior commissar to a position that was, in effect, the political dictatorship of the XV Brigade. Apparently he hoped to create, through rigorous discipline, an elite corps out of the skeptics and malcontents about him. His objective was laudable, but his methods were mis-

---

[1] A photograph of Walter and his mascots was circulated in the United States in the pages of *Life* magazine.

185

guided. Unfortunately Doran always sought political solutions to military problems. What his men needed were better weapons, capable officers, coordinated staff work; what they got were lectures on "discipline" and warnings that deserters would be shot. Furthermore, Doran consistently overlooked the highly individualistic nature of the men he commanded. They were not Turks or Bulgars with a tradition of unquestioning obedience to their officers. Of the Doran period, a University of Michigan man concluded, "Like most Americans, I could not stomach the know-it-all, party-line dogmatism of the Polit-Commissar system, which had originally developed in armies of illiterate peasants." Others recall their deep antipathy toward doublethink, half truths, and sacred lies. How they yearned, sometimes, to hear the truth—even if it struck them dead—rather than the endless reams of roseate propaganda. Yet they were caught in a vicious circle: the more they sloughed off Doran's political indoctrination, the more he heaped it upon them. Paradoxically the goal of "education," as Doran conceived it, was the total collapse of all intelligence on the part of his men. He demanded that the mind be a *tabula rasa,* upon which he could then write.

The result was that too much time at Albares was frittered away in promulgating claptrap, in political voodoo, in exorcizing demons. Over a texture punky with demoralization, Doran laid down thick coats of fresh paint. Rallies, pep talks, and mimeographed directives exhorted the brigade to win the war by learning how to salute, by improving dress, by studying Spanish, and by obeying officers. An article in *Our Fight,* the weekly news sheet, explained that the salute was not pukka-colonel nonsense:

> A salute is the military way of saying hello. A salute is not undemocratic. . . . A salute is a sign that a comrade who has been an egocentric individualist in private life, has adjusted himself to the collective way of getting things done. . . . A salute is proof that our Brigade is on its way from being a collection of well-meaning amateurs to a precise instrument for eliminating Fascists.

The Winter Palace had not been stormed by men saluting one another: the American volunteers felt that saluting defiled the egalitarian promise of the International Brigades, and they resisted it with cold determination. Moreover, the recent emphasis upon proper uniform impressed only the popinjays of the brigade. Captain Detro adamantly refused to surrender his sloppy turtleneck sweater, even after Doran returned from Madrid wearing a resplendent tailored outfit. He was a sight to behold—stiffly wired garrison hat, silk-lined opera cape, knee-top boots, and cavalry spurs. (Suitable for driving water trucks?) He dared to wear the spurs only once, but the cape remained.[2]

A growing problem was how to assimilate the large numbers of Spanish replacements into the brigade. Few Americans bothered to learn Spanish, beyond a few expressions like *cajones* and *maricón* with which to pepper their slang. Unable and even unwilling to communicate with one another, the men tended to cluster together in national pockets without much interest in trying to understand one another. In order to forge a sense of identical interests, Doran urged each American to "adopt" a Spanish recruit and to live, eat, and train with him; but the Spaniards resented this contrived comradery as much as did the Americans. Language remained a barrier despite compulsory Spanish classes. Most of the Americans stayed as monolingual as the company commander, who, when asked for the time by an Albares native, replied, "It's una o'clocka."

As a morale prop, Doran pressed the Historical Commission of the XV Brigade to complete, in time for distribution at Christmas, an illustrated yearbook called *Book of the Brigade*. It consisted of participants' accounts of battles (no hint of the Jarama mutiny, of course), abundant photographs, and dozens of biographical sketches (often highly fictionalized). Doran submitted to the editors a list of men who were to be "played up." The list was divided into three categories to indicate the amount of prominence (and space) allotted to a particular volunteer. In category one were Copic, Merriman, Nelson, and Doran, among others. Detro and Law rated category two, Hourihan and Seacord category three, while Harris and Stember rated no mention whatever. All of this was "press agent stuff," one of the editors confessed years later. The book, which provided a carefully expurgated record of events from Jarama to Fuentes de Ebro, was said to have been appreciated by the men—or at least by those who found their name or picture in it.

Meanwhile *The Volunteer for Liberty,* house organ of the Anglo-American section of the Interbrigades, manufactured whipsaw bits of

---

[2] Doran's publicity photograph at this time makes him appear like a Byronic figure standing on a mountain peak. The lens of the camera had been placed on a level with his shins and pointed upward almost vertically.

humor calculated to raise morale by lowering the boom on the enemy. There was, for example, the cartoon featuring two Spanish charwomen: "Funny stink in Room 402, isn't there, Conchita?" "Oh, that's the room Franco slept in one night six years ago." There were frequent Hitler-Goebbels jokes, such as the one in which Hitler, motoring in the country, ran over a pig. He dispatched Goebbels to inform the farmer and was puzzled when his minister returned, loaded down with fruit and vegetables. "What did you tell him?" Hitler asked. "Hardly anything," replied Goebbels. "I just said, 'Heil Hitler! I have the swine run over and killed.' " *The Volunteer for Liberty* gave detailed accounts of the twentieth anniversary of the Russian Revolution, minor polar explorations by Soviet scientists, and obscure archaeological discoveries in the Valley of the Don, but American holidays like the Fourth of July or Thanksgiving passed without mention. Its pages provided an opportunity for André Marty to denounce the Spanish Anarchists as "scum stealing arms from the front." Always the editors found more enemies to denounce than causes to uphold.

Perhaps Doran's greatest *coup* was his kidnaping of Clement Attlee and two other British Labour Party Members of Parliament. They had been visiting battle sectors of Spain but had refused an invitation to inspect the British Battalion at Mondejar, perhaps because they feared that this might be construed as an endorsement of an illegal organization. On December 6, Doran staged his seizure. A XV Brigade automobile and chauffeur waited outside Attlee's hotel until the dignitaries appeared. Saluting smartly, the chauffeur explained that his car was at their disposal, courtesy of the Republic. Once inside, they were whisked out to Mondejar (a few miles west of Albares), where they found the British Battalion standing at attention in the winterish gloom, singing "God Save the King." Under these circumstances the dignitaries could hardly demand to be returned immediately to Madrid. In the upper rooms of a mill beside the Tajuña, Attlee was feted by Doran and the XV Brigade staff, who told him that henceforth the First Company of the British Battalion would be known as "The Major Attlee Company." Warming to this flattering ceremony, Attlee confessed that the Nonintervention Agreement seemed to be a farce. When Miss Ellen Wilkinson, one of the MPs, asked Doran about his duties as a brigade commissar, Doran thought a minute before saying pleasantly, "Well, I could have any of these men shot." At the end of the fiesta they sang the "Internationale," although Major Attlee had to lipsync because he did not know the words. A torchlight procession escorted the delegates back to their automobile. Before he departed, Attlee bungled his attempt to use a Republican slogan when he called out, *"No Pasaremos!"* (*we* shall not pass).[3]

All this tomfoolery ended a week later when the XV Brigade got orders to move out. A new Republican offensive had been planned against Teruel, a Nationalist salient only seventy miles from the Mediterranean. They climbed aboard trucks and shouted to familiar village faces, "We'll be back!" The folk of Albares and Mondejar had learned to look upon the goings and comings of the Anglo-Americans as though they were migratory fowl. A season would pass, a battle would be won or lost, and the *extranjeros* would reappear in their village. This time they were wrong. The brigade never came back.

The convoy of trucks bounced eastward on the Valencia highway, deeply potholed after a year and a half of wartime use and no peacetime repairs. At Motilla del Palancar a highway arrow at the crossroads read VILLANUEVA DE LA JARA—14, but this meant nothing to most of the volunteers on the trucks. They careened down and up the hairpin road at Contreras Canyon, the bottom of which was strewn with shattered automobiles and camions—monuments to the notorious recklessness of Republican drivers. In the purple twilight they flashed past snug little villages, all of them with blue-tiled church domes, and dropped down to the coastal plain through groves of carob, olive, and finally orange trees. They slept overnight in the Valencia *plaza de toros*. "In Spain," an American remembered, "they always bedded us down in the bullrings and shot us from the church towers." The next morning they swung aboard a businesslike troop train mounting antiaircraft guns on the carriage roofs. It was sunny and warm as they crossed the greensward of the Levantine *huerta* where oranges hung ripe on trees. Once upon a time laborers had bombarded their coaches with fruit, but the old enthusiasm for war had waned. On this trip the Anglo-Americans had to invade orchards and "organize" oranges for themselves. One Briton found a melon,

---

[3] Attlee's visit to the XV Brigade was widely publicized by the British Communist Party, without, however, indicating how he came to make the visit. A recent history of the Lincoln "Brigade" has this to say: "That Attlee accepted this signal honor is indicative of the healthy orientation of the British Labour Party of that day."

but as the train had pulled out and was gaining speed, he began dropping behind. The men cheered him on, but it was no use. He had to throw the melon away and sprint for the train.

There was a serious shortage of coal in Republican Spain, and the train poked from one woodpile to another. As it ascended the coastal mountains, men jumped off, sauntered cross country, and met the locomotive at summits with plenty of time to spare. Once in the mountains the climate changed radically. In this coldest winter in a generation, the lacerating gusts of wind sweeping down from the Pyrenees could knock a man off his feet and slice him like a knife. Upper Aragon might as well have been the North Pole. Those who recalled the fierce heat during the Quinto campaign had difficulty in believing they were in the same region.

From Caspe, an Ebro town perched on a cliff, the XV Brigade marched south across a totally uninhabited region of wind-etched monadnocks to Alcañiz. (Four months later they would retrace their steps along this road under very different circumstances.) Deep in the hill country of the Maestrazgo region, one of the wildest in Iberia, they garrisoned stone-rubble hamlets. The Lincolns drew Agua Vivas, a village so hopelessly poor that windowpanes were a rarity. It was often impossible to differentiate between houses and stables, except that the latter were warmer. Albares was bustling and metropolitan when compared with Agua Vivas. Some of the houses were of such primitive construction that windows had been chiseled out of rock walls after the basic shelter had been completed. The Mac Paps were quartered nearby at Mas de las Matas, which they translated ominously (and erroneously) as "More of the Killed." While in these villages the brigade learned that the Republican thrust at Teruel, sixty miles southwest, had been successful. The city had been surrounded and cut off from Nationalist Spain, and the enemy garrison was trapped inside. Since the Ministry of War intended Teruel to be an entirely Spanish operation, no Internationals had been employed. There was immense enthusiasm in the Republic: never before in the war had they captured a provincial capital in a military campaign. (And never would they take another one, as events proved.)

The battle developing in sub-zero temperatures at Teruel had, for the moment, only an abstract bearing upon the men of the XV Brigade quartered in the Maestrazgo, three mountain chains distant. As Christmas approached they received food packages sent by the FALB. The boxes were a strange grab-bag of incongruities. They contained cans of orange juice, bottles of olive oil (greeted with hooting and booing), crates of toilet tissue (newsprint was said to cause piles). Yet there were also cartons of cherished Lucky Strikes and Hershey bars. After the brigade quartermaster produced some bottles of champagne and hogsheads of vile *coñac,* they had a Christmas party. The men distributed candy bars to the children of Agua Vivas, who had never heard of Santa Claus, never seen a candy bar, never received a gift from a stranger. Over at the medical unit there was a big party featuring grain alcohol and American nurses.[4] Only officers were invited.

Christmas Day closed out a year for the Lincoln Battalion, but the significance of this day probably passed unnoticed among the Americans at Agua Vivas. It is even doubtful that any of the first seventy-six who had embarked on the *Normandie* a year before were still campaigning with the Lincoln Battalion. Names like Bart, Harris, Stember, Seacord, and Scott belonged to an almost prehistoric age. The battalion and the battles continued, but the names and faces changed. No one knew how many Americans had come to Spain as volunteers, but the figure exceeded three thousand.

On December 29, 1937, the Nationalists unleashed a counteroffensive to regain Teruel. The Republic promptly abandoned its resolve not to employ the International Brigades. On December 31 the XV Brigade was ordered to move up immediately to buttress the right flank in the Sierra Palomera, which ran due north from Teruel.

Philip Detro held on to the Lincoln command, even though racked by some obscure illness that had converted him into a walking skeleton. Since Carl Geiser had been wounded at Fuentes, his place as battalion commissar was taken by Fred Keller, a twenty-three-year-old who was often billed as "a young altar boy from Brooklyn." Lincoln folklore records that Keller had been an elevator operator at the FALB office in New York. Conversations with passengers had aroused his curiosity about Spain until he resolved to volunteer. Like Geiser, he was forthright and popular, although some party stalwarts opined that his "political level of comprehension was at rock bottom." It is alleged that on one occasion when Doran sent him two well-connected politicos with instructions to put them to work,

---

[4] According to the testimony of an American nurse in Spain, just before leaving New York "they gave us four packs of prophylactics at the medical bureau. The doctor said it was to care for our emotional life, that we were going away from our sweethearts and husbands."

Keller handed them some posters and said, "O.K., fellas, here's a political job for you. Go mix some paste and hang up these posters around town." [5] The Mac Paps, who had suffered most heavily at Fuentes, were reorganized. Captain Robert Thompson, said to be ill with fever and probably out of favor with the high command, had been repatriated to the United States.[6] His place was taken by Edward Cecil-Smith of Canada, a pudgy little man with a toothbrush mustache. Dallet's friend, Saul Wellman of New Jersey, was now Mac Pap commissar. The big three on brigade staff continued to be Copic, Doran, and Merriman. Men were betting that it was just a matter of time before Merriman took over the XV Brigade.

Even to reach the front was a major battle of men pitted against nature. The mean altitude was always over three thousand feet, snow drifted three feet deep on portions of the highway, and the temperature dipped as low as eighteen below zero. (Centigrade readings always made it seem colder than it was.) Roads leading toward Teruel from the Mediterranean were clogged with tanks, troop carriers, supply trucks, ambulances. At each hamlet and road junction, the brigade staff became yelling and cursing traffic cops trying to untie the snarl of vehicles. Late afternoon brought fresh snow, the flakes dropping horizontally and cutting visibility to distances measurable in mere feet and inches. Many of the Republican drivers,

[5] Keller proved to be very useful to the Popular Front image of the battalion because liberal journalists like Ernest Hemingway and Herbert L. Matthews trusted him and depended upon him for material. But a few months later Keller left the battalion to attend Special Cadres School, after which he was assigned duties never publicly discussed. Late in 1939 he was subpoenaed to testify before the House Un-American Activities Committee, where he repeatedly denied that he had been "political commissar" of the Lincoln Battalion; he called his position "war commissar."

[6] During World War II, Thompson served as a noncom with the Thirty-second Division in New Guinea, where he won the Distinguished Service Cross for bravery during the Buna campaign. When a United Press correspondent asked him what his peacetime job was, Thompson replied, "Maybe you won't believe me, but I'm a Young Communist League organizer for Ohio." After the war he became a member of the National Board of the Communist Party. Sentenced to a three-year term for conspiracy in 1950, he jumped bail and disappeared for three years. When finally apprehended he was held in West Street Jail of New York, where a Yugoslav being held for deportation, doubtless hoping to make a good impression upon the authorities as an anti-Communist, attacked Thompson with a hammer and nearly killed him. When Thompson died in 1966, his widow requested permission to have his burial in Arlington National Cemetery this was refused. Subsequently burial was approved.

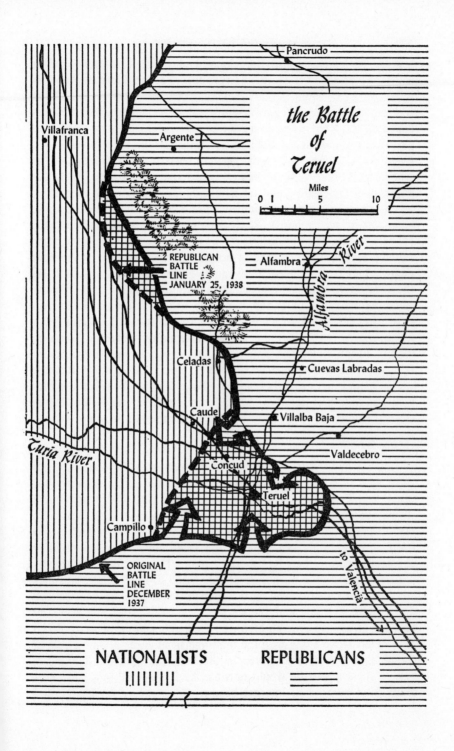

the Battle
of
Teruel

Miles

0 1   5   10

Pancrudo

Villafranca

Argente

REPUBLICAN
BATTLE
LINE
JANUARY 25, 1938

Alfambra

Alfambra River

Celadas

Cuevas Labradas

Caude

Villalba Baja

Turia River

Valdecebro

Concud

Teruel

Campillo

to Valencia

ORIGINAL
BATTLE
LINE
DECEMBER
1937

NATIONALISTS   REPUBLICANS

natives of Valencia and Barcelona, had never seen snow before, much less driven in it. On the hairpin curves in the Sierra de San Just, a first skid was often the last. Disabled vehicles, after being stripped of tires, bolts, and other salvageable parts, had to be shoved off the roads to make room for hundreds of others behind them. The waste was shocking but irremediable. One American driving a rebuilt 1928 truck with a brake functional on only one wheel painfully had to watch brand-new vehicles being pushed over precipices simply because they had stalled and no mechanic was on hand to start them again. Ingenious drivers patched their vehicles with barbed wire, scraps of string, leather belts, chewing gum. The wake of the convoy to Teruel, recalled an American, was littered with "cigarette butts, brandy bottles, and the stink of hot oil and frozen sweat in the deep tire tracks." Yet some veteran campaigners professed gratitude for the unbearable weather: it grounded enemy bombers.

At nightfall they unloaded in a rocky field of deepening snow outside a hamlet called Argente. A few miles west lay the Sierra Palomera, a sawtooth chain of barren mountains stretching south to Teruel, twenty-five miles distant. The front was beyond these mountains, but the Republican lines were being eroded steadily. Because enemy planes methodically bombed villages behind the front, the Lincolns, already half-numb in the cold wind, were instructed to sleep in the open fields. By the following morning one man in every ten was the victim of frostbite or "Teruel fever"—a rheumatic ague. It was New Year's Day, 1938.

Nothing happened. The front did not collapse. They froze. After three days of hiding behind lee walls in Argente, trying to escape the bitter winds raging across their valley, the Lincolns were shifted farther south to the neighborhood of Cuevas Labradas, ten miles north of Teruel. Already the brigade medical unit had established a hospital in an unheated villa in the small town and was treating casualties from other Republican units. The doctors worked by candlelight and with pocket flashlights taped to their heads, and they sterilized their instruments on the kitchen stove. Patients were bedded down in their mud- and blood-caked uniforms, for there were no changes of clothes or even blankets. Shell-shocked cases were placed next to the stove along with the limb and head cases. It was a rule of thumb that if a man wounded in the head survived the ambulance ride to the hospital he would not die. Abdominal wounds were normally fatal because of internal hemorrhaging caused by jarring and bucking of the ambulances. Stacked like cordwood against an outer wall, corpses did not rot, they froze—and that was a relief. The view from the balcony of the villa was as sharp as a steel engraving: ice-glazed poplars lined the banks of the brook-sized Alfambra River and looked like dead-flower arrangements.

The amenities of Cuevas Labradas—or "Caves of Labrador," as the men called it—were not for the Lincoln Battalion, which bivouacked on the other side of the Alfambra in the tunnel of an uncompleted railroad. The railroad had everything that a railroad ought to have—graded embankment, station houses, watchmen's huts: everything, that is, except tracks, ties, and locomotives. (Someone dubbed it "The Great Teruel and Mañana Line.") The tunnel, slightly curved inside, seemed at first to be a God-given barracks and air raid shelter, until the men learned, to their dismay, that the battering winds instead of sweeping over the ridge took a shortcut through the tunnel. When they built fires inside, the floor turned into slush and icicles hanging from the roof plummeted down like sheets of broken glass. The men were not warned that in sub-freezing temperatures wet feet or sweat could be as lethal as an enemy bullet.

After one night in the tunnel, Captain Detro gathered his men and moved up to the front. They filed up a sinuous mule-path into the Sierra Palomera, a flattish wilderness of nameless stubble and uncharted *barrancas,* and dug in on the lip of a ridge facing the village of Celadas, which consisted of a rich Renaissance church surrounded by squalid huts. The Nationalists were using Celadas as an assembly point for a counteroffensive against the Alfambra River line. From their ridge, a mile or more away, the Americans could see movements of trucks and men in the village. The front, at this stage of the battle, was little more than batches of men trying to fortify widely spaced strongpoints. The men dug as deeply as they could in frozen ground and piled up cairns of rock as protection against both wind and steel. Urine crystallized almost as soon as it struck the ground. They called this position "The North Pole."

On their second day above Celadas, the Lincolns watched as a Nationalist force attempted to storm Republican positions located on similar ridges to the south. The advancing troops were visible as distant specks crossing the open, snow-covered valley while their artillery and bombers pounded the ridge. This movement was beyond the range of American rifle and machine-gun fire, and their antitank guns were elsewhere. They could do nothing but watch helplessly and hope fervently that their flank would not be rolled up. The attack was beaten off but resumed the next day. Clusters of the enemy managed to seep through some dead ground between the Lincolns and their skittish comrades to the south. Detro dispatched First Company to plug the gap. After a short fire-fight at long range, the enemy troops backed down into the valley again.

In the days that followed, the massive Nationalist counterstrokes probed along a twenty-mile front running north from Teruel, while the Republicans tried to hold on to territory seized during the first days of the battle. Whereas the Republicans had taken Teruel by manpower, the Nationalists meant to retake it by fire power. Fire power meant incessant waves of Junkers, Capronis, and Fiats whose most innocuous missile was a bullet that could blow a hole four inches deep in a dirt road. It meant artillery barrages productive of a "95 percent killing zone." It meant seeding incendiary bombs over the front until virtually every object capable of burning burned. It meant, on clear days, fighter planes skywriting the Falange emblem— yoke and arrows—in white smoke against a blue sky. Shells bursting in the chalky foothills raised up geysers of powdered stone and white snow beautiful to look at. Bomb-torn telephone and power lines drooped across hillsides like towropes at a ski resort. Shrapnel hissed like a human voice as it buried itself in snow. Thawed mud oozed up from fresh bomb-craters and froze again.

The Americans helplessly endured this highly tooled, "mechanized doom." They passed the time in trying to count the enemy planes, a most demoralizing pastime. "Never saw more than eighty-four Fascist planes overhead at any one time, but, of course, I couldn't see beyond my ridge." They examined the ignition panel of a downed Fiat and bitterly noted that the writing was in Italian. When the incoming planes strafed them, they dug into the numbing earth, placing their backs toward the sky through some instinct—erroneous, of course— that backs were more impervious to bullets than chests. They carried their wounded and their bad cases of frozen feet through snow-drifted *barrancas* to the hospitals that had sprung up overnight, like horrible mushrooms, in the wide canyon of the Alfambra River. But the greatest agony was the dehumanized pounding they had to endure. Men were nothing more than victims within a shrieking universe of solids and noise conspiring to tear them to pieces.

After a week in the Sierra Palomera, the Americans were relieved. The temperature had risen, and they slogged through thawed muck on their way back to the railroad tunnel outside Cuevas Labradas. Here they devoured a tub of mule stew, their first hot meal since leaving Agua Vivas. And for breakfast they had the standard Teruel fare, oranges roasted over hot coals. (A volunteer called this dish *orange flambé*.) Though casualties had not been high, Celadas seemed worse than Brunete, and Brunete had been worse than anything before. (Jarama had been a killer, but the dead do not remember; Brunete and Teruel were torturers.) Yet the battle was only commencing.

Teruel, a city renowned for its mules and its Mudéjar architecture, sits on a high knoll above the confluence of the Turia and Alfambra rivers and is surrounded by a geological potpourri of scragged gorges, tooth-shaped peaks, and twisted ridge fingers. West of town, however, the Calatayud highway runs up a slight gradient to a palm-flat plain around the village of Concud, three miles out. The Nationalists used Concud as the base for their counteroffensive against Teruel, pushing their armies downhill on both sides of the Calatayud road.

On January 14 the XV Brigade joined the defense of the city, marching by night down the Alfambra gorge. The British were positioned in the cemetery of Santa Barbara, a promontory high above the Alfambra which overlooked the plain about Concud. They barricaded their Maxims behind broken marble tombstones and soberly watched thousands of headlights on the Calatayud highway, where the enemy were assembling men and material. The Mac Paps held a precarious position along a spur leading up to a furiously contested rounded peak known as El Muletón (Big Mule), the key point in the fighting on the west side of the Alfambra. For the Canadians it was hold or die, for at their backs there was a seventy-foot cliff hanging over the river valley. The Lincolns and the 24th Battalion were strung out across the Calatayud road, on lower ground that was within a few yards of the city limits on the west. They were particularly vulnerable to sniper fire, which came from the top of the long slope facing them. They established a firing line in outlying huts, the *manicomio* or asylum for the insane, and among the trenches inherited from the troops they had relieved. Their left flank was anchored by a flat-topped ridge known as La Muela (The Tooth), where the Republic had massed its artillery batteries. Behind them loomed the broken towers and smashed walls of old Teruel.

For the first three days it was a sniper's war. For the Lincolns, the creature comforts, after Celadas, were considerable. They slept in wrecked houses and stables, and they had hot stew and hot coffee from the cookhouse established close at hand. They broke into abandoned shops and replenished wardrobes from stock on hand. Even Fred Keller, Lincoln commissar, outfitted himself with striped morning trousers tucked into black riding boots, a sheep-lined great-coat, and a black sombrero.

On January 17 the Nationalists attacked across a wide front from El Muletón to La Muela in an effort to break across the Alfambra River. The XI Brigade was decimated and routed on El Muletón and the Mac Paps pinned against the edge of the gorge as the enemy came on, not in skirmish lines but in columns. The antitank battery and British machine gunners in the cemetery behind the Mac Paps fired over their heads and stopped the attack. But the Canadians were subjected to an artillery barrage that filed down the lip of their trenches to a depth of six feet in some places. In the midst of this merciless pounding, half the Spaniards in their Second Company threw down their rifles in terror and raced to the doubtful safety of the enemy lines. Clouds of chalk dust settled upon the defenders, turning their hair white and jamming guns, which were cleaned and fired and jammed again.

Although enemy artillery pounded the lines of the Lincoln Battalion on the edge of Teruel, the men had better protection in huts and buildings and their casualties were less alarming. They learned that the more a city is gutted the better it can be defended. Unlike other battles that the Lincolns had fought in, Teruel was a holding action. It became almost as routine as dawdling over morning coffee, picking up one's rifle, and walking down the street to work. It was comparatively comfortable fighting. A hut and the men in it might be splintered by a shell or a man's head taken off by a sniper bullet, but for the predominantly city-born Lincolns these hazards were preferable to the vast, empty distances of Brunete or Aragon. They always felt more at ease among roads and houses—shattered though these were.

Captain Philip Detro seemed to be on the verge of collapse. His long frame had worn down to skin and bones, and his fine irony had soured to sarcasm. Instead of crawling through the narrow communication ditch crossing the Calatayud highway, he defied snipers by bolting across high ground in full view. He said he disliked to stoop. One day a sniper got him as he ran across. At the dressing station, they found a compound fracture of the right femur, a bad but not fatal wound. Yet six weeks later Detro died in a Murcia hospital.[7] His adjutant, Lieutenant Leonard Lamb, a New York social worker, took over command of the Battalion.[8]

The Nationalist counteroffensive against Teruel in mid-January failed to break the Alfambra line, and collected to try again. The brigade took stock. The Lincolns counted eighty casualties thus far, the Mac Paps, a hundred and fifty. World War veterans, who had consistently pooh-poohed comparisons between the Spanish War and "the big war," were beginning to confess that the artillery barrages at Teruel were the worst they had ever seen. Whole city blocks had been shell-brushed and streets had disappeared under heaping mounds of broken stones, splintered wood, and crumbled plaster. The men were worn down. Whatever semblance of military bearing they had had, had been filed away by three weeks of battle. An American runner arrived at General Walter's headquarters with a message. En route he had bloodied his face in a motorcycle crash, he had not bathed or shaved since Agua Vivas, and he chewed a thick cud of tobacco. Shoving over a pile of maps on the General's table, he perched himself on the edge and delivered his message. General Walter, having tried to stare him down unsuccessfully, remarked archly, "You Americans—very odd people."

During the lull in the fighting, Mrs. Charlotte Haldane arrived for a tour of the front and was honored for her work with the Paris office by a party held in Colonel Copic's candlelit bunker.[9] There was a fine dinner with excellent wine, followed by singing. "I sing, even at the front," Copic proudly told his visitors. He had a fine baritone and

[7] The cause of his death is not known. It is variously reported as 1) gangrene, 2) malaria, 3) pneumonia, 4) "defeatism and fatalism."

[8] Leonard Lamb, a twenty-seven-year-old Cleveland native, had commanded the Lincoln Battalion for a short time after Amlie had been deposed. He was wounded after Belchite while inspecting a captured Italian pistol that exploded in his face, at which time Detro took over the battalion. For reasons unknown —though doubtless political—Lamb was never made a permanent commander, though he compiled a brilliant battle record in Spain.

[9] Mrs. Haldane had come to Spain as guide and interpreter for Paul and Eslanda Robeson. Robeson sang "Old Man River," "Lonesome Road," and "Fatherland" before enthusiastic crowds of Americans at Benicasim (Interbrigade hospital), Albacete, and Tarazona. Robeson was the only American entertainer to visit the volunteers during the course of the war. (But he did not sing in the trenches of Teruel, as is sometimes reported.) Before he left Spain, he and his wife were given a highly romantic account of Oliver Law by an American commissar.

once had considered music as a career. Copic's *soirées* customarily opened with revolutionary anthems and gradually shifted over to bawdy songs as the night wore on. The entertainment was interrupted when a soldier brought the Colonel a heavy silver salver taken from a private house nearby. Copic explained that all valuables were held in custody by his staff in order to avert looting. "Looters," he added menacingly, "are shot on the spot." A week later, in the Barcelona headquarters of the Communist Party, Mrs. Haldane was interviewing "La Pasionaria" when a gift package arrived for the "Red Virgin." It turned out to be the same salver that Mrs. Haldane had seen in Copic's bunker under Teruel.

On February 3 the XV Brigade was withdrawn from Teruel after five weeks in the line and marched down the Valencia road. As far as the eye could see there were wrecked, blackened tanks, strafed trucks, demolished staff cars, and rock piles marking the sites of houses. Yet the road was crammed with vehicles still pumping men, munitions, and optimism into the seven-week battle. It was like throwing good money after bad, for the Nationalists recaptured Teruel on February 22.

The brigade boarded an ailing freight train bound for Sagunto, the first stage on their way back to the rest villages of the Tajuña Valley. On one uphill grade the men looked out of the windows and saw that they were slipping backward. So they were ordered outside to help push the faltering, wood-burning locomotive up an incline. A few kilometers farther on, the train broke down. Doran and Merriman herded the men across stony meadows to a hollow deemed safely distant from the often-bombed railroad. As they huddled together in the cold, Doran told them that a visitor from the States had arrived to see them. Having heard that Paul Robeson was in Spain, the men perked up. A figure heavily wrapped in a black-leather coat stepped in front of them. To everyone's surprise it was Earl Browder, General Secretary of the CPUSA.

The men listened respectfully while Browder spoke of recent labor victories in the United States, of his hope that President Roosevelt would soon permit arms to be shipped to the Republic, and of his conviction that fascism would ultimately be defeated in Spain and elsewhere. Having uttered these pleasantries, Browder might better have quit while still ahead. But Minor and Doran had told him about "demoralized elements" in the Lincoln and Mackenzie Papineau battalions, and Browder was troubled. With a stern face he warned that men with "unhealthy attitudes" had to shape up promptly or else they would be sent home. A ripple of laughter greeted this reprimand, followed by throaty cheers. "Save me the first boat!" shouted someone. "Take me!" piped in another. At first, the men thought Browder was spoofing them, but when they saw from his expression that he was in earnest, they drowned out further speech with hooting and catcalling. The leader of the American Communist Party no longer spoke the same language as the American volunteers. Earl Browder did not address them a second time.[10]

The Lincoln Battalion was well on its way back to the Tajuña Valley when an urgent order reached them: the Nationalists had broken the Alfambra line and the XV Brigade was recalled to the front. The news arrived while the Lincolns were waiting at a railroad siding in Valencia province, and they felt a sense of bitter outrage. They took out their frustration on a tun of brandy sitting on a flatcar. When the train commander complained, Commissar Keller explained that because water froze in a minute or so up at Teruel, the men had collected antifreeze for their guns. Thus fortified, the Lincolns entrained for the North Pole once again. If the Lincolns frothed in disappointment, they were nevertheless more fortunate than the Mac Paps, whose train had been so balky that they never got down for a thawing-out in Valencia at all.

To divert Nationalist forces from the city of Teruel, the Republican command planned a series of dagger-like blows against isolated enemy strongpoints far to the north. The XV Brigade drew Segura de los Baños, a remote hill town lying sixty miles from Teruel. They were to make a surprise night attack upon scattered outposts in the Sierra Pedigrossa. Once these had been subdued, the path would be open for a sweep down the mountain valley to Vivel del Rio, five miles south, the most important road junction between Teruel and Belchite.

How the XV Brigade got from the Teruel-Sagunto railroad to Segura de los Baños or how many days elapsed in the journey, no one seems to know. Yet somehow they crossed three mountain ranges, dodged bulges in the front, and traversed an alpine wasteland seldom

[10] According to one witness, Browder was jeered not because he had threatened to send malcontents home but because he had stated that all of them would be required to serve in Spain until the end of the war. The same informant reports that after this session, some of the officers and commissars were assigned personal bodyguards.

seen by any Spaniard beyond those few souls who are indigenous to the region. Republican transport, never very good, reached the nadir of its efficiency during the Battle of Teruel. (One American truck driver remembered an eighteen-mile traffic jam on the Valencia road.) All the villages—when there were villages—looked alike, even though they did not really look like villages at all. At a distance they resembled fanciful rock-piles blending against stony hillsides as though they were made of transparent glass. Moving closer, one could pick out an elephantine church, constructed in what might be called post-neolithic style, which dwarfed the surrounding houses in the manner of a Marxist poster illustrating the oppression of the church. It was a pitiless region more hospitable to pigs and sheep than to man. The climate was harsh: winter sunshine could be blotted out by a blinding blizzard within a few minutes' time.

Segura de los Baños lay in a ravine underneath two sharp peaks crowned with ruinous castle towers, between which ran the Belchite road. The towers provided excellent observatories for surveying the projected field of battle. Two miles to the west rose the ridges of the Sierra Pedigrossa, which the Nationalists occupied. In between was a fallow valley cut by a trickle of ice and water somewhat pretentiously known as the Rio Martín. Throughout most of the war the belligerents had done nothing more aggressive than train binoculars on one another, neither having shown much eagerness to venture out into the exposed valley lying between their respective eyries. This state of affairs was due to be changed. The Lincolns and Mac Paps were to push across the valley to the sierra, while the British and 24th were to move down the valley toward Vivel.

Morale had never been worse. The attack had been hurriedly patched together without regard for logistics. Since supplies of food had not been ordered or had been lost en route, the men tried to supplement iron rations by foraging in the manner of a medieval army. But the peasants had even less to eat than they. A schism had already rent the brigade when Commissar Doran forced the Mac Paps to stand in the road until he had confiscated the mattresses of the village for his headquarters company. A Philadelphia tough named "Butch" Goldstein stormed into headquarters and told Doran to "go screw himself." He was promptly arrested, but when the Mac Paps rallied to his support, brigade staff feared that a mutiny might be building up. Major Merriman convinced Goldstein that he should make an apology to Doran, which he did, but the episode festered like an open sore. Goldstein was treated like a dragon slayer for having "told off" Doran.[11]

For two days the volunteers lay hidden in stony huts of the village, unable to build fires because smoke might arouse suspicion among the enemy. Then, on the night of February 16, as snow flurries lashed the frozen valley, they moved to attack. Butch Goldstein was handed a pair of wire cutters and assigned the task of cutting through the barbed wire surrounding the enemy machine-gun emplacements. Undaunted, he brandished them above his head and shouted as though proving a point, "Hey, fellas! Ya see what happens when you tell a commissar to go screw himself?" The Mac Paps were ordered to seize Mount Atalaya, the highest promontory; the Lincolns, a crest farther south. In the darkness they crisscrossed other Republican units bound for other crests, other hills. "Thousands of little men—little ghosts," recalled an American, "none of them ever seen again."

After five confusing hours of maneuvering through empty space, the Mac Paps got on the slopes of Mount Atalaya and crept upward without having been observed. They cut through the enemy wire and charged upward amid a chorus of yells and grenade bursts, quickly overrunning the fortified sheep-cotes of a panic-stricken enemy. But this sudden explosion of flame, shots, and curses on Atalaya served to alert other outposts along the mountain. These bowled grenades and fired nervously into the valley. The Lincoln machine-gun company, now commanded by David Reiss of Paterson, New Jersey, had become lost and did not arrive at the foot of the ridge assigned to them until daylight. While the Mooney guns fired upward, the Third Company under William Titus fanned out to attack from the rear. Insults passed up and down the slope: Reiss was heard shouting, "*Camaradas, camaradas, somos hermanos!* Surrender, you bastards!" It was a slow-motion fight until Titus led the rush upon the enemy parapets. With two grenades clutched in his hands, he was killed immediately. Almost as though they were horrified at what they had done, the Nationalists surrendered minutes later.

After Lieutenant Milton Wolff of brigade staff had taken hold of

[11] There seems to be a certain validity in the accusation by some members of the Mackenzie Papineau Battalion that they drew the most hazardous assignments and disagreeable duties. They never had the representation among the brigade staff which the Lincolns possessed. Even though their battalion contained more Americans than Canadians, it was nevertheless sponsored by Canadian agencies, which, of course, were far less powerful than the American equivalents.

the enemy commander and "booted his ass down the side of that hill in full view of his troops," the Lincoln Battalion found itself the possessor of a barren hillside strewn with rusty tin cans, a Fiat machine gun or two, a small group of petrified Nationalist soldiers, and a large supply of tinned octopus. This was victory.

For two more days similar hills were attacked, shelled, bombed, cursed up, and cursed down. It was fatiguing and noisy, but relatively safe. Brigade had ordered a "diversion" at Segura de los Baños, and a diversion is what they got. It had no effect whatever upon the main battle at Teruel. It was a fight that might have injured a great many people but fortunately did not. Despite accounts of "massive enemy fortifications" and "ceaseless bombardment" and "expectations of counterattack," the overriding impression one has of Segura de los Baños is that no one had much stake or interest in the battle then—or now.

One of the most beguiling accounts of the Spanish Civil War is found in the official history of the British Battalion where the author discusses the fight at Segura de los Baños:

> In the course of the day, three heavy and two light guns fired over 40,000 rounds, and not a round was wasted. The fire of the other guns with the infantry companies was no less deadly and efficient. All rounds were fired at carefully observed objectives. The objective had been secured, but at the cost of two British lives.

If battles were evaluated by the harmlessness of their outcomes, then Segura de los Baños would figure prominently in the history of war.

II

⌘ The Retreat to Caspe

The goddamn Fifteenth Brigade. Does it ever
do *anything* right?

—Battalion refrain (1938)

By early March both sides were claiming Teruel as a victory—the
Republicans because they had captured the city in December, the
Nationalists because they had recaptured it in February. After
seventy days of furious fighting, the lines had been stabilized approximately where they had been before the battle began. Under such circumstances, 25,000 corpses could be resurrected as statistics to support whatever definition of victory formed in the mind of the analyst
or commentator, irrespective of his politics. Yet if the cairn of rubble
and bone marking the site of Teruel offered no positive testimonial to
the significance of the battle, the events immediately following lent
themselves to two hypotheses: Teruel had temporarily used up the
military resources of the Republic, and Teruel had mobilized the Nationalist forces in a single sector. Within twenty days of retaking the
city, the armies of General Franco launched an offensive that, as
events proved, was the most decisive and devastating of the war—a
lightning attack through the heart of Aragon to the Mediterranean,
the result of which was that the Republic was cut in half.

The XV Brigade had been pulled from the front altogether and
sent north to Azaila for rest. They felt secure. Six months before, they
had camped outside this village before their romp at Quinto. Hence
the setting had for them no malign connotations. Furthermore, there
were hints of spring: thin blades of wheat pushed through pebbly soil,
and pear trees blossomed in the irrigated valley bottoms. The men
bathed in knee-deep ditches and picked off their lice in sunny orchards. The nights were cold but no longer did their rifles freeze tight,
as they had at Celadas and Teruel.

The aura of peace was so pervasive that most of the ranking officers of the brigade wrote out passes for themselves and went on leave. Colonel Copic slipped away to Barcelona. Doran left word that he required a sinus operation and disappeared. The acting Lincoln commander, Captain Leonard Lamb, went on hospital leave, and his commissar, Fred Keller, had business somewhere. Others went off for "dental appointments," which rarely had anything to do with teeth. Thus it was that as the Nationalists prepared their biggest offensive of the war, the XV Brigade had to function with a crippled chain of command. Major Robert Merriman seemed to be left unofficially in command of the brigade, although a Russian *sovietnik* named "Nicholai" came down from divisional headquarters to look in now and then. Few leaves were authorized for the *hors ranqués,* who remained behind to reap the whirlwind.

Several hundred replacements from Tarazona arrived. They had left training camp on Lincoln's birthday amid cries of "See ya in Zaragoza!" and "Bring us Franco's balls!" With them was DeWitt Parker, who had at last been permitted to leave his old post in Paris. Although he had never been in battle, he was at once installed as commissar of the Lincoln Battalion. The frail, balding commissar was beyond his depth, but the men appreciated his nonautocratic manner. Temporary commander of the battalion was Lieutenant David Reiss, a veteran machine-gunner of Teruel but a figure so lackluster that few men later could remember what he looked like or how to spell his name. Both Reiss and Parker had been selected merely to keep the shop open until the prime movers returned from leave.

On March 6, 1938, the Lincoln Battalion marched twelve miles west to Belchite, where old-timers pointed out to rookies the principal landmarks of the city that they had captured exactly half a year before —Nelson's factory, Dead Man's Point, Doran's church. Grotesquely picturesque, Belchite was a rubbish pile of crumbled brick, charred wood, and dangling wires. Brass plaques above doorways indicated that most houses had been insured against fires by a Zaragoza agency. The place was populated by stray cats and a few old people with no other place to go, scuttling creatures clad in black who camped out in crannies among the ruins. Belchite was spooky and it still stank. The Americans slept at night in wrecked houses and listened to the wind banging doors and rattling blinds, but during the day they spread out in the more hospitable olive grove north of town. If, in Spain, olive branches had nothing to do with peace, they provided a fairly effective screen against enemy airplanes. Meanwhile, the other three battalions of the XV Brigade moved into arid hill-country near Lecera and Letux, half a dozen miles south and southwest. All commanders were told that "a strong enemy push was expected within the next few days" from the west, but Merriman's information was that his brigade was part of a third or fourth line. The front, twelves miles west, had been dormant since October. The Republican command expected a powerful enemy move somewhere around Teruel, some seventy miles south, not at Belchite.

At six thirty in the morning of March 9, three separate Nationalist armies swept like an uncontrolled forest fire over the Republican defensive line scratched out between Vivel del Rio and the Ebro River. The northernmost wing comprised the crack Army of Morocco, predominantly Moors and Legion, supported by forty-seven artillery batteries and the air power of the Condor Legion. The timetable of General Juan de Yagüe was as methodical as that of a well-run railroad —Belchite in two days, Hijar in four. It called for the total destruction of all Republican units of the Army of the East between Lecera and Fuentes de Ebro. His plan of attack was so sophisticated that Belchite, "our martyred city" as it was called in Nationalist dispatches, would be "liberated" by columns advancing not from just one position but from three. The main thrust came from Fuentetodos —the birthplace of Goya—twelve miles due west from Belchite. The XV Brigade, which idly waited an order to be withdrawn to a rest village, lay supinely across the path of this Juggernaut, completely unprepared for what was to come.

Within three hours of the opening guns of battle, the Republican line had been ruptured, and widely scattered troops were streaming to the rear. Resistance, where it existed, consisted of mere companies or sections dug in along the piny mountains west of Belchite trying to hold back the enemy while their ammunition dried up and their flanks were overrun. There was no panic as such, only an irresistible flood of men flowing eastward like quantities of water from an exploded dam. Many of them held on to their fiber suitcases; artillerists carried the breech blocks of abandoned field pieces. When stopped on the road by reserve patrols, they invariably gave out the story that they had been ordered to fall back to Belchite, where a new defensive line was being prepared for them. Who issued this order they could not say. The Lincoln Battalion, whose headquarters was in Belchite, knew nothing of such a line. In almost all cases, the highest ranking officers found among the retreating Spaniards were sergeants. Whether their commissioned officers had deserted to the enemy, been abandoned in the mountains, or been shot while trying to stop the retreat, no one cared to say. The flow to the rear could not be stopped. At Letux, Major Edward Cecil-Smith of the Mac Paps attempted to hold back great throngs of them at gunpoint, but those toward the rear fanned out and slipped around his armed patrols like busy ants circumventing an obstacle cast in their path.

Against this inundation the Republic command remained bewildered, even stupefied. Contact between headquarters and the front all but vanished. The Lincoln Battalion, to mention but one case, received no orders at all until eighteen hours after the front had been broken. Telephone communication between division and brigade broke off abruptly when divisional headquarters moved suddenly without warning brigade transmissionists. While the enemy pressed forward with *blitzkrieg* efficiency, Major Merriman rode back and forth between his widely separated fragments with the anachronistic bravado of a Roman general. Paradoxically, the enemy seemed to be everywhere, yet could not be found.

It was shortly before midnight of March 9–10 when the Lincoln Battalion was told to take up defensive positions around the Hermitage of El Puego, three miles west of Belchite on the Fuentetodos road. Commander Reiss ordered his men to march out with bayonets fixed, an ominous-sounding order that helped no man's morale. The Hermitage, a bulbous pseudo-Byzantine monstrosity, was situated on a hill overlooking the highway and was said to be held by a Republican brigade possessing antitank guns collected to halt any armored column moving on Belchite. What no one knew at the time was that the Republican force, if it had ever been there at all, had pulled out and that the higher ridges around the Hermitage were already being occupied by the Nationalist advance guard. The eastern horizon was already a leaden glare when the Lincolns, who still believed they occupied a reserve line, settled into shallow rifle-pits surrounding the Hermitage. Mercifully none of them knew what daylight would bring.

After setting up his command post in a concrete cave behind the Hermitage, Commander Reiss sent patrols beyond his plateau to the series of ridges rising above them to the southwest. But most of these were caught in the troughs between the lines and driven back at once. The men were so surprised by this fire that at first they thought Republican troops had shot at them by mistake. But when it dawned upon them that these were enemy positions, they were aghast. Had the enemy made a terrible blunder, or had they? It was a solitary place they held. Ahead, to the west, the Fuentetodos road ran straight as a shot across an empty, colorless plain until it met the mountains three miles distant; behind, the same plain reached back to the big olive forest just north of Belchite. Had it not been for foothills rising three hundred feet above them on their south, the Hermitage knoll would have been a formidable position. As it was, the Lincolns were barely in place before a harassing small-arms fire poured down upon them like sheets of pelleting rain. Joe Bianca, a peppery New York seaman with handle-bar mustaches, set up his Maxim on the far left flank and began to answer the enemy fire. Paul MacEachron of Oberlin College led his rifle squad out of sight into the hills and was never heard from or seen again.

The sun was barely over the horizon before they were buzzed, bombed, and strafed by enemy planes, which swirled around the Hermitage like maniacal wasps. They even attacked a member of the brigade commissariat who heard the racket around the Hermitage and tried to walk out from Belchite to see what was happening. Although by himself on the plain, hardly worth the attention, three planes made two strafing passes at him. Flat-trajectory shells began to explode about the Lincoln hilltop. Against high explosives they had one machine gun operational. It was ridiculous to look around and to see men clutching rifles with bayonets still fixed into place.

From his culvert command-post, Reiss sent out runners, who, if they arrived anywhere, failed to report back. The telephone connection to Belchite went dead. At about nine o'clock Major Merriman arrived in an armored car and reassured them that the situation was not grave: the Mac Paps held the left flank solidly and the British occupied a reserve position in the olive grove to their rear. Before departing, Merriman promised that the British would be sent up during the next lull in the battle. But no lull occurred.

A short time later, an enemy armored column appeared on the Fuentetodos road and moved warily upon the Hermitage. Men began yelling "Tanks!" and falling back to battalion headquarters. They had no antitank guns to contest this armored wave. While Reiss and his staff stood at the mouth of the culvert debating what to do, a shell

zeroed in on top of them, one of those million-to-one shots. Half a
dozen men, including Commissar Parker, were killed outright. An
equal number were hideously wounded. Commander Reiss had been
flung to one side like a rag doll, his stomach torn open. Vernon Selby,
a West Point soldier-of-fortune, collected three men and started carrying him downhill toward Belchite. After a quarter of a mile they
looked down and found him dead. Shocked, they dropped him and
dashed for the olive grove, shells bursting all around them as they
ran.

Everywhere groups of Lincolns were breaking from the line, plunging down Hermitage Hill and running toward Belchite. No one ordered a retreat, yet no one tried to stop them. It took an uncommonly
brave man to watch his fellows deserting while he held on. Within
minutes everyone was in retreat except for those squads and sections
unaware of the flight behind them. Some men of Third Company isolated beyond intervening ridges on the left flank learned of the disaster only when a wounded man scrambled back with the bitter news
that the first-aid station had pulled out. As twenty tanks fanned out in
the valley below them, they hightailed it to the rear. The gun crew of
Joe Bianca, which almost alone had been clattering since sunup, left
Hermitage Hill last. Many men at remoter outposts were never notified of the retreat. They formed, by necessity rather than desire, last-
ditch pockets of resistance, covering the flight of their comrades until
overwhelmed. Survivors would later rhapsodize about the heroism of
men like Paul MacEachron, whom they abandoned ignominiously
while holding the enemy at bay.

The plain was specked with figures running, stumbling, and in
some instances crawling toward Belchite while enemy tanks on the
high ground shell-sniped the remnants of the crippled battalion.
Overhead, Fiat fighters seemed to hang stationary in the air while
strafing them. Like drowning men they tore off or threw away articles
bulky or heavy—blanket rolls, ammunition belts, mess kits, rifles,
machine guns. "On all sides," remembered a survivor, "men were retreating, looking straight ahead and not seeing anything." Those
along the highway were pursued by ricocheting machine-gun slugs
and shells that bounced off the macadam surface with great slamming
clangs. Those seeking a haven in the olive grove ran a gantlet of
shellfire that tore entire trees from the ground and shook down thousands of olives in a purple rain. There was no accounting for the behavior of particular men. Staggering through geysering shell-bursts, a

team of eight men carried a stretcher bearing a comrade whose foot had been nearly blown off—shock was his only sedative—for they doggedly refused to abandon a job promised and begun. Yet nearby, a man cradled a slightly red palm and ran to the rear bellowing, "I'm bleeding! God! I'm bleeding!"

On the western edge of Belchite there was a brief rally. A mixed group of Spaniards and Internationals set up machine guns along the bank of a stagnant pond serving as the town reservoir and in the windows of Nelson's factory. Here they held back the tanks for a brief period. But by four thirty in the afternoon, a *bandera* of Moors penetrated the town and opened fire upon the defenders from the rear. The wild scramble commenced again. Men got lost in the olive grove, wandered in circles, and were picked up by enemy patrols. Since Nationalist units were penetrating Belchite from three different directions, the main line of escape lay along the Azaila road, due east. (Merriman was trying to rally the brigade midway between Belchite and Lecera, to the south, but egress from Belchite in that direction was virtually impossible.) The British Battalion, led by an ex-sailor named Sam "Moscow" Wild,[1] managed to hold together and even to perform some solid work as a flank guard on the retreat to Azaila. But the Lincoln Battalion, which had received the breakthrough head-on, was in a state of collective shock. They wanted to get away and made no bones about it. Panicked fugitives reported having personally seen ditches full of Internationals who had surrendered to the Moors and had been castrated and shot.[2] On the Azaila road bands of stragglers climbed on top of ambulances, and when the tops were packed they pulled out the wounded and piled into the van. It was dog-eat-dog. The road was jammed with thousands of fugitives from other Republican units, all mixed in together. They escaped extermi-

---

[1] Sam Wild had, like Fred Copeman, taken part in the Invergordon mutiny of the Royal Navy (protesting a pay cut) in 1931. On the second day of fighting at Jarama when the British Battalion fell back, Sam Wild's Lewis-gun section was the last to withdraw, prompting Copeman's remark to two British army veterans, "Thank God we've got a Navy." Later Copeman became critical of Wild when he heard that Wild was executing British volunteers for desertion.

[2] Customarily International prisoners were executed as outlaws by the Nationalists rather than accorded treatment due regular prisoners of war. During the breakthrough of March, 1938, however, numerous Internationals were accepted as prisoners. Thirty-one Americans picked up at Belchite were eventually freed by the Nationalist authorities. An Argentine doctor reported that these men bitterly denounced and cursed their officers and comrades for having left them behind during the retreat.

nation only because the pursuers were by this time as exhausted as the pursued. While the Lincolns fled toward Azaila under cover of darkness, the Nationalists paused briefly at Belchite. General Yagüe's timetable of invasion was accurate almost to the minute.

The breakthrough had been so swift and from so many directions that the Republican command found it impossible even to keep track of overrun positions, much less organize viable lines of defense. As we have seen, in the afternoon of March 10, Major Merriman tried to assemble the XV Brigade at Lecera, a village in the plain seven miles south of Belchite, but at the time this order was issued the highway between was already being cut by enemy patrols. At one point Merriman's armored car was ambushed, and he escaped capture only through the breakneck daring of the driver, who spun off the highway and churned cross country to safety. While more than half of the Lincoln Battalion fled to Azaila and Hijar, the others dutifully collected at Lecera and joined a motley group of Internationals and Spanish Republicans in establishing a line.

The Mac Paps reached Lecera in the morning of March 11. What had befallen them illustrates the paucity of Republican staff work at this time. For twelve hours on March 10 they had been shelled, bombed, and strafed in their position in the hills west of Azuara (twelve miles northwest of Lecera). Major Merriman pulled out the 24th (Spanish) Battalion,[3] which had been with the Mac Paps up to this time, but left the Mac Paps beyond the Cámaras River. By midafternoon all Republican forces had been recalled east of the river, except the Mac Paps, and the Azuara bridge had been blown up. The only reinforcements Major Cecil-Smith received were some men from the XV Brigade machine-gun company, but these arrived not only without their machine guns but without rifles. Late in the day Major Cecil-Smith heard that the XIII (Slavic) Brigade was coming to his aid. (They never arrived, and the patrol he dispatched to locate them never returned.) Night fell, but still no orders came from Merriman. Finally the Major, on his responsibility, pulled his battalion back across the Cámaras River over the demolished bridge and placed them in the red cliffs along the eastern bank. With them were a con-

---

[3] The International battalions had been renumbered as follows: 57th (British), 58th (Lincoln), 59th (old 24th), 60th (Mackenzie Papineau). To avoid confusion, I have retained the original numbering when alluding to the Spanish Battalion.

tingent of Spanish marines. Cecil-Smith then hurried off to General Walter's headquarters to obtain explicit instructions on what he was supposed to do. Walter ordered him to bring his battalion to the halfway point on the Lecera-Belchite road.

The Major got back to the Mac Paps at daybreak of March 11 and found that the enemy artillery was already shelling the cliffs. The marines had vanished during the night. Hastily gathering up his men, Cecil-Smith evacuated his cliffside line. One Mac Pap machine-gun crew in a high cave was not informed of the withdrawal. Its gun, commanded by Lieutenant Leo Gordon (Joe Gordon's brother) covered the retreat of the others. None of the crew was ever heard of again. In open march formation, the Mac Paps passed several hills already occupied by enemy troops, but these, doubtless mistaking them for their own, did not molest them. Instead of leading his battalion to the assigned point of rendezvous, Major Cecil-Smith reported directly to brigade headquarters at Lecera, because, as he later expressed it, "it was evident that considerable changes had taken place in our front line since the night before"—a remark that is surely the classic understatement of the campaign. His premonition was sound, for the Lecera-Belchite highway had been cut even before General Walter issued the order. The Mac Paps verged upon total exhaustion: they had dug all night and had marched twelve miles since sunup. At Lecera they were permitted a two-hour rest before entering the line again.

The motley group assembled at Lecera had by no means lost its cutting edge. When the Nationalists arrived on the outskirts of town during the afternoon of March 11, they met a brisk fire covering an orderly retreat eastward to Albalate del Arzobispo, where a defensive line was being established along the Rio Martín. Had it not been for incredibly stupid staff work, Lecera might have held out longer than it did. Within fifteen minutes, Major Cecil-Smith received three different, and conflicting, sets of orders: had he obeyed all of them literally, he would have performed the remarkable feat of being simultaneously in three different places. In the end, he took up a hillside position south of Lecera and assisted in beating off a tank and infantry attack. But in the midst of the fighting, another staff officer arrived and, producing a neatly annotated map, showed Cecil-Smith that he was firing upon the XIII Brigade and not the enemy at all. This was absolutely false, as the Major knew, but he had to withdraw his men and watch the enemy take the town. Nor was he able to have the acerbic pleasure of "I told you so," because the headquarters officer had long since moved on to other assignments in conducting an "orderly withdrawal."

By midnight Lecera had been evacuated. The Mac Paps provided the rear guard on the ten-mile hike eastward to Albalate del Arzobispo. Not a man among them had thrown away his rifle. They even managed to salvage the brigade water-truck despite its bullet-punctured radiator: a soldier straddled the hood, pouring in water from a hose connected to the immense tank. But somewhere on the night march they lost other paraphernalia—like General Walter. Many days later he reappeared. "Maybe he went to Barcelona to look for Copic," suggested one man.

By the morning of March 12 those Anglo-Americans not yet killed or captured found themselves somewhere among the Republican units halfheartedly fortifying the far bank of the Rio Martín between Hijar and Albalate del Arzobispo. But a retreat once begun was difficult to halt. Men who had been buffeted for three days had lost confidence in themselves and in their officers. Squads assigned to defend hillsides doubted that anyone else would hold: the result was a climate encouraging desertion through an inability to trust anyone beyond oneself. In these marathon retreats the brave and the obedient soldiers, like Paul MacEachron and Leo Gordon, were victimized, for they covered the getaway of others unwilling to defend themselves. Unfortunately for the Republic, however, the supply of sacrificial lambs had been depleted through overuse.

Albalate lay in the trough of a network of eroded hollows easily approached by the Nationalists and difficult to defend. As soon as the first enemy skirmishers appeared, the Republican line folded up and panicked men surged northward to Hijar. Trucks, ambulances, and staff cars raced through the stragglers, occupants leaning out of windows shouting, "The Fascists are behind us!" Such havoc-criers might as well have joined the Nationalist column. Pedestrians were knocked down and run over, wounded men were abandoned, rifles were thrown away. Even the Mac Paps, who thus far had adhered to one another with remarkable self-control, were broken apart in the knockdown avalanche of men bent solely upon escape. Before the column reached Hijar, Nationalist cavalry cut the road. When Major Cecil-Smith called for his Maxims, he learned to his dismay that the guns had been put aboard a truck for safekeeping and the vehicle could not be found. The retreating mass then swung cross country to the Hijar-Alcañiz highway, the main route east. Here they were joined by other groups, including the Lincolns, which had evacuated Hijar. Once again, while the best men braced themselves to slow down the enemy advance, the worst fled eastward to Alcañiz, twenty miles away.

For the moment, however, the Nationalists were too preoccupied with mopping up pockets remaining in their newly gained territory to pursue fugitives with great energy. There was breathing space for the remnants of the XV Brigade to regroup on a crest three miles east of Hijar. Their rifle pits overlooked hairpin curves of a road dropping down to an open plain across which the enemy would have to come. It was a fine defensive position: they could be outflanked perhaps, but not frontally attacked. Too exhausted to move or to eat, they fell asleep on their guns—those who still retained guns. It was here that Commissar Doran rejoined his brigade. He found that 75 per cent of his men were missing in addition to nearly all the heavy equipment from Maxims to mortars. One of the first things he did was to issue an order warning that henceforth any man who threw away his weapon or abandoned an assigned position would be shot. The reaction of the haggard men to this edict can be imagined.

Throughout March 13 the XV Brigade, or what was left of it, remained in the hills back of Hijar. By this time the men assumed that the worst was over. The day was deceptively quiet, as though the Nationalists planned to press no farther eastward. (On this day the total number of casualties reported by the Army of Morocco consisted of two men wounded.) Since there were reports of enemy patrols on the far flanks, the Republican command ordered all units to fall back upon Alcañiz in the morning. What no one seemed to know was that the entire center of the Franco offensive—for the most part Italians of the CTV (Cuerpo de Tropas Voluntarios)—was converging upon Alcañiz by a different road coming from the southwest. Once again the XV Brigade was ordered to march into the jaws of a trap.

The twenty-mile stretch to Alcañiz was bad terrain for men in retreat. It sagged and buckled. From the top of one naked hillock one could see only identical hills cresting like waves on the surface of a disturbed sea. It was perfect country for cavalry, which might approach to concentration points within a few hundred yards of the macadam road, now teeming with men and vehicles in retreat. Except for clumps of spiky gorse and occasional locust trees fringing the highway, there was no protection whatever. While Doran and Merriman zoomed ahead in staff cars, the men straggled down the lonely road, scanning the hillsides for signs of danger. The most reliable men, all of them party stalwarts, scouted the hills on both flanks. Before departing, Merriman had told one of his commissars in a low voice, "There is nothing between us and the Fascists except those few scouts." The Mac Paps were assigned the rear guard—doubtless their reward for having held together better than other battalions. But even they straggled badly, the stronger men outpacing the weaker until separated by nearly a mile. Adopting an ambulance for a staff car, Major Cecil-Smith drove back and forth, urging the laggards to speed up and the pacers to slow down. One thing was clear, no one wished to be last.

Three miles from Alcañiz, the Major's ambulance rounded a curve and found a Fiat tank sitting on the road, fifty yards ahead. Beside it, a crew in blue uniforms were setting up a machine gun. The CTV had cut the road. The two groups blinked at each other for a moment. "Come over here!" shouted a tall, blond blue-shirt. "Wait a minute, we're coming right back!" someone called from the ambulance. The reflexes of the driver were quicker than those of the tankist. He hit the accelerator, and the ambulance spun off the highway to the north and careened down a cart road, billowing dust and pebbles behind. Shells from the tank were cracking overhead when they learned that the road led into a *cul-de-sac*. A small factory reared up; beyond was a shallow lake ringed with reeds and duck blinds. The only way out was by foot to dunelike ridges half a mile north. The Major shouted, "Direction Alcañiz! Every man for himself!" and took the lead. A medic was killed while debating where to run. The others raced for the hills and escaped.[4]

Up and down the line of retreat, Nationalist patrols began to seize portions of the highway and to open fire upon the Republicans. Like a wave shaken in a taut rope, a spasm of panic swept through the long column. No one had warned them that they should expect an attack from the south, and no one knew at the time that enemy forces effecting the penetration were insignificant. The cry "Fascists!" trig-

---

[4] Major Cecil-Smith was justifiably furious with brigade staff for allowing this trap to be sprung upon him, after having escaped so many others during his retreat from Azuara. Alluding to the CTV movement that cut the column west of Alcañiz, he wrote in his official report, "From what I have heard since, the brigade staff was in a position to know of this [movement] fairly early, but they failed to notify our battalion of the fact."

gered a collective reflex ejecting them northward in a pell-mell flight. A few officers had the presence of mind to fire shots above the heads of their men to attempt to stop them, but by and large they joined, and even led, the stampede.

An American commissar, Sandor Voros, quickly outrun by the others, found a haven beside a Soviet tank. The observer was scanning the hillsides to the south with binoculars. Suddenly he cursed and shouted orders down to the driver. On a far ridge had appeared six cavalry scouts, obviously the enemy. Voros expected to see the gun barrel swing around to the target and figured one shell might get them all. But, to his surprise, the tank shifted around and began to scurry to the rear. Seeing that he would soon be left alone, Voros tried to climb aboard, but the tankist ordered him off. "I am a comrade!" he hollered, while the Russian hammered at his fingers with a pistol until he let go and dropped in the road. The tank soon disappeared, but fortunately for Voros, so did the enemy scouts.

Alcañiz, a picture-postcard town on a crag, was moated on three sides by a loop in the Guadalope River. Its defensive potency had been well established in the Middle Ages but was largely ignored by the Republican command, which evacuated the place with only token resistance by machine gunners in the Templars castle on the peak. Just five days before, Alcañiz had been a backwater supply depot some forty miles behind the front lines; now the CTV and Army of Morocco were breaking into the western outskirts. The only two escape routes—north to Caspe and east to Gandesa—were clogged with men and vehicles. Heads craned skyward, watching for bombers that could have obliterated this dense, helpless mass. Miraculously none appeared, although an American caught in this stalled logjam recalled that a flock of birds, mistaken for distant planes, stampeded men into roadside ditches. Throughout this bedlam of strangled motion and this babel of tongues, the cacophonous bells of the collegiate church tolled incessantly, their clangor spreading the alarm of a doomed town to citizens and soldiers already frenetic in their effort to escape.

The XV Brigade, which had been haphazardly splinted together in the hills behind Hijar, had pulled apart once more. Some moved toward Gandesa, forty miles east, while others, including most of the men cut off on the Hijar road, crossed the Sierra de Vizcuerno toward Caspe, eighteen miles north. Many veterans remembered their march across this desolate, horse-opera landscape back in December when they had gone up to Teruel. It was an awesome, desolate mountain range encrusted with red granite boulders, some of them as large as houses. There was no time to pause, for the men had no assurance that the enemy would not reach Caspe ahead of them, via a direct road paralleling the Ebro. Orders came down that Caspe, a railroad center surrounded by defensible crags, had to be defended until fortified lines could be thrown up farther east as a last dike to stop the Nationalist surge toward the sea. In the absence of Copic, Commissar Doran was given the authority to employ all Internationals who were located or strayed into the sector. The Albany gang-scrapper at once plunged into the work of mobilizing his ragtail army to do battle with the vanguard of two crack Nationalist divisions.

Every man and vehicle passing into the Caspe perimeter was set to work. The human material was none of the best. Few retained weapons, most had lost blankets. Their retreat across the rough Sierra de Vizcuerno had literally torn uniforms from bodies. One fugitive showed up with his trouser legs ripped off: whenever he walked his scrotum bobbed like a broken spring. Few had eaten a decent meal in six days. Any of them might have served as an adequate model for a party poster labeled "Arise, ye wretched of the earth." To feed them, Doran broke into the food stores of the brigade staff mess, a hoard formerly guarded jealously by Colonel Copic. To clothe them, he sent Commissar Sandor Voros to demand equipment from the "yellow bastards" at the brigade *intendencia*. Voros found the quartermaster readily enough, but when he demanded 150 blankets, trousers, tunics, boots, and canteens, the officer in charge absolutely refused to fill the order without a written order from Doran. Vainly Voros argued that he was Doran's personal envoy. Nor was the officer upset when Voros sneered, "Put a Communist in charge of a load of goods and you get a Capitalist!" Finally Voros signed Doran's name next to his own and delivered an ultimatum, "If those blankets aren't there by ten o'clock, I'll be back again, *but for you!*" All of Doran's talk about having men shot began to pay dividends. The gear arrived promptly.

Probably less than three hundred men of the XV Brigade rallied around Doran at Caspe.[5] For the past week they had occupied the center of a collapsing, malign universe. All alternatives had failed.

_____

[5] There is great confusion about the defense of Caspe. At least two battalions of the XIII Brigade were also present and remnants of the XI (German) Brigade, which had been nearly exterminated on El Muletón at Teruel. It is unlikely that Doran commanded more than five hundred men.

They had tried to fight but had been overwhelmed; they had tried to flee but had been hounded to earth. Now Doran lectured them, and they sat too weary to protest the old "comic-star" screeds, in which optimistic jargon was directly proportionate to impending disaster. He spoke of massed waves of fighter planes promised by the Soviet Union and of artillery promised by France. The men heard these things and knew that they were lies, but in the chill dawn of Aragon as the Fascists closed in upon them they wanted to believe in Doran because there was nothing else to believe in. The meat of Doran's discourse was seasoned with excremental images that, for that place and time, considering what they felt toward the enemy, toward themselves, and toward Doran himself, became a kind of vulgar eloquence. Even his mad-dog threats to execute deserters struck them as vaguely comforting, for, after all, the turned flank had been the overriding menace during the long retreat. Moreover, it was even possible that those who hated Doran most passionately had a special object in staying with him to the bitter end: once and for all, they could test him against themselves and prove that he was the lesser man. One Doran-hater expressed his feelings this way, "If that little bastard can take it, so can I. But if he runs out on me, I'll follow him wherever he goes and kill him with my bare hands." For whatever reason, they rose from the dead and formed a line.

It is a well established barnyard fact that a cock fights best on his own dunghill. Caspe had become Doran's.

From the barren highlands southwest of Caspe, the ground slopes gradually down, yielding to olive groves that carpet the plain surrounding the town. Just behind the cubes of houses lies the Guadalope River, which joins the mighty Ebro a mile to the north. The black line of the Zaragoza-Barcelona Railroad crosses the Guadalope on a high trestle on the northern edge of Caspe and disappears in the warty countryside to the east. The pivots of the defense were two hilltops commanding lines of enemy approach. On the southern edge of town lay Castle Hill, a high cliff overhanging the river crowned by a modern castle; on the western edge, Reservoir Hill, commanding the railroad and Ebro River road. Advancing Nationalist skirmishers, preceded by tanks, quickly pressed back the Internationals from exterior lines to these dominating positions and to the houses and factories along the western perimeter of Caspe. At this stage, in midmorning of March 15, the defense stiffened.

The fight for Reservoir Hill continued throughout the day. It was defended by Captain Nilo Makela, a leathery Finn from Canada, who in better times had led the Mac Pap machine-gun company. With him were perhaps two hundred men, a mixed group of Americans, Canadians, and British. They had obtained a few Maxims without undercarriages. The gunners, most of them Finnish-Americans known in the brigade as "the eighth wonders of the world," set up their guns on rock supports and repeatedly beat back the enemy skirmish lines. Down on lower ground to their rear, a British contingent under "Moscow" Wild barricaded themselves in the railroad station and dispersed enemy troops attempting to infiltrate Caspe through the railway cut. The only escape route from the town lay across the railroad trestle spanning the Guadalope. Doran placed a heavy guard here with instructions to fire upon any Republicans attempting to leave Caspe without authorization. There was plenty of ammunition: the castle contained enough munitions to demolish the town.

The Nationalist commanders of the Thirteenth and Fifth Divisions moving upon Caspe from the west expected the town to fall with only token resistance. In the opening hours of the battle, they sent in skirmishers. When these were beaten back, companies were sent in, with scarcely better results. Finally whole battalions were hurled into the attack. They were so astonished at the firmness of the defense that they concluded then, and earnestly believed afterward, that all five International Brigades held Caspe. With a fury goaded by frustration, they shelled, bombed, and strafed Reservoir Hill throughout the afternoon. Tanks and swarms of infantry pressed up the wooded slopes on the west. Outgunned, outmanned, and nearly cut off from the town, Captain Makela ordered a withdrawal at dusk. It was while he was standing on a knoll directing the fall back that a tank shell exploded at his feet, tumbling him down an embankment. He bled to death on a hospital train.

Although Reservoir Hill had been defended with remarkable élan and dogged courage, Doran was not in the mood to offer congratulations. He had not ordered evacuation of the hill, and he demanded that the hill be recaptured before dawn. Major Cecil-Smith, who had just arrived in Caspe after a twenty-four-hour trek through the mountains, was assigned to lead the attack. Dutifully he collected a scruffy force, variously estimated at somewhere between one and two hundred men, some of whom were unarmed skulkers and *inutiles* rounded up by Doran's guards. Three tanks were drawn up to shell the hill while the attackers climbed the slope. They had two light machine guns but no grenades. The Three companies belonging to the Fourteenth (French) Brigade, just arrived in Caspe, were instructed to assist them, but they refused to budge because, as Cecil-Smith reported later, "their captain adjutant had gone back to town."

For three hours the force of Major Cecil-Smith worked up the slope of Reservoir Hill by the light of a full moon, while tank cannon battered the summit. "All we could really do," recalled one attacker, "was to throw rocks and yell at them." The covering fire from the tanks was noisily effective, even though many shells exploded upon the Internationals. Yet, much to the surprise of everyone, they not only occupied the hill but also captured thirty prisoners, ten mules, three Fiat machine guns, and a range finder. What is even more remarkable, at five in the morning the Nationalist division west of town received an emergency alert and was ordered to stand by to repel a major counterattack from the Republicans. For the first time since the breakthrough around Belchite, the Army of Morocco sounded an alarm.

Meanwhile, in the western districts of Caspe, International patrols probed streets and alleyways looking for enemy patrols, which, in turn, were looking for them. Greenish explosions flickered about odd corners of the town as they tossed grenades at one another. At one point "Moscow" Wild was captured by a Nationalist patrol, but when his guard tried to rifle his pockets, he kicked him in the shins and got away. Near brigade headquarters, a small group with Captain Milton Wolff walked up to a tank, assuming it to be Republican. When only a few feet away, Wolff saw it was a Fiat. The gunner stuck his head out of the turret and asked, in bad Spanish, "What part of Spain, you?" Wolff said, "Salamanca" and yelled for his men to take cover. Italian curses echoed through the street as the gunner slammed down his turret hatch and opened fire at point-blank range. Wolff scrambled to safety, but some of his men were caught in the road. The dead and wounded were crushed by the treads of the tank as it rumbled up the street.

At first light, when it became clear that only a small group of Republicans held Reservoir Hill, the Nationalists pressed forward rapidly. Doran's master-stroke proved in the end to be only a whimsical *tour de force*. The Internationals who had taken it were unable to hold it longer than a few hours. When Cecil-Smith found enemy fire battering him from the rear, he dispatched a runner to Doran, requesting permission to retire. He got no reply. Finally, on his own authority, he fell back along the railroad track. Before he reached the town, a message reached him, ordering him back to his hill. He could not obey it: he had lost control of his men, who were, as he later understated it, "somewhat upset."

By midday of March 16 the Internationals had been thrust back into the northern quarter of Caspe, where they held on to the Guadalope bridge, the railroad station, and a plateresque convent. Making use of a ready-made position in a railroad cut, they held the enemy at bay despite what a Jarama veteran called "the most intensive fire we ever experienced." The entire rim of Reservoir Hill, now fortified by the Nationalists, crackled, boomed, and sputtered like a fireworks display. Doran was enthralled. He watched the battle from Castle Hill, on the other side of town, coming and going along a steep pathway used in Fourteen-Stations-of-the-Cross ceremonies at Eastertime. On one occasion, as the battle raged under him, he turned to an assistant commissar and announced proudly, "Just look at *my* battle."

Toward dusk Doran authorized the evacuation of Caspe via the railroad trestle. Squads could no longer cope with battalions. Many men who had fought so well never received orders to pull out. They were simply abandoned. Some of them were one-time deserters and "demoralized elements" whom Doran had charitably armed and sent into battle instead of executing on the spot. Human débris, as he viewed them. By letting them die at Caspe, Doran gave them an opportunity to salvage their honor.

In the mellowing perspective of thirty years, many Lincoln veterans would point to their defense of Caspe as the sublime moment of the war. For two days a handful had forced two enemy divisions to pause. And for one hour—between five and six in the morning of March 16—they had made the enemy brace itself against a possible counterattack. If militarily this amounted to little, existentially it was everything. It was an eye-boggling counterpunch by a runt who had been knocked around the ring for fifteen rounds. Yet this is the boast of hindsight. What the men felt at the time is better reflected by the scene at the bridge as Doran supervised the evacuation of the town. Among the tail of the column were a group of spectral creatures, unkempt and bleary-eyed. They were Anglo-Americans who had stormed Reservoir Hill and had watched and cursed as Fascist steel cut down every second man. Spotting Doran, they crowded around him, screaming in his face, "You dirty, filthy murderer! You butcher!" A burly Britisher squared off in front of him and unleashed a torrent of obscenities, begging Doran to lift his fists or to reply. But Doran did nothing except turn his back and walk across the bridge. He was a zealot. He saw what others did not see; he did not feel what others felt. Whatever Caspe was or became, it would be his.

In the early morning hours of March 17, while the XV Brigade was hiking eastward through oak forests to Batea, two prisoners were brought into the headquarters of the First Bandera of the Falange of Navarre. They had been found among the defenders of the railroad station, where they had been abandoned by Doran. Both were badly wounded. One was a fifty-year-old American oozing blood in the chest; the other was a red-headed Scotsman hit in the leg. Since neither spoke any Spanish, an Argentine doctor attached to the Bandera interpreted for them. "I came to Spain," said the elderly American, "because I was told that I would spend a few agreeable months without any danger. As the trip was free and would give me an opportunity to see a beautiful country like Spain, I enrolled in the Red Army. I took this trip just like a tourist would take a Cook's tour." The speaker was a frightened, broken old man. He wanted only to live, and to live meant to please his captors, and to please them meant that he had to lie with finesse. His interpreter was moved to pity. No one else was.

Both prisoners were shot.

12

ꛯ The Rout at Corbera

No more Fifteen Brigada—all killed—all
dead—You got to smoke? Sure I run—you
run, too. All over—all gone—no use no
more—Brigada gone. Only a couple get
away. Me.

—Finnish-American near Batea

When news of the Aragon debacle reached Albacete, the Interbrigade training-camps were swept clean of recruits in a frantic attempt to plug gaps. It was pitch black in the morning of March 14 when barracks lights were switched on in Tarazona de la Mancha and the trainees ordered to stand by. "Yow! We're moving!" somebody yelled. "So's your bowels," chimed in another. Night maneuvers or the real thing? One by one the men were summoned into the barracks office and asked a perfunctory question, "Are you fit to go to the front?" Then their names were checked, and they were on their way. Before they boarded boxcars in Albacete, Major Allan Johnson came down to make a speech. "What you lack in training," he said, "you make up in enthusiasm and anti-Fascist conviction. The first Internationals who helped to save Madrid, had no training at all." After letting this sink in, he added, "I wish I could be with you. Good luck." Rations were handed out—packs of French cigarettes, loaves of bread, cans of Argentine beef. As they pulled away from the platform, a band blared out "Himno de Riego," but as the train crept down the track to Valencia, the men inside sang old bourgeois favorites like "Just a Song at Twilight." These were the last recruits to pass through Tarazona de la Mancha.

Though dispatched with all speed to the front, they required four days to reach there. The delay resulted from a confusion so cataclysmal that no single *responsable,* much less trainmaster, had, in these parlous times, a clear idea of where the Republicans were or the Nationalists were not. The replacements were drawn up into the high tundra of Teruel province and dropped out at a deserted railroad siding. The ground nearby was pock-marked by bomb craters, which, as one rookie said, "put the fear of God into us." They whiled away half a day here without sign of friend or foe except for a few distant shepherds—who seemed to be neither. Then trucks picked them up and carried them back down to the coast at Sagunto—through which they had passed the previous night—and up to Tortosa, where hundreds of trucks moved through yellow fog toward the front. At dawn of their third day they bivouacked in an olive field, each squad assigned to a different tree. Commissars warned them not to start fires for fear of attracting enemy bombers and lectured them not to pay heed to "weak elements." In the afternoon they saw columns straggling along the road—"ragged, unarmed soldiers, their faces streaked with dirt, their beards long, a look of desperation in their eyes." These men had retreated from Hijar, Alcañiz, Caspe, and dozens of other places that the new men had never heard of.

Shortly after midnight of the fourth day, the replacements marched nine miles to XV Brigade headquarters at Corbera, a village three miles northeast of Gandesa. They were shocked to see campfires by the hundreds burning in the valleys—deliberate violations of front-line security as taught by Major Johnson. They were split up among the four battalions and discovered that they outnumbered those who had survived the harrowing retreat. The Lincoln Battalion, for example, consisted at this time of about a hundred ragged down-and-outers who greeted the new men with sarcasm or ignored them altogether. Eager questions were answered with reluctant grunts or lashing expletives. The veterans heaped mountains of verbal excrement upon Merriman, Doran, and Copic (who had at last returned to his Brigade and was angrily demanding to know why they had retreated). Some of the most vitriolic remarks came from a man who subsequently confessed, as though he were ashamed of it, that he was presently commander of the Lincoln Battalion. This was Al Kaufman, a New Yorker who had begun the retreats as a rear-rank machine-gunner and had inherited the battalion by default, after nearly every other officer had been killed, wounded, or captured. When a recruit asked about food, the veterans broke into hysterical laughter. Food?—there was no food. There had been no food for five days. They admitted—one might even say they bragged—that they had been running since

Belchite and wanted an excuse to run to Barcelona, or even farther. A smug youth, Irving Somebody, interrupted these seditious mutterings. "But comrades," he said, "that's cowardice. . . . Don't you realize that it's impossible to retreat from fascism; that unless we lick fascism all over the world it won't be long before . . ." "Crap!" broke in a voice. Haggard men glowered at the upstart, a zealous squirt who apparently had read so many copies of the *Daily Worker* that they had ruptured his brain. They spat. One of them said menacingly, "Comrade, we've been through hell the last few days, and do I understand you're accusing us of being cowards." Irving backed down. "Well," he put in apologetically, "I don't want to be misunderstood . . ." "Haul your ashes," broke in Joe Bianca, resuming the post-mortem.

To uplift morale, Edwin Rolfe, editor of *The Volunteer for Liberty* (now printed in Barcelona instead of Madrid), bombarded the front lines with two-page broadsides exhorting the Internationals to hold their ground. Immense headlines fairly screamed:

ATRAS LOS INVASORES DE ESPANA!
(Drive out the invaders of Spain!)

NO CEDER UN SOLO PALMO DE TERRENO AL ENEMIGO!
(Don't yield an inch of ground to the enemy!)

FORTIFICAR ES VENCER!
(To fortify is to win!)

Vets who took the *Volunteer* with a few grains of cynicism pointed out that the implication buried beneath the bold type was that the higher-ups were really alarmed, or else they would not suggest that the war could be won merely by holding ground.

In Rolfe's news sheet appeared learned articles of a how-to-do nature like the one explaining that good soldiers could defend themselves against tank attacks even if they lacked armor-punching weapons. The recipe was given in detail. "If time allows" one should dig a pit 180 centimeters deep and 60 centimeters wide. Place into this pit two well-seasoned and steady men armed with grenades and liquid explosives—preferably phosphorous bombs, but if these are not handy, gasoline bottles will do. When the tank approaches within eight or ten meters, the men should rise up suddenly and throw their grenades at either the caterpillar treads or the fuel tank. One thing must be borne in mind: one ought not panic and run away from a tank "because it has guns." If it is not possible to knock out the tank as it passes over or near the pit, one should not become fretful or disappointed, for usually tanks return by the same route and there would be an opportunity to destroy it on its way back. ("Oh yeah!" commented a sarcastic veteran. "No tank will ever get past me, because I'll outrun it, no matter how fast it goes!")

What ought men to do when support on their flanks melts away and the enemy infiltrates behind their position? Veterans found the answer in an article written for the *Volunteer* by "Gallo" (Luigi Longi), inspector general of the International Brigade. At the alarm "Our flanks have been broken!," soldiers panicked unnecessarily. Cool reflection would show that if the enemy broke your line and got behind you, your situation might be improved. For even though it was true that he had outflanked you, at the same time you had outflanked him! (The next logical step might be for the adversaries to push past each other so rapidly that neither engaged the other at all.) At first, the men fumed at what they termed "a la Pasionaria" propaganda and win-the-war articles in the *Volunteer* prepared by scribblers fighting the good fight from behind their desks in distant Barcelona, but in time the newspaper did, in fact, help morale by providing them a weekly target for their derisive laughter. Although not so intended, the *Volunteer* became a sort of gag bag, cheering them up by what Sandor Voros called "back-ass propaganda."

Meanwhile, in the concrete nave of the movie house at Corbera, once the setting for countless Class-C Hollywood dreadfuls, Commissar Doran was staging one of his own. The euphemistic title of this spectacle was "Reorganization and Re-education," a worn scenario at best. It featured courts-martial, sentences, denunciations, and admonitions. The upshot was that Doran, who served both as prosecutor and judge, sentenced "a number of our comrades," as one witness later expressed it, to death for desertion and cowardice. It is vividly recalled that he rolled the verdict through his twisted jaw with apparent relish as he proclaimed to each man, "You are condemned to *die* before a firing squad!" It happened that one of the prisoners was a prominent Young Communist Leaguer from Cleveland named Jack Cooper. Cooper's offense was no greater than anyone else's: during the retreat he had abandoned his weapon. But because he was a machine gunner, Doran pressed the point that his weapon was more valuable to the Republic than those of riflemen. At this stage a junior commissar testified that he had encountered Cooper during the retreat and recalled him as "nothing but a walking corpse intent only on saving the few survivors of his company." Others joined in with their protests until the court-martial became a shouting match. Ultimately Colonel Copic's deep-lunged baritone entered the dispute on the side of the prisoners. He said he feared that news of executions would leak out and alienate journalists like Ernest Hemingway and Herbert L. Matthews, who were regular visitors to the brigade and whose dispatches had always favored the Republic. Copic demanded reinstatement of the accused in the name of solid public relations, and presumably his point prevailed, despite Doran's grumbling that the decision smacked of "rotten bourgeois degeneracy."

Less forgiveness was shown to twenty-two long-distance deserters who had fled all the way from Belchite to Barcelona. One of them, John G. Honeycombe, a former field organizer for the Communist Party in California, applied to the War Ministry for a repatriation permit but was told that the Interbrigades were not responsible to the Republican government. The official at the Ministry added, "Frankly, I would like to see all of you get out of Spain," implying that he was disgusted with the Comintern network in Spain. Some men tried to stow away aboard ships; others sought help from the United States consulate.[1] But the police agents of Tiny Agostino rounded them up and returned them to Corbera, where they were put into a labor battalion. They were billeted under guard in an olive grove, refused fire and blankets, and fed a daily ration of lentil soup and two pieces of bread. The intention was to put them between the lines when the brigade next went into action.[2]

Widespread shuffling took place with the command structures of the various battalions. The Mac Paps, backbone battalion during the retreats, lost both commander and commissar. Major Edward Cecil-

---

[1] On March 29, Vice Consul Flood cabled Washington, suggesting that his office be authorized to issue emergency documents of travel to France for American fugitives from the Interbrigades. It was perfectly clear to the consular officers that these men had lost all rights and were being punished with totalitarian thoroughness by the brigades. But two days later Hull cabled back that no assistance should be given to American volunteers "unless they are able to obtain discharge from military service of the Spanish government and permission of Spanish authorities to leave Spain."

[2] One of the prisoners was the West Pointer Vernon Selby. Wounded and in shock, he was separated from the others and hospitalized. A week or so later Selby made his peace with Doran and returned to duty on battalion staff, where his military training and experience (in Central America) were desperately needed.

Smith suffered a singular accident: while cleaning his pistol it had gone off, blowing a hole in his foot. (Men wondered whether the wound was self-inflicted. Was there a charge pending for his momentary lapse at Alcañiz?) His place was taken by Hector García, a Spaniard, since North Americans now comprised a minority in the battalion. Carl Geiser, erstwhile Lincoln commissar at Fuentes de Ebro, replaced Wellman as political *chargé* of the Mac Paps.

The greatest changes affected the Lincoln Battalion. The new commander was Captain Milton Wolff, who had worked up through the ranks as a machine gunner in the Washingtons and had fought in every campaign since Brunete. *The Volunteer for Liberty* billed him as "the young Lincoln," a comparison with surface merit, for Wolff's prominent cheek bones, aquiline nose, and shock of unruly black hair did suggest the namesake of the battalion. Politically and ethnically they had nothing whatever in common. Unmistakably Brooklyn, Wolff was as tall as Detro but with more sinew and stamina. By trade the twenty-two-year-old commander was a shipping clerk, but before coming to Spain he had toughened himself by a six-month stint in the C.C.C. He resolutely denied that he was a member of either the Communist Party or the Young Communist League.[3] Largely self-educated, Wolff was nevertheless a natural intellectual: in his knapsack he carried Thomas Mann's *Joseph in Egypt,* which he read during lulls in campaigning. Napoleonic style was not the style of Milton Wolff, for he detested elegant uniforms and patrician mannerisms. He wore baggy trousers, a stained leather jacket, no hat whatever, and rarely an insignia other than the three-pointed star of the Interbrigades. In rainy weather he donned a wool poncho—not a silk-lined opera cape. As commander of an Old Testament host, Wolff might have done very well indeed. He was intelligent, egalitarian, blunt, and

---

[3] A year later there was the following exchange between Wolff and the chairman of the House Un-American Activities Committee:

CHAIRMAN: In the event of a war between the United States and the Soviet Union, which side would you support?
WOLFF: Is there such a war today?
CHAIRMAN: You certainly would know. You went over and fought in Spain.
WOLFF: Is there such a war today?
CHAIRMAN: If there were such a war.
WOLFF: Is there a war today between the United States and Soviet Russia?
CHAIRMAN: If a war should break out between the United States and the Soviet Union, would you support this Government?
WOLFF: If war should break out between the United States and the Soviet Government, I would be glad to give my answer.

fearless. Most of the men admired him enormously. To the Spaniards of the brigade he was always *El Lobo* (The Wolf).

The new Lincoln commissar was John Gates (*né* Sol Regenstreif), the twenty-four-year-old son of a candy-store proprietor on Fordham Road, The Bronx. Stubborn (as a kid he would drink his chocolate milk only when his mother stirred it clockwise) and brilliant (honor society at DeWitt Clinton High School and Regents scholarship to City College), Gates quit college to join the Young Communist League. He was posted to Warren, Ohio, as a party organizer in the steel industry. The mayor there once had him arrested on the court-house steps for "making loud noise without permit" and publicly called him a "young snotnose." If Wolff was wolf, Gates was terrier. He was pint-sized, wiry, and spunky. In 1933 he led a hunger march to Columbus at a time when nervous deputies met the marchers at each county line with shotguns. Eastern Ohio was Joe Dallet country. Dallet called Gates "insignificant" yet worried about his rise in the party. Gates, on the other hand, found Dallet a poseur: "He always wore a flannel shirt, never a suit or tie—this was not the way prole-tarians dressed, only the way Dallet thought they dressed."

When Gates learned of the existence of the Lincoln Battalion he volunteered and was accepted with the proviso that he recruit four unmarried men from his district. This done, he became celebrated as "the first volunteer from the state of Ohio." He prepared himself for Spain by taking pistol lessons at the Youngstown YMCA. In transit to Spain he found ten thousand French francs in his Paris taxicab, whereby some anonymous capitalist inadvertently donated a wad to support the fight against fascism in Spain.

At a period when most American volunteers were being sent to Jarama, Gates was sent to the Cordoba front with the Twentieth (International) Battalion, an experimental group composed of men from twenty different nationalities. The idea was to see whether chauvinism could be rooted out of the Interbrigades by mixing up volunteers from divergent countries. The experiment failed in much the same way that the Tower of Babel failed, but Gates, who was fluent in Spanish, attained the position of acting brigade commissar, with a rank equivalent to lieutenant colonel. Within a few months in Spain, Gates had advanced farther in the Interbrigades than any other American except Steve Nelson. (In a letter to his wife, Dallet wrote slightingly of Johnny Gates's startling career.) When William Law-rence was recalled to the States in early autumn, Gates assumed his job as American representative to the Base. But he hated this work—

fending off disgruntled veterans who echoed the same plea, "When is my turn to go home? Bill Lawrence promised me. . . ." Moreover, Gates became increasingly unpopular for establishing the policy that volunteers had enlisted for the duration of the war (not for six months) and would be repatriated only because of physical disability.

The desk work at Albacete never suited Gates. In February, 1938, he joined, with neither rank nor privileges, the XV Brigade during the Segura de los Baños campaign. Doran assigned him to drive a mule, panniered with explosives, up a hillside under shellfire. When he found that the men on top had a plethora of ammunition, Gates could have concluded that Doran wished either to test him or to kill him. During the retreat from Belchite, Gates took charge of the men falling back to Azaila. Then, during the final hours of fighting at Caspe, Doran ordered a group under Gates to hold back the enemy advance until instructed to withdraw. For twelve hours Gates waged a back-to-the-river fight. No retirement order came from Doran. Just before he was about to be overwhelmed, Gates, on his own authority, retreated. Purportedly he was the last American to leave Caspe.

Since a week of spring rains had broken the momentum of the enemy advance, it was possible to hope that their offensive would not soon be resumed. Physically the men had recovered from their grueling retreat, but the psychic effects lay dormant in their skulls like tumors. They were apprehensive without understanding why. To perk them up, Commissar Doran organized a grand *fiesta* outside Corbera on March 29. Around a huge bonfire, they were treated to bottles of acerbic champagne, baskets of almonds, and Colonel Copic's baritone. Imported from Barcelona for the occasion were female representatives of the Unified Socialist Youth, who delivered fiery speeches under the eyes of wary chaperones. Ten men, one of whom was Joe Bianca, were commended for bravery and received billfolds and wristwatches.[4] (In view of what they would undergo in the days to

---

[4] It has been alleged that one of these men cited was Herman Bottcher, a gnomish and taciturn figure of twenty-nine who spoke English through a thick German accent. He had emigrated to the United States from Germany in 1931 and worked as a gardener while attending San Francisco State College. A few months before graduation he quit college to fight in Spain. After the Spanish Civil War, Bottcher returned to the United States and joined the U.S. Army prior to Pearl Harbor. Sent to New Guinea, he was ecstatic over the exotic vegetation he found there. To a friend he wrote: "I love the jungle. . . . It intrigues me, no, it bewitches me. You should see the multitude of beautiful butterflies, brilliant in color or the gorgeous plumage of the birds

come, pocket compasses would have been more suitable gifts.) But the rank-and-filers were restive, scenting trouble ahead with a kind of sixth sense. "We must be moving," said one of them sardonically. "When they throw a *fiesta* for you, it never fails."

Even Commissar Doran, never one for sentimentality or defeatism, seemed affected by gloomy forebodings, for on this day he wrote his wife what for him was an extraordinary letter. Gone were the lurid phrases about "filling Fascist bellies with lead" and the heavy committee-report tone he employed even with his wife:

> Please do not worry, darling, some day I am coming home to you, nestle close, and let nothing ever take me away from you. I have fashioned a real lifelike picture of yourself in my mind and somehow even in the most difficult moments I feel your presence close by. I hope you have not changed much. I want you to be nearly exactly as you were. You must know, darling, that at moments just thinking of you, as you were, serves to fire and inspire ever so much. Nothing can ever rob me or make me forget memories of the two of us, nothing can ever impel me to blot out the burning desire within me to once more be at your side. I believe the entire Brigade knows about us, dear. Do you mind if I tell?

Tell what? That he, Commissar Doran, was guilty of loving a woman like lesser mortals? Underneath the mawkish phraseology of the letter is the voice of a man faced with the specter of the ultimate change— his own death. Marx provided a tough, outer shell; inside, Doran was yolky with mysticism.[5]

---

or the exquisitely fragrant flowers." A short time later he wiped out a line of Japanese pillboxes, received a battlefield promotion to captain, and was awarded the Distinguished Service Cross. The Army publicized him as the "One-man Army of Buna"; his men called him "The Jungle Killer." During the Leyte Campaign Bottcher spent forty-eight days behind Japanese lines, specializing in terror attacks upon outposts. He died on January 1, 1945, after a mortar shell blew off his leg.

It is curious that no contemporary account of the Lincoln Battalion in Spain mentions Bottcher and that the VALB did not lay claim to him until after he had distinguished himself and after he had been killed. He is known to have been "depressed" by his experiences in the Spanish Civil War and always refused to talk about them. In any event, Bottcher acquired considerable posthumous popularity among the Lincoln veterans.

[5] Because the tone and substance of the letter differ so markedly from the progress reports that Doran customarily submitted to his wife, one should not exclude the possibility that it is a forgery, composed later to "humanize" the Hero of Caspe.

The vague restiveness within the XV Brigade, founded though it was upon intuition rather than information, accurately mirrored concurrent developments at the front. At that moment the Nationalists were breaking through the Republican lines farther west and resuming their drive to the Mediterranean. While the First Division of Navarre swept east from Caspe to Gandesa, the CTV moved along a converging route from Alcañiz to Gandesa. At Gandesa the two armies were to link up before forcing a pathway through the Sierra Pandols to Tortosa and the sea. The XV Brigade was situated in the vertex of the angle formed by lines of the enemy approach. And, once again, liaison and reconnaissance proved to be so inadequate that brigade staff never possessed an accurate idea of the identity or strength of other Republican units stationed on their flanks.

On March 30, 1938, at five in the morning, the men were shouted awake and armed hurriedly. All day they moved cautiously westward through a region of red hills, stubbly vineyards, olive groves, limestone terraces. Enemy airplanes swarmed overhead, seeking out bigger game in the rear—convoys, depots, armor. As the day wore on, the rumble of artillery in the west grew audible, sounding to rookies who had never heard it before like the menacing approach of a summer squall. The storm was coming nearer but the eye of it was undetermined miles distant.

Daybreak of March 31 (Thursday) found the XV Brigade, mixed in with its "sister" brigade, the German XI, still feeling its way westwardly through a five-mile arc lying between the Gandesa-Alcañiz and the Gandesa-Caspe highways. With each kilometer of advance, their frontal line, of course, became thinner. To the left, the British followed the Alcañiz road; in the center the Mac Paps and 24th (Spanish) moved by mule paths and terrace walls through a succession of tree-mantled hills; to the right, the Lincolns straddled the Caspe road a mile or so northwest of Batea. By this time Gandesa lay six to nine miles behind them. First contact with the Nationalist vanguard came unexpectedly and jarringly.

The British passed through Calaceite at dawn. Since Merriman's information was that the closest enemy troops were twelve miles farther west, the British straggled in a long file, their heavy weapons bringing up the rear. What they did not know was that the CTV had slipped through a gap in the Republican line and had cut the Alcañiz-Gandesa road. Without having fired a shot, a large Italian column had got between the British and the front. Lining up whippet tanks, machine guns, and antitanks in the neck of a horseshoe curve, they waited quietly for their first victims. They had not long to wait.

The first company of the British Battalion walked past the CTV line-up, apparently mistaking Italian lettering on the tanks for Spanish. The head of the column passed unsuspectingly through the jaws of the trap. As the light improved, a voice in the second company split the quiet air, "Tanks!" which, in effect, provided the signal for the Italian open-fire. They cross-stitched the road with a pointblank fire that dropped the drowsy Britons where they stood in dumb surprise or propelled them in a clawing flight up the rocky cliffside to the south. The slaughter was prodigious. Tanks throttled up and darted back and forth along the road, "their guns rattling like motor bikes." One tank tried to run down a squad of Britons paralyzed with indecision in the roadway; they dodged in time, but the tank crushed wounded men writhing in its path.

Within half an hour the British Battalion ceased to exist. A cluster of perhaps thirty men briefly rallied on a promontory above the road and pecked at the Italians below them. But they quickly melted away when Italian soldiers deployed to surround them. In tiny bands, the survivors of the Calaceite massacre, probably none of whom had maps, fell back toward Gandesa through the barren Sierra de Pesells. It is by no means certain that brigade staff learned what had happened to them until the following morning, for their line of retreat was far to the south. In this brief fight the British lost 150 men killed and wounded, and another 140 were captured.[6] Calaceite was the most humiliating defeat an English force ever suffered at the hands of Italians.

Pressure upon the other three battalions built up steadily throughout Thursday afternoon, but the mounting skirmish fire was easily contained. Refugees streamed eastward. Their two-wheeled carts were heaped high with sticks of furniture, bed ticks, frying pans as large as shields, and always the family dog, tied with a piece of twine, ran along between the wheels. Behind the refugees came the advance patrols of the enemy. Bullets snapped overhead as the two adversaries established tentative lines. There were many confusing and fatiguing movements and countermovements as brigade staff tried to smooth out the wobbly defensive arc. Contact between battalions

---

[6] In contradistinction to the Spanish Nationalists, the CTV sought opportunities to take International prisoners, because these could then be traded for Italian prisoners held by the Republicans.

existed only through brigade headquarters. The result was that each functioned as an autonomous force without clear ideas of what was occurring on the flanks. By the end of the day's probing activity there existed vacuums between companies as well as battalions, a condition conducive to piecemeal destruction. At night the western sky was illuminated by the headlights of hundreds of vehicles as the enemy carried men and matériel up to the front in complete disregard of convoy security. With their immense resources of manpower and firepower, what need did the Nationalists have of secrecy?

"We knew," said one volunteer, "that daylight would be a bitch."

Friday was April Fools' Day.

The battle opened before dawn when Major Merriman ordered the Mac Paps to advance against unidentified troops occupying a high wooded ridge. Merriman believed them to be members of the XI Brigade. Sniffing disaster, the Mac Paps showed a notable reluctance to obey the order. Their commissar, Carl Geiser, collected a light machine-gun squad and pushed ahead on his own. Beyond a clearing he saw several hundred men hunched over campfires cooking breakfast. "Come on over. We're your friends," came a voice in a perfect Brooklyn accent. Reassured, Geiser holstered his automatic (he had no cartridges for it anyway) and led his squad across. Up close he saw unfamiliar uniforms, then shoulder patches designating 23rd of March Division, and finally three machine guns trained on him. They were the CTV. The voice belonged to an Italian soldier who had once spent a year in New York, working as a short-order cook.

An Italian captain put a pistol against Geiser's spine and walked him over to the brow of a hill overlooking the Mac Pap position. "Call those men up here," he demanded. "I can't do that," Geiser replied. In his pocket were credentials identifying him as political commissar—a clear-cut death warrant. He did not doubt that he would be executed: it might as well be then as later. Across the valley the Mac Paps, sensing something was wrong, opened fire, and in the developing battle the Italian captain lost interest in Geiser. He and the other prisoners were marched off to the rear. For over a mile they passed bivouacs of Italians casually breaking camp and preparing for the day's work. The woods seemed to be packed with soldiers, tanks, trucks, and artillery in cornucopian abundance. Halting this mass was the job of the Mackenzie Papineau Battalion, and scraps of the XI Brigade—if Merriman ever located them.

At a farmhouse girdled by whitewashed walls, a young Italian lieutenant shared his breakfast of broiled fish and wine with the American commissar. He was most curious to have the duties of a commissar explained to him, for in his army there was no such officer. Geiser said he functioned as political chaplain to his men. The officer appreciated the analogy. While eating, they discussed the war as dispassionately as though it had taken place centuries before, in Carthaginian times perhaps. Both agreed that Spain was a testing ground in the ideological struggle between fascism and communism and that the major battle would be fought elsewhere, on a wider scale, in the years ahead. The lieutenant considered the war in Spain nearly over. "Next will be France," he said. The lieutenant hoped that the CTV might be permitted to invade France on their way back home to Italy. He asked Geiser no questions of a military nature. Perhaps as a gentleman he disliked to embarrass his guest; or perhaps as an officer of *Il Duce* he gave no serious thought to the rabble ahead of him. He volunteered the information, presented in a businesslike manner, that the northern arm of the offensive comprised thirty thousand men who were expected to be in Gandesa by noon, in Tortosa by sundown, and at the sea by the following evening. Then, with fine courtesy, he bade farewell to Geiser and turned him over to a firing squad to be shot.

The prisoners were lined up against a wall in the courtyard. A priest came out and mumbled something in Latin from a tiny Bible. A squad of riflemen took their places. On the road beyond the open gate a limousine raced past, braked, and backed up. An officer leaned from the window and shouted, "No executions!" and drove on. The firing squad strolled away, the priest wandered back inside the farmhouse, and the men looked at each other. The day turned sunny. All day long new prisoners arrived until by nightfall the little courtyard was quite full.

Meanwhile, the Mac Paps were engaged in a series of rear-guard actions that were a paradigm of the Republican resistance in the vicinity of the Alcañiz-Gandesa road. Repeatedly they fell back to hilltops, where no sooner had they set up a firing line than they discovered that their flanks were gone. Throughout Friday morning they withdrew with textbook precision, contesting every yard of relinquished territory; but by early afternoon the defenders began losing contact with one another and control over themselves. Stretcher-bearers, runners, ammunition carriers dispatched to the rear failed to return. Companies dissolved, squads carried on. Thus far the battle had been fought with mortars, machine guns, and rifles. Wooded valleys and ridges crackled and popped like a forest fire. "It was like playing cowboys and Indians," reported a Mac Pap, "except there were too many Indians."

In the middle of the afternoon a Mac Pap squad led by Lawrence Cane of New York City abandoned its hilltop after Nationalist flags blossomed from hills on their flank. They pulled out and fell back again. Quite by accident their route of retreat passed through XV Brigade headquarters just west of the crossroads where the road from Caspe joined the road from Alcañiz. They were intercepted by an officer yelling and waving a machine gun. It was Colonel Copic, who seemed dumbfounded to hear that the Mac Paps no longer occupied positions, several miles west, so clearly marked on his headquarters map. "And who gave you the order to retreat?" demanded the Colonel. "What are you asking me for?" Cane snapped back. "All I know is that we got out with a whole ass." Still brandishing his machine gun, Copic shouted, "Why didn't you stay and fight?" The Colonel got his answer a few minutes later when two Fiat tanks broke through a copse and began shelling the command post from forty yards away. According to Cane, "Copic jumped fifteen feet." With this running start, he quickly outpaced the others and disappeared in the direction of Gandesa, three miles down the road. (Once on the far shore of the Ebro, at Mora la Nueva, Copic reported to divisional headquarters and said he had come to request reinforcements. He did not return to his brigade, which was trapped on the other side.)

The vertex of the defensive angle had caved in. Tanks and skirmishers seemed to be everywhere. What was left of the Mac Paps and the 24th Battalion broke and ran. "It looked like the world had come to an end," remembered one. Yet compared with the Lincolns, the Mac Paps and Spanish were fortunate, because most of them reached Gandesa ahead of the CTV, which was pushing rapidly down the Alcañiz road. But the Lincolns were still five miles northwest, their line of retreat cut off, when Major Merriman raced his staff car up the Caspe road to warn them that the enemy had gotten behind them.

Disaster overtook the Lincoln Battalion but slowly. On Thursday (March 31) they had established contact with the enemy in the ragged hill country a mile or so northwest of Batea. Twigs and severed leaves drifted down upon them as Nationalist machine-gunners opened fire. But the only casualty was a Spanish rookie who crawled across exposed ground toward a Lincoln gun crew. They tried to wave him back, but he came on, calling out, "I want to see the machine gun working." Seconds later he was hit in the groin and thrashed about, shrieking, *"Mama mia! Ai! Mama mia!"* He was beyond the range of stretcher-bearers. Meanwhile the Americans fanned out and opened fire. The woods turned blue-gray from the fumes of discharged cartridges; hot gun barrels blistered their hands. For the new men this was a nontraumatic initiation into war, less like a battle than a target-shoot—except that there was no visible target. After nightfall Captain Wolff sent patrols to probe the flanks. A mongrel dog followed one group of green men, barking now and then. Fearing the noise would give their position away they resolved to kill it, but since no one had the nerve to bayonet it, they left the dog alone, hoping it might go away.

Friday morning was so quiet that most of the Lincolns slept off their exhaustion after a night of waiting and watching for an enemy attack that failed to materialize. They lay on pine-scented hillsides, studied local insect life, and wondered what the folks were doing in the U.S.A. Food trucks came and went, no more molested than the morning milk-truck back in Allentown. "The war seemed very far away," mused one volunteer, who also remembered that artillery rumbles were so far away that they sounded "musical and harmless." They had not been told that the British Battalion had been routed the day before, or that the Mac Paps and Twenty-Fourth were fighting for their lives just five miles south of their bucolic groves. What was worse, as events proved, was that they were ignorant of enemy movements in their own sector. The Navarese division that they had been fighting on Thursday had bypassed them and was at that moment pushing east toward Villalba de los Arcos to pick up a road leading into Gandesa from the north. In other words, by Friday afternoon the Lincoln Battalion had been nearly surrounded. Not even the chronic pessimists among them had any inkling of just how bad their situation was. They were in the deceptively quiet eye of the storm.

The scales fell from their eyes in late afternoon when Merriman's bullet-spattered staff car arrived with news that the Gandesa-Alcañiz road had been taken by the CTV. Even as Merriman drove north to Batea, enemy snipers had fired at him. A queasy flutter went through the men as they heard this. Hovering over his map with Doran and Wolff, his professorial glasses drooped far down his nose, Merriman

advised them that they move cross country to the hills north of
Gandesa, where they could pick up the main highway leading to the
Ebro bridge at Mora de Ebro. (Merriman had no information concerning the Navarese division that was then moving south across his
projected line of retreat.) Doran, who is said to have been death-
oriented at this point, insisted that they remain where they were, fortifying and fighting to the last man. His insane proposal seems not to
have been overruled: it was just ignored. There was not a minute to
lose. Captain Wolff was calling out, *"Batallón! A formar!* Let's go!" It
was getting dark.

Men poured off the hillsides and assembled in the road. Some of
them naïvely assumed that they were preparing a night attack against
the enemy. Yet when they began marching away from the sunset, they
sensed something terrible had happened. "No one said anything, no
one asked any questions, but we knew we were moving, moving fast."
Armorers stood in the road trying to hand out extra rounds of
ammunition and grenades to the men filing past in the fading light.
But sensing trouble ahead, the men avoided carrying anything that
would slow them down. One man muttered over and over, "Never
again! Never again!" It was not clear what he was referring to, but
there was a wide world of meaning in what he said.

On Merriman's topographical chart the route of their anabasis
seemed clear enough: they simply had to follow a road labeled
camino viejo de Batea a Gandesa until it intersected another *camino
viejo* (old road) passing north toward Corbera. But on a Spanish
chart an "old road" meant that it might have been a bustling thor-
oughfare at the time of the Visigoths but that nowadays it was apt to
be a faint rut intersected by cart roads and mule paths, none charted.
Road signs did not exist in this hinterland, and even during the daytime an experienced map-reader would have had difficulty picking the
correct route out of the profusion of intersecting lanes.[7] Moreover,
the necessity for rapid movement precluded close contact between
marchers, who in the deepening blackness either collided with one
another or straggled widely apart. The night was filled with whispers,
rising to angry shouts, emanating from all directions, "Contact.
. . . CONTACT! Goddamn it to hell, where *are* you?" Terrace
walls were mistaken for the road: men plunged down cul de sacs only
to bump into walls. Those separated in this manner found a little

---

[7] A search of this sector in 1967 revealed no trace of a road whatever,
only rutted lanes winding about in all directions.

thing in the brain dragging them ineluctably closer to the brink of panic. It was terrifying to contemplate being left alone behind enemy lines—claustrophobic suffocation and burial in empty space. Piece by piece, men began throwing equipment away. Those behind stumbled over machine-gun pans, blanket rolls, mess tins left by those ahead; they cursed the waste and cowardice, then seeing the wisdom of it, began throwing away equipment of their own.

Within a short time the Lincoln Battalion had fragmented into perhaps half a dozen clusters of hapless men, all of them bent upon getting as far east as possible before sunup brought discovery. Except for the staff, none had compass or map. One band of about eighty men, among them a New York novelist named Alvah Bessie, strayed northeast toward the hamlet of Villalba. A line from a song drummed monotonously in the back of his mind—"Be it ever so humble, there's no place like home." In the stupefying, exhausting night march Bessie became aware that his tongue was hanging out, like an animal's; he clamped his mouth shut, plodded on, and found his tongue hanging out again. Just before dawn they spotted the lights of a town but hurried on, few caring what place it was or who held it. The road began to be strewn with abandoned equipment—blankets, knapsacks crammed with such items as toothbrushes and stinking codfish and love letters, and cartridge belts full of ammunition. Whoever had been there before them had left in a hurry. Then an abandoned truck loomed in the middle of the path with Soviet rifles leaning against the tailgate. Someone said, "I wonder if the damned thing will run," and climbed into the cab. The motor turned over with a roar and men clambered aboard. As the truck started to roll, Bessie stood for a moment on the running board, but not wanting to get ahead of the column, he jumped off. The red taillight bounced down the path and disappeared.

On the outskirts of the unknown town (it was Villalba de los Arcos), they passed silhouetted figures on the road. Wrapped in blankets and holding rifles, they stood by and did not challenge the Americans slipping across the cordon to the fields beyond. Suddenly Bessie's squad leader dropped his rifle and began to run. "Tabb!" called Bessie in alarm, "Where are you? I can't see you?" They were in a field humped with bundles of sleeping men. Bessie tripped over a soft obstruction on the ground—a man sat up and cursed, "*Coño!*" The Americans had wandered into a Nationalist bivouac! The darkness came alive with a din of noise—horses whinnying, pots and pans clanking, pounding footsteps in all directions. The Americans dashed blindly through the campment, tripping over aroused bundles as frightened as themselves, and scaled a series of terrace walls on the far side of the field. From behind came strident shouts, *"Alto! Los Rojos! Alto los Rojos!"* Bullets snapped over their heads. Moaning with exhaustion, Bessie and three others reached the top of the ridge at first light. They were alone—the others having been shot, captured, or dispersed. Ripping off the red-star emblems on their caps, they hurried eastward. Late in the day they reached Mora de Ebro, where they fell in with a platoon of Mac Paps. "Where's the Lincoln?" asked a Mac Pap. "We're the Lincoln," one of the four replied. "Pleased to know you," said a Canadian.

Far to the west they could hear the thunder of artillery at Gandesa and the whine of diving airplanes. In the middle of this holocaust was the main body of the Lincoln Battalion.

On Saturday morning (April 2) the main column of the Lincoln Battalion, reduced to perhaps two hundred men, reached a scrub-pine ridge about a mile from Gandesa. In eight hours they had covered less than seven miles of rough hill country: they had failed to reach and to cross the Gandesa-Corbera highway before daybreak. Now, with sinking hope, they watched the landscape below them unfold in the candescent dawn like a print emerging from a photographer's tray. A series of terraced vineyards descended like a broad staircase to a wide valley, beyond which lay the peaks and folds of the Sierra Caballs. Due east was Gandesa, a slate-colored town resembling neatly piled rocks in the green plain. To their right the CTV along the Alcañiz highway were launching their morning attack on the town. But to the Americans' consternation, they saw concentrations of the enemy moving upon Gandesa from the north as well. (These were the Navarese moving down from Villalba.) They were in a bag, with the drawstring being pulled tight even as they watched. Black smoke hung over Gandesa, which was being shelled to drive out the remnants of the Republican rear-guard.

The only way out was to cut their way though the enemy encirclement in order to join the Republicans still remaining in Gandesa. After several hours' delay, the Lincoln Battalion started down, although a great many men adamantly refused to budge from the hill. Except for a few almond trees there was practically no cover on the terraces, and the rock retaining-walls faced the wrong direction. They were spotted almost immediately. Machine-gun fire broke their advance. While some men milled about futilely seeking protection, others scrambled back up the hill. It is alleged that a few Americans ran the gantlet of fire unscathed and slipped into Gandesa, but if this is so, the survivors failed to chronicle their exploit. The experience of George Watt, an assistant battalion commissar, typified countless others. When the machine-gun fire became unbearable, he took refuge with a half-dozen men in a *barranca* coursing downhill toward the enemy lines. To Watt it seemed like a deathtrap—a natural pathway up to the Lincoln hilltop whenever the Nationalists decided to press their attack. He stripped himself of all equipment. For a fleeting moment he wondered what to do with a packet of his wife's letters— then threw them away. His men refused to fall back to the hilltop with him. Watt got back safely but never saw those men again.

On two adjacent hills the Lincolns frantically employed bayonets to scratch out rifle pits in earth the color of old bloodstains. Since no retreat was possible, they set up the few Dichterev machine guns that they had retained along a circular outer rim and waited, like Custer, to fight the last battle of their lives. A few shells ranged overhead, but for the most part, the enemy was vastly more interested in breaking through to Gandesa than in mopping up an insignificant force in their rear. There was a long period of agonized calm until the hope grew that they might be forgotten or ignored until sundown, at which time it might be possible to get away to the Sierra Caballs. They followed the path of the sun across the sky with empathic absorption. It was the longest day of their lives.

Late in the afternoon a line of enemy horsemen gathered in the valley below and trotted, as though on parade, up the slope toward the Lincoln hilltops, weaving in and out among the maze of terrace walls. With their guidons fluttering gaily, they charged the American positions but were beaten back after a crackle of fire from the ridges dropped perhaps a dozen of the riders off their horses in fine Hollywood style.[8] Veering away, the cavalry galloped northward. They

---

[8] This story has improved with age. The primordial history of the Lincoln Battalion (1939) says "it took no more than a few minutes to convince the attackers that their charge was futile" and mentions no casualties whatever. The "definitive" history (1967), basing its account primarily upon an interview with Fred Keller in 1965, talks about "four or five hundred cavalry," led by an Italian officer who "shouted to the Americans to surrender in the name of Il Duce," being "cut down by the Lincoln heavy machine guns so that the slopes of the hill were covered with the dead and dying." It is interesting that

flushed small clusters of Lincolns out of *barrancas* farther down the slope and pursued them through the vineyards. When the trapped men tried to surrender they were chopped down with sweeping saber strokes. Among those who died in this manner was Al Kaufman, a short-term commander of the Lincoln Battalion. Witnessing this butchery, the Americans above realized the futility of surrender and resolved to break out at whatever cost as soon as darkness fell.

At dusk, battalion scouts searched for a feasible route that would cross the Gandesa-Corbera road and lead into the sierras to the east. Ironically it was Vernon Selby, the rehabilitated deserter, who found a likely path. They moved out at once, so rapidly indeed that many men never learned of the withdrawal until the staff had vanished in the gloom.[9] The group of thirty-odd fugitives who left the others far behind included Doran, Merriman, Keller, Wolff, Lamb, and a scout who called himself "Ivan" (John Gerlack of Chicago). This meant that all the stratocrats responsible for leading their men to safety were inexplicably bunched together in a small group far in the lead, with but two exceptions—John Gates and George Watt.[10] The night was pitch black. The men straggling behind soon lost contact with one another and separated into smaller groups. The smart ones tried to orient themselves by the stars or by the reddish glow hanging over Gandesa. They picked their way delicately through enemy campments, at times close enough to hear scraps of conversation and snoring.

It was nearly midnight (April 2–3) when Doran-Merriman's group of thirty emerged from a trenchlike sunken road that struck the Gandesa-Corbera road within half a mile of the latter place. Gerlack, in the lead, had just started across when a figure reared up out of nowhere and challenged him. *"Manos arriba!"* (Hands up!) came a frightened voice, followed by a wailing cry, *"Cabo de guardia!*

Herbert L. Matthews interviewed Keller on April 11, 1938, and received a detailed account of the attempt by the Lincolns to break out of the Gandesa encirclement. Yet Keller said nothing about the cavalry charge.

[9] It has been alleged that Merriman was overheard saying to Doran, "It's time for us to get out of here." Depending upon how one stresses the word "us," several quite different meanings may be construed. Some veterans are convinced that Merriman and Doran slipped away from the column in order to increase the possibility of their own escape.

[10] A letter to John Gates in 1968 asking whether it may be possible that Merriman-Doran's group abandoned the rank and file on the hilltop above Gandesa draws no answer. The failure to reply could be interpreted as 1) tacit assent or 2) disdain for the question.

Rojos!" A rifle went off. Gerlack shouted, "This way!" and bolted across the highway, followed by Lamb. They jumped down an embankment on the other side and ran. Someone else yelled, "No, get back!" More shots were fired. "Somebody" thought he saw Doran shot in the leg. (The identity of "Somebody" is unknown.) In this instant of startled confrontation with equally startled enemy sentries, every semblance of order and discipline utterly vanished. No one gave the order to return the fire and rush across the road. Every man had to cope with his own reflexes, and these commanded him to flee.

Afterward none of the survivors told exactly the same story. Blackjacked unexpectedly in the dark, no man was certain of the sequel. Some insisted that the headlights of a car or a tank suddenly floodlit them; others said the scene was acted out in total darkness. Merriman and Doran were together. Some thought they ran up the highway toward Corbera. They vanished as completely as if the earth had swallowed them up.

The Lincolns scattered in all directions. A few dashed across the road after Gerlack, but most fell back and fled through the vineyards and orchards north of Corbera. A University of Michigan student wandered alone for many hours until he found himself on the edge of a village that he took to be many miles northwest of Corbera. He worked down backstreets until he came to a sign identifying the place. His heart jumped when he saw CORBERA. He escaped by dashing east to the Sierra Caballs.

The Lincoln Battalion as a military organization dissolved. It was every man for himself as they bolted away from the clamor and shots on the Corbera road. Most of them were accustomed to city streets and roads and were ill-prepared to strike out alone through open fields marked only by sinuous cow-lanes. Few had ever seen a map of the region through which they were to pick their way. Rifles were anchors dragging them back: they were better thrown away. Darkness was an enemy, for it confused and separated them; yet when darkness ended, they would be hunted like animals.

Commissar John Gates managed to collect a few dozen men and fled north. It was a man-killing hike through hill country. Just as they filed through a narrow valley before dawn, a voice on the ridge above shouted down, *"Alto!"* A Nationalist patrol had spotted them. At once a Spaniard with them named Copernico shouted back, *"Alto!"* The voice above called, *"Quien es?"* And Copernico echoed back, *"Quien es?"* Faint shapes collected on the brow of the hill. While the others hurried through the valley, Copernico remained behind, echoing the voices on the ridge. Then he hoisted a white handkerchief and wound up the hill to surrender.[11] He had parleyed with the enemy long enough to permit the others to escape. By the time the Nationalists had brought up a machine gun to rake the valley floor, Gates' group was gone. A few miles farther on they overtook a group of Lincolns led by Lieutenant Melvin Offsink, First Company commander. Offsink was in a bad way: his legs had given out. He lay like a gasping fish while they cajoled, threatened, and cursed him to make him continue. But he refused. They left him where he lay. A used-up CCNY student named Ralph Wardlaw remained behind with him. Neither was ever seen again.

Beginning at dawn on Sunday (April 3), Nationalist patrols stalked remnants of the Republican Army squeezed into the ten-mile neck of land lying between Gandesa and the Ebro. The hunted men slept in patches of prickly gorse by day and sought to find the river by night. They had no food. Sometimes local *campesinos* fed them and guided them over obscure trails to the river; at other times they turned them over to Nationalist patrols. The safest course was to approach a quiet farmhouse, take food at gunpoint, and depart quickly. Some Lincolns made the river easily without seeing an enemy patrol, while others found themselves nearly trapped countless times.

Under the pressure of the chase, normal patterns of behavior were often reversed. Within the first hours an unusually stanch veteran ran amuck and had to be abandoned. On the other hand, John Cookson, who customarily behaved like "a hysterical old lady," was transmogrified into a daring leader of his transmission squad. In the darkness he hooked onto the tail of a passing Nationalist column, learned their password, and marched with them down a road he figured would lead to the Ebro. Three days later he was ferried across the river not only with all his men but also with telephones still hanging about his neck.

On Sunday morning the Republican command ordered the evacuation of Mora de Ebro. What the villagers did not carry across the great iron bridge, hordes of starving fugitives carried off for themselves. Newsreel cameramen caught on film the grubby pathos of

---

[11] A few months later Copernico wrote a letter to the Lincoln Battalion, explaining that he had been taken prisoner but had managed to escape to the Republican lines. The purpose of his letter was to collect his back pay.

retreat. Soldiers without rifles hugged live chickens, rabbits, and pigeons as they jogged across the bridge. A tattered man wearing captain's bars slung a ewe over his shoulder and tippled. Boxes of dynamite lay stacked along the girders of the bridge. Then there was a detonation that shook the earth, a black cloud spumed up, and the bridge toppled on its side into the yellow river.

In this way the Republic prevented further enemy penetration east of the Ebro. Cataluña was safe. But all the Americans fleeing from the rout at Corbera were thereby trapped on the far side. There was no other bridge within thirty miles.

With enemy patrols dogging their heels, survivors stood in canebrakes along the right bank of the Ebro and peered at the turbulent, flooded river carrying stumps, bloated animals, and tons of yellow mud to the sea. Beyond, granitic mountains promised safety. At only a few places were cable ferries set up to haul small groups of men across; elsewhere a man had to cross the river as best he could. The flooded condition of the Ebro gave even strong swimmers pause—but not for long. They plunged in and swam, or failed to swim, across. But the Lincoln Battalion contained an unusually large number of nonswimmers—there are no swimming holes in The Bronx—and these gaped helplessly at the swirling water and roamed the shore vainly seeking some way across. Many men who had survived the fatigue and terror of their flight from Corbera were gunned down by enemy patrols combing the right bank with the zeal of duck hunters. (A favored diversion was chasing unarmed men into the river in order to target-shoot them like bottles or tin cans as they floated downstream.)

When Commissar Gates reached the Ebro late Sunday night, his large group had been reduced to two men, counting himself. During the day they had been bombed by a small airplane, shelled by artillery, and finally split asunder when they ran into an enemy patrol. Gates and a comrade ducked behind a stone wall and scuttled away from the others. It was dark when they reached the river, and they decided to swim over at first light. As they approached a small hut to catch some sleep, a voice inside cried out in alarm. It turned out to be George Watt and six other Lincolns. Here all of them slept for the first time in over forty-eight hours. On Monday morning they ripped the wooden door off the hut and dragged it to the water. After stripping naked—in the excitement Gates kept his hat on—they pushed off, the four nonswimmers holding on to the door. When the current caught them, the latter panicked and tried to climb upon the door, which sank. They drowned. Only Gates, Watt and two others gained the opposite shore. On bare feet they crossed a field of cockleburs and dropped, naked and exhausted, along a roadside "too beat to care." A short time later an automobile drew up and three correspondents got out—Ernest Hemingway, Herbert L. Matthews, and Sefton Delmer (London *Daily Mail*). They had rushed down from Barcelona when they heard that the Lincoln Battalion had been annihilated. After interviewing the four survivors, Hemingway shook a burly fist at the far shore and shouted, to hills devoid of auditors, "You Fascist bastards haven't won yet. We'll show you!" [12]

With countless variations, the saga of Commissar Gates was repeated up and down twenty miles of riverbank. Lieutenant Leonard Lamb, who did not swim, attempted to crawl across the partially submerged skeleton of the bridge at Mora but had to turn back when he reached a yawning gap in the middle. Farther downstream he was ferried across by Spanish guerrillas. Fred Keller swam the Ebro not once but three times in order to show reluctant men how easy it was. Easy for him, not them—because they could not swim. He saw them machine-gunned by a Fascist patrol on the west bank. One small group luckily found a small boat and pushed off. Once afloat they discovered that the oars were missing. Paddling with their arms, they managed to reach the other shore but only after a five-mile ride downstream. A painstaking midwestern student with a scientific turn of mind constructed a raft for his clothes and equipment and pushed off into the current. On the far shore he noted with satisfaction that his clothes were perfectly dry. After dressing, he let the raft drift downstream and moved "inland." A few steps later, he found that he had landed on an island! He swam the remaining distance in full regalia. Most members of the Lincoln Battalion, however, never made it across the Ebro. There were hundreds of unchronicled personal tragedies the details of which can never be known.

On the hillsides around Darmos, two miles east of the Mora bridgehead, survivors of the Lincoln Battalion set up a dreary little

---

[12] A short time later, according to Delmer, Hemingway hailed an American Negro on the Tortosa road and gave him a sermon on how good soldiers returned to battle: "Look, Comrade. We all of us got to die once. So we may as well die clean as die s . . . ty." Temporarily inspired, the "Boogy Comrade," as Hemingway called him, did turn back toward the front, although Delmer later saw him in Tortosa.

camp. Brigade trucks scoured the river roads of the east bank questioning Republican soldiers, *"Quince Brigada? Ha visto la Quince?"* At the end of the first week in April, the mail clerk arrived. His sacks bulged with letters and packages and he reeled off hundreds of familiar names. Only fifteen Lincolns were on hand to claim their mail. Initially, the men present answered "Dead" or "Missing" to names called out, but this became so depressing that they fell silent. The clerk's cheery cries sounded a roll call of the dead.

As though to compensate them for what they had endured (and he had avoided), Colonel Copic sent the men at Darmos bottles of *coñac* and champagne. "Blood liquor," commented one man bitterly. They drank out of tin cans—not to celebrate anything but to forget all. (Doubtless there would have been joyous toasts had they known that the Colonel was soon to be recalled to the Soviet Union—and not for the purpose of receiving a medal.[13]) For about a week additional survivors trickled into the Darmos compound, having just got across the Ebro or having fallen in with other units down, or up, the river. No one seemed to know where the Fascists were, and few cared—so long as they kept far away from Darmos. "The bastards are driving to the sea," opined an American truck-driver, a man with a road map and the leisure to study such matters. "If France don't come in now, we're frigged ducks. *Mucho malo. Mucho* friggin' *malo.*" (France did briefly open its frontier for the shipment of war matériel, then clamped it shut again. Smelling salts to perk up a dying man.)

On April 15, 1938, the Nationalists reached the Mediterranean at Viñaroz, thirty miles south of Tortosa, where troopers of the Army of Galicia were photographed cavorting in the sea with their leather boots on. (A posed film, obviously, for no good soldier would allow his shoes to get wet in this way.) On the same day, at Darmos, the Lincoln Battalion abandoned its hope that additional stragglers would cross the Ebro. A roll call counted 125 men present of the approximately four hundred who had gone into action at Batea two weeks before. It was the same old story, but no less tragic for being recounted once more: the Lincoln Battalion had gone into battle and had been destroyed. Yet the consequences were probably worse than those in the past. Jarama, for example, had slaughtered the innocents but in a legitimate battle. However, the retreat from Batea had turned willing soldiers into frenzied animals, had broken their collective

---

[13] Copic, like Gal, is supposed to have perished in the military purges, *c.* 1940.

identity, and had forced them to consider that the Republic was doomed to lose. No survivor of that horror, that nightmare-come-true, would ever forget his total helplessness as his world smashed to bits around him; nor would there be, as there were after the Jarama massacre, new replacements to retissue the deep psychic wound. From this time on, with few exceptions, the war in Spain was less a war to win than a disaster to escape from.

There were diversions. Mr. John Little (*né* Picallo), the New York Executive Secretary of the Young Communist League, a busy man with an important title, arrived in Spain with a gift of a million cigarettes for the XV Brigade. Mr. Little had originally hoped to turn over the cigarettes at a ceremony honoring Commissar Dave Doran, the most famous Leaguer in Spain. Doubtless he was shocked to learn that Doran had vanished at Corbera. On his return to the United States, his office produced, with amazing speed, a forty-five-page pamphlet titled *The Life and Death of an American Hero*. Dave Doran thereby became a Marxist martyr. (The author, one Joseph Starobin, admired Doran enormously but had never had the privilege of serving under him in Spain.) Soon, at rallies of the party, the League, and the Pioneers, crowds were singing:

> Oh, we have come together
> From the forest and the plain.
> We are marching for our future—
> Hand in hand.
> With the banner—
> Of Dave Do-ran.

Oblivious to all this hagiolatry, the men at Darmos meanwhile enjoyed the cigarettes. For the first time there were enough to go around.

13

⊞ Prisoners of Starvation

> If your fellow-countrymen must come all the
> way over here to fight in a war that concerns
> only Spain, they should realize that their
> chances of being killed may be greater than
> of being sent home after a paternal scolding.
>
> —Nationalist officer to American
> journalist (May 29, 1938)

As a result of their Aragon offensive, which had gained the sea and cut the Republic in half, the Nationalists were exultant and optimistic. On April 20, 1938, from his administrative headquarters in Burgos, General Franco announced that "the war is won." [1] Just two days later, under a press release titled A TOWER OF BABEL, Burgos authorities issued a specific count of XV Brigade prisoners captured during their offensive. These included 141 British, 49 Americans, 21 Canadians, 18 Cubans, 12 Argentinians, 4 Filipinos, 1 Mexican, 1 Icelander, and 1 Chinese. Names were not given. The announcement came as a surprise. In the past, the Nationalists had customarily denied that Internationals existed in their prisons, because admitting their presence was tantamount to assuming some kind of responsibility for them. However, since General Franco considered that the war was practically over, it is likely that he planned to barter these prisoners for diplomatic recognition on the part of the countries concerned. Unfortunately for the men being held, they had become commodities whose value could be determined only after a long period of diplomatic horse-trading and haggling.

Early in May, Charles S. Bay, the U.S. consul at Seville, was in-

---

[1] The General seemed to enjoy the sound of this sentence, since he had used it before when the Alcázar was relieved, when Malaga was captured, when Bilbao fell, and when the Republicans were forced to evacuate Teruel.

vited to come to Burgos. Presumably the Nationalists wished to purchase forty American schoolbuses for an odd purpose: they wished to
inaugurate a series of "Battlefield Tours" commencing in June. An
influx of international visitors (non-Comintern) was anticipated, for
as the newly appointed director of tourism said, "It is not often that a
country at war invites tourist travel." [2] Indeed, it was not. The Department of State had instructed Bay to inquire about the American
prisoners while in Burgos, even though the Government repetitiously
and earnestly denied "official" interest in or responsibility for them.
Whether it was suggested, during Bay's conference, that forty American lives might be traded for forty American schoolbuses is not
known, but it was not unlikely. In any event, nothing was accomplished: Franco did not obtain his schoolbuses, nor did Bay visit the
prisoners. There is strong evidence that the Department of State refused to believe that the Nationalists had more than a dozen Americans: their claim of holding forty-nine sounded preposterous.

All the while, in the United States, there was a buzz of interest
in—but certainly no clamor about—the Nationalist *communiqué*
announcing the existence of American prisoners. It was to be expected that the *Daily Worker,* with no specific information whatso-
ever, would print several lurid *exposés* of "Fascist atrocities in the
concentration camps of Franco's Spain." These made good reading,
but were, of course, barren of relevant facts: how many men were
prisoners, who they were, how they might be released. Three months
passed and no additional news came to light about them. Since no
diplomatic representatives or war correspondents had seen them,
there was no guarantee that they existed at all. Whenever the subject
came up, the Nationalist authorities hid behind a hedge of silence,
probably because they had failed to win the war as had been expected
and because they could not decide what the prisoners should be
traded for. The Department of State maintained only a perfunctory
interest in the matter, largely because the prisoners, if they existed,
further tangled the delicate web of nonintervention in the Spanish

[2] This announcement prompted Thomas Wolfe to write, with baleful irony:
"I should like, if opportunity presents itself, to visit the various craters and
ruined masonries throughout the town of Barcelona, paying particular attention to the subway entrance where a bomb exploded, and where one hundred
and twenty-six men, women, and children were killed in one economical
gesture. I should like . . . to pay a visit of devotion and respect to the
Chapel . . . where General Franco's wife and daughter go to offer prayers for
the success of the Defender of the Faith."

Civil War. The presence of American volunteers was embarrassing enough to the United States: the existence of American prisoners was a diplomatic nightmare. If the captives were repatriated to the United States, the Government might have to prosecute them for military service with a foreign power. More embarrassment. If the Government tried to recover them, would not American Rightists raise a storm of protest? More trouble. It was more convenient to ignore the problem and hope that it might evaporate.

The person most responsible for publicizing the plight of the prisoners and for oiling the apparatus of repatriation was William B. Carney, *The New York Times* correspondent in Nationalist Spain. It was ironical that "General Bill," as he was called by his detractors —and there were many of them—was regarded by most Lincolns as a Fascist sympathizer.[3] In truth, Carney was not unsympathetic to Nationalist points of view, especially as these pertained to the role of the Church in Spanish affairs. Not only was he favored by Franco's press officers, but he also had access to a variety of "unofficial but usually dependable" sources of information. But he was foremost an energetic journalist with a keen nose for a good story.

As early as March 14, Carney had spoken briefly to four American prisoners captured at Alcañiz and had subsequently learned that they had been executed, without trial, by an officer of the *Tercio*. Then on April 3, he interviewed six Americans picked up in the Gandesa area. They had been brought to the General Military Academy in Zaragoza and expressed their great surprise, not only at being taken alive but also in having been brought to Zaragoza in the comparative comfort of trucks and boxcars. Five of them fervently denied that they had ever been combatants—the customary ruse to avoid execution. But John Logan, a thirty-three-year-old sailor from Boston, bluntly swore that he would "fight to the end in this war against world Fascism." These men were sent, Carney learned later, to a monastery near Burgos, but he did not believe the *communiqué* claiming forty-nine American prisoners of war. His own sources put the figure at eighteen. For weeks he badgered Burgos authorities for permission to visit the prison but encountered only courteous evasion. Finally, early in

---

[3] Among other things, it was alleged that Carney, who had covered the Republican zone for *The Times* before Herbert L. Matthews appeared on the scene, had once written a dispatch explaining the location of Republican batteries in the Madrid sector. I have not been able to find this dispatch in *The Times* file.

July, his visit was authorized. He collected eighteen cartons of cigarettes and drove out to see his fellow countrymen.

The abandoned monastery of San Pedro de Cardeña rears its squat
limestone bulk out of a remote hollow in the hill country six miles
southeast of Burgos. Exclusive of the subterranean dungeons along
the northern side, the main building consisted of vast, empty naves
and three stories of monastic cells. Tiny windows with broken panes
and rotting sills looked out over the medieval walled enclosure of
dovecotes, toolsheds, crumbling stables, chicken coops, and dung
heaps. A low wall of bleached stone surrounded the establishment,
taking in a fine stand of walnut trees on the hill behind the monastery.
Outside the not very formidable wall stood ramshackle hostelries
once used by pilgrims, now used by guards. San Pedro sometimes
rated footnote recognition in Spanish history as the burial place of El
Cid Campeador until Burgos city-fathers carted off the bones to the
city hall.[4] An equestrian statue of the celebrated Moor-killer (how *he*
would have been surprised at General Franco's *entente* with Spain's
ancient enemies!) still remained over the main gate, although the
hand and sword of his outstretched arm had been broken off by anti-
clerical protesters in the 1830s.

Carney was met by a doleful commandant, a major well past the
age of retirement, who had a long list of grievances against his American prisoners. He said that they were "rebellious against all discipline," that they objected to compulsory attendance at mass because
they were not Catholics, and that they discussed "political and social
doctrines almost to the exclusion of every other topic." Worse than
this, they employed what bad Spanish they knew to make disrespect-
ful gibes at Nationalist leaders, politics, and religion. (Among other
things, they baited their guards by claiming that the stubby arm on
the statue of El Cid was making the clenched-fist salute of the Popular Front!) The major deeply regretted that his guards perforce had
beaten some of them for saluting the Nationalist banner "with upraised fist rather than open palm." The Americans, opined the major,
were shameless incorrigibles who failed to understand the criminality
of their professed political beliefs. Fearing that the three thousand

---

[4] While it is hardly a pressing point, one might mention that the well-
traveled bones of El Cid returned to San Pedro de Cardeña following the
Spanish Civil War. It would have been ironical had El Cid and the International prisoners inhabited the same abode, but they missed each other by a
few years. Since San Pedro suffered a devastating fire early in 1967, there is
no telling where the bones are now.

Spanish prisoners also incarcerated in San Pedro might be polluted, the International captives had been isolated from them.

A succession of massive wooden doors opened and banged shut before Carney reached the inner courtyard of the monastery. Here the major left him alone, surrounded by tiers of seemingly empty windows. A ground-level door swung open, and the American prisoners shuffled out into the morning sunshine. As though on parade, they formed silent lines facing him, glowering with sullen hostility. Carney could scarcely believe his eyes. Having expected only eighteen, he counted eighty. But their appearance, even more than their number, shocked him. At the front he was no stranger to the misery and grubbiness of men in war, but as he later wrote, "I was not prepared for the rough aspect of the ragged, dirty, mostly unshaven crew confronting me." It was like a preview of Dachau or Buchenwald. Grimy flesh lay visible through rents in grimier rags. To obtain tobacco and extra morsels of food, they had long since sold every decent stitch of apparel they had possessed. Most were barefoot because guards had forced them to trade shoes—Nationalist leather being worthless stuff. Some were merely skin and bones, barely able to stand. Realizing that the power of publicity might be able to pry open the doors of San Pedro, Carney asked them to write their names and hometowns in his notebook. Five prisoners, who made no secret of their contempt for "General Bill," refused. One man signed what must have been a comic pseudonym—Luis Busto Bango of Grasselle, West Virginia. All but three of the prisoners had been picked up within a two-week period of Aragon retreats, four months before. No one had any news about what had happened to Merriman beyond having heard that he had been "cut off while defending a hopeless position." [5]

Their primary interest lay in discovering whether there was any effort being made to free them. Two weeks before, an American consul had come to San Pedro, but he seemed to them to be unsympathetic to their grievances (including, among others, a protest against being forced to salute the Nationalist flag).[6] They urgently needed

[5] There had been rumors that Merriman was imprisoned in the Jesuit Commercial College in Bilbao. Carney did not ask about Doran.

[6] Charles S. Bay came to San Pedro on June 24 to talk with twenty prisoners selected by the warden. His confidential report to the Department of State said that the men were in "good condition," their food was "plain and nutritive," their hospital facilities were "adequate" although latrines and lavatories were "distinctly insufficient." According to him the "only criticism was about permission to write letters for money." From his report the Depart-

decent food, medicine, and surgical services. Since their arrival, one American had died of dysentery, one of pleurisy, and two of appendicitis. Many men still carried bullets and pieces of shrapnel in their limbs and bodies. With them were several surgeons who had begged the authorities for instruments and anesthesia, but these requests had been turned down on the ground that these items were required at the front. The only medication available was aspirin, which had to be requested five hours in advance. One of the worst cases was Charles Barr of Steubenville, Ohio. His left eye had been blown out by shrapnel at Belchite, and lodged next to his right eye was a tiny piece of metal that had to be removed, lest a jolt sever the optical nerve and blind him permanently. The men were bitter about the way guards had buried one of their comrades: "just dumped him in a hole in the field by the river" even though they had taken up a collection to buy him a wooden coffin.

When Carney asked who would pay their fare back to the United States in the event they were released, their spokesman said the money should be paid out by the same agencies that sent them over. (Only five men in the group had paid their own way.) At first, no one would say who supplied these funds, for they understood that such persons or agencies would be liable for prosecution and they had sworn not to divulge the source. But when Carney explained that prosecution depended upon proof of written contract, they told him they had been sent by the Communist Party or by "one of the organizations working with the party such as the North American Committee or the Friends of the Abraham Lincoln Brigade." The five men whom Carney had interviewed previously at Zaragoza now denied that they had enlisted because they needed a job: political reasons were the sole factor.

Before the interview ended, Robert Steck of Davenport, Iowa, pulled up his shirt to show red welts on his back, the punishment for not kneeling in church. Among the last questions put to Carney were who Joe Louis would fight next and whether John L. Lewis had formed a third party. "Anything else?" Carney asked. "Yes," said Charles Barr, "why aren't you wearing your Fascist uniform?" Carney laughed. "Do you really believe I am a Fascist or have ever worn any Fascist uniform?" Most of them grinned. One man said, "Skip it." As

ment would necessarily have concluded that the conditions at San Pedro, while not comfortable, were far from wretched. Carney would not have concurred with this summation.

he turned to leave, he wished them good luck. One of the unregistered, hostile five spoke for the first and only time: "I don't want any of your luck!"

On July 11, 1938, *The New York Times* ran on its first page WRITER SEES 80 AMERICANS HELD IN SPANISH REBEL CAMP. Carney's article listed seventy-five names followed by their hometowns. Immediately there was a powerful outcry on behalf of the prisoners. On the following day a *Times* editorial reflected the national mood by declaring that these men were "more Americans than Internationals." Far from the stereotype of the bomb-throwing Bolshevik, they sounded "like homesick and stranded Americans, concerned about what's going on back home and how to get there." On another page of the same newspaper, David McKelvey White, a former Brooklyn College professor who had briefly fought at Brunete before taking over the FALB, denied flatly that his organization had at any time recruited men for Spain. But he did go on to say that the FALB was prepared to post funds with the Department of State to finance the return of the prisoners. (His fund-raising campaigns were clearly not hurt by this new publicity.) And within two weeks, prodded by Carney's dispatch, the Department of State announced that negotiations were in progress to obtain their release.

Even though the negotiations were to drag along slowly, without the initiative of the much-abused William B. Carney they might have commenced too late or not at all. The prisoners were known by name. Burgos was now responsible for them.[7] They could not "disappear" like so many other International prisoners. The Department of State was now responsible for negotiating for their return; the FALB, for assuming the financial burden. Yet Carney, the best friend the men at San Pedro ever had, continued to be libeled as a "pro-Fascist." [8]

The dean of the American prisoners at San Pedro de Cardeña was Louis Ornitz, a twenty-seven-year-old organizer for the Amalgamated Clothing Workers Union of New York. As one of nine children in a destitute immigrant family, he had learned elementary survival in an East Side slum, but in Spain he had escaped death only through

[7] Responsible morally, not legally. Since the war in Spain was a civil commotion, both sides dealt with prisoners as political criminals rather than ordinary prisoners of war.

[8] After the war Carney received a decoration from the Knights of Columbus but nothing from the Franco government.

downright good luck. Way back at Brunete (July, 1937) Ornitz had driven a salvage truck that collected shell fragments: the Republic needed the iron. When the front collapsed, he was ordered to haul away two artillery pieces from a threatened sector, but no sooner had he loaded them on his truck when a company of Moors surrounded him. One grabbed his head and forced his mouth open while another examined his teeth. Fortunately for Ornitz, he had never had a cavity in his life. As they marched him to the rear, he watched them straddling the bodies of dead and wounded, employing little rocks to peck out gold fillings. The sergeant in charge, a Spaniard, edged near and pointed to his ring, which had a red star enameled to a gold background. Ornitz promptly passed it over: Moors were said to cut fingers from hands to obtain rings. The sergeant warned Ornitz never to admit that he was a combatant—only an ambulance driver assigned to drive a truck against his will. Otherwise: the Spaniard pointed to a ditch, where human feet protruded through a shallow covering of earth.

At headquarters an officer with a perfect Oxford accent asked him how many Americans were fighting in Spain. "Fifty thousand," replied Ornitz, "with tanks and planes arriving every day." The officer lacked a sense of humor. While a guard twisted Ornitz' arm behind his back, the Oxford voice continued, "We know all you fellows who believe in communism are Jews." Yet unaccountably they seemed to accept his ambulance-driver disguise. Other International prisoners with whom he shared cells were dragged out and shot, but Ornitz, though beaten up repeatedly, escaped execution.[9] After a series of provincial prisons and castle dungeons near the Portuguese frontier, he was sent up to Santander with fifteen other Internationals for incarceration with twelve hundred Spanish Republicans. Once each week the prisoners were turned out into a large pen and permitted to receive visitors. On their first Sunday the Internationals collected four gunny sacks of tobacco, sausage, chocolate, and bread from friendly local people, until guards dispersed the crowd.

In the spring of 1938, Ornitz was sent to San Pedro, which housed about two thousand Spanish prisoners undergoing an intensive program of political purification. Pupils who passed this course were released from prison on condition that they enlist in the Nationalist

[9] Ornitz later said that he was beaten whenever the Nationalists received a setback in the war and that, for this reason, he looked forward to being beaten. But one suspects that this is masochism recollected in tranquility.

Army. (The course was not offered to International prisoners.) Since the major in command of San Pedro spent most of his time in the *casino* at Burgos, a stocky sergeant known as El Palo (The Stick) ruled the prison with a hardwood club slightly smaller than an ax handle. His Spanish was so rapid and idiomatic that few Internationals could understand it, yet failure to respond instantly meant a drubbing across the head or shoulders. El Palo harbored no particular grudge toward the prisoners: he beat his own men the same way, for this was a time-honored custom of the Regular Army.

During his nine months of internment in twelve different prisons, Ornitz met no other Americans until mid-April of 1938, when he was awakened by a commotion in his cellblock. "What's going on?" he shouted. The answer, in English, startled him, "What the hell do you think is going on!" The voice belonged to an old comrade, Matthew Dykstra of Los Angeles, a truck driver picked up among the British fugitives at Calaceite. There were so many new arrivals that Ornitz at first thought the entire XV Brigade had been captured at one swoop. In all, there were 450 Internationals from twenty-five different countries, most of whom had been taken during the Aragon retreat.

They were bitter, debilitated, demoralized, and apprehensive. Erratically fed, endlessly photographed, repeatedly threatened with execution, they had been paraded like Roman slaves through the streets of a dozen Nationalist towns in their bloodstained rags and had been compelled to salute with outstretched palm the Nationalist flag at patriotic rallies. Through fear and despair, some captives had already tried to curry favor with their captors in order to win a morsel of extra food or to gain a promise of survival. A hierarchy of "rats," as the stalwarts called them, worked as go-betweens and informers. A Portuguese volunteer named Lieutenant Fuentes, once of the Mac Paps, who knew that he would be executed if he were ever returned to Portugal, had eagerly divulged the number and location of the XV Brigade when he was captured on April 1. And a German known as "Rin Tin Tin" sought to please his captors with a tale of how he had ridden a white horse through the lines to escape the Communist oppressors of the Interbrigades. Military discipline had been replaced by jungle law, and hyenas were king beasts.

Commissar Carl Geiser, who was among the group at San Pedro, was in grave danger. When the Italians had confiscated his *livret militaire* near Batea, he assumed that execution was a certainty. But as the days passed by and the prisoners were shifted from one Aragon town to another, it dawned upon him that his papers had been lost or misplaced, perhaps permanently, and that his captors thought he was an ordinary soldier. At Alcañiz, where they stayed briefly in the church, the men voted not to reveal that he was a commissar. But shortly after their arrival at San Pedro, Lieutenant Fuentes and a Cuban prisoner were overheard talking between themselves about the possible advantages that might accrue to them if they turned Geiser in. Such divisive poison required a harsh antidote before it infected everyone. The medicine came in the form of a committee who backed the "rats" into a corner and warned that if anything happened to Geiser, neither would leave San Pedro alive. Nothing is better for unity than discovery of a secret enemy within. Next they cast out the go-betweens and instituted a tougher line of resistance to the regimen of the prison. (None of the Dartmouth pranks of Joe Dallet at Ceret, however, for they knew that no sympathetic photographers were waiting outside.) If a man were beaten, they clamored in chorus, which seemed to take the fun out of it for the guard. If cudgeling did not cease, it nevertheless diminished. Years of party discipline and warfare with armed goons on the picket line had taught these men that timid acquiescence to wrongs served only to perpetuate them.

After the first week at San Pedro, Geiser found more difficulty in restraining the men from rash acts than in making them buck up and resist. Each day, for example, the Internationals were lined up outside facing a fenced-off plot containing an immense map of Spain created from growing plants (the Republican zone in dull green grass, the Nationalist in brilliant, multicolored flowers). Here they earned their right to breakfast by engaging in a cheerleader exchange of patriotic shouts with a prison officer.

"*España!*" shrilled the officer, his palm shooting into air.

"*Una!*" (one) intoned the Internationals.

"*España!*"

"*Grande!*" (great) mumbled the chorus.

"*España!*"

"*Libre!*" (free) yelled the Internationals in a thunderous battle-cry, the point of which was not lost upon the Spanish prisoners, whose cellblocks reverberated with defiant shouts of "*Libre! Libre!*" as though this were a call to arms. It was a grand moment—tattered men in poor health, without legal protection or even human rights, breaking out in revolutionary defiance against a hated ideology. But the warden speedily broke the mood, not by creating martyrs of a few but by withdrawing food from them all. San Pedro de Cardeña was not a bourgeois jail but a totalitarian penal colony that ground down prisoners by the solemn weight of a massive indifference to their welfare. The men were far too hungry to engage in hunger strikes.

The monotony of the prison routine suggested the recurring images of a feverish dream. Breakfast was unvarying—a *gazpacho* consisting of hot water, vinegar, garlic, olive oil, and bread crumbs. At first, many men refused it because it aggravated their dysentery, but on cold mornings they had to have a hot drink and there was no other choice. Then came a course in elementary Christianity taught by a priest who seemed to think that Karl Marx was a Protestant theologian. On the wall was a map of Spain with a hand-lettered inscription Above Spain Only God. To bait the priest was often dangerous, for the prelate could invoke the secular arm of El Palo. To question him about a point of doctrine was a waste of time, for it brought forth a lecture prefaced by "It is a complicated world—you do not understand these things and must obey those of us who do. . . ." At the end of every six-week period the course ended; then at the beginning of every seventh week it began again with the same scholars, none of whom ever seemed to pass. Like God, the course was eternal.

Lunch meant a bowl of lentil soup, which passed through innards like gravel, with an occasional topping of a single sardine per man. "Those sardines saved us from starving," remembered a survivor. "The oil was so rich." Afterward there was free time—too much of it. In the whole prison only one English book existed, *Lawrence of Arabia*. Since everyone wanted to read it, the pages were torn out and divided among section leaders for oral reading to their men. It was not an ideal book for men locked up in prison. When Geiser requested reading matter printed in English, he received reams of anti-Communist propaganda. Joyously the men ripped them apart and fashioned packs of cards. This enraged the successor of El Palo, the lieutenant known as "Tanky". (He had been wounded in a tank by a shell fired from a XV Brigade antitank gun and actively disliked the Anglo-Americans.) He demanded that someone read one of the pamphlets aloud while the others listened. There were no volunteers. Finally a Welshman, encouraged by the bull-pizzle in Tanky's hand, was prodded to the front, where he struck a lyceum stance and opened a pamphlet. While Tanky and the priest watched over his shoulders, the Welshman solemnly read in English—"Mary had a little lamb, its fleece was white as snow, and everywhere that Mary went, the lamb was sure to go. . . ."

Afternoon was an endless period in which the men were aware of their own rotting condition. Five hundred men had to share five cold-water taps and five "egyptian" toilets—noisome holes. It was never possible to bathe or to wash clothes, which stiffened on them like suits of cardboard. Twice during their long residence at San Pedro they were marched to bathe in a distant icy stream. Although their heads had been shaved to the skull, they were never deloused. Fastidious prisoners rolled up their blankets in the morning to trap the lice inside, then employed the afternoon unrolling slowly and crushing them with their fingernails. There was infinite time to contemplate their misery and wretchedness. The prison at San Pedro was worse than that at Bilbao, where inmates learned simple trades like crutch making, or Belchite, where they trucked away rubble, but at least it was better than the camp at nearby Lerma, which was filled with cripples, faceless creatures, and ghastly human relics neither fully alive nor wholly dead.

Dinner was a plate of beans and some bread—although twice a week they got a stew made of bones, sausages, and beans. During the entire period of their imprisonment they received lettuce only twice and other green vegetables not at all. In summer they could buy, if they had money, braided strings of onions from *campesinos* hawking their truck in the vicinity. Teeth loosened and fell out, gums became pulpy, sores festered, and rheumatic agues known as "San Pedronitis" wracked their bones. Five hundred Internationals lived in two long halls and slept on straw pallets lying on the flagstone floor. In summer they nearly suffocated in the rank, foul air. In winter they stuffed rags and paper into broken windowpanes and bedded down in groups of two or three to keep warm. Their infirmary consisted of a raised wooden dais at the far end of their hall. Elsewhere in the prison there was a fifty-bed hospital run by nuns, but this was regarded as nothing more than a dying place. Six out of every ten hospital cases never recovered. An American with lung cancer begged his comrades not to send him to the hospital. He wanted to die among friends. So they kept him there, carrying him around like a child until he became a husk and died.

To combat the deadening ennui that was endemic to San Pedro, Geiser and others organized SPIHL, an acronym for San Pedro Institute of Higher Learning. Originally the Institute provided courses in contemporary history, heavily slanted toward Marxist interpretations (probably the only such courses in Nationalist Spain). But the men were sick and tired of polemics and propaganda, and most of them boycotted the courses. Beginning in September, SPIHL offered a revamped curriculum billed as "free—non-sectarian" in which the "unpopular courses have been dropped" in favor of nonpartisan offerings. The institute began its fall semester in the black, with 169 *pesetas* in cash, a dictionary, a six-book reference shelf, and a ream of paper. Eventually there were twenty-one courses in eleven languages taught by instructors ranging from a member of the British Zoological Society to an Indian fakir whose specialty was palm reading. Each class was assigned a section of whitewashed wall as blackboard; students sat cross-legged on the stone floor. The priest seemed dismayed by this competition to his theological seminars.

The commissars had fair success in keeping spirits up by collective activities. Robert Steck founded a newspaper called *Jaily News,* and a short time later an opposition sheet called *Undercrust* appeared. They made chessmen out of soap, masticated paper, and bits of wood carved with sharpened spoons. Even Tanky developed a grudging admiration for the prisoners when Hy Wallach, a New Yorker, defeated thirty men simultaneously in a chess tournament to which the guards were invited.

But as weeks turned into months, temporary diversions palled. No news came concerning their release, and the war dragged on and on.

During their first months at San Pedro, the International prisoners feared that they might be executed before the outside world even learned of their existence; later they feared that they would all perish of debilitation and disease before anything would be done. Visitors began to arrive, but still nothing happened. Whenever Red Cross or diplomatic delegations came to see them, guards issued knee-length smocks to cover their nakedness. To reveal the true condition of their apparel, some of the British tucked the smocks into their trouser rags on an occasion when Sir Robert Hodgson of the British Mission to Burgos came out to San Pedro. Sir Robert had the surface mannerisms of a Colonel Blimp, but he was horrified to find fellow Englishmen treated this way by Spaniards—of all people. Stopping in front of a tattered Scotsman, he blurted out, "Rather ghastly—what?" To which, in his best Oxbridge accent, the Scotsman replied, "Rawther!" Doubtless because of Hodgson's protests to Burgos, the prisoners soon received shirts, trousers, and rope-soled sandals.

German prisoners suffered the worst harassment at San Pedro, because as anti-Fascists they were enemies of their own government, which had intervened on the Nationalist side. Alone among the International prisoners they did not want repatriation, for the conditions at San Pedro were not as bad as those in German concentration camps. All prisoners were privately examined by a plainclothesman whom the men assumed to be the Gestapo agent-in-residence.[10] He took their head measurements to prove that they were of degraded, non-Aryan stock, and his photographer took their pictures, many of which were published in Nationalist Front periodicals in neutral countries.[11] While this agent had only a perfunctory interest in the Americans, he spent a full day with each German prisoner and boasted that his organization had assembled a file of two million "Reds" in Spain. His photographer, however, had no stomach for this work; he drank heavily and sometimes surreptitiously passed on a ten-*peseta* note to the prisoners.

San Pedro was poorly, even absurdly, guarded, but among the International prisoners only six Germans attempted a prison break. They climbed out of a window one night while the others sang noisily to distract the guards. At the morning rollcall Tanky discovered that six men were missing and demanded to know where they were. No one answered. From the ranks he pulled "a mousy little Pole who never did anything" and formed a firing squad. In the nick of time somebody reported the window. In an ungovernable rage, Tanky picked out four men at random—two were Americans—stripped them naked, and lowered them into a deep cistern below the courtyard. By this time everyone was frightened, even the guards. The Dogberry comedy evoked at first by Tanky's befuddlement had soured. As soon as the major learned what had happened, he hurried over, ashamed and horrified, and had the victims hauled out. None of them was physically hurt, but it is alleged that one of the Americans

---

[10] In view of General Franco's very Spanish distrust of foreign meddling into domestic affairs, it is unlikely that this official belonged to the Gestapo. Nationalist Spain was never a puppet state of Nazi Germany.

[11] Usually pictures of Negro and Jewish prisoners labeled "typical International prisoners taken by the Nationalist Army." Their magazine in the United States was *Spain,* published in English by the National Spanish Relief Association, which also sponsored a propaganda broadcast, *The Hour of Spain,* over WHN (New York) every evening except Wednesday at 11 P.M.

lost his mind. Days later the bodies of two of the escaped Germans were dragged in for the prisoners to see, although it was rumored that the other four had safely reached France.

Late in September the prison was stirred by rumors that release was in the offing. Hopes soared but drooped again when only fourteen Americans were selected for repatriation. These were long-termers like Louis Ornitz, dangerously ill like Charles Barr, or family men like Sam Romer. They were to be exchanged for fourteen Italians held by the Republic.

On October 9, 1938, the fortunate fourteen, dressed in warm but seedy clothing, filed across the International Bridge at Irun without looking behind them. On the French side of the bridge waited a swarm of cameramen, reporters, diplomats, and spectators. Receipts were signed and countersigned before the gaunt men were turned over to David Ameriglio (alias Leeds), the representative in France of the FALB, which had arranged for their passage home. In the washroom of the Hendaye station, Ameriglio had the men don brand-new Republican Army uniforms. But as they came out, *gendarmes* drove them back inside again: in France, they were told, wearing the military uniform of another power was forbidden. Balked by red tape from advertising the International Brigades, and reluctant to let them wear Nationalist gifts, Ameriglio shopped in Hendaye and bought blue-denim overalls, which they put on over their uniforms. For a time, French medical authorities threatened to quarantine them, but after a short hassle the men were vaccinated there and then for smallpox. Finding no other legal technicalities or restrictions applicable, the French allowed them to continue to Le Havre.

Disembarking from the *Queen Mary* in New York on October 18, the former prisoners found two hundred sympathizers with a band. They were not free men—not yet. The FALB hierarchy escorted them crosstown to a dinner at the Commodore Hotel, which kicked off a new fund-drive for $150,000 to bring home all members of the Abraham Lincoln "Brigade." One of the ex-prisoners, Norman Dorland, made a speech that was so impassioned that it was amplified and published in *New Masses*. In it, he told how the Fascists collaborated with the Gestapo, shot and beat prisoners, and deprived sick men of medical attention. Dissemination of this *exposé,* considering that more than sixty Americans still remained incarcerated at San Pedro, was a shocking example of the kind of cynicism that places more value upon a few pieces of silver than upon human lives.[12] Doubtless angered by reading this account of their war crimes, the Nationalists abruptly broke off negotiations with the Department of State for releasing other Americans.[13] And that was how matters stood until the end of the war.

In November the first snows fell upon San Pedro de Cardeña. Not until April 22, 1939, did the next group of seventy-one men cross into France. On August 25, eleven more passed over. Franco's prisons were finally emptied of remaining Americans when eight men, including the ill-fated Whitey Dahl, were released in March of 1940.

Among the last American prisoners of war to leave Spain was Lawrence Doran of Los Angeles. He had spent two years in jail because the Nationalist authorities could not be sure that he was not Commissar Dave Doran, formerly of Albany, New York.

[12] Louis Ornitz also wrote a monograph titled *Captured by Franco* sponsored by FALB, but this was sensibly withheld from publication until May, 1939, at which time most of the other prisoners had been released from San Pedro.

[13] Part of the delay resulted from the timidity of the Department of State in accepting responsibility for the American prisoners. At one point in the negotiations all the Americans could have been released *en masse* had the American Government been willing to supply a warship for the return of an equal number of CTV prisoners waiting at Alicante. Washington was horrified at the suggestion that an American naval vessel might be employed in transporting Italian combatants from Republican Spain. As a result of this policy of "scrupulous nonintervention" in Spain, both the Republicans and Nationalists became irritated with the United States official. Thus it came about that American prisoners of war were held back long after other International prisoners.

14

ꙮ The Sixth Column

When soldiers desert twice they get
shot.

—Lincoln officer to Herbert L.
Matthews (April 9, 1938)

In the aftermath of the Corbera disaster, at least a hundred American volunteers, taking advantage of the widespread dispersion of Republican forces in the Ebro zone, deserted the front altogether.[1] Mingling with the thousands of refugees who choked the roads leading south to Valencia or north to Barcelona, the deserters sought not only to evade Fascist patrols but also to escape the hawkish eyes of SIM officers, the Republican secret service, whose job it was to compel others to keep up the good fight. They fled on foot, rode freight cars, hitched rides on trucks, hoping that in the present disintegration of the Republican Army they could find a haven in France, in Gibraltar, in North Africa. Every nerve and muscle told them that they had been outmanned, outgunned, and outgeneraled. Wherever they looked they saw doom, disaster, and defeat. If the fifth column consisted of Nationalist sympathizers among the civilian population and army, these constituted a sixth column who added to the confusion and demoralization by attempting to secede from it. They were not defeatist but defeated.

From Le Havre to Casablanca the waiting rooms in the United States consulates filled up with bitter men who had escaped Spain and

---

[1] The exact number will never be known. I have compiled a list of forty-eight men who deserted *successfully* (that is to say, who reached the United States) between April and July of 1938. Yet my list is by no means definitive. It is not unreasonable to estimate that for every man who escaped, at least one other tried.

266

now sought passports and passage home. (Consulates in Spain were now regularly watched by SIM agents, who apprehended deserters in the shadow of the American flag drooping from exterior windows.) Nearly every vessel departing from the Channel ports carried stowaways. When the *Normandie* docked in New York on May 30, its passengers included Ernest Hemingway, who told reporters that the war in Spain was becoming a bore, and four Lincoln stowaways, who were hustled off to Ellis Island. Two Americans got as far as Cork, Ireland, where they were jailed for vagrancy. French frontier guards estimated that six hundred Internationals had crossed into France immediately following the Aragon retreat.

Escaping from Spain often required more cool nerve, and always more ingenuity, than was required in meeting the Fascists headlong. A Milwaukee volunteer stole a small launch in Valencia harbor and rowed it at night far offshore to minimize the possibility of attracting patrol boats. Just before sunrise, he opened the engine hatch and found nothing inside except a pile of moldering ropes! He hailed a French ship, which waved back gaily. On the second night he rowed the launch back into the harbor, moored it where it belonged, and got away by train to Cartagena. There he found a British ship bound for Gibraltar. A brash Californian bought an elegant, but second-hand tweed suit in Barcelona and rode to Port Bou in fine style, where he bluffed his away across the frontier with a seaman's card and a tale that he had been left behind by his ship while carousing in Barcelona. A deserter from Frederick, Maryland, walked across the Pyrenees. He traveled by night and holed up in culverts by day. It took him eleven days to cover the final twenty-five miles. Another volunteer, apprehended in the Pyrenees, clung stubbornly to his ridiculous story —that he had been told that the Lincoln Battalion had been sent up there for "reorganization."

Most of these who escaped from the International Brigades and returned to the United States slipped quietly into the anonymous stream of American life. Though they had done what they felt they had to do, they were nevertheless not proud of having quit. They did not intend to play into the hands of Franco apologists and Red baiters, whom they loathed, by disparaging the Lincoln Battalion or Republican Spain. They sat tight and kept their mouths shut. Yet there were a handful so embittered by their experiences in Spain, particularly by the role of the Communist Party in a *soi-disant* People's Army, that they willingly, even eagerly, recounted their adventures in print or testified before the House Un-American Activities Committee, chaired by Martin Dies of Texas. The tenor of their denunciations, as might be supposed, was that the leaders of the brigades were, as one witness expressed it, "political Capones" who "paraded under the guise of an ideal appealing to the highest social and moral feelings of men." The rectitude of the Republican cause was never the issue: only the cynicism and opportunism of the Communist Party policies in Spain.

Typical of the testimony before the Dies Committee was the tale of Alvin I. Halpern, an ice-cream worker from Boston. (It is not clear whether he acquired his nickname "Hot-Air Hal" before or after his defection from the Lincoln Battalion.) Recruited by one Mannie Blanke at the CP headquarters on Essex Street, Halpern had gone to Spain in June, 1937, with the understanding that he could return after six months of service. His passport was confiscated at Albacete and never seen again. At Tarazona during the Dallet regime *The New York Times* was banned from camp because of its "Fascist tendencies." During the autumn Halpern fought in the Aragon offensive as a runner for Major Robert Merriman—"Murderman we called him." He said that if a volunteer protested against the policies of the battalion he was called a "Fascist provocateur" and was sent to a detention camp where "they would shoot you down." He had never witnessed an execution, but he had seen undesirables assigned to labor battalions and sent into no man's land for the enemy to pick off. When battalion authorities refused to repatriate him after six months' service, he resolved to escape.

When the Nationalists broke through in Aragon, Halpern was in a hospital near Sagunto, recuperating from a wound. He slipped across the Mediterranean to Oran only to learn that the United States consul had died two weeks before and the French authorities wanted to expatriate him to Spain. In desperation he clung to the British consul, who arranged for his passage to the States. Still wearing his Republican uniform, Halpern confronted Mannie Blanke on Essex Street. Blanke called him a deserter. Halpern retorted by asking why Blanke had never gone to Spain. Blanke insisted that he had flat feet. Halpern came back with, "I saw guys going over the mountains into Spain with wooden legs, and other men aiming rifles who couldn't see ten feet beyond the barrel." The upshot of this dialogue was that Blanke promised him fifty dollars for a suit of clothes and money to have his wound treated, but when Halpern bought the suit he could not collect the money. Irate, he revenged himself by selling his story to the Hearst press. A few days later he was blacklisted by his union, an affiliate of the CIO.

Much less spectacular was the testimony of Abraham Sobel, another *protégé* of Mannie Blanke. A twenty-three-year-old night-schooler at Northeastern University in Boston, Sobel had met Blanke at the Ukrainian Workers Club and had been intrigued by the prospect of "taking a crack at Hitler"—Blanke's major pitch. In applying for a passport, Sobel was instructed to say that he was bound for Australia; a friend of his posed as a theological student going to Palestine. Before leaving Boston, Blanke told him, "You can leave Spain whenever you like." Sobel was stalked by misfortune. He was aboard the *Ciudad de Barcelona* when it sank off the Catalonian coast. After barely reaching shore alive, Sobel resolved to drive a truck in Spain in order to come out alive. But at Brunete his ammunition truck blew up under him. At Teruel he went into the line, against his will, and was wounded on his first day in action. He learned of the Aragon debacle while hospitalized at Mataró, a coastal town north of Barcelona. Patients were being asked to volunteer to brace the crumbling front. Sobel quickly dressed and hiked cross country to France. Once home, he wanted to make the Communist Party "pay through the nose" for what he had gone through. Americans in Spain, he claimed, were virtually prisoners and most of them would return immediately if they could.

Other testimonials like the foregoing were given, briefly publicized, and generally forgotten. Sobel did not speak for Joe Gordon; Halpern did not reflect the experience of Douglas Roach. But these antipathetic case-histories nonetheless serve as a reminder that to volunteer for Spain was not necessarily to enlist in a holy cause. Behind the mask of idealism lurked methods as tyrannical as those that men came to Spain to destroy. The greatest misfortune is that to cope with attacks from deserters like Halpern and Sobel, all too many "stalwarts" of the Lincoln Battalion overreacted. They became habituated to a single-dimensioned interpretation of their Spanish experience. Details that somehow darkly mirrored the cause—whether party or Republic—they buried within themselves. Loyalty in time became a virtue more prized than truth. And the pity is that many men were willing to accept outrageous distortions only because, in so doing, they reaffirmed their loyalty. [2]

[2] In the words of one veteran: "Of course, we all knew of bad things which happened in Spain, but I would not defile the memory of good things by telling you these."

Just after the stragglers of the Lincoln Battalion established their camp at Darmos in April, 1938, an order came down to John Gates from division headquarters: court-martial all deserters and execute some of them as examples. Massive desertion must never be allowed to happen again. Accordingly, Gates held a trial attended only by members of the brigade commissariat and party cadres. Three deserters received death sentences: an Algerian, a Spaniard, and an American seaman named Paul White. White, whose real name is said to have been John Quincy Adams, had deserted the battalion at least once before. The executions were carried out that same night. According to the testimony of Major Humberto Galleani,[3] the firing squad was commanded by a "very excitable" New Yorker known as "Ivan."

Some of the Lincolns bivouacked in an olive grove heard shots in the night, followed by silence. Then four of them were shaken out of their blanket rolls by one of Tiny Agostino's henchmen, who handed them shovels and said, "Follow me, and don't ask questions." They dug a trench in the hillside and dumped in a body. Needless to say, they asked no questions. By morning everyone in the battalion knew that someone had been shot without knowing who. Later in the day the men were told that Paul White had been executed as a deserter "by the unanimous decision of the battalion." It was frightening. They, the men of the battalion, had decided nothing, much less decided it unanimously. On the next day, according to John Gates, a countermanding order came down from division, but it arrived too late for Paul White.[4]

[3] Humberto Galleani, an officer in the Italian Army during the World War, was a naturalized American citizen who had come to Spain in October, 1936. As an officer in the Garibaldi (Italian) Battalion, he had taken part in the defense of Madrid that autumn. During the spring of 1937 he engaged in a propaganda tour throughout the United States, where he was called by *Newsweek* "the first American volunteer." Upon his return to Spain in September, 1937, Galleani was assigned to the staff of the XV Brigade and became increasingly disaffected by the Communist domination of the Interbrigades. After the war, objecting to what he considered the Moscow orientation of the VALB (Veterans of the Abraham Lincoln Brigade), Galleani attempted to found an opposition organization of International veterans. He set up his headquarters in the office of *Il Martello*, an Italian-American newspaper with Anarchist leanings, but many veterans who agreed with Galleani ideologically could not abide him personally. "A first-class prima donna," recalls one of these. The group fell apart.

[4] As it happened, many Lincolns disliked White for personal reasons and were less disturbed by his death than they might otherwise have been. (Per-

In view of the massive waves of desertions throughout the International Brigades, André Marty established a prison in a ruinous castle situated on a crag above Castelldefels, a resort town south of Barcelona. From April, 1938, to January, 1939, the warden was none other than Tiny Agostino, whose goon squads ransacked Barcelona, picking up suspected deserters. Since fugitives usually headed for either the American consulate on the Plaza de Cataluña or the Hotel Majestic, headquarters of the international press corps, these places were kept under surveillance at all times. On one occasion the German poet Ernst Toller was mistaken for a deserter. One of Agostino's guards, a hulking American Negro, backed him against a corridor wall with the muzzle of his machine gun and demanded that Toller establish his identity. "Let's hear your friggin' poems!" Toller recited and proved who he was. It was probably the most earnest reading he ever gave. Even Agostino himself was often seen prowling the halls of the Majestic, looking for men who might wish to spill all to American journalists. Once, during his absence, his second-in-command at Castelldefels, a rummy from Texas, wrote *salvo conductos* for everyone in prison, including himself, and led an abortive prison break.

Early in April there was a brutal execution outside of Tarragona. Several hundred stragglers from the International Brigades had been rounded up and herded into a minimum-security corral north of town while commissars sorted them into three categories: 1) those to be returned to their units, 2) those to be placed into labor battalions, 3) those to be imprisoned at Castelldefels. Bored with this rigmarole, three Finns—Oskar, Niemin, and Kulksinem—broke out at night and went on a drunk in Tarragona. Jailed by civil authorities, they promptly escaped and returned to the compound early in the morning. There was a court-martial, but few men took it very seriously. At dusk all the inmates of the camp were marched down to the beach and lined up facing the sea. An ambulance arrived and from the van stepped down the three Finns, cheered as though they were celebrities. Commissars thrust rifles in the hands of eighteen prisoners, all of them either British or Americans, and ordered them to serve

haps the commissariat singled him out for this reason.) It is common nowadays to find Lincoln veterans denying any knowledge of the White affair and affirming their opposition to executions generally. Yet a poll of three hundred veterans, published in 1940 under the title *Fear in Battle*, reveals that 70 percent of them agreed that a two-time deserter ought to be executed.

as a firing squad. Everyone seemed to enjoy this spectacle enormously and waited for the finale—a commissar dashing in from the wings with a last-minute reprieve. Even the three Finns regarded the affair as melodrama. But suddenly shots were heard—the indecisive crackle of rifles not fired simultaneously. Someone yelled, "My God! They're killing them!" Two of the Finns writhed on the sand, but Niemin had been only nicked. He stood upright like a bewildered animal as bolts rattled nervously in rifles. Even after the second volley, Niemin, who looked as though he had been splashed with red varnish, still stood on his feet. Then he lifted his right fist, shook it, and toppled over. Was that last gesture a Popular Front salute or a challenge? A vast stillness fell over the watchers as a Boston Irishman went forward to fire three pistol shots into the prostrate bodies. Three Finns had come to Spain in the name of Liberty and had perished in the name of Discipline.

How was international solidarity to be maintained in the growing atmosphere of despair and vindictiveness? As though the Fascist Army in their front were not menace enough, the Lincolns now had to contend with the police agents in their rear. Under certain circumstances a sacred word can become a monstrous oath. There was the case of the American volunteer on leave in Barcelona who encountered an old friend from training camp. "Hello, Comrade," he said congenially. But his friend grabbed him by the lapels and hissed, "If you ever call me that again, I'll *kill* you!"

For years names of volunteers circulated underground, surfaced now and then, and finally became time-encrusted and forgotten. There was always a whispered hint, never anything proved, connecting the name with execution in Spain: Harry Perchuk, Marvin Stern, Vernon Selby, Edward Scheddin, Albert Wallach, Abraham Eisenberg, Harry Crain, Bernard Aronofsky, Lester Jacobs, Edward Montmarquette, Moritz Matz, George Wilbur, Pete LaMotte, Mike Bartulla, and others never whispered about because their imprisonment and disappearance were never known. Like the volunteers swallowed up in the areas of rapid Nationalist penetration, these men, too, were the tombless unknown soldiers of the Spanish Civil War.

If dead men told tales, this chapter would be longer.

15
◧ The Far Shore

"The men don't know it, but we're
expecting a large-scale attack at three
in the morning. The Fascists have
brought up five or six divisions."
"Oughtn't they to know it?"
"They will if it comes off; if it
doesn't, it's better that they don't."

—Commissar, First Company,
to acting adjutant

On the sunny hillsides around Darmos, the Lincoln Battalion regrouped to pick up its pieces. Several times each day a preposterously huge railroad gun poked its snout out of a tunnel that passed under the village like a subway. It fired an angry salvo at some target miles out of sight beyond the Ebro and then ducked back inside its hole again. The gun, which fired a missile nearly as large as a small automobile, was a blustering, useless museum-piece, but its thunderous noise was somehow heartening. The old Republic seemed to have a bang or two left in her. Yet among the Lincolns, more fundamental weapons were in such short supply that rifles had to be collectivized so that sentries could be armed. A section leader wore a cavalry sword tucked in his belt. The men had no more equipment than a comparable number of hobos. During the first weeks of April, 1938, Darmos was less like a military camp than a Hooverville.

No one was quite sure who commanded the battalion, and no one much cared. Probably it was Aaron Lopoff, a twenty-four-year-old New Yorker who used to write pulp fiction. At Batea, one short week before, Lopoff had been only an adjutant company commander; but at Darmos he found himself the highest-ranking officer in the camp. He was short, dark, and swarthy—the kind of bayou chieftain one could imagine rallying around Jean Lafitte. The men thought the world of him: he had no truck with newfangled theories or utopian nonsense. Instead of "Dear Comrade" lectures, Lopoff had his men build *chavolas* out of cane and pine boughs to ward off the sun and rain, and he let them work the bile out of their systems. "Re-education" was out of the question: men who had swum the Ebro had earned the equivalent of post-doctoral degrees in survival. They would have found "comic-star" lessons a trifle jejune. They responded to orders like a pack of snapping curs. Lopoff let them snap.

They were, confessed one man later, "a crummy bunch." Soldierly appearance seemed to have been washed away as completely as military discipline in the bitter waters of the Ebro. As much as anything else they resembled a paramilitary force badly whipped in a border incident. Gaunt, ragged, and unshaved, they might have served as models for cartoon Bolsheviks as featured in the Hearst press. There was a Puerto Rican who, whenever planes came over, had to clamp a stick between his teeth to keep from biting his tongue. There was an eighteen-year-old who invariably prefaced his comments with "I'm dumb, yellow, and worthless." There was an old miner, broken in mind and body, who sat for hours engaged in furious argument with some antagonist locked within his own brain. And there was a youth who ran amuck, shouting with hysterical wisdom, "They kill all the good guys. They're all dead and gone with their guts hanging out. I seen guys died had more room between the eyes than they got across the shoulders." Some of the favorite conversations dealt with how they could steal a truck and hightail it to the French frontier or whether they could make North Africa in a small sailing craft.

Within a few days of their escape across the Ebro, Vincent Sheean of the *Herald Tribune* hitchhiked down from Barcelona to see them. The arid, rolling landscape reminded him of New Mexico except that it was jammed with people, refugees largely, whose overloaded carts clattered eastward. Everywhere he found an army of shreds and tatters, subsisting on implausible hopes germinated in very dry soil. Everyone was anxious. Prospects seemed always to be prefaced with "Maybe . . ." or "If only . . ." Those men with a penchant for *weltpolitik* grasped at the Czechoslovakian crisis, hoping for a world war that would compel the democracies to aid Spain. They would break off personal narratives in mid-passage to ask eagerly, "What is Chamberlain going to do?" Sheean knew that Czechoslovakia was being sacrificed to Hitler, but not wishing to compound their despair, he said nothing about it.

On the periphery of the Darmos compound, a few *campesinos* worked in the fields among almond trees in pink blossom. But the pastoral landscape was suddenly darkened by the wings of Italian bombers, Savoia-Marchettis, which scattered bombs nearby. Someone counted fifty enemy planes—and not a single Republican fighter in the sky. An American lieutenant, who had quit law school to come to Spain, said, "When I start to make laws, I'm going to make a law abolishing all airplanes. Anybody who makes an airplane or sells one or flies one will be put in jail." All concurred. Each man had a story about his own encounter with a Fascist plane during the past month of retreats. A tall Tennessean who wore, without clowning, a clown's costume so ragged that even his patches were patched, had the last word: "All airplanes are Fascist airplanes, until you know different." After Belchite, all Lincoln men looked upward.

Moving on to the brigade autopark, Sheean found a strange assortment of vehicles, half of which belonged in junkyards and the other half in automotive museums. Because of an uncanny knack in picking the bones of abandoned vehicles and "organizing" parts from other outfits, the XV Brigade normally rolled when other brigades walked. (Mechanics liked to boast that some of their rolling stock consisted of the trucks that had carried the first Americans up to Jarama, even though no individual part, nut, or bolt was still the same.) But this period was past. Almost everything had disappeared during the retreats. Lieutenant Louis Secundy chewed a piece of grass and grinned while squawks came through his telephone, demands for transport that did not exist. What he now had were "old rattletraps held together with safety pins and string." A Jewish lad of seventeen working on an engine told Sheean, "I promised my mother I would be home for Passover, but I guess I won't get there now." The brigade ambulances were no better. Both sides regularly employed them as staff cars and ammunition vans; therefore ambulances were regularly shelled and strafed. They cluttered the courtyards of hospitals, punctured with bullet holes and rarely with a pane of window glass intact. There was one exception—a brand new ambulance in green-yellow camouflage stenciled "From Workers in Barre and Montpelier, Vermont."

On April 8, Vincent Sheean revisited the Lincolns and found a semblance of order gradually returning. On the main highway a sign, painted in neat letters, read LINCOLN BATTALION. The rags were gone and men had shaved. Food had improved, for Comrade Archer, a Negro cook, was back in the kitchen, where he magically turned dried salt cod into crab-meat salad. Sheean was sitting in the command post when shouts were relayed up the line of *chavolas* as an angular figure, all legs and beard, jogged up the hill. Spanish voices shouted, *"El Lobo!"* The wolf had come back. He had to bend double to enter the shelter. "You built this thing plenty low," gruffed Captain Milton Wolff. "I guess you guys didn't think I was coming back." He shook hands with his men brusquely, as though trying to ignore how glad they were to see him. Wolff had wandered alone for five days before swimming the Ebro far downstream. With his resurrection to command, wounds and scars began to heal.

The Ebro front, except for random bombing and barrage, was dead. The Nationalist offensive had swerved south along the sea toward Valencia. The Republicans north of the Ebro were far too weak to attempt anything beyond counting their greatest blessing— the presence of the river as a moat between them and the enemy. Even after hospitals and labor camps had been swept clean of convalescents and skulkers, the Lincoln Battalion numbered only two hundred Americans. "Maybe we'll be sent home," went the latest rumor, soon proved erroneous. To bring the battalion up to paper strength, five hundred Spanish *quintos,* or draftees, arrived in Darmos. With zealous illogic George Watt, the new Lincoln commissar, explained to the Americans that the International Brigade was about to assume the role that had always been planned for it: foreign volunteers were to be instructors and models for Spanish soldiers. (The men recognized this as a glaring rationalization: *quintos* replaced Internationals only because the sources of the latter had dried up.) The new men, Watt warned, might lack "political convictions" because they had been denied "the opportunity for education." The old hands were to assist the new men in developing an understanding of the anti-Fascist crusade. What this came to, in essence, was that Americans were expected to explain to Spaniards why Spaniards should fight their own war. Probably at that very moment, on the other shore of the Ebro, Nationalist officers were employed in identical chores—explaining to moon-faced peasants why they had to fight in *their* war.

The *quintos* were primarily girlishly soft, lazy youngsters of the late-acne stage who had been forced into manhood by possession of uniforms and weapons. The run of them expected, like most Spanish youths, to become bullfighters. Along with their regulation kits, they brought cardboard suitcases and gunnysacks stuffed with the accouterments of barracks-room apathy: eau de Cologne, hand-knit sweaters, stacks of writing paper and little bottles of multicolored ink, bags of nuts, and even live rabbits. For them war was a homesick interlude made tolerable by playing el futbol, strumming guitars, and writing countless letters home. They enjoyed feeling and firing weapons—Hollywood had taught them that much—but in the manner of children engaged in imaginative sham-battles. Even though officially absorbed into squads and pelotones with the original Lincolns, they kept to themselves in xenophobic enclaves, no more interested in crossing the cultural and language gap than were the Americans. What did either group really have to communicate to the other? What shackle could be found that would link the worlds of Youngstown and Villafranca del Cid? Unlike the Republican militia of an earlier period, most of whom had been the products of rigorous indoctrination by trades-union organizations in the cities, the quintos were primarily rural or village youths uprooted from uncomplicated environments and transplanted into a politically convoluted war. What did they care about the Czechoslovakian crisis, the theories of Carlos Marx, the dangers of Trotskyite deviationism, or even the complacency of Alfonso XIII? Why should they be grateful to the extranjeros for coming to Spain in order to teach them how to kill other Spaniards? They made no trouble, they listened politely while commissars tried to teach them the ABCs of dialectical materialism, and they asked no questions—probably because the issues were not important enough to them to justify a question. Given time and a few battles, those among them with harder grains would acquire a conventional attitude of hatred toward "the enemy" in the manner of any soldiers, in any war, at any time. What they actually were—as everyone knew but no one would say—was fodder for cannon to feed on. Or, as the Spanish express it much more metaphorically, they were carne de cañon (cannon meat).

No more Americans were being recruited for Spain. Instead, the FALB was raising funds to bring home the badly wounded.[1] Since the

[1] Wounded men had been returning home surreptitiously since Jarama, usually with the help of an independent Paris group chaired by Louis Bromfield called the Emergency Committee for American Wounded from Spain.

Soviet Union had stopped shipments of war matériel to Spain, the FALB sensed that the International Brigade would soon be written off and phased out. When the time came to repatriate the Lincolns back to the United States, the New York organization would require every dollar it could raise, unless the United States government could somehow be maneuvered into picking up the tab.[2] They did send, for booster purposes, six Jarama veterans back to Spain, including one-eyed Joe Gordon. On their arrival, they were widely photographed drinking wine from a *purrón,* smoking foul antitanks, and bucking up the younger men. Asked how he thought the war would turn out (a defeatist query), Gordon said, "We're here, aren't we? And we certainly don't think we'll be on the losing side." He went on to say that he was sick and tired of playing war games with salt cellars and toothpicks in a beanery behind the FALB office and that he would have come back to Spain even had it meant stowing away on a garbage scow. But these six Jarama veterans were the last leaves of a dead branch.[3] Spain was no longer the conscience of the Left. When the Soviet Union lost interest, most American Liberals became bored with the Spanish struggle. The avant garde of the party talked nowadays about whether international brigades might be organized to fight the Germans in Czechoslovakia or the Japanese in China.

The last volunteer was perhaps the most atypical of all. He was twenty-three, wore horn-rimmed glasses, was educated at Andover and Harvard, and was the son of Ring Lardner. With press credentials from the *Herald Tribune,* James Lardner had come to Spain originally as a fledgling war correspondent. He toured the Ebro front

When this source dried up, the FALB openly solicited funds for wounded veterans. On July 3, 1938, the first publicized group of wounded Lincolns, eighteen men, arrived in New York.

2 By no means as far-fetched as it sounds. In April, 1938, when it appeared that the Republic was ready to collapse, Secretary Cordell Hull, fearing that several thousand Americans would be imprisoned and/or executed by the Nationalists, notified his *chargé* at Paris that the cruiser *Raleigh* was standing by at Villefranche and would evacuate *all* Americans from Spain in the event of a sudden Nationalist victory. When the Republic held, the *Raleigh* went elsewhere.

3 Although the FALB sponsored no more American volunteers, a few individuals continued to go to Spain and to join the Lincoln Battalion, making their own arrangements and paying their own way. Probably the last would-be volunteers were seven Americans (four of them from Brooklyn) who were jailed in Le Havre on August 23, 1938, for having stowed away on the *Normandie.* Their pooled resources included $17.85, 3 Spanish *pesetas* (Republican), 30 French *centimes,* and 5 Estonian *kroons.* After jail terms they were deported to the United States.

in April and interviewed General Lister, but when his dispatch was edited away to virtually nothing, he seemed to lose his appetite for reporting. Within a week he showed his friends Ernest Hemingway and Vincent Sheean his list of nineteen reasons for joining the International Brigades, methodically divided into two headings: first, why he wished to aid the Republic, and second, what this experience could do for him. Sheean guessed that the Brigades would accept him in order to publicize him as Ring Lardner's son and would then put him in some safe spot far to the rear. Hemingway, on the other hand, tried to dissuade him, arguing that enlistment at such a late period seemed utterly wasteful.[4] Even Martin Hourihan, on his way home after nine months in Spanish hospitals, tried to talk Lardner out of it. Laughing at these objections, Lardner bought khaki trousers and a leather windbreaker (the Republic was short on uniforms, and Lardner felt a little guilty about taking one) and signed up. He left Sheean his books—*Fighting Planes of the World,* a stack of Lenin's pamphlets, an oversize Shakespeare, and a sheaf of Republican songs.

Lardner was sent out to Badalona and put into a camp containing *inútiles de guerra,* men deemed unfit for frontline service because of thievery, chronic demoralization, or habitual cowardice. For four days he lay about on a straw pallet listening to them cursing Doran, Merriman, and Wolff. Then Lardner deserted—to the front. Stopping off at the Majestic for a bath in Sheean's room, Lardner left him all his tinned food and cigarettes. When Sheean suggested that these might be more welcome at the Lincoln Battalion, Lardner said, "I don't want to go bearing gifts." Purged of his old self, he departed for Darmos, where he asked for no favors and got none. George Watt was very much impressed with the new volunteer, telling Wolff, "You know who he is—Ring Lardner's son." But Wolff, egalitarian to the bone, retorted, "Yeah, I know! What do you expect me to do about it? Put him in Company Three." The men accepted him easily, much to Sheean's surprise, for there were as he knew "some prize roughnecks in the brigade." Lardner never complained, behaved like a model soldier, and became corporal on his own merit. Party publi-

---

[4] After the Republic lost Caspe, Hemingway knew it was through. On March 30, he called upon Ambassador Claude Bowers to see about the immediate evacuation of all American wounded from Spain. According to his canvass, there were 30 in Barcelona, 382 in Benicasim and Saelices, and 125 in Murcia, all of whom could be evacuated in six days. He feared that if the Nationalists won a rapid victory, these men would be massacred in their hospital beds.

cists, however, capitalized on Lardner's presence in the battalion, for here was an all-American youth from a distinguished family—a perfect Popular Front news-story.[5] They would later discover that a Lardner wounded merited announcement in most American dailies, a Lardner dead was worth a column.

The four months following the Corbera encirclement were as quiet and as uneventful as the four months of the previous year following the Jarama massacre. On May Day the Mac Paps tried to stir up apathetic Fascists on the far bank of the Ebro by floating small rafts downstream bearing provocative signs like Los Españoles Nunca Sera Esclavos De Fascismo (Spaniards will never be slaves of Fascism). The Lincoln camp had been moved to Marsa, six miles east of Darmos. In the open fields outside town, May Day took on a county-fair atmosphere as the *quintos* won most of the contests in grenade throwing, infiltration (crawling without employing knees), and wheelbarrow races (of questionable utility in combat). The winners carried away boxes of Sunshine crackers and bars of Hershey chocolate as well as the approving smiles of a trades-union delegation which had come down from Barcelona to meet the famous Internationals and found, to their surprise, that most of them were Spaniards. Among the visitors was a busload of young girls of Anarchist persuasion who called themselves *Mujeres Libres* (Free Women). It had been hoped that they would live up to their name, but all of them pretended not to know what sex was. "All they were interested in was talking politics," recalled a disappointed volunteer. (A bathing-suit snapshot of one of these girls, a little on the beefy side, later appeared in the *Volunteer for Liberty,* the closest thing to a pinup ever to appear in its proletarian pages. Yet even this photography served a political purpose, for the young girl was "defying enemy aviation as she takes a dip in the blue Mediterranean.")

Late in May the brigade was suddenly called up, issued rifles, and trucked northward to the Lerida sector, where the Republic had launched an offensive to relieve pressure on the Valencia front. They were held in reserve to mop up enemy pockets after the enemy line

---

[5] *The Volunteer for Liberty,* for example, twice featured stories about James Lardner, once when he enlisted and again when he was promoted. Asked why he had joined the Lincoln Battalion, Lardner replied, "The cause is so plainly a worthy one that the question which the young men of the world should be putting to themselves is what justification they have for staying out of the struggle."

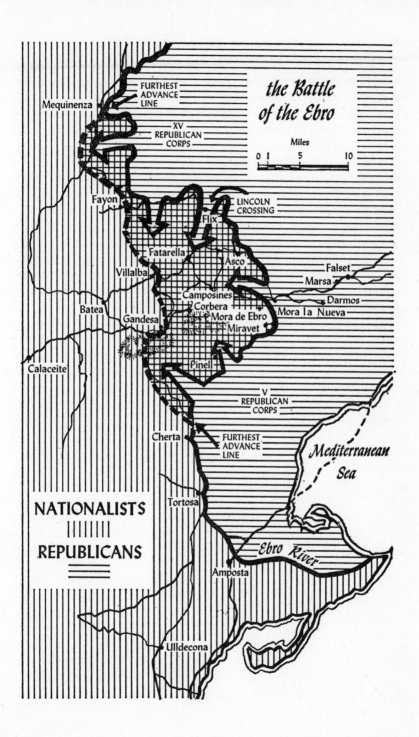

the Battle
of the Ebro

Miles
0 1   5   10

FURTHEST
ADVANCE
LINE

XV
REPUBLICAN
CORPS

Mequinenza

Fayon

LINCOLN
CROSSING

Flix

Fatarella

Asco

Falset

Villalba

Marsa

Camposines

Darmos

Batea

Corbera

Mora la Nueva

Gandesa

Mora de Ebro

Miravet

Calaceite

Pinell

V
REPUBLICAN
CORPS

Cherta

FURTHEST
ADVANCE
LINE

Mediterranean
Sea

Tortosa

NATIONALISTS

REPUBLICANS

Ebro River

Amposta

Ullidecona

had caved in. For a time they camped in a fine forest of pines, where two platoons of *quintos* tried out their new 7.65-mm rifles on a solitary squirrel, which escaped. When the rains came, they moved into big cattle-barns on the outskirts of Mollerusa, where they had a good time. They were snug, and warm, and a little high from the local wine. They sang funny bawdy songs and reverted to horse-laughing schoolboys. Some of the bitterness of the past months passed out of their systems. Artillery rumbled at the front, twelve miles west, but they moved no closer. The offensive was inexplicably called off, and they returned to Marsa. Odds went higher that the Lincoln Battalion would never again be used in battle. But John Gates, who had assumed Doran's post as brigade commissar, promptly scotched that rumor. "I hear men say that the XV Brigade will never go into action again. But I am here to tell you that it will . . . and when it does, it will maintain its tradition of sacrifice and courage." Gates' arm was as long as Doran's, but the fist was gloved.

June and July were hot, long months of monotonous waiting— whether for battle or repatriation no one knew. In the heat of the day not a breath of air stirred through the olive groves where the volunteers stripped down and lay baking in their reed *chavolas,* fighting a losing battle against flies. This was an epoch to be notched in their minds by flies, and a volunteer named Hank wrote an "Ode" to them:

> The fly, the fly
> Oh me. Oh my,
> It gets in my hair
> It sits in my chair.
> In spite of all "Flit"
> It gets in your s . . . .
> And then in soup,
> Oh my, what a scoop!
> It is on terms
> With all sorts of germs . . .
> When left in the open
> It's ill disposed.
> And therefore, *amigo,*
> Your fly—Keep It Closed.

Dysentery reached epidemic proportions, and the perennial jokes —"I could hit a dime at ten meters"—were no longer funny. Mail was irregular, men wrote insulting marginal notes to the censor, food worsened (little bread these days), and tobacco all but disappeared. The brothels along the beach at Tarragona did a booming business with the front so near, but overnight passes were hard to obtain, because these were too often a ticket for desertion. Each day from battalion headquarters near Marsa, a red-stucco villa with fifteenth-century vaulted cow-barns, the orders of the day came down with relentless monotony—target practice, maneuvers over hot terraces, scaling devil-tower mountains. But in the stifling heat it was difficult to implement such orders. Herbert L. Matthews came down from Barcelona in mid-June to watch three companies attacking a fourth, which defended the Darmos railroad tunnel. While the men sweated up the terraces, he stayed below with Wolff and the battalion staff, who offered the opinion that the tunnel would be captured, but not before suppertime—which meant cold meat and potatoes. They all agreed that this was a pyrrhic victory, at best.

June was also the month when Colonel Vladimir Copic was relieved from command of the XV Brigade. He departed so suddenly that he had no time for a swan song. Earlier, in a speech commemorating Dave Doran, the Colonel had taken a swipe at the Lincolns because they "refused to obey military procedures as to saluting and discipline." Little things like that mattered a great deal to Colonel Copic. Doran was his kind of man. (Although insiders claimed that Copic had never forgiven Doran for breaking into his hoard of edibles to feed the rank and file at Caspe.) The new commander, Major José Antonio Valledor, was a veteran of the Asturias fighting, where he had been captured and subsequently imprisoned in Pamplona. He helped to engineer a massive prison-break at Pamplona and escaped to France. Quietly efficient and unhistrionic, he was "less an opera star" than Copic.

To bring back the revolutionary luster of the Lincoln Battalion, George Watt, a wiry towhead whose political earnestness sometimes bordered on mystical devotion, instituted an elitist movement known as "Activism." He proposed a series of pep rallies and an Activist Congress by which "the military and political work of our brigade may reach new high levels of combative efficiency." To become a full-fledged Activist, one went through a Tom Sawyerish ceremony in which he vowed to obey ten commandments including, "Not to rest as long as there remains a soldier who is not an activist" and "To struggle without rest against pessimists and provocateurs." (Watt was restless, to say the least.) Some of the *quintos* rallied to the banner of *el activismo* with the zeal of youthful pledges of Sigma Chi, but most Americans shook their heads and referred to the movement as "scoutmasterish." They liked Watt personally, but they thought him hyperthyroid. They dubbed him "Kilowatt" and made up a rime about George Watt not knowing "what's what." Some men needled him by pretending they had formed an antiactivist order known as FONICS—Friends of the Nonintervention Committee—dedicated to the immediate withdrawal of all foreigners from Spanish soil, beginning with themselves. Scribbled on walls and etched on trees, FONICS was the KILROY of the Spanish Civil War. But all this was less subversive than good-humored. Their favorite song of this period had nothing to do with proletarian fervor, regret for dead comrades, or aspirations of the wretched of the earth. It was curt and nasty, and it was sung with mingled curses and laughter:

> March-ing, march-ing, march-ing,
> Always f . . . ing well march-ing.
> God send the day—
> When we'll—
> F . . . ing well march no more!

They cursed but did not whimper. They were a battalion of Falstaffs.

One night early in July there was an ominous night maneuver that left them "breathless and somewhat terrified." They moved out of camp with full equipment, marched nine miles across rough country, and at dawn reached a dry riverbed. Here they split into squads, paddled across the pebbled bottom in imaginary boats, and assaulted a mountain from which came harrowingly realistic rifle and machine-gun fire. Every day thereafter they crossed imaginary rivers and attacked deeply entrenched "enemy" positions. No explanation was given for these training maneuvers, but none was required. "Aha! We're going to cross a river," said one man, with mock puzzlement. "Now what river do you suppose *that* could be?"

Concurrently came a fresh rumor "straight from the horse's mouth" that the Internationals were to be separated from the Spanish troops in order to be counted and withdrawn from Spain. It was common knowledge that wounded men were being repatriated without reporting back to the battalion—a sign, perhaps, that this time the rumor might be true. Gates and Wolff repeatedly denied it, but in order not to dash their hopes, should the rumor not be true, they had to take a negative line. A question-answer routine made the rounds like a vaudeville exchange: "You heard the news?" "Sure, they're going to withdraw the volunteers from Spain." "No crap, and here I was planning to get married and grow up with the country."

There was now a single, overwhelming question: Which would come first, crossing the Ebro or withdrawing from Spain?

In the third week of July, 1938, the XV Brigade began a two-day march that led them into a thick canebrake near the Ebro river-town of Ascó. The men had not seen the river, but they could smell it close by. The brigade photographer, whose duties usually kept him in Barcelona, was on hand with bags of equipment. Obviously this was no training maneuver. On July 24, Captain Milton Wolff assembled his battalion and explained the plan of attack. They were part of a force of eighty thousand men who would cross the Ebro and, traveling light and rapidly, overrun the Nationalist positions between the river and Gandesa. The enemy lines were overextended, and their troops were very green. The first waves would cross in small fishing skiffs that had been hauled up overland from the Mediterranean; later waves would cross on pontoon bridges. Until these bridges were constructed, no tanks or artillery would be available to support them. (If the enemy air force knocked out the bridges, then what?) For the first couple of days they would have to live on iron rations carried with them or on captured enemy *intendencias*. If successful, the offensive would compel Franco to abandon his attack toward Valencia in order to meet this new threat against his rear.

It was an audacious plan. In effect they would be breaking the enemy line with nothing more formidable than infantry. But few of the Americans gathered around Milton Wolff in the twilight had much desire to add pages to Spanish military history. There was a pause. Thousands of frogs drummed in the marshes. Then Morris Micklenberg, a Jarama survivor and currently ringleader of FONICS, raised Everyman's question: How were they to get back across the Ebro? As with most old campaigners, it naturally seems to have occurred to Micklenberg that this offensive, like all the others, was doomed to fail. Wolff's brusque reply was a *double entendre:* "We're not coming back!" That was exactly what troubled Micklenberg.

In the remaining hours, veterans threw away all nonessentials. Even the *quintos* seemed to understand that where they were going was no place for guitars and suitcases. When the canteen came up on the supper truck, men bought overalls with big, roomy pockets (sixty *pesetas*—three days' pay) and filled them with chocolate bars, packs of cigarettes, and extra ammunition clips. Few men wore leather shoes. Most were shod in rope-soled *alpargatas* which laced up the ankles like ballet slippers and resembled, with trouser cuffs down, tennis shoes. The future was not bright, but at least their agonized period of suspense had ended. Men changed fatalistic grins. They had long ago abandoned hope of winning a war, and though they doubted they could even win a battle, they gamely congregated for another bloody round. They passed one another slips of paper on which were jotted names, streets, towns—just in case. (The battalion secretary rarely notified wives or parents when a volunteer was killed or wounded, because casualties produced a bad impression back home.)

Before daybreak they moved down to the riverbank, sensing rather than seeing the raw muscle of mule trains, columns of men, and trucks pulling skiffs and scows to the crossing points. Just at dawn the coffee truck bumped down a streambed, bringing a last delivery of mail. A few shells shrieked overhead and exploded in the hills far behind them. Already the first wave had crossed the Ebro. Crushing down the cane, the Lincolns reached the eastern shore. The wide river was spotted with colorful little rowboats that looked as though they had been picked up from a Catalonian tunnel-of-love. "It's Prospect Park in the summertime!" shouted the usually prosaic Lieutenant Lopoff. Climbing into the bow of a craft named "Muy Bien," Lieutenant Lamb struck a mock-heroical pose as Washington crossing the Delaware while his crew shoved off. It was July 25, the feast day of Santiago, the patron saint of Spanish infantry.

As the first group piled into the boats, an Italian trimotor, painted a nearly invisible pale-blue, droned down the river at an altitude of a hundred feet and scattered a load of bombs along the shore. Minutes later it returned, strafing the canebrake. On its third pass, nearly every man had a rifle or Dichterev ready and opened fire. The plane bounded upward, like a startled bird, and swung away. The men cheered and cursed. "That's the way to treat those bastards! Let him come back, the son of a bitch; we'll put some lead in his ass!" On the far shore a volunteer picked up a jagged hunk of shrapnel and examined it with admiration. "Boy, that could make a hole in you; *hombre,* that could do a thing or two!" But they had crossed the unlucky river without a casualty. Exultant, they pushed through red hill-country toward Gandesa, just twenty-one kilometers southwest.

The crossing came as a complete, dumbfounding surprise to the

Nationalists, who had not a remote idea that the Republican Army of the East had sufficient power or daring to fight a major battle with the Ebro at their back.[6] Within hours, Republican troops were pouring through gaping holes in the Nationalist line, the swath of their advance marked by billowing clouds of yellow dust. The Lincoln Battalion pushed warily across a wooded terrain, which some of them recalled from their flight to the river four months before. Behind them they heard bombers pounding the pontoon bridge points. Enemy observation planes buzzed them as they marched but dropped no bombs. Some men waved cheerfully to the surprised pilots; others sniped at them. As at Brunete, their worst enemy on this first day was dirt, sweat, and heat. Canteens were quickly emptied. Enervated by the torrid heat, weaker men dropped behind. Recollections of the trap that had been sprung upon them at Corbera forced them to proceed with inordinate caution, even though they failed to contact enemy patrols. Dusk found them on a piny ridge slightly east of Fatarella, no more than ten kilometers from the Ebro.

Before first light of July 26, Lieutenant Leonard Lamb led First Company into Fatarella and flushed out the enemy garrison, which surrendered *en masse*. The Lincolns breakfasted on captured chocolate, cookies, tinned fish in tomato sauce, and Italian cigars. When they learned that their captors were *internacionales,* the prisoners were petrified. Huddling together, dirty and dejected, they refused to lower their hands when ordered, for they assumed that this was an excuse for their captors to shoot them. Always they had been told that the Internationals killed their prisoners: that had always been given them as the reason why they were supposed to kill Internationals.[7] Instead of impounding them with a few guards, Captain Wolff dispatched them to the river, escorted by two entire sections of Third

[6] When General Franco heard the news, he said he was tempted to allow the Republicans to penetrate as far as they wished, then destroy them. Later in the day, while his staff watched in silence, he picked up a notebook and jotted down numerous calculations. Finally he said, "It is impossible for a fisherman in Galicia [his native region] to live decently on his present rate of pay." A short time later, however, he became deeply frightened when his forces were unable to push the Republicans out of the Gandesa salient. One of the civilians on his staff recalls that he once overheard Franco weeping, late at night, behind the walls of the Pullman compartment in which he traveled.

[7] A prisoner taken a few weeks later improved upon this story. He said that Nationalist officers told their men that the Reds fed their prisoners to the lions in the Barcelona zoo. When a XV Brigade captain asked him, "Suppose we were to shoot you?" he answered with a grin, "That would be the first truth Franco ever told."

Company. Few of these men returned to the battalion promptly, for on their way back they walked into an ambush.

Meanwhile Captain Wolff continued the advance toward Villalba de los Arcos, seven kilometers farther southwest, without making contact with the enemy, which had fallen back in apparent rout. Had liaison between the battalions been less imperfect, the Lincolns would have learned that the Mac Paps and British were then being engaged against Hill 481—soon to be known and ever to be remembered as "The Pimple"—which overlooked Gandesa two kilometers east of town and which had to be taken before Gandesa could be invested. But the Lincolns were in a byway of the developing battle. Never entirely certain where the enemy was, they continued to move timidly. By dusk of the second day they had failed to reach Villalba. Although their sunburnt skin scaled off in layers, the night turned so cold that the men slept dovetailed to one another in an olive grove.

Earlier in the day Lieutenant Jack Cooper of the brigade headquarters company had been ordered to set up his Maxims on a ridge near Venta de Camposines, the main crossroads between Gandesa and the Ebro. It was known that large pockets of Nationalists had been bypassed and isolated by the rapid Republican advance: when they attempted to break out, the odds were that they would appear in the vicinity of "The Crossroads." Since it was surrounded by jagged knolls overgrown in pine scrub, it was a poor position to hold with a small force. Late in the afternoon Cooper heard voices yelling *"Viva Franco!"* and sporadic rifle shots nearby. Before he could withdraw his guns, Cooper was overrun by swarms of Nationalists. Along with seven *quintos* he was taken prisoner and interrogated. "Where are your forces?" asked an officer. "Way ahead." "How many?" "Five army corps," lied Cooper. The enemy officers were unnerved at this information. For days they had been bedeviled by Republican patrols and had been subsisting on nuts and fruits picked off trees. Collecting their prisoners, the beleaguered Nationalists hid themselves in a thicket. In the morning an officer deferentially approached Cooper and said, "We surrender."

At midday of July 27, Lieutenant Cooper, who had once been sentenced to a firing squad by Dave Doran, marched into Brigade headquarters followed by 208 prisoners. "I didn't know until that minute that we had taken so many," he said modestly. Earlier he had been stripped of his pistol, bullet clips, and fountain pen. The most lethal weapon in his pocket was a soiled handkerchief.

On the third day, July 27, in the wooded hills near Villalba the Lincolns ran into their first serious resistance. Moors willing to fight had thrown up a line blocking the Villalba-Gandesa highway. The region was studded with scruffy hummocks sticking up like small islands above patchy fields planted in olive and vines. Without tanks or artillery to knock out opposing machine-gun nests it was poor country to attack across. Bullets whipped overhead as the volunteers deployed on lee slopes and crawled to the brows of hills to locate the enemy fire. To the north, in the direction of Villalba, a flash battle raged; to the south, toward Gandesa, were thunderous intonations.

Spearheaded by Lamb's First Company, the Lincolns quickly drove enemy snipers off the nearest hummocks and approached a valley several hundred yards wide. Fig trees and stony terraces separated them from an array of enemy machine-guns on the next ridge, a clean hump of earth like an Indian mound. Officers in front, the Lincolns attacked frontally, dodging downhill and using warped fig trees for cover. Once in the valley, officers picked out possible avenues to approach the enemy positions, only to learn that whole sections of the *quintos* had refused to follow them down. Mortar shells began to stalk terrace walls behind which they crouched. The attackers soon fragmentized into autonomous splinter groups. Men were being hit, and almost invariably these were the best men, those who had obeyed the order to attack. Lieutenant Lamb, the most experienced company commander, was shot through the hip. Pinned down in the valley, they could do little except wait until those behind them turned the enemy's flank. This was not done. A volunteer drifted back with a dangling red hand. "Does it hurt you?" asked a stretcher-bearer, a notorious malingerer. "No! It feels good—for Christ's sake!" blurted out the wounded man.

With each passing hour the firepower arrayed against them perceptively increased. Their three-day hike had ended: the enemy was establishing a front. Not until nightfall was Captain Wolff able to unify his command. In three days they had covered about eight miles.

Beginning at dawn of July 28 the Lincolns delivered three attacks upon the ridge, all of them beaten back. A thickset Negro from San Francisco named Luchells McDaniels bombed a pathway up the slope to within fifty yards of the first enemy gun before being forced to retire through lack of support. The *quintos* proved to be disappointing. Trying to force them over, Lieutenant Lopoff shot two of them in front of the others, but this extremity but frightened them more. Most of them cowered and refused to budge; they seemed indifferent to the mode of their execution—whether Nationalist planes strafed them, mortar shells doom-cracked about them, or officers kicked and goaded them. Taking that ridge was of absolutely no importance to them: they were perfectly content where they were. Nor were most of the Americans much more interested in advancing. They obeyed orders and did not desert—but all too many delayed, evaded, and lagged behind. During a mortar barrage Frank Stout, battalion scout, dropped down wearily beside Alvah Bessie, adjutant of Second Company. "I'm hoping to get hit," he said. "I've been wanting a nice little blighty for some time." A shell exploded almost on top of them, heaping them with dirt as though from a shovel. "Hurray, I'm hit!" he yelled exultantly. Eagerly groping his side, he examined his hand for blood, but there was nothing on it but dirt. "Shucks, I guess it was a stone," Stout said. (Four days later he was disemboweled by shellfire.)

Explosions rent the brittle fig trees, showering the men with green fruit warm from the sun. Figs passed through intestines like bits of sharp glass, but this was the only food available. In the middle of the afternoon shouts went up and down the line, "They're coming!" It was a Nationalist counterattack. They got behind knolls and frantically lobbed grenades over the crests, awaiting the imagined shock of long bayonets bearing down on them from the skyline. Men without grenades emptied clips into the smoke and dust ahead of them without picking out targets. The sole object was to surround their positions with a cordon of lacerating metal. The attack was beaten off. As the sun declined, the firing died down. In the past thirty-six hours the battalion had not advanced one foot. The element of surprise had been forever lost.

Elsewhere conditions were the same, or worse. The British Battalion had been cut to pieces on the slope of Hill 481, and the Mac Paps had finally been halted within sight of the soccer field on the northern edge of Gandesa.[8] The underlying fallacy of the offensive had become tragically clear: soldiers could be transported across wide rivers more readily than the heavy equipment necessary to supply and to

---

[8] Killed while serving as a company commissar of the Spanish Battalion was Arnold Reid, once in charge of the Paris operations. A top British Communist told Charlotte Haldane that Reid was killed on orders of "a member of the Politbureau of the American Communist Party." She never learned why.

support them. The Nationalists dominated the air. Far upstream, the enemy opened floodgates, putting the Ebro in spate and sweeping away pontoon bridges. Ambulances were so far down on priority lists that none was allowed to cross the river until the third day of the offensive. Those wounded in the first days had to be evacuated by hand, hauled on supply trucks, or dragged on *artolas* (crude litters) by mules. They accumulated on the western shore awaiting transportation on small boats, while their wounds clogged with the fine dust raised by hundreds of vehicles passing bumper to bumper on the roads. Survivors told shocking stories of how wounded men were robbed openly as they lay helpless on the riverbank and how stretcher-bearers picked through piles of wounded, taking men belonging to their outfit and ignoring the others.

Among the Lincolns, June 29 was a day marked by little activity of any kind. A diarist recorded: "Other attacks. None successful. Quiet day." The best the men could do was to snipe at the now-familiar ridge that had blocked them for three days. There were thousands of hills in Spain that looked exactly like that one. It had no special name—not even an elevation number on the topographical chart. If they took it there would be another one almost the same on the far side. It was a wart, a nodule, a bump—hardly worth making all this fuss about. Yet in the evening brigade told Wolff that it was the only point holding up the advance upon Gandesa from the northeast. It had to be taken.

July 30 was memorable for the breakfast—coffee, marmalade, ham, corned beef, and plums. It was the kind of rich fare given to condemned men before they walk the last mile. Two Spanish battalions attacked through the Lincoln lines and were slaughtered in the pale mist of first light. After this, handfuls of Americans ran down into the valley and took cover behind humps of dead and wounded. Wolff came over and demanded that the ridge be taken. Lopoff said it was impossible. "The kids won't go over. They're scared stiff."

"What'ya mean they *won't* go over?" demanded Wolff, in an ugly voice. "We've *got* to take that hill—brigade's orders." The phrase "brigade's orders" seemed to impress no one very much. They were not about to march into the jaws of death because some military genius running his eyes across the contour lines of his chart two miles behind the line had decided that the failure of the Lincoln Battalion to occupy one ridge had deprived the Republic of victory not only in this offensive but also, perhaps, in the war. Readers of

Tennyson might have been moved—but they were not. Wolff's instinct told him his men were right. For a long time he talked on the telephone with brigade; for a longer time he hunched over his maps. In the end he called it off. After nightfall they dragged their wounded from the bloodsoaked valley. Then they were relieved.

For another week the Lincoln Battalion was shifted about the sector between Villalba and Corbera in a "reserve" status. To be in reserve during the developing Battle of the Ebro meant that instead of being machine-gunned at close quarters, one was shelled by impersonal agencies at long range. The Nationalists had begun to pull their artillery from the Valencia front; and lining up their guns almost hub to hub, they laid down a wall of flying shrapnel to block the Republican thrust upon Gandesa. This Technique was appropriately termed *aplastamiento* ("plastering"), and the concussions were colossal and stupefying. Air-bound shells sounded like loosely coupled boxcars lurching through the sky or like empty garbage cans crashing down concrete alleyways. The explosions spumed up earth in the shape of instant trees, which broke apart in the air and rained down like metallic vomit. The earth shimmied like shook jelly, and shells blew a hole in it six feet wide and four feet deep. Amid such cosmic carnage and clatter the screams of the wounded seemed strangely detached annoyances, picayunishly irrelevant to the more important business of holding on to one's own head, or arm, or mind. As the earth exploded about them what happened to others was only pathetic, what happened to oneself was tragic. The men huddled together like sheep in a storm, vaguely hoping that the flesh of others might somehow cushion their own.

They called this place "Death Valley." (The ancient name was Venta de Fusil—or "Rifle Market.") It was a *barranca* leading up toward "The Pimple," which they were supposed to storm as soon as the barrage slacked off. Bad as it was, they were probably better off with the barrage than without it, for the slopes of "The Pimple" were already cluttered with bodies minced by shellfire. As it happened, there was never a lull in the barrage.

Thirteen days after crossing the Ebro, the Lincolns were ordered back to Mora de Ebro for rest and reorganization. The men were so overjoyed to leave "Death Valley" that they ran most of the way back to the Corbera road. Everyone knew that the offensive had been stopped; their own losses stood at 50 percent. The Ebro battle was conforming to the pattern of all other Republican efforts—Brunete,

Aragon, Teruel—in which a sharp spearpoint was filed away by attrition. Only the scenery differed.

In the moonlight the XV Brigade marched through Corbera, a deserted village of cardboard fragility except for the church, which still loomed enormously on the hill. Most of the buildings, where they stood at all, had been reduced to two-dimensional walls like the false props of a Hollywood town. Festering leather carcasses of mules and horses lay in the streets, but the solitary trace of humanity was the rotten-sweet smell of the invisible dead buried under the broken litter of the town. It had taken many centuries to fashion Corbera out of stone, and wood, and clay, but it took less than two weeks to bring it down.

For a week the Lincolns rested in terraced olive groves near Mora de Ebro. They received threadbare but clean clothes, and at night they bathed in the lukewarm river. The delousing machine could not be used because it puffed a telltale cloud of black smoke. During the day they lay on their backs watching the hawklike descent of enemy bombers upon the pontoon bridgeheads. One day airplanes dropped leaflets containing politely worded invitations to surrender:

> COME OVER TO US, with your officers or alone. Nothing will happen to you if you surrender: if not, you will all die, for you have no more bridges. In Franco's Spain, justice reigns; there is abundance, peace, and liberty. Come over to your brothers. Come over to our lines.

The *quintos,* whose initiation into battle had not been happy, read the leaflets reflectively, but the Americans chuckled over them. "Ain't got no union label—scab printing," said one. "Good ass-paper," said another. "We've run out of the *Daily [Worker].*" Nevertheless brigade caught wind of a rumor that fifth columnists planned an attack upon the Internationals, and Lincoln officers were instructed to carry pistols with them at all times.

Petitions to leave Spain continued to be passed on to Brigade Commissar John Gates, who reiterated that all the American volunteers would leave Spain together, or not at all. Once upon a time, no volunteer worth his salt had been willing to work on the staff of *The Volunteer for Liberty,* but now men who had written a line or two for high school yearbooks eagerly sought a job. The Battle of the Ebro was taking a bad turn—the Nationalists were counterattacking furiously—and men knew that soon they would be fitted into a quaking sector somewhere. The battalion doctor, William Pike, seemed to have the appropriate attitude—comic fatalism. As he told a veteran who reported to him with scabies, "It won't make any difference if you cure 'em; you're gonna get bumped off anyhow, and no one will look at you and say, 'Why how disgusting—he's got a skin disease.' " To buttress sagging morale, staff officers reported that the nature of the casualties in the recent campaign had changed radically: fewer men had been killed, more had been wounded. Here was food for optimists.

They waited, bored but at the same time conscious that boredom was preferable to what lay ahead after boredom ended. Louis Fischer of *The Nation,* who had helped to organize the Interbrigades at Albacete two years before, turned up at the rest camp. While the men sat cross-legged and respectful, Fischer, who was a liberal, pulled cigarettes out of a pack and distributed them much in the manner of a Santa Claus passing out gifts to underprivileged children.

The New York Times reported that James Lardner had been wounded in the back by shrapnel. (Actually he had been wounded in the rear end while escorting the prisoners from Fatarella, after he had climbed an apple tree for fruit.) There were other bits of news. A prominent plastic surgeon of New York, preparing to sail for Nationalist Spain, was enthusiastic about the opportunities lying ahead for his profession; he estimated that there were twenty-five thousand cases requiring plastic surgery in the Nationalist zone. Joe Cuban was dead. He had been among the eight Americans in Bill Harvey's squad at Jarama, the first Lincoln group to engage the enemy; a few weeks before, he had returned to Spain with Joe Gordon. And when Joe Louis knocked out Max Schmeling, some of the guys chipped in to cable congratulations for "kayoing the myth of Aryan Racial Superiority. You have joined us in dealing a blow against the enemies of democracy." Their limbo ended on August 14, when an order came to fill in latrine pits, turn in picks and shovels, and to stand by with battle kits.

Moving downstream by a back road to the cubistic hamlet of Pinell de Bray, they picked up the macadam road winding up through the Sierra de Pandols toward Gandesa, six miles northwest. After nightfall they turned off along a mule path that scaled upward toward peaks out of sight above them. This was alpinist work. How, they wondered, were food and water and ammunition to reach them at this isolated outpost? At daybreak of August 15, they found themselves on the spine of a saddleback hump known as Hill 666 of the Sierra Pandols. It was a windswept and treeless section of bare rock the color of bleached bone. Originally vegetated thinly with mountain gorse and stunted holly, the mountain had been burnt by incendiary bombs dropped by Nationalist airplanes to roast the living and the dead among the Republican troops that the XV Brigade had just relieved. They faced west, as though straddling the backbone of a colossal, scaly dinosaur. From higher elevations enemy machine-guns raked their position across a dip in the saddleback ridge. To their north was a perpendicular drop three hundred feet down to a mountain valley; from this cliff edge there was a bird's-eye view of Gandesa, only two miles away and eleven hundred feet below them. The view of the Gandesa valley was breath-taking. The whole battle was laid out beneath them like a scale model. It was immediately clear why the Nationalists wished to possess the long spine of the Sierra Pandols. If the mountain were ever lost, enemy artillery would be able to sweep the entire plain of battle far below.

The slopes were strewn with unburied dead. For the past two weeks there had been ferocious fighting here, and the stench of semi-baked, putrescent flesh gagged and choked the living. *Sanidad* sent up camphor bags, which the men hung around their necks to deaden olfactory nerves. No burial was possible: the men could not dig even rifle pits.[9] It would have required pneumatic hammers to penetrate the calcite bedrock; picks and shovels made no more dent than spoons and helmets. The only recourse was to find a crevice and to build a barricade of loose rocks. Hill 666 was a geological nightmare, as hostile to man as the surface of the moon. During the day the bare rock acted as a reflector for the sun, and they broiled; at night they shivered as cold winds whipped across the razor-like crest. There was, however, one major consolation: the position favored defense. If the Nationalists attacked, they would have to cross exposed rock slides in full view. Moreover, the volunteers' right flank was absolutely secure; anything threatening them from that direction would have to have wings.

On their second day in the Pandols, the Lincoln Battalion, which held the right flank next to the cliff edge, was ordered to attack a Moorish outpost several hundred yards down the ridge. Artillery and

[9] The dead were never buried. Thirty years later the slopes around Hill 666 are still littered with heaps of human bone.

air support was promised. Two hundred men readied themselves. At three in the afternoon, Republican shells whistled over and exploded brittly among the bedrock enemy parapets. Then five Soviet *chatos*— one of them with a picture of Mickey Mouse on its rudder—screamed down and strafed for five minutes. They left, but no order came up from headquarters to attack. A Nationalist observation plane circled high above, buzzing like a sluggish fly. Then enemy artillery opened up from far down in the Gandesa Valley, their shells exploding among the British reserve positions in a bowl below the Americans. Gradually the shell bursts crept up the hillside toward the Lincolns. Shrapnel clattered on the rocks, ricocheting crazily. "This is a hell of a way from Wall Street," muttered a volunteer. One shell landed squarely on two men coming up the hill, erasing them. Because of the barrage, the attack was postponed.

After dark, two Lincoln companies filed out under Lieutenant Lopoff, who said cheerily, "It'll be a cinch. A handful of men could do it." For half an hour those men left behind in reserve heard and saw nothing. Then, in the distance, there was sudden yelling and firing, followed by pink grenade explosions that backlighted tiny fig-ures scrambling up a slope toward the Moorish outpost. As though a fuse had blown, silence and blackness fell again. Once more there was a brief fire-cracker eruption that died out. Half an hour later survivors of the attacking companies dribbled back. Some were sobbing—others were gasping.

"Christ! It was hell up there," blurted out one man. "They had machine guns—they had barbed wire: why didn't they tell us they had barbed wire? How were we to know they had barbed wire?" No one had given them wire cutters, and they had not learned of the wire until entangled in it. Large numbers of men had refused to attack: hidden by the darkness, they deliberately held back. A Spaniard handed an officer at the Lincoln command post a bloody automatic and announced, a little theatrically, *"La pistola del commandante."* Lopoff had been hit in the eye while leading the attack. Since he walked part of the way to the dressing station, everyone thought he would live. (They were wrong: he died six weeks later.) Brigade sent the British in to take the outpost. They attacked before dawn and were beaten back with heavy losses. Only then did brigade decide to hold, not advance, the positions they had.

On the days that followed, the initiative passed to the Nationalists. It was not uncommon to see overhead a squadron of twenty Junkers bombers escorted by sixty Fiat pursuit planes—without a single Republican aircraft in the sky. They sowed their bombs up and down the Sierra de Pandols. And on the ground, Moorish antitank guns and mortars systematically demolished Lincoln parapets. Mules brought up great quantities of empty sandbags, but along the rocky summit of Hill 666 there was barely a grain of loose earth to fill them with. (A company commander telephoned Captain Wolff and suggested that pocket handkerchiefs might be more useful. "I got a bad case of sinus," he said.) High-velocity shells caromed across rock outcroppings, spraying men with lethal rock splinters. It was possible to see a shell bounce several times before coming to rest. Commissar Watt named their position "The Ping-Pong Hills."

When the eight-hour barrage ceased, Moors attacked and were beaten back by grenades. For almost an hour the enemy tried to infiltrate up the rocky slopes of Hill 666. In the middle of the fighting, Lieutenant Donald Thayer of Rochester, Minnesota, was asked what support his Third Company could give to a company on his flank. Thayer, who was having problems of his own, replied testily, "Well, I can give you my heartfelt sympathy." In the end the Moors took a bad drubbing and fled back to their lines.

The Nationalists repeated their bombings, shellings, and assaults on succeeding days. Their antitank guns sniped at Lincoln parapets from a higher peak half a mile away. Emanuel Lanzer, commander of Fourth Company, was literally blown out of his clothes by a mortar shell but was not seriously hurt. But his best machine-gunner, Joe Bianca, was hit in the groin by a piece of shrapnel. "See you in Sunday School," Bianca had time to say before he died. After one attack had been repelled, the commissar of First Company led his men singing "The Star-Spangled Banner." It was badly rendered by parched throats, but they croaked it to a conclusion before the next barrage began.[10] They did not advance, they did not retreat. They held.

After eleven days in the Sierra de Pandols, the XV Brigade came down and the 43rd Division, tough Pyrenean soldiers, went up. They

[10] On this same day, in Washington, the House Un-American Activities Committee voted to submit to the Attorney General evidence they had accumulated to show that the Lincoln Battalion was a subsidiary of the Red Army. While the men in the Sierra de Pandols hurled back fresh attacks, a new series of battles, which would be fought for thirty years behind barricades constructed of lawyers' notes, obscure laws, and the Fifth Amendment, was beginning at home.

cheered each other as they passed in the dusk. The brigade had been cited for its "magnificent defense of Hill 666," but so far as the men were concerned, the military honor mattered far less than leaving behind the blighted mountain peak. "We came down," wrote one man, "a whole lot faster than we had gone up." Near Pinell de Bray, reduced since they had seen it to cubistic ruins, they camped in a bower not far from the Ebro. Thinking back on their recent experience, they felt proud of themselves. For "a crummy bunch" they had fought pretty well. There was plenty of grit left.

16
▟▙ La Despedida

I, want to go ho-ome,
I, want to go ho-ome.
Machine guns they rattle,
The cannons they roar.
I-don't-want-to-go-to-the-front any more.
Send me over the sea,
Where the Fascists can't get at me-ee.
Oh my—
I'm too young to die.
I, want to go HOME!

—Battalion song

September was a month of brutal fighting during which the Lincoln Battalion hurled itself into breaches and plugged gaps in a continually breaking line around "The Crossroads" at Venta de Camposines. Men were poured like putty into the leaking seams of a moribund "offensive" whose slogan had become a double-think phrase, "To Resist Is to Win." They fought on hilltops and they waited in caves. At times the massed rows of enemy troops, pushing like a city mob down the road from Corbera, were near enough for an American volunteer to read the divisional emblems stitched on their tunics. But more often than not, the enemy artillery barrage, that cursed *aplastamiento*, was so awesome that even the Nationalist infantry feared to budge. The air was laden with thick sulphurous fumes, as acrid as a city smog. The sun shone but looked like the moon. If the Republicans retook a hundred yards of lost territory, the event made headlines in the Barcelona papers. It had become that kind of war.

On September 21, 1938, in the litter-free city of Geneva, Juan Negrín, Prime Minister of the Spanish Republic, announced before the League of Nations that all international volunteers would be withdrawn from the front immediately in order to be counted, sorted by nationality, and repatriated to their country of origin. Even as he spoke, the XV Brigade was being rushed, once again, into a ruptured sector a few hundred yards west of "The Crossroads." Only 280 men were at this time listed on the rolls of the Lincoln Battalion, of which about 80 were Americans. News of the imminent withdrawal reached the brigade staff early in the morning of September 22. Since the men had already been committed to battle, nothing was to be done until division headquarters ordered them back. Commissar Gates prohibited all newspapers from circulation in the brigade. No man would fight well if he knew that he would be permanently withdrawn within a few hours. Besides, Gates wanted to leave Spain with, as he put it, "the taste of victory on our lips."

The Lincoln Battalion had deployed in a thin line south of the Corbera road to help repel an enemy thrust against "The Crossroads." Beginning at dawn, artillery pounded their sector so unmercifully that individual shell-bursts could not be distinguished. "This sounds like the World War," remarked an American volunteer who had fought in it. An observer behind the lines counted three hundred enemy planes in the sky at one time, or so he claimed. Late in the afternoon Captain Wolff got an urgent appeal from a Polish battalion holding a small knoll half a mile north of the highway: the enemy was breaking through. The Lincolns went over to help. It was growing dark, and the terrain was obscure. Wolff sent out patrols to reconnoiter the wooded hillsides, all of which looked exactly alike. Corporal James Lardner with two men, a Spaniard and a New Yorker named Tony Nowakowsky, was sent to determine whether a knoll farther to the northwest was occupied. Lardner's patrol reached the foot of the hill. From the top came down the noise of spades and shovels. Lardner went up alone to investigate. Nowakowsky heard a shout of alarm at the top and Lardner's voice challenging in Spanish. Then came yells, popping grenades, and the clatter of machine guns. Finding his Spanish companion dead, Nowakowsky fled. Lardner was either killed on the hill or executed later. It was ironical that only a few days previously George Watt had vetoed a request that Lardner be sent to Barcelona to work on the *Volunteer for Liberty*. Watt had said, "I don't think he's a very good writer yet. He's learning things now that will mature him."

After positioning his men on hills behind the Poles, Captain Wolff called a meeting of the Lincoln officers. Gates had told him that they had to hold for just one more day. "Get it? One more day!" Then they could pack up and go home. The news of their imminent withdrawal had already leaked to the men. No one was willing to be shot or killed during the final hours. "The last day was psychologically very bad," remembered one volunteer. "Everybody wanted to live."

In the memorably succinct words of one combatant, September 23 was a "f . . .-up." The Fourth Company had assumed a position far behind where it was supposed to be. Scores of *quintos* vanished completely, deserting to the enemy or skulking behind the lines. After a five-hour softening barrage, the enemy walked through the Lincolns as easily as though parading through high grass. The Nationalists found a punky flank and rolled the whole battalion back to the Corbera road. A hundred yards south, running parallel to the road, a deep *barranca* wound downhill toward "The Crossroads." The temptation to use it as an escape tunnel was irresistible. Most of the men jumped into it and hightailed it to the rear. The breakthrough happened so suddenly that Wolff did not hear of it until too late. He and Commissar Watt climbed out of their command post and gazed out upon a network of trenches filled with impedimenta but emptied of men. Looking northward across the scored ground, they saw swarms of enemy soldiers flooding the abandoned trenches. If his men had not run, Wolff could have made a stand without great difficulty. It was a heartbreaking *dénouement*.

Collecting a dozen stalwarts, Captain Wolff fell back several hundred yards and set up two machine guns. But the enemy pressed no farther. Perhaps another Republican outfit filled the hole. No one ever knew. This microscopic remnant of the Lincoln Battalion waited in frustration and in bitterness until midnight, when the order reached them that they had been relieved. "If the gulley had not been there, the guys might not have run," Wolff said.

It was already daylight on September 24, 1938, when the last Americans tramped across the wooden planks of the pontoon bridge at Mora de Ebro and climbed up the long hill on the far shore. From the summit it was impossible not to look back at the wide yellow river and the ruffled landscape beyond, obscured by the dirty haze of war. They were now merely spectators. It was possible to want to leave and, at the same time, want not to have left what was being thrashed out on that field of battle. Men wept, without shame. For them the war was finished.

While a League commission took its census of the Internationals scattered in camps and hospitals through Cataluña and the Levante,[1] the Lincoln Battalion waited at Marsa. Billeted in houses, stables, and farms nearby, the men luxuriated in the creature comforts of an almost forgotten civilization, for Marsa contained not only a cinema and soccer field but also a splendid big bar with a terrace looking out across a valley of almond trees to barren peaks shaped like scoops of ice cream. A hospital was set up in an arcaded barn a mile from town, and men fatally wounded were buried in disused common land beside the small creek that runs through the valley.[2] Early in October the XV Brigade, consisting solely of Spaniards, was called back to the Battle of the Ebro. On the soccer field at Marsa, Milton Wolff— now major—drew up his old battalion for the last time. Then he ordered the Americans to fall out and to form in a far corner of the field. The Spaniards marched away to war and the Americans had their picture taken. The demobilized Lincolns, standing or sitting cross-legged like a varsity club in a high school yearbook, smiled into the lens. Not counting the villager who hurriedly climbed the wall behind them to be included in the picture, one counts fifty-nine faces.

On October 17 the XI and XV brigades held a farewell *fiesta* at Marsa. A parked truck in a field outside the village provided a reviewing stand for Luigi Longi and Ludwig Renn as the Internationals marched past. André Marty, who missed the parade, arrived in time for the banquet spread upon planks mounted on sawhorses at a farmhouse nearby. The walls were decorated by Republican streamers and a photograph of Lenin. Longi and Renn spoke movingly of the International Brigade, which on this day, the eve of its disbandment, celebrated its second anniversary. Marty, however, delivered a fist-shaking tirade concluding with the words, "With a mad dog, we cannot fool. We must annihilate it. Fascism is a mad dog, and we shall kill it." There were no allusions to Trotsky in his speech. After two years of war, André Marty seemed to have learned, at last, who the real enemy was.

On October 29 the brigade was bussed into Barcelona to take part in the parade of the International volunteers down the sycamore-lined

[1] No accurate statistics exist concerning the total number of Americans who were enlisted in the Lincoln-Washington Battalion. The figure given is 3,200, of which 1,500 were killed. The actual number is probably higher.

[2] A traditional gravestone marked with his name, rank, and brigade marks the burial spot of John Cookson of Cobb, Wisconsin. This is the only known grave of an American volunteer killed in Spain. It is grown up in weeds.

Diagonal (today known as Avenida del Generalísimo Franco). This was *La Despedida* (Farewell), but it was something of a victory march as well. Groups representing twenty-six nations—from Algeria to Yugoslavia, but no Russians—tramped down the broad avenue as thousands of spectators lined the curbs, climbed lampposts, and waved from balconies. Plaques listing the names of outstanding Internationals lined the route. (The only American so honored was Dave Doran.) The marchers carried no weapons. Their uniforms ranged from spit-and-polish to business suits. Compared with the Rakosi (Hungarian) and the André Marty battalions, who were decked out in new uniforms with stiffly wired garrison hats, the Lincolns resembled a group of border marauders. With blanket rolls slung over their right shoulders, with every kind of foot gear known to man, and with patched uniforms bronzed with age, they swept past, some grinning and others dead-serious, eight abreast and nearly in step. "They were not clad in spic-and-span uniforms; and they could not seem to keep in step or in line," wrote Herbert L. Matthews, who watched them. "Those men had learned to fight before they had learned to parade." Near the end of the parade, girls broke through the crowd and doused them with flowers and clung to their necks. Major Wolff, who had had such a close haircut for the occasion that he was nearly unrecognizable, later told Vincent Sheean, "We've never been what you call very good at parade marching, and when we got on those streets with flowers up to our ankles, I guess we did a kind of shag."

In a farewell speech, Premier Negrín, with tears in his eyes, promised citizenship to any of them who returned to Spain after the war. Finally La Pasionaria delivered an unforgettable speech:

> Comrades of the International Brigades! Political reasons, reasons of State, the welfare of that same cause for which you offered your blood with boundless generosity, are sending you back, some of you to your own countries and others to forced exile. You can go proudly. You are history. You are legend. You are the heroic example of democracy's solidarity and universality. We shall not forget you, and when the olive tree of peace puts forth its leaves again, mingled with the laurels of the Spanish Republic's victory—come back!

Through La Pasionaria, a volunteer could recover the vanished innocence of communism. A military band burst forth with "Himno de Riego." Few Internationals knew the words, but they sang it lustily, for the last time. No man caught up in the collective pageantry of *La Despedida* could doubt, at that moment, that the battle had been fought in vain.

At only one other time during the war did the populace of Barcelona turn out with such wild enthusiasm to greet an army of strangers. That was on January 26, 1939, the day the Nationalists entered the city.

In early November the American volunteers moved to Ripoll, a Pyrenean town thirty miles from France. It was the site of a remarkable assemblage of Romanesque statuary completely invisible behind double layers of sandbags. Initially the French government insisted that disbanded Internationals embark at Spanish ports on vessels that would carry them direct to countries other than France, because ·Rightists did not want to have 12,763 Popular Front warriors cross their country. But finally the French agreed to issue transit visas provided that transportation be paid for in advance, that the ex-soldiers travel on sealed trains, and that each of them carry documentation proving that his respective country would accept him. For the Americans this meant that the Department of State had to certify each man's citizenship.

So far as financial arrangements were concerned, the FALB, which had had no difficulty raising money to ship men over, claimed insolvency when the time came to bring them back. Special funds were solicited from such private donors in the United States as Bernard Baruch, who personally contributed ten thousand dollars to bring the men home. In November, however, the FALB deposited the required funds for repatriation with French authorities without publicizing that the Spanish Republic had defrayed all expenses.[3]

The men waiting at Ripoll had been originally scheduled to go over the frontier on November 11, but they were delayed for three more weeks because Lincoln officers and the Department of State were each trying to outmaneuver the other in the matter of supposedly lost passports. On November 6, Quero Molares, the Republican official in charge of evacuating Internationals, was told by XV Brigade authorities that 272 Americans at Ripoll waited with valid passports. The

[3] In December the Republican chargé in Washington called upon Pierrepont Moffitt, Chief of the Division of European Affairs at the Department of State, and inquired whether the United States would be willing to reimburse the Republic for its expenditures in bringing home the American volunteers.

United States consulate at Barcelona accordingly sent three officers up to Ripoll on November 10 with instructions to stamp each passport "Valid only for direct return to the United States." But on reaching the Lincoln camp, the consuls found 420 Americans and only 40 passports. Battalion officers claimed all the others had been lost between Albacete and Barcelona. The result was that information about each volunteer had to be cabled to Washington, innumerable affidavits sworn to and forms filled out, and the Lincolns lost their opportunity to cross the frontier on November 11. The Department feared that volunteers from other countries would take advantage of the confusion prevailing at the time in order to enter the United States illegally. Moreover, it was widely believed that the missing passports had been handed over to various Comintern agencies for use in espionage activities throughout the world. When it became clear that volunteers might be held back for months at Ripoll, some 201 passports miraculously turned up and were submitted to the Barcelona consulate ten days later. What happened to the others remains a mystery.

On December 2, the first group of 326 Americans left Ripoll at eight in the morning aboard a special train festooned with evergreen wreaths, whether decoration or camouflage they never knew. (Fifteen men missed the train because it left on time.) The townspeople gathered to see them off with the Popular Front salute. When a Spanish officer on the platform dabbed his eyes with a handkerchief, an American leaning out of a broken window of the train shouted, "Hey, guys, pipe that captain going tragic on us!" As the train pulled out of Ripoll, Milton Wolff saw Malcom Dunbar, Merriman's successor. Imitating his Oxbridge accent, Wolff called out, "Hi, Dunbah. Cheerio!" Dunbar looked up and answered in Brooklynese, "Coit'nly." They crossed a barren alpine waste, a cold corner of Spain not to remember, to Puigcerda, the Spanish frontier town. On the station were placards reading "1938—AÑO DE LA VICTORIA." But the year had almost run out.

The men sang their way into France, at Bourg-Madame. They had arrived two hours earlier than expected, and as they stood at the railroad station they watched five Junkers unload bombs on the Puigcerda station across the wide valley. "They were looking for us," said Wolff to Herbert L. Matthews, who had come up from Barcelona to chronicle their arrival. "I hope they won't still be looking for you when I drive back down," replied Matthews. The Americans trooped through the station, whooping like schoolboys on holiday. They gorged upon butter, bread, and chocolate; they chain-smoked their way through packs of French cigarettes. Matthews noted that by habit they nipped off the ends of cigarettes and dropped the stubs into coat pockets. They had forgotten what abundance was. The Republic had provided each man with bizarre pin-stripe suits. But they had no overcoats and shivered in the thin wintery air. Fifty men still wore *alpargatas,* leather shoes being hard to find in Spain. Battalion officers told Matthews that probably 350 American volunteers still remained in Cataluña and about a hundred more in Valencia. An additional fifty or so were questionable cases: they had lived in the United States but had never taken out citizenship papers. Even though some of these had wives or children in the States, they had been told that they must await openings on immigration quotas. Perhaps the most pathetic case of all was Joe Morrison, a middle-aged American Indian who had no passport, no registration of birth, and no friends or relatives at home able to identify him.

The Paris train, which departed Bourg-Madame at 4:44 P.M., turned into a joyous bedlam of singing and drinking as it rolled northward through the night. *Gardes mobiles* were stationed at each door, but they were not unfriendly. One of them even contributed a bottle of cognac to the party. Lincoln officers traveled in first class, their men in third. Morning revealed compartments of dozing men and empty bottles wobbling from side to side as the train arrived in the outer yards of Paris. Fearing a recurrence of the tumultuous demonstrations that had marked the entry of French volunteers a month previously, the Government arranged to shuttle subsequent trainloads of Internationals around Paris on a wide detour. But at each switch and at every station of the drab outer *arrondissements,* small groups of Frenchmen saluted the train with clenched fists.

At Le Havre, the Lincolns were met by a small army of gendarmes and an official from the Compagnie Générale Transatlantique, who explained that the *Normandie* would not sail as scheduled because of a seaman's strike. *"Faut marcher au Parc de la Heve,"* he told them. "Park?" shouted an American. "Who the hell wants to go to the goddamn *park?"* The local prefect had buses on hand to transport them to a dingy compound four kilometers outside of town, the Le Havre equivalent of Ellis Island. It consisted of brick hutments enclosed by a link fence with loops of barbed wire at the top. "They give us the bum's rush around Paris, and now a concentration camp," complained a volunteer. The mattresses were filthy; there were no facilities for bathing. The director warned them that he expected order in his camp; if they made trouble, he would have to call in the gendarmes patrolling outside the eight-foot fence. Le Havre was on the verge of civil insurrection because of the bitter strike; the authorities feared that the presence of *les voluntaires d'Espagne* might act as a militant catalyst for the working class of the city. Wolff calmed his men down by asking that they set an example "in the face of the hostility of the French Government." Then, echoing La Pasionaria's farewell speech, he added, "We have a history and a tradition and will maintain it till we disband in New York."

News of the strike came as a hard blow to the Americans. They eagerly desired to return home, but if they sailed on a ship manned by scabs, their voyage would mock the basic principles that had sent them to Spain. In the evening, a delegation from the seamen's union came out to the Parc for a meeting in the communal mess hall. They had proposed to the company that they would agree to crew the *Normandie* for the express purpose of carrying the American volunteers home, provided that all other passengers be excluded. This proposal had, of course, been rejected. The union was worried about the plight of the volunteers, but it could not cancel a strike solely for their benefit. Therefore they arranged with the authorities for the Lincolns to ship out on the *Paris,* due to depart on December 6, manned by a crew from the French Navy. The only scabs aboard would be in the stewards' department. "Then we won't sail," interrupted Wolff. But the union spokesmen explained that they had no choice: their transit visas would otherwise expire and they might then be returned home, not in honor but under arrest. He went on to say that his union had "granted permission" for the anti-Fascist fighters to embark on the *Paris;* indeed, they requested them to do so. Lifting his clenched fist, the delegate shouted *"Salud!"* and the mess hall exploded with excited approval. A college boy shouted, *"Viva la France et les pommes de terre frites!"* Two men began singing "Le Marseillaise" and another called out, "Anybody we catch tipping the fink stewards goes over the side!" On the spot, the Americans took up a collection for the strike fund.

Conditions in Le Havre became so volatile that the *Paris* moved over to Cherbourg, where passengers and stewards could be taken aboard in a calmer atmosphere. Because of a backlog of passengers stranded in France by canceled sailings, only 148 Lincolns at Parc de la Heve could be accommodated. These traveled to Cherbourg by train. Much to their mortification, they embarked behind a thick cordon of gendarmes who held rock-throwing crowds at bay. Their instinct was to attack the police from the rear, and they went aboard angrily. At Cherbourg, an American reporter needled Milton Wolff about his contribution to the defeat of the labor movement in France. Wolff tried to explain that his men really had no choice about it. Yet the come-down left a bad taste in their mouths. The crossing was stormy the whole way, but much to their delight, the scab stewards were seasick from shore to shore.

On December 15, 1938, the *Paris* docked at its 48th Street pier in New York, bringing back the first group of disbanded American volunteers from the Spanish Civil War. Immigration officers held back the Lincolns until all the other passengers had gone ashore. Photographs on their passports or temporary travel documents were carefully compared with faces in the flesh, the men were finger-printed, and their documents were confiscated. "When will I get my passport back?" asked one man. "Never—I hope," came the reply. The customs shed was nearly empty when they came down the gang-plank. Outside, they saw massed policemen, mounted and on foot, keeping a welcoming crowd of two or three thousand people on the far side of Twelfth Avenue. Cheering and clapping broke out as the Lincolns stepped out of the pier building and crossed over. The Brighton Beach Community Center Junior Drum and Bugle Corps played in honor of George Watt, native son (who had been left behind at Le Havre).

The FALB had arranged for a parade. Led by Milton Wolff, the Americans, once again in uniforms of the Spanish Republic, marched crosstown. At their head waved flags of the United States, the Repub-lic, and the Lincoln Battalion. There were no hammers and sickles, no portraits of Lenin, no red banners. On their flanks mounted po-licemen rode like a cavalry escort. Behind came the great throng of sympathizers and well-wishers carrying banners that read

LIFT, LIFT THE EMBARGO ON SPAIN
and
DOWN WITH DALADIER DECREES

As in Barcelona, people dashed from the curb to embrace them or applauded as they passed by. Many bystanders, however, stared in puzzlement, wondering who these men were and perhaps reflecting that they looked terribly young really to be veterans of the Spanish-American War. At random points along the line of march, somber figures—mothers, fathers, wifes, and lovers—held up crudely fashioned signs that begged the men passing by for a word:

WHAT HAPPENED TO X
ANYONE KNOW Y? LOST AT JARAMA
PLEASE TELL ME ANYTHING ABOUT Z

A wet-eyed woman of middle age held up an enlarged photograph with her query. The picture looked vaguely like Paul White, but no one stopped to see.

By the time the procession reached Madison Square, many Lincoln veterans had dropped out and slipped away forever. Milton Wolff was left with a hard core of disciples. A FALB sound-truck boomed out a speech of welcome. Four veterans stepped forward carrying a wreath labeled "In Memory of Those Who Died for Democracy" to lay it at the base of the Eternal Light in the park. But their way was barred by Lieutenant Charles Maura of the New York police department, who informed them that they needed a permit to place the wreath. Some Lincoln veterans lurched forward angrily and were pulled back. The police bristled and closed ranks. For a moment it looked as though the homecoming might turn into a free-for-all in the faint penumbra of the Eternal Light. But a FALB official rushed over to say that the Lincoln Battalion did not desire to make a scene. The wreath was dropped outside the railing of the light. No permit was required for that. Somebody played "Taps."

Epilogue

⚑ Premature Anti-fascists and All That

Milt, my feeling is that you guys sort of bought this anyway. You hired out to be tough and then somebody gets hurt and says they can't do this to me. I liked you very much when you were a kid in Spain and as you started to grow up. Now I haven't seen you for a long time. . . .

> —Hemingway declines Wolff's invitation to chair the Tenth anniversary meeting of the Lincoln Brigade (1946)

Mr. Moulder: Mr. Nelson, in the event of war between the United States and Russia, to which country would you owe your allegiance and loyalty in such a conflict?
Mr. Nelson: I refuse to answer that question.

> —Steve Nelson hearing before HUAC (1949)

It was a war without pensions and without medals. The only decorations which most of them brought back were their wounds, although these were plentiful enough. There was no mustering-out pay, no military hospitals. Ninety per cent of the veterans needed jobs, 70 per cent required some form of medical attention, and 5 per cent were totally disabled and beyond rehabilitation.[1] The stalwarts, of course, could fall back upon the resources of the party. But for most of the sixteen hundred veterans, nothing stood between their homeless homecoming and the wintry air except the Friends of the Abraham Lincoln Brigade, with national headquarters at 125 West 45th Street. This was their equivalent of a Veterans Administration— it was not much, but all they had. The men flocked to this eternally

---

[1] Among these were Douglas Roach, dying of tuberculosis, and Robert Raven, blinded at Jarama. In 1948 one blind veteran protested to the party that he had been swindled: during the war he had been a featured attraction on fund drives, but now he was destitute and forgotten. As a bonus or as hush-money, he was given funds to purchase a small shop in New York City.

poor-mouth organization, which had collected money in the name of all the Americans who had fought in Spain and disbursed it in favor of a privileged minority. (No malcontents, demoralized elements, or FONICs need apply; some doubtful cases were sent downtown to party headquarters on 12th Street for political clearance.)

If a man had a good record in Spain and showed promise of good work within, or on the fringes of, the party, the FALB could arrange for expensive medical treatment, free housing and board, and night courses for the crippled. There were introductions to well-connected personages in trade unions, and there were parties to meet zealous young women prepared to befriend "the conquering heroes of the revolutionary class who slew the ugly beast of Fascism," as a FALB handout quaintly described them. But if a man showed "political immaturity," that is to say if he articulated dissenting attitudes toward the leadership of the International Brigades or the party, then he would be brushed off with a ten-dollar bill and a Greyhound ticket to Bartlesville, Oklahoma, or wherever he had come from. And any veteran who "ratted" was apt to find his name in the *Daily Worker* as an "enemy of the working class," which could mean a blackball by his old union. Veterans who registered at the FALB headquarters had no difficulty in determining where and how they stood in the eyes of the leadership. If important, they got money to buy a suit; if insignificant, they had to root through piles of hand-me-downs stored in a back room. One Boston veteran with twenty months service in Spain who had failed to learn the habit of echoing the everlasting yea emerged from the storeroom clad in an oversized, double-breasted "zoot suit" of pale pink hue, but he took it in good humor. An Ohio veteran was offered the loan of an apartment in far-off Brooklyn until a FALB worker learned that he had once written for the *Daily Worker;* then he was given an apartment for two weeks in the Village. As in all organizations, the hierarchy functioned to look after the hierarchy. The difference was that the FALB had to answer not to the public nor to the law, but only to itself.

Wounded men were not necessarily a liability, for they could be used as persuasive exhibits in fund campaigns. Bill Harvey, who had been cut down at Jarama by an enemy bullet which lodged permanently in his neck next to the spinal cord, regularly and successfully solicited money from uptown college groups and Long Island ladies' societies. The publicity brochure which preceded him featured the profile of a youth whose head was braced by an elaborate contraption of metal rods and leather straps. The FALB photographer, however, had airbrushed his nose, because he thought it "too Jewish"—the emphasis, in those days of the Popular Front was upon the "American-ness" of the boys in Spain. Even the dead were resurrected and put to work. Friends and relatives of deceased veterans received letters in which the opening paragraphs contained sentimental recollections and the concluding parts solicited funds.[2] An FALB official took aside Jim Lardner's best friend in the battalion and urged him to dun the family for money. Outraged by this scheme for emotional blackmail, the friend refused. It was the first step toward his disillusionment with the Lincoln hierarchy. But others plunged into this work.

Some veterans, disaffected with the Lincoln organization even before they arrived in the United States, slipped away as soon as their ship docked and vanished permanently. For others, disenchantment proceeded more slowly. During the early spring of 1939, for example, when thousands of International volunteers from Fascist-controlled countries were stranded in French concentration camps near Argeles-sur-Mere, certain Lincoln veterans begged the FALB to do something to help them. With some justification, the FALB officials declared that their funds were small and their obligations large. Then would not the FALB be willing to petition the Soviet Union to offer asylum to all "exiled victims of Franco?" It was known that many key Spanish Communists like "La Pasionaria" and the military leaders Modesto and Lister had been accepted by the Soviet Union. The officials were shocked by this proposal—how could the FALB ask for the admission of these so-called Interbrigade veterans when it was possible that among them were spies, saboteurs, and counter-revolutionaries? Indeed, why should such *lumpenproletariat* be allowed to worm their way into the sacred soil of the Soviet Union? For many Lincolns, such Stalinoid suspicion and ingratitude seemed to be a contemptible way to view former comrades-in-arms who, like themselves, had fought fascism in Spain. In the end, nothing was ever done about the German volunteers who had twice saved Madrid.[3]

[2] On one occasion this scheme backfired. Maxwell Wallach, whose son Albert had been executed in Spain, collected letters from FALB officials and veterans and then turned his collection over to HUAC in an effort to discover how his son had died and who was responsible. This was the closest to a "war-crimes" trial that ever occurred in connection with the Lincoln Battalion. Nothing was ever proved.

[3] Some of these men were evacuated to North Africa prior to Hitler's blitzkrieg through France in the spring of 1940; others were turned over to the Nazi authorities by the Vichy government.

The burnish was beginning to wear off the blade. It was becoming clear that the FALB cared more about the sensibilities of the Kremlin leadership than about the good fight in Spain or the welfare of the men who fight there. Some Lincoln veterans began to feel that an old capitalist slogan might be fittingly scrawled above the door on 45th Street—"Nothing is too good for the working class, and *Nothing* is what it gets."

On August 23, 1939, came the Hitler-Stalin Pact, which for so many American Communists marked the beginning of their long retreat from Moscow. With Stalin's unilateral decision to abandon his crusade against fascism, the Popular Front collapsed. A few days later, Hitler launched his war against the western democracies, while in the United States the party called for its members to support the slogan, "Keep America Out of an Imperialist War." The new policy seemed to mock all those who had signed "anti-Fascist" in their military books at Albacete. Here was a zigzag in Comintern policy that many Lincoln veterans could not follow. One of them, a worker in a Communist-dominated New York union, was fired when he refused to sign a "loyalty oath," in other words, a pledge to support the spirit of the pact. As a Jew he believed that making deals with Hitler was not only insane but obscene. In open rebellion he carried a hand-lettered sign through the Garment District:

LAST WEEK A HERO OF THE SPANISH CIVIL WAR
THIS WEEK A VICTIM OF THE STALIN-HITLER PACT

A "spit-brigade" gathered around him to insult and to spit on him. Once feted as an enemy of fascism, he was now an "enemy of the people."

Late in 1939 the FALB rotted and died, because the alliance against fascism, which had germinated it and sustained it, was in disrepute. By this time events in Spain were as irrelevant to the world situation as indignities in Ethiopia. David McKelvey White, national chairman of the FALB, acquiesced in the dissolution of his organization in favor of a smaller cadre, comprising only Spanish veterans, known as the Veterans of the Abraham Lincoln Brigade (VALB). In December, VALB held its first national convention in New York and installed Milton Wolff as its national commander.[4] The VALB never

---

[4] The VALB had existed as a kind of loose assemblage prior to 1939. As early as December 1937, fifty veterans had attempted an organizational meeting and had agreed upon a slate of officers. But it did not intrude upon the domain of the FALB—which had established an efficient fund-raising system

had a democratic base. Decisions came down from above, and in its thirty-year history there is no record of a policy *opposed* to the Kremlin–*Pravda*–*Worker* line. Members have at times been summarily expelled for violating constitutional clauses against "slandering IB leadership" and "attempting to form secret groups in the VALB." [5] (It is interesting to note that the constitution contains provisions for expulsion of members but not for their resignation!) The VALB has never been much more than a paper organization with an ambitious mailing list. Publication of its newspaper, *Volunteer for Liberty* (in recent years renamed *The Volunteer*), has proceeded irregularly. In moments of financial crisis, the part-time executive secretary makes personal appeals for the men to chip in. Except for the early years, it is unlikely that its active membership has ever consisted of more than one-tenth of surviving veterans.[6]

As might be expected, the VALB was rigorously pacifistic during the tenure of the Hitler-Stalin Pact, but when Hitler invaded the Soviet Union in June 1941, it promptly reverted to militant antifascism once again. Members participated in the "Smash Hitler Rally" at Madison Square Garden in July, and a few months later Milton Wolff authored a pamphlet entitled *Western Front Now. The Volunteer for Liberty* gave great attention to the "major phase" of the Allied war effort—in other words, the Soviet effort—and urged veterans to engage themselves in a war which miraculously was "imperialistic" no longer. Some six hundred Lincoln veterans (who were not necessarily VALB members) joined the armed services or the merchant marine during the Second World War, or roughly half the

based upon a list of fifty thousand donors—until the Politburo decided to dissolve the earlier organization. Not until January 1940, did the VALB file a certificate of incorporation with the Secretary of New York State and thereby become a legal organization.

[5] The leadership was disturbed when dissenting veterans, rankled by the Kremlin agreement with Hitler, attempted to found the Anti-Totalitarian Friends of Spain, an opposition organization that advocated American support of Britain and France. The leadership need not have worried, for this group, chaired by Humberto Galleani, fell apart through failure to obtain financial support.

[6] At the 1967 convention, for example, attendance amounted to three hundred people, of whom only forty had actually fought in Spain, as against the six hundred Lincoln veterans said to be still living. At this meeting Steve Nelson succeeded Milton Wolff as national commander, the latter having held that post for twenty-eight years. A major order of business was condemnation of the United States role in Vietnam. Copies of Mao's quotations were peddled at the door; a refreshing departure from the laborious Moscow orientation of three decades.

number of those who survived the Spanish war. Sixty-five are alleged to have become commissioned officers; twenty-five were killed.[7] Two men—Herman Bottcher and Robert Thompson—earned the Distinguished Service Cross. A handful which included Milton Wolff served with General William Donovan's O.S.S. in northern Italy, doubtless in connection with anti-Mussolini partisans. Perhaps the most singular career was that of George Watt, who was among an air force crew shot down in southern France, forced to climb the Pyrenees, and interned temporarily in Franco's Spain. Yet because the Dies Committee (HUAC) had tried to establish relationships between the International Brigades and the Comintern in dozens of well-publicized hearings, more often than not the service record of a Lincoln veteran was stamped S.O.D. ("Suspected of Disloyalty"). Fighting in Spain was a taint. To be a fervent anti-Fascist during the Second World War was acceptable; but to be a "premature anti-Fascist" was to be guilty of excessive fervency.

The mood of exultation among the Lincolns as a result of the defeat of the Axis powers was short-lived, for the pursuit of Communists in the United States during the McCarthy era brought interrogation and harassment to most of the Spanish veterans. It was an epoch of suits, subpoenas, and hearings during which party stalwarts barricaded themselves behind the Fifth Amendment and bid defiance to what they termed "The Federal Bureau of Intimidation." The authorities were interested in rooting out Communists, not in punishing men for having fought in Spain; it was just that in some cases there were ample grounds for suspecting that the two things were not unrelated. Under the Smith Act, which made it illegal to conspire to overthrow the United States government—or out of contempt of court charges growing from it—half a dozen veterans went to jail. No one was ever jailed simply for having fought in the Lincoln Battalion, although the literature issued by VALB sometimes made it appear so. And no one was ever shot out of hand, like the volunteers at Marsa and at Castelldefels, for voicing minority opinions.

Finally in 1953, under the McCarran Act, which required registration of Communist-front organizations, the Attorney General filed a petition with the Subversive Activities Control Board for an order requiring the VALB to so register. The case dragged on for two years and required 4,576 pages of transcripts and 306 supporting docu-

[7] Among the dead was Joe Gordon of Jarama, who perished as a seaman on the Murmansk run.

ments before the petition of the Attorney General was upheld. The evidence is convincing: it shows that the VALB faithfully parroted the Kremlin line for a period of fifteen years and that most of its leaders were members of the Communist Party. Yet reading the transcripts today, one must feel an overwhelming outrage, not because of sympathy for the VALB but because of the senselessness in expending such enormous accumulations of data, dollars, and hours in order to substantiate such an insignificant point. The logic of proof is subverted by the illogic of the effort. One might as well destroy corn borers by artillery barrage. By unleashing a flood of sympathy for the VALB, the Government indirectly undid its own purpose. People and factions which had virtually forgotten the existence of the VALB now rushed to its defence. Such organizations get fat upon their wounds, the bloodier the better, and the VALB had long experience in the wherewithal of obtaining plasma.

The concluding remarks of the Subversive Activities Control Board, which have sometimes been conveniently forgotten by patriots of the Right and partisans of the Left, should be engraved somewhere and used to exorcise witches: "This report and the findings herein relate to the VALB as an organization and should not be considered as embracing all veterans of the war in Spain. The record shows that some Americans fought there on behalf of the Republic out of motivations completely alien to Communist purposes. Further, it is clear that many veterans of the Spanish War are not members of the Respondent or in any way represented by it." The result of placing the VALB on the Attorney General's list, however, may be readily imagined. Ignoring the fine print, Rightists used the decision to bludgeon former members of the Lincoln Battalion who had nothing whatever to do with VALB, while Leftists rallied strength to annul the decision which was supposed to have impugned all men who had fought in Spain.

The high-level histrionics were by no means over. In 1962 the Emergency Civil Liberties Committee (ECLC) offered its services to carry the VALB counter-petition to the United States Supreme Court. The occasion was the twenty-fifth anniversary meeting of the Lincoln Battalion, a "Fight Back Rally" held at Palm Gardens in New York. (Palm Gardens was no Ukrainian Workers Hall—and the audience was bourgeois in mood and in dress.) On a sleek stage were two three-pointed stars cut out of pasteboard and flanked by the American flag. Red-lettered signs read: REPEAL THE McCARRAN ACT and

AMNESTY FOR FRANCO'S POLITICAL PRISONERS. Bosses came and went, platforms were raised up and demolished, but the rhetoric was ever the same. Metaphors knocked heads together just as they had in the good old days, twenty-five years before. The featured speaker said: "We have traveled a hard road seeing our liberties whittled away, our own tradition of freedom trampled upon. . . . Heroes and patriots, yes patriots, are today hounded as victims of the hateful McCarran Act. . . . The warmongers in order to achieve their goal of world holocaust must have conformity of the so-called mass mind. . . . Political prisoners rot in medieval Spanish dungeons. . . ." And so forth. The ECLC spokesman called for a follow-up meeting at the New Yorker Hotel on April 13 to celebrate Thomas Jefferson's birthday and to call for the repeal of the McCarran Act. (First Lincoln, then Washington, now Jefferson.) Pete Seeger sang old Lincoln songs (omitting the gamier ones). Then the hall went dark and scenes of the Spanish Civil War flickered against a screen. The hall was hot and stuffy, the atmosphere prickly and faintly paranoid. But there was more sanity indoors than outside, where fifteen pickets from the Nationalist Party carried signs which read:

RED ANIMALS INSIDE
and
ABE LINCOLN BRIGADE MURDERED NUNS

The upshot was that on April 26, 1965, the Supreme Court vacated orders requiring registration of the VALB as a Communist-front organization on the grounds that the evidence was "too stale," most of it deriving from moldering dossiers of two decades before. The date was memorable: it was one of the few times in its history that the Lincoln Battalion had won a battle.

Meanwhile, the VALB continues to picket and to protest. They march in front of Spanish consulates, carry placards on wharves overlooked by Spanish ships, boycott Spanish dance and song groups. Like all protesters they give the bystander a nagging, indefinite sense that something somewhere might be wrong. Perhaps their most successful demonstration in recent years occurred in front of the Spanish pavilion at the New York World's Fair in 1964. Since placards were prohibited on the premises, the demonstrators wore four-inch, blue and white buttons labelled AMNESTY FOR ALL POLITICAL PRISONERS IN SPAIN. The Fair police were stumped; there was no law covering the ejection of visitors wearing buttons. As soon as the protestors reached the Spanish pavilion, excitable employees rushed out to do verbal battle. On the terrace the veterans belabored the employees, but less personally than perfunctorily. Now and then the groups shouted "Fascists!" or "Communists!" at one another. "We don't tell you what's wrong with the United States," shouted a Spanish lady. "We read about it in the newspapers every day, but we just keep our mouths shut." Strolling players, the *tunas,* from the University of Madrid tried to subdue the demonstration by playing guitars and singing student songs. Bystanders were genuinely perplexed. "What's going on?" one asked. "Must have something to do with integration," another replied. Led by a blind vet, the VALB attempted to present a petition to the manager of the Pavilion, who said he would receive it as a courtesy but not as an official duty. In the end, tempers cooled and cameras were busy. A *New York Times* reporter was on hand to cover the story. And it was noted that many employees of the Pavilion quietly pocketed amnesty buttons as *recuerdos* of their confrontation with *el batallón lincoln.* The use of buttons was regarded as a tactical *coup* by other groups who had attempted to demonstrate at the World's Fair.

In her farewell speech at Barcelona, La Pasionaria said of the International volunteers, "You are history. You are legend." So far as the Lincolns are concerned, she was half-right, for the Americans who fought in Spain have passed beyond history and become legend. For the new generation becoming radicalized and activated in the 1960s, the Lincolns are spiritual godfathers who fought the good fight before they were born. Historical documentation is virtually helpless in containing the growth of mythic accretions. Symbolically the Lincolns are bigger-than-life figures, roughly sketched but instantly recognizable Agamemnons of a far-off but meaningful war. During the march on the Pentagon in the fall of 1967, a small group of Lincoln veterans materialized among the vast crowd, were identified, and were greeted by cheers and applause. They surged with the others across the green fields of Arlington County just as they had climbed up the black hill at Jarama or had dropped down into the parched valley of Brunete three decades before. But Spain was far behind them, Franco only an old man like themselves. Ahead was a newer Fascist symbol, the Pentagon, a Kafkaesque metaphor of another war. Not too far away was the national headquarters of the American Nazi Party, and hooked-cross armbands fringed their line of march. Even though the Lincolns were all men of fifty-plus, the New Left, who knew only the legend not the history, found them representatives of an ancient cause with which they could identify. It was like an apostolic succession—a laying on of hands.

Sources

Mere lists of books consulted are more often pretentious than useful. What follows instead is a summary of essential sources directly employed in writing the present work. It is not intended to be an exhaustive bibliography relating to American volunteers in the Spanish Civil War.

The Lincoln Battalion has been the exclusive subject of two studies, both written by former volunteers, Edwin Rolfe's *The Lincoln Battalion* (New York: Random House, 1939) and Arthur H. Landis' *The Abraham Lincoln Brigade* (New York: Citadel Press, 1967). Both are deliberately partisan books. Yet if one is willing to acquiesce in a *mariage de convenance* between history and apologia and prepared to recognize that certain subjects will be left undiscussed, then both become indispensable collections of material.

Other veterans have written memoirs. The best of these—one might argue, indeed, that it is the finest personal narrative in the vast literature of the war—is Alvah Bessie's *Men in Battle* (New York: Charles Scribner's Sons, 1939). It is regrettable that Bessie's narrative covers frontline service only between late March and August of 1938; but for this period it is a classic memoir of a soldier in the ranks of the Lincoln Battalion. Sandor Voros' *American Commissar* (Philadelphia and New York: Chilton Company, 1961) has been attacked by numerous veterans, but one suspects that this animus owes more to his defection from the party than to misstatements of fact. As a commissar in the Historical Section of the IB, Voros had access to widely varied sources of information; his battlefield experience, however, was limited to the period of the Aragon retreats. Steve Nelson's *The Volunteers* (New York: Masses and Mainstream, 1953) is valuable for the period between Brunete and Belchite, even though it contains some fictionalization. John Gates' autobiography, *The Story of an American Communist* (New York: Thomas Nelson & Sons, 1958) contains a strong section about his service in Spain.

Despite its obvious one-sidedness, *Book of the XV Brigade* (Madrid: Commissariat of War, 1938), cast in a "yearbook" mold, is a major document for the period from Jarama to Fuentes to Ebro, containing as it does short accounts of the battles written by the combatants and photographs unavailable elsewhere. The French version of this project, *Combats contre le Fascisme: Le Livre de la 15eme Brigade Internationale*

320

(1937) adds fresh material about Jarama. The sixty-three issues of *The Volunteer for Liberty,* official organ of the XV Brigade, were published in facsimile by the Veterans of the Abraham Lincoln Brigade in 1949, making an invaluable record readily accessible. *Our Fight,* another brigade newspaper, is equally rich in information; a bound file is available in the Hemeroteca Municipal in Madrid. *News Bulletins of the International Brigades,* which was published simultaneously in a dozen languages, is useful in showing what kinds of foreign and domestic news were approved by the censors and passed on to the international volunteers; the city hall at Valencia contains a complete file.

Letters of American volunteers during the Jarama period are collected in Marcel Acier's *From Spanish Trenches* (New York: Modern Age, 1937). Other accounts by veterans are found in Alvah Bessie's miscellany, *The Heart of Spain* (New York: Veterans of the Abraham Lincoln Brigade, 1952), which boycotts Hemingway deliberately, however. Robert Payne's *The Civil War in Spain* (New York: G. P. Putnam's Sons, 1961) is a well-edited anthology concerning some previously unpublished material, notably entries from his diary as well as Edwin Rolfe's during the Ebro period. Stephen Spender's *Poems from Spain* (London: Hogarth Press, 1939) prints many poems written by volunteers, most of which retain their literary value apart from the propaganda purpose, which underlay the collection. Representative poems and sketches by American volunteers are found in Alan Calmer (ed.), *Salud!* (New York, 1938).

The most accurate general study of the International Brigades is Verle B. Johnston's *Legions of Babel: The International Brigades in the Spanish Civil War* (University Park and London: The Pennsylvania State University Press, 1967), which also contains a comprehensive bibliography. Vincent Brome's *The International Brigades* (New York: William Morrow, 1966) contains an appalling number of factual errors. A Spanish Nationalist interpretation is Adolfo Lizón Gadea's *Brigadas Internacionales en España* (Madrid: Editora Nacional, 1940), which seems to have been written in haste and in mild hysteria. However, the anonymous booklet, *The International Brigades: Foreign Assistants of the Spanish Reds* (Madrid: Spanish Office of Information, 1948) contains captured documents and photographs available nowhere else. The standard history of the British Battalion is William Rust's *Britons in Spain* (London: Lawrence and Wishart, 1939).

Personal narratives by non-American volunteers that have proved to be useful are the following: George Orwell, *Homage to Catalonia* (London: Seeker and Warburg, 1938); Tom Wintringham, *English Captain* (London: Faber and Faber, 1939); Fred Copeman, *Reason in Revolt* (London: Blandford Press, 1948); John Sommerfield, *Volunteer in Spain* (New York: Alfred A. Knopf, 1937); Keith Scott Watson,

Single to Spain (London: Arthur Barker, 1937); Gustav Regler, *The Owl of Minerva* (New York: Farrar, Straus and Cudahy, 1959); Jef Last, *The Spanish Tragedy* (London: George Routledge, 1939). The only book-length memoir of an American pilot in Spain is F. G. Tinker's *Some Still Live* (New York and London: Funk and Wagnalls, 1938). Pro-Nationalist accounts bearing upon the International Brigades are Peter Kemp's *Mine Were of Trouble* (London: Cassell, 1957); Hector Colmegna's *Diario de un Medico Argentino en la Guerra de España* (Buenos Aires: Espasa-Calpe, 1941); Captain de Diego *et al, Belchite* (Barcelona: Editora Nacional, 1939); and Harriet Castle, *Viva la Muerte* (manuscript).

Among the pamphlets published by one or another of the agencies supporting the Popular Front, the following contain valuable information about the American volunteers: Joe Dallet, *Letters from Spain* (New York: Workers Library Publishers, 1938), Dallet's letters to his wife; Joseph Starobin, *The Life and Death of an American Hero* (New York: Young Communist League, 1938), a biography and letters of Dave Doran; *Ben Leider: American Hero* (New York: Ben Leider Memorial Fund, n.d.), biography of Ben Leider; *Story of the Abraham Lincoln Battalion* (New York: Sheridan Square Press, 1937), a vivid and accurate account of Villanueva de la Jara and Jarama authored by an anonymous volunteer (probably Eli Biegelman); *They Did Their Part, Let's Do Ours* (New York: Friends of the Abraham Lincoln Brigade, 1939), plans for care of the American wounded returned from Spain; and Lou Ornitz, *Captured by Franco* (New York: Friends of the Abraham Lincoln Brigade, 1939), the fullest account of the prisoners of war at San Pedro de Cardeña.

Accounts of the Lincoln Battalion by journalists and observers in Spain include the following: Virginia Cowles, *Looking for Trouble* (New York & London: Harper and Brothers, 1941); Herbert L. Matthews, *Two Wars and More to Come* (New York: Carrick and Evans, 1938) and *The Education of a Correspondent* (New York: Harcourt, Brace and Company, 1946); Vincent Sheean, *Not Peace But a Sword* (New York: Doubleday, Doran and Company, 1939); Sefton Delmer, *Trail Sinister: An Autobiography,* Vol. I (London: Secker and Warburg, 1961); Charlotte Haldane, *Truth Will Out* (New York: Vanguard Press, 1950); Stephen Spender, *World Within World* (New York: Harcourt, Brace and Company, 1951); Joseph North, *No Men Are Strangers* (New York: International Publishers, 1958); Henry W. Buckley, *Life and Death of the Spanish Republic* (London: Hamish Hamilton, 1940); Sidney Franklin, *Bullfighter from Brooklyn* (Englewood Cliffs: Prentice-Hall, 1952); Ernest Hemingway, *By-line: Ernest Hemingway* (New York: Charles Scribner's Sons, 1967); Josephine Herbst, "The Starched Blue Sky of Spain," *The Noble Savage,* No. 1 (New York, 1960), pp.

76–117; H. Edward Knoblaugh, *Correspondent in Spain* (London & New York: Sheed and Ward, 1937); Martha Gellhorn, "Madrid to Morata," *New Yorker* (July 24, 1937) and "Men Without Medals," *Collier's* (September 9, 1937).

The case against the Lincoln Battalion is disclosed in the testimonies printed in the U.S. Congress, House of Representatives, *Hearings Before a Special Committee on Un-American Activities* (1938, 1939, 1940). Additional evidence was presented in Subversive Activities Control Board, Docket No. 108–53, *Herbert Brownell Jr., Attorney General of the United States, Petitioner, vs. Veterans of the Abraham Lincoln Brigade, Respondent* (1955). State Department dispatches pertaining to the Lincoln Battalion are published in *Foreign Relations of the United States: Diplomatic Papers* (1936, 1937, 1938, 1939).

The best general study of the Spanish Civil War is Hugh Thomas' *The Spanish Civil War* (New York: Harper and Brothers, 1961). For military history there are Manuel Aznar's *Historia Militar de la Guerra de España* (Madrid: Ediciones Ideal, 1940), and Luis-María de Lojendio, *Operaciones Militares de la Guerra de España* (Barcelona: Montaner y Simon, 1940). Studies of campaigns in which the Lincoln Battalion fought are almost nonexistent. The exceptions are Robert Colodny's *The Struggle for Madrid* (New York: Paine-Whitman, 1958), which contains a superb analysis of Jarama, and Luis María Mezquida y Gené, *La Batalla del Ebro* (Tarazona: Disputacion Provincial, 1963), a detailed chronicle with excellent maps. A valuable collection of military folklore pertaining to both armies is Rafael García Serrano, *Diccionario para un Macuto* (Madrid: Editora Nacional, 1966).

Of greatest relevance among studies of a specialized nature are David T. Cattell's *Communism and the Spanish Civil War* (Berkeley and Los Angeles: University of California Press, 1956); Allen Guttmann's *The Wound in the Heart: America and the Spanish Civil War* (New York: The Macmillan Company, 1962), a remarkable analysis of the various attitudes in the United States toward the Spanish war; Stanley Weintraub's *The Last Great Cause* (New York: Weybright and Talley, 1968), a study of how writers and intellectuals responded to the war; and Murray Kempton's *Part of Our Time: Some Ruins and Monuments of the Thirties* (New York: Simon and Schuster, 1955), which devotes a chapter to the Lincoln Battalion. Of passing interest is John Dollard's *Fear in Battle* (New Haven: Yale University, Institute of Human Relations, 1943), a statistical study of fear symptoms based upon data compiled from questionnaires filled out by three hundred veterans of the Lincoln Battalion.

There is a considerable body of fiction treating the International Brigades, the most famous of which is Ernest Hemingway's *For Whom the Bell Tolls* (New York: Charles Scribner's Sons, 1940). At least four veterans of the XV Brigade wrote novels in which they made use of their experiences in the war: Ralph Bates (English), *Sirocco* (New York: Random House, 1939); Humphrey Slater (English), *The Heretics* (New York: Harcourt, Brace and Company, 1947); Alvah Bessie (American), *The un-Americans* (New York: Cameron Associates, 1957); and William Herrick (American), *The Itinerant* (New York: McGraw-Hill, 1966).

The most important depository for ephemera such as press clippings, pamphlets, broadsides, and pamphlets pertaining to the Lincoln Battalion is the David McKelvey White Collection at the New York Public Library. The Sherman-Grinberg Film Libraries in New York has generously allowed me to view relevant newsreels. The Ministry of Tourism and Information (Sección de Estudios de la Guerra de España) in Madrid has made available their collection of photographs, Nationalist and Republican, treating the war; The Instituto Geografico y Catastral has provided 1:50,000 topographical maps of the battlefield areas. Lincoln Battalion songs, expurgated, have been recorded on the Folkways album "Songs of the Spanish Civil War." As background for the period I read the New York *Times* and *New Masses* from cover to cover for the period, 1936–1939. Between January 1967 and April 1968 I traveled about ten thousand miles in Spain and visited, to my knowledge, every town, camp, and battleground associated with the Lincoln Battalion.

Without any doubt my greatest fund of information has come from interviews of the veterans. These include: Moe Fishman, John Gates, Robert Gladnick, William Harvey, Martin Hourihan, Sheldon Jones, Dave Mates, Steve Nelson, Lester Rowlson, Elman Service, Harold Smith, Robert Taylor, Saul Wellman, Neil Wesson. By deputy I have reached Oscar Hunter and George Watt. Taped interviews of Lawrence Cane and Carl Geiser have also been made available.

Chapter Notes

The purpose of these notes is to cite the source of *printed* materials employed in my text. I am not at liberty to indicate the source of data obtained verbally from individual veterans. Some men consented to be interviewed with the understanding that their names would not be used as conveyors of certain items of information.

The working basis for any book about the Lincoln Battalion consists of *Book of the XV Brigade*, Rolfe's *The Lincoln Battalion*, and Landis' *The Abraham Lincoln Brigade*. These are partisan accounts prepared by volunteers loyal to their cause and protective of it. They contain invaluable historical information without being legitimately historical, in any final sense. I allude to them here so as not to cite them repetitiously below.

Full bibliographical citations are provided only for those items not listed in the preceding section, "Sources."

CHAPTER 1

Chapter heading quoted in Guttmann's *The Wound in the Heart*. Consuls' reports, *Foreign Relations of the United States* (1937). Nationalist view of the Lincolns, Gadea's *Brigadas Internacionales en España*. Composition and text of "The Marching Song," *New Masses* (April 20, 1937); variant "revolutionary" ending, William G. Ryan testimony, *Hearings before a Special Committee on Un-American Activities* (1938), hereafter *HUAC*. Comintern use of IB passports, W. G. Krivitsky, *In Stalin's Secret Service* (New York and London: Harper and Brothers, 1939). Marty clique and Albacete bureaucracy, Regler's *The Owl of Minerva;* Wintringham's *English Captain;* Louis Fischer's *Men and Politics* (London: Jonathan Cape, 1941); and Ilya Ehrenburg's *Memoirs: 1921–1941* (Cleveland and New York: World Publishing Company, 1963).

CHAPTER 2

Chapter heading, quoted in Acier, *From Spanish Trenches*. Villanueva customs, Tinker's *Some Still Live*. A slightly different version of the power struggle for commissar is recounted by Voros, *American Commissar*. Training difficulties among the British, Wintringham and Copeman's *Reason in Revolt*. Bart's problems at Albacete are discussed by Voros, who calls him "Brodsky." The anonymous pamphlet, *The Story of the Lincoln Battalion* is excellent for the Villanueva period. Dr. Fogarty, town records, Villanueva de la Jara. Lincoln musicale, *New Masses* (April 20, 1937). Merriman biography, Voros; *Delta* [magazine of Sigma Nu] (December, 1937); and University of Nevada alumni records. Robert Merriman as Robert Jordan, *American Literature*, xxxviii, (November, 1966). Joseph Selligman, Swarthmore College alumni records.

CHAPTER 3

Chapter heading, quoted in Acier. Battle of Jarama, Colodny's *The Struggle for Madrid* and Aznar's *Historia Militar de la Guerra de Espana*. British Battalion at Jarama, Wintringham and Copeman. "Suicide Hill" and attack of February 23, *The Story of the Lincoln Battalion;* the letters quoted in Acier; Merriman's account recorded by Voros. American deserters, *Foreign Relations* (1937). Joe Gordon's story, *Book of the XV Brigade*. (In September, 1967, an American veteran of the battle conducted me through the sector between Chinchon and the trenches occupied on February 23.)

CHAPTER 4

Hyndman poem in Spender's *Poems from Spain*. The fullest characterization of Gal is found in Cowles, *Nothing But Trouble;* Hemingway's summation of Gal, introduction to Gustav Regler's *The Great Crusade* (New York: Longmans, Green and Company, 1940); Matthew's analysis of the Gal attack, *The Education of a Correspondent*. Evacuation from Spain of French deserters, *Foreign Relations* (1937). My account of the February 27 massacre is primarily based upon the testimony of five survivors. Only one of these has been able to tell me about the "Jarama Mutiny"; Voros alludes to but does not discuss it. Estimates of losses, Matthews' *Two Wars and More to Come*. Stember's admonition, *Notre Combat* [XV Brigade news-sheet] (March 3, 1937). Lincoln desertions, *Foreign Relations* (1937). For confessions of avowed deserters see Herbert Kline, "Conversations in the Trenches," *New Masses* (July 20, 1937).

CHAPTER 5

Hawthorne's visit, "The Yanks under Fire in Spain," *New Masses* (May 4, 1937); veterans protest his account, *New Masses* (July 20, 1937). Other visitors, as follows: Spender, *World Within World;* Gellhorn, *New Yorker* (July 24, 1937); Cowles, *Looking for Trouble;* Herbst, *The Noble Savage.*

Our Fight editorials, Stember (March 10); Dr. William Pike (April 8). Levinger poem, Kempton, *Part of Our Time.* March 14 counterattack, Copeman. How Raven was blinded, letter printed in Rolfe; Hemingway interviews Raven, New York *Times* (April 25, 1937) and reprinted in *By-Line: Ernest Hemingway.* Recollections of Raven at Villa Paz, Richard Rees, *A Theory of My Time* (London: Secker & Warburg, 1962).

Madrid during the spring of 1937, Delmer, *Trail Sinister: An Autobiography;* Franklin, *Bullfighter from Brooklyn;* Buckley, *Life and Death of the Spanish Republic;* Malcolm Cowley, "To Madrid," *New Republic* (October 6, 1937); Cowles; Herbst. Hemingway's aversion to commissars, North, *No Men Are Strangers.* "Whitey" Dahl's career, Carlos Baker's manuscript on Hemingway and files of the New York *Times* (1937–1956). Jeff Davis Battalion, James Hawthorne, "American Fliers in Spain," *New Masses* (June 8, 1937). Lincolns during bombardment of the Florida, New York *Times* (May 23, 1937).

Americans at Jarama during trench vigil, Matthews' dispatch in the New York *Times* (May 24, 1937) and Nelson's *The Volunteers.* Letters home (headings inserted), Acier. May Day parade, Nelson. Text of "The Valley of Jarama", *Book of the XV Brigade;* militant version, Weintraub, *The Last Great Cause.*

CHAPTER 6

Public opinion polls, James Hafer, "The Communist Party of the United States and the Spanish Civil War," American University thesis (1956). Guttmann's analysis of American response to the war in Spain is definitive. North American Committee, various testimonies in HUAC (1938 and 1939) and Eugene Lyons, *The Red Decade* (Indianapolis and New York: The Bobbs-Merrill Company, 1941). Leider biography, *Ben Leider: American Hero* and Ruth McKenny, "In Memoriam, Ben Leider," *New Masses* (March 16, 1937); Leider funeral, New York *Times* (August 19, 1938). Announcement of fund drives and rallies, *New Masses,* passim. Sullivan County Red camp, New York *Times* (May 26, 1937). Debs column, *American Socialist Monthly* (February, 1937).

Maison des Syndicats, Haldane, *Truth Will Out* and Nelson. Wallach's biography has been pieced together from fragments in HUAC, Voros, and Haldane. *Ciudad de Barcelona* sinking, Abraham Sobel testimony in HUAC and Voros. Perpignan jail and Ceret trial, Nelson and Joe Dallet, *Letters from Spain*. Additional Dallet information comes from Dartmouth College alumni records. All quotations from his letters are taken from *Letters from Spain*. Interbrigade prison at Albacete, Spender.

CHAPTER 7

Chapter heading from *Book of the XV Brigade*. Copic's speech, *ibid.* Nelson's alleged political activities were the subject of an inquiry by HUAC in 1949. Albares rest period, Nelson. Military operations at Brunete and subsequent campaigns, Aznar, *Historia Militar de la Guerra de España* and Lojendio, *Operaciones Militares de la Guerra de España*. Caballero's alternative plan, Johnston, *Legions of Babel*. Villanueva de la Cañada and Mosquito Ridge, Copeman, Nelson; see also Harold Smith's account in Bessie (ed.), *The Heart of Spain*. Oliver Law poem (courtesy of Allen Guttmann), Boris Todrin, *Seven Men* (New York, 1938). Rally at the "Pearly Gates", Nelson.

CHAPTER 8

Chapter heading from *New Republic* (January 12, 1938). Quarrels in the British Communist Party, Copeman. Communist penetration of the Republican army and government, Frank Borkenau's *European Communism* (New York: Harper and Brothers, 1953). Prieto's directive on the IB, *The Volunteer for Liberty* (September 23, 1937). For current ramifications of the Fuqua visit, *Cronica de la Guerra Española*, No. 71 (Madrid, 1968).

Quinto, *The Volunteer for Liberty* (December 27, 1937), *Our Fight* (September 15, 1937), Nelson, and Wintringham. Pulburrel Hill, Rust, *Britons in Spain*, and Nelson. Belchite, both Nelson and *Book of the XV Brigade* are especially informative on this battle. Nationalist version of Belchite, Diego, *Belchite*. Street fighting, *The Volunteer for Liberty* (October 4, 1937). Gellhorn visit to the Brigade, "Men without Medals," *Collier's* (September 9, 1937). Detro biography, *The Volunteer for Liberty* (December 6, 1937) supplemented with the alumni records of Rice University and University of Missouri.

CHAPTER 9

Chapter heading and other Dallet quotations, *Letters from Spain*. American desertions, *Foreign Relations* (1937) and HUAC (1938).

Doran biography, Starobin, *Life and Death of an American Hero.*
Mackenzie-Papineau information, Victor Hoar manuscript on Canadian
volunteers. Thompson sequel, Kempton. Landis was a participant in this
battle and his account is one of the better sections of his book.

CHAPTER 10

Albares rest period, *The Volunteer for Liberty* (December 20, 1937).
Attlee visit, *The Volunteer for Liberty* (December 13, 1937), Gates' *The
Story of an American Commissar,* and Rust. Landis' claim that Keller
was apolitical is not supported by testimony given before the SACB in
Attorney General vs. Veterans of the Lincoln Brigade (1955). Move-
ment up to Teruel front, Edward K. Barsky account in Bessie, *Heart of
Spain* and James Neugass, "Spanish Diary," *New Masses* (June 14,
1938). XV Brigade hospital, Leo Eloesser, "Doctors in War," *ibid.*
(June 29, 1939). Paul Robeson visit, diary of Eslanda Robeson in
Bessie, *Heart of Spain.* The Landis account of Browder's visit is at vari-
ance with the testimony of John C. Honeycombe in HUAC (1938).
Segura de los Baños, Voros and Rust. Goldstein anecdote, Landis.

CHAPTER 11

Nationalist offensive in Aragon, Aznar. A major document concerning
the retreat to Caspe is the report of Major Edward Cecil-Smith, courtesy
of Victor Hoar, Mac Pap historian. For other accounts of the retreat see
Rust. Copeman, Voros, *The Volunteer for Liberty* (April 23, 1938) and
(August 13, 1938). International prisoners at Caspe, Colmegna, *Diario
de un Medico Argentino en la Guerra de Espana.*

CHAPTER 12

Chapter heading, Bessie, *Men in Battle.* Tarazona recruits to the
front, *ibid.* Headlines from *The Volunteer for Liberty* (March 17, March
21, March 25, 1938). Courts-martial in the Brigade, Voros and Honeycombe testimony, HUAC. Deserters seek refuge in consulates, *Foreign
Relations* (1938). Gates' biography, Voros and Gates', *The Story of an
American Communist.* Bottcher biography, *Liberty* (July 3, 1943),
German-American (February 1, 1945), and *Yank* (March 2, 1945).
Doran letter to his wife, Starobin.
Calaceite defeat, Rust. The fullest "inside" narrative of the retreat
from Batea is that of Bessie's *Men in Battle.* Debacle at Corbera, Mat-
thews' dispatches in the New York *Times* (April 3 and April 12, 1938)
and Hemingway's dispatch in *New Republic* (April 27, 1938). Copernico

episode, *The Volunteer for Liberty* (August 26, 1938). Cookson's escape, *ibid.,* (October 6, 1938). Hemingway at the Ebro, Gates and Delmer. Survivors at Darmos, Bessie. One million cigarettes, *The Volunteer for Liberty* (April 9, 1938).

CHAPTER 13

Chapter heading, New York *Times* (May 29, 1938). Thomas Wolfe letter, *The Nation* (May 21, 1938). Carney's dispatches in the *Times* (April 2, April 4, May 29, 1938). Consul Bay's visit to San Pedro, *Foreign Relations* (1938). Prison life in San Pedro, Ornitz, *Captured by Franco* and Norman E. Dorland, "In Franco's Prison Camp," *New Masses* (November 22, 1938). FALB arrangements for sponsoring prisoners' return, *Foreign Relations* (1938).

CHAPTER 14

Chapter heading, New York *Times* (April 10, 1938). My estimate of the number of deserters is based upon joining together testimonies in HUAC, consuls' reports in *Foreign Relations,* news stories in the New York *Times,* and lists in the consulate archives, Valencia. See also William G. Ryan, "Escape from Loyalist Spain," *American Mercury* (April, 1939). The HUAC testimonies contain numerous allusions to executions; e.g., the Tarragona affair. See also Voros, Copeman, Spender, and Haldane. Ernst Toller at Hotel Majestic, Stanley Payne, *The Civil War in Spain.*

CHAPTER 15

Chapter heading, Bessie, *Men in Battle.* Darmos campment, Bessie and Sheean, *Not Peace But a Sword.* Return to Spain of Jarama veterans, *The Volunteer for Liberty* (June 30, and August 13, 1938). The last would-be volunteers, New York *Times* (August 23, 1938). James Lardner, Sheean and Ring Lardner, Jr., *Somebody Had to Do Something* (Los Angeles: James Lardner Memorial Fund, 1939). May Day fiesta, Voros and *The Volunteer for Liberty* (May 25, 1938). Ode to the fly, *The Volunteer for Liberty* (July 19, 1938). Training maneuvers for Ebro crossing, Bessie and Matthews' dispatch in the New York *Times* (June 14, 1938). "Activism," *The Volunteer for Liberty* (July 19, 1938). Valledor biography, *ibid.,* (June 30, 1938). Crossing the Ebro, Bessie; *The Volunteer for Liberty,* passim; Matthews' *The Education of a Correspondent.* Cooper's prisoners, *The Volunteer for Liberty* (September 5, 1938). Attacks on "The Pimple", Rust. "Death Valley", Bessie and

diary of Edwin Rolfe in Payne. Death of Arnold Reid, Haldane. Evacuating the wounded, *The Volunteer for Liberty* (November 7, 1938).
The Sierra Pandols, Bessie and *The Volunteer for Liberty* (October 6,
1938). Death of Bianca, *New Masses* (August 15, 1938).

CHAPTER 16

The only adequate account of the last battle at Camposines is that in
Landis. Lardner's death, Sheean and *Somebody Had to Do Something.*
La Despedida, Sheean and Matthews, *The Education of a Correspondent.*
Speech of "La Pasionaria", Bessie, *Heart of Spain.* Negotiations for
withdrawal, *Foreign Relations* (1938 and 1939). Crossing the frontier,
Rolfe, *The Lincoln Battalion* and Matthews' dispatch in the New York
Times (December 3, 1938). Delays at Le Havre, New York *Times*
(December 4, 7, and 8, 1938) and Bessie, *The un-Americans.* Madison
Square demonstration, New York *Times* (December 16, 1938).

EPILOGUE

Chapter heading, Milton Wolff, "We Met in Spain," *American Dialog*
(October–November, 1964). Medical needs of the veterans, *They Did
Their Part, Let's Do Ours* (pamphlet) and *Francis J. Gorman Talks
About America's Soldiers of Liberty* (pamphlet, New York: FALB, n.d.).
Albert Wallach investigation, HUAC (1939). FALB refuses to petition
the Soviet Union, Voros. Evidence that VALB was a Communist-front
organization is summarized in SACB, *Attorney General vs. Veterans of
the Abraham Lincoln Brigade;* see also issues of *The Volunteer for Liberty*
published during these years. Veterans in Second World War, introduction to bound facsimile of *The Volunteer for Liberty* (1949). National
convention of 1967, Johnston, *Legions of Babel.* The McCarthy mood as
it affected two veterans, Gates, *The Story of an American Communist*
and Bessie, *Inquisition in Eden* (New York: The Macmillan Company,
1965). Twenty-fifth anniversary meeting of VALB, *The Volunteer*
(March, 1962). Supreme Court vacates order requiring registration, New
York *Times* (April 26, 1965) and *The Volunteer* (April–June, 1966).
World's Fair confrontation, New York *Times* (July 19, 1964) and *The
Volunteer* (July–August, 1964). A sympathetic account of the veterans
since the war is found in Brock Brower's "The Abraham Lincoln Brigade
Revisited," *Esquire* (March, 1962).

Index

About the Author

CECIL EBY, professor of English at the University of Michigan, has twice been awarded travel and teaching fellowships to Spain. The first produced his well-received *The Siege of the Alcázar* (Random House, 1965); the second, *Between the Bullet and the Lie*. He has also published numerous articles on American literature and history.